FIELDING'S
WESTERN
CARIBBEAN

Other Fielding Titles

FIELDING'S WESTERN CARIBBEAN

The adventurer's guide to the exotic Western Caribbean

By
Joyce Wiswell

Fielding Worldwide, Inc.

308 South Catalina Avenue

Redondo Beach, California 90277 U.S.A.

Fielding's Western Caribbean
Published by Fielding Worldwide, Inc.
Text Copyright ©1995 Fielding Worldwide, Inc.
Icons & Illustrations Copyright ©1995 FWI
Photo Copyrights ©1995 to Individual Photographers

FIELDING WORLDWIDE INC.

PUBLISHER AND CEO	**Robert Young Pelton**
GENERAL MANAGER	**John Guillebeaux**
MARKETING DIRECTOR	**Paul T. Snapp**
ELECTRONIC PUBLISHING DIRECTOR	**Larry E. Hart**
PUBLIC RELATIONS DIRECTOR	**Beverly Riess**
ACCOUNT SERVICES MANAGER	**Christy Harp**
PROJECT MANAGER	**Chris Snyder**
DATABASE PUBLISHING MANAGER	**Jacki VanderVoort**

CONTRIBUTING WRITERS

David Swanson   **Nick Tonkin**

EDITORS

Kathy Knoles   **Linda Charlton**

PRODUCTION

Martin Mancha   **Gini Sardo-Martin**
Ramses Reynoso   **Craig South**
Janice Whitby

COVER DESIGNED BY	**Digital Artists, Inc.**
COVER PHOTOGRAPHERS — Front Cover	**Mark Lewis & Donald Nausbaum/Tony Stone Images**
Back Cover	**Julie Houck/Westlight**
INSIDE PHOTOS	**Carol Lee, Benford Associates, Grenada Tourist Office, Karen Weiner, Escalera Associates, Robinson, Yesavich & Pepperdine, Inc., Saba Tourist Office, Trombone Associates, Corel Professional Photos**

Inquiries should be addressed to: Fielding Worldwide, Inc., 308 South Catalina Ave., Redondo Beach, California 90277 U.S.A., ☎ *(310) 372-4474*, Facsimile *(310) 376-8064*, 8:30 a.m.–5:30 p.m. Pacific Standard Time.

ISBN 1-56952-072-0

Printed in the United States of America

Letter from the Publisher

The Caribbean can be a daunting place when it comes to choosing the perfect island getaway. Our focus is making sure you get the best experience for your time and money. To assist you we have created handy comparison tables for accommodations and restaurants complete with best buy and highest rated listings so you can get the most for your money. You'll also find the introductions tighter and with a definite accent on the romantic and adventurous.

Author Joyce Wiswell, faced with covering and reviewing hundreds of "tropical getaways on white sandy beaches," brings a youthful enthusiasm along with a true love of the Caribbean to this book. She has tackled the daunting task of giving the reader a balanced overview of the region as well as highlighting the unique personality of each island. In these 500-plus pages you will find the famous, the hidden and the overlooked all rated and reviewed in our new easy-to-use format. Supporting her efforts have been the staff and researchers at Fielding Worldwide who have done an impressive job of gathering, checking, sorting and compiling more than 1000 attractions, hotels and restaurants. Special thanks to our staff for making it all come together. If it helps you find that one perfect place for your once-a-year getaway, then we have done our job.

Today, the concept of independent travel has never been bigger. Our policy of *brutal honesty* and a highly personal point of view has never changed; it just seems the travel world has caught up with us.

Enjoy your Western Caribbean adventure.

RYP

Robert Young Pelton
Publisher and CEO
Fielding Worldwide, Inc.

ACKNOWLEDGEMENTS

So many people assisted in this project it is impossible to list them all, but you know who you are and how much I appreciate your help. In particular, special thanks to Richard Kahn and Stephen Bennett of Kahn Travel Communications who assisted in planning my itinerary and Fielding's John Guillebeaux and Kathy Knoles. Cheers to all the hoteliers, tourist board personnel, restaurateurs, bartenders, waiters, locals and tourists who befriended a wandering traveler and made her feel at home.

ABOUT THE AUTHOR

Joyce Wiswell

Joyce Wiswell has been writing about travel for more than 15 years. Various writing assignments have taken her to nearly every state in the union, as well as China, Hong Kong, the Philippines, Thailand, Europe, and, of course, throughout the Caribbean. Her work has appeared in numerous magazines and newspapers. Wiswell is also the author of *Fielding's Las Vegas Agenda*, *Fielding's Caribbean* and *Fielding's Eastern Caribbean*.

A native of New Jersey, she is a magna cum laude graduate of Connecticut's Quinnipiac College. After paying her dues as a magazine writer and editor in New York City for eight years, she fled for life in California, where she lives happily in Santa Barbara. When not traveling, she putters in the garden and pampers her cats, and worries unduly about both when on the road.

Fielding Rating Icons

The Fielding Rating Icons are highly personal and awarded to help the besieged traveler choose from among the dizzying array of activities, attractions, hotels, restaurants and sights. The awarding of an icon denotes unusual or exceptional qualities in the relevant category.

RATINGS
- Fielding Award
- Author Selection
- Money Saver
- Expensive
- Quality
- Warning
- Danger
- Inexpensive
- Spacious
- Cramped
- Mild Disapproval

CULTURAL
- Museum/Art
- Interesting Architecture
- History
- Book Reference
- Artistically Important
- Musically Interesting
- Cultural Archeology
- Crafts
- Theatre
- Festivals

SIGHTS
- Picturesque
- Great Scenery
- Market
- Beaches/Resorts
- Cultural
- Fortress
- Castles
- Church

WHERE TO STAY
- Simple
- Luxurious
- Cottage
- Bed & Breakfast
- Scenic
- Business
- Honeymoon
- Chateau

TRAVEL TIPS
- Arrival/Departure
- By Air
- By Water
- By Train
- By Car
- Bus/Local Transit
- Barge
- River Boat
- Calendar
- Itinerary
- Compass
- Kids

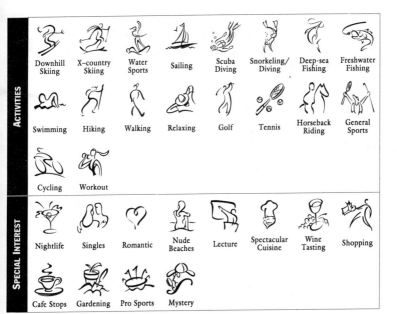

ACTIVITIES

Downhill Skiing	X–country Skiing	Water Sports	Sailing
Scuba Diving	Snorkeling/ Diving	Deep-sea Fishing	Freshwater Fishing
Swimming	Hiking	Walking	Relaxing
Golf	Tennis	Horseback Riding	General Sports
Cycling	Workout		

SPECIAL INTEREST

Nightlife	Singles	Romantic	Nude Beaches
Lecture	Spectacular Cuisine	Wine Tasting	Shopping
Cafe Stops	Gardening	Pro Sports	Mystery

What's in the Stars

Fielding's Five Star Rating System for the Caribbean

★★★★★ Exceptionally outstanding hotels, resorts, restaurants and attractions.

★★★★ Excellent in most respects.

★★★ Very good quality and superior value.

★★ Meritorious and worth considering.

★ Modest or better than average.

Restaurants are star rated and classified by dollar signs as:

$	Inexpensive	$1–$9
$$	Moderate	$9–$15
$$$	Expensive	$15 and up

A NOTE TO OUR READERS:

If you have had an extraordinary, mediocre or horrific experience we want to hear about it. If something has changed since we have gone to press, please let us know. Those business owners who flood us with shameless self-promotion under the guise of readers' letters will be noted and reviewed more rigorously next time. If you would like to send information for review in next year's edition send it to:

Fielding's Caribbean
308 South Catalina Avenue
Redondo Beach, CA 90277
FAX: (310) 376-8064

TABLE OF CONTENTS

LIST OF MAPS

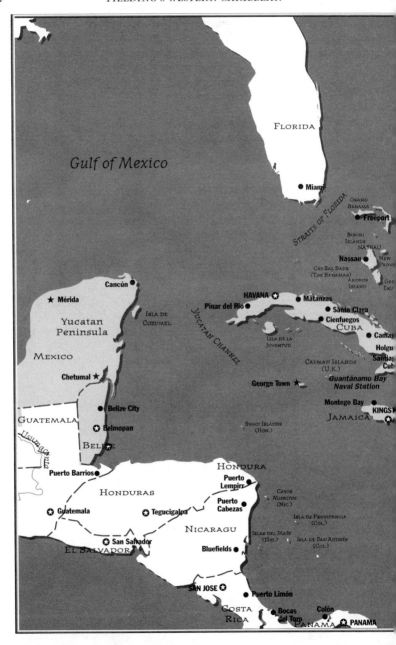

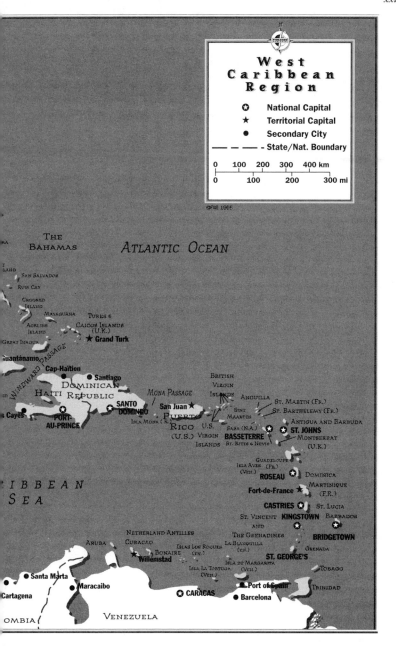

WESTERN CARIBBEAN INTRO

While the many islands of the Eastern Caribbean are strewn closely together as if a giant tossed a handful of land into the sea, those of the West are generally much more spread out, with miles of deep blue sea between landfalls. These destinations are famed for their superior diving and untamed natural beauty. Some, such as Belize, Haiti and the Dominican Republic, are very poor, which means cheap prices for tourists but also accompanying pangs of conscience.

With the notable exception of hot, humid weather and that alluring crystalline sea, Aruba has no more in common with the Mexican Yucatan than Arkansas has to California. See "Island Snapshots" to determine which jewel of the Caribbean is right for you.

Caribbean Planner

By Air

Many airlines fly to the Caribbean, though for island-hoppers, American and American Eagle are probably the best bet, as they service many destinations and give good deals on multi-island tickets. (On one swing, I hopped to eight islands, and the fare was only about $1250, including round-trip from California.) On the other hand, many flights connect through San Juan, Puerto Rico, which means it can take many hours to get where a crow can fly in minutes. TACA is also good for short hops between islands.

Other airlines with service from the U.S. to the Caribbean are Aeromexico, Air Jamaica, ALM, Avensa, Avianca, BWIA, Cayman Airways, Continental, Delta, Dominicana, Lacsa, LanChile, Mexicana, Northwest, TWA, United, USAir and Viasa.

How much you'll pay depends on how demanding you are. If you're counting pennies, obviously you'll fly coach. If you're willing to spend more upgrade to business or first class—but be aware you'll pay dearly for the wider seat and better food, in most cases, several hundred dollars more. When island hopping, you'll be on small craft with no separate classes of service.

To save money, buy your ticket as far in advance as possible, and be on the lookout for special promotions. It's cheaper all the way around to travel to the Caribbean in the summertime—everything from air to hotels are generally discounted. Also consider a package deal that includes air, transfers, hotel accommodations and sometimes meals and a rental car. Charter flights are also worth investigating, but have the distinct disadvantage of extremely limited schedules and a disturbing propensity to cancel flights. Unlike commercial carrier, if your charter flight is canceled, you're usually left on your own to scramble for an alternate.

The Affordable Caribbean, *(8403 Colesville Road, Silver Spring, MD 20910* ☎ *(301) 588-2300)* is a monthly newsletter that reports on last-minute deals and other Caribbean bargains. If you travel to the Caribbean frequently and have a flexible schedule, it's well worth the $49 annual subscription cost.

By Sea

There's nothing like a cruise for relaxing and really getting away from it all. These floating hotels pamper guests and provide lots of on-board activities for those who get bored just laying on deck soaking up the rays. Cruise ships stop at virtually every island, and several, such as Princess, have their own private islands where passengers spend the day enjoying watersports and beach barbecue.

Life at sea is so pleasant it can be hard to drag yourself off the ship at the ports of call. Obviously you're not going to soak up much island flavor in five or six hours, but there's still plenty to do and see—besides the requisite shopping—at each island. (See the chart on Island Excursions for ideas. And take note that if you sign up for one of the official cruise line excursions, you'll pay much more than if you venture off alone. The disadvantage is that if you don't get back on time, you're in trouble—ships sail exactly when they say they will, and don't take a head count first. Always bring your passport ashore just in case you literally miss the boat.

A cruise can be as short as three days and as long as several weeks; seven day trips are most popular in the Caribbean. What you pay varies widely upon what type of cabin you snag. The most expensive are the suites with balconies—a true treat if you can afford it—while the cheapest fares go to those who have a tiny inside cabin (no window) on a lower deck. Generally the higher up you are, the higher the price. Watch the papers for deals on

st-minute cruises—cruise lines will slash fares a few weeks out rather than
l empty.

Once you cruise with a line, it will try hard to get you back. The major lines
ward frequent cruisers with deep discounts and two-for-one fares. While
s fun to try out different cruise lines, these promotions go a long way to as-
re brand loyalty. Also note the loyalty of your travel agent (cruises are vir-
ally always booked through an agent rather than directly through the line).
good travel agent will send flowers and/or a bottle of wine to your cabin.
you've used the same agent a few times and have not received these perks,
s time to try an agency that will let you know your business is appreciated.

For general information on cruising, contact the **Cruise Lines Association**
00 Fifth Avenue, New York, NY 10110; ☎ *(212) 921-0066)*. Also see Field-
g's *Worldwide Cruises* for frank reviews of each ship and line.

By Land

Some islands are so tiny you'll easily get around on foot. Others, such as
lize's Ambergris Caye, use the golf cart as the preferred mode of transpor-
tion. Several have excellent bus systems and good taxi fleets (Jamaica in
rticular)—it varies widely by island. For details, see the "Getting Around"
ction in the directory in the back of each island chapter.

The biggest decision will be whether or not to rent a car. Chain and locally
vned rental companies are available on virtually every island, and summer
tes are often cheaper than during the prime winter season.

If you're staying at an all-inclusive resort and plan to rarely leave the prop-
ty, there's no need to rent a car. If, however, you plan to explore and try
fferent restaurants each evening, you're often better off renting a car than
ying lots of taxi fares. You'll also be more independent.

Road conditions vary from island to island. Some have modern paved
ads, but too often, the roadways are narrow, rutted and filled with hairpin
rns. Driving is often on the left side of the road, which can be dangerous if
u're not used to it. On the plus side, most islands have few major roads so
tting lost is rarely a problem. Consider renting a convertible so you can
ak up every possible ray of sunshine, or a four-wheel drive to easily navi-
te the often torturous roads on some islands.

A few tips on car rentals: Always reserve as far in advance as possible, as the
rs do get snatched up during prime tourist seasons. Check to see if they'll
liver the car to your hotel—many do at no extra charge, and it's a nice
rk. Before leaving home, check your car insurance policy to see if rental
rs are covered. They often are, and this allows you to refuse the rental com-
ny's outrageously priced insurance, which saves big bucks. If you're not
vered, seriously consider buying the rental insurance, as island drivers can

be wackier than even those in Boston, and, as stated, the roads are often a
ful.

Taxi service also varies. Some islands have metered cabs, but many mc
use standardized fares. In those cases, always ask what the trip will cost b
fore you get in. If you're hiring a cabbie for a day's sightseeing, you'll usua
be able to negotiate a fare. On some islands fares increase dramatically
night. In others, they disappear by midnight. If you're relying on taxis,
sure you'll be able to catch a cab if you plan to stay out late. Always tre
your cab driver with courtesy and respect. You should anyway, but it can
pecially pay off when you hit it off and the cabbie—virtually always a native
turns you on to interesting facts and places you'd never otherwise find.
you're a business traveler on an expense account, tote along a small not
book for receipts, as most cabbies don't carry them.

Lodging

Some of the world's best resorts are found in the Caribbean. So, alas,
some sleazy and roach-ridden dumps. Most fall in between, but on the poc
er islands, remember that "luxury" is relative.

Once you decide on an island—no easy choice in itself—your next task is
pick accommodations. The choices are immense—luxury resorts that ca
to every whim, all-inclusive properties when everything from soup to nuts
included in the price, glamorous villas with your own butler and pool, bu
get motels with limited amenities, atmospheric inns with rich history a
often colorful owners, cheap guest houses where you'll get little more tha
clean (or not so) room, and apartments and condominiums where you c
save money by preparing your own meals.

Many hotels offer the same rates for single and double occupancy, with
surcharge for a third or fourth person in the room. Children under 17 or
(it varies by company) often stay and even eat for free. Larger resorts off
supervised children's activities during the high season, and it's often comp
mentary. They can also arrange for a nighttime baby-sitter for a nomir
charge.

Always ascertain if you are paying for the Full American Plan (FAP, thr
meals), Modified American Plan (MAP, two meals), Breakfast Plan (BP, f
breakfast), Continental Plan (CP, continental breakfast) or European Pl
(EP, no meals). The latter is the most common. Many resorts offer option
meal plans that for, say, $40 to $60 a day, include three meals. Unless y
really have no plans to venture off-site, eschew these since it can be terri
dull to eat all your meals at the same spot, no matter how good the foo
Also, unless you're a very hardy eater, you can probably save money by d
ing a la carte. As you spend a few days on your vacation, you'll inevitab

ear about some great restaurant you must try, so it's better not to be locked with a meal plan.

Also be sure exactly what is included in the rates. Watersports are some-mes complimentary, but often not, and that snorkel equipment and float n really add up. Other non-motorized watersports are free, but you'll pay rent a jet ski or take a sunset cruise. Even the coffeemaker in your room n't be taken for granted. It's usually free to make a cup of joe, but some-mes (and ironically, at the most expensive resorts) you'll get a charge cked onto the room. When it comes to the minibar, assume that you're aying (dearly) for anything you use. Some hotels and resorts, however, will ck a bottle of champagne or wine in your refrigerator as a welcome gift. If doubt, call the front desk. (I once assumed a delicious box of bonbons was raciously supplied to each guest, until I saw the $20 charge on my final tab hen checking out.)

No matter what class of lodging you choose, you can generally assume u'll pay a premium for an oceanfront room. Slightly less are rooms with a ew of the sea, though not necessarily on it. Cheapest are the "garden view" oms—but beware—that "garden" may actually be a parking lot. In cases here rooms are on multiple levels, request a unit on the upper floor(s) for creased privacy and better views.

Never assume a hotel has air conditioning—it's not nearly as common in e Caribbean as throughout the U.S. You can usually count on having a iling fan—and trade winds often do a good job in keeping things cool— t if you're set on air, be sure to ask. Some places charge a $10 or $20 daily e for the use of air conditioners. Also keep in mind that central air is very re; most hotels use individual units that can be quite noisy, enough to rown out the soothing sounds of the surf. Television and telephones are so not often available—if it's important to you, ask first.

All-Inclusive

One fast-growing Caribbean trend is the all-inclusive property, which eans that for one price, you get lodging, all meals, drinks, activities and en-rtainment. They also frequently include gratuities and surcharges.

Sounds great, but there are definite disadvantages to such a resort. Gener-ly, as with Club Meds, the rooms are quite basic and nothing to get excited out. There are usually just a few restaurants (and sometimes only one), so eals can become routine. Some can overdo the camaraderie angle to the oint where you're made to feel almost guilty if you don't join in corny roup activities.

The biggest drawback is that when everything is made so easy and accessi-le, it can be hard to tear yourself off the grounds. This is fine if you're just oking to escape the world for a while, but if you're interested in really get-

ting to know an island and its people, it won't happen at an all-inclusiv
Often they have fences and guards to keep the locals out—good for securi
but hardly conducive to a cultural exchange. Many times all-inclusives are s
generic they could be located anywhere—the same feel on Jamaica (whe
they are extremely popular) as in Cozumel—two very distinct destinations

Resorts like Sandals and Couples (whose logo, oddly enough, is a copula
ing pair of lions) accept only same-sex couples. Honeymooners and oth
lovers staring dreamily into each other's eyes and making out in the pool
the norm. At the other extreme, the properties that cater to singles, such
Jamaica's Hedonism, are tropical meat markets where scoring with the o
posite sex is a top priority. Club Med, which started the whole all-inclusiv
phenomenon nearly 30 years ago, used to be known as the premiere singl
spot, but lately is courting families with lots of special activities for kids.

Several all-inclusives are quite luxurious and cater to the well-heele
crowd. Others are relatively tiny (Turks' Windmills Plantation for instance
and you'll really get a chance to know the staff and your fellow guests. Mo
fall in between, with a hundred or so rooms, several restaurants and dece
nightlife. Nearly all have well-manicured grounds and a wealth of wate
sports, arts and crafts activities, talent shows, sports competitions and then
nights. Most also offer diving and sightseeing excursions that cost extra, an
a few don't include alcohol in the price. Be sure to ask exactly what you'
getting before making your reservations.

The biggest thing to keep in mind is that if you're not interested in socia
izing, don't stay in an all-inclusive! If, on the other hand, you only have a s
amount of money to spend and don't want to worry about carrying cash, a
all-inclusive can be perfect for a relaxed, hassle-free holiday.

Lots of properties throughout the Caribbean offer all-inclusive packages i
addition to European and American plans. In these cases, you're probab
better off booking your room under the European Plan (no meals), then se
ing how you feel once you check the resort out in person. It's the rare hot
that won't let you switch to an all-inclusive plan, but rarer still the ones th
will let you get out of it once you make the commitment.

Packing the Suitcase

First and foremost, try to pack lightly enough so you can carry your lug
gage on the plane, as opposed to checking it in. That way you'll whis
through customs (where applicable) well ahead of your fellow travelers wai
ing forlornly at the luggage carousel. Everything goes slower in the Caribb
an—and luggage retrieval is certainly no exception. Most airlines will only l
you carry on two bags (and sometimes one on a very crowded flight) th
measures no more than 62 inches (width plus length plus height). In all ca
es, carry-ons must fit under your seat or in the overhead compartment. Th

impossible on the tiny planes that hop from island to island, but if you and your bag to them on the runway rather than check it, you'll still get it back more quickly.

As humidity is quite high throughout the Caribbean, bring natural fabrics; lightweight cotton is the best. Casual clothes are fine just about anywhere both day and night (when it's not, it's noted in the hotel or restaurant description). An exception are historic churches, which generally have a no-shorts rule. Respect this custom; it's especially easy for women, who can wear a light sundress.

The nights are generally warm and sultry, but some clubs and restaurants will invariably overdo the air conditioning, so tuck in a jacket or sweater. If you're gong to be trekking through the jungle or rainforest, obviously you want sturdy shoes and The nicer hotels equip their rooms with umbrellas; you may want to tuck in a small portable one just in case. Don't forget to bring a beach bag to hold your suntan lotion, hat or visor and a few dollars for lunch (your carry-on bag can serve this purpose).

Bring sandals or flip-flops for the beach (the sand gets hot!) and good sneakers for touring around. Lots of villages have cobblestone streets, and the old forts usually have dubious pathways, so you'll appreciate sturdy shoes. Unless you're into tottering around on high heels, you can leave them at home; flat dressy sandals will do even at the finer resorts.

Consider buying a sarong once you arrive. These large, colorful pieces of rectangular cloth can be tied in a variety of ways, from halter dress to shirt, fold up into practically nothing, are easy to hand wash and make great souvenirs to boot. You'll find them in all the shops and marketplaces.

You'll also find lots of hats, mainly straw, and it's a good idea to pick one up. The sun is very strong throughout the region, and just because you are dutifully sightseeing rather than lazing on the street doesn't mean you won't get burnt.

The sunbathers on many islands go topless; whether or not you do too is a personal choice. However, it's considered rude to go to a nude beach and keep your clothes on. In any event, wearing swimsuits anywhere but the pool or beach is generally a no-no, and men, please spare us the sight of your hairy (or otherwise) chest in public places.

Other essentials include mosquito repellent, a portable water bottle, strong sunscreen and film. You'll generally save a lot of money by buying these items stateside rather than on the island. Smokers, on the other hand, can usually score cigarettes much cheaper on the islands, often even compared to the duty-free shops. For instance, a carton of American cigarettes in Belize costs only $9. (Remember you can legally bring only one carton back into the U.S.)

Finer hotels outfit their bathrooms with hairdryers, shampoo, conditione and body lotion, but these products are usually cheap, so if you're particula bring your own. It's well worth checking out the "introductory" or trave sizes of personal care items at the drug store or supermarket, or buying sma plastic containers to fill. There's no need to lug your whole bottle of Prel just bring what you'll need for your length of stay.

Women should pack a few tampons or sanitary pads…just in case. Als bring a small sewing kit, extra eyeglasses, condoms if you're planning to g extra friendly with new acquaintances and motion-travel wristbands or med ication if you're prone to seasickness and will be boating. There's nothin like the fit of your own snorkel mask, so bring that along, too. Men who us electric shavers may need an electric converter (see the "Directory" und each island for electrical currents). Prescription medications and eyeglasse should always be carried on your person when traveling, not checked wit your luggage.

What not to bring: travel iron (virtually all hotels supply one on request– and besides, this is the Caribbean and wrinkles are acceptable), expensiv jewelry (Why add to the myth that Americans are all rich, and the possibilit of getting ripped off?), cowboy boots (too hot) and beach towels (unles you're staying in the cheapest of guest houses). Rather than dragging you whole address book along, which you'd hate to lose anyway, copy the ad dresses of friends to whom you plan to send postcards and tuck it into you wallet.

Fanny packs are excellent for carrying your money and camera, and a lc cooler than backpacks. Always lock your passport, extra money, plane ticke and other valuables in the in-room safe or check them at the front desk.

Remember, unless you're extremely fashion conscious, it's inevitable you' wear the same comfortable clothes again and again, so pack lightly. And b sure to leave room in your suitcase for souvenirs!

Money Managing

Unless you plan to bring huge sums of money with you or are staying very long time, it's much more convenient to NOT bring traveler's check There are two reasons for this advice: many establishments tack on at least 5 percent surcharge when cashing them; and worse, many places don't tak them at all. On the other hand, you always run a risk when carrying cash, s it basically comes down to a personal decision. If you do opt for traveler' checks, be sure to carry the numbered receipts separately from you money—you'll need them for a refund in the event of loss or theft. Membe of the Automobile Club of America (AAA) can get free traveler's checks, a can American Express cardholders.

A credit card is essential, even if you don't plan to use it. Most hotels won't give you a room without a credit card imprint, even if you're paying in cash. The same is true for car rental companies. This may be annoying, but perfectly understandable as hotels get ripped off constantly and with a credit card, they at least have a chance of recouping their losses. Also, you never know what emergencies may arise, so always carry a credit card. Visa and MasterCard are the most widely accepted and American Express is often honored, but the still relatively new Discover card has yet to make much of an inroad in the Caribbean.

Except for Puerto Rico, each destination has its own currency, but U.S. dollars are accepted virtually everywhere. In most cases, you won't even need to change money. If you do want to convert to local dollars, you're best off doing so at a bank, where the rate of exchange is invariably better than at hotels. In all instances, avoid the black market. In poor nations such as the Dominican Republic, you're setting yourself up for scams or outright robbery.

Unless you're a whiz at division and multiplication, it's a good idea to carry a small calculator when shopping to figure out how prices translate into U.S. dollars. The calculator can also be used to communicate and negotiate when you're dealing with someone who doesn't speak English.

Automatic Teller Machines (ATMs) are becoming more common throughout most islands, but not so that you can really rely on them, except in San Juan. If you're island hopping and need cash, seek out the ATM at the San Juan airport. It's also a good idea to tuck a few blank checks into your wallet—if you really get into trouble cash-wise, some major hotels will cash one for you (after a lot of begging). If you're really stuck, you can always get a cash advance on your credit card at a casino, but be warned that the service charges are exorbitant (about $17 for each $100).

When traveling about the island, always carry small bills. They are much more convenient for paying taxi and restaurant fares. Plus, it's rude to dicker over a price at the marketplace, get the seller down from $18 to $9, then present a $20 bill. Keep a supply of singles for tipping doormen and other personnel at your hotel, as necessary.

Above all, use your in-room safe (they are becoming increasingly standard) or check your valuables with the front desk. Nothing will ruin a vacation faster than getting ripped off—it's worth the few minutes of hassle to play it safe.

Documents

Each island requires some sort of identification to enter; details are given in the directory at the back of each chapter. Generally, you're best off with a passport, though some nations accept a photo I.D. such as a driver's license. (Often, expired passports are also acceptable.) Visas are generally not re-

quired for citizens of the U.S., Canada and the European Economic Cor
munity, but again, rules vary by island.

You'll often need to show proof that you're just a visitor and are not pla
ning to make the island your new home, often in the leave of a return pla
ticket. Sometimes you're even required to prove you have enough funds f
your length of stay.

When you purchase your plane ticket, the agent will inform you of any sp
cial documents needed. If he or she fails to volunteer this information, as
Cruise ship passengers need to bring a passport along, but usually don't ne
to show it at ports of call. Still, it's a good idea to take it along with you whe
debarking the ship, just in case.

Customs and Duties

As if coming home from a glorious Caribbean holiday isn't depressin
enough, you have to go through customs, unless Puerto Rico was your v
cation spot. (In that case, you don't pass through customs and can brin
back as much stuff as you want.) You'll fill out a simple form stating ho
much you spent on goods you're bringing back—if it's over $400, you
have to list each item. When shopping in duty-free stores, be sure to save th
receipts to show proof of purchase.

If you stay on an island less than 48 hours or have been outside the U.
within 30 days of your current trip, you can only bring back $25 worth
duty-free goods (except, again, for Puerto Rico).

If you've gone over the limit, you'll be taxed at a flat rate of 10 percent c
the first $1000 of merchandise. Except for gifts under $50 sent directly
the recipient, all items shipped home are considered dutiable.

Some people try to beat customs by wearing their new Rolex or emera
earrings and acting as if they've always owned them. This is not especia
recommended—you may need to show proof you did indeed leave the U.
with these expensive items. Conversely, if you're traveling with a Rolex
huge rock on your finger, it's a good idea to bring the receipt along to pro
you already owned it.

A NOTE ON DRUGS:

*Don't even think of trying to get illegal drugs into an island or back to the
U.S. It's just not worth the risk, and while few people busted in the Caribbean have "Midnight Express"-style horror stories to tell, remember you are
in a foreign country and you're under its rules. Carry prescription drugs in
their original containers to avoid hassles.*

For more information on duty-free allowances, contact the U.S. Customs ervice *(P.O. Box 7404, Washington, DC 20044; for taped information, call* ☎ *(202) 927-2095).*

Insurance and Refunds

You can insure everything from your valuables being stolen to your rental ar crashing to bad weather ruining your trip—it's up to you and how much f a gambler you are. A must: car rental collision insurance, unless your car wner's policy covers rental cars (many do, and it's well worth checking be- ore you leave home, as this is a big savings).

Always check the small print when booking a hotel and airline ticket. These ays most airlines charge anywhere from $30 to $50 (and more) if you hange your flight times; if you decide to scrap the whole trip, airline tickets re often nonrefundable. Most hotels require at least 48 hours' notice (and s much as two full weeks in the high season) to refund your deposit. When ruising, consider the optional insurance policy that lets you cancel at the last ninute, for any reason, and still get a refund.

When to Go

Common holidays such as Christmas and Easter are celebrated throughout he Caribbean. In addition, virtually every island has a large carnival, usually 1 February before Lent. These giant parties consist of parades, imaginative ostumes, food festivals, sports competitions and general fun. Trinidad's and Martinique's carnivals are among the most elaborate. The following guide sts the holidays and festivals unique to each island.

Aruba

Carnival is mid-to-late February, an island-wide celebration with street lancing, parades, live bands and the crowning of Carnival Queen. Aruba lso celebrates Good Friday, Easter Monday, National Anthem and Flag Day March 18), Queen's Birthday (April 30), Labor Day (May 1) and Boxing)ay (December 26).

Belize

St. George's Caye Day, Independence Day and Pan American Day are all elebrated nationwide with special events. The Cashew Festival (May) in Crooked Tree Village pays homage to the tasty nut. The Sea & Air Festival 1 San Pedro, held each August, is a musical extravaganza with competing •ands from across Central America.

Public holidays include Baron Bliss Day (March 9), Good Friday, Holy aturday, Easter Monday, Labor Day (May 1), Commonwealth Day (May !4), St. George's Caye Day (September 10), Independence Day (September 1), Columbus Day (October 12), Garifuna Settlement Day (November 19) nd Boxing Day (December 26).

Bonaire

Carnival takes place in February, which each October sees the annual sail
ing regatta. Other holidays include Coronation Day (April 30), St. John's
Day (June 24), St. Peter's Day (June 28) and Bonaire Day (September 6).

Cayman Islands

Pirate's Week, held late October, is a grand affair of swashbucklers ho-ho
hoing throughout George Town. Other holidays include Ash Wednesday,
Good Friday, Easter Monday (third Monday in May), Constitution Day
(first Monday in July) and the Monday after Remembrance Sunday (Novem
ber).

Cuba

Carnival is held each July in Havana and Santiago; the fun reaches a climax
on July 26. You'll also find local festivals throughout the country each sum
mer.

Curaçao

Carnival starts in late January with parades, dancing, music and other
events. In March, the Regatta attracts boat racers from the world over.
Other holidays are Chinese New Year (January), Harvest Festival (March),
Good Friday, Easter Monday, Queen's Birthday (June 30), Labor Day (May
1), Curacao Flag Day (July 2) and Boxing Day (December 26).

Dominican Republic

There's a big Merengue Festival each late July-August where locals per
form and dance to the spirited music in Santo Domingo (a smaller one is
held each October in Puerto Plata.) Holidays include Our Lady of La Alta
gracia (January 21), Durate's Birthday (January 26), Independence Day
(February 7), Restoration Day (August 16) and Our Lady of Las Mercedes
(September 24).

Haiti

Port-au-Prince's Carnival has declined in recent years, but it still happens
each year before Lent, with the three days before Ash Wednesday especially
riotous (literally, knife fights are not uncommon). Jacmel's Carnival, which
occurs at the same time, is a more traditional affair with good costumes.
After Carnival comes Rara, the "peasant carnival" with colorful bands roam
ing about seeking handouts. Again, the celebration can get too rowdy. On
All Saints Day and Day of the Dead (November 1 and 2), some residents
roam about dressed like corpses.

Jamaica

Carnival happens islandwide in April with costume parades, reggae and ca
lypso concerts and dancing in the streets. Negril has its own carnival each
May with a float parade, concerts, a mento band competition and Jonkanoo
and gereh dancing. Each August, the Reggae Sunsplash International Music

Festival in Montego Bay draws flocks of people. Jazz fans have a similar party in June in Ocho Rios. Public holidays include Ash Wednesday, Good Friday, Easter Monday, Labor Day (May 23), Independence Day (first Monday in August), National Heroes Day (third Monday in October) and Boxing Day (December 26).

Puerto Rico

In January, the annual San Sebastian Street Festival turns Old San Juan into a giant fiesta. Carnival happens each February with parades, costumes, coronations of queens and the traditional coastal burial of the sardine. Festival Pablo Casals celebrates the Spaniard (who lived here many years) with cultural concerts each June. Inquire upon arrival about the numerous patron saint and folklore festivals that take place throughout the year in various villages. Public holidays include those observed in the U.S., as well as Three King's Day (January 6), Eugeio de Hostos' Day (January 9), Martin Luther King's Birthday (January 16), Emancipation Day (March 22), Constitution Day (July 25) and Discovery Day (November 19).

Turks & Caicos

The big annual happenings are the celebration of the Queen's Birthday (second weekend in June), when all ex-servicemen wear their uniforms and metals are awarded; and the Provo Summer Festival (end of July) with boat races, beauty pageants, a carnival and a float parade. Public holidays are New Year's Day (January 1 and 3), Commonwealth Day (March 13), Good Friday, Easter Monday, National Heroes' Day (late May), Queen's Birthday (June), Emancipation Day (August 1), Columbus Day (October 9) and Boxing Day (December 26).

Yucatan Peninsula

Carnival is celebrated for three days before Ash Wednesday in both Cancun and Cozumel with all the usual merriment. On Holy Cross Day (May 3), construction workers mount decorated crosses on unfinished buildings, with fireworks and picnics at building sites. Christmas celebrations generally start on December 16. Public holidays include Constitution Day (February 5), the birthday of Benito Juarez (March 21), Labor Day (May 1), Battle of Puebla (May 5), Independence Day (September 16), Day of the Race (October 12) and Revolution Day (November 20).

Secret Tips for Caribbean Survival

Duty Free Does Not Necessarily Mean Cheaper

The term "duty-free" (a shopper's best friend) means that retailers are not required to pay import taxes on certain items, so they can pass these savings directly along to the consumer. Often that translates to prices 30 to 40 percent cheaper than in the U.S. Even islands not officially duty-free still often have duty-free shops at the airport or around the island, such as in Belize. Furthermore, on your way to an island, you can shop duty-free in major U.S. airports by showing your boarding pass.

While most duty-free items are truly a bargain, it isn't always necessarily so. Cigarettes, for example, often cost close to $17 per carton at airport duty-free shops, and you can often do better on the island itself (and even in some U.S. supermarkets). If you're planning to buy expensive French perfume or a good piece of jewelry, do some comparison shopping before leaving the U.S. to see how prices stack up. And remember, if the product is defective, you'll have a much easier time getting satisfaction from your local store than a little shop in the Caribbean.

Good duty-free bargains can generally be found on French perfumes, Dutch porcelain, Swiss crystal, fine bone china and woolens from England, linens and gemstones, especially emeralds.

Those Damn Surcharges

Most folks are genuinely amazed when checking out of a hotel and seeing their final hotel tab. Where did all these charges come from? What's this government tax? What on earth is a "service charge?"

While it's always a good idea to go over your bill with a fine-tooth comb, most of these charges, alas, are legitimate.

All hotels (even all-inclusive) charge a government tax of anywhere from 5-10 percent of your nightly room rate. The service charge, which averages 10-15 percent, is supposedly for maids and other staff—whether they actually ever see it or not is another matter. Still, don't feel obligated to tip extra if the service charge is included. Many hotels automatically tack on a service charge whenever you charge a meal or drink to your room, and room service checks virtually always include a service charge. In these cases, it's not necessary to tip the bartender or waiter. If you're not sure, ask. Energy surcharges are sometimes added to the bill to help defray the costs of electricity when prices are quite high. Note that all these charges are rarely, if ever, mentioned in the brochure or when you inquire about rates.

The biggest killers are the telephone surcharges. Ironically, it seems the more expensive the hotel, the higher the telephone rates. Many charge around $1 per local phone call, even if you're calling an 800 number to use your credit card. If you dial direct to the U.S., be prepared for exorbitant fees—double or triple the amount of your call. If you must call the States direct, have your party immediately call you back—you'll save a lot of money that way. Also consider buying a phone card, which are springing up all over the islands, wherein you pay a flat fee (say, $10) for a prescribed amount of ime. When you can use your stateside carrier's credit card (such as ATT, Sprint and MCI) you'll invariably save, but note that their 800 access numbers are often not reachable from the Caribbean, even with operator assistance.

Beware of the minibar—that tempting bottle of Red Stripe probably costs double or triple the usual price. If you don't trust your will power regarding raiding the fridge and gobbling down all those $5 candy bars (which cost 50 cents in the store) leave the minibar key at the front desk.

If you're a drinker, you'll really drop dead when you get your cruise ship bill. (Most lines give you a preliminary statement a few days before the end of the trip to help ease the final shock.) The cruise fare usually doesn't include drinks—alcohol and otherwise—and while the prices are reasonable, they really add up. You'll also pay port taxes (about $75 per person), any shopping you did aboard, those tempting pictures snapped by the ship's photographers, casino chips charged to your cabin (an especially dangerous habit to fall into) and any ship-run shore excursions.

The biggest expense, and one you must plan for, are the tips given out at the end of the cruise. Most cruise lines hand out printed guidelines and even give formal talks on the art of tipping, but the general rule of thumb is that waiters and cabin stewards get $3 per day per person and busboys (they're rarely female) and wine stewards get $1.50 per day per person. You may be tempted to skip the tips, after all, you're leaving and will never see these people again—but keep in mind that the service staff's salary is virtually nil, with tips making up the vast majority of their income. So bring aboard enough cash for tips, then forget about it until the last night, when tips are usually distributed in envelopes provided by the cruise line. You may also want to tip the bartender and maitre'd if he took special care of you, but that's completely optional. It's never necessary to tip those higher up the chain such as the cruise director and shore excursions manager.

Ten Ways to Save Money

1) Choose a cheap destination.

Just as a vacation in the Midwest is usually a lot cheaper than one in New York, prices vary widely from island to island. Among the cheapest in the West are the Dominican Republic, Haiti and Belize. (Conversely, among the most expensive are Jamaica and Turks.) And remember, just because it costs less, it doesn't mean you're settling for second best. See the descriptions of each island to see if you're a good fit.

2) Consider a self-catering holiday.

Securing lodging with a kitchenette or full kitchen can save you big bucks over eating in restaurants. Food establishments at resorts can be particularly expensive—you may pay as much as $10 just for a bagel and cup of coffee. Be sure to ask exactly what the kitchen contains before making your reservation. Some come equipped with microwaves, dishwashers and high-quality dishes and cookware, while others consist of little more than a hot plate and refrigerator.

3) Go with another couple.

If you're a couple chummy with another twosome, consider taking your holiday together and staying in a two-bedroom condo or villa. You'll save big on lodging and also a rental car, but be sure you like these people enough to spend your hard-earned vacation with them.

4) Swap houses.

This requires a lot of lead time (generally a year) but can be well worth it if you find a Caribbean homeowner who wants to swap houses or apartments for a week or two. Two organizations (**Intervac**, ☎ *(800) 756-4663* and **Vacation Exchange Club**, ☎ *(800) 638-3841*) publish a directory of interested homeowners. It costs from $46 to $60 to be listed. These services will also supply you with guidelines—obviously, you want to check out the person carefully to avoid getting ripped off and want to get as many details as possible about their home.

5) Travel in the off season.

You'll save big on airfare, lodgings and even rental cars if you travel to the Caribbean during the summertime. Yes, it can be very hot, but then again you have that splendid sea in which to spend the day. Off-season travel also has the distinct advantage of sharing the beaches, museums and attractions with fewer people. But note that many shops and restaurants reduce their hours in the summer, so your choices may be more limited. Jamaica's all-inclusive offers great summer deals.

6) Book a package deal.

Virtually every resort offers packages that include meals, rental cars, sightseeing and so on. Divers especially should look to properties that cater to them—Bonaire's Harbour Village and Captain Don's come to mind—while golfers can be kept happy with packages on Jamaica and Puerto Rico that include greens fees.

7) Don't be too quick to sign up for the meal plan.

Major hotels and resorts often offer, and heavily promote, meal plans that keep their guests on site, which keeps stockholders happy. But they are not necessarily such a great deal. Just as importantly, buying a meal plan locks you into eating in the same restaurant or two night after night—hardly the way to get to know the island. If you're unsure about the meal plan, wait until you arrive and can scope out the scene before committing.

8) Try a guest house.

Sure you'll sacrifice room service, free postcards and usually a swimming pool, but you'll gain a wealth of island flavor and lots of inside tips, assuming the owner is friendly and chatty (most are). Puerto Rico's government-sponsored paradores can be especially charming, and several on Belize's beach towns offer great savings over full-service hotels and resorts. You'll especially save if you're willing to share a bath

If you're unsure about the property, ask to see a room before checking in—no reputable operation will refuse.

9) Be flexible.

If you're lucky enough to have a schedule that allows for last-minute trips, you can score big in the savings department. Scan the travel sections of your local newspaper for promotions and ask your travel agent to be on the lookout for good deals. This can especially pay off with cruises—lines hate to sail empty, so will often offer deep discounts a few weeks out.

10) Stock your refrigerator.

Even most of the cheapest hotels outfit their rooms with a refrigerator; if not, invest in a Styrofoam cooler. Keep it stocked with beer, wine, juice and soft drinks and you'll save a lot of money over using the minibar or room service. If the hotel has jammed your minibar to the gills (most do), buy identical drinks at the liquor or grocery store and simply restock it yourself. Carry your cooler to the pool or beach so you don't have to buy drinks from the roving waiters. Buying a sackful of groceries such as donuts, cereal, fruit, bread and cheese can save big bucks on breakfast and lunch.

Health Precautions

There are very few health risks throughout the Western Caribbean. In many cases the water is safe to drink (even if it doesn't taste so great); always inquire at your hotel if you're not sure. They'll give you an honest answer—the last thing these people want is a bunch of sick guests on their hands.

The biggest health threat in the Caribbean—as, alas, the world over these days—is from AIDS and other sexually transmitted diseases. Use condoms! It's best to bring them from home because they are not always as readily available on smaller islands as we've grown accustomed to seeing them in the U.S. Latex condoms offer much more protection than those made of lambskin.

It's always a good idea to carry along a small bottle of stomach medicine such as Mylanta, diarrhea aids such as Pepto Bismol, Imodium and pain relievers like aspirin or Tylenol. Don't assume you'll be able to find such items on the island. (No problem in Jamaica, but lots of luck on Cuba.) If you require injections, bring your own sterile syringes and consider buying disposable ones from a U.S. pharmacy before you leave.

Fortunately, malaria is generally no longer a threat (except possibly in the Dominican Republic and Haiti), which is good news, since you can count on providing lots of free meals for mosquitoes and no-see-ums.

Watch out for the sun, it's going to be a lot stronger than you think, especially on overcast days when you may forget to apply sunscreen. Though getting a killer tan is high on many tourists' list of things to do, start slowly with a strong sunscreen, then once you work up a good base tan, gradually switch to a lower number. (Of course dermatologists recommend no tan at all, bu let's deal with reality.)

The high humidity will probably make you perspire more than usual. Drink lots of fluids to avoid dehydration (water is best) to replace the ones you're oozing through your pores.

Guests at all-inclusive properties invariably go wild the first night with al those free drinks—then pay dearly for it the next day. Keep that in mind as you order your fourth pina colada.

Buying prepared food from street vendors is generally safe, but do check out the operation. Is the meat kept refrigerated? Are the utensils clean When buying bottled water, especially on the street, check that the tamper proof band is intact. Some unscrupulous vendors will refill bottles with tap water; be especially wary in Mexico.

Illegal Drugs

If you're a recreational drug user, you'll generally have no problem scoring high-quality marijuana (called ganga on many islands) at prices much cheap er than the U.S. In Jamaica you'll be deluged with dealers offering illega substances. We're not endorsing this, but if you are intent on buying drugs use common sense and stay away from dim alleyways, deserted parking lot and the like. You can often ask your trusty bellboy or bartender where it's OK to score. Bring your own pipe or rolling papers because they can be hard to find on some islands. It's incredibly stupid to buy anything stronger than pot because heaven only knows what they are lacing cocaine, crystal meth and other potent drugs with. As stated earlier, don't even think of trying to bring drugs into another country or back into the U.S.—it's just not worth the risk.

Weather—or Not

Californians cope with earthquakes and mudslides, East Coasters deal with blizzards and ice storms and Midwesterners have bitter cold and flash floods In the Caribbean the enemy is the hurricane.

Hurricane season is an annual event that generally runs from June to Sep tember. Most turn out to be little more than pesky rainstorms or dramatic electrical displays, but some are deadly and should be taken dead serious Thirty years ago, Hurricane Hattie was strong enough to literally rip a Bel izean island in two, and Hurricane Hugo devastated St. Croix, St. Eustatius and other islands in 1989. In September 1995, Luis and Marilyn wreaked havoc on several Caribbean islands, including the Puerto Rican island Cule bra. Heed the warnings of locals who know of what they speak when it comes to threatening weather.

Mother Nature's other biggest drawback is the high humidity that lingers on the islands all year long and is especially uncomfortable in the summer. It won't kill you (though it sometimes feels like it will) but take care to avoid overexertion and drink lots of water to keep hydrated.

Island Etiquette

While some of your best vacation photos will be candid shots of locals, keep in mind that many folks—older ones especially—often don't appreciate being part of your tourist experience. Always ask before snapping someone's photo and take a refusal with grace. Kids, on the other hand, usually love to get the attention and will often ask YOU to take their picture. Indulge them, even if you're down to your last shot (better to fake taking the picture than hurt their feelings), and besides, you'll probably get some really cute shots.

Carry small bills when dealing with street vendors and in marketplaces where you'll be negotiating prices.

In museums and restaurants, keep your negative feelings to yourself (or at least whisper them to your companion) about the lousy artwork or crappy food. You may find you just hate conch, but remember that it's a staple in many island diets, so try not to be judgmental. On the other hand, if the food is truly inedible, you have every right to send it back.

No one should have to endure lousy service, but extra patience will be required in the Caribbean. Everything is on a slower pace, and that, alas, includes waitresses and cooks.

Respect local rules and customs regarding the formality of dress. In most cases shorts and T-shirts are just fine, but most churches ban them, even if you're just ducking in for a quick peek. Bathing suits are nearly always improper anywhere but on the beach or at the pool. If you want to go topless, make sure it's considered acceptable on the island.

Make a genuine effort to speak the language on places such as the Dominican Republic, where English speakers are relatively rare. No matter how terrible your syntax or pronunciation, such efforts are greatly appreciated, and people will be much more apt to help you out than if you just walk up expecting them to speak your language.

Above all, do your fellow countrymen a big favor, and don't act like the Ugly American. It's no wonder everyone thinks we're all rich the way some U.S. travelers flash around large bills and expensive jewelry. (And actually, if we can afford a Caribbean vacation—even on the cheap—we are pretty rich compared to most locals.) Be sensitive to the fact that on most of these islands, life is much simpler and less materialistic. Remember, too, that you are a guest in this foreign land. Sure, you're paying for it, but that doesn't mean you've bought the right to impose your values on people of different cultures.

Here's a huge generalization, but it does apply: Islanders are usually quite reserved and will often avoid eye contact, especially on the street. However, it's amazing how far a smile and a "good day" will go. Try it, and you'll be pleasantly surprised and left all atingle in good feelings.

WEST CARIBBEAN
SNAPSHOTS

From the jungles of Belize to the arid shores of Aruba, the Western Caribbean has great diversity—and great things in store for visitors. Here's a quick look at each destination's highlights.

Aruba

This Dutch Leeward island, located 18 miles from Venezuela, is certainly not among the Caribbean's prettiest islands, but it still does a smashing business with watersports enthusiasts who come to dive, windsurf and snorkel in its calm waters. The island is quite dry and receives very little rain, so you can usually count on hot, sunny days. Accommodations are sophisticated and nightlife is good in the many casinos and discos. The people are prosperous and very accommodating.

Belize

Belize is not an island, but its Central America location along the shores of the Caribbean Sea and vast popularity as a dive site make it well worth including in these pages. Belize is a poor (though democratic) Third World country, so accommodations are often somewhat lacking. Not lacking at all, however, are things to do besides dive and snorkel among the huge coral reefs—jungle trekking, caving, sportsfishing and exploring ancient Maya ruins, to name just a few. The people are friendly and English-speaking. Another bonus: It's cheap!

Bonaire

Word is out on this small island, near Aruba and part of the Dutch ABC chain (as in Aruba, Bonaire and Curacao), as a prime diving destination. The result is a building boom that loyalists fear will sink it right into the sea—or at the least, ruin its peaceful charm. So come now! The 112-square-mile island has just 11,000 residents and extremely diverse topography, with green hills and rocky beaches adding interest to the flat, almost desertlike terrain of the south. The island is relatively affordable and the people are gentle souls intent on keeping their paradise intact despite the development.

Cayman Islands

This complex of three islands—Cayman Brac, Little Cayman and Grand Cayman—is due south of Cuba and just an hour's flight from Miami. Most of the tourist action takes place on Grand Cayman's West Bay Beach, a glorious place to unwind and forget the real world. Diving is the big attraction in the Caymans—Sting Ray City, where you can pet the little buggers, is especially popular. Caymanians have a high standard of living and are courteous and helpful to visitors.

Cuba

Residents of the U.S. are forbidden by law to visit the land of Fidel Castro, but that doesn't stop many from flying in through Canada or Mexico to see what all the fuss is about (just make sure they don't stamp your passport in Cuba, or you'll be answering to the State Department when you get back home). This last bastion of communism is heartbreakingly poor, but the people are nonetheless filled with an exuberance and love of life. With its excellent beaches, Cuba was a favorite playground of Americans until the Castro-led revolution resulted in a Cold War between it and the U.S. Today's tourists will find most accommodations merely adequate and food somewhat hard to come by, but a visit to Cuba remains a feather in the cap of well-seasoned travelers.

Curaçao

Like its siblings, the C in the Dutch ABC chain has excellent diving, though Europeans are much more hip to this fact than Americans. Located off the coast of Venezuela, the landscape is drab and arid, but man-made structures, especially in the capital city of Willemstad, are so colorful and pic turesque that the island has a genuine charm. Besides exploring the dazzling underwater marine park, tourists visit the several interesting historic structures and museums; good beaches, however, are rare. Locals, a varied mix of nationalities, are relatively well off.

Dominican Republic

Prices are cheap in this Spanish-speaking nation, which covers more than two-thirds of the Island of Hispaniola (the rest is comprised of Haiti). Santo Domingo is the oldest city in the Western Hemisphere, and history buffs go crazy exploring its many excellent museums and old churches. The beaches are great and there are 14 national parks and seven reserves to be trekked. The people are very poor but have a genuine friendliness and a great passion for dance, particularly the merengue. A high crime rate and the aura of general poverty can mar a vacation for inexperienced travelers.

Haiti

Occupying the western third of Hispaniola (the rest of the large island belongs to the Dominican Republic), Haiti is home to some seven million people, mostly Creole-speaking. This is the Caribbean's most mountainous country and its once luxurious rainforest has been slashed and burned almost to extinction. Life here is grindingly poor—the country is vastly overpopulated, most people are illiterate and life expectancies are low. Despite all their hardships, residents are friendly and have a great sense of humor. But Haiti's infamous and often violent political struggles make this a destination only for the most savvy traveler looking for a completely different adventure.

Jamaica

Long one of the Caribbean's most popular destinations, Jamaica is a beautiful country complete with mountains, rivers, stunning waterfalls and sophisticated resorts (all-inclusive are especially prevalent here). Located just 90 miles south of Cuba, its glorious beaches are the main lure. Jamaicans are friendly, outgoing and worship Bob Marley and his reggae offshoots; the island's large population of Rastafarians are a peaceful people whose sometimes intimidating look merely masks a gentle soul. The biggest problems for tourists are a high crime rate and the overwhelming pushiness of vendors selling everything from cheap jewelry to potent ganga.

Puerto Rico

Most first-time visitors to this American territory are happily surprised by its gorgeous scenery, excellent beaches and fine resorts. San Juan sees most of the tourist action and has a charming historic district and excellent museums to supplement its glorious stretches of sand. Rugged mountain ranges and lush rainforests are also in abundant supply. Puerto Rico offers tourists one of the most well-rounded vacation experiences, and has great duty-free shopping to boot. The people are Spanish speaking but many also speak English; many wish for independence. Crime can be a problem, especially in the cities, so use the same precautions you'd use anywhere.

Turks and Caicos

These two groups of more than 40 islands form an archipelago north of Haiti. Seven-square-mile Grand Turk is the seat of government and has a handful of small historic hotels and nice beaches. Most tourists head for 37 square-mile Providencials (formerly known as Provo and still called that), the most developed and home to an excellent golf course and the splashiest resorts, including a Club Med. The limestone islands have more than 200 miles of white sand beaches and excellent diving among its offshore reefs.

Yucatan Peninsula

The Yucatan Peninsula, located in southeast Mexico and bordered by the Caribbean Sea to the east, draws its fair share of vacationers looking for dazzling beaches, scenic natural lagoons and colorful coral reefs. The main sun-and-fun destinations are Cancun and Cozumel, each nicely developed for tourists with fine hotels and resorts and sophisticated restaurants. Inland you'll find tropical jungles and ancient Maya ruins. The people are generally warm and welcoming, and English is spoken in the major tourist centers.

WESTERN CARIBBEAN ADVENTURE

By David Swanson

On Foot

It may surprise some readers, but it actually snows in the Caribbean. Not in quantities that are enough to ski, and certainly not with any regularity, but the lofty 10,370-foot summit of **Pico Duarte** in the Dominican Republic usually receives one or two dustings of snow each winter. I point this out by way of establishing that hiking in the Western Caribbean can yield the truly unexpected. A flip side of the multi-day ascent of Pico Duarte might be the walking excursion to **Cayman Brac's eastern tip**, where a verdant limestone bluff rises to a modest 140 feet above sea level and provides a home to the elusive Cayman Brac parrot and a boisterous colony of brown boobies.

The sharp cry of the eco-tourism monster is ringing through the region and, for reasons good, bad and inconsequential, government tourism offices are groping about blindly to try and cash in on the latest rubbernecking craze. The effects aren't usually bad, and sometimes they are spectacularly successful on a number of levels. But so often it seems that the end result—a better educated visitor and/or indirect financial support of the environment—is a mere afterthought in the process. Ideally, eco-tourism is a con-

cept whose time has come, even if the idea needs polishing by a fe
opportunistic governments. As this book goes to press, a greater quantity o
trails and paths are being utilized and promoted than ever before, and mor
are being developed to cater to the increasingly eco-conscious visitor.

Most of the hikes we've listed can be made on your own. On occasio
there will be recommendations regarding the use of local guides, obtained
either through a guide service or, sometimes, by inquiring in the vicinity o
the trailhead. By and large, on the more impoverished islands, there is le
government money to spend on trail upkeep and markers, making guides
prerequisite for first-time visitors. In some areas, however, island tourism o
fices will strongly encourage using a guide for trails of only moderate diff
culty; the hidden agenda, obviously, is indirect support of the loc
economy.

There are at least three main reasons for using a guide. The guide will he
lead you through genuinely difficult or exposed areas. A good guide will ad
to your trek by explaining the natural environment you are exploring and th
historical significance of ruins you may encounter, as well as provide an in
side glimpse into the local character of the island. And hiring a guide con
tributes to the local economy by directly supporting an individual, some o
whom spend a good deal of their "spare" time maintaining trails.

There are also at least three reasons against hiring guides. Some of the trai
where guides are recommended by tourist offices are not that difficult fo
hikers of reasonable ability. The well-meaning conversation a guide will en
gage in may detract from your solitude or desired enjoyment of the natur
environment. And for those of us visiting the Caribbean on a budget, guide
are usually expensive; it's not uncommon to spend over a hundred dollars o
more for a guide on a major trail, which can add up after a few hikes.

While the quality of guides available on various islands differs greatly, w
urge you to use your own judgment, keeping in mind that a good guide wi
do much more than point you to your destination, and can greatly add to th
experience of the hike. If you plan to hike several major trails on an islan
hire a guide for at least the first day so that you gain a sense of the difficulti
you will be encountering, as well as an appreciation for the plant life and hi
tory of the area. You may decide that you'll want to use that guide's servic
for the remainder of your visit.

There are a few precautions hikers should take before embarking on an
trail. First, carry plenty of fresh water. Rivers, as clean and refreshing as the
may appear, are not generally safe to drink from. The parasite bilharziasis
frequently found in some slow-moving streams and lakes, and the illness
causes can even be deadly. Let the heat and humidity of the tropics be a con
stant reminder to drink bottled water regularly while exercising. If you fe

dehydrated at the end of the day, slightly increase the salt in your diet, which will help you retain fluids when exercising.

If you're walking through areas where shade is minimal, the sun will be intense. The hot "ABC islands" (Aruba, Bonaire and Curacao) are particularly exposed, and the Caymans, Turks and Caicos can also be remiss in throwing you shade. Even in moderate doses of an hour or two, the sun can cause severe sunburns that will crimp your style for an entire vacation and, in extreme cases, can cause sunstroke (and we won't even start on the skin cancer topic). For the former, use sun block at all times, taking into account that much of the lotion will drip off during sweat-inducing activities. For the latter, minimize your time in the sun, particularly at the start of a trip, wear sunglasses and a tasteful wide-brimmed hat and, again, always drink plenty of fluids. If you plan to do more than a day or two of hiking, consider bringing along a Gatorade-style drink (available in powdered form) which will help replace lost electrolytes. For severe cases of dehydration, consult a doctor.

Watch out for the ghastly manchineel tree. Its fruit, which looks something like a green crab apple, is very poisonous. But problems with the tree don't end there: if you stand under a manchineel during rainfall, the runoff from the leaves can cause blisters. Like the fruit, the tree's sap is also quite potent and was once used by Carib Indians to dip their arrowheads in before heading out for a missionary slaughter. In more heavily traveled areas, particularly around beaches, locals will frequently post warning signs on the trees (some manchineels are marked with red paint). However, in more remote areas, you're on your own. Have an islander point out the tree shortly after arrival so you can avoid it on your explorations. Also note that the sap from the oleander is also poisonous.

Snakes are not generally a problem in the Caribbean. Although there are many local varieties, none are considered poisonous, and the intimidating boa constrictors found on a few islands are content to leave humans alone. One problematic encounter is that with a scorpion, recognized by the stinger arching over its back. Although generally not fatal, scorpions boast a painful defense strategy and are best avoided; they are usually found in hot, dry areas. Finally, two mere nuisances are mosquitoes and sand-flies, found principally in areas of stagnant water and on beaches, respectively. They are best combated with insect repellent, although moving out of the afflicted area usually does the trick.

Wear appropriate clothing for your treks. It may be difficult to conceive of in the balmy Caribbean, but temperatures drop as one climbs into cloud-wrapped mountains. Combined with perspiration, brisk wind, and humidity or rain, these conditions can be ideal for hypothermia. The hike to the summit of Pico Duarte, or even to the 7402-foot Blue Mountain Peak of Jamaica, attain altitudes where temperatures can drop below freezing in the winter months. For any hike ascending elevations above 3000 feet, we recommend packing a pair of long pants and a light windbreaker jacket. Although heavy hiking boots aren't really necessary in the Caribbean, a sturdy pair of walking shoes, broken in before your trip (to avoid blisters), is generally sufficient. Before you invest a chunk of change on a tasteful pair of new shoes, remember that you may be hiking on muddy paths or through streams that are sure to alter the appearance of the most colorful designs! As appealing as it might be at some points, walking barefoot is not a good idea; hookworms can penetrate skin.

By Pedal

It makes sense that, following the explosion of mountain biking in the U.S., it would catch on sooner or later in the Caribbean. And why not? What could be more inviting than riding through charming island villages, past rolling fields of sugarcane and down to silky white beaches? Those interested in more demanding explorations will find an ample quantity of steep hills and challenging forest trails on the mountainous islands. The sport is still in its nascent stages—you will be observed as a distinct curiosity on most islands—but there are biking organizations beginning to develop on some of the larger islands, as well as an increasing quantity of rental shops carrying a variety of the better brands known at home.

It is possible to ship your bike into the Caribbean on the same plane you are arriving on, although the disadvantages may far outweigh the relative ease of renting from a local shop. If your bike uses exotic parts, you may want to bring the unique items and a tool kit with you. Don't ship anything fragile (like a top-of-the-line road bike) that you wouldn't want banged around. I watched as one island baggage handler tossed a boxed bicycle onto the airport's baggage conveyer-belt hard enough to have the handlebars puncture the cardboard. Moments later, as the bike turned a corner, it flopped sadly off the belt and onto the floor where it sat unattended while its owner stood trapped in a long customs line.

The rental agencies we've listed on each island differ greatly in what they provide. Most of the businesses we've listed are set up specifically to cater to tourists, while a few are stores which focus primarily on sales to locals, renting to visitors as a way of supplementing business. The number of bikes the shops carry also varies significantly. If the popularity of biking continues to increase, the number of bikes available to rent in the Caribbean could easily double in the next couple of years.

In a few cases, the rental stores have well-staffed repair shops and can handle virtually any problem you may encounter with your own bike on the island. On other islands, the shops may be strictly a rental agency and are limited to servicing only what they rent in their repair facilities. Some of the better shops are happy to substitute your peddles and clips if you are bringing your own shoes, but call in advance if you want to count on it.

When renting a bike, check to make sure the seat and handlebars are adjusted for your height. Discovering that your bike doesn't "fit" a few miles from the shop is annoying. Verify that tires are adequately filled and learn how to use the air pump for the bike you are renting (it may be foreign to what you are used to at home). If you don't know how to patch a tire, have someone in the shop spend a few minutes showing you how; if you're planning a long ride, carry a spare tube, if possible.

As with hiking, bicycling comes with some warning precautions. In addition to carrying plenty of bottled water, "hydrate" your body by guzzling a quart or two of water before you hit the road. You may find it helpful to bring along energy bars or powdered drinks which help maintain your stamina and replace electrolytes. Heed prior warnings concerning the sun, which can be relentless on some treeless roads (see "On Foot"). Helmets are an essential component of safe riding; although most or all of the shops provide them, bring one from home if you can.

Bike and Cruise Tours

☎ *(503) 667-4053.*
If you are willing to dedicate your entire Caribbean vacation to cycling, Linda Thompson offers biking tours in conjunction with Norwegian Cruise Line sailings out of Puerto Rico. Bikes are provided in Puerto Rico, loaded onto the ship, and a leader and preset riding itinerary averaging 20-25 miles each day greets cyclists on each island. Group size varies but usually averages a couple dozen riders; prices start at about $1850 (from the east coast) including airfare, seven-day cruise, bike rental and port taxes.

Underwater

When divers dream of the Caribbean, typically they fantasize about Bonaire, the Caymans, Belize, Cozumel, and the Turks and Caicos Islands.

These four destinations alone are among the world's great underwater challenges, but the entire Western Caribbean offers a veritable smorgasbord of dive possibilities.

Each area has its specialties. In addition to the famed **Blue Hole**, Belize has three atolls off its 175-mile barrier reef, each featuring remote lodges catering specifically to dive visitors. For better or worse, **Grand Cayman** has perfected the dive vacation and offers a well-organized diving infrastructure which appeals to those who are new to the sport; it doesn't hurt that the Caymans have a series of magnificent walls and dozens of sites to tour (and don't forget the region's best animal encounter, **Sting Ray City**). **Bonaire** is the environmentalist's choice, matching its spectacular reefs with a strictly enforced underwater protection plan. This same island offers one of the world's best collections of shore dives, allowing you to visit Bonaire for a couple of weeks, and dive two or three times daily without ever getting into a boat: just park and dive. In **Cozumel**, drift diving is the specialty, letting divers glide swiftly through spectacularly carved valleys and mountains which seem to be scaled down versions of the Grand Canyon. Freshwater diving has also developed a niche on the east coast of the **Yucatan Peninsula,** at **Akumal**, where an extensive series of underground limestone caverns beckon cave enthusiasts. The **Turks and Caicos Islands** are a less-publicized destination, but offer several breathtaking walls; the Turks have the added bonus of being a front-row seat for the annual winter migration of 3000 humpback whales. Wreck lovers will find real and man-made sites off **Aruba**, home to the *Antilla*, a WWII relic scuttled by her German captain to avoid capture, which maintains a secure post as one of the Caribbean's finest, and most popular, wreck dives. **Curacao** and **Puerto Rico** are relatively new dive frontiers, particularly for Americans, but both offer excellent reefs and walls.

Or perhaps your dive dreams are simpler; let's say, just trying it, for starters. Learning to dive is a less complicated and more available exercise than many people imagine. You've probably heard of hours spent in a classroom obtaining certification. While this in itself probably appeals to no one, you can try diving in a much easier fashion by signing up for a resort course. These half-day introductions into the world of diving are available through most major dive shops, generally for around $75. While there is some classroom-style information, the course culminates, usually in a pool or shallow reef, with actual diving in full regalia.

If you are certain that diving is something you're willing to fall in love with, then you'll want to obtain certification—your "C" card—which allows you to dive on your own without needing an instructor to tag along (although all diving should be done with a buddy). You can take the entire course at home spread out over several weeks or months (usually starting in a pool, graduating to a lake or ocean dive), or you can do it all in the Caribbean, concentrated into five or six days. An increasingly popular option is a combination of the two, allowing you to review the classroom material at home (usually via video), and save the actual water training for your vacation. Another route is to obtain your certification one dive at a time spread over several vacations and different destinations; NAUI calls this their "Passport Diver" program and it allows you to pick up the course wherever you left off, spread out over a period of months or even years.

Another new option is the fleet of "live-aboard" vessels which ply the waters of the Western Caribbean with increasing popularity. The advantage, obviously, is that you can maximize your actual diving time on a vacation (up to four or five dives per day), and minimize the hassle of traveling to and from dive sites. Additionally, live-aboards generally visit more remote areas, like the **Blue Hole in Belize**, **French Cay** in the **Caicos**, or the **West Wall of Grand Cayman**, which are difficult to reach by day boats. Like a cruise ship, the live-aboards are all-inclusive (though BC, regulators and computers must be rented if you don't bring your own); also like a cruise ship, you are hostage to a fairly strict itinerary and you'll have little or no interaction with island life. However, for divers who just can't get enough, the one-week live-aboard trips are a very popular option. It's also possible to become certified on the live-aboards; for an extra charge, you may obtain open-water certification on the Peter Hughes boats, or the entire classroom and open-water course on the Aggressor trips. The chapters in which you'll find live-aboard choices are Belize, the Cayman Islands, and the Turks and Caicos Islands; trips start at about $1495, plus airfare.

It goes without saying that diving is a serious, potentially dangerous sport. There are universal risks, which won't be addressed here, and there are those which are fairly unique to the Caribbean. One that isn't a hazard, fortunately, is sharp-toothed creatures. The ferocious shark activity common in the Bahamas is actually rare in the Western Caribbean. Nurse sharks are spotted throughout the region, but they are typically shy and unproblematic, content to nap under ledges. On rare occasion, hammerheads will be seen where deeper waters approach dive sites (like sea mounts), but they tend to stay their distance. The huge, graceful whale shark is observed in the Western Caribbean in only one location, southern Belize, and infrequently at that; the timid creature is affably tolerant of human interaction. Barracudas and moray eels, both of which can pack a powerful punch, also tend to be shy and won't usually bite unless provoked or cornered.

On the other hand, there are several, more innocuous creatures which do create problems. One is fire coral, which is found throughout the region, and remains most deserving of its name. Although the nasty sting you'll feel after touching it will eventually go away, it can be inflamed by scratching the area of your skin that came into contact (quickly fanning your hands around the affected area while underwater helps to dispel the coral darts which cause the pain). On the same theme, avoid the beautiful fireworm, which also defends itself with bunches of tiny daggers. Another tough customer is more obvious: the black sea urchin has dozens of sharp needles protruding from its body like a pincushion. These spines can grow up to a foot long and will back up their sting with a dose of venom. More serious still is the scorpionfish, which frequently appears to be just another rock, until it's stepped on, at which point it releases a potentially fatal toxin; medical attention should be sought immediately.

In listing dive operators, we've identified their major diving affiliations, i.e PADI, NAUI, SSI, etc. The reality is, association with one of these organizations does not ensure that the outfit is indeed good. Dive shops pay a fee to obtain these affiliations, and many in the dive community are annoyed by the cache these names carry. If you are making arrangements to dive exclusively with a single shop on you trip, it's probably wise to get feedback from other divers on a particular operator.

The dive sites we have listed are by no means comprehensive, and aren't necessarily "the best" a given island has to offer. We have tried to create a representative sample of the kinds of dives available, avoiding, what one operator referred to obliquely as "proprietary" sites which aren't known to others. Where we've graded sites as being suitable for beginners, note that few if any, of these locations are appropriate as a first dive. A beginner or novice site is usually for divers who have completed their certification or, at least, are in the company of a trained instructor.

CRUISE PORTS

Cruising can be so addicting that it's sometimes hard to even get off the ship at a port of call. If you do choose to do so, you have several options for exploring that day's island. The cruise company will try hard to get you to take one of their organized shore excursions, which often include lunch. The advantage is that you'll be shown around safely and you'll always be back on time to catch the ship. The drawback, however, is that their prices can be quite high, often as much as 100 percent above what you'd pay on your own. If you're adventurous, it's better to explore on your own, but keep a sharp eye on the time, as cruise ships set sail promptly as scheduled with or without straggling passengers.

Aruba

Island Tour

A tour for landlubbers focusing on the island's markets, historical sites and scenic vistas. Highlights are the Frenchmen Pass and St. Ann's Church in the village of Noord.

Atlantis Submarine

A 30-minute cruise aboard a catamaran takes you to the dive site on the island's southeast coast. A 50-minute tour of the ocean floor follows and includes looks at coral reefs and associated marine life.

Seaworld Explorer

The semi-submarine Seaworld Explorer tours the spectacular Arashi Reef and the wreck of the *Antilla*, a German freighter that went down during World War II, leaving behind the largest shipwreck in the Caribbean. Other tours aboard the vessel also are offered.

Snorkeling

A catamaran takes you from the dock to the snorkeling site of Arashi, the west point of the island.

SCUBA

Certified divers only are invited to view the wreck of the *Pedernalis*, torpedoed during World War II by a German submarine. The dive site may change due to weather conditions.

Belize

Cruise ships do not stop at the port in this country.

Bonaire

Washington National Park

Nature lovers will be intrigued by this 13,500-acre preserve that offers excellent hiking and birding opportunities.

Bonaire Marine Park

Both snorkelers and divers will enjoy this underwater marine park that descends to a depth of nearly 200 feet. Divers have dubbed it one of the best scuba areas in the world, so you won't be disappointed.

Cayman Islands

Combination Island Tour

It's a trip to Hell and back, but there's nothing remotely evil about this tour, which emphasizes land and sea. Observe marine life at the underwater observatory at Sting Ray City, then visit the Cayman Turtle Farm, local historic sites, and Hell, named for the eerie rock formations that surround it.

Island Tour

See the island's historic sites, the Cayman Turtle Farm, and the unspoiled Seven Mile Beach. Stop at Hell's post office to send that special someone a postcard from Hell.

Seaworld Explorer

View Grand Cayman's underwater world without getting wet aboard the *Seaworld Explorer*, a semi-submarine (glass-bottomed boat) that allows you to view coral reefs, tropical fish, and even a shipwreck in air-conditioned comfort. A guide provides commentary.

Submarine Atlantis

If "semi-submarines" just don't do it for you, dive to depths of 150 feet in the Atlantis I, an air-conditioned, pressurized submarine.

Deep-Dive Submarine

This little excursion will put a definite dent in your wallet, but this may be a once-in-a-lifetime adventure. Board a two-passenger research submarine for an 800-foot-deep dive down the Cayman Wall.

Flight Seeing

View Grand Cayman from the air aboard the twin-engine "Otter."

Catamaran to Stingray City

The Cockatoo, a 60-foot racing catamaran, takes you on a 45-minute trip through the North Sound to the Southern Stingray Playground. After you've watched the rays being fed, don snorkeling gear and join the fun.

Jolly Roger Cruise

The Jolly Roger, an authentic replica of a 17th century Spanish Galleon, provides a Disneyesque look at pirates as it "attacks" another ship, fires its cannon, and engages its "pirates" in sword fighting and plank walking.

Deep-Sea Fishing

You could find wahoo, tuna, or marlin at the end of your line on this excursion. All fishing gear is provided, and an experienced captain will lend a hand.

Snorkeling

Everything is provided on this snorkeling adventure, which takes place just off Parrot's Landing. Other snorkeling adventures take place at the Stingray City Sand Bar and at Cheeseburger and Cemetery reefs.

SCUBA

Coral reefs, tropical fish, shipwrecks, and other enticing sights await both certified and noncertified divers at various locations on the island.

Golf

Play the 18-hole, par-57 executive course at the Britannia Golf Course, designed by Jack Nicklaus.

Cuba

Cruise ships do not stop at the port on this island.

Curaçao

Island Tour

See the distillery where Curacao liqueur is produced (samples provided), then see the island's historical sites and the fascinating Curacao Seaquarium.

Seaworld Explorer

The semi-submarine *Seaworld Explorer* takes you on a guided tour of the island's coral reefs. Fish feeding makes for great photo ops. Some tours include a stop at the Seaquarium.

Trolley Train Tour

Board the Willemstad Trolley Train for a narrated tour of the island's architectural and historic sites.

Snorkeling

Snorkeling near the Seaquarium provides a colorful look at local marine life around a sunken tugboat. Equipment included.

SCUBA

The Curacao National Underwater Park, offering 3000 acres for exploration, is one of the island's most popular dive sites. The Seaquarium also offers scuba diving.

Dominican Republic

Santa Domingo

A bus tour of Santo Domingo acquaints you with the island's historical sites as well as modern buildings. Highlights are the Alcazar, a house built in the 1500s and occupied by Columbus and his bride; Casas Reales, a 16th-century restoration of the tongue-twisting Palacio de la Real Audiencia y Chancilleria de Indias y el Palacio de los Governadores y Capitanes Generales de la Isla Espanola (basically, the house where the governor and captains lived); the city's grand cathedral, and the Columbus Lighthouse.

North Coast

Bus tours are available in the town of Puerto Plata, near the shore where Columbus first landed. Although there's not that much to see here, it's an option if you're interested in local history.

SCUBA

There are plenty of opportunities for diving, but most are meant for experienced divers only. Try La Caleta Reef or reefs off Playa Palenque, both popular local sites.

Haiti

Port-au-Prince

Tour this large island city by bus, taking in sites such as the Parc des Heroes, the Presidential Palace, Jane Barbancourt Castle and several interesting museums.

Cap Haitien

A tour of this area includes a look at the ruins of the Citadelle la Ferriere, one of Haiti's most famous landmarks. Perched 3000 feet, it offers spectacular views of the surrounding area. Ruins of the Sans Souci Palace, an opulent estate constructed in the early 1800s, also are worth seeing.

Snorkeling

Sand Cay is one of the island's most popular dive sites, and half-day trips can be arranged.

Jamaica

Montego Bay Tour

Take the Howard Cook Highway to the Rose Hall Great Plantation for a tour. Stops at the City Center Shopping Plaza and the Jamaican Craft Market. Other city tours include a visit to the Greenwood Great House, filled with antiques, rare books, and musical instruments.

Mountain Valley Rafting

Low-key water rafting from Lethe through the island's lush landscapes.

Freestyle Sailing

Fun in the sun on the trimaran *Freestyle*, where you can snorkel, sail, swim, or just enjoy a cruise of the harbor at Montego Bay.

Dunn's River Falls

If you don't take the tour, do Dunn's River Falls on your own. The 600-foot waterfall is stunning—and one of the most famous sights on the island. You're welcome to climb, but be sure to wear rubber-soled shoes.

Ocho Rios

View the local flora and famous historic sites on your journey to Ocho Rios and Dunn's River Falls, which you can climb with the help of an experienced guide. Also available are tours that focus specifically on local plantations.

Rafting on the Martha Brae

Scenic tour includes historical landmarks and rafting two miles down the Martha Brae River aboard a 30-foot bamboo raft. See bamboo groves, staghorn ferns, exotic orchids and tropical birds.

Horseback Riding

A trail guide will accompany you on this horseback excursion, where you'll ride in the saddle until you get to the beach, where the saddle is removed and you'll ride bareback along the edge of the sparkling water.

Sundancer Yacht Cruise

It's all aboard for a cruise along the island's coast on the 75-foot Sundancer, which also stops at Dunn's River Falls.

Photography Tour

A professional photographer accompanies you on a photo excursion to Montego Bay's most famous landmarks and scenic overlooks. Highlights include the Rose Hall Great House, St. James Parish Church and a look at the island's various architectural styles.

Helicopter Tour

Tour Montego Bay aboard a helicopter while the pilot narrates your excursion. The view is spectacular, and you'll soar over landmarks such as the Rose Great Hall and the Half Moon Bay Golf Club.

Shop 'Til You Drop

It's duty-free shopping at more than 100 stores in Ocho Rios. Tour buses take you to downtown, Soni's Plaza, and Taj Majal, and a shopping map serves as a guide to local shops.

Kingston

Your tour of the Kingston area should include the National Gallery, Devon House, the Bob Marley Museum and St. Peter's Church, located in Port Royal. Also worth a stop is the Archaeological Museum at Fort Charles.

Sportfishing

Deep-sea fishing is available in Montego Bay, where the captain and his mate will help you as much as needed. Fishing gear is provided.

Snorkel

A yacht transports you to Sunset or Sergeant Major reefs for snorkeling (equipment provided) and fish feeding.

SCUBA

Both certified and noncertified dives are offered in the area, and all dives are supervised by a certified divemaster or instructor. Dive sites depend on local conditions on the day of the dive.

Golf

Spend the day golfing in the Jamaica hills at the 18-hole, par-72 Runaway Bay Country Club, or opt for a game at the 18-hole Half Moon Bay Golf Club, designed by Robert Trent Jones.

Puerto Rico

City Tour

Both the old and the new San Juan are explored on this tour, which includes El Morro Fort, Carnegie Library, the Capitol, Condado Lagoon and other scenic landmarks.

Museo Pablo Casals

This museum pays homage to the famous cellist, who left Spain to live out most of his later life on the island. Included are tapes, musical scores and the master's cello.

El Yunque Rainforest

It's a one-hour drive to El Yunque Rainforest and Luquillo Beach, each one of the island's natural wonders. A great option for photographers and serious nature lovers.

Arecibo Observatory

Operated by Cornell University, this observatory, about a two-hour drive from San Juan, has an impressive telescope and is part of the National Astronomy and Ionosphere Center. Tours are given on a regular basis.

Parque de las Cavernas del Rio Camuy

This area in the limestone hills on the island's northwest coast is especially popular with spelunkers, who will enjoy exploring the huge caves. Guided tours are available.

Bacardi Rum Distillery

Watch the process whereby sugarcane becomes rum, then sample the results, or visit the Bacardi shops and museum.

Barrachina Center

Whether you take a scheduled excursion or make the trip yourself, you won't want to miss this shopper's paradise. Get good deals on jewelry, perfumes, and other items, with an extra 10 percent discount for ship passengers.

Nightlife Tour

Nightlife tours may include shows at the Sands Hotel or at other locations in the city. Some allow time for a visit to the casino.

Golf

Play either the Cerromar Beach North or Cerromar Beach South course, both par-72 courses nestled amid island scenery.

Turks & Caicos

These islands are generally not on the cruise ship itinerary, but if you elect to visit (access is by plane or boat), you may wish to see the National Museum, housed in the former Guinep Lodge on Grand Turk.

Yucatan Peninsula

Island Tour

See several Mayan archaeological sites, including the ruins of San Gervasio. Other tours focusing on Mayan ruins include a guided excursion to Tulum (one hour away by bus from Playa del Carmen), or combine a tour of San Gervasio with a folkloric show or Playa del Sol Beach Club.

Tulum

Archaeology buffs won't want to miss an excursion to the ruins of Tulum, part of the lost civilization of the Maya, and Xel-Ha, the sacred lagoon.

Cancun

The drive to Cancun takes approximately one hour. Once there, you're on your own for sightseeing, shopping or visiting the resort's beaches.

Cultural Excursion

The music and dance of Mexico's various regions are highlighted in this folkloric show.

Fiesta Party Boat

Party on, dude! Margaritas and rum flow freely, a live band provides the music, and you can enjoy a 90-minute stop at Playa Sol before returning to the ship.

Sub-See Explorer

This underwater viewing craft takes passengers on a tour of Cozumel's underwater reefs without ever leaving the boat.

Fury Sail & Snorkel Tour

The *Fury* takes passengers on a one-hour sail to a snorkeling site, where equipment and instruction are provided. A guided tour of the waters includes feeding the fish. Beverages are provided, and the tour ends with sunbathing or swimming on the powder sand beach. Several variations on the snorkel tour for both experienced and novice snorkelers are available to various parts of the island.

SCUBA

Proof of certification is required for this tour, which offers diving at several spectacular local sites within Palancar National Park.

ARUBA

Windsurfing is Aruba's most popular sport.

With the highest percent of repeat visitors in the Caribbean, there is something definitely addictive about Aruba. Something habit-forming *had* to inspire *Bon Appetit* readers to elect the smallest, but most developed of the ABC Islands, their all-time favorite destination in the Caribbean. Sure, there are nice beaches, dry sunny weather, and cool breezes, but how do you explain honeymooners who return *18 years in a row* to the same hotel? Only 50 years ago, Lago Oil workers, Dutch seamen and Norwegian whalers prowled the streets and busted up barrooms; today those besotted sailors have been replaced by half a million sunburned tourists a year, who seem to thrive on the big resorts, the 10 casinos, the 100 restaurants, and what seems to be the zillion duty-free shops. Simply, Aruba has raised the island packaged vacation to a strange, but wonderful art. If you stay at a big all-inclusive resort in Aruba, you can sleep, surf, sun, soak, wine, dine and shop without ever leaving the property.

Aruba is not exactly a pretty island, unless you've got a yen for tough scrubby land with lots of cacti. What it does have are temperate blue waters that give way to nearly every watersport imaginable—from parasailing and game fishing to jet skis, snorkeling and scuba. Because of the constant trade winds, windsurfing has become the number one sport, particularly during the end of May and the beginning of June, when the never-say-die converge for the annual Aruba Hi-Winds Pro-Am Windsurfing Competition. Even during the year, the die-hard surfers are a sight to behold, as they make their daily pilgrimage to the beach, en masse across Lloyd G. Smith Boulevard, their sails held high over tight gleaming muscles.

Bird's Eye View

The smallest of the ABC islands, Aruba lies 16 miles off the northeast coast of Venezuela, about a four-hour plane ride from New York. Sprawling over 74.5 square miles, the 20-mile-long island looks like a slab of ham pointing northwest to southeast toward South America. Like Bonaire and Curaçao, its sister islands, Aruba has scant vegetation, yet its outback, called *cunucu*, is a soul-stirring landscape. As the paved road gives way to gravel and finally to coral dust, a stark and arid terrain appears, punctuated by upended boulders, mauve dunes, crashing waves and an array of scrubby Aruban vegetation, from cacti *(kadushi)* tomnesquite *(kwihi)* to the wind-bent divi-divi trees *(dwatapana)*.Tiny bright red flowers called *fioritas* provide one of the few splashes of color. On the northwesternmost tip, at Kudarebe, the sand dunes make for excellent warm-weather sledding.

Dutch-gabled and pastel-pretty, Oranjestad, the capital, called Playa, is a dazzling yellow brick town. Shops line the main shopping street of Nassaustraat and Wilhelminastraat. About 7500 hotel rooms stretch along the five-mile strand of pure white sand on Palm Beach and in the smaller Eagle Beach and Druif Bay (both south of Palm, near Oranjestad). During the year, more than 540,000 tourists add to the native population of a mere 71,000.

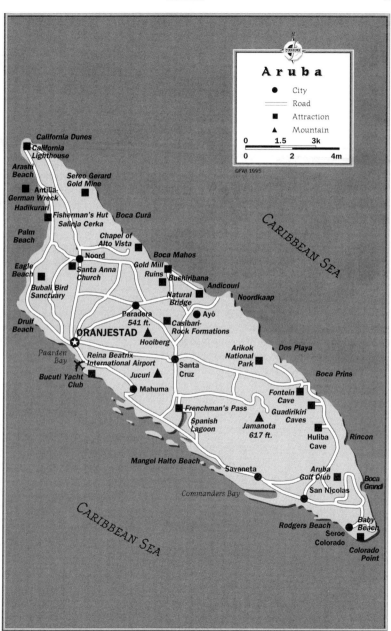

Aruba

● City
═ Road
■ Attraction
▲ Mountain

0   1.5   3k
0   2   4m

©FWI 1995

CARIBBEAN SEA

California Dunes
California Lighthouse
Arashi Beach
Sereo Gerard Gold Mine
Antilla-German Wreck
Hadikurari
Fisherman's Hut
Salinja Cerka
Boca Curá
Palm Beach
Chapel of Alto Vista
Noord
Boca Mahos
Eagle Beach
Santa Anna Church
Gold Mill Ruins
Bushiribana
Andicouri
Bubali Bird Sanctuary
Natural Bridge
Noordkaap
Druif Beach
Paradera 541 ft.
Ayó
Casibari-Rock Formations
ORANJESTAD
Hooiberg
Paarden Bay
Reina Beatrix International Airport
Jucuri
Santa Cruz
Arikok National Park
Dos Playa
Boca Prins
Bucuti Yacht Club
Mahuma
Fontein Cave
Frenchman's Pass
Guadirikiri Caves
Spanish Lagoon
Jamanota 617 ft.
Huliba Cave
Rincon
Mangel Halto Beach
Savaneta
Aruba Golf Club
Boca Grandi
Commanders Bay
San Nicolas
Rodgers Beach
Baby Beach
Seroe Colorado
Colorado Point
CARIBBEAN SEA

History

When Spanish explorers arrived in the 15th century, the Caiquetios, a tribe of Arawaks, may have already been living on Aruba for more than 4500 years, having migrated there from their ancestral homes in Venezuela. The Spanish exiled most of them in 1513, though more immigration occurred around 1640, when the Dutch permitted the Indian population to live a free—if difficult—life in Aruba. Though the last full-blooded natives died out in 1862, remains of their villages, workshops and cemeteries can be glimpsed throughout the Aruban countryside. Many place names still retain their Indian origins, such as Arashi, Daimari, Jamanota and perhaps the name Aruba itself, which some think is Arawak for "guide." Even the faces of modern Arubans—with their high cheekbones and tawny complexions— strongly reflect their native ancestry.

After being discovered by the Spanish explorer Alonso de Ojeda in 1499, Aruba was deemed useless along with its sister island Bonaire and Curaçao, and ignored for years. After the Spanish shipped off the resident male Indians to work the salt mines of Hispaniola, they began a limited colonization, turning the dusty mote into a large ranch and introducing horses, donkeys, sheep, dogs, goats, pigs, cats and chickens. In 1636, the Dutch took over and continued ranching. The English and the Spanish duked it out from 1792-1816, though the Dutch remained in control. Aloe cultivation and gold mining became important industries

In 1824 a lowly goat herder discovered the first gleaming nuggets of gold and started a tropical gold rush. Smelters were built and miners flooded the island. When the going got rough, major smelters shut down in 1914, but today there are those who still find nuggets. The real gold of Aruba became aloe vera, brought over from North America via Jamaica in the mid-19th century, a hardy succulent that adapted well to the climate. By 1900 Aruba had become the largest exporter of aloe vera, earning itself the nickname of Island of Aloe, for producing more than 90 percent of the world's supply. Today every Aruban home boasts its own small crop, using it as a natural laxative and wound-healer.

In 1924, oil refining arrived, ushering in an unprecedented era of prosperity. By 1985 the oil boom had gone bust, and the country's biggest employer Exxon went home, leaving the country its worst crisis, with 60 percent of the foreign exchange lost, 70 percent of the harbor space empty, and 40 percent of the population unemployed. In 1986, Aruba separated from its sister islands of the Netherlands Antilles (Curaçao, Bonaire, Sint Maarten, Saba and Statia), but still remained part of the Dutch Kingdom. This was a move favored by Arubans, but the time couldn't have been less favorable. It forced the island to totally depend on tourism. Government guarantees were given to the Hyatt, Sheraton and Holiday Inns—a plucky move that worked. Today tourism is Aruba's biggest industry, employing about half the population.

People

Expect to find some Dutch customs and windmills on Aruba.

Arubans have legendary smiles and sunny dispositions—character traits tailor-made for tourism. In fact, Arubans are sometimes so helpful that they fight among themselves over who gets to help you. Acts of kindness are considered a way of life. Sociopsychologists have attributed this collective congeniality to several historical factors, including the relative absence of slavery and the benign Dutch intervention. Even the government has shown itself to be enlightened, and there seem to be no overt inequalities in service. As such, Arubans have a high standard of living, often earning as much as visiting tourists, so there is little resentment over spending habits (the downside of this is that nothing is cheap). About three-quarters of the people living full-time on the island are native-born. Racial intermingling has also had a long history here, starting with the Indian base, and adding 16th-century Spaniards, 17th-century Dutch, 18th-century Portuguese and French Huguenots and 19th-century African and Italian gold diggers, not to mention Americana oil technicians in the 20th century. The majority of Arubans are Roman Catholic.

Beaches

Several yachts and catamarans offer cruises along Aruba's coast.

Of the three ABC Islands, Aruba has the most beautiful beaches. All are open to the public free of charge. Avoid swimming on the east side because the surf can get dangerously rough. **Palm Beach**, considered by some to be one of the 10 best beaches in the world, is the hub of Aruban beachlife—interpret that as *crowded*—but it is also excellent for swimming and other watersports. **Fishermen's Hut**, north of the hotel strip, is the favorite hangout of the windsurfing crowd. Here you'll see a lovely view of neon sailboats bobbing madly in the wind. **Rodger Beach** is notable for its lovely palm trees, and **Baby Lagoon** on the west is unusually calm. A truly wondrous wide stretch of strand, **Manchebo Beach** seems to magically inspire women to fling their tops off. Other good beaches are **Bachelor's Beach** and **Boca Grandi** in the east, which is good for windsurfing.

Underwater

Perpetually consigned to the impressive shadow cast by Bonaire and Curacao, Aruba will never attain premier status as a dive destination. There is a decent barrier reef extending between Oranjestad and the southern tip, but with all dive operators located a long boat ride away, visitors don't always hear about it. One does need to be wary of a brisk current, but there are lovely sites along this reef (two of them below) which are worthy of exploration. Shore diving is possible, but there is usually a maze of cuts and channels which must be negotiated in order to access the main reef; the current also allows for some drift dives, but these, too, can be difficult to locate. If you really want to experience the island's limited reef and wall diving, your best bet is to hook up with a dive shop that knows this area. What the island does offer is a bevy of wrecks, including one of the Caribbean's very finest, the *Antilla*, a WWII remnant which sits close enough to the surface to be explored by snorkelers. There's also a tug, a 200-foot freighter, a pair of rusting airplanes and, off the rugged northern tip, the remains of the *California*, which is notorious as the ship that didn't respond to the Titanic's S.O.S. signals. The best area for snorkeling is probably **DePalm Island**, a small resort served by a free ferry every half-hour.

Baby Beach Reef

One of Aruba's delightful shore dives, Baby Beach is a beautiful reef (20 to 70 feet) which receives few visitors (it lies near the southern tip of the island) and has maintained a relatively pristine state. Crabs, octopuses and lobsters are found amid the forests of elkhorn and sheet coral and the nearby depths usually showcase bigger animals like turtles and rays.

Mangel Halto

Just south of Barcadera Harbor, Mangel Halto descends gradually off the beach down to a depth of 110 feet, passing a diverse palette of hard and soft coral growth, grooved brain coral, sea anemones, tube and vase sponges and deep water gorgoneans. Copper sweepers, queen angels, blue tangs and schools of yellowtails are among the regular visitors, with occasional appearances by octopuses, green morays and nurse sharks further down. An excellent shore dive.

Wreck of the Antilla

Nicknamed "the ghost ship," this 400-foot German freighter was scuttled (brand new) in 1940 when Holland was invaded by Germany. The ship, broken in two parts, lies on its port side in 60 feet of water, with sections of its structure reaching above the surface. The vessel's large compartments allow easy penetration, and the hull is covered with tube sponges and orange cup coral. The Antilla is easily the most popular wreck in the ABCs, and several dozen divers can be exploring the ship at once (all local dive shops visit the site regularly). The rare wreck that's both stimulating for the experienced and accessible for beginners, the Antilla is a Caribbean legend.

Dive Shops

Aruba Pro Dive

Costa Linda Resort, Oranjestad; ☎ *(297) 8-25520.*
Explores south coast area between Spanish Lagoon and Seroe Colorado via shore dives; wreck dives in the afternoon. Four-hour resort courses taught from beach $70; single tank dive $35 from boat or shore. Keeps small groups limited to ten; no service charge on dive prices. PADI, NAUI, SSI and IDD. Snorkel trips to Antilla and two reefs $45 with lunch.

Red Sail Sports Aruba

Oranjestad; ☎ *(297) 8-61603.*
One tank dive, $30, two tanks, $54, plus rental equipment . Two dives scheduled daily, focuses on wrecks; resort courses daily in pool $77. PADI and NAUI, training to Divemaster. High-volume operation with huge boats.

Scuba Aruba

Noord; ☎ *(297) 8-34142.*
One tank dive, $30; two tank dive $55, including equipment. Caters to beginners (resort courses, $50). Maximum group size 16. All-Caribbean staff.

On Foot

With an average annual rainfall of only about 20 inches, Aruba's interior is scraggly and desolate, with a series of low rolling hills that snuggle against the middle part of the northern coast. The island's highest elevation is **Yamanota Hill**, a rise of 617 feet near the center of Aruba. Its summit can be reached by car, and a series of trails trickle down the slopes, but hikers should be cautious in their explorations as a unique, venomous rattlesnake inhabits his rugged territory. **Arikok National Park** encompasses a triangle of land between San Fuego and Boca Prins (on the eastern coast); a group of short rails surround the park's focal point, **Mt. Arikok**, Aruba's second highest summit. Also worth on-foot investigation is **California Point**, the island's northern tip, where sand dunes reach toward the sea and brown pelicans nest.

Wind-bent divi-divi (watpana) trees are a common sight on Aruba.

Hooiberg (The Haystack)

This peculiar, 541-foot volcanic mound lies straight east of Oranjestad, and its summit is reached via a climb up several hundred steps. The trailhead is marked, located just off the main highway between Oranjestad and Santa Cruz, and ascends through cactus, white manjack and sage. The top yields views of almost all of Aruba and, on the near horizon, of Venezuela, less than 20 miles away. Allow an hour round-trip.

By Pedal

Offering an excellent escape from the pulse of resort activities concentrated on the leeward coast, most of Aruba's landscape is relatively flat and ideal for either road or mountain bike riding. The major consideration (as on Bonaire and Curacao) is the heat and sunlight, which can be ferocious; carry plenty of water and sunscreen. Using the roads closest to the shore, a circuit of the island is roughly 50 miles, though there are several ways to shorten the route you desire; the south coast is entirely asphalt, while the north coast is comprised of varying degrees of dirt roads. If you get lost, look to the divi divi trees to serve as a compass of sorts (winds keep them pointed southwest).

Bike Rental Shops

Pablito Bike Rental

> *Oranjestad;* ☎ *(297) 8-78655.*
> Rents Taiwanese mountain bikes. Full day, $12, or $45 for a full week; hourly rate also available.

Tri Bike Aruba

> *Santa Cruz;* ☎ *(297) 8-50609.*
> Olympian Gert Van Vliet's triathlon and pro mountain bike sales and repair shop anticipates entering the rental business in late 1995 after receiving a shipment of Trek 930s and other high-quality models.

What Else to See

On the jagged, windy northern coast, the **Natural Bridge**, the largest in the Caribbean and Aruba's most noteworthy natural formation after the beaches, is one of the island's biggest attractions. Every bus and jeep stops here, so expect crowds. Honeymooners like to pose for photos as the waves surround the gaping coral bridge. The culturally starved can head for a trio of small but fascinating museums. The **Archaeology Museum** features artifacts from the island's Indian past. The **Numismatic Museum** showcases more than 30,000 coins from all over the world, including the rare jotin from 1798. (Brazil should have taken notice how the governor of the Netherlands Antilles Johan R. Lauffer solved a coin shortage at the time by cutting one coin into four pies; the word *jotin* is taken from the French *guillotine*.) The **Historical Museum** is housed in the island's oldest building, **Fort Zoutman**, built in 1796 by the Dutch. It's also the site of the weekly **Bonbini Festival**, held every Tuesday evening, featuring local music, dance, crafts and food.

BEST VIEW:

Schooner Harbor is a great photo op for its colorfully docked sailboats and open market where fishermen and boatpeople hawk their wares in open-stall markets.

City Celebrations

rnival

Various locales around Aruba, Oranjestad.

This yearly party starts two weeks before Lent (usually in February). Don't miss the Grand Parade, held on the Sunday before Lent. Other festivities include street dancing and the crowning of the Carnival Queen.

zz and Latin Music Festival   ★★★★

Various venues, Oranjestad.

This yearly festival, begun in 1988 and run under the auspices of the Aruba Tourism Authority, is a local favorite. Held every June, it attracts some big names.

Historical Sites

rt Zoutman   ★★★

Off Lloyd G. Smith Blvd., Oranjestad.

The fort, built in 1796, is the island's oldest building. The Willem III tower was added in 1868 and served as a lighthouse for decades. On the grounds is Museo Arubano, a historical museum in an 18th-century home that displays relics and artifacts found around Aruba.

Museums and Exhibits

uba Archeology Museum   ★★★

Zoutmanstraat 1, Oranjestad.

Artifacts from the precolonial period—including some skeletons 2000 years old—are on exhibit at this small museum. Its founder, Martin Bloom, conducts interesting island tours (see "Special Tours/Excursions").

Man Shell Collection   ★★★

18 Morgensten St., Oranjestad.

The De Mans are proud owners of one of the world's largest private shell collections. Call ahead and if they're free, they'll let you check it out.

mismatic Museum   ★★

Irausquin Plein 2A, Oranjestad.

More than 3000 pieces of coins and currency from 400 countries from the private collection of J.M. Odor.

Tours

antis Submarines   ★★★★★

Seaport Village Marina, Oranjestad.
Hours Open: 10 a.m.–3 p.m.

Not for the claustrophobic, but a great excursion for everyone else in a modern submarine that goes as deep as 150 feet below the sea to observe coral and fish along the Barcadera Reef. Trips depart every hour on the hour, and reservations are essential. The fee is $48 for adults, $34 under 16; children under four not permitted.

Palm Tours   ★★★

L.G. Smith Blvd. 142, Oranjestad.

If it involves showing tourists around Aruba, they're happy to oblige at De Palm. On- and off-road excursions start at $49.95 and include lunch and snorkeling;

three-hour treks for hikers cost $25; deep-sea fishing starts at $220; horseback rid
are $30 for two hours. They also do boat tours and snorkel excursions, with pric
starting at $22.50.

Martin Booster Tracking   ★ ★

Diamontbergweg 40, San Nicolas.

Martin Booster, an archeologist who founded the Archeology Museum, personal
conducts these interesting tours that explore the island's pre-Columbian roots. V
jeep, he'll take you far into the interior and regale you with tales of Aruba past ar
present. The tour generally departs at 8:30 a.m. and goes until 3:30 p.m.; the $4
price includes lunch.

Sports

Aruba's temperate blue waters give way to nearly every watersport—fro
parasailing to game fishing to jet skis, snorkeling and scuba, but the No
sport here is **windsurfing**. Consistent year-round winds and shallow flat w
ters make it one of the top sailboard destinations in the world, particula
good for beginners and intermediates. For 300 days of the year, guarante
winds blow up to 20 knots. The prime location is **Fisherman's Huts**, north
the Holiday Inn on Palm Beach. For those not up to high winds yet, quiet
waters are available farther south on Palm Beach, where there is also equi
ment and instructors. The most advanced head for **Bachelor's Beach**. Durin
the end of May and the beginning of June, the hail-and-hearty conver;
here from around the world for the annual **Aruba Hi-Winds Pro-Am Windsur
ing Competition**. Aruba is a haven for all watersports, but golf and tennis fir
lots of takers. Companies dedicated to well-organized sports activities can
found in major hotel lobbies. **Scuba diving** is probably Aruba's best-kept s
cret, and nowadays, many operators offer one-tank dives so you will ha
time for all your other pleasures. (For more information, see "Dive Site
above.) **Sport-fishing** is big on the island, and half- and full-day charters c
be arranged through one's hotel or directly from local operators. Less thar
mile from shore, the sea is rich with kingfish, tuna, bonito, wahoo and bl
and white marlin. **Boat excursions** for picnics and sightseeing are available o
catamarans and glass-bottom vessels for viewing the corals—check with yo
hotel. Though yachting is not a big pastime here yet, there is a nautical cl
at the mouth of the Spanish Lagoon. **Horseback riding** is available daily o
trails throughout the countryside, on paso fino horses imported from Sou

merica; the mounts of these finely trained horses are known for an unbe-
evably comfortable ride.

ruba Golf Club

Golfweg 82, San Nicolas.

This desertlike course has nine holes and lots of sand traps and goats to keep things interesting. It is located on the island's southeastern part, and open only to members on Saturday and Sunday. Greens fees are $7.50 for nine holes, $10 if you want to go around twice. Hopefully, a long-awaited 18-hole championship course will open this year along the west end; inquire at your hotel.

ruba Sail Cart

Bushire 23, Oranjestad.
Hours Open: 10 a.m.–7 p.m.

Can't quite get the hang of windsurfing? This goofy sport is easy to learn instead. You'll be whisking about in no time on special carts equipped with a windsurf-type sail—fun! Costs about $15 for a half-hour.

ancho El Paso

44 Washington, Oranjestad.

Here's the spot to come for trail rides on beautiful paso fino horses.

ed Sail Sports

Seaport Marketplace, Oranjestad.

The island's largest selection of watersport rentals, including scuba instructions and packages. One-tank dives start at $30.

Where to Stay

Fielding's Highest Rated Hotels in Aruba

★★★★	Aruba Marriott Resort	$156–$450
★★★★	Aruba Sonesta Hotel	$115–$530
★★★★	Hyatt Regency Aruba	$205–$300
★★★	Americana Aruba Hotel	$175–$185
★★★	Amsterdam Manor Beach	$90–$140
★★★	Aruba Hilton Int'l Hotel	$125–$880
★★★	Aruba Palm Beach	$115–$255
★★★	Costa Linda Beach Resort	$270–$430
★★★	Divi Aruba Beach Resort	$135–$195
★★★	La Cabana Beach Resort	$95–$640
★★★	Playa Linda Beach Resort	$115–$605

Fielding's Most Romantic Hotels in Aruba

★★★	Amsterdam Manor Beach	$90–$140
★★★	Divi Aruba Beach Resort	$135–$195
★★★★	Hyatt Regency Aruba	$205–$300

Fielding's Budget Hotels in Aruba

★★★	Amsterdam Manor Beach	$90–$140
★★	Best Western Manchebo	$100–$180
★★	Holiday Inn Aruba	$121–$170
★★	Best Western Talk of The Town	$85–$215
★★★	Divi Aruba Beach Resort	$135–$195

What you get on Aruba are either high-rise, glitz-and-glitter beach resorts, low-rise garden-like resorts, or time-share apartments and condominiums. The number of rooms available in Aruba has skyrocketed in recent years, probably shooting beyond 8000 by now. Most of the hotels are situated on L.G. Smith Boulevard, west of Oranjestad. Moderate-priced accommodations with good quality are hard to find, families sometimes suffer in Aruba unless they go in for apartments or time-shares. Whatever you do, don't arrive in Aruba without a reservation, especially during high season (mid-December to mid-April). In any case, you must give the name of your hotel to the immigration officer when you arrive. Condominiums give you the option of cooking your own meals, but are usually housed in modern, unattractive buildings. If you want a bargain, go off-season and save up to 45 percent. You can also take advantage of packages offered by some hotels.

Gambling is a major attraction on Aruba and there are many casinos.

Hotels and Resorts

If you have a taste for the Vegas life, stay in one of Aruba's many top-class resorts that will serve your every need; between the health club, the casino, the lagoon-style pool and the full deck of restaurants, you'll never have to leave the premises. High-rises, of course, give you a better view of the sea; low-rises seem more intimate and are usually planted around fabulous gardens. Some hotels, such as the Sonesta, offer some of the best shopping malls on the island.

| Americana Aruba Hotel | $175–$185 | ★ ★ ★ |

J.E. Irausquin Blvd. 83, Palm Beach, ☎ (800) 447-7642, (297) 8-64500, FAX (297) 8-61682.

Single: $175–$185. Double: $175–$185.

Situated directly on Palm Beach with its own full casino, this well-managed property consisting of twin high-rise towers is a busy spot, with lots going on and a social hostess to see that it stays that way. Most guests are from the U.S. and Canada. Accommodations are decent if not spectacular, with air conditioning, bamboo and wood furniture, cable TV and hair dryers; some overlook the "fantasy" swimming pool with waterfalls and spas. A great spot for kids with special supervised activities, though not exactly teeming with island flavor.

Aruba Beach Club $130–$290   ★ ★

J.E. Irausquin Blvd. 51-53, Palm Beach, ☎ *(800) 445-8667, (297) 8-23000, FAX (297) 8-68217.*

Single: $130–$290. Double: $130–$290.

This time-share resort is on the sea at Druif Beach, and shares facilities with the Casa Del Mar Beach Resort, including three restaurants, three pools, three bars and four tennis courts. Accommodations are decent enough with air conditioning, cable TV, kitchens and balconies. The atmosphere is casual and lively.

Aruba Hilton Int'l Hotel $125–$880   ★ ★ ★

J.E. Irausquin Blvd. 77, Palm Beach, ☎ *(800) 445-8667, (297) 8-64466, FAX (297) 8-68217.*

Single: $125–$880. Double: $135–$880.

Hilton has taken over this former Concorde Hotel and $42 million later, has turned it into a decent and efficient operation. Accommodations are in a high-rise and nicely decorated with all the modern touches; all balconies have full ocean views. The grounds include a new watersports center, two pools (one for kids), very nice public spaces, a health club, two tennis courts and a full casino. Splurge on the VIP floors if your budget allows; the extra bucks buy a hair dryer, minibar and more space to move around.

Aruba Marriott Resort $156–$450   ★ ★ ★ ★

L.G. Smith Blvd., Palm Beach, ☎ *(800) 223-6388, FAX (297) 8-60649.*

Single: $156–$450. Double: $156–$450.

The new Marriott is a smashing full-service resort, with a magnificent pool, huge casino, spiffy health spa, tennis and all the usual watersports. Lots of bars, restaurants and shopping on-site to keep visitors happy, though as with all these mega resorts, genuine island atmosphere is scarce.

Aruba Palm Beach $115–$255   ★ ★ ★

J.E. Irausquin Blvd. 79, Palm Beach, ☎ *(800) 345-2782, (297) 8-63900, FAX (305) 427-7481.*

Single: $115–$255. Double: $115–$255.

This eight-story Moorish-style beachfront hotel is set amid exquisitely landscaped tropical grounds. Rooms are spacious and come with all the usual amenities, though their balconies are quite small, and not all have an ocean view. Walk-in closets are a nice touch. They offer all the expected recreational diversions, from tennis to water sports. A choice spot.

uba Sonesta Hotel   **$115–$530**   ★ ★ ★ ★

L.G. Smith Blvd. 82, Oranjestad, ☎ *(800) 766-3782, (297) 8-36389, FAX (297) 8-34389.*

Single: $115–$530. Double: $115–$530.

No beach, but boats depart every 20 minutes to a private island seven minutes away where all sorts of watersports await. Located in the heart of Oranjestad in the Seaport Village complex, which offers some 85 shops and restaurants. After entering through an impressive atrium lobby, guests are brought to their very nice rooms, which have all the usual amenities plus minibars and tiny balconies. The children's program is free and highly rated, and the casino is huge and happening. A great spot, but only for those who don't mind being well off the beach.

est Western Bucuti   **$115–$235**   ★ ★

J.E. Irausquin Blvd., Eagle Beach, ☎ *(800) 528-1234, (297) 8-31100, FAX (297) 8-25272.*

Single: $115–$235. Double: $115–$235.

This casual lowrise has very nice accommodations with sitting areas, sofa beds, microwave ovens, refrigerators, TVs and pleasant furnishings. It shares facilities with the adjacent Best Western Manchebo Beach Resort, with all the usual watersports, tennis, pools and casino. The beach is large and wide, and Aruba's only sanctioned topless spot.

est Western Manchebo   **$100–$180**   ★ ★

L.G. South Blvd. 55, Palm Beach, ☎ *(800) 528-1234, (297) 8-23444, FAX (297) 8-32446.*

Single: $100–$180. Double: $115–$180.

This sprawling lowrise, located on one of Aruba's best beaches, has guest rooms that are comfortable if unexciting; each has a refrigerator, which is always welcome. It's a sister property to the adjacent Best Western Bucuti, and between the two, guests are kept busy with all the typical resort amenities. Lots of Europeans like this spot.

est Western Talk of The Town   **$85–$215**   ★ ★

L.G. Smith Blvd. 2, Oranjestad, ☎ *(800) 528-1234, (297) 8-82380, FAX (297) 8-20327.*

Single: $85–$215. Double: $95–$215.

This lowrise motel near the airport has traditional guest rooms, some with microwaves and refrigerators, as well as apartments of one or two bedrooms and full kitchens. There's a good restaurant and two pools on-site; beach lovers are transported to a nicer beach than the one across a busy street. A good choice for budget travelers, as the service is quite caring.

ashiri Beach Hotel   **$230–$330**   ★ ★

L.G. Smith Blvd. 35, Oranjestad, ☎ *(800) 462-6868, (297) 8-25216, FAX (297) 8-26789.*

Single: $230–$330. Double: $230–$330.

Aruba's first all-inclusive resort is physically nondescript, but excellent service (this is a training school for budding hoteliers) makes up for the lack of atmosphere. There's tons to do—watersports, gambling classes, sightseeing excursions, tennis,

sailing—and lots of young people frequent this busy property. Rates are quite rea
sonable since everything is included—including all you can possibly drink, and the
some. Parents can stash their kids in the supervised programs.

Divi Aruba Beach Resort $135–$195   ★★

J.E. Irausquin Blvd. 47, Palm Beach, ☎ *(800) 554-2008, (297) 8-23300, FAX (297)
34002.*
Single: $135–$195. Double: $135–$195.

Located on glorious Druif Beach, this popular lowrise is nicely casual and ver
friendly. Standard accommodations are in motel-like wings and feature tile floor
ceiling fans (as well as air), and small balconies. Concrete casitas offer more privac
Other rooms front the ocean and have tiled patios and larger bathrooms, while th
newer Divi Dos rooms include refrigerators and Jacuzzis. Lots of honeymooners a
this spot, which comes highly recommended more for the excellent beach than fo
the property itself.

Holiday Inn Aruba $121–$170   ★

J.E. Irausquin Blvd. 230, Palm Beach, ☎ *(800) 465-4329, (297) 8-63600, FAX (29
8-65870.*
Single: $121–$170. Double: $121–$170.

It's a Holiday Inn, after all, so don't come looking for anything special. Rooms a
acceptable but could really use a refurbishing; on the other hand, the outdoor ga
dens are quite nice. There's lots to keep you occupied, including watersports, s
tennis courts, horseback riding, a large pool, health center and, of course, the ubic
uitous casino.

Hyatt Regency Aruba $205–$300   ★★★

J.E. Irausquin Blvd. 85, Palm Beach, ☎ *(800) 233-1234, (297) 8-61234, FAX (297)
61682.*
Single: $205–$300. Double: $205–$300.

Set on 12 acres fronting Palm Beach, this sprawling high-rise resort is known for i
famous pool, a giant, multilevel swimming hole with waterslides, waterfalls and a
sorts of bells and whistles. Rooms are all the same size (the view determines th
price) with Southwestern decor, oversized baths and loads of amenities, though th
balconies are disappointingly tiny. The grounds are lush and lovely with all the usu
sporting diversions, a pretty lagoon dotted with black swans and lots of eaterie
Grand, glorious and Aruba's best.

La Cabana Beach Resort $95–$640   ★★

J.E. Irausquin Blvd. 250, Eagle Beach, ☎ *(800) 835-7193, (297) 8-79000, FAX (29
8-77208.*
Single: $95–$640. Double: $95–$640.

All accommodations are suites at this beachfront resort located five minutes fro
Oranjestad. Choose from studios or apartments with up to three bedrooms; all hav
full kitchens, whirlpools, hair dryers, and private balconies. Besides having the mo
rooms in Aruba, the hotel also boasts the biggest pool and biggest casino. One o
the three pools has a 120-foot waterslide; another has a waterfall. The Club Cabar
Nana ($80 per week) keeps kids out of the way. There's always something happen
ing at this very fun and well-serviced resort.

amarijn Aruba Resort $145–$190 ★★

J.E. Irasquin Blvd. 41, Palm Beach, ☎ (297) 8-24150, FAX (297) 8-24150.
Single: $145. Double: $190.

This all-inclusive resort is a sister property to the Aruba Divi Beach Resort, with golf carts whisking guests to and fro. The Dutch-style architecture consists of two-story townhouse-style units with the typical furnishings and amenities inside. The grounds include two tennis courts, restaurants and bars, watersports, and mountain bikes. Guests can get free admittance and transport to the Alhambra Casino. Lots of honeymooners here.

Apartments and Condominiums

Families and couples will find the best bargains in this section. Some complexes even throw in a rental car; if you don't plan on driving, make sure you are near an accessible bus route. Some of the most inexpensive deals can be found in the Malmok district.

msterdam Manor Beach $90–$140 ★★★

Eagle Beach, ☎ (297) 8-31492, FAX (297) 8-71463, FAX (297) 8-71463.
Single: $90–$140. Double: $90–$140.

This complex is marked by its authentic Dutch style, with gabled roofs and inner courtyards, though it desperately needs some landscaping. Accommodations range from studios to two-bedroom apartments, all with pinewood furniture and full kitchens. The nice pool is set right on the road and lacks privacy. Eagle Beach is across the street, and guests can arrange watersports at various nearby properties. Not a top choice, but decent enough for the price. Lots of Europeans here.

aribbean Palm Village $85–$290 ★★

Palm Beach Road, Noord Village, ☎ (297) 8-62700, FAX (297) 8-62380.
Single: $85–$256. Double: $85–$290.

Located a mile from Palm Beach, this low-rise apartment complex is off the beach and away from shops and restaurants, so you'll be using the rental car that's included with the rates. Accommodations are in suites with two baths, living and dining areas and kitchens, and very nicely decorated. There's a decent Italian restaurant on-site, plus two pools and supervised programs for the kiddies.

asa del Mar Beach Resort $135–$400 ★★

J.E. Irausquin Blvd. 53, Palm Beach, ☎ (297) 8-23000, FAX (297) 8-26557.
Single: $135–$400. Double: $135–$400.

This time-share resort has two-bedroom suites both on the beach and offshore, all with full kitchens. A social hostess keeps kids busy for parents who want some time alone. Facilities are shared with the Aruba Beach Club and include three restaurants, three bars, three pools, four tennis courts, watersports and a fitness center.

osta Linda Beach Resort $270–$430 ★★★

J.E. Irausquin Blvd. 59, Oranjestad, ☎ (800) 346-7084, (297) 8-38000, FAX (305) 670-4948.
Single: $270–$430. Double: $270–$430.

This attractive beachfront resort consists of nicely appointed two- and three-bedroom suites with Roman tubs, full kitchens and two TVs. Two tennis courts, a large

pool and three restaurants and bars with nightly entertainment round out the facil
ities. Supervised children's activities are offered during high season.

Dutch Village $145–$415 ★ ★

L.G. Smith Blvd. 39, Oranjestad, ☎ *(800) 367-3484, (297) 8-32300, FAX (297) 8
20501.*
Single: $145–$414. Double: $145–$415.
This stylish complex consists of time-share studios and apartments of one to three
bedrooms, all with full kitchens. There's a pool, tennis and watersports on-site, bu
you'll have to cook in or go elsewhere for meals; several restaurants are within walk
ing distance at the Aruba Divi and Tamrijn Aruba.

Mill Resort $105–$550 ★ ★

J.E. Irausquin Blvd. 330, Palm Beach, ☎ *(297) 8-67700, FAX (297) 8-67271.*
Single: $105–$325. Double: $175–$550.
This condominium hotel is a five-minute walk from the beach; management wil
take you there if you're feeling lazy. The lowrise complex consists of studio and
suites, most with full kitchens, Jacuzzis and patios; all are air conditioned. No res
taurant on-site, but the very good Old Mill is next door. The grounds include two
pools, a kid's pool and two tennis courts. A good choice for families.

Playa Linda Beach Resort $115–$605 ★ ★ ★

J.E. Irausquin Blvd. 87, Palm Beach, ☎ *(800) 346-7084, (297) 8-61000, FAX (297) 8
63479.*
Single: $115–$605. Double: $115–$605.
This time-share complex has a great location on a great beach. Accommodations are
in studios and one- and two-bedroom apartments, tropically decorated and with
modern kitchens and private verandas. There's an open-air restaurant, beach bar
snack bar, health club with masseuse on call and a neat swimming pool complete
with falls and whirlpools. Each week they throw a cocktail party for guests.

Where to Eat

Fielding's Highest Rated Restaurants in Aruba

★★★★	Chez Mathilde	$16–$33
★★★★	Papiamento	$20–$33
★★★★	Valentino's	$16–$26
★★★	Brisas del Mar	$10–$30
★★★	Die Olde Molen	$15–$30
★★★	La Dolce Vita	$11–$32
★★★	Mi Cushina	$12–$24
★★★	Old Cunucu House	$14–$27
★★★	Que Pasa?	$12–$26
★★★	Talk of the Town	$18–$20

Fielding's Special Restaurants in Aruba

★★★★	Chez Mathilde	$16–$33
★★★★	Papiamento	$20–$33
★★★	Bali	$10–$20
★★★	Charlie's Bar	$7–$22
★★★	Old Cunucu House	$14–$27

Fielding's Budget Restaurants in Aruba

★★★	Steamboat	$7–$15
★★★	Bali	$10–$20
★★	Buccaneer Restaurant	$7–$23
★★★	Charlie's Bar	$7–$22
★★★	Mi Cushina	$12–$24

With more than 100 international restaurants, Aruba is becoming a Disneyland of cuisines. French, German, American, Swiss, Spanish—all are at your fingertips in Aruba. Plentiful supplies of Dutch cheese have inspired *keshi yena*—a stewed chicken-or-meat stuffed Gouda cheese pocket. From Indonesia, a former Dutch colony, came the lavish *rijsttafel* (rice table), an array of savory meat and vegetable dishes served with rice. From Spain, via nearby Venezuela, comes the delicious caramel dessert *flan quesillo*. You can, however, also eat strictly Aruban specialties, such as *sopi di yuana*—iguana soup—which tastes strangely like mom's chicken soup. *Funchi* (cornmeal bread) and *pan bati* (Aruban griddle bread made with cornmeal) are Amerindian specialties that accompany every Aruban meal. At the atmospheric Papiamento mi Cushina in Cura Cabai owned by native Wijke Maduro, a 10-minute drive from Oranjestad, you can go true Aruban—with specialties such as *keri keri* (finely minced fried shark) or *bestia chiquita stoba* (stewed lamb served with delicious freshly baked pan bati.) Other local delights worth trying include *pastechi* (cheese or meet-filled turnovers), wild hare stew and *cabrito* stew, a traditional seasoned feast of goat meat. When you get tired of exotica, head for the hotel coffee shops for American-style grub.

Arubans enjoy the people-to-people contact tourism has brought them.

Bali   **$$**   ★★★

Lloyd G. Smith Boulevard, #11, Oranjestad, ☎ *(297) 8-20680.*
Asian cuisine. Specialties: Indonesian Rijstaffel.
Lunch: Noon–3:30 p.m., prix fixe $10–$20.
Dinner: 6–11 p.m., prix fixe $10–$20.
Feast on almost 20 different Indonesian specialties while bobbing gently on the sea in this intricately decorated houseboat in Schooner Harbour. In what could be

Aruba's most exotic dining experience, servers present dishes of varying intensity (but nothing is overly spicy), including *nasi goreng* or *bami goreng*, rice and noodles with egg, peas, chicken or beef. Lighter meals are also served, including Western-style sandwiches. No lunch is served on Saturday.

Boonoonoonoos　　　　　　$$$　　　　　　★★

Wilhelminastraat 18A, Oranjestad, ☎ (297) 8-31888.
Latin American cuisine. Specialties: Ajaka (chicken in banana leaves), Jamaican jerk ribs.
Lunch: Noon–5 p.m., entrees $5–$13.
Dinner: 5:30–10:30 p.m., entrees $13–$33.

No, the eyes do not deceive, there really are four pairs of oo's in the name of this downtown restaurant, which means "extraordinary" in Jamaican patois. Located in a restored colonial home that's been brightly splashed with paint, cuisine covers the Caribbean in a large nutshell as conceived by Austrian chefs Kurt and Jacky Biermann. Signature dishes include Jamaican jerk ribs and a silky pumpkin cream soup; hungry diners will be more than satisfied with the Carib Combo platter, groaning with eight or nine dishes representing several Caribbean islands. The service is as good as the food. No lunch is served on Sunday.

Brisas del Mar　　　　　　$$$　　　　　　★★★

Savaneta 22A, East Oranjestad, ☎ (297) 8-47718.
Seafood cuisine. Specialties: Broiled lobster, catch of the day.
Lunch: Noon–2:30 p.m., prix fixe $10–$30.
Dinner: 6:30–9:30 p.m., prix fixe $10–$30.

Bustling and jammed with locals, especially on music-filled weekends, Brisas del Mar is about 20 minutes away from downtown Oranjestad, but well worth the trek for spanking fresh seafood and some of the finest local dishes on the island. Reservations at this folksy beach shack are required because there are only 10 or so tables. A recurring special is a flavorful fish stew, loaded with whatever's fresh, in a tasty broth. Groups can order the Aruban special, a potpourri of lightly fried fish cakes, spiced minced shark, hot relishes, plenty of rice and corn pancakes.

Buccaneer Restaurant　　　　　　$$　　　　　　★★

Gasparito 11-C, East Oranjestad, ☎ (297) 8-66172.
Seafood cuisine.
Dinner: 5:30–10 p.m., entrees $7–$23.

Moderately priced seafood generally satisfies the crowds of diners who come back again and again to this aquarium-laden, cozy restaurant located just a short jog from the large hotel strip in Noord. I've heard some complaints, though, about overcooked fish, so buyer beware. If you don't want to eat, there's a popular bar, and plenty of swimming marine life at which to gaze. European-style meat dishes are also available for seafood-hating companions. No lunch is served on Mondays.

Chalet Suisse　　　　　　$$$　　　　　　★★

J.E. Irausquin Boulevard, Palm Beach,
International cuisine. Specialties: Dutch pea soup, veal in cream sauce.
Dinner: 6–10:30 p.m., entrees $15–$30.

For a change of pace, enjoy Old European specialties in a wood-panelled dining room that's a cool, comfortable spot protecting diners from the glare of the sun outside. Homey and rib-sticking dishes like Dutch split pea soup, veal and steak offer few surprises, but are exceptionally well prepared.

Charlie's Bar $$ ★★★

Main Street 56, San Nicolas, ☎ *(297) 8-45086.*
American cuisine. Specialties: Grilled shrimp, churrasco.
Lunch: Noon–4 p.m., entrees $7–$18.
Dinner: 4–9:30 p.m., entrees $7–$22.

You too can become a part of history by hanging a hankie or old tennis shoe to join the hundreds of other artifacts on the ceiling of this 50-plus-year-old bar. It's located in the once-thriving ghost town of San Nicolas, former headquarters of The Standard Oil Company. Charlie's served as a watering hole for workers (no women were allowed then) and it now overflows with tourists seeking a cold brew (or something stiffer) and a simple lunch or dinner of fresh seafood or steak. Overseeing all this activity is Guus Dancker, who has manned the circular bar for more than 40 years.

Chez Mathilde $$$ ★★★★

Havenstraat 23, Oranjestad, ☎ *(297) 8-34968.*
French cuisine.
Lunch: 11:30 a.m.–2:30 p.m., entrees $16–$25.
Dinner: 6–11 p.m., entrees $19–$33.

Every Caribbean island must have a bastion of haute cuisine, and this elegant and intimate beauty in a 19th-century town house is IT in Aruba. Dishes are prepared in the classic French style by a Dutch chef, including thick and juicy lamb or veal chops, pate, bouillabaisse, tournedos with peppercorns and lobster thermidor. The romantic setting comes complete with candlelight, fine tableware and classical music. No lunch is served on Sunday.

Die Olde Molen $$$ ★★★

J.E. Irausquin Boulevard, Palm Beach,
International cuisine.
Dinner: 6–10:30 p.m., entrees $15–$30.

Until the brisk winds that blow on the islands constantly threatened to ruin them, this authentic Dutch windmill among the high-rise hotels in Palm Beach sported real sails. Reassembled from an 1800s-era mill that was shipped over from the old country, this tourist attraction is now a restaurant serving international food with Aruban touches. Shrimp is often featured, prepared in a savory cheese sauce, as is pepper steak and liqueured ice cream desserts. Worth a visit for the aesthetic value.

La Dolce Vita $$$ ★★★

Palm Beach 29, Oranjestad, ☎ *(297) 8-65241.*
Italian cuisine. Specialties: Veal, snapper.
Dinner: 6–11 p.m., entrees $11–$32.

Life is truly sweet here, especially for weary shoppers hoofing it down the fashionable Caya Betico Croes, where this well-known Italian restaurant is located. After several hours perusing the almost duty-free jewelry and clothing shops, snag a table (after reserving ahead) in this refurbished private home for veal and red snapper prepared in different ways, or pastas and authentic Italian desserts and coffee drinks.

La Paloma **$$$** ★★

Noord 39, Noord, ☎ (297) 8-62770.
Italian cuisine. Specialties: Conch stew with pan bati, caesar salad, red snapper.
Dinner: 6–11 p.m., entrees $13–$28.

A nice place to take the family for American-style Italian food, La Paloma is always full of patrons who like the huge menu chock full of pasta with red sauces and huge steaks, the brisk service and old-fashioned decor (chianti bottles!). The restaurant is housed in a low-rise building in the Noord area. If you want peace and quiet, this place isn't it. The bar is a popular watering hole.

Mi Cushina **$$$** ★★★

Noord Cura Cabai 24, San Nicolas, ☎ (297) 8-48335.
Latin American cuisine. Specialties: Bestia chiquito stoba, pan bati.
Lunch: Noon–2 p.m., entrees $12–$24.
Dinner: 6–10 p.m., entrees $12–$24.

There are a handful of charming small restaurants serving home-style Aruban cuisine, which is not readily available outside of the islands; one of the best is Mi Cushina, or owner Wijke Maduro's "kitchen" and family museum. Occasionally, Maduro serves iguana soup or goat stew, but usually there is fresh fish like grouper or shark served lightly fried in cake form or minced with tangy sauce. A specialty is *bestia chiquito stoba*, or lamb stew in a Creole sauce. Entrees are reasonably priced because of the hearty portions, which include some of the best pan bati on the island.

Old Cunucu House **$$$** ★★★

Palm Beach 150, Palm Beach, ☎ (297) 8-61666.
International cuisine. Specialties: Pan fried conch, cornmeal, pan bati.
Dinner: 6–10 p.m., entrees $14–$27.

Experience the Aruba of bygone days in this 1920s-style dwelling with a restaurant whose name means "old country" house. Tasty seafood is featured, as well as New York steaks and a few Aruban specialties. The atmosphere here is very relaxed and informal, amidst modern high-rise hotels that dwarf it. Even if you don't come to eat, there's a rustic bar with live and local entertainment on weekends.

Papiamento **$$$** ★★★★

Washington 61, Noord, ☎ (297) 8-64544.
Latin American cuisine. Specialties: Meat or fish cooked on hot marble, clay pot seafood.
Dinner: 6–11 p.m., entrees $20–$33.

This is possibly one of Aruba's "don't miss" experiences if only for the exquisite surroundings. Dining here is like being invited to a gracious private home—which this is. Lenie and Eduardo Ellis design their own handwritten menus, garnish their Continental dishes with fresh garden herbs, and have decorated the various dining areas with distinctive plantings and antiques. You can dine by the pool or request a single honeymoon table. Perennial favorites are available on the ever-changing menu.

Que Pasa? **$$$** ★★★

Schelpstraat Street 20, ☎ (297) 8-33872.
International cuisine.
Dinner: 6 p.m.–2 a.m., entrees $12–$26.

Hang with the locals at this funky cafe/art gallery in an eclectic Dutch house. The imaginative menu features dishes from all over the world—especially good are the pasta specialties, fresh fish, homemade soups and interesting appetizers such as bitterballen and sate ajam.The portions are huge and the service friendly. The walls are adorned with colorful Haitian art; if one strikes your fancy, you can buy it on the spot. This fun spot is a real winner.

Steamboat $$ ★★★

Lloyd G. Smith, Oranjestad, ☎ *(297) 8-66700.*
International cuisine. Specialties: Buffet Brunch.
Lunch: Noon–5 p.m., entrees $7–$10.
Dinner: 5:30–11 p.m., prix fixe $15.

One of Aruba's best bargains is this buffet foodery in a shopping center near all the hotel action. Steamboat serves a large breakfast or brunch for under $8, and large sandwiches are available for lunch. Dinner is another all-you-can eat buffet that draws crowds (understandably) for $15 per person.

Talk of the Town $$$ ★★★

L.G. Smith Boulevard 2, Oranjestad, ☎ *(297) 8-23380.*
American cuisine. Specialties: Prime rib, steaks.
Dinner: 5:30–11 p.m., entrees $18–$20.

This is an excellent stop for people with big appetites, with superb beefsteaks and prime rib feasts on Saturday nights for under $20. Located near the airport in a Best Western resort of the same name that resembles a Spanish hacienda, it's a surprisingly nice spot for quiet, intimate, candlelit dinners, and possibly the only restaurant in the Caribbean that's been awarded membership in the prestigious Chaine de Rotisseurs culinary society.

Valentino's $$$ ★★★★

Palm Beach Road, Noord, ☎ *(297) 8-64777.*
Italian cuisine. Specialties: Mozzarella in carozza, penne del pastor.
Dinner: 6–11 p.m., entrees $16–$26.

Arubans like to come here to celebrate special occasions along with residents and guests at the chic Caribbean Palm Village Resort in Noord. The reason is delicious pastas—especially fettucini with salmon—intimate tables and gracious, friendly service. Before dining, patrons can unwind with drinks, then ascend to the second-story courtyard restaurant overlooking the pool and cooled by evening breezes.

Where to Shop

Oranjestad, the capital, is a shopper's haven. Shops line the main shopping streets of Nassaustraat and Wilhelminastraat, selling mostly duty-free products (minus the 8 percent duty), such as liquor, jewelry, electronics, crystal, china, perfumes and designer fashions. Shopping malls—**Holland Aruba Mall**, **Seaport Village Mall** and the **Strada Complex**—make for one-stop shopping while **Harbour Town** and **Port of Call Marketplace** cater to the cruise crowd. The best free-port shopping can be found at **Caya G. F. Betico Croes**.

Aruba Directory

ARRIVAL AND DEPARTURE

American Airlines flies nonstop to Aruba from New York's JFK Airport and Miami daily. The flight takes about 4-1/2 hours from NYC. ALM, United and Air Aruba fly nonstop from Miami to Aruba. If you book recommended accommodations and flights at the same time through American, you can receive substantial discounts. You can also save money by reserving your flight 14 days in advance, as well as flying Monday through Thursday. ALM also flies to Aruba six days a week from Miami. The Venezuela airline VIASA flies three times a week from Houston. Aruba's national carrier Air Aruba flies from Newark, Baltimore and Miami. Air Canada offers flights from Toronto or Montreal to either Miami or New York, and then transfer to American or ALM. The departure tax is $10.

BUSINESS HOURS

Shops open Monday–Saturday 8 a.m.–6 p.m. Alhambra Bazaar is open 5 p.m.–midnight. Banks open Monday–Friday 8 a.m.–noon and 1:30–4 p.m.

CLIMATE

Dry and sunny, Aruba boasts average temperatures of 83 degrees F, though trade winds make the heat seem gentler. Mosquitoes get frisky in July and August, when it is less windy.

DOCUMENTS

U.S. and Canadian citizens need to show some proof of citizenship—birth certificate, passport or voter's registration plus a photo ID; driver's license is not accepted. You must also show an ongoing or return ticket.

ELECTRICITY

Current runs at 110 volts, 60 cycles, as in the U.S.

GETTING AROUND

Taxis are plentiful, but the lack of meters requires firm negotiations with the driver before you take off. Drivers often know the city as well as private guides. Ask your hotel to recommend one. A dispatch office is also located at **Alhambra Bazaar and Casino** ☎ *(297) 8-21604*. You can also flag down taxis from the street. Rates are fixed (no meters) but you should confirm the price before you set off. All Aruban taxi drivers are specially trained guides; an hour's tour will run about $30.

Cars are easily rented on the island; you will need a valid U.S. or Canadian driver's license to rent a car; different agencies have various age requirements. You will save money if you rent from a local agency rather than from one of the well-known agencies. Among the best are **Hedwina Car Rental** ☎ *8-26442* and **Optima** ☎ *8-36263*. Avis, Budget and Hertz are all available at the airport.

Scooters are the best vehicle to toot around the island and are the most economical. You'll save money renting for two days or longer. **Ron's** ☎ *8-62090* and **George's** ☎ *8-25975* will deliver to the airport.

Inexpensive buses run hourly between the beach hotels and Oranjestad. The main terminal is located in South Zoutmanstraat, next to Fort Zoutman. A free Shopping Tour Bus departs hourly from 9:15 a.m.– 3:15 p.m., starting at the Holiday Inn and making stops at all the major hotels on the way toward Oranjestad.

LANGUAGE

Arubans are pleasantly multilingual. The official language is Dutch; also spoken are English, Spanish, Portuguese and the local dialect called Papiamento.

MEDICAL EMERGENCIES

Horacio Oduber Hospital ☎ *8-24300* is a modern facility near Eagle Beach, with an efficient staff. Ask your hotel about doctors and dentists on call.

MONEY

The official currency is the Aruban florin (also called the guilder), written as Af or Afl. American dollars are accepted at most establishments, but it might be cheaper to pay in florins.

TELEPHONE

To call Aruba from the U.S., dial ☎ *011+297+8* followed by the five-digit number. Forget calling home from your hotel—surcharges can hike the price of an overseas call to exorbitant levels. Instead, head for SETAR, the local company, with several locations in Oranjestad and near the high-rise hotels in Palm Beach. From here, you can make phone calls using a card you purchase, and also send and receive faxes.

TIME

Aruba is on Atlantic Standard Time, year round.

TIPPING AND TAXES

Aruban custom is to charge a 10–15 percent service charge and 5 percent government tax. The total of these two charges is usually written into the "tax" slot on credit cards. If you want to give more for service, feel free, but it is not expected. Hotels add 11 percent service charge.

TOURIST INFORMATION

Aruba Tourism Authority, *A. Shuttestraat 2, Oranjestad, Aruba, N.A.* ☎ *011+297+82-3777*, FAX *83-4702.* From the U.S. call ☎ *(800) 862-7822.*

WHEN TO GO

New Year's is celebrated with an explosion of fireworks set off by the hotels and serenaded by strolling musicians and singers. Carnival is a blowout event, which starts two weeks before Lent, and culminates with a Grand Parade on the Sunday preceding Lent. National Anthem and Flag Day on March 18 is celebrated by displays of national dancing and folklore. A weekly Bonbini show in the courtyard of the Fort Zoutman museum on Tuesdays 6:30–10:30 p.m. also presents island folklore, song, and dance. The International Theatre Festival is an annual event; contact the tourist board for exact dates.

ARUBA HOTELS		RMS	RATES	PHONE	CR. CARDS
Oranjestad					
★★★★	Aruba Marriott Resort	413	$156–$450	(800) 223-6388	A, D, DC, MC, V
★★★★	Aruba Sonesta Hotel	299	$115–$530	(800) 766-3782	A, D, DC, MC, V
★★★★	Hyatt Regency Aruba	360	$205–$300	(800) 233-1234	A, CB, DC, MC, V
★★★	Americana Aruba Hotel	419	$175–$185	(297) 8-64500	A, MC, V
★★★	Amsterdam Manor Beach	72	$90–$140	(297) 8-31492	A, DC, MC, V
★★★	Aruba Hilton Int'l Hotel	479	$125–$880	(800) 445-8667	A, D, DC, MC, V
★★★	Aruba Palm Beach	200	$115–$255	(800) 345-2782	A, D, DC, MC, V
★★★	Costa Linda Beach Resort	155	$270–$430	(800) 992-2015	A, DC, MC, V
★★★	Divi Aruba Beach Resort	202	$135–$195	(800) 554-2008	A, DC, MC, V
★★★	La Cabana Beach Resort	803	$95–$640	(800) 835-7193	A, DC, MC, V
★★★	Playa Linda Beach Resort	194	$115–$605	(800) 346-7084	A, DC, MC, V
★★	Aruba Beach Club	131	$130–$290	(800) 445-8667	A, D, DC, MC, V
★★	Best Western Bucuti	63	$115–$235	(800) 528-1234	A, MC, V
★★	Best Western Manchebo	71	$100–$180	(800) 528-1234	A, DC, MC, V
★★	Best Western Talk of The Town	63	$85–$215	(800) 528-1234	A, DC, MC, V
★★	Bushiri Beach Hotel	150	$230–$330	(800) 462-6868	A, MC, V
★★	Caribbean Palm Village	170	$85–$290	(297) 8-62700	A, DC, MC, V
★★	Casa del Mar Beach Resort	147	$135–$400	(297) 8-23000	A, D, DC, MC, V
★★	Dutch Village	97	$145–$415	(800) 367-3484	A, DC, MC, V

ARUBA HOTELS		RMS	RATES	PHONE	CR. CARDS
★★	Holiday Inn Aruba	600	$121–$170	(800) 465-4329	A, DC, MC, V
★★	Mill Resort	102	$105–$550	(297) 8-67700	A, D, DC, MC, V
★★	Tamarijn Aruba Resort	236	$145–$190	(297) 8-24150	A, CB, MC, V

ARUBA RESTAURANTS		PHONE	ENTREE	CR. CARDS
Oranjestad				
American				
★★★	Charlie's Bar	(297) 8-45086	$7–$22	None
★★★	Talk of the Town	(297) 8-23380	$18–$20••	A, DC, MC, V
Asian				
★★★	Bali	(297) 8-20680	$10–$20	A, MC, V
French				
★★★★	Chez Mathilde	(297) 8-34968	$16–$33	A, D, DC, MC, V
International				
★★★	Die Olde Molen		$15–$30••	A, DC, MC, V
★★★	Old Cunucu House	(297) 8-61666	$14–$27••	A, DC, MC, V
★★★	Que Pasa?	(297) 8-33872	$12–$26••	MC, V
★★★	Steamboat	(297) 8-66700	$7–$15	A, MC, V
★★	Chalet Suisse		$15–$30••	A, DC, MC, V
Italian				
★★★★	Valentino's	(297) 8-64777	$16–$26••	A, DC, MC, V
★★★	La Dolce Vita	(297) 8-65241	$11–$32••	A, D, MC, V
★★	La Paloma	(297) 8-62770	$13–$28••	A, MC, V
Latin American				
★★★★	Papiamento	(297) 8-64544	$20–$33••	A, MC, V
★★★	Mi Cushina	(297) 8-48335	$12–$24	A, DC, MC, V
★★	Boonoonoonoos	(297) 8-31888	$5–$33	A, DC, MC, V
Seafood				
★★★	Brisas del Mar	(297) 8-47718	$10–$30	A, MC, V
★★	Buccaneer Restaurant	(297) 8-66172	$7–$23••	A, D, DC, MC, V
Note:	• Lunch Only			
	•• Dinner Only			

BELIZE

Mayan ruins throughout Belize continue to fascinate all who explore them.

Belize is not usually thought of as a Caribbean destination, located as it is in Central America between Mexico and Guatemala. But its huge barrier reef, second-largest in the world, makes it a haven for divers and fishermen. Add to that the mysterious appeal of well-preserved Mayan ruins, thick jungle teeming with exotic wildlife (including monkeys and jaguars), waters swum by the giant and gentle manatees and a system of caves beckoning to be explored, and it's no surprise that Belize has become *the* hot eco-tourism destination.

It's a designation Belizeans take seriously. As tourism continues its inevitable march through the country, both the government and concerned citizens are intent on ensuring that Belize remains wild and untamed. No one

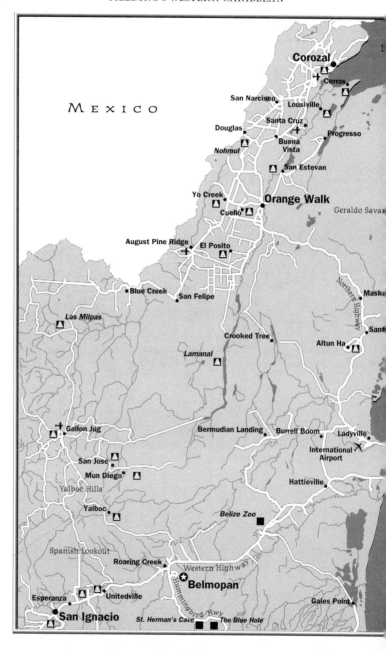

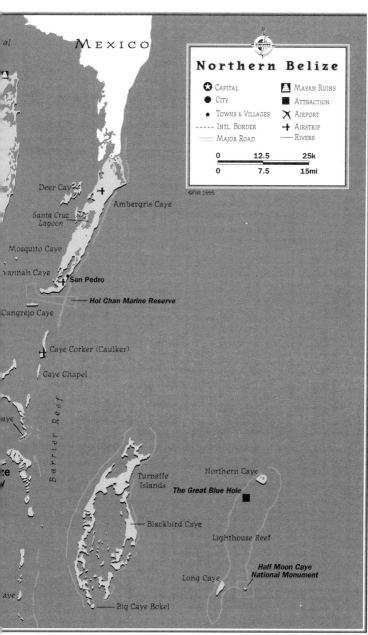

MEXICO

Northern Belize

⭐ CAPITAL
● CITY
• TOWNS & VILLAGES
----- INTL. BORDER
—— MAJOR ROAD

🏛 MAYAN RUINS
■ ATTRACTION
✈ AIRPORT
✛ AIRSTRIP
—— RIVERS

| 0 | 12.5 | 25k |
| 0 | 7.5 | 15mi |

©FWI 1996

Deer Cay
Ambergris Caye
Santa Cruz Lagoon
Mosquito Caye
vannah Caye
San Pedro
Hol Chan Marine Reserve
Cangrejo Caye
Caye Corker (Caulker)
Caye Chapel
aye
Barrier Reef

Turneffe Islands
Northern Caye
The Great Blue Hole
Blackbird Caye
Lighthouse Reef
Half Moon Caye National Monument
Long Caye
Big Caye Bokel
aye

wants to see this nature-rich country succumb to the miles of concrete and luxury hotels that have overrun such spots as St. Martin and St. Thomas.

First-time visitors should keep in mind that Belize is about as Third World as they come. Even the "luxury" hotels of Belize City leave much to be desired when compared to the tony resorts that have become a Caribbean mainstay. It's best not to drink the water in most places, eschew ice in drinks and you should don enough insect repellant to kill a small army. Many roads are made of hard-packed sand filled with giant ruts, even the paved streets are horrendous, air conditioning is a rarity and the domestic airlines will give heart attacks to those who fear flying. Leave your memories of pampering trips to the Caymans and Martinique far behind, and prepare for an adventure of an entirely different ilk.

The democratic nation has two main parties, the United Democratic and the People's United, which local wags say exist only to throw the other out of power, mostly by exposing corruption. Sounds more than a bit similar to the United States, but in Belize, elections are really mainly by personalities and skeletons in closets—not issues. While some claim that enough money can open up any sensitive ecosystem to development, most hoteliers say they were pleasantly surprised that they never had to grease a palm to build their properties. The general consensus is that both parties are sincerely dedicated to preserving the country's natural assets. But Belize is a young and decidedly Third World nation, and it's fervently hoped that good intentions will not be forgotten in the heady lure of tourist dollars.

You, as a visitor, can help. Always stay on the trails, don't remove or disturb plants, don't touch or kick sand on coral, respect wildlife, use local guides when available and, very importantly, don't buy any sea turtle products; reptile skins and leather; birds, their feathers or skins; and furs of spotted cats (you'll never get them past customs anyway). As Belizeans struggle to cope with an influx of tourists, it's imperative visitors show them that they like the country just as it is. Belize will never have the sophistication of a San Juan or a Charlotte Amalie—and viva la difference!

Bird's Eye View

Sandwiched between the Mexican Yucatan and Guatemala, Belize is a small country, totaling just 8866 square miles (about the size of Massachusetts). It borders Guatemala to the west and the Caribbean Sea to the east. The counry is well known for two features, one the work of nature and the other left by ancient man.

Lying just offshore is a large barrier reef, the longest in the Western Hemisphere and second in the world only to Australia's Great Barrier Reef. The reef stretches 200 miles from the Yucatan Peninsula to the Guatemalan border and is visable (as breaking waves) from most points on the mainland. There are also three coral atolls—**Turneffe Islands, Lighthouse Reef** and **Glover's Reef**—that give divers a total of 350 miles of reef to explore. Add more than 200 cayes (pronounced "key"), mostly uninhabited, and you have a true diver's paradise. The reef is also good for snorkelers, especially **Hol Chan Marine Reserve**, a five-square-mile underwater park with depths from 3 to 30 feet, located off the coast of San Pedro in **Ambergris Caye**.

The "other" Belize is on the mainland, an area rich in ruins from the remarkable Mayan civilization that lived in the area from 2000 B.C. to A.D. 1000. No one is quite sure what happened to these flourishing, advanced peoples, but a visit to at least one ruin is *de rigueur*.

In the north, the land is mostly flat, while the southern regions encompass the craggy **Maya Mountains**. Many rivers meander through the land, their banks lined with monkeys, parrots and toucans in the trees, their waters filled with manatees, crocodiles and trophy-size fish.

Much of the country is given over to jungle and rainforest, and numerous sanctuaries provide safe havens for howler monkeys (locally called baboons), jaguars, tapirs, pumas, ocelots, hundreds of bird species and other exotic creatures. There are caves to be spelunked, rivers to cruise, mangrove swamps to be explored and giant waterfalls to splash about in.

The Cayes

Belize's 100 or so cayes (pronounced "key") are mostly uninhabited, but several, notably **Ambergris Caye** (see separate section) and **Caye Caulker** cater to tourists, especially divers eager to explore the surrounding crystal-clear waters.

Located just 19 miles northeast of Belize City, Caye Caulker is a peaceful little island (five miles long and a half-mile wide) with streets of sand. The island is sliced in two by a narrow passageway called the **Split**, which was created by Hurricane Hattie in 1961. While tearing the island in two, Hattie created a small beach and excellent snorkeling.

The north section is given over to mangrove swamps and nesting birds; there's a total of 139 species, with more than 20 percent indigenous to Belize. It's in the south end where all the action takes place—though "action" is a relative word in such a quaint, laid-back place.

A handful of streets are lined with boutiques, clapboard houses, inns and wooden, slat-style lobster pots. There are only a few cars—most folks get around on golf cart (even the taxis), bicycle or foot.

The barrier reef is visible from most points in town and is the reason divers and fishermen flock here. **Hol Chan Marine Reserve** (also excellent for snorkeling), the famed **Blue Hole at Lighthouse Reef**, and a recently discovered underground cave system keep divers fascinated. Other nearby prime diving sites include **Pyramid Flats, Long Caye, Coral Caverns** and **Sergeant's Caye**. A popular day trip is to **Goff's Caye**, a tiny tropical island with exactly 13 palm trees.

History

It's interesting to think that when Jesus walked the Earth as man, some 750,000 Mayas lived in what is now Belize. They planted corn everywhere and built impressive cities and ceremonial centers of limestone. But, a thousand years later, as Europe entered the Dark Ages, the Maya civilization collapsed, for reasons still unclear.

Five centuries later, the Spanish captured Mexico and Central America, and the few Maya left were kept in virtual slavery. Today's jungles and rainforest developed and mahogany flourished. British pirates (called logcutters, then later, Baymen) arrived in the 1600s and went to work harvesting the highly valued mahogany. The Spaniards sent troops to kick the British out, but five tries later, the logcutters remained.

Finally, Spain signed a treaty with England granting the Baymen the right to cut wood between the Honro and Belize rivers. But when the Spanish governor of Yucatan tried to remove the Baymen from the Hondo River, England intervened with a fleet of ships and soldiers under the command of Admiral Sir William Burnaby.

No violence was necessary; the dispute had already been settled before the admiral arrived in 1765. Before leaving, though, he crafted Burnaby's Code, a constitution-like document that established the public meeting as the supreme lawmaking body. This code was honored until 1862, when Queen Victoria granted the settlement English colonial status, and the area became known as British Honduras. In 1870, British Honduras was named a Crown Colony.

Meanwhile, Maya refugees from Mexico began flooding into Belize and, among other things, introduced sugarcane. But sugar prices crashed in the

880s, and World War I effectively killed the demand for mahogany. The colony became entrenched in poverty. It wasn't until after World War II, when Belizean soldiers came home with new ideas for the colony's future, that things started looking up.

On December 31, 1949, the British Government devalued the British Honduras dollar. That sparked the Movement of Liberation—formed the very next day—which finally succeeded in 1964, when the colony became a self-governing nation. The name was officially changed to Belize in 1973—it had been called that for years, though no what knows exactly where the word comes from or what it means. On September 21, 1981, Belize became an independent nation.

Today, the country is a democracy that belongs to the United Nations, the Commonwealth and the Non-Aligned Movement. The government is dedicated to opening the country to tourism while at the same time preserving its rich natural assets.

Mayan Ruins

Hundreds of years later, the scientific community continues to be baffled by the ancient Mayan civilization that lived in Mexico and Central America. Who were they? How did they erect such impressive buildings? And where did they all go?

Mayans inhabited the area from 2000 B.C. to 1000 A.D. They were a remarkably advanced people, well-honed in science, trade and art, and built sophisticated cities and temples. Between 250 and 900 A.D., the peak of the Classic period, literally millions of Mayans lived in Belize, which was considered the heart of the Mayan Empire. Mayan ruins are found throughout the country, some remarkably preserved—and many more, undoubtedly, sleeping far beneath the jungle floor. You'll easily find the major ruins on tourist maps or by asking at your hotel. The ruins feature incredibly steep steps—the reward for climbing to the top is awesome views, but take great care, as the stones are often quite slippery.

Located 31 miles north of Belize City, **Altun Ha** (Water of the Rock) is one of the easier explored ruins. It's also one of the country's most important, as the jade head found here is the national symbol of Belize. The head, the largest carved jade object in the entire Maya area, represents the sun god, Kinich Ahau, and is on the corner of every Belize dollar. Altun Ha was a major ceremonial center in the Classic Period and a vital trading center with Maya centers in the interior.

One of the most significant ruins is **Caracol** (The Snail), located south of San Ignacio. It wasn't until the 1980s that archeologists realized its importance as the "supreme" Maya city, after unearthing an elaborately carved altar stone that describes a victory by Caracol over Tikal, once considered the most important Maya metropolis. The impressive ruins include a *canaa* (sky palace) that rises 140 feet—the tallest man-made structure in Belize.

Located on the New River Lagoon, **Lamanai** (Submerged Crocodile) is one of the nation's largest ceremonial centers and had a long occupation, from 1500 B.C. to the 19th century, when the Spaniards came. Among the ruins are a sugar mill and two Christian churches.

La Milpa, in the Rio Bravo Conservation Area in northwestern Belize, is Belize's third-largest site, featuring more than 85 structures and 24 courtyards, including the enormous **Great Plaza**.

Cahal Pech (Place of the Ticks), located in the Cayo District on the west bank of the Macal River, is a medium-sized Maya center. The best reason to come here are the fantastic views of San Ignacio and the Belize River Valley

Other important sites include **Lubaantun** (Place of Fallen Stones), a late Classic ceremonial center northwest of Punta Gorda (a 20-minute walk from the road); **Cerros**, a short boat ride from Corozal Town in the Bay of Chetumal, an important coastal trading center during the late Pre-Classic period (100 B.C.–A.D. 250); and **Xunantunich** (Maiden of the Rock), a major ceremonial center on a natural limestone ridge, located near the western border across the river from San Jose Succotz.

People

Belize's 200,000 residents are a blend of Creole (the majority at 60 percent), Maya, Mestizo (a mix of Spanish and Indian), Mennonites (conservative farmers and furniture makers), immigrants from India, and Garifu (black Carib Indians who perform ritualistic dances). There are expatriates from Europe, Asia and the United States.

Education is a top national priority, and 90 percent of the population is literate, though school is mandatory only until age 14. After that, student must pay to attend high school, a price out of reach of most Belizean families.

The people are generally friendly and open. A smile is invariably returned, and children who bump into you on the street will offer a sincere and polite apology. Though crime is a serious problem in Belize City, the rest of the nation is relatively safe—though, of course, care should always be taken when engaging strangers in conversation and carrying valuables.

Beaches

Belize has ancient ruins, renowned sportsfishing and wonderful diving—but not, alas, great beaches. Much of the coast is given over to mangrove swamps. Even on Ambergris Caye, which has a sandy coast dotted with swaying coconut trees, you generally can't swim off the beach unless you don't mind mucking about in sea grass and the guts of fish stripped clean by those who caught them. (Good swimming can generally be found at the end of the boat docks that jut from nearly every hotel.) To the south, Placencia has picturesque beaches, but again, sea grass keeps most swimmers out.

Underwater

Marked by a thin, rippling necklace of mostly unbroken waves, the **Belize Barrier Reef** stretches from the south end of the Yucatan Peninsula to a point near the southern border of Belize, 175 meandering miles away. As such, it is second in length only to the Great Barrier Reef off Australia. If the diving were limited to this extended site, Belize would be a fine dive destination. But three separate atolls east of the main reef provide most of the country's best dives. Add in a phenomenal deep blue sinkhole—the largest in the world—and you have the recipe for one of the Caribbean's very best underwater adventures.

The barrier reef was formed along a fault line and extends from the Mexican town of **Xcalak** (a few miles north of the Belize border), winding roughly south and parallel to the coast to a conclusion around **Hunting Caye**, near the Guatemala border. This wall creates one of only three faro reef systems in the world. The barrier reef averages a distance of between 8 and 15 miles over most of its length, but comes within a mile of **Ambergris Caye** and the town of San Pedro, where most of the dive operators are based. San Pedro, in fact, owes much of its relative prosperity to the dive industry, with roughly a dozen outfits set up to serve the country's many diving visitors. The downside is that crime and petty theft have increased dramatically over the past decade, causing many visiting divers to steer toward live-aboard situations or to the almost uninhabited outer reefs (see below). However, **Ambergris** is the only Belize island to offer much in the way of creature comforts, which pretty well guarantees its position as dive central into the foreseeable future. **Hol Chan Marine Reserve**, just off the southern tip of Ambergris Caye, is a mere 10- to 15-minute boat ride from most of the San Pedro operators. The reserve was established in 1987 after overfishing had substantially depleted the area's marine life; since then, fish have started returning and over 40 moored dive sites now exist. The reserve contains three distinct areas: Zone A, comprised of the barrier reef immediately south of San Pedro; Zone B, a sandy flat of sea grass covered in conch and visited by seahorses and rays; and Zone C, the mangrove swamp. Visibility inside the barrier reef averages 50 feet, but regularly exceeds 100 feet on the outside.

The barrier reef continues south, passing Belize City, St. George's Caye, Man-O-War Caye and the town of Placencia before petering out at Hunting Caye. The southern stretch of the barrier past Gladden Reef, is infrequently visited, but offers the best chance of encountering an exciting, if sporadic, local visitor, the somnolent 30-foot whale shark.

Belize's most exciting diving, however, is located around the three atolls which lie to the east of the barrier reef: **Lighthouse Reef**, **Turneffe Island** and **Glovers Reef**, each of which have one or two dive operations on their tiny specs of land. Though it lies the farthest offshore, Lighthouse is easily the most famous of the three, due largely to the magnificent **Great Blue Hole**, one of the world's most renowned dive sites. The all but perfectly circular hole was once a cave which collapsed about 10,000 years ago, creating an underwater sinkhole 1000 feet across and 480 feet deep. Popularized by Jacques Cousteau in a television special, the unique site has understandably become the must-do dive of Belize, although it's not for all tastes. Served by a small airstrip, Lighthouse is also home to **Half Moon Caye National Monument**, a nesting area for endangered red-footed boobies. **Turneffe Islands** is the largest of the atolls, and the closest to Belize City. The area surrounding **Big Caye Bokel**, at the southern tip of Turneffe, is the location of most of the best dive sites, and **Blackbird Caye** is home to a dolphin research station; manatees are also known to frequent these waters, feeding in the grassy flats of mangrove swamps. The third, most remote, and somewhat overlooked atoll is **Glovers Reef**, which lies off the coast from Dangriga and offers a wall that plunges quickly to over 2000 feet; there is ample room for virgin sites to be located along this 14-mile-long atoll. Visibility on the three atolls typically ranges from 120 to 150 feet.

Lighthouse and Turneffe are visited by the San Pedro dive operators but both are a very long trip, three hours each way via boat (overnight camping trips are popular). However, a number of Belize's return visitors base themselves at one of the five resorts on these far-flung outposts; although there's little to do while on land, you are considerably closer to the superb diving. All of these resorts book one-week, all-inclusive visits only, and do not offer shorter packages or individual dives. Another approach worth investigating is using a live-aboard to explore Belize's extensive waters (see **Belize Aggressor II** and **Wave Dancer**, below). The few wreck sites Belize has to offer are primarily off the east side of Lighthouse Reef, but as many of these ships were washed onto the crest of the reef (and, therefore, are above the water) as lie below. A few additional wrecks lie off the northeast side of Glovers Reef which, not coincidentally, was named after pirate John Glover.

The Elbow

Easily the most-requested site on Turneffe, Elbow Reef lies at the southern end of the atoll, just off Big Caye Bokel. Currents can be tricky (it's generally an advanced location), but sometimes permit a drift dive starting at 90 feet, descending to 130 feet. Huge gorgonians, yellow tube sponges and a rich quantity and variety of both reef fish and larger pelagics parade through the spur-and-groove formation.

Elkhorn Crossing

Giant elkhorn and other corals abound through this appealing shallow dive (to 25 feet), popular as an easy late afternoon site. The depth allows more light onto the reef, making the coral more vivid, but Elkhorn is also a terrific night dive, when octopus, spiny lobsters and starfish come out to play.

The Great Blue Hole

A series of now-submerged caves lies under the middle of Lighthouse Reef, and the long-collapsed roof of the Great Blue Hole provides a gaping entrance. Aerial photos display the surface image best (like a striking blue eyeball gazing into space), but words cannot prepare a diver for the thrill of dropping over the sandy lip into a chilly, deep purple abyss. Then, about 130 feet down, a new landscape appears: cathedral-like caverns adorned with dozens of stalactites. There's essentially no fish or coral life to be seen on this dive. Instead, it's the unique experience of investigating a cave which became known only through a cataclysmic, ice-age event. Although the dive is relatively effortless, the short bottom time (about 8 minutes) and depth makes this dive strictly for the experienced. Visitors should be cautioned that, in view of the effort which goes into reaching this site, a number of divers think it's overrated; others will find the Great Blue Hole just their cup of tea. Either way, there's nothing else like it.

Half Moon Caye Wall

Perhaps Belize's most spectacular wall, this group of sites lies off the east end of Half Moon Caye, starting at only 40 feet below the surface. The sheer wall offers dramatic caverns and swim-throughs, and Half Moon is the only sheltered, east-facing reef (on the atolls), which provides a magnet for bigger pelagics, including lemon, whitetip, blacktip and even bull sharks, drawn in from the depths.

Hole in the Wall

A series of coral spurs lead to a hole (at 50 feet) inside the reef, frequently thick with thousands of silversides; this swim-through descends to 80 feet and leads to the outer reef where gorgonians sprout from the reef. The landscape and architecture of this Glovers Reef site are fascinating.

M and M Caverns

A popular deep dive (80 to 100 feet) just off San Pedro, the M and M Caverns lie in a surge channel which slices through the barrier reef formation, providing access to swim-through caverns and fissures. The walls are decked out in deep water fans and colorful tube sponges.

Silver Caves

Named after the great quantities of silverside minnows which seasonally invade, this group of fissures, caves and overhangs lies just west of Half Moon Caye and also attracts occasional spotted eagle rays and tarpon. There's also a vivid array of sponges displayed in all shapes and colors, but the real reason you go is for the minnows, who school by the thousands in tight, shimmering curtains which part in unison in front of you, and come together behind you in a harmonious rush.

Dive Shops

Amigos Del Mar

San Pedro, Ambergris Caye; ☎ *(501) 26-2706.*
PADI outfit handling day-trips to Hol Chan area and nearby sites; actively involved in reef protection program. Two-tank dive, $45.

Belize Aggressor II

☎ *(800) 348-2628 or (504) 385-2628.*
Seven-day, all-inclusive trips, $1495, including all meals and five-and-a-half days of diving. The boat holds 18 passengers and beginners may obtain their certification while on the cruise (additional charge). Extensive photo/video facilities on-board. The boat is based in Belize City and leaves every Saturday for Lighthouse and Turneffe, with a trip to the Great Blue Hole weather permitting.

Coral Beach Hotel and Dive Club

San Pedro, Ambergris Caye; ☎ *(501) 26-2013.*
This 20-year-old, locally-owned PADI and NAUI outfit arranges overnight trips to the Great Blue Hole ($240, including all food and five dives). Two-tank dive, a rock-bottom $38.

Lighthouse Reef Resort

Lighthouse Reef; ☎ *(800) 423-3114 or (813) 439-6600 (no Belize number available).*
Seven-night, Saturday-to-Saturday package includes flight from Belize City, three dives daily, all meals and an air-conditioned room: $1350 for cabanas or $1500 for suites. The Great Blue Hole is eight miles away and included in package price, along with one night dive. 11 rooms. Sea kayaks also available.

Manta Resort

Southwest Caye, Glover's Reef; ☎ *(800) 342-0053 or (813) 594-8022 (no Belize number available).*
A truly isolated location on the least-visited of Belize's three atolls, Manta is situated on a privately-owned 12-acre island on the southern end, right next to the 2000-foot wall. Seven night package with three dives per day, all food and accommodations, $1295 (discounted to $995 during summer months).

Ramon's Village

San Pedro, Ambergris Caye; ☎ *(800) 624-4215 or (501) 26-2071.*
A PADI and NAUI outfit started in 1988, Ramon's limits dive groups to eight. Two-tank dive, $45. Also assembles day trips to the Great Blue Hole several times a week (three dives, $165), and once a week to the Turneffe Islands (three dives, $125).

Turneffe Flats Lodge

Turneffe Islands; ☎ *(800) 815-1304.*
Started as a fishing lodge in 1985 and gradually shifting to dive activities; located on the northwest end of Turneffe. Snorkeling and fishing available for nondivers. Seven-night, Saturday-to-Saturday package with three dives daily, all food and accommodations, $1295; includes trip to Great Blue Hole, weather permitting.

Turneffe Island Lodge

Turneffe Islands; ☎ *(800) 338-8149.*
12-room inn, situated at Caye Bokel, minutes away from most of Turneffe's best sites. Seven-night package, $1295, including all food, accommodations and three dives daily; day trip to Great Blue Hole extra. Underwater camera and video service available; also features kayaks and windsurfing.

Wave Dancer/Peter Hughes Diving

☎ *(800) 932-6237 or (305) 669-9391.*
One of Belize's two all-inclusive, live-aboard dive boats. The 20-passenger Wave Dancer visits Turneffe and Lighthouse Reefs and, weather permitting, the Great Blue Hole. The seven day trips are priced at $1495-1645 (depending on type of berth you select; all have private bathroom/shower). The boat operates year-round and departs every Saturday out of Belize City. Instructor available on all trips and beginners with referrals may obtain their open-water certification on the trip for $198.

On Foot

Although Belize is aggressively promoting itself as a nature destination, relatively few trails exist at this time for visitors to take advantage of on their own. Most hiking is done with the several guide outfits that explore the jungles of hardwood and plush tropical foliage blanketing much of the interior. **Victoria Peak**, the nation's highest point, rises to 3675 feet above the **Cockscomb Basin Wildlife Sanctuary**, but no marked trails climb to its summit; you'll need a guide to make the long two-day round-trip from Cockscomb. This area is also home to the **Jaguar Sanctuary**, and there are a few trails that explore its reserves, resplendent with wildlife (although jaguar sightings are few and far between). The spectacular **Mountain Pine Ridge** has lots of impromptu hiking options; the area is at its driest—no small consideration—during the springtime. The **Planti Trail**, a short path through an area of traditional Native American medicinal plants, begins immediately next to the Chaa Creek Cottages (see "Where to Stay"); there is a $5 donation ($7.50 with a local guide). The poisonous fer-de-lance snake can be found throughout much of Belize's interior; tapping a stick in front of your path will usually scare it away. Boa constrictors, though rare, have also been spotted in the Belizean mountains. Some of Belize's informal guide services advertise at Eva's Restaurant in San Ignacio, and offer tours to some of the region's many caves, as well as excursions into Mountain Pine Ridge. However, do not use guides who make themselves available in Belize City, many of whom are con men.

Blue Hole National Park and Saint Herman's Cave

Not directly related to the famous Great Blue Hole out on the barrier reef, this park was established in 1986 and surrounds another collapsed sinkhole, this one containing the headwaters of the Siban River, and creating a superbly cool swimming hole. A rugged one-and-a-half mile "Nature Trail" leads from the Blue Hole to St. Herman's Cave, which is entered through the bottom of another sinkhole. Pottery, spears, torches and other Mayan artifacts have been located here and are now being studied by the local Department of Archeology.

By Pedal

With the exception of the moderately busy 50-mile stretch between Belize City and Belmopan, Belize's roads are very lightly traveled, although they vary substantially in how well they are surfaced. Generally, the **Western Highway** leading to the Guatemala border, and the new **Northern Highway** to Mexico are in good shape, and suitable for road bikes. Heading south beyond Dangriga, however, will require a mountain bike capable of negotiating bumps and potholes, where the road is paved. If you are heading south, note that a new road (not yet shown on all maps) heads southeast to Gales Point, from the La Democracia junction a few miles past the Belize Zoo. Although this route's scenery is not quite as spectacular as the traditional track via Belmopan, it cuts out about 40 miles of hilly travel along the Hummingbird Highway (note, however, that this is rugged and remote country with few fellow travelers, much less any cyclists). A particularly nice area to have a mountain bike is in lovely **Placencia**, where the road down a thin, 16-mile spit of sand connects the town to the mainland. **San Ignacio** is an excellent base for exploring **Mountain Pine Ridge**, where fire trails and jeep paths provide access to the country's most remote jungles; a guide is advised for any extensive exploration. The ruins of **Xunantunich** make for a beautiful 19-mile round-trip from San Ignacio, and the **Yalbac Hills** to the north would appear to have superb mountain biking potential. A more ambitious ruin trip is **Altun Ha**, which lies about 35 miles northwest of Belize City (two miles off the Old Northern Highway). At this writing, Belize's only bike rental shop has closed down, but a new agency may be open soon. If stopping in Belize City, make sure your bike is securely locked, and even that may not be enough in this rough town.

What Else to See

Belize may be small in size, but it's full of things to do and see. One of the more popular activities for visitors is swimming with manatees. Belize is said to have the largest population of the playful, shy sea cows in the world. **Excalibur's** *(59 Barrier Reef Drive (Front Street), San Pedro,* ☎ *(501) 26-3235)* offers a trip to **Goff's Caye**; en route, the boat stops to let snorkelers frolic among the manatees, which the company says are "100 percent guaranteed."

Caving is also popular; the rutted **Hummingbird Highway**, which links Belmopan and Dangriga, has several along its route. At **Caves Branch**, you can float on an inner tube through miles of underground river caves, many with Maya artifacts and wall carvings. Professional guides are mandatory; call ☎ *(501) 2-33903*. Also worth exploring is **St. Herman's Cave**, where spears, torches and pottery have been recovered. To get there, take the trail from Blue Hole, but beware, it's a killer. There are also caves to explore around San Ignacio in the Cayo District, including the Chumpiate Maya, a limestone cave with enormous Maya pottery that's been untouched for eons.

River trips through mangrove swamps are available from most destinations throughout the country. One of the best is along the **Monkey River**, south of Placencia. Chances are good you'll spot manatees, iguanas, howler monkeys and lots of exotic birds during the five-mile float. Part of the Bladen River Reserve, the Monkey is Belize's largest protected river.

If you're into butterflies, they've got them by the bushel at San Ignacio's **Butterfly Breeding Centre** *(*☎ *(501) 92-2037)*. The chief attraction here is the blue morpho, known as the "Belizean Blue."

Wildlife of a wilder kind can sometimes be spotted at the **Cockscomb Basin Sanctuary** near Dangriga. This is the world's first and only jaguar preserve. The cats are nocturnal, so you probably won't see them by day, but overnight excursions can be arranged by calling ☎ *(501) 2-77369*.

Parks and Gardens

Belize Zoo   ★ ★ ★ ★

Mile 30, Western highway, Belize City.

Hours open: 10 a.m.–5 p.m.

The Belize Zoo and Tropical Education Center was opened in 1983 by Sharon Malota, who was seeking a home for a small group of animals no longer needed by a natural film producer. Today the zoo totals 28 acres and has more than 100 species of native animals, including many endangered species such as the jaguar, tapir and howler monkey. The zoo is small by U.S. standards, but internationally respected for the good care its animals receive and the emphasis on education and conservation. Animals are enclosed in thatch-roof cages with lots of natural bush, so you'll go to some effort to spot them. Frustrating perhaps, but not nearly as depressing as a visit to a zoo where the poor creatures sit bored in concrete cages. The biggest attraction is April, a 500-pound tapir (Belize's national animal) who resides in her own pond and is a big hit with the many schoolkids who pass through.

Tours

Community Baboon Sanctuary ★ ★ ★ ★ ★

Bermudian Landing, near Belize City.
Hours open: 8 a.m.–5 p.m.

Don't come expecting large black monkeys thumping their chests—the animals here are the small howler monkeys (locally known as baboons). Called an "experiment in grass-roots conservation," the sanctuary comprises 20 square miles of eight villages, where some 130 landowners have voluntarily left trees intact at riverbeds and boundary lines to give the thriving population of howler monkeys a viable habitat. After touring the small but crammed museum on the Belize ecosystem, a guide takes you into the jungle, where chances are excellent you'll spot a family of the little rascals. The father of the group lets out a strange howl that sounds like water going down a rusty drain—hence the name. You'll also spot leaf-cutting ants industrially going about their business, and, alas, more mosquitoes than imaginable. Wear lots of repellant and bring your camera.

Crooked Tree Wildlife Sanctuary ★ ★ ★

two miles off the Northern Highway, near Belize City.

Located 33 miles northwest of Belize City, this bird sanctuary is home to the jabiru stork, the largest bird in the Western Hemisphere with a wingspan of eight feet. You'll also spot snail kites, snowy egrets, and five species of kingfisher, among other feathered friends. The 3000-acre park, founded by the Belize Audubon Society, has swamps, lagoons and waterways. Hire a local guide at the village of Crooked Tree for the best views of this fascinating slice of nature.

Tour Companies

Belize City.

Melmish Mayan Tours (☎ *(501) 2-45551)* in Belize City offers a variety of tours of Maya ruins, the Baboon Sanctuary, into the jungle and caves and along rivers. They're highly reputable and a pleasure to deal with. Other major tour operators in the city include **Mayaland Tours and Travel** (☎ *(501) 2-30515)*, **Belize Travel Adventures** (☎ *(501) 2-33064)*, **Belize Land Air Sea Tours** (☎ *(501) 2-2-73897)* and **Discovery Expeditions Belize** (☎ *(501) 2-30748)*. **Tubroos Tree Adventures** (☎ *(501) 2-33398)* offers specialty tours on natural history and archaeology, while **Native Guide Systems** (☎ *(501) 2-75819)* can tailor special tours for birding, kayaking and sightseeing. In San Pedro on Ambergris Caye, tour companies include **Island Adventures** (☎ *(501) 26-2697)*, **Rocks Inn** (☎ *(501) 26-2362)* and **Belize Visitor & Tours** (☎ *(501) 26-2728)*. In Placencia, Ellis Burgess is a laid-back guide who will take you just about any place you want to go in his plush red van. He's easy to find just by asking around. Other tour guides include **P.I. Tours** (☎ *(501) 62-3291)* and **Seahorse Guides** (☎ *(501) 62-3175)*. On Caye Caulker, try **Cari Search LTD** (☎ *(501) 2-22178)* for tours with marine biologists. The **Caye Caulker Tour Guide Association** (☎ *(501) 2-22285)* and **Harrison Tours** (☎ *(501) 2-22263)* offer general excursions, while **International Cultural Tours** (☎ *(501) 2-22285)* conducts tours with an emphasis on culture, ecology and local customs.

Sports

Besides trekking through the jungle, most athletic pursuits in Belize take place off its shores in the Caribbean Sea. Diving, of course, is the biggest attraction, But sports fishing is also immensely popular, and fishermen from the world over love to tell tales of the ones that got away—and the ones that didn't—in Belize.

Bonefishing takes place year-round along the coast and at offshore cayes. The most popular fishing spots are **Ambergris Caye** (where the fish averages three pounds), **Turneffe Islands** (where you can expect sizes of five pounds), **Tobacco Caye** and **Glover's Reef**. Trophy size is considered eight pounds. Fly fishing is the preferred method; a nine-weight fly rod, nine-weight floating rod and small fly are recommended. With spinning gear, use a six- to eight-pound line and small jig or hook and hermit crab as bait.

Placencia is the best spot to fish for permit, also found year-round closer to the reef and drop-offs on the flats. They average about 10 pounds, with trophy sizes about 30 pounds. Fly fishers should use a 10-weight rod, weight-forward floating line and 14- to 15-pound leader.

Other game to try for include tarpon (found April through November along the flats and cayes and June and July on the reef at Ambergris Caye), snook (found on flats close to the mainland from November through March), and, along the barrier reef, mutton and yellowtail snapper, grouper, jack crevalle and barracuda

Belize's many rivers—particularly the Sibun and Belize—also offer up great rewards. The quarry here is snook, tarpon, cubera snapper and jewfish, which can grow to 200 pounds. All can be found year-round, through the best time for tarpon is April and May when the fish spawn.

Fishing the flats costs about $100 to $250 for a half or full day. Full-day deep-sea fishing trips start at $350. River excursions go for $125 to $250 for a half or full day. A tip of $20 per full day of fishing is considered the norm.

Bring your own equipment, as tackleshops are few and far between. You'll have no problem finding a guide—the country teems with them. For more information, contact the **Belize Game Fishing Association** at ☎ *(501) 2-77044*. Also pick up *Destination Belize*, the nation's official visitor magazine, which supplied information for this section and contains a wealth of detailed tips for reeling in the big one.

The **Belize River Lodge** *(☎ (501) 25-2459 and 800-748-3715)* in Belize City specializes in fishing packages in the lodge, which dates back to 1961, or on three live-aboard yachts from 40 to 58 feet. On Ambergris Caye, fishers flock to the **El Pescador Hotel** *(☎ (501) 26-2398)*, a 12-room colonial-style lodge that caters to sports fishermen.

Diving

Belize City.

There are more mosquitoes on Belize than diving companies, but not many more. The list of operators is far too long to include in these pages, but here are some of the larger companies. Ambergris Caye (San Pedro): **Old Island Divers** *(☎ (501) 26-2151 and (800) 258-3465)*, **Amigos del Mar** *(☎ (501) 26-2706)*, **Excalibur Dives** *(☎ (501) 26-3235)* **Blue Hole Center** *(☎ (501) 26-2982)*, **Tortuga** *(☎ (501) 26-2804)* and **Belize Dive Center** *(☎ (501) 26-2797)*. **Reef Seeker** *(☎ (501) 26-2804)* offers glass-bottom boat trips for snorkelers (rent your equipment before departing), and is unique in that even if just one person signs up, they'll still make the trip. Placencia: **Placencia Dive Shop** *(☎ (501) 62-3227)*, **Deep End Dive Shop** *(☎ (501) 62-3295)*, **Rum Point Divers** *(☎ (501) 62-3239)* and **Seahorse Guides** *(☎ (501) 62-3166)*. Belize City: **Blackline Marine Service** *(☎ (501) 2-33187)*, **Western Caribbean Live Aboard** *(☎ (501) 2-32810)* and **Blue Planet Divers** *(☎ (501) 26-76770)*. Caye Caulker: **Belize Diving Service** *(☎ (501) 2-22143)*, **Caye Caulker School of Scuba** *(☎ (501) 2-22292)* and **Frenchie's Diving Service** *(☎ (501) 2-22234)*.

Fishing

Belize City.

Fishing is big business in Belize, and you'll have no problem finding a guide to take you to the hot spots, be it along the barrier reef, off an atoll or along a river. Here are some of the major operators. Ambergris Caye (San Pedro): **Deep Sea Charter Fishing** *(☎ (501) 26-2911)*, **Amigos del Mar** *(☎ (501) 26-2648)*, **Captain Morgan's Retreat** *(800-447-2931)*, **El Pescador Hotel** *(☎ (501) 26-2398)* and **Excalibur Tours** *(☎ (501) 26-3235)*. Placencia: **Blue River Guiding** *(☎ (501) 62-3130)*, **Kingfisher Sports** *(☎ (501) 62-3175)*, **P&P Sport Fishing** *(☎ (501) 62-3132)*, **Seahorse Guides** *(☎ (501) 62-3166)*, **Southern Guide** *(☎ (501) 62-3277)* and **Westby Sportsfishing** *(☎ (501) 62-3234)*. Belize City: **Belize Travel Adventures** *(☎ (501) 2-33064)*, **Belize River Lodge** *(☎ (501) 2-52002)*, **Discovery Expeditions** *(☎ (501) 2-30748)*, **Ramada Royal Reef Marina** *(☎ (501) 2-32670)* and **Zippy Zappy Boating Service** *(☎ (501) 2-75033)*. Caye Caulker: **Roque's Fishing and River Tours** *(☎ (501) 2-22014)* and **Allan Nunez Reef Trips** *(☎ (501) 2-22285)*.

Belize City

Blessed are those who expect nothing, for they shall never be disappointed. Keep that in mind when you visit Belize City, the nation's only urban area that's home to some 80,000 residents. Though it has some decent accommodations and a few sites worth seeing, the city is rundown, grungy and not especially worth visiting. Many folks leave immediately after clearing customs at Philip S.W. Goldson International Airport—and they're not missing much.

Still, the city does have some charms. It's cut in two by the narrow (and quite polluted) Haulover Creek, with three bridges spanning its width. The charming one is the **Swing Bridge**, which dates from the early 1900s. Nine men labor to open the bridge by hand crank each day at 5:30 a.m. and 5:30 p.m. Hours before, an array of boats, including some dubious-looking makeshift skiffs, line up and "park." It's a colorful sight.

Downtown's two main streets are called Albert and Regent. They're lined with cafes, shops, offices (it's strange to hear the clatter of typewriters) and outdoor vendors displaying a curious collection of goods—a typical stall has cheap tableware, pots and pans, racy comic books and large quantities of sexy lingerie. These entrepreneurs are mellow, letting passersby peruse their wares without the obnoxious pushiness that plagues Jamaica and the Bahamas.

What does plague the city is crime. Muggings and purse snatchings are all too common, and virtually every structure—even the expensive homes in the Caribbean Shores district—has bars on the windows. It's hoped the addition of tourism police and a new quick trial system with harsh punishments will put a dent in youthful crime. Recently, two boys aged 17 and 19 were sentenced to 14 years apiece for hitting a woman while stealing her gold chain.

Though it fronts the Caribbean Sea, the city has no beaches. You can stroll the seafront promenade and gaze with awe at the giant pelicans that hang out in the **Fort George** area. Also here is the **Baron Bliss Lighthouse**; Bliss, Belize's greatest benefactor, is entombed in front.

Sites to see in the city include the **Commercial Centre**, located at the southeastern corner of the Swing Bridge. This large, open building has vendors selling fruits, vegetables and some tacky souvenirs. A sign above its large planters begs, "please don't sit on the plants. Give them a change to grow." Apparently people do indeed park themselves atop the greenery because the poor things are struggling.

Government House, a green-roofed colonial structure, is one of the city's prettiest buildings. Located on the sea at the end of Regent Street, it houses visiting dignitaries. Nearby is **St. John's Cathedral**, the oldest cathedral in

Central America. Built in 1812–20 from bricks used as ballast on English ships, four Mosquito Coast kings were crowned here.

If you're dying to get pampered, make tracks for the **Acupuncture & Massage Center** at *3 Cork Street* in the Fort George area. The charming Chinese couple that owns the place gives a marvelous, hour-plus massage for just $20. They're also skillful acupuncturists; call ☎ *(501) 2-31017* for an appointment.

The city is currently undergoing an ambitious, $50-million beautification project. The money is being spent to redo roads, add sidewalks, revamp the fetid canal system and fund loans so property owners can fix up—or at least paint—their facades. As a banner on City Hall declares, "Belize City Council and Citizens Working Together for a Cleaner and Healthier Belize by the Year 2001." They have their work cut out for them, but also a fine spirit that's not to be discounted.

Ambergris Caye

Belize's biggest tourist region is on the island known as Ambergris Caye (pronounced "key"), located far to the north, just a few miles from the Mexican Yucatan. San Pedro, its biggest town, is a fun and funky place where the streets are made of sand, many shops and restaurants have sand floors and the preferred mode of transportation is the golf cart. Since the carts are incredibly expensive to rent ($15 an hour, $70 a day, $275 a week), most folks get around on foot—usually bare ones at that.

Tiny San Pedro has two main streets that only in the past few years were officially given names. Front Street is now Barrier Reef Drive but no one seems to recall the new name they gave Middle Street—which gives you an idea just how casual life here is. The town is small, but it's crammed with hotels, restaurants, an incredible amount of liquor stores and a slew of watersports centers for the chief attraction—diving. Nearly 50 wooden piers jut out from the shoreline to accommodate the many fishing and diving boats active in town.

San Pedro has no real attractions, just a gloriously laid-back aura characterized by people strolling about in the most casual of outfits with beers firmly clenched in hand. The beaches are pretty but not especially swimmable due to an overwhelming abundance of sea grass. If you're dying for a dip, just walk to the end of a pier and jump in where the sea is clear.

The town has a great nightlife, and, interestingly enough, Belize's only casino: an unassuming little joint called **Palace Video** *(*☎ *(501) 26-3570)* where they have a handful of video poker and slot machines. It's open daily from 1 p.m. to 2 a.m. They don't serve liquor and a sign outside warns against bringing in firearms.

One very cool spot is **Tarzan's** (☎ *(501) 26-2947)*, a disco whose sand floor gives way to a lighted dance floor. Two balconies upstairs overlook the action and a silly automated waterfall adds to the surrealness of the spot. It opens each night at about 8 or 9 and closes Monday-Wednesday at midnight and Thursday-Sunday at 3 a.m. If it's crowded enough, the owner will flick on the air conditioner. Music varies from reggae to disco to hard rock, while occasional entertainment features the likes of male strippers and wet tee-shirt contests. (They have to import the "talent" from Belize City as the locals watch, but don't participate.)

At the **Pier Lounge** at the Spendrift Hotel, they have crab races on Mondays (hermit crabs trying to maneuver an obstacle course) and the chicken drop on Wednesdays. This dubious event consists of blowing on a chicken's behind, then dropping it onto a numbered grid in hopes it will defecate on your number.

More sedate types make tracks for the **Sunset Bar** above the Lagoon restaurant. Open only from 5–7 p.m., it's simply a bunch of tables and chairs on the roof where you can lazily sip a beer and watch the sun drop. Also worth a visit is **Fido's**, where they serve the coldest beer in town. The restaurant is not great, but the bar, overlooking the beach and sea, is nice and casual. Resist the urge to play the two video poker machines here—they're a royal rip-off.

San Pedro is one of the few spots in Belize where you'll see conspicuous signs of prostitution. These working girls come over from Belize City looking for tourists willing to pay for a good time. Use caution: AIDS has infiltrated Belize, just like everywhere else.

Placencia

You know you're in for something different when the plane drops you at Placencia "airport." The word is in quotes because the facility, if it can be called that, consists of an airstrip, shaded bench and sign with the name of the town. That's it—no baggage handlers, no gift shop, no taxi line—just a few iguanas sunning themselves and the roar of the plane as it lifts off the tiny runway, just in the nick of time.

Welcome to Placencia, one of the most laid-back places on Earth—and also one of the hardest to leave. It's here you'll find Belize's best beaches (though they're still not great compared to other Caribbean islands), a Garifuna village with its own distinctive culture dating back centuries and the happiest bunch of expatriates ever to plant their roots in a new land. The locals, mostly Creoles, peacefully coexist with these American and European entrepreneurs—mostly older hippies, younger deadheads, and others seeking the good life—but view them with a bit of bemusement. Most of the hotels here are owned and run for foreigners, but as long as they respect and employ the local community and treat nature with respect, no one seems to mind.

Placencia Village, which has about 500 residents, has earned its spot in the *Guinness Book of World Records* by having the world's narrowest street. The publishers must have been in a good mood when they made the entry—undoubtedly swept away by the area's charms—since this "street" is nothing more than a concrete sidewalk that winds past restaurants and though people's yards. It lasts just a mile or so, then ends abruptly and nowhere in particular. And that about sums up Placencia.

Visitors to the region would be remiss if they failed to make a visit to the neighboring town, **Seine Bight**, located four miles to the north. This Garifuna community follows ancient cultural traditions from Africa, speaks its own language (**Garinagu**) and generally keeps to itself. Visitors are welcome to wander through its maze of simple huts on stilts, however, and even participate in a healing dance if one's occurring. This ritual, performed only on "prescription" by the traveling Garifuna medicine man, involves the family of the ill dancing for three days and three nights straight. Afterwards, selected family members spend seven days and six nights in the temple—a wooden shack to the uninformed—and may not leave until that time has passed. As stated, tourists are welcome to watch and even dance, but must cover their head in a bandana and show respect for a ritual taken very seriously by those who practice it. Some 765 people, mostly related to one another, live in Seine Bight.

Like the Creoles, the Garifuna don't seem to mind the creeping stretch of tourism right in their backyard. Most of the area's nicest lodging is found just outside the village but so far the two distinct worlds live peaceably, with a good deal of mutual respect.

Visitors to Placencia are big on diving—there are 40 cayes offshore with colorful coral and teeming schools of fish. Catch and release fly-fishing for bone fish, snook and trophy-size permit is big. Also popular are excursions up the Monkey River, manatee watching in Placencia Lagoon (which separates the peninsula from the mainland) and night trips to the **Cockscomb Basin Wildlife Sanctuary** in hopes of spotting the elusive jaguar.

Placencians know how to party! Fun night spots include **De Tatch**, where they'll let you scribble your thoughts on the wall; the **Flamboyant**, where folks gather around picnic tables under a giant yellow flamboyant tree; **Tentacles**, a bar and restaurant on stilts right over the sea; and the **Dockside Bar**, where the breeze and the music is always good. People are friendly, the kids are adorable (they love getting their picture taken) and it takes just a few hours in this southern town to feel the stresses of the real world slip away in favor of the what-the-hell, live-and-let-live Placencian state of mind.

Where to Stay

Fielding's Highest Rated Hotels in Belize

★★★★	Belize Yacht Club	$125–$300
★★★★	Hotel Casablanca	$60–$90
★★★★	Mayan Princess	$75–$125
★★★★	Nautical Inn	$65–$99
★★★★	Rum Point Inn	$150–$112
★★★★	Victoria House	$95–$130
★★★	Belize Biltmore Plaza	$100–$100
★★★	French Quarter	$85–$110
★★★	Ramada Royal Reef Resort	$105–$147
★★★	Ramon's Village	$115–$245

Fielding's Most Romantic Hotels in Belize

★★★	Colton House	$33–$45
★★★★	Hotel Casablanca	$60–$90
★★★	Kitty's Place	$33–$108
★★★	Ramon's Village	$115–$245

Fielding's Budget Hotels in Belize

★	Seaside Guest House	$8–$18
★	North Front Street Guest House	$15–$25
★★★	Colton House	$33–$45
★	Martha's Hotel	$30–$60
★★	Barrier Reef Hotel	$40–$65

Belize City

The city has a fair sprinkling of good hotels with meeting space and business services—notably the **Radisson Fort George**, **Ramada Royal Reef** and **Biltmore Plaza**—as well as some excellent guest houses where you sacrifice room service but gain an insider's view by staying with locals. The **Colton Guest House** is highly recommended for its pretty, clean rooms and gracious hosts.

Hotels and Resorts

Belize Biltmore Plaza　　　　　　　　**$100**　　　　　　　　★★★

Mile 3, Northern Highway, ☎ (800) 333-3459, (501) 2-32302, FAX (501) 2-32301.
Single: $100. Double: $100.

Don't be put off by your first impression; it's quite nice inside this property (but looks awful from the outside). Rooms are quite modern and have all the usual creature comforts (air conditioning, TV, direct-dial phones) and look onto a courtyard with a nice pool complete with swim-up bar. Other facilities include a bar, restaurant and business services. This hotel is located close to the international airport—a plus—but there's not much within walking distance—a definite drawback.

Bellevue Hotel　　　　　　　　**$79–$83**　　　　　　　　★★

5 Southern Foreshore, ☎ (501) 2-77051.
Single: $79. Double: $83.

This family-run hotel has been around since the early 1900s. It shows its age but accommodations are pleasant enough with air conditioning and telephones. There's a pool, restaurant, bar, disco and tour company on site, and service is warm and caring.

Gallows Point Reef Resort　　　　　　　　**$50–$95**　　　　　　　　★★

seven miles offshore, ☎ (501) 27-5819, FAX (501) 27-4007.
Single: $50–$95. Double: $50–$95.

Located just seven miles from Belize City but, as they say, a whole world apart, this small island offers up accommodations in the economical Wave Hotel and the more expensive Buccaneer House. There's also "Tent City" for campers ($10 per person per night). Activities include diving, snorkeling, glass-bottom boat rides and caye hopping.

Radisson Fort George　　　　　　　　**$99–$139**　　　　　　　　★★★

2 Marine Parade, ☎ (800) 333-3333, (501) 2-77400, FAX (501) 2-73820.
Single: $99–$139. Double: $99–$139.

This is one of Belize City's most luxurious hotels—but keep in mind that Belize is a Third-World country, so luxury is relative. Rooms are nicely done and quite modern, but could use some renovation. The nicest are in the executive "tower" (it's just six floors high); these include minibars and sea views. The hotel has a decent restaurant, hopping bar, good gift shop and a not-terribly-inviting pool. Service is professional.

Ramada Royal Reef Resort　　　　　　　　**$105–$147**　　　　　　　　★★★

Newtown Barracks, ☎ (800) 228-9898, (501) 2-32670, FAX (501) 2-32660.
Single: $105–$135. Double: $117–$147.

One of Belize City's best choices, the Ramada is convenient to downtown. Rooms are pleasant with air conditioning, ceiling fans, modern baths and direct-dial phones. Facilities include two restaurants, three bars, a salon and a full-service marina. Favored by business travelers.

Inns

Colton House   **$33–$45**   ★★★

9 Cork Street, ☎ *(501) 2-44666, FAX (501) 2-30451.*
Single: $33–$38. Double: $40–$45.

This 1928 colonial-style wooden house is a real find. Situated next to the Radisson Fort George Hotel, it offers four guest rooms so amazingly clean you'd swear you were in Japan! Two share a bath while two have their own private bathroom. All are very nicely done with polished wooden floors, high ceilings and antique reproductions; each has its own separate entrance. There are no air conditioners, but ceiling fans generally do the job. There's also a new efficiency unit with a microwave and air conditioner. Very, very nice.

Fort Street Guest House   **$45–$60**   ★★★

4 Fort Street, ☎ *(501) 2-30116.*
Single: $45. Double: $60.

This restored Victorian home is a favorite with those who like a decent room—complete with modern art and mosquito netting—and don't want to pay through the nose for it. You'll share a bath, but it's clean. The on-site restaurant is excellent and has a decidedly Casablancan air.

Low Cost Lodging

North Front Street Guest House   **$15–$25**   ★

124 North Front Street, ☎ *(501) 2-77595.*
Single: $15. Double: $25.

Obviously, at these rates, the rooms are nothing to write home about, and you'll be sharing a bath. Still, the accommodations are decent enough at this friendly and funky guest house. The Caye Caulker boat dock is a block away.

Seaside Guest House   **$8–$18**   ★

3 Prince Street, ☎ *(501) 2-78339.*
Single: $8–$13. Double: $15–$18.

There's no hot water or private baths at this colonial-style guest house, but you sure can't beat the price, especially if you opt for the four-bed dormitory room. The American owner is friendly and accommodating, and the location, three blocks from central square, is good.

Ambergris Caye

There's a slew of hotels in and around San Pedro, the island's chief tourist area. The nicest ones, such as **Victoria House** and the **Belize Yacht Club**, are a few miles out of town, which is a distinct disadvantage unless you rent a golf cart or keep early hours (taxis generally disappear by 11 p.m.). In town, **Ruby's** offers fairly decent and Spartan rooms, while **Casablanca** is well worth the extra money for its air-conditioned and fanciful accommodations. **Ramon's Village** is the splashiest resort and less than a mile from downtown.

Hotels and Resorts

Barrier Reef Hotel   **$40–$65**   ★★

San Pedro, ☎ *(501) 26-2075.*
Single: $40–$48. Double: $48–$65.
This rambling guest house, built in 1907, is conveniently located on Front Street, across the street from the beach. Rooms are basic and include ceiling fans or air conditioners and private baths. One of the town's few pools is on site.

Coral Beach Hotel   **$45–$65**   ★★

San Pedro, ☎ *(501) 26-2013, FAX (501) 26-2864.*
Single: $45. Double: $65.
Despite the name, this hotel, located on Front Street, is not on the beach, though it's only a few minutes' stroll away. If you can live without air conditioning, you can deduct $15 off your room rate per night. Meal plans are available for $20 or so extra. The hotel has a popular dive shop that arranges excursions to outer isles and atolls.

Holiday Hotel   **$60–$94**   ★★★

San Pedro, ☎ *(510) 26-2014, FAX (501) 26-2295.*
Single: $60–$94. Double: $69–$94.
All rooms at this simple hotel are right on the beach. Each is quite basic but very clean; refrigerators and air conditioners are available for a small extra charge. There's an on-site restaurant and deli, as well as a dive shop, good boutique and a cute bar. The Wednesday night barbecues (about $6) are fun with live music and good food. The Front Street location puts you in the heart of San Pedro's nightlife.

Mayan Princess   **$75–$125**   ★★★★

San Pedro, ☎ *(501) 26-2778, FAX (501) 26-2784.*
Single: $75–$115. Double: $85–$125.
This beachfront property, opened in 1992, is one of downtown San Pedro's best choices. The cement building houses very nice rooms with full kitchens, rattan furnishings, living rooms, and large furnished balconies. They are set up like a railroad flat and include extras like cable TV, direct-dial phones and ice makers. Request a room on the second or third floor for privacy from beach strollers.

Paradise Resort Hotel   **$50–$140**   ★★★

San Pedro, ☎ *(501) 26-2083, FAX (501) 26-2232.*
Single: $50–$140. Double: $70–$140.
The Paradise, located downtown right across the street from the power plant (some rooms suffer from its noise), is one of San Pedro's largest properties. Rooms are in thatched cabanas situated around a courtyard on the beach. They are basic but nice, with hardwood floors, simple rattan furniture, ceiling fans, air conditioners in some and shower-only baths. Request a second-floor unit for better views and more privacy. Cabana number one has a cute little porch and is right on the sea, but has no air conditioner. Some units have a kitchenette. As with most operations in town, there's no pool.

Ramon's Village   **$115–$245**   ★★★

San Pedro, ☎ *(501) 26-2071, FAX (501) 26-2214.*

Single: $115–$245. Double: $115–$245.

Ramon's is the closest San Pedro comes to a full-service resort, and it's a cute one at that. Accommodations are in picturesque private cabanas with thatched roofs; the basic rooms are nothing too exciting, but the suites are quite nice. Only a handful of units face the sea, but all are just steps from the beach. There have been some complaints of too-thin walls and ceiling fans hung dangerously low, but the beach is among San Pedro's best. On-site facilities include two restaurants, a nightclub, an Olympic-size pool and a dive shop.

Spendrift Hotel $53–$165 ★★

San Pedro, ☎ (501) 26-2174.
Double: $53–$165.

Another of San Pedro's many Front Street hotels, the beachfront Spendrift offers standard rooms with or without air conditioning. There's also a one-bedroom apartment with kitchenette, living and dining area, and a two-bedroom unit with a huge kitchen, but no ocean view. The decent Little Italy restaurant is on the premises.

Victoria House $95–$130 ★★★★

San Pedro, ☎ (800) 247-5159, (501) 26-2076, FAX (501) 26-2429.
Single: $95–$115. Double: $110–$130.

This deluxe choice is located right on the beach, a few miles south of San Pedro. Guests are accommodated in air-conditioned hotel rooms or stone and thatch casitas. There are also villas with two or three bedrooms. The grounds are quite lovely, and the bar and restaurant are both excellent. There's also a good on-site dive shop.

Apartments and Condos

Alijua Hotel Suites $72–$104 ★★★

San Pedro, ☎ (501) 26-2791, FAX (501) 26-2362.
Single: $72–$88. Double: $88–$104.

This newer property, located on Front Street in the heart of San Pedro, has six full suites and one "semi-suite" with just a small refrigerator and coffeemaker rather than the fully stocked kitchenettes in the others. Each unit has two beds in the bedroom, a nice bathroom with tub and shower and the small kitchenette, which is incorporated into the living/dining area. Amenities include cable TV and ceiling fans, with air conditioners only in the bedroom. All are located on the second floor; downstairs are shops and restaurants. The beach is across the street, but there's an on-site sun deck with lounge chairs, hammocks and barbecue grills.

Belize Yacht Club $125–$300 ★★★★

San Pedro, ☎ (501) 26-2777, FAX (501) 26-2768.
Double: $125–$300.

This resort complex of red-roof Spanish-style villas is quite upscale by Belize standards. Units come with one to three bedrooms and are very nicely done, with complete modern kitchens, tropical furnishings, nice baths and air conditioners in the bedrooms. There's an excellent gym, small but inviting pool and an outdoor bar that serves light fare at lunchtime. No beach, but there is a dock handy for boaters.

Decent, but the locale, about a mile from downtown San Pedro, is a bit out of the way.

Bed and Breakfast

Hotel Casablanca   **$60–$90**   ★ ★ ★ ★

San Pedro, ☎ *(501) 26-2327, FAX (501) 26-2992.*
Single: $60–$90. Double: $60–$90.
Casablanca gets my vote for San Pedro's most unique hotel. Its five rooms, located above the gourmet Lagoon restaurant, are just fantastic, with air conditioners, ceiling fans, high-quality furnishings, fanciful art deco touches and wonderful original art painted right on the walls. The third floor is given over to the rooftop Sunset Bar, and the beach is just a block away. The rates include breakfast served by owner Dion, an interesting combination of Oklahoma and Manhattan, who will more likely than not appear in her feather-and-silk robe and stilettos from Victoria's Secret to pour coffee.

Low Cost Lodging

Martha's Hotel   **$30–$60**   ★

San Pedro, ☎ *(501) 26-2053, FAX (501) 26-2589.*
Single: $30–$40. Double: $55–$60.
You'll get hot and cold water and a private bath, but not much else besides a clean and basic room at Martha's, located in the heart of town.

Ruby's Hotel   **$14–$38**   ★ ★

San Pedro, ☎ *(501) 26-2063, FAX (501) 26-2434.*
Double: $14–$38.
The location, right on Front Street, is good, and it's well worth the few extra dollars for a second- or third-floor room, which have private baths and nice sea breezes. Don't expect much in the guest rooms—they are very plain and as basic as they come, but do include fans and are fairly clean. You can save bucks by sharing a bath. The bakery right next door is wonderful.

Placencia

All properties in Placencia are tiny affairs—usually less than 10 rooms—and generally consist of individual wooden cabanas raised on stilts. Most are owned and operated by American expatriates. **The Nautical** has sparkling clean rooms and well-tended grounds. the new **French Quarter** should prove to be a winner and the **Rum Point** is wonderfully imaginative. All, unfortunately, are out of an easy walk's reach to Placencia village. **Kitty's Place** offers up fine, comfortable digs and is just a mile from town.

Hotels and Resorts

French Quarter   **$85–$110**   ★ ★ ★

Seine Bight Village, ☎ *(800) 641-6665.*
Double: $85–$110.
Kathleen Eschenburg, Glenn McCullough and three of their four kids fled life as hoteliers in Ocean City, Maryland, to open their dream resort in Belize in the fall of 1995. The brand-new resort has five individual cabanas made of solid mahogany with interiors of rosewood, mahogany and ironwood. Each unit is raised eight feet off the ground and has a veranda, huge bathrooms with tub and shower, original art

and pretty Guatemalan fabric curtains and bedspreads. The resort features the village's only pool, as well as a restaurant, bar and book and video library.

itty's Place $33–$108 ★ ★ ★

Near the airstrip, ☎ *(501) 62-3227, FAX (501) 62-3226.*
Single: $33–$63. Double: $43–$108.

Kitty's is a charming enclave of wooden cottages with porches on a picturesque beach. Accommodations come in a variety of styles, from rooms sharing baths to large sea-view units with private baths to two apartments with kitchens. All are cooled by ceiling fans. The property is run by American expatriate Kitty Fox, who, on request, flicks on the satellite TV at the independently owned bar and restaurant. Also on the premises are a decent gift shop and a cute little duck pond. Placencia Village is a mile and a half away.

autical Inn $65–$99 ★ ★ ★ ★

Seine Bight Village, ☎ *(501) 62-2310.*
Single: $65–$89. Double: $75–$99.

The Nautical takes its name seriously—there are all kinds of sea touches around this very nice property. Guest rooms are comfortable and sparkling clean, with wooden walls, beamed ceilings, blue fabrics and comfortable beds. All have ceiling fans, and air conditioning is available for an extra charge. Second-floor rooms have balconies, so are the better choice. Run by a charming couple from Arizona, the Nautical has a guests-only restaurant and a perfectly situated hammock located at the end of a dock complete with gazebo. Quite impressive, and they even have purified water!

um Point Inn $93–$175 ★ ★ ★ ★

☎ *(800) 747-1381, (501) 62-3239, FAX (501) 26-3240.*
Single: $93–$112. Double: $150–$175.

Igloos in Central America? Don't laugh—it works at this very unique resort. Guests are housed in cement cabanas, each with its own different-shaped windows cut all through the structure. Inside, they are very spacious with skylights, ceiling fans, nice furnishings and large bathrooms. Really cool! The main lobby is a comfy area where guests can hang out and watch videos or peruse the excellent library. Many opt to laze on hammocks that dot the huge wooden porch. The rates include all meals but not drinks.

nging Sands Inn $50–$89 ★ ★

Maya Beach, ☎ *(800) 617-2673, (501) 62-2243.*
Single: $50–$79. Double: $60–$89.

This newer property has cute but basic cabanas with thatched roofs, clean baths, cheap paneling on the walls, ceiling fans and pretty little flower gardens in front on each. The biggest drawback to this spot is that the cabanas are practically on top of one another, so be sure to request one at the end for a bit more privacy. There's a bar and restaurant on site.

Inland

Lodges located right in the heart of the jungle and long rivers are sprinkled throughut Belize. Here's a rundown of some of the best known.

Belmopan

Banana Bank Lodge (☎ *(501) 8-23180)* is located an hour west of Belize City o
4000 acres that lie along the Belize River. Accommodations are in the five-bedroom mai
house and five two-bedroom cabanas. Activities include horseback riding, canoeing, bird
watching and jungle treks. **Cave's Branch Jungle Camp** (☎ *(501) 8-22800),* located 1
miles south of Belmopan off the Hummingbird Highway, specializes in expeditior
through the jungle and three underground river cave systems. Lodging is in Mayan-styl
screened and thatched cabanas. There's no electricity (all lighting is with kerosene lamps
latrines are used and bathing is in the river, so this spot isn't for everyone.

Crooked Tree

The Bird's Eye View Lodge (☎ *(501) 2-32040)* is set in the heart of the Crooked Tre
Wildlife Sanctuary, 33 miles northwest of Belize City. The Belizean-owned lodge is step
from the lagoon, where birdwatching is particularly good from October through earl
May, the dry season.

San Ignacio

Windy Hill Cottages (☎ *(501) 92-2017)* at Graceland Ranch has comfortable cottage
with verandas, hammocks and ceiling fans. It's also unique in having a registered nurs
on-site (she's the co-owner.) Features include a pool, private nature trail, horsebac
riding and canoeing. **Black Rock Jungle River Lodge** (☎ *(501) 92-2341)* Set on th
banks of the Macal River and accessible only by a 20-minute walk from the road. Gues
are housed in private, screened cottages. Activities at this rustic spot include hikin
through the jungle, horseback riding, canoeing, caving and birdwatching. **Caesar's Plac**
(☎ *(501) 92-2341)* Accessible by car and has more modern conveniences. Set on fiv
landscaped acres on Barton Creek, rooms are pleasant and have hot water. There's also
campground with full RV hookups. **Maya Mountain Lodge** (☎ *(501) 92-2164)* House
guests in gaily decorated thatched-roof cottages. Activities at this fine spot include horse
back riding, canoeing, browsing through the excellent reference library and jungle expe
ditions.

South of San Ignacio, the **Five Sisters Lodge** (☎ *(501) 92-2985)* is located in the sce
nic Mountain Pine Ridge Forest Preserve. The lodge takes its name from the five wate
falls and numerous pools that empty into the Privassion River. Guests are housed i
thatched cabanas with richly varnished mahogany interiors. Each has hot water, verand
and hammocks.There's a good restaurant on site, as well as guided tours to **Rio Fr
Caves** and the **Caracol** ruins.

In the Orange Walk District, the **Chan Chich Lodge** (☎ *(800) 343-8009)* is general
considered the nation's premier eco-tourism property. It's located within a 125,000-acr
nature reserve and bordered to the north by another 150,000 acres of protected lan
The main lodge and 12 cabanas are nestled within the lower plaza of an ancient May
city. Each cabana, constructed entirely of materials from the surrounding jungle, has ho
water and electricity. Activities include swimming in the nearby river, touring archaeolog
ical sites, horseback riding, canoeing and guided night walks. Rates are $100–$115 dou
ble occupancy; meal plans and all-inclusive packages are also available.

Other Orange Walk properties include **Lamanai Outpost Lodge** *(☎ (501) 2-33578)*, which is set on the banks of the New River Lagoon and overlooks the Lamanai Maya ruins; and **Maruba Resort** *(☎ (501) 3-22199)*, which offers luxurious accommodations and a spiffy health spa right in the heart of the jungle.

The Cayes

Among the budget accommodations on Caye Caulker (under $25) are **Caye Caulker Guest House** *(☎ (501) 22-2249)*, **Jiminez Huts** *(☎ (501) 22-2175)*, **Martinez Caribbean Inn** *(☎ (501) 22-2113)* and **Tom's Hotel** *(☎ (501) 22-2102)*. More relatively upscale lodging ($25–$50) can be found at **Chocolate's Guest House** *(☎ (501) 22-2151)*, **Rainbow Hotel** *(☎ (501) 22-2123)*, **Tropical Paradise** *(☎ (501) 22-2124)* and **Vega Inn** *(☎ (501) 22-2142)*.

Lodging on other cayes and atolls:

Turneffe Islands: **Blackbird Caye Resort** (budget, *☎ (501) 2-73129)*, **Turneffe Flats** (moderate, *☎ (501) 2-30116)* and **Turneffe Island Lodge** (expensive, *☎ (800) 338-8149)*.

Tobacco Caye: **Fairweather & Friends** (budget, *☎ (501) 5-22201)*, **Ocean's Edge Lodge** (moderate, *☎ (800) 967-8184)*, **Island Camps** (budget, *☎ (501) 2-72109)* and **Reef End Lodge** (budget, *☎ (501) 5-22171)*.

Glover's Reef Atoll: **Glover's Reef Atoll Resort** (budget, *☎ (501) 8-23505)* and **Manta Resort** (expensive, *☎ (800) 342-0053)*.

Where to Eat

★★★★★	De Tatch	$3–$8

Fielding's Highest Rated Restaurants in Belize

★★★★★	De Tatch	$3–$8
★★★★★	Lagoon	$8–$17
★★★★	Brenda's	$3–$10
★★★★	Fort Street Restaurant	$7–$14
★★★★	Maxime's	$5–$22
★★★★	Micky's Place	$4–$19
★★★	Elvi's Kitchen	$3–$17
★★★	Franco's Restaurant	$5–$7
★★★	Little Italy	$4–$17
★★★	Tentacles	$6–$16

Fielding's Special Restaurants in Belize

★★★★★	De Tatch	$3–$8
★★★★★	Lagoon	$8–$17
★★★★	Brenda's	$3–$10
★★★	Elvi's Kitchen	$3–$17

Fielding's Budget Restaurants in Belize

★★★★★	De Tatch	$3–$8
★★★	Franco's Restaurant	$5–$7
★★	Flamboyant	$3–$10
★★★	Elvi's Kitchen	$3–$17

Belize City

While the quality of water may be dubious, the food is not, and Belize City's restaurants run the gamut from gourmet rooms in hotels to tiny shanties on the side of the road. Most vegetables, meat and seafood are produced locally. Belizean food is generally spicy with a generous dose of peppers and cilantro. Some of the county's most famous dishes are *escabeche* and *relleno*, hardy soups of vegetables and chicken served with corn tortillas. You'll also see *granacho* on lots of menus—a corn fried tortilla piled with refried beans, cabbage, cheese and hot sauce. You may also spot *gibnut*, a small, furry animal that Queen Elizabeth bravely tried when she visited the country a few years ago.

A note to vegans: You'll have a terrible time trying to eat well in Belize. Bring your own food or prepare to live on salads of iceberg lettuce. Vegetarians who eat seafood fare much better.

Calypso Bar & Grill $ ★★★

Newtown Barracks, ☎ *(501) 2-32670.*
American cuisine.
Great views from this hotel restaurant built right over the sea. The menu offers American and Belizean dishes in a casual atmosphere. There are live bands on the weekends, when the joint stays open until 2 a.m.

Fort Street Restaurant $$ ★★★★

4 Fort Street, ☎ *(501) 2-60116.*
International cuisine.
Lunch: 11 a.m.–2 p.m., entrees $7–$8.
Dinner: 6–10 p.m., entrees $12–$14.
This intimate dining room pays homage to the film classic *Casablanca*, with a large poster of Humphrey Bogart standing guard. The eclectic menu features Continental and Belizean specialties such as lobster and steaks, as well as fresh seafood and vegetarian dishes. Save room for their famous "Death by Chocolate" cake. Also open for breakfast from 7–10 a.m.—don't miss the luscious french toast.

GG's Cafe and Patio $ ★★★

2-B King Street, ☎ *(501) 2-74878.*
International cuisine.
This charming restaurant in downtown Belize City has a pleasant courtyard where you dine under Belikin beer umbrellas. Owner George Godfrey makes great hamburgers, steaks and local dishes like skewered pork and rice and beans. Reasonable prices make this spot a winner.

Maxime's $$ ★★★★

2 Marine Parade, ☎ *(501) 2-77400.*
American cuisine.
Dinner: 6–10 p.m., entrees $5–$22.
Located on the fifth floor of the Radisson Fort George, this gourmet room has large picture windows overlooking the city and sea. Next door is a comfortable bar with a nice open-air balcony. The large dining room doesn't have much atmosphere— yellow walls, simple artwork, ceiling fans—but the service is decent and the food quite good. The menu offers a large selection of soups, salads and seafood. There's also pork and beef from the Cayo Hills and chicken from Mennonite farms. Most dishes cost $12 to $14.

Ambergris Caye

Long before tourism became the economic mainstay, San Pedro was a sleepy fishing village. Today's fishermen realize they can make more taking tourists out on deep-sea excursions than on fishing themselves, so ironically enough, local restaurants have a hell of a time getting fish. Nonetheless, you'll probably find a fair amount of tasty sealife on the menus, as well as luscious lobster dishes and the ever-popular rice and beans. **Elvi's Kitchen** may have turned into a tourist trap, but it still serves decent fare. For gourmet dining, try the upscale (but any standards) **Lagoon**. Great baked goods await at **Ruby's Cafe** on Front Street.

Elvi's Kitchen $$ ★★★

San Pedro, ☎ (501) 26-2176.
International cuisine.
Lunch: 11 a.m.–2 p.m., entrees $3–$17.
Dinner: 5:30–10 p.m., entrees $3–$17.

Elvi's has been open for 18 years, making it a San Pedro institution. Locals resent that it's become so popular and touristy, but the food is still quite decent and reasonably priced. The restaurant is quite atmospheric with a sand floor, picnic-style wooden tables, ceiling fans and a high thatched roof. The huge menu lists tons of seafood, chicken, meat and burgers. Don't miss the rice and beans. There's live music on Thursdays (Caribbean) and Saturdays (Mexican). They close each October for two weeks, so if you're in town then, call ahead.

Lagoon $$ ★★★★★

San Pedro, ☎ (501) 26-2327.
International cuisine.
Dinner: 6–10 p.m., entrees $8–$17.

Wonderful food and professional service are the hallmarks at Lagoon, San Pedro's only true gourmet restaurant. The eclectic menu features international specialties, but this place is best known for its tasty seafood and lobster dishes. Lobster Lagoon comes with sweet butter liqueur creme sauce restuffed in the shell and served with mashed potatoes to die for, while lobster curry has a sweet coconut cream sauce with artichokes, mushrooms and onions, served on a bed of rice with almonds, raisins and bits of pasta. Also luscious is the green salad with pico de gallo and creamy Parmesan dressing. The restaurant has cute ice cream parlor-style wrought-iron chairs, cloth tablecloths and napkins, waiters in black tie (in San Pedro!) and the funkiest bar in Belize. Don't miss it. If you come early enough, go up to the third floor to the Sunset Bar, open only from 5:00-8:00 p.m., where the views are great and the drinks potent.

Little Italy $$ ★★★

San Pedro, ☎ (501) 26-2866.
Italian cuisine.
Lunch: 11:30 a.m.–2 p.m., entrees $4–$17.
Dinner: 5:30–9 p.m., entrees $4–$17.

Keep in mind that this is not Italy, and you'll be satisfied with the Italian fare at this waterfront restaurant. You can sit outside overlooking the beach or in a large dining room with plastic red-checkered tablecloths, ceiling fans, candles and Italian operas on the stereo. You can order spaghetti for just $5, then add sausage, fresh fish or shrimp for another $4 to $12. The a-la-carte menu also features sandwiches, burgers, pizzas and lots of salads. There's a decent wine list, and good desserts like Caribbean Coupe—vanilla ice cream with fresh fruit and papaya rum. Service is excellent.

Ricky's Place **$$** ★ ★ ★ ★
at the Hotel Playador in San Pedro, ☎ *(501) 62-2223.*
International cuisine.
Lunch: Noon–2 p.m., entrees $4–$10.
Dinner: 6–10 p.m., entrees $9–$19.
Located a few miles outside downtown San Pedro, near the Belize Yacht Club, this casual beachfront restaurant is a great choice for tasty lunches (the lobster salad is excellent) or romantic dinners. The menu features salads, seafood, steak, chicken and pork. Locals flock here on Thursdays, when they serve a huge Mexican platter of tacos and enchiladas.

Placencia

Placencia is primarily a fishing village, so you can expect lots of good seafood. You'll also have no trouble finding American-style burgers and sandwiches. **Brenda's** offers up ethnic fare as well as the antics of its owner, while breakfasts (and the house specialty drink) are killers at **De Tatch**. Italian prix-fixe dinners can be found at **Franco's**.

Brenda's **$** ★ ★ ★ ★
☎ *(501) 62-3137.*
Belizean cuisine.
The hours tend to vary at Brenda's, named for its owner, a wild and crazy young woman who deserves her own comedy special on HBO. The food's just great and the servings huge at this rustic wooden eatery. The menu varies but usually features local seafood, chicken and beef dishes. Brenda takes special requests and will keep you thoroughly entertained while you wait. Count on spending about $7 or $8 for an unforgettable meal.

De Tatch **$** ★ ★ ★ ★ ★
in the village,
American cuisine.
Lunch: from 6 a.m., entrees $3–$8.
Dinner: to 2 a.m., entrees $3–$8.
They don't come much cooler than De Tatch, a great bar/restaurant where locals congregate to listen to the great collection of 150 cassettes—everything from reggae to blues and jazz to folk, and especially Belizean punta music. The floor is sand and the walls are decorated with graffiti from travelers passing through, funny tee-shirts and the "Lost Souls of the Caribbean" collection of orphan shoes found on the beach outside. Besides the usual burgers and sandwiches, they have great coffee and yummy dishes like stuffed fry jacks (deep-fried flour dough stuffed with scrambled eggs, bacon, beans and cheese). If you're feeling daring, try a "Bye Yama"—a drink named after a big storm that has two shots of rum and cranberry juice. As they say, it comes out of nowhere, kicks you in the back and leaves. Be careful, because it takes exactly like Kool-Aid and goes down easy.

Flamboyant　　　　　　　　　$　　　　　　　　★★

in the village, ☎ *(501) 62-3322.*
International cuisine.
Dinner: to about midnight, entrees $3–$10.
Eat inside the cute little restaurant, or, better yet, outside under the giant flamboyant tree strung with Christmas lights from which this restaurant takes its name. The menu offers up Creole and American dishes such as burgers, chicken, lobster and shrimp. Like most Belize restaurants, the cole slaw is a treat!

Franco's Restaurant　　　　　　$　　　　　　　★★★

at Kitty's Place, near the airstrip, ☎ *(501) 62-3237.*
International cuisine.
Lunch: 11:30 a.m.–5 p.m., entrees $5–$7.
Dinner: 7–9 p.m., prix fixe $15.
Located upstairs with great views of the beach and sea, Franco's is a casual spot for simple sandwiches by day and pasta, seafood or meat four-course fixed-price dinner at night. The restaurant is spartanly decorated with such eclectic items as golf clubs, U.S. license plates and a portrait of Bob Marley. You can catch up on the news on the satellite TV at the bar, or just soak up the local gossip by eavesdropping on the chatty staff.

Tentacles　　　　　　　　　$$　　　　　　　★★★

☎ *(501) 62-3156.*
Seafood cuisine.
Dinner: 6–10 p.m., entrees $6–$16.
Locals favor this thatched-roof cafe set on stilts on the water's edge. Dine on seafood, local dishes and even Italian fare at this very pleasant spot.

Where to Shop

Belize is not much of a shopper's paradise, though it's great fun to divide prices by two (one U.S. dollar equals $2 Belize), giving the feel that everything is on a giant 50 percent off sale.

The international airport in Belize City has a duty-free shop in both the departure and arrival lounges with great prices on designer perfumes, premium liquors and cigarettes. In the city itself, several hotels, notably the **Biltmore**, Radisson and Fort Street, have decent gift shops. Local artwork can be found at **Emory King's Art Gallery** and at **Rachel's**. The **National Handicraft Center** (☎ *(501) 2-33636)* has a wide array of zericote wood carvings, black slate carvings, jippi joppa baskets and other crafts made by Belizean artisans. **G Tees** (☎ *(501) 2-74082)* is a quaint, art deco-style shop with good Belizean art, clothing and gifts. On Fridays, Mennonite farmers bring their handmade furniture into the city; ask at your hotel to find them.

Shopping is decent at **San Pedro** on Ambergris Caye. Among the better hotel gift shops are those at the **Holiday Hotel** (where among the tee-shirts saying "you better Belize it!" are salves made from jungle plants that reduce the itch of mosquito bites or ease a stomach ache) and the **Belize Yacht Club**, where they sell very fine shirts with the resort's logo. Jewelry crafted from protected black coral, which grows just a quarter- to a half-inch in diameter every 100 years, can be found at the **Little Old Giftshop on Front Street** (☎ *(501) 26-2924)*, while ceramic iguana figurines, pottery, masks and original paintings, all done by artist John D. Westerhold, are at **Iguana Jack's** (☎ *(501) 26-2767)*, which also has the best logoed T-shirts in the country. Also well worth a visit is **Belizean Arts** (☎ *(501) 26-3019)*, located off Front Street next to Fido's Bar, where they have an excellent selection of jewelry, wood-carved animals and local artwork.

In the San Ignacio area, **Caesar's Place** (☎ *(501) 92-2341)* has a wide selection of arts and crafts, many made on the property; you can take a free guided tour of the workshop. Products from the rainforest and other Central American countries can be found at **San Iggy Gifts** (☎ *(501) 92-2034)* at the San Ignacio Hotel.

Belize Directory

All prices are in U.S. dollars.

ARRIVAL

Belize is serviced by **American Airlines** (flights depart from Miami), Continental (though Houston) and **TACA** (from Los Angeles, San Francisco, Houston, Miami, New Orleans, Washington, D.C. and New York). All flights land at Phillip S.W. Goldson International Airport in Belize City.

CLIMATE

It's a subtropical climate, with constant trade winds from the Caribbean Sea. Summer temperatures average 75–85 degrees F, while winter is about 60–80 degrees F. Saltwater temperatures range from 75 and 84 degrees F. The rainy season is between June and August. The best time to come is October through May, though March can be overwhelmingly windy. Average humidity is 85 percent.

BUSINESS HOURS

Stores open weekdays 8 a.m.–noon and 1–5 p.m. Some also open Saturday. Banks open Monday–Thursday 8 a.m.–1 p.m. and Friday 8 a.m.–1 p.m. and 3–6 p.m.

DOCUMENTS

A passport and proof of return is required for entry. Visas are not necessary for citizens of the United States, Canada and nations of the European Economic Community. (Rules for other countries vary, so consult your local Belizean embassy or consulate.) Visitors are allowed to stay a month without extension.

ELECTRICITY

Current runs at 110 volts, the same as the United States and Canada.

GETTING AROUND

The best way to explore the mainland is by rental car—preferably a four-wheel drive (the roads are generally awful). If you're heading south, a four-wheel drive is mandatory. Prices start at about $65 per day. Virtually all rented vehicles have manual transmission and no air conditioning.

Taxis are cheap and plentiful. There are no meters but rates are standardized, so be sure to ask before you get in. Cost from the airport to Belize City is $15, and it's just $2.50 for most short trips.

Belize has a good and inexpensive bus system that connects all major towns, with buses leaving Belize City hourly to major towns in the north and west. It costs just $10—but it takes many hours to travel from Belize City to Punta Gorda. Most buses are now relatively modern and air conditioned, but if you tend toward car sickness, don't get near one! Most roads are filled with potholes and deep ruts, and also quite curvy.

Intra-country air service is excellent and also relatively cheap. (Round-trip flights between Belize City and Ambergris Caye, for instance, are just $35.) Local carriers include **Maya Airways** *(☎ (501) 02-44234)*, **Tropic Air** *(☎ (501) 02-45671)* and **Island** *(☎ (501) 26-2435)*. The latter is not especially recommended as it has a spotty safety record. While Tropic has the nicest planes, Maya is generally considered the safest and most reliable.

Prepare yourself for an adventure when flying domestically. The planes are small and noisy, and with the exception of flights to Ambergris Caye, tend to hop, rather than make a beeline, to your destination. It's sort of like taking a flying bus, with many stops both scheduled and unscheduled. Don't be surprised to land in a tiny airstrip so someone can run off to buy mangos, or head south to pick up more passengers, even though your final destination may be well to the north. Bring aboard lots of patience, a bottle of water and a camera, as the sights from the air make the kooky trip worthwhile.

Scheduled boat service is also available from Belize City to the Ambergris and Caulker cayes.

LANGUAGE

English is the official language and spoken by virtually everyone. You may also hear Spanish, Maya, Creole and Garifuna. All media is in English.

MEDICAL EMERGENCIES

Belize City has a large hospital (☎ *(501) 02-32723)*. There are also hospitals in Orange Walk, Corozal, Dangriga, Punta Gorda and San Ignacio. To reach the police, dial 911. To get the fire department or an ambulance, dial 90.

MONEY

The local currency is the Belize dollar (BZ), though U.S. dollars are accepted everywhere. One U.S dollar equals BZ $2, a rate that is fixed. Unless specified otherwise, always assume posted and quoted prices are BZ. (If you say "U.S.?" the answer may just be yes, and you'll end up paying double.)

TELEPHONE

Belize's excellent telephone system belies its Third World status. Direct-dial service is available to virtually anywhere. For directory service, dial 113. For local and regional operators, call 114. For international operator assistance, dial 115.

TIME

Central Standard Time. Belize does not observe daylight savings time.

TIPPING AND TAXES

Service charges are generally not included on restaurant checks; 10 percent is the norm, with 15 percent for outstanding service. That's also true for taxis and tour guides. There is a seven percent government hotel tax, and a Value Added Tax (VAT) is expected to be implemented in 1996. Departure tax is $11.25.

TOURIST INFORMATION

The Belize Tourist Board (☎ *(212) 563-6011 and (800) 624-0686)* at *421 Seventh Avenue, Suite 701, New York, NY 10001* can supply information. Be sure to request *Destination Belize*, the official government tourist magazine, which is filled with good information. In Belize City, the Tourist Board is located at *83 North Front Street;* ☎ *(501) 2-77213*.

WHEN TO GO

In February (one week before the start of Lent), the Fiesta de Carnaval is celebrated nationwide, with an emphasis on cultural traditions. Groups compete in special dances called *comparsas*. February also sees the International Billfish Tournament and the San Pedro Carnaval, a Mestizo carnival made up of competing comparsas and lots of craziness. On March 9, Baron Bliss Day is a national holiday with horse and cycle races and a regatta. In May, the Cashew Festival in Crooked Tree Village pays homage to the cashew harvest season with live punta music, cashew wine, and Caribbean-style meals and games. May 24 is Commonwealth Day, which is celebrated nationwide as the Queen's birthday with lots of special events. Each June sees the Dia de San Pedro, a three-day festival honoring St. Peter, the patron saint of San Pedro. Activities include a boat parade, fiesta, jump ups, and the blessing of the fleet. San Pedro also hosts the International Sea & Air Festival each August, when bands from Mexico and Central America compete nightly. September is the most happening month, with Independence Day celebrated with cultural, religious and sporting activities, including the crowning of Miss San Pedro. St. George's Caye Day commemorates a 1798 battle in which the Spanish were defeated by slaves, Baymen and British soldiers. There are lots of parades, carnivals and concerts held throughout the nation. October sees the Belikin Spectacular, a billfish tournament, and Pan American Day in Orange Walk and Corozal with fiestas that celebrate Mestizo culture. In the southern regions, Garifuna Settlement Day occurs each November 19 with cultural dancing and festivals. Both Christmas and Boxing Day (December 26) are celebrated in Belize.

BELIZE HOTELS		RMS	RATES	PHONE	CR. CARDS
Ambergris Caye					
★★★★	Belize Yacht Club	22	$125–$300	(501) 26-2777	MC, V
★★★★	Hotel Casablanca	5	$60–$90	(501) 26-2327	MC, V
★★★★	Mayan Princess	23	$75–$125	(501) 26-2778	A, MC, V
★★★★	Victoria House	26	$95–$130	(800) 247-5159	A, MC, V
★★★	Alijua Hotel Suites	7	$72–$104	(501) 26-2791	A, MC, V
★★★	Holiday Hotel	16	$60–$94	(510) 26-2014	A, D, MC, V
★★★	Paradise Resort Hotel	24	$50–$140	(501) 26-2083	A, D, MC, V
★★★	Ramon's Village	61	$115–$245	(501) 26-2071	A, MC, V
★★	Barrier Reef Hotel	11	$40–$65	(501) 26-2075	A, MC, V
★★	Coral Beach Hotel	19	$45–$65	(501) 26-2013	MC, V
★★	Ruby's Hotel	19	$14–$38	(501) 26-2063	A, MC, V
★★	Spendrift Hotel	10	$53–$165	(501) 26-2174	
★	Martha's Hotel	14	$30–$60	(501) 26-2053	MC, V
Belize City					
★★★	Belize Biltmore Plaza	90	$100–$100	(800) 333-3459	A, MC, V
★★★	Colton House	5	$33–$45	(501) 2-44666	

BELIZE HOTELS		RMS	RATES	PHONE	CR. CARDS
★★★	Fort Street Guest House	8	$45–$60	(501) 2-30116	MC, V
★★★	Radisson Fort George	106	$99–$139	(800) 333-3333	A, MC, V
★★★	Ramada Royal Reef Resort	118	$105–$147	(800) 228-9898	A, MC, V
★★	Bellevue Hotel	37	$79–$83	(501) 2-77051	A, MC, V
★★	Gallows Point Reef Resort	40	$50–$95	(501) 27-5819	
★	North Front Street Guest House	8	$15–$25	(501) 2-77595	
★	Seaside Guest House	6	$8–$18	(501) 2-78339	

Placencia

★★★★	Nautical Inn	12	$65–$99	(501) 62-2310	A, MC, V
★★★★	Rum Point Inn	10	$150–$112	(800) 747-1381	A, MC, V
★★★	French Quarter	5	$85–$110	(800) 641-6665	MC, V
★★★	Kitty's Place	8	$33–$108	(501) 62-3227	MC, V
★★	Singing Sands Inn	7	$50–$89	(800) 617-2673	A, MC, V

BELIZE RESTAURANTS		PHONE	ENTREE	CR. CARDS
Ambergris Caye				
Continental				
★★★★★	Lagoon	(501) 26-2327	$8–$17	
Italian				
★★★	Little Italy	(501) 26-2866	$4–$17	A, MC, V
Caribbean				
★★★★	Micky's Place	(501) 62-2223	$4–$19	A, MC, V
★★★	Elvi's Kitchen	(501) 26-2176	$3–$17	A, MC, V
Belize City				
American				
★★★	Calypso Bar & Grill	(501) 2-32670		MC, V
Continental				
★★★★	Fort Street Restaurant	(501) 2-60116	$7–$14	MC, V
★★★★	Maxime's	(501) 2-77400	$5–$22	MC, V
★★★	GG's Cafe and Patio	(501) 2-74878		None

BELIZE RESTAURANTS	PHONE	ENTREE	CR. CARDS
Placencia			
★★★★★ **De Tatch**		$3–$8	
★★★★ **Brenda's**	(501) 62-3137		
★★★ **Franco's Restaurant**	(501) 62-3237	$5–$7	MC, V
Creole			
★★ **Flamboyant**	(501) 62-3322	$3–$10	None
Seafood			
★★★ **Tentacles**	(501) 62-3156	$6–$16	
Note: • Lunch Only			
•• Dinner Only			

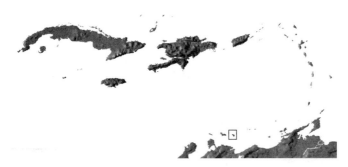

BONAIRE

Horseback riding is a good way to view Bonaire's diverse landscape.

Once sleepy Bonaire, the B in the ABC islands of the Netherlands Antilles, is now being battered by jackhammers and chainsaws. In the past three years, a building boom has hit this tiny Dutch isle like a hurricane from which it may never recover. Once the scuba diver's rough-but-ready paradise—in the 1980s, it was *the* place to dive—Bonaire is finally moving into the modern age, and if you've been gone for a few years, the change will be startling. For the first time in Kralendijk, the island's capital, there are traffic jams, big yellow cranes and parking that's becoming a chore. Two new shopping malls—pretty pink and mellow yellow—adorn the harborside, with two more slated soon for production. A recent cleanup campaign called "Tene Boneiru Limpi" (Keep Bonaire Clean) got rid of debris in the countryside and the project has become an islandwide contest. Unfortunately, illegal drugs have infiltrated the country, and petty crime, mostly theft of rental cars (particularly four-wheel drives) is on the rise. Still, more and more cruise liners are docking in port, and Americans continue to lead the pack of dive fanatics, with Europeans closing the gap of annual visitors. Despite the modernization, new buildings are being designed to tastefully reflect the native colonial Dutch style, and the dive sites, thanks to the die-hard diving ecologists who first "founded" the island, have kept the blue waters pure and the dive sites pristine. These days, Bonaire is being touted as the place to go, even if you *don't* dive (though, to take full advantage of the island's vast underwater treasures, including 86 offshore dive sites, at least one of you in the couple should be obliged to dive!)

Bird's Eye View

Bonaire is the "B" in the ABC Islands that include Aruba and Curaçao, and the second largest of the five islands that make up the Netherlands Antilles. Fifty miles north of Venezuela, it sprawls over 112 square miles in a shape that resembles a boomerang. With a population of a mere 11,000, it rates as the most sparsely populated island in the Caribbean. The island itself is formed from the tip of a 24-mile-long (three-mile wide) volcanic ridge that pokes out of the sea, buffeted on the windward side by trade winds blowing from the northeast. In contrast, the leeward side embraces a protected harbor surrounded by calm waters. The diversity in topography throughout the island is startling—from the northern green hills of the Washington-Slagbaai National Park to the flat, almost desertlike terrain of the south. The highest ridge is the 790-foot **Brandaris Peak** located in the park. Gritty, rocky beaches stretch around the island, though calmer conditions on the leeward side attract the most divers; most of the island's development is here. The scenic, seahugging road north of the main hotel has been recently closed to make way for the development of private homes in the area, though it has been replaced by a stunning new road that rises up from a scenic view and then travels inland through Bonaire's stark stubby *kunucu* countryside.

Bonaire's uninhabited kid sister, **Klein Bonaire**, all 1500 square acres, is tucked into the curve of the main island, just one-half mile offshore and protected from wind and waves. Both islands receive little rainfall, which accounts for the desertlike vegetation, such as cacti, divi-divi trees and other

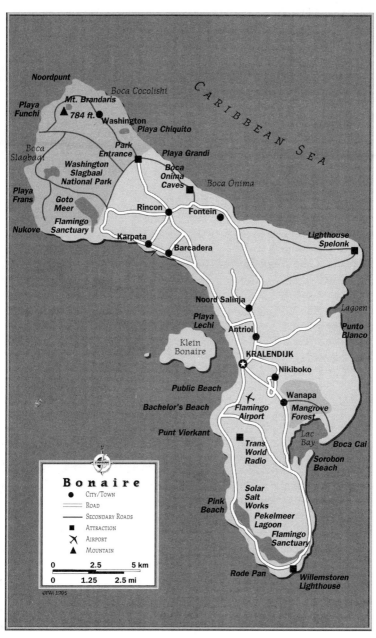

Noordpunt
Boca Cocolishi
CARIBBEAN SEA
Playa Funchi
Mt. Brandaris
▲ 784 ft. Washington
Playa Chiquito
Boca Slagbaai
Park Entrance
Playa Grandi
Washington Slagbaai National Park
Boca Onima Caves
Boca Onima
Playa Frans
Goto Meer
Rincon
Fontein
Nukove
Flamingo Sanctuary
Karpata
Barcadera
Lighthouse Spelonk
Noord Salinja
Playa Lechi
Lagoen
Antriol
Punto Blanco
Klein Bonaire
KRALENDIJK
Nikiboko
Public Beach
Wanapa
Bachelor's Beach
Flamingo Airport
Mangrove Forest
Punt Vierkant
Trans World Radio
Lac Bay
Boca Cai
Sorobon Beach
Solar Salt Works
Pink Beach
Pekelmeer Lagoon
Flamingo Sanctuary
Rode Pan
Willemstoren Lighthouse

Bonaire
● CITY/TOWN
ROAD
SECONDARY ROADS
■ ATTRACTION
✈ AIRPORT
▲ MOUNTAIN

0   2.5   5 km
0   1.25   2.5 mi

JFWH 1995

desert succulents, that dot the landscape. The entire coast of both Bonaire and Klein Bonaire are lined with coral reefs, which inspired ecologically committed legislators to protect all the reefs within the marine park.

The Dutch-influenced capital city of **Kralendijk** stretches along a wide, sheltered cove with boutiques, restaurants, bars and government offices occupying most of the buildings. Both to the north and south of this small city are resort developments that serve all kinds of tourists.

History

Bonaire has one of the largest flamingo colonies in the world. The birds build their mud nests in the salt pans.

Ever since the Spanish explorer Amerigo Vespucci discovered Bonaire in 1499, entrepreneurs have been toying with how to exploit it. Failing to discover gold on the island, the Spanish turned to extracting salt from the seas, stripping the forests of hardwoods and dyewoods, and hunting wild goats and sheep. Neither the Dutch, who arrived in 1623, nor the British, who took control in the early 19th century, could discover any successful ventures. A U.S. merchant named Joseph Foulke, to whom the British leased the land in 1810, also failed to make good. When the Dutch returned six years later, they ventured into shipbuilding, brickmaking and stock raising with little success. In recent years, many of Bonaire's natives were forced to find work off-island in the oil refineries of Venezuela, Curaçao and Aruba. As news of Bonaire's natural wonders became disseminated by the emigration, tourists began to trickle onto the island: fishermen who gloried in the abundance of marine life and untouched coral reefs and bird-watchers who were astounded by the glorious flocks of pink flamingos at Goto Meer and Pekel Meer. But it wasn't until the first scuba divers arrived around 1962, when there were only two major hotels, that the island began to discover where its real treasures lay—right underwater.

Beaches

Brilliant white is the color of most beaches in Bonaire, but most are gritty and full of coral. Hence, they are not really suitable for long strolls. Beaches on the leeward coast tend to run narrow. All the major hotels are located on beaches (managements have tried to beef up the sand there) but some of the best ones are along the southern coast, such as the clothes-optional Sorobon or Boca Cai on Lac Bay, full of mangroves at the north end of the bay. At Playa Chiquito, the surf is treacherously strong (too dangerous for swimming), but the strand is good for sunbathing, though there are few places for shade. Pink Beach, south of Kraldendijk, is good for swimming but gritty for strolling. Snorkelers head for Playa Funchi, but the absence of facilities has left the beach in smelly disrepair. Lots of tour boats end up in Boca Slagbaai where you can see flocks of flamingos dipping their long legs in the water. Stop there if you have just trekked through the National Park.

Underwater

Sometimes, dive operators can be a little uncooperative with journalists. Objectivity—particularly when comparing their island's sites and qualities with another—frequently flies headlong out the window. Other times, in asking opinions on the best dive sites available on a given island, outfits will list a few unfamiliar locations which, in fact, turn out to be sites only they can take you to because no one else knows/visits/cares about them. Speaking with Kitty at Bruce Bowker's Carib Inn on Bonaire, I was punished with a new style of reporter harassment. When asking what her three or four favorite dive spots on the island were, she sighed, and replied simply, "No, I'm not going to do that." She explained that Bonaire has many great dive sites and, although there are a few which are just a little better than the others, magazines keep writing about those few. "Divers come to the island and these spots are the only places they want to visit." With obvious frustration, she added, "we have to talk them into trying anything new."

The local dive operators can afford to be a little arrogant. Simply put, Bonaire offers one of the world's great dive locations, possibly the best in the Caribbean. The island is well outside the hurricane belt (which plagues most other Caribbean islands), allowing the coral reef wrapping the island to thrive and provide a dynamic playground for more than a thousand species of marine life. Although big creatures are few and far between, reef fish are in good supply and macro life is gloriously showcased (it's a perfect destination for photo enthusiasts). The angle of drop-offs rarely exceeds 60 degrees, so you won't find much in the way of walls. But the reef, which generally starts less than a hundred feet from shore along the island's leeward coast, is sublime. Rain averages 12 inches a year, visibility a reliable 60 to 80 feet, but sometimes reaches 100 feet or more. Currents are almost nonexistent—one diver referred to the whole leeward coast as "like a big lake"—but diving on the choppy windward side is rare (limited to occasional calm days in the fall). And, if you like shore diving, well, hop in the car and look for one of the painted yellow stones which mark the island's 30 or so "official" shore dive locations. Yes, you could park and dive for two weeks without visiting the same spot twice.

The reef is terrific, but Bonaire also has a leg up on the competition because it has long been a leader in marine conservation. In fact, what have become standards on the more progressive Caribbean islands—permanent mooring systems, bans on spearfishing, etc.—have been in effect here since the late '60s. Anchoring of any kind is illegal around the entire island, except for the harbor immediately in front of Kralendijk. In sum, because these practices have been in effect for decades here, the island is years ahead of most other Caribbean locales in terms of a genuinely protected undersea environment. When you arrive, you'll pay a $10 admission fee to the **Bonaire Marine Park**, which includes a one-hour orientation session by your dive shop. There are a few sites (Knife, Petrie's Pillar, Twixt and Valerie's Hill), which are currently off-limits to divers; these areas were overdived and local operators are giving them time to rejuvenate. For overachievers, there is a recompression chamber available at the island's San Francisco Hospital.

Scuba die-hards sometimes forget about snorkeling, but they shouldn't miss the shallow terraces which line shores. It's a whole 'nother world. Diver of not, you'll find outstanding snorkeling all along the west coast. **Klein Bonaire** is terrific, particularly Jerry's Jam (where the coral grows up to the surface) and Leonora's Reef. Other great sites on the main island are **Thousand Steps**, **Nukove**, **Playa Funchi** and **Windsock** (so named because it lies at the foot of Bonaire's airport runway). One other, albeit unpredictable, snorkeling possibility occurs for a few days each year (usually late summer or early fall) when krill swarm the placid Bonaire waters, followed by whale sharks and mantas which feed gleefully on the red crab larvae. While it's almost impossible to set a vacation to their schedule, in September 1995, the phenomena occupied local attention for an unprecedented 10-day stretch, as divers and swimmers donned snorkel and mask to swim with the big guys.

Don't limit yourself to this selection of dive sites; make sure you see some of the island's other great spots. For further information (and more sites), pick up a copy of the *Diving and Snorkeling Guide to Bonaire* by Jerry Schnabel and Suzi Swygert.

Jerry's Jam (aka, Ebo's Special)

This favorite, just off Klein Bonaire (facing Kralendijk); offers a series of caves and caverns amid huge pyramidal formations of mountainous star coral. Big groupers park at cleaning stations while thick green morays and nurse sharks inhabit the crevices and cracks (20 to 150 feet).

Forest

The dive starts at 15 feet and leads to an unusually steep drop-off (to more than 200 feet). The site is named for the high density of black coral at 40 to 90 feet, with queen triggerfish, morays, tiger groupers, parrotfish and trumpetfish exploring their forest; mantas are known to hover out in the deep blue beyond.

Rappel

Set against seaside cliffs and traditionally a boat dive, but named after a more exotic method of access—Rappel may also be reached by a swim from nearby Karpata. The site begins with a dramatic drop-off at the cliffs to sea-level notches created by wave action and erosion; underwater, the notches form shallow caverns growing red cup (*tubastrea*) coral. Nurse sharks and young barracudas sometimes lurk nearby, but orange seahorses, marbled grouper and spiny lobster are among the regulars. Further out, wire corals and formations of mountainous star coral punctuate the drop-off (to 130 feet).

Town Pier

Perhaps Bonaire's most talked-about location is suffering a local p.r. backlash. True, you may be sharing the pier with a number of other divers at once. Regulations now require that you dive with a local operator, and only on nights when there's no boat traffic docked. And the layer of dock trash blanketing the floor beneath the pier is hardly pretty. But, despite the negatives and the hype, Town Pier remains one of the

Caribbean's great night dives, and excellent for shutterbugs. The pilings are quite beautiful, bedecked in sponges, corals and anemones, and seahorses, octopus and moray eels are dependably present.

Wreck of the *Hilma Hooker*

If, somehow, you tire of Bonaire's stunning reefs, head for this 1000-ton, 235-foot steel-hulled freighter that sits just off the shore next to Angel City Reef. The ship has a notorious reputation—it was seized by the Antillean Coast Guard in a 1984 drug raid and then began to sink—but now rests peacefully on a sandy floor, 90 feet down. Encrustation is occurring slowly, but you can penetrate the cargo hold and pose for pictures at the dramatic port propeller. The *Hilma* boasts the added benefit of being one of the Caribbean's few wrecks accessible from shore.

Dive Shops

Bruce Bowker's Carib Inn

Kralendijk; ☎ *(599) 7-8819.*

One of the smallest shops on Bonaire is also a unique operation which opened in 1980. Single-tank boat dive, $25 (not including equipment); second dive the same day, $19. A PADI Five Star facility and SSI-affiliated, with a nine-room inn popular among divers. Huge repeat business means rooms are booked up many months in advance.

Captain Don's Habitat

Kralendijk; ☎ *(599) 7-8290.*

A PADI five-star facility with courses through Instructor (also handles NAUI referrals). In operation since 1975, but Captain Don started diving in 1962. Tanks available 24 hours. Single-tank boat dive $33; includes unlimited shore dives the same day; unlimited shore diving $14, or $44 for two boat dives and unlimited shore dives (all plus 10% service charge). Also, mountain bike rentals. Rodale's Scuba Diving survey named Captain Don's as its reader's favorite resort/operator in the Caribbean.

Sand Dollar Dive and Photo

Kralendijk; ☎ *(599) 7-5252.*

Since 1986, and now the largest on the island with 15 instructors and an extensive photo/video department. PADI, NAUI, SSI affiliated; courses through instructor. Arranges two tank, all-day trips to sites off Washington/Slagbaai National Park, $65. Single-tank boat dive, $28 (plus 10% service charge); shore dives, $8 per tank. Runs four or five boat dives per day, and scheduled Wednesday night boat dives. Good choice for families.

Sunset Beach Dive Center

Kralendijk; ☎ *(599) 7-8330.*

PADI five-star facility; NAUI and SSI referrals. Single tank boat dive and unlimited shore diving (the same day), $33. Six days of unlimited shore dives, $109. Several other combination packages available.

On Foot

Some Bonaire tours include the huts where salt mine slaves lived.

While Bonaire's interior isn't as colorful and diverse as its submarine display, the island's environmental awareness extends to the **Washington/Slag-baai National Park**, which occupies most of Bonaire's northern end. The 13,500-acre wildlife sanctuary is laced by dirt roads, and on-foot exploration is easy, as long as you're equipped with sun block and plenty of water. The area was once occupied by a plantation which produced aloe, charcoal and goats, and it was turned over to the government in the late 60s. After paying your $3 entry fee, you'll be handed a map detailing three tracks: the yellow route is a 22-mile circuit of the of the park, while the green route is a shorter, 15-mile track through the center (the two routes overlap at points). A dotted green track is actually a trail, which climbs to the top of **Brandaris Hill**, the Bonaire's 784-foot high-point; allow two hours round trip. Another area which deserves impromptu exploration is the solar salt pans which loom mysteriously on the horizon south of Kralendijk. You can spend a few minutes or a few hours here, depending on your curiosity. The nearby **Pekel**

Meer Lagoon is a colorful, 135-acre flamingo sanctuary, which serves as home to as many as 10,000 greater flamingos.

By Pedal

Bonaire features over 200 miles of quiet dirt roads which create wonderful opportunities for mountain bike touring. One important consideration is the island's sun and heat, which can be oppressive. It's important to carry lots of water, and to liberally apply sun block before any extended riding.

Bike Rental Shops

Cycle Bonaire

Kralendijk; ☎ *5997-7558.*

The island's solitary cycling shop, with 15 Trek mountain bikes available for rent. $15–20 per day (higher for 930s with shocks), including first-aid kit, water bottle and patch kit.

What Else to See

Visitors to Bonaire come to revel in the natural sights, but the small capital of Kralendijk deserves a perusal, recently spruced up by well-supported restoration projects. Traversing the town is easy since there are only two main roads. The **fish market** is always a hoot, located today near the Hotel Rocha line, and historical buffs will find interesting **Indian artifacts** at the Instituto Folklore Bonaire. Guides will want to drag you out to see the slave huts on the southwestern coast, which is only interesting if you like imagining how two grown men could fit into the tiny hovels. Whatever you do underwater, don't miss visiting the Washington/Slagbaai National Park, in the northwest of the island (see "On Foot" above).

Museums and Exhibits

Instituto Folklore Bonaire   ★★

Ministry of Education, Kralendijk.

If you happen to be in the neighborhood (don't bother otherwise), drop in for a look at local artifacts and musical instruments from the pre-Columbian days. The cramped and poor exhibits prevent this small museum from reaching its potential.

Parks and Gardens

Bonaire Marine Park

The entire coastline, Kralendijk.

To keep its world-famous reefs intact, this government-run park, which includes the entire coastline of Bonaire and neighboring Klein Bonaire, has enacted strict rules for snorkelers and divers. You may not step on or collect the coral, and anchors are forbidden—patrolling marine police see that the rules are enforced. The undersea world includes some 80 species of colorful coral and 270 species of fish. The Visitors Center offers up brochures, slide shows and lectures. The $10 fee allows for one calendar year of diving.

Washington/Slagbaai National Park

Northwest Territory, Boca Slagbaai.
Hours Open: 8 a.m.–5 p.m.

This 13,500-acre national park, dedicated to preserving the island's natural landscape, is well worth a visit. Opt for the short route (15 miles and marked with green arrows) or the longer version (22 miles and yellow arrows); if you're driving, a four-wheel drive is essential for navigating the dirt roads. Once a plantation of divi-divi trees and aloe plants, the park has been a wildlife sanctuary since 1967, with additional acreage added in 1978. The roads take you past dramatic seascapes, freshwater lakes and lowland forest that is home to 130 species of birds (bring your binoculars) and a few mammals like donkeys and goats. There's a small museum at the gatehouse; just past it colorful flamingos roost on a salt pond from October to January. Plan on at least a few hours in this special spot.

Tours

Bonaire Sightseeing Tours

Kralendijk.

If you prefer exploring Bonaire in the hands of professional guides, they'll take care of you. Excursions, via jeep or minivan, are offered to the northern coast, the low-lying south or Washington/Slagbaai National Park. Prices range from $12 to $45.

Cruises

Various locales, Kralendijk.

A few hours' excursion on the sea is always a wonderful way to unwind. A few companies offer such jaunts. The Bonaire Dream, a glass-bottom boat, lets you see underwater life without getting wet; catch it at the Harbour Village Marina. Sunset and snorkel cruises are offered by the **Woodwind** (☎ *(599) 7-607055)*. Don't forget the sunscreen!

Sports

Diving, of course, is the king sport on Bonaire (for more information, see under "Dive Sites" above). Recently, however, boardsailing and **windsurfing** have also become the rage in Bonaire. Head for the windward coast of Bonaire, where the trade winds from the Guinea-Bissau end their transatlantic blow in Lac Bay. This is Jibe City, a four-square-mile lagoon where the trade winds blow at 12-35 knots year round. Beginners can feel assured by water that only reaches waist high and the steady onshore winds mean no one ever worries about being blown out to sea. The company Wind Surfing Bonaire stocks 50 state-of-the-art BIC boards with carbon masts, new Aerotech sails with Windsurfing Hawaii, and Chinook booms—all rigged and ready to launch.

For more information: **Windsurfing Bonaire**, *P.O. Box 301, Bonaire;* ☎ *(599) 7-5363 or (800) 748-8733, rentals $25 per hour; $40 per half day lesson $20 plus board.*

Sailing has enjoyed a 15-year tradition in Bonaire, with a major regatta race held in October. These days it's an islandwide party. The tourist office can supply more details. For longer expeditions, hang out at the marina at Harbour Village and negotiate with crews. Your hotel can also arrange water-skiing. Full and half-day charters for **fishing**, complete with all the provisions are available through hotels. The offshore fishing grounds beyond the Marine Park are abundant with wahoo, mackerel, tuna, barracuda, swordfish and many others. Boating of all types can be seen from the harbor at Kralendijk, and many offer day trips to Klein Bonaire for lunch and snorkeling. The **Bonaire Sailing Regatta** attracts sailors from all over the Caribbean to compete in various categories, including yachts, sailfish, dinghies, windsurfers, hobie cats, fishing sloops and others.

Horseback riding can be arranged by your hotel through **Rini's Stables**.

A few tennis courts are located at major resorts, including the Sunset Beach Hotel, Harbour Village, Divi Flamingo Beach and the Sand Dollar.

Deep-Sea Fishing

Various locales, Kralendijk.

This outfit will take you out for a half- or full day of fishing. **Piscatur Charles** *(*☎ *(599) 7-8774)* offers reef fish excursions aboard a 15-foot skiff.

Scuba Diving

Various locations, Kralendijk.

Bonaire's rich reefs make for excellent diving; in fact, it's considered one of the top three spots in the world for scuba. Many outfits offer lessons, equipment rentals and excursions. Best known is **Captain Don's Habitat Dive Center** *(Kaya Gobernador N. Deprot,* ☎ *(599) 7-8290)*, a PADI five-star training facility. Also check out: **Dive I** and **Dive II** *(Divi Flamingo Beach Resort,* ☎ *(599) 7-8285)*; **Bonaire Scuba Center** *(Black Durgon Inn,* ☎ *(599) 7-8978)*; **Sand Dollar Dive and Photo** *(Sand Dollar Condominiums,* ☎ *(599) 7-5252)*; **Neil Watson's Bonaire Undersea Adventures** *(Coral Regency Resort,* ☎ *(599) 7-5580)*; **Great Adventures Bonaire** *(Harbour Village Beach Resort,* ☎ *(599) 7-7500)*; and **Bruce Bowker's Carib Inn Dive Center** *(Carib Inn,* ☎ *(599) 7-8819)*. Personalized tours for twosomes are offered by **Dee Scarr's Touch the Sea** *(☎ (599) 7-8529)*.

Windsurfing Bonaire

Great Southern Travel & Adventures, Kralendijk, ☎ *(800) 748-8733.*

This is a great spot for both beginners and experts. Lessons start at $20 an hour, and they'll even pick you up at your hotel.

Where to Stay

✦	**Fielding's Highest Rated Hotels in Bonaire**	
★★★★	**Harbour Village Resort**	$170–$400
★★★	**Captain Don's Habitat**	$150–$245
★★★	**Coral Regency Resort**	$150–$230
★★★	**Divi Flamingo Resort**	$85–$140

♡	**Fielding's Most Romantic Hotels in Bonaire**	
★★★★	**Harbour Village Resort**	$170–$400
★★	**Sorobon Beach Resort**	$110–$165

	Fielding's Budget Hotels in Bonaire	
★	**Sunset Inn**	$60–$105
★★	**Carib Inn**	$64–$124
★★	**Sunset Beach Hotel**	$80–$140
★★★	**Divi Flamingo Resort**	$85–$140
★★	**Buddy Dive Resort**	$80–$165

Bonaire's accommodations are geared for divers, the serious kind who need casual but efficient service delivered with an amiable hospitality. Some serious divers who know the area well tend to stay in condominiums, apartments or crowd into the more casual guest homes. A new phase in Bonaire's development was marked by the recent opening of the Harbor Village Beach resort, a paradise of lush landscaping that acts as a haven for wealthy Venezuelans, Europeans and Americans. In the past several years Bonaire has seen a minor explosion of affordable apartments, inns and guesthouses.

Hotels and Resorts

All hotels face the sea. All you need to do is choose whether you want to stay in town or in the countryside. Perhaps the liveliest hotel is **Captain Don's Habitat**, due to the wildcat personality of its owner, Don Stewart, who has been rumored to shoot a mosquito with a pistol. **Divi Flamingo Beach Hotel** has the best restaurants, the Chibi-Chibi and the Calabase Terrace, plus a casino that draws crowds. **Sorobon Beach Resort** is infamous for its clientele who like to take advantage of the nearby "clothes optional" beach.

Captain Don's Habitat $150–$245

Kralendijk, ☎ *(800) 327-6709, FAX (305) 371-2337.*
Single: $150–$245. Double: $150–$245.

The clientele at this casual spot is mostly scuba divers and the facilities cater to them well, with instruction, seven boats and an underwater photo shop. Landlubbers are kept happy, too, in two-bedroom cottages with kitchens or oceanfront rooms or villas. The beach is tiny, but the pool is nice, and kids are kept busy in supervised activities during high season. The atmosphere here is informal and fun, especially when Captain Don stops by to spin tall tales.

Divi Flamingo Resort $85–$140 ★ ★ ★

J.A. Abraham Blvd., Kralendijk, ☎ *(800) 367-3484.*
Single: $85–$140. Double: $85–$140.

Despite the need for at least a fresh coat of paint, the Divi remains a popular choice due to its friendly staff and lively atmosphere. The original buildings housed German prisoners of war during World War II, but from that dubious start the resort has grown into a pleasant and fun spot. Accommodations are merely adequate and desperately in need of a redo, but the grounds are nice with tennis (including a resident pro), extensive dive facilities (with special programs for the handicapped), casino and lots of after-dark entertainment.

Harbour Village Resort $170–$400

Kaya Gobernador Debrot 71, Kralendijk, ☎ *(800) 424-0004, FAX (305) 567-9659.*
Single: $170–$400. Double: $170–$400.

Catering to divers, this Iberian village-style complex offers both traditional guestrooms and condos with kitchens; all are spacious, nicely decorated and have air conditioning. The beach is wide by Bonaire standards, and the diving facilities are choice. There's also a spiffy fitness center, a pool and traditional watersports free of charge. The grounds are quite pretty and the digs luxurious, but maintenance is sometimes lacking.

Sunset Beach Hotel $80–$140

Kaya Gobrenador Debrot 75, Kralendijk, ☎ *(599) 7-5300.*
Single: $80–$140. Double: $80–$140.

Located on one of the better beaches, the Sunset's accommodations are, unfortunately, set far inland, so ocean views are scarce. Rooms are quite plain, but do offer such extras as coffee makers, refrigerators and air conditioning. The extensive grounds, which could use more landscaping to reach their potential, include two tennis courts, a good dive center and a small pool. The friendly staff can't make up for the fact that this place is screaming for renovation.

Apartments and Condominiums

One- and two-bedroom apartments are often chosen by visitors to Bonaire who want to save a little money, but you may empty your wallet anyway if you stock up on staples in Bonaire; the prices can be exorbitant. In most cases, you may need a car. For more information about housekeeping units, contact **Hugo Gerharts** *(Kralendijk, Bonaire, N.A.;* ☎ *(599) 7-8300)* or **Harbourstown Real Estate** *(Kaya Grandi 62, P.O. Box 311,* ☎ *(599) 7-5539, FAX (599) 7-5081).*

Buddy Dive Resort $80–$165   ★★
Kaya Gobernador Debrot, Kralendijk, ☎ *(800) 359-0747.*
Single: $80–$165. Double: $80–$165.
Accommodations vary from small apartments with no air conditioning to newer and more spacious units with air conditioning and kitchens. Primarily serving divers, this no-frills complex provides clean towels daily, but maid service only once a week. There's a pool and bar, but no restaurant. A decent choice for those who don't mind fending for themselves and are seeking budget quarters.

Coral Regency Resort $150–$230   ★★★
Kaya Gobernador Debrot 90, Kralendijk, ☎ *(800) 327-8150, FAX (599) 7-5680.*
Single: $150–$210. Double: $150–$230.
This time-share resort (beware of hard sells) puts up guests in studios and one- and two-bedroom suites in two-story buildings arranged around a free-form pool. Units are attractive with large sitting areas, air and full kitchens. There's a recreation center and dive shop, as well as a bar and restaurant—but no beach to speak of.

Sand Dollar Beach Club $160–$350   ★★
Kaya Gobernador Debrot 79, Kralendijk, ☎ *(800) 288-4773, FAX (599) 7-8760.*
Single: $160–$350. Double: $160–$350.
Accommodations at this beachfront condominium complex include studios and apartments from one to three bedrooms, all with air conditioning, full kitchens and pleasant contemporary furnishings. Each is differently done as these units are individually owned. There's an excellent on-premise dive center, as well as two tennis courts, supervised children's programs during high season, a restaurant and a tiny beach strollable only during low tide. A nicely elegant spot.

Sorobon Beach Resort $110–$165   ★★
Lac Bay, ☎ *(599) 7-8050.*
Single: $110–$165. Double: $110–$165.
Bonaire's only "naturalist" resort means that clothes are optional—and many guests take advantage of this fact. Accommodations are in cabinlike structures and consist of one-bedroom units with small kitchens and simple furnishings. The grounds include a small family-style restaurant, bar and private beach—the better to bare all on. The remote location also assures privacy, and a daily shuttle into town assures diversion. A nice, simple spot for the carefree set who don't mind forgoing air conditioning.

Sunset Oceanfront Apartments $60–$190   ★★
P.O. Box 333, Kralendijk, ☎ *(599) 7-8448.*
Single: $60–$190. Double: $130–$190.
This small apartment complex is across the street from the ocean, but a half-mile from the beach. Accommodations are in one- and two-bedroom apartments that overlook the sea; each has a small kitchen, contemporary furnishings and air condi-

tioning only in the bedrooms. There's a small pool on-site, but little else in the way of extras. Restaurants and a casino are within an easy walk.

Inns

These are inns dedicated to serving the committed diver. Furnishings are usually very basic and require a no-nonsense attitude. **Sunset Inn** probably has the best location for walking to the city's restaurants and shops.

Carib Inn $64–$124   ★ ★

J.A. Abraham Blvd., Kralendijk, ☎ (599) 7-8819.
Single: $64–$124. Double: $64–$124.
This intimate scuba resort, founded by American diver Bruce Bowker, attracts those who love the sport and are seeking simple lodgings without a lot of extras. Seven of the nine units have their own kitchen; all are air-conditioned and were recently redone. There's a pool but not much else; you'll have to cook in or walk to a nearby restaurant to be sated. Bowker runs a pleasant inn, with lots of repeat guests, so reserve early. The dive center is excellent.

Sunset Inn $60–$105   ★

Kaya C.E.B. Hellmund 29, Kralendijk, ☎ (599) 7-8291.
Single: $60–$105. Double: $60–$105.
Located within walking distance of a few dive centers, the back-to-basics Sunset has air-conditioned rooms with kitchenettes and coffee makers, though not much else. Its central location makes exploring Kralendijk on foot easy.

Low Cost Lodging

To save money in Bonaire, travel with several people and share the cost of an apartment or condominium. The tourist board can also supply names of private homes that will rent out individual rooms. Also, try to travel during low season (mid-April through mid-December), when rates are slashed.

Where to Eat

Fielding's Highest Rated Restaurants in Bonaire

★★★★	Classic Eatery	$5–$25
★★★	Chibi-Chibi	$15–$26
★★★	China Garden	$5–$24
★★★	Den Laman	$11–$22
★★★	Green Parrot	$5–$20
★★★	Mona Lisa	$12–$23
★★★	Raffles	$11–$25
★★★	Red Pelican	$4–$35
★★★	Richard's Waterfront	$13–$28
★★★	Toys Grand Cafe	$5–$23

Fielding's Special Restaurants in Bonaire

★★★	Chibi-Chibi	$15–$26
★★★	Mona Lisa	$12–$23
★★★	Raffles	$11–$25
★★★	Red Pelican	$4–$35
★★★	Toys Grand Cafe	$5–$23

Fielding's Budget Restaurants in Bonaire

★★	Kilumba	$8–$15
★★★	Green Parrot	$5–$20
★★★	Toys Grand Cafe	$5–$23
★★★	China Garden	$5–$24
★★★★	Classic Eatery	$5–$25

Bonaire is a fish-eating culture; practically everything else has to be shipped in. Perhaps that's one of the reasons costs can run high. A few hotels, such as the Divi Flamingo Beach Hotel and Harbour Village, have good restaurants, but most diners head for the city of **Kralendijk** when the hour to feast arrives. Among native specialties are local fish such as wahoo, dolphin (not the Flipper kind), and conch, fungi (a thick pudding made from cornmeal), goat stew, and a fine array of Dutch cheeses. Indonesian cuisine adds a little exotica to the local fare; especially good is the new **Toy's Grand Café**, which serves Indonesian delicacies in a funky retro atmosphere. For a real change of pace, head for the base of the customs pier, and indulge in schnitzel and fries while enjoying the bay view at a cute little eatery called **'t Ankertje** ("little anchor" in Dutch). Some of the best hamburgers on the island are found at **The Green Parrot** at the Sand Dollar Resort.

Beefeater   **$$$**   ★★
Kaya Grandi 12,
American cuisine. Specialties: Steaks, scampi, homemade ice cream.
Dinner: 6:30–11:30 p.m., entrees $15–$25.
In the center of town is this restored, authentic Bonaireian town home, very intimate, serving rather dear beef and seafood dishes, as well as vegetarian cuisine. But the surroundings are lovely, with a courtyard view. It's nice to see how old Bonaire might have looked. Desserts are homemade and utilize local fruit.

Chibi-Chibi   **$$$**   ★★★
J.A. Abraham Boulevard, ☎ (599) 7-8285.
International cuisine. Specialties: Antillean onion soup, fettuccini flamingo.
Dinner: 6–10 p.m., entrees $15–$26.
Like the tropical bird that is its namesake, the Chibi-Chibi is positioned prettily on stilts, and for an experience like none other, the sea below is lit at night so diners can watch the vivid marine life below their tables. (Not surprisingly, you must reserve in advance.) Cuisine is familiar to American tastes, with fresh fish available, but local specialties are also on hand, including keshi yena, a whole Edam cheese stuffed with chicken and spices.

China Garden   **$$**   ★★★
Kaya Grandi 47, ☎ (599) 7-8480.
Chinese cuisine. Specialties: Goat Chinese-style, lobster in black bean sauce.
Lunch: 11:30 a.m.–2 p.m., entrees $5–$24.
Dinner: 4–10 p.m., entrees $5–$24.
Housed in a grand restored home downtown, this popular restaurant is possibly the best Chinese eatery from a handful of choices. In typical island hodgepodge style, the China Garden combines Cantonese specialties with local favorites like goat, with a few American sandwiches thrown in. Everything is generously portioned, so you get what you pay for and then some. All sweet-and-sour and black-bean sauced dishes are recommended, and the seafood is fresh.

Classic Eatery   **$$$**   ★★★★
1 Kaya L.D. Gerharts 4, ☎ (599) 7-8003.

International cuisine. Specialties: Fresh fish, duck a l'orange, sweet red pepper soup.
Lunch: 9 a.m.–4 p.m., entrees $5–$15.
Dinner: 4–11 p.m., entrees $5–$25.

This is a French salon in the true sense of the word—without the snob factor. Because it's such a small restaurant (less than 10 tables), everyone gets individualized attention. The classic French menu, with some innovative touches, always includes duck a l'orange and a soup of roasted sweet peppers. If you don't want to eat, stop by for a drink at the enormous mahogany bar where the local arts community holds court regularly.

Den Laman $$$ ★ ★ ★

Kaya Gobernador,
Seafood cuisine. Specialties: Red snapper Creole, conch flamingo, kingfish.
Dinner: 6–11 p.m., entrees $11–$22.

Seafood doesn't get much fresher or better prepared on the island than in this indoor-outdoor restaurant. Red snapper lightly grilled or prepared Creole style is a best bet and is usually available. Decor is piscatorial, with a huge aquarium providing a running conversation piece; it can be fun for kids. Closed September.

Green Parrot $$ ★ ★ ★

Kaya Gobernador, ☎ (599) 7-5454.
International cuisine. Specialties: Onion string appetizer, barbecue.
Lunch: 11:30 a.m.–3 p.m., entrees $5–$10.
Dinner: 4:30–10 p.m., entrees $10–$20.

Homesick Americans will like this jumping place, which has frothy and fruity margaritas, juicy burgers, barbecue and, familiar to habitues of the Tony Roma's chain, an onion string loaf. The view is great at sunset since it is situated on a hotel pier that is open to the breezes. It's a good place to grab a reasonably priced lunch when coming from or going to the airport, which is only a few miles away. There is a buffet on Sunday with barbecued meats and lively entertainment.

Kilumba $$ ★ ★

Kaya L.D. Gerharts, ☎ (599) 7-5019.
Seafood cuisine. Specialties: Stewed goat, catch of the day.
Lunch: entrees $8–$15.
Dinner: entrees $8–$15.

Bonaireians like this seafood-Creole spot north of town, named after an African sea god. Why? Because the atmosphere at the bar is mellow, and everyone knows everyone else; a good place to schmooze. Goat stew is recommended at lunch, and in the evenings, usually quite busy, fish dinners are given the spotlight.

Mona Lisa $$$ ★ ★ ★

Kaya Grandi 15, ☎ (599) 7-8718.
International cuisine. Specialties: Pork tenderloin sate with peanut sauce, wahoo.
Lunch: Noon–2 p.m., entrees $12–$23.
Dinner: 6–10 p.m., entrees $15–$23.

Absorb some local color in this popular bar and restaurant, where the Dutch-born chef personally oversees each table. The Mona Lisa's bar, decorated with a profusion of hometown knickknacks, is a riot of activity. Copious snacks are served there until very late. The pretty restaurant wears a more demure face, with a diverse menu of Indonesian, Dutch and French favorites. An ongoing special is pork sate (tenderloin marinated with garlic, sesame oil, soy and other spices) served with peanut sauce, but a popular French onion soup is always available.

Raffles $$$ ★★★

Kaya C.E.B. Hellmund 5, ☎ (599) 7-8617.
International cuisine. Specialties: Seafood platter Caribe, salmon cascade.
Dinner: 6:30–10 p.m., entrees $11–$25.
Bonaire has a number of old homesteads, but Raffles, with a red London phone booth as its landmark and mascot, roosts in one of the oldest of the old. Patrons have more than a hope for an intimate conversation in the indoor dining room, along with Caribbean entrees, French-style desserts and soft jazz playing. There's also a terrace for people watching. *Pescado de mariscos*, a Latin bouillabaisse, is usually available; also chicken and steaks. Make room for the mousse made with two kinds of chocolate.

Red Pelican $$$ ★★★

Kaminda Sorobon 64, Lac Bay, ☎ (599) 7-8198.
Seafood cuisine. Specialties: Seafood stew, marinated fish salad.
Lunch: Noon–2 p.m., entrees $4–$6.
Dinner: 7–10 p.m., entrees $20–$35.
A sophisticated, intimate spot, the Red Pelican is very close to being the toniest restaurant on the isle, with a location a little ways off the tourist track, on the windward coast in Lac Bay. Decor is island-tropical and cuisine is International. Expect herring, stews and chicken dishes.

Rendez-Vous Restaurant $$$ ★★

3 Kaya L.D. Gerharts, ☎ (599) 7-8454.
International cuisine. Specialties: Chicken apricot, keshi yena.
Dinner: 6–10:30 p.m., entrees $14–$26.
The livin' is easy at this midtown eatery which, like most on the island, has two dining areas—indoor and out. But wherever you sit, it's cozy, and a loaf of home-baked bread gets things off to a nice start. Local dishes are well represented, and *keshi yena* (Edam cheese stuffed with meat) is prepared picadillo style, with raisins. Otherwise, there's always good seafood, with a daily special, and vegetarians needn't feel slighted. Good fruit desserts, patisserie and espresso.

Richard's Waterfront $$$ ★★★

60 J.A. Abraham Boulevard, ☎ (599) 7-5263.
Seafood cuisine. Specialties: Conch al Ajillo, grilled wahoo, seafood soup.
Dinner: 6:30–10:30 p.m., entrees $13–$28.
The food is usually stellar at this friendly waterfront charmer, especially when attentive owner Richard Beady, from Boston, is around to check on things. The daily special, on a blackboard, regularly features fresh fish of the day; wahoo is recommended. There won't be many surprises, like extra hot pepper in the popular fish soup, which is a favored starter. Both conch and shrimp are often prepared with garlic-butter sauce. The bar is a favorite with locals and others, especially at sunset, for all the usual reasons.

Toys Grand Cafe   **$$$**   ★★★

J.A. Abraham Boulevard, ☎ *(599) 7-6666.*
International cuisine. Specialties: Snails in blue-cheese sauce, nasi goreng.
Lunch: 11:30 a.m.–2 p.m., entrees $5–$15.
Dinner: 5–10 p.m., entrees $10–$23.

Someone with a touch of whimsy created this eclectic restaurant on the main drag in Kralendijk. The walls are covered with familiar figures from the cartoon and entertainment worlds. Not grand in cuisine, but in concept; it's mostly fun. Not really for kids (maybe grown up ones), as the interesting and creative menu is peppered with Indonesian favorites, meats and shellfish with vivid sauces. At certain times of the day, a few meals are available at a substantial discount.

Zeezicht Restaurant   **$$$**   ★★

Kaya Corsow 10, ☎ *(599) 7-8434.*
Seafood cuisine. Specialties: Ceviche, local snails in hot sauce, seafood soup.
Lunch: 9 a.m.–4 p.m., entrees $5–$9.
Dinner: 4–11 p.m., entrees $9–$25.

See the *zee* (sea) at this waterfront eatery with a front porch at the water's edge. A good American breakfast is served from 9 a.m., and lunch is usually local fish and conch sandwiches, which are recommended. There are Indonesian specialties, including a mini-rijstaffel for those who can't handle the usual 16-dish feast. Whether eating inside or out, there is something for everyone here, food and ambience-wise. Service can be slow at peak times.

Where to Shop

Shopping in Bonaire is for the bored spouse who doesn't like diving. You can, however, find some bargains, up to 50 percent, on gemstone jewelry, ceramics, liquor and tobacco. Most stores will accept American cash, credit cards and traveler's checks, but make sure prices are quoted in U.S. dollars. An easy stroll down Kaya Grandi in Kralendijk will take you past most of the interesting shops. Locally wrought jewelry and batiks from Indonesia are a little extra special at **Ki Bo Ke Pakus** in the Divi Flamingo Beach Resort Casino. Dutch cheeses can be found at **Littman's Gifts** next door to Littman's Jewelers, a longtime establishment.

Bonaire Directory

ARRIVAL AND DEPARTURE

ALM offers nonstop flights to Bonaire from Atlanta (twice a week) and from Miami (once a week). **Air Aruba** also has a direct flight from Newark, New Jersey, three times a week (these flights first touch down in Aruba before flying onto Bonaire). **American Airlines** flies daily to Curaçao from Miami, allowing passengers to make immediate transfers to Bonaire, usually on ALM, which makes 4–5 daily nonstop flights to Bonaire from Curaçao. A plus for flying on American Airlines is that you can sometimes receive a discount if you book your hotel at the same time you make your flight reservation.

The departure tax is $10. There is also an inter-island departure tax of $5.65.

BUSINESS HOURS

Stores open Monday–Saturday 8 a.m.–noon and 2–6 p.m. Banks open weekdays 8:30 a.m.–4 p.m.

CLIMATE

Temperatures average 82 degrees F and vary only 6 degrees between summer and winter. Water temperatures range from 76–80 F. Bonaire gets less than 20 inches of rainfall per year. Bonaire is below the Hurricane Belt and is rarely bombarded by storms or heavy seas.

DOCUMENTS

U.S. and Canadian citizens need show only proof of citizenship (passport, original or notarized birth certificate or voter's registration with photo ID), and an ongoing or return ticket.

ELECTRICITY

Current runs 127 volts, 50 cycles. American appliances will work slower; best to bring an adapter.

GETTING AROUND

Expect to take a taxi from the airport to your hotel—about $10. Rates are established by the government, and most honest drivers will show the list of prices if you ask. Note that rates are higher (25 percent) after 8 p.m., and from 11–6 a.m. (50 percent).

Driving in Bonaire is on the right side of the road. Unless you are an experienced driver, tooting around Bonaire in a scooter or moped can be dangerous since roads are often strewn with rocks or full of holes. The best way to see the Washington National Park is in a Jeep, van or automobile. To rent a car, you will need to show a valid U.S., British, or Canadian driver's license.

Budget, Avis and Dollar Rent a Car all have booths at the airport.

LANGUAGE

Papiamento is the unofficial island language, Dutch the official. English is almost unilaterally spoken. Spanish is also well known.

MEDICAL EMERGENCIES

St. Francis Hospital in Kralendijk ☎ *8900* is run by well-trained doctors who studied in the Netherlands. Divers will be happy to know it comes equipped with a decompression chamber.

MONEY

Official currency is the Netherlands Antilles florin or guilder, written as NAf or Afl. Most establishments list prices in guilders, but will accept dollars (giving change in guilders). U.S. dollars and traveler's checks are accepted everywhere.

TELEPHONE

From the U.S. dial 011 (international code), plus 5997 (country code), plus the 4-digit local number. Few lodgings have room phones, so most people head down to the Landsradio office in Kralendijk. The airport also has telephones.

TIME

Bonaire is on Atlantic Standard Time.

TIPPING AND TAXES

Most hotels and restaurants add a 10–15 percent service charge. The government also requires hotels to add a $4.10-per-person daily room tax. Feel free to tip more for especially good service.

TOURIST INFORMATION

The Tourism Corporation of Bonaire is located at *12 Kaya Simon Bolivia;* ☎ *8322* or *8649*, FAX *8408*, weekdays only. Or from the United States call Tourism Bonaire ☎ *(800) 826-6247.*

WATER

Tap water is safe to drink since it comes from distilled seawater.

WHEN TO GO

Carnival takes place in February. Coronation Day is April 30. St. John's Day is June 24. St. Peter's Day is celebrated in Rincon on June 28. Bonaire Day is Sept. 6. Annual Sailing Regatta are a series of races celebrated with a festive air in mid-October.

BONAIRE HOTELS	RMS	RATES	PHONE	CR. CARDS
Kralendijk				
★★★★ **Harbour Village Resort**	72	$170–$400	(800) 424-0004	A, DC, MC, V
★★★ **Captain Don's Habitat**	43	$150–$245	(800) 327-6709	MC, V
★★★ **Coral Regency Resort**	28	$150–$230	(800) 327-8150	A, DC, MC, V
★★★ **Divi Flamingo Resort**	145	$85–$140	(800) 367-3484	A, DC, MC, V

BONAIRE HOTELS	RMS	RATES	PHONE	CR. CARDS
★★ Buddy Dive Resort	30	$80–$165	(800) 359-0747	A, DC, MC, V
★★ Carib Inn	9	$64–$124	(599) 7-8819	A, MC, V
★★ Sand Dollar Beach Club	24	$160–$350	(800) 288-4773	A, MC, V
★★ Sorobon Beach Resort	20	$110–$165	(599) 7-8080	MC, V
★★ Sunset Beach Hotel	145	$80–$140	(599) 7-5300	A, DC, MC, V
★★ Sunset Oceanfront Apartments	12	$60–$190	(599) 7-8448	A, DC, MC, V
★ Sunset Inn	7	$60–$105	(599) 7-8291	A, MC, V

BONAIRE RESTAURANTS	PHONE	ENTREE	CR. CARDS
Kralendijk			
American			
★★ Beefeater	(599) 7-7776	$15–$25••	A, MC, V
Chinese			
★★★ China Garden	(599) 7-8480	$5–$24	A, MC, V
International			
★★★★ Classic Eatery	(599) 7-8003	$5–$25	MC, V
★★★ Chibi-Chibi	(599) 7-8285	$15–$26••	A, DC, MC, V
★★★ Green Parrot	(599) 7-5454	$5–$20	A, MC, V
★★★ Mona Lisa	(599) 7-8718	$12–$23	A, MC, V
★★★ Raffles	(599) 7-8617	$11–$25••	A, MC, V
★★★ Toys Grand Cafe	(599) 7-6666	$5–$23	MC, V
★★ Rendez-Vous Restaurant	(599) 7-8454	$14–$26••	A, MC, V
Seafood			
★★★ Den Laman		$11–$22••	A, MC, V
★★★ Red Pelican	(599) 7-8198	$4–$35	A, MC, V
★★★ Richard's Waterfront	(599) 7-5263	$13–$28••	A, MC, V
★★ Kilumba	(599) 7-5019	$8–$15	None
★★ Zeezicht Restaurant	(599) 7-8434	$5–$25	A, MC, V

Note: • Lunch Only

•• Dinner Only

CAYMAN ISLANDS

Cayman Brac's 180-acre Brac Parrot Reserve is home to 500 rare parrots.

Cayman Islands is a scuba Eden. Due south of Florida and Cuba, the three small Cayman Islands were eclipsed for centuries by Jamaica (180 miles to the southeast), but have today zoomed into world-class status as divers, snorkelers, saltwater anglers, and beach-loving layabouts learn to love the high standard of living (20 percent higher than in the U.S.), the low crime rate, and the ingratiating good manners. The islands also draw travelers who need little nightlife and revel in the ease, peace and thriftiness of renting a condo by the beach. Reports of the Caymans having the best dive sites in the world have attracted more than 75,000 scubaniks a year (out of the 400,000 tourists who visit annually); the Cayman walls, particularly in the north, are said to rank next to Australia's Great Barrier Reef and the Red Sea in the excellence and accessibility of their sites. Money does seem to find its way here. *The Firm*, Hollywood's recent Tom Cruise movie about money-laundering on the Caymans, brought the Caymans a newfound publicity, at the same time erroneously suggesting an island lacking in moral conscience. What *is* conspicuously absent here are the traditional Caribbean straw-hat markets and open-air produce stands; instead, expensive Italian sandals have replaced the traditional bare feet, and native vendors have been usurped by sophisticated ex-pats who run the trendy boutiques. Still, the simple life can still bleed through on the Caymans, when the town's rooster is heard daily crowing from the veranda of the Old Courts Building at dawn.

Bird's Eye View

Grand Cayman, 22 miles long and eight miles wide, is the principal island of a complex that includes Cayman Brac and Little Cayman. About an hour's flight from Miami, Grand Cayman covers 76 square miles of land mass, though half of that is swamp. About 89 miles to the northeast of Grand Cayman lies Cayman Brac (the name means "bluff" in Gaellic), a limestone bluff rising from sea level to a height of 140 feet. Five miles west of Cayman Brac, the mile-wide Little Cayman lives up to its name, with a land mass of a mere 10 square miles.The capital of the islands is George Town, on the west side of Grand Cayman. No rivers cross the islands, but the vegetation is lush and tropical, dotted with coconut trees, thatch palm, Australian pine and seagrape.

West Bay Beach is the hub of tourism in Grand Cayman, an exquisite strand that gently curves around the western shore. Here, you'll find most of the resorts and hotels. An enormous coral reef surrounds North Sound, a massive bay in the west. Sting Ray City is the shallow habitat of two dozen western Atlantic stingrays whom Caymanian divers have fed and tamed to eat out of their hands.

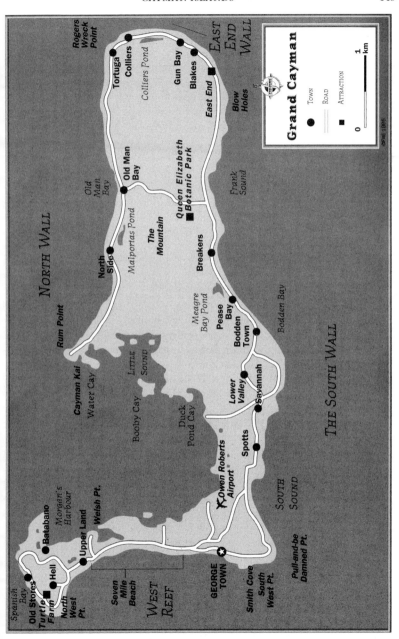

History

Columbus discovered the Caymans in 1503 and dubbed them *Las Tortugas* for the enormous numbers of tortoises that would provide sustenance to English, Dutch and French sailors for centuries. (Las Tortugas somehow evolved into Los Caimanes, the Spanish name for a kind of tropical American crocodile). For a good 150 years after being sited, the Caymans were almost entirely avoided. They were remote, perilous to approach by sea, and their interiors were inhospitable—swampy and mosquito-infested in Grand Cayman, and hard and scrubby on Little Cayman and Cayman Brac. Among the few creatures that thrived here were crocodiles, called *caymanas* in the language of the Carib Indians. For a time the critters shared the island with such buccaneers as Sir Henry Morgan and Edward Teach (the original Blackbeard) who hid out in the islands while preying on Spanish and French ships. (Cayman history abounds with stories of sunken treasure and derring-do.) The abundance of meaty sea turtles made the islands a convenient provisioning stop, but by most accounts, the first real settlers didn't arrive until 1655, when deserters from Oliver Cromwell's army abandoned their platoon in Jamaica as the English were taking it from the Spanish. In 1670, Spain ceded both Jamaica and the Caymans to Great Britain. A century later, Grand Cayman had 933 residents, most of whom were slaves. After emancipation by Britain in 1835, the island became home to many other freed slaves; their descendants gradually becoming part of the families of the island, paving the way for the harmony that still exists today.

Just 33 years ago Jamaica chose independence, but the Caymans stayed on a British Crown Colony. The first tourists started to arrive in the Caymans during the 1950s while the roads were still bad, the insects voluminous and the electrical supply iffy. Legislation creating tax-investment havens in 1966 favored offshore banking and trust companies whose executives began seeing vacation promise in the islands. A tourist board, established in 1966, began strictly supervising hotel inspections, which has succeeded in raising and maintaining a high standard of service. About half a million people visit the Cayman Islands each year.

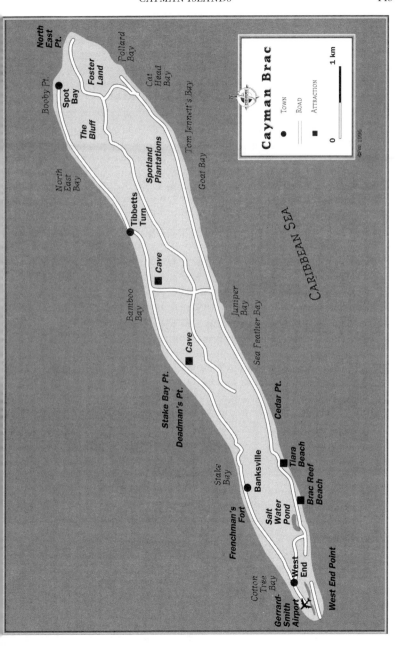

People

Nearly all the 30,000 Caymanians live on Grand Cayman, a fourth of them in George Town. About 1650 live on Cayman Brac and a mere 50 on Little Cayman. Their ancestry is an ethnic mix from 50 countries, including Jamaica, the U.S., and the U.K. The lilting brogue is a leftover from British seafarers centuries ago. The utter lack of racial tension on the island stems from the fact that neither sugar plantations or long-term slavery was part of the island's history, and the mixing of races seems to have been more fluid here than on other islands. In 1841, an observer noted that Caymanians were "strictly honest and industrious," and that even the wealthy were prone to walk around without shoes on. Today the simple life still seems to prevail though Caymanians enjoy the highest standard of living in the Caribbean There is little serious crime. And if the Caymans are short on native culture locals make up for it for being congenial and tolerant.

Today lots of offshore investors park their money here because taxes and fees are few and client's identities are usually shielded by law. So profitable are the ventures that there are more than 50 banks and $435 million in assets here. Though the recent movie *The Firm* and its plot about money-laundering in the Caymans almost smudged the reputation of the island, locals insist such a scam can't happen here. They claim that anyone trying to deposit lots of U.S. cash would raise eyebrows among local officials.

Beaches

The beaches of the Caymans can be described in a few short words—powder-fine white strands with a handful of birds. **Seven Mile Beach** is considered one of the most fantastic beaches in the Caribbean, marked by a beautiful crescent shape and clear turquoise blue waters. Public buses operate hourly down the strand. North of the Holiday Inn, where most of the watersport facilities are based, is a public beach with small cabanas and tables and chairs Most memorable sunsets can be seen from the beach at **Rum Point**, at the

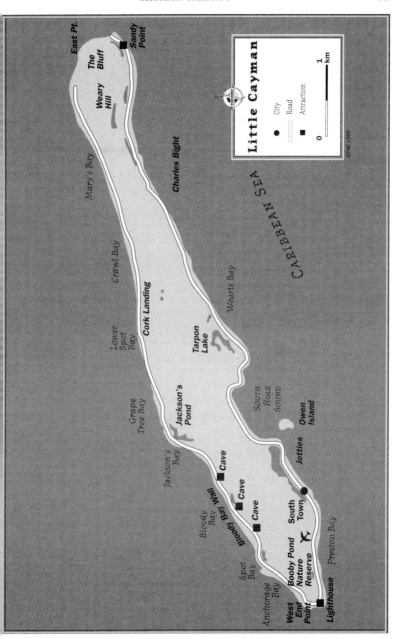

Little Cayman

- ● City
- Road
- ■ Attraction

0 km 1

©1995

East Pt.

The Bluff

Sandy Point

Weary Hill

Mary's Bay

Charles Bight

Crawl Bay

CARIBBEAN SEA

Lower Spot Bay

Cork Landing

Wearis Bay

Tarpon Lake

Grape Tree Bay

Jackson's Pond

SOUTH HOLE SOUND

Jackson's Bay

Cave

Owen Island

Bloody Bay Wall

Cave

Jetties

Bloody Bay

Cave

South Town

Spot Bay

Booby Pond Nature Reserve

Preston Bay

Anchorage Bay

West End Point

Lighthouse

northeastern tip of North Sound, a sleepy little community of private home
and condos. **Little Cayman** is known for its long white beaches with nary a
footprint to mar their beauty. For some reason, locals don't use the beache
much for sunbathing or swimming, so most of the strands are exquisitely pri
vate and not crowded.

Underwater

Make no doubt about it, diving is an industry in the Cayman Islands
Spurred on by magnificent underwater scenery, the islands have single-hand
edly captured the press, accolades and repeat business to secure a position a
one of the two or three top dive destinations in the Caribbean. A series o
immense walls, dropping to 6000 feet or more, line the islands and create
ideal diving conditions. The downside is that dive operators are frequently
accused of running a cattle show; as the number of shops on the island ha
increased over the last decade, competition has heated up and operators have
begun using larger boats to increase their efficiency. Groups of 15 or 20 are
the rule, but some operators will carry more, particularly when cruise ship
dock. Some more-experienced divers, unaccustomed to crowded dive site
and stringent safety rules, disparagingly refer to the Caymans as "the Mc
Donald's of dive destinations." The good news is that the diving, from 11
permanent mooring sites off Grand Cayman alone, and with visibility some
times approaching 200 feet, is still among the world's best.

The structure of the Cayman Reef formation is relatively simple. Each o
the islands represent the (possibly volcanic) summits of immense mountain
which rise thousands of feet from the floor of the Caribbean Sea. Leading
out from the shoreline, the first region is a very gentle sloping plane of sand
usually covered in turtle grass, which leads to a fringing reef of elkhorn o
staghorn corals. The next section is a moderate incline of alternating chan
nels of patch reef and sand, referred to as a spur-and-groove system, which
leads to a steeper drop-off. With the exception of Little Cayman's wall
(which starts at only 20 or 30 feet), the sheer escarpment usually begin
about 50 or 60 feet below the surface (diving on Cayman Brac and Little
Cayman is discussed in more detail below). As a rule, depth approaches
staggering 6000 feet less than a mile off shore, continuing down on th
south side of the islands to the Cayman Trench, 24,720 feet below the sur
face—the deepest part of the Caribbean. Divers are kept to a firm depth limi

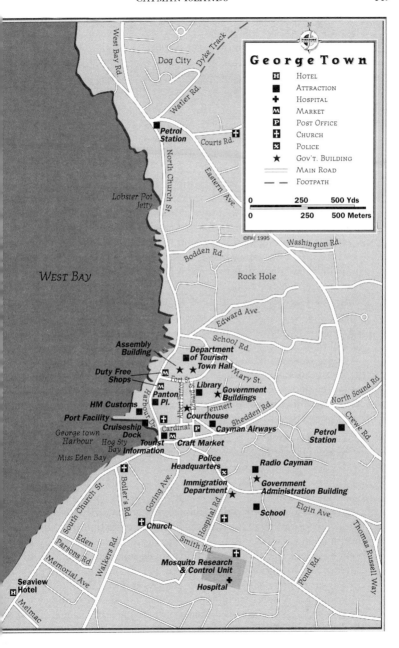

George Town

H	Hotel
■	Attraction
+	Hospital
M	Market
P	Post Office
✚	Church
☒	Police
★	Gov't. Building
	Main Road
– –	Footpath

0   250   500 Yds
0   250   500 Meters

©FWI 1995

Dog City

West Bay Rd.
Watler Rd.
Dyke Track

Petrol Station

Courts Rd.

North Church St.

Eastern Ave.

Lobster Pot Jetty

WEST BAY

Bodden Rd.

Washington Rd.

Rock Hole

Edward Ave.

School Rd.

Assembly Building

Department of Tourism
Town Hall

Duty Free Shops

Mary St.

Fort St.

Library

North Sound Rd.

Panton Pl.

Government Buildings

HM Customs

Jennett

Port Facility

Courthouse

Shedden Rd.

Crewe Rd.

Cruiseship Dock

Cardinal

Cayman Airways

Petrol Station

George town Harbour

Hog Sty Bay

Tourist Information

Craft Market

Miss Eden Bay

Police Headquarters

Radio Cayman

Harbour Dr.

South Church St.

Boiler's Rd.

Immigration Department

Government Administration Building

Goring Ave.

Hospital Rd.

School

Elgin Ave.

Eden

Church

Thomas Russell Way

Parsons Rd.

Walkers Rd.

Smith Rd.

Memorial Ave.

Pond Rd.

Mosquito Research & Control Unit

Hospital

Seaview Hotel

Melmac

of 110 feet by shops who are members of the Cayman Islands Watersport Operator's Association (CIWOA), which regulates universal safety standards for the plethora of dive shops on the islands.

Four separate walls, named after the compass points, surround Grand Cayman. The **West Reef** structure stretches along **Seven Mile Beach** and offers the best visibility and access, and some of the most famous dives. Since the majority of dive operators and tourist accommodations are located along the beach, its sites are more heavily trafficked than most of the others on the island. The vast **North Sound** is the breeding ground for Grand Cayman, which in turn spills into the Caribbean at low tide, attracting bigger fish to the **North Wall** (on the flip side, the rich effluent can sometimes decrease visibility, however); the diving here is exciting and somewhat more advanced, and summer months draw Caribbean reef and hammerhead sharks to the area for breeding. Sometimes referred to as "the last frontier," the rugged **East End Wall** has some of the island's most pristine, and least-visited dives—56, by one count—featuring a great concentration of tunnels and caves. The main drawback is that the eastern reef is a solid two-hour boat ride from **West Bay** dive shops, but that's also its attraction. It's also worth noting that wind usually approach the island from the southeast, making the walls on the south and east sides somewhat more weather dependent. Several noteworthy wrecks lie at opposing ends of the island; the *Ridgefield*, on the eastern tip, offers excellent snorkeling. It's possible to locate good snorkeling locations off almost any beach, but the south end of West Bay provides a number of sites close to shore. Snorkeling the channels which lead through reefs fringing North Sound, along Sand Cay and at Pedro Point is possible, but they should be approached with caution due to unpredictable currents (check around locally before visiting these areas).

Beside the island's glorious walls, Grand Cayman's most famous site well-nigh the single most-visited dive location in the Caribbean, perhaps anywhere: **Stingray City**. Even the most jaded divers continue to be seduced by this open-water petting zoo, sometimes referred to as "the world's greatest 12-foot dive." The site is an underwater sandbank that is frequented by a docile group of up to 100 southern Atlantic stingrays who have become accustomed to human interaction (though they are fed, they have yet to negotiate a cut of the huge financial dividend this attraction generates). Every dive shop on Grand Cayman visits Stingray City; most, but not all, tack on a $5 or $10 surcharge above their normal single tank price. They can afford to. The demand for this dive is tremendous and it's not unusual to see a hundred divers or more congregating on the rays at once. Although the interaction provided is not as swooning, you may also snorkel Stingray City, at another sight just east, named **Sandbar**, where the water is generally shoulder-level depth, allowing you to stand and feed the rays.

There are currently around 30 dive operators on Grand Cayman alone. The competition makes two-tank dive prices reasonable by Caribbean standards; single-tank dives, however, priced anywhere from $5 to $20 less than two tanks, are not generally a good deal by comparison. The four operations we've listed (plus a live-aboard) are those which consistently crop up favorably in reader surveys and local recommendations. It is by no means a comprehensive list of the only decent shops on the island. Given the variety of services and differing styles of operation available, your best bet is to shop around and solicit more opinions to make the selection which works best for you; it's worth inquiring if they are a member of the CIWOA. Finally, if a quieter atmosphere stirs your diving fantasies, head east to **Cayman Brac** or **Little Cayman**. The sites on these smaller islands frequently rival those of Grand Cayman, yet they exist off the shores of remote backwaters which have thus far not been overrun.

Babylon

One of the best of the East End sites, Babylon's astonishing wall starts at 40 feet and drops through crevices and cathedrals, winding around a pinnacle blanketed by tube sponges, strands of black coral, strawberry vase sponges and huge gorgonians. Large pelagics frequent the area, and even pilot whales are spotted during the summer months. A dramatic dive with spectacular vistas.

Big Tunnels

Located just north of Seven Mile Beach, this site is anchored by a 50-foot coral arch which leads to an exciting series of intermittent tunnels, ledges and swim-throughs, including one area referred to as the Chapel. Eagle rays and the occasional moray will glide by, but the real attraction beyond the landscape is smaller: tarpon, pufferfish and grunts, with a colorful array of tube and basket sponges, gorgonians, sea fans and branching corals.

Eagle Ray Pass

It's the one everyone talks about and, somehow, it still lives up to its reputation. The Pass is an alley for marine life shuttling in and out of the sound; it serves as a feeding station and is visited by a number of eagle rays as well as turtles, hammerheads and reef sharks. A tunnel on top of the reef begins at about 65 feet and descends to 110 feet where it exits out on the wall, adding to the drama of this spectacular location.

Orange Canyon

Known for one particularly huge elephant ear sponge, this is one of the West side's most colorful sites, accented by a group of orange sponges set against a deep swim-through canyon. The top of the reef starts at 45 feet, marked by enormous parapets that overlook the wall; the abundant small life includes shrimp, arrow crabs, sea cucumbers and brittle stars.

Trinity Caves

The 45-foot reef at this site is sliced by a maze of deep, narrow channels (60 to 100 feet) which eventually lead to the most spectacular part of the West Wall. The topography is exciting, and a menagerie of groupers, squirrel fish and turtles live in the three cathedral-like rooms that give the site its name.

Wreck of the *Oro Verde*

It's difficult to imagine anyone tiring of the Cayman walls, but if you must do a wreck, the *Oro Verde* is probably the best, conveniently located in front of the Holiday Inn on Seven Mile Beach. A Panamanian cargo ship which ran aground in 1976, the Oro Verde was cleaned up for diving (hatches, jagged edges, glass removed, etc.) before being sunk as an artificial reef, making it a safe location for beginners; it now rests on a sand bank 50 feet down. Because the site is fairly new and visited by dozens of divers daily, encrusting is taking place at a very slow rate and may never fully develop like other famous sinkings. Still, the Oro Verde is a delightful introduction to the world of wreck diving.

Dive Shops

Bob Soto's Diving Ltd.

George Town; ☎ *(809) 949-2022.*

Oldest operation on the island (since 1957) is also the oldest in the world. PADI five-star development center, also NAUI and SSI affiliated. Two-tank dive, $60. Maximum group size, 20. Runs an East End "safari" via bus, $70 (including lunch and two dives). Night dives scheduled Tuesday and Saturday, $55.

Cayman Aggressor III

☎ *(800) 348-2628 or (809) 949-5551.*

Popular, all-inclusive live-aboard boats; $1495 for the seven-day trips, which feature five-and-a-half days of diving (up to five dives daily including a night dive). Generally sticks to the less-visited East End Wall of Grand Cayman but, weather permitting, will also swing over to Little Cayman. The boat sleeps 18 and operates 52 weeks a year, departing every Saturday afternoon. Instructor available on all trips and beginners may obtain certification over the course of the week.

Don Foster's Cayman Ltd.

George Town; ☎ *(800) 833-4837 or (809) 949-5679.*

One of the island's better-established outfits, with groups limited to 20. PADI, NAUI and SSI affiliated; courses to divemaster. Two tank dive, $60, snorkeling trips $25.

Parrots Landing

George Town; ☎ *(800) 448-0428 or (809) 949-7884.*

Refers to itself as an "elite" dive operation, Parrots opened in 1988 and is PADI, NAUI and SSI affiliated. Maximum group size, 20. Two-tank dives, $60. Night dives Tuesday and Friday, $50.

Sunset Divers

George Town; ☎ *(800) 854-4767 or (809) 949-7111.*

A 23-year-old operation, PADI, NAUI, SSI affiliated, courses to Divemaster. Two-tank dive, $60. Computer diving available on all boats, with regular trips to remote east-end sites. Group size, 20 maximum, but also has smaller boats.

Cayman Brac - Underwater

Although many residents consider Brac the loveliest of the three Caymans topside, the island's dive sites—which would be rated excellent most anywhere else in the world—are always compared against the glories of Grand and Little Cayman. Yet Cayman Brac's wall, which starts at a depth of 50 to 60 feet, actually offers drama comparable to the better known Bloody Bay Wall. Tunnels and crevices abound throughout many sites, and fine diving is found on both sides of the island. Winter winds from the northwest can sometimes play havoc, but year-round visibility is roughly comparable to the 100+ foot average found on the sister islands. At popular **East Chute**, a small 1986 wreck sits placidly on the sand floor near the lip of the wall and has begun to develop soft corals and sponges on her hull. **Bert Brothers Boulders**, on the less-dived eastern tip of the island, is a spur-and-groove reef structure featuring beautiful swim-throughs and gorges. **Windsock Reef**, off the island's western tip, offers excellent snorkeling among forests of elkhorn and pillar coral, while the nearby barrier reef also provides good snorkeling possibilities.

Dive Shops

Dive Tiara

Cayman Brac; (809) 948-1553.

A 10-year-old operation, PADI, NAUI and SSI-affiliated. Two-tank dive, $66. Tiara also runs trips to Little Cayman four times a week (40-50 minutes to Bloody Bay Wall).

Little Cayman - Underwater

From the air, an almost insignificant 11-mile strip of sand, Little Cayman anchors what is possibly the single most spectacular wall in the Caribbean. The top of the formation starts at only 20 or 25 feet below the surface on the northern coast of the island, then plunges to a pulse-quickening depth of over 6000 feet, sometimes at a dead-vertical, or even inverse, angle. The three-mile stretch actually encompasses two areas which are slightly different near the crest; **Bloody Bay Wall**, to the west, is a sheer drop from 20 or 30 feet down, whereas the **Jackson Bay Wall** (on the east) is more typical of the spur-and-groove structure found on Grand Cayman. One unique aspect about Little Cayman is that virtually all sites along the cascading wall are accessible for beginners, weather and depth permitting. Although visibility averages 100 feet year-round, conditions are better from spring through fall, and can secure visibility approaching 200 feet in the placid summer months. Shore diving is possible from a number of points but, with very limited medical services no closer than Cayman Brac, local operators frown on it. The Bloody Bay Wall is also a spectacular setting for snorkelers, with coral heads rising to within 10 feet of the surface at some spots.

As if to literally portray the difference between Grand and Little Cayman diving, the noted animal show here is not a slew of southern stingrays, but a single, graceful manta named Molly who sports a 10-foot wingspan. Molly does not inhabit the Jackson Bay area year-round, but dive shops claim that she puts in an appearance about 95 percent of the time during their summer night dives. Molly is attracted by dive lights—which seduce a rich bounty of plankton for her to feed on—and she swoops, circles and plays with divers in appreciation. The local operators are very protective of Molly, who has been interacting with them since 1991, and she in turn has established a bond, even allowing them to sever nets and ropes she became entangled in on two separate occasions.

Three years ago, very few divers made it to Little Cayman, primarily due to transportation and accommodation considerations. However, airline service has increased and several new resorts have opened with a keen eye toward accommodating dive business. The government has stepped up the conservation effort at the island and limits each shop to a strict maximum of 14 weekly boat trips to the Jackson/Bloody Bay area, with no more than 20 divers on board each boat. So far, a backlash has not occurred, but the potential for disappointed visitors certainly exists. Still, with barely a hundred year-round residents on the substantially uninhabited island, this is a remote dive destination with an extraordinary payoff.

Fisheye Fantasy

Just outside the marine park and Bloody Bay Wall, this is the island's must-see site, a twisting and turning series of overhangs, swim-throughs and tunnels, capped off by a donut-hole passage. Red rope sponges drop from the roof of the overhangs, with an abundance of black coral, soft purple fans and vivid encrustations decorating the walls, and wrasse, angels and snapper touring the caves.

Marilyn's Cut (Hole in the Wall)

Set at the intersection of the Bloody Bay and Jackson walls, Marilyn's Cut begins with a vertical chimney that leads down through the interior of the reef. After the drop into darkness, the hole angles out to the wall about 60 feet down, where colorful hard and soft corals abound. Ostensibly taking a cue from Molly, a 25-pound grouper named Ben is a frequent companion to divers at one point on this dive, mugging endlessly for cameras and rolling over for visitors to stroke his stomach.

Meadows

This site is fine during the day, with stovepipe and strawberry vase sponges elegantly trimming the drop-off, but at night, the area comes alive with another cast of characters, including Molly (see above). If the friendly manta is on a holiday elsewhere, spotted eagle and stingrays can usually be seen in the sand chutes, along with groupers, large parrotfish and swarms of silversides. Located at the "hinge" where the wall heads away from the island into open waters.

Dive Shops

Paradise Divers

Little Cayman; ☎ *(800) 450-2084 or (809) 948-0004.*

The island's only independent outfit, Paradise keeps groups to a maximum of 16. PADI affiliated. Two-tank dive, $60. Night dives, $35.

Reef Divers

Little Cayman; ☎ *(809) 948-1033.*

Tied in to Little Cayman Beach Resort, Reef Divers is the island's busiest and largest outfit with three dive boats working the shoreline; PADI affiliated. Two-tank dive, $63.

FIELDING'S CHOICE:

Stingray City, the world-famous dive site, in North Sound, is less than an hour's catamaran ride from the Hyatt Regency's dock. The surprise is that you can actually scuba and snorkel with a large family of stingrays, who, years ago, learned to bump a diver's mask so the diver would drop his bag of squid. Those who have done it have been scared out of their minds but have come back glowing.

On Foot

Cayman Islands Governor Michael Gore is an ardent bird-watcher, which has helped ensure protection for the island's 180 species. Some of the better known are the snowy egret, the bananaquit, many species of heron and, of course, the Cayman parrot. There are a series of mosquito control dikes on the peninsula at West Bay which are explored (repellent well in hand) by keen birders and there is a book, *Birds of the Cayman Islands*, available locally for die-hards. Trails on Grand Cayman are limited, but the Ordnance Survey map sold at the Land and Survey Department in George Town details the starts and stops of a number of possibilities. Among them are sporadic paths along the north shore, an area inhabited by the nearly extinct Cayman Iguana. There is also an interpretive nature trail, just under a mile long, that tours wetlands, logwood swamp, air plant woodland and a cactus thicket; this trail is located in the **Queen Elizabeth Botanic Park** (admission $3 for adults). A newly-restored 200-year-old footpath also explores the woodlands at the heart of Grand Cayman. The two-mile trail can only be done with a wildlife guide, **Albert Hines**, who offers a two-and-a-half hour tour Monday

through Friday at 8:30 a.m. and 3 p.m., Saturdays at 8:30 a.m. only; th
price of the excursion is $30 and profits are used to maintain the path (*rese*
vations required: ☎ *(809) 949-1996*).

Cayman Brac - On Foot

Brac distinguishes itself among the Caymans by having the most interes
ing interior landscape. In particular, a limestone bluff (a "brac" in Gaeli
rises to an elevation of about 140 feet—the highest point in the Caymans-
and provides the islands' best hike. The 180-acre **Brac Parrot Reserve** is loca
ed on the bluff and serves as home to about 500 of the rare birds, a uniqu
subspecies of the Amazon parrot. Also located on the bluff is a series c
caves, which are said to have once held pirate treasure. Most vehicular traff
is concentrated along the paved coastal roads, however, a dirt track follow
the island's spine (between the north and south coasts) and provides secluc
ed walking potential. Hikers should be on the alert for the maiden plu
prevalent around the bluff, which can cause a skin rash if brushed against.

Cayman Bluff

While several tracks meander towards the top of this limestone plateau, a wel
defined farmer's path begins in Spot Bay, passing caves as it winds to the summi
The trail continues along rockier ground to the island's east-end lighthouse, hom
to a noisy flock of brown boobies. White-tailed tropic birds can be spotted most c
the year around the nearby caves, where they build nests. The setting is ideal for
special Caribbean sunrise; allow two hours round-trip.

Little Cayman - On Foot

The smallest of the Caymans is a mostly undistinguished flat of sand a
cented by scrub and mangroves. Just past South Town is the 200-acre **Boot
Pond Nature Reserve**, nesting grounds for roughly 3500 mating pairs of rec
footed boobies; the island is also home to great blue herons, black-necke
stilts and even some magnificent frigatebirds. The truly adventurous ca
head east along the island's coastline for solitude and exploration, or tw
simpler paths depart from the airport just outside town; one heads west t
the lighthouse, while the other, referred to as **The Nature Trail**, crosses the i:
land to the northwest and leads to **Spot Bay** (allow an hour round-trip for e
ther of these walks).

By Pedal

With a maximum elevation of just 60 feet above sea level, riding on Grand Cayman can hardly be considered difficult, that is, unless you attempt the approximately 55-mile round-trip from George Town to **Rum Point** (and that's utilizing the north-south cut at Old Man Bay; the eastern coast scenery along the Queen's Highway is less appealing). This ride explores a good chunk of the island, including the lovely beaches at Rum Point, and is suitable for good cyclists who are equipped with sufficient water and stamina. Alternatively, you can also take the ferry which travels between the Hyatt and Rum Point; there's no charge for bikes and this reduces the riding to under 30 miles one way. Another area which is nice for cycling lies in the vicinity of Hell and the Turtle Farm; from George Town, a ride to the northern tip and back would come in under 10 miles.

Bike Rental Shops

Cayman Cycle Rentals
George Town; ☎ *(809) 947-4021.*
Owns a burgeoning collection of Huffy 10-speeds. $12 per day, or $20 for a pair of bikes.

What Else to See

There is little to dazzle the eye in regards to historical settings in Grand Cayman, but a jaunt around George Town should include a trip to the **Cayman Islands National Museum**, on the waterfront at Hog St. Bay, where you can view some 2000 artifacts about the island's history. If you get bored, the little library on Edward Street stocks English novels and magazines. To see more of Grand Cayman, you might consider renting a bike, motorbike or even a car. You can start out driving along Seven Mile Beach, past the residence of the island's governor and onto the West Bay. A stop at **Hell**, a formation of jagged burnt charcoal-colored rocks called iron-shore, has spawned a cottage industry of products imbued with "hell" themes. There is even a post office nearby where you postmark letters "from Hell." At the **Cayman Turtle Farm**, you can watch reptiles being hatched and raised (28,000 yearlings released into the sea last year) and scour the gift shop for turtle paraphernalia. Along the **South Sound Road**, you'll drive past some of the most attractive old wooden houses on the island. Bat fanatics can stop at their own **Bat Cave** (take the dirt road off the main road, to Bodden Town, heading east). A cliff overhanging the sea houses numerous caves; just beware where you walk. At the **Cayman Islands National Botanic Park**, you can hike over a 1.5-mile marked trail. The *Submarine Atlantis* at George Town Harbour—considered the stretch limo of the Caribbean—makes a sightseeing dive on a sophisticated vessel by a Creole pilot whose assistant entertains as you browse 100 feet down, among puffers, parrot fish and the reef life.

City Celebrations

Pirates' Week   ★ ★ ★ ★ ★

Various locations, Georgetown, ☎ *(809) 949-5078.*

To celebrate its history as a pirate haunt, this islandwide festival, held in late October, brings out the buccaneer in locals. There are costume parades, fishing tournaments, treasure hunts and the ever-popular kidnapping of the governor. Lots of ho-ho-hoing, and more than a few bottles of rum.

Museums and Exhibits

Cayman Brac

Brac Museum   ★ ★

Stake Bay.
Hours open: 9 a.m.–4 p.m.
This small museum exhibits local antiques and relics from shipwrecks.

Grand Cayman

Cayman Islands National Museum   ★ ★

Harbour Drive, Georgetown, ☎ *(809) 949-8368.*
Hours open: 9 a.m.–5 p.m.
Housed in an 1833 West Indian building on the waterfront—which in previous incarnations was a jail, courthouse and dance hall—this museum exhibits more than 2000 items detailing the history of the islands and its peoples. Students & Seniors $2.50.

Treasure Museum   ★ ★ ★

West Bay Road, Georgetown, ☎ *(809) 947-5033.*
Hours open: 9 a.m.–5 p.m.
This small museum specializes in recovered artifacts from shipwrecks, with lots of pieces from the Maravillas, a Spanish galleon that sank in 1656. Among the exhibits are a seven-pound gold bar, dioramas of the islands' seafaring history and an animated Blackbeard the Pirate, who regales visitors with long-ago tales that may or may not be true.

Parks and Gardens

Queen Elizabeth II Botanic Park

Center of the island, Georgetown.

Hours open: 7:30 a.m.–5:30 p.m.

This new interpretive woodland trail is less than a mile long, but packs a lot in a relatively small space. The trail passes through more than a dozen Caymanian landscapes, from wetlands to cactus thicket, logwood swamp to woodland and mahogany trees. There's also an iguana habitat partially funded by the World Wildlife Fund that is home to the endangered native blue iguanas, a crocodile swamp with 300-year-old fossil bones and a pond housing small freshwater turtles found only in the Caymans. Bird-watchers may spot Grand Cayman parrots, Northern Flicker woodpeckers, Vitelline warblers, Zenaida doves and Bananaquits. The Botanic Park is the first of several ambitious projects to protect the Caymans' environment. Future plans call for a network of preserves on Grand Cayman and a blufftop tract atop Cayman Brac.

Tours

Atlantic Submarines Cayman ★★★★★

Goring Avenue, Georgetown, ☎ *(809) 949-7700.*

Not for the claustrophobic but memorable for everyone else, this modern submarine seats 46 people in air-conditioned comfort. It travels along the Cayman Wall at depths of up to 90 feet, giving nondivers a taste of the fascinating underwater sights. Night dives are especially recommended. Prices range from $79–$90; half that for kids under 12 (children under four are not permitted). Atlantis also operates two research subs that go as deep as 800 feet and carry just two passengers at a time. This trip costs $275 per person; a highlight is the wreck of the cargo ship Kirk Pride.

The 12,000 green turtles at Cayman Turtle Farm on Grand Cayman range in size from two ounces to 400 pounds.

Cayman Turtle Farm ★★★

West Bay, Georgetown, ☎ *(809) 949-3893.*
Hours open: 8:30 a.m.–5 p.m.

The island's most-visited tourist attraction houses more than 12,000 green turtles, from hatchlings to giant specimens weighing 600 pounds. It's the world's only green sea turtle farm, and while it supplies turtle meat to local restaurants, it also strives to replenish their numbers in the wild. You can taste turtle dishes at the cafe, but skip the gift shop, as U.S. citizens can't import anything made of these endangered critters. Children 6–10 are half price and under 6 are free.

Sting Ray City

North Sound.

Some two miles off the northwest tip and 12 feet down live several dozen stingrays that await handouts from divers and snorkelers. They are relatively tame, but beware of their stinger tails! One of the Caribbean's most popular dive sites.

Sports

Watersports are the bread and butter—or is that the fish and crabcake?—of the Caymanian experience. Scuba is king, and there are three dive shops that have the capability of serving 75,000 divers annually. (For more information, see "Dive Sites"). The less-athletically inclined should definitely take a cruise on the island's famous submarine, the 28-passenger *Atlantis* ☎ *(809) 949-7700*, which dives up to 150 feet both day and night. Also consider a glass-bottom-boat trip—contact the Holiday Inn for information. Deep-sea fishing has caught on with a great passion in recent years. Blue marlin, bluefin and yellowfin tuna, wahoo, dolphin, tarpon, groupers, snappers, barracuda and the occasional shark are all potential catches. The prime fishing season runs from November-March, but fishing year-round remains good. In June, there is a Million Dollar Month sport-fishing competition, with a one-million-dollar prize (where *do* they get that money?) awarded to the angler who breaks the current world record for Atlantic blue marlin (the odds are probably longer than the New York Lottery). On Grand Cayman, Sunfish and Hobie Cats can be rented as well as 60-foot catamarans chartered with crew. Seven-Mile Beach receives the most cruises. North Sound, Spots Bay and Hub Bay have all proved safe for anchors, but boats must first register at the Port Authority in George Town if they want to come ashore. A yacht race is held annually in the spring for locals and visitors. Some hotels and condo complexes have tennis and there is an unusual 18-hole golf course called the Links. You can also do as the British bankers do—take in cricket, or polo, with all the gusto of an ex-pat.

Deep-Sea Fishing

Various locations, Georgetown.

Several outfits offer charters and excursions for deep-sea, reef, bone and fly fishers: **Crosby Ebanks** *(☎ (809) 947-4049)*, **Capt. Eugene's Watersports** *(☎ (809) 949-3099)*; **Charter Boat Headquarters** *(☎ (809) 947-4340)*, and **Island Girl** *(☎ (809) 947-3029)*. Serious fishermen and women should plan to visit Grand Cayman in June, when the Million Dollar Month fishing tournament is held, featuring international competitors and cash prizes. For details, contact Box 878, West Wind Building, Grand Cayman.

Golf

Two locations, Georgetown.

The island's newest course is the **Links at Safehaven** *(☎ (809) 947-4155)*, a par-71, 6519-yard championship course designed by Roy Case. Duffers can also tee off at **Britannia**, designed by Jack Nicklaus, which includes a nine-hole regulation course, an 18-hole executive course, and a Cayman course, in which special short-distance balls are used. Green fees are $25–$50; ☎ *(809) 949-8020.*

Mastic Trail   ★ ★ ★ ★ ★

Off Frank Sound Road, Georgetown, ☎ (809) 949-1996.

This newly restored 200-year-old footpath winds through a two-million-old woodland in the heart of the island. Just reopened in 1995, the trail is located west of Frank Sound Road, a 45-minute drive east from George Town. The two-mile trail showcases the Mastic Reserve's scenic wonders, including a mangrove swamp, woodland area, and traditional farms. Birders should be on the lookout for the Grand Cayman parrot, Caribbean dove, West Indian woodpecker, Cuban bullfinch, smooth-billed Ani and Bananaquit. The new nonprofit reserve now numbers 200 acres, with the plan of adding 800 more acres as funds become available. Guided tours, which are not recommended to children under six, the elderly and the infirm, last 2.5 hours and are limited to eight people, so reservations are essential. They are available Monday through Friday at 8:30 a.m. and 3 p.m. and on Saturday at 8:30 a.m.

Scuba Diving

Various locations, Georgetown.

Chances are excellent that your hotel will have its own dive center, or check out one of the following: Grand Cayman: **Dive Cayman BVI** *(☎ (809) 947-5133)*, **Parrot's Landing** *(☎ (800) 448-0428 or ☎ (809) 949-7884)*, **Quabbin Dives** *(☎ (800) 238-6712 or ☎ (809) 949-5597)*, **Sunset Divers** *(☎ (809) 949-7111)*, **Bob Soto's** *(☎ (809) 947-4631)*, **Don Foster's** *(☎ (809) 949-5679)* and **Red Sail Sports** *(☎ (809) 949-8745)*. Cayman Brac: **Divi Tiara** *(☎ (809) 948-1316)* and **Brac Aquatics** *(☎ (809) 858-7429)*. Little Cayman: **Southern Cross Club** *(☎ (809) 948-1099)*. Prices are generally about $40 for a single-tank dive; $55 for two tanks.

Windsurfing

Various locations, Georgetown.

Chances are good your hotel can set you up, but if it lacks facilities, try **Cayman Windsurf** *(☎ (809) 947-7492)* or **Sailboards Caribbean** *(☎ (809) 949-1068)*.

Where to Stay

★★★★★	**Clarion Grand Pavilion**	$155–$455
★★★★★	**West Indian Club**	$130–$365
★★★★	**Beach Club Hotel**	$125–$265
★★★★	**Hyatt Regency Grand Cayman**	$180–$500
★★★★	**Little Cayman Beach**	$118–$137
★★★★	**Radisson Resort**	$165–$390
★★★★	**Spanish Bay Reef North Wall**	$160–$218
★★★★	**Treasure Island Resort**	$160–$275
★★★	**Holiday Inn Grand Cayman**	$238–$832
★★★	**London House**	$235–$750

★★	**Divi Tiara Beach Resort**	$95–$200
★★★★	**Hyatt Regency Grand Cayman**	$180–$500

Fielding's Budget Hotels in Cayman Islands

★★★	**Ambassadors Inn**	$60–$80
★★★	**Island Hill Resort**	$60–$80
★★	**Seaview Hotel**	$65–$105
★	**Brac Reef Beach Resort**	$106–$147
★★★★	**Little Cayman Beach**	$118–$137

About half of the 3000 rooms in the Cayman Islands are situated not i
hotels but in rental condos, which look like sitting ducks, almost none high
er than a palm tree, as regulated by law. A good book to get is the *Rates an
Facts* booklet put out by the tourist board. The chain establishments o

Grand Cayman's Seven Mile Beach are big and well equipped with restaurants and recreational facilities. Most folks like to settle into one of the hotels or condos on West Bay because it is easy to walk up and down the strip for meals, shopping, etc. without ever needing a car. If you want to avoid the hustle of George Town and Seven Mile Beach, stay on the north side or east side. Many prefer the flexibility of renting a one- to three-bedroom apartment with a fully equipped kitchen and daily maid service.

Hotels and Resorts

The big chain hotels, including **Holiday Inn**, **Radisson** and **Ramada**, give good service here and particularly lean toward providing package tours, some specifically for divers. The **Hyatt Regency**, luxurious and lushly landscaped, is known for being the hub of lively social activities, especially at night. (Hyatt's private villas come with their own pool, Jacuzzi and cabaña.) The **Spanish Bay Reef**, the first all-inclusive property on Grand Cayman, rates as the island's most secluded—a true dive hotel. **Pirates Point Resort** is run by a Cordon-Bleu educated-chef. The Beach Club Colony should be avoided if you don't care for your personal beach space to be invaded by loads of cruise passengers.

Cayman Brac

Brac Reef Beach Resort   **$106–$147**   ★

West End Point, ☎ *(800) 327-3835, (809) 948-7323, FAX (813) 323-8827.*
Single: $106–$147. Double: $106–$147.

Divers like this casual hotel and its all-inclusive package rates that include all drinks, transportation from the airport and three buffet meals daily. Dive packages are available at additional cost. The rooms are basic but at least air cooled, and recent renovations have added decks or patios as well as new carpeting and wallpaper. There's a pool and tennis court to keep nondivers occupied.

Divi Tiara Beach Resort   **$95–$200**   ★★

West End Point, ☎ *(800) 948-1553, (809) 948-7553, FAX (809) 948-1316.*
Single: $95–$185. Double: $100–$200.

Set on a fine beach, this pleasant hotel appeals to those who want to avoid crowds. Rooms are typical but do offer air conditioning and were recently redone; a few have Jacuzzis to boot. There's a pool and tennis court, and most meals are served buffet-style. Good service. The dive center is excellent.

Grand Cayman

Beach Club Hotel   **$125–$265**   ★ ★ ★ ★

Seven Mile Beach, West Bay, ☎ *(800) 223-6510, (809) 949-8100, FAX (809) 947-5167.*
Single: $125–$240. Double: $125–$265.

Dating back to the 1960s (making it one of the island's oldest resorts), the Beach Club resembles a colonial plantation villa. Accommodations are strung along the beach and include standard and unexciting guest rooms and villas. Watersports cost extra, and there's a great dive shop on-site. Lots of cruise passengers converge here when their ship is in port, so don't expect tranquility.

Clarion Grand Pavilion   **$155–$455**   ★ ★ ★ ★ ★

West Bay Road, West Bay, ☎ *(809) 947-5656.*

Single: $155–$455. Double: $155–$455.

This spot was reopened in February 1994 by new Cayman owners after extensive refurbishing. Accommodations are tasteful and well appointed, and all have central air and such extras as coffeemakers, minibars, a trouser press (do you really need creases in the Caribbean?) and hair dryers. The pool is found in a lovely garden courtyard complete with lush foliage and a cascading waterfall. Other facilities include a fitness center, tennis courts, a 24-hour business center and nearby watersports. Parents can stash the kids in supervised programs all year round.

Holiday Inn Grand Cayman $238–$832   ★★★

Seven Mile Beach, West Bay, ☎ *(800) 465-4329, (809) 947-4444, FAX (809) 947-4213.*

Single: $238–$298. Double: $238–$832.

Lots of action at this busy and pleasant hotel. Guest rooms are air-conditioned and nicely done, though only some boast views. There's a full dive shop, twice-weekly barbecues by the great pool and all sorts of watersports for rent (though prices are a tad high). One of the hotel's best assets is its picturesque location on Seven Mile Beach. It's not too close to the cruise ship port, so guests are not overrun with day-trippers. Not a lot of island flavor—-this is, after all, a Holiday Inn—-but the lodgings are dependable and the two restaurants, two bars and a comedy club keep the doldrums away. Current renovations are spiffing up all guest rooms and adding an exercise room and Jacuzzi.

Hyatt Regency Grand Cayman $180–$500   ★★★★

Seven Mile Beach, West Bay, ☎ *(800) 233-1234, (809) 949-1234, FAX (809) 949-1234.*

Single: $180–$400. Double: $225–$500.

This is a world-class resort all the way, and definitely Grand Cayman's finest resort. Accommodations are in British Colonial-style buildings surrounding a central courtyard, and are simply fabulous, with expensive furnishings, original art, air conditioning (of course) and Italian marble baths. Landscaping is lush, and guests can choose from four pools, four tennis courts, a dive shop, all watersports and 18 holes of golf designed by Jack Nicklaus. Lots of bars and lounges, including one seen in The Firm. Elegant!

Radisson Resort $165–$390   ★★★★

Seven Mile Beach, West Bay, ☎ *(800) 333-3333, (809) 949-0088, FAX (809) 949-0288.*

Single: $165–$240. Double: $165–$390.

Set on a scenic spread of beach, the Radisson is a five-story hotel with comfortable and contemporary guest rooms. A very nice deck houses a pool, bar and Jacuzzi set among potted plants. All the usual watersports, plus a dive shop and health club, keep guests busy, and the disco hops once the sun goes down. A truly pleasant spot, with lots of elegant touches.

Sleep Inn $90–$197   ★★

Seven Mile Beach, West Bay, ☎ *(800) 627-5337, (809) 949-9111, FAX (809) 949-6699.*

Single: $90–$185. Double: $197.

This modern hotel, set right on the beach, has air-conditioned guest rooms with all the typical amenities. Eight suites have kitchenettes. The grounds are basic, with just a pool and Jacuzzi for recreation, but watersports can be found nearby.

Spanish Bay Reef North Wall $160–$218

West Bay Road, West Bay, ☎ *(800) 223-6510, (809) 949-3765, FAX (809) 949-1842.*
Single: $160–$218. Double: $160–$218.
Situated on a private coral reef on the island's isolated northwest tip, this all-inclusive resort houses guests in air-conditioned rooms with Caribbean decor. Popular with divers, it offers good facilities for scuba, as well as other watersports and the typical resort pool. The rates include all meals and activities. The atmosphere is nicely casual, but service is not always up to par.

Sunset House $90–$190   ★★

South of GeorgeTown, ☎ *(800) 854-4767, (809) 949-7111, FAX (809) 949-7101.*
Single: $90–$185. Double: $95–$190.
Great diving and snorkeling right offshore, but there's no beach to speak of at this casual hotel that dates back to the late 1950s. Accommodations are in standard guest rooms and two efficiencies; all are nicely done and air-cooled. Two pools help make up for the lack of beach, and there's a full-service dive shop, with a fleet of six boats, on-site. A really nice spot.

Treasure Island Resort $160–$275   ★★★★

Seven Mile Beach, West Bay, ☎ *(800) 327-8777, (809) 949-7777, FAX (809) 949-8489.*
Single: $160–$195. Double: $160–$275.
One of the island's largest resorts, this former Ramada fronts the beach and situates its guest rooms around a courtyard with two pools, a Jacuzzi and a gurgling waterfall. Accommodations are larger than usual and nicely done with minibars and sitting areas. There's live music in the nightclub six nights a week, and by day lots to keep busy with, including two tennis courts, a dive shop and all watersports. A good choice for those who like a lot of action.

Westin Casuarina Resort $180–$385

Seven Mile Beach, ☎ *(800) 228-3000.*
Single: $180–$385. Double: $180–$385.
Just opened in September 1995, the new $50-million Westin is the largest resort in the Cayman Islands. The eight-acre beachfront property was originally conceived as a Marriott. Facilities include a dive shop, tennis courts, two freshwater pools, two whirlpools, a swim-up bar and fitness center. The spacious guest rooms are done up in Caribbean style and feature oversized bathrooms with hair dryers and French doors opening onto balconies. Should prove to be a winner.

Little Cayman

Little Cayman Beach $118–$137

Blossom Village, ☎ *(809) 948-1033, FAX (809) 948-1040.*
Single: $118. Double: $128–$137.
This newer resort, opened in 1993, has a nice sandy beach off a reef-protected bay. Air-conditioned guest rooms are a cut above the competition on the island and

attractively furnished. Guests keep busy diving (they have an excellent shop), hanging out by the pool, riding bikes, or playing pickup volleyball games. The bar and restaurant are good and popular with locals.

Southern Cross Club $125–$285   ★★

Crawl Bay, ☎ *(800) 899-2582, (809) 948-3255.*
Single: $125–$185. Double: $215–$285.

This 1950s cottage resort sits on a pretty beach. Rooms are basic and rely on ceiling fans to keep things cool. The rates include three family-style meals a day and watersports. Most who come are into deep-sea fishing, with the hotel arranging excursions. The bar attracts lots of tale-swapping fishermen and women.

Apartments and Condominiums

Lots of visitors who come to the Caymans come for rough and rugged adventure underwater, so they're used to taking care of themselves. More and more self-catering accommodations are appearing every year. The downside is that if you plan to cook for yourself, food costs are extremely high; this year at least the markets seemed to be getting better stocked. Amid the action on Seven Mile Beach, a short walk from restaurants and a supermarket, are **Pan Cayman** in the Caribbean Club; here you'll find a better beach and a lot more peace and quiet. Golfers congregate in the **Britannia Villas**, which is part of the Hyatt complex, at the golf course. The **Indies Suites** are a good bargain for travelers who spend most of their time underwater and shut their eyes the minute their head hits the pillow (one plus is the free breakfast).

Grand Cayman

Beachcomber Condos $190–$395   ★

Seven Mile Beach, West Bay, ☎ *(800) 327-8777, (809) 947-4470, FAX (809) 947-5019.*
Single: $190–$395. Double: $190–$395.

This condo complex has two-bedroom, two-bath units with air conditioning, fully equipped kitchens and a balcony or patio with ocean views. Several units have dens that can convert into a third bedroom if needed. There's a pool on-site, and maid service is available, but you'll have to dine elsewhere.

Caribbean Club $160–$425   ★★★

Seven Mile Beach, P.O. Box 30499, West Bay, ☎ *(800) 327-8777, (809) 947-4099, FAX (809) 947-4443.*
Single: $160–$280. Double: $160–$425.

This colony of villas includes one- and two-bedroom units (only six are actually on the beach) in a secluded atmosphere. The pink cottages are air-conditioned and include large living/dining areas, full kitchens and attractive, comfortable decor. The restaurant is popular with visitors as well as locals. There's a tennis court, but no pool. No kids under 11 during the winter season.

Cayman Kai Resort $140–$220   ★★

North Side, East of Rum Plantation, West Bay, ☎ *(800) 223-5427, (809) 947-9055, FAX (809) 947-9102.*
Single: $140–$215. Double: $150–$220.

Situated in a 20-acre grove along the secluded north shore beach, this secluded resort houses guests in one- and two-bedroom lodges and villas, all with kitchens but only some with air conditioning. The beach is not great for swimming, but the snorkeling is great. The property caters primarily to divers, but is a bit more formal than the island's other dive resorts. A restaurant, bar and three tennis courts keep nondivers occupied.

Christopher Columbus Apts $190–$390   ★★

Seven Mile Beach, West Bay, ☎ *(809) 947-4354, FAX (809) 947-5062.*
Single: $190–$390. Double: $190–$390.
Popular with families, this condominium resort offers individually decorated two-bedroom, two-bath units with air conditioning, small but complete kitchens and light, tropical furnishings. As expected, the penthouse units are by far the nicest (and most expensive). No restaurant or bar, so guests congregate at the pool, tennis courts and sandy beach.

Colonial Club $230–$500   ★

West Bay Road, West Side, ☎ *(809) 947-4660, FAX (809) 947-4839.*
Single: $230–$455. Double: $255–$500.
Built in the Bermudian style with a pink and white exterior, this condo complex has comfortable two- and three-bedroom units with central air, complete kitchens and maid service. Located on an especially nice stretch of beach, extras include a pool and lighted tennis court. No restaurant on-site, so you'll have to cook in or venture out.

Discovery Point Club $145–$315   ★★

Seven Mile Road, West Bay, ☎ *(809) 947-4724, FAX (809) 947-5051.*
Single: $145–$285. Double: $145–$315.
Located on Seven Mile Beach, this well-appointed resort offers one- and two-bedroom condos with all the modern conveniences, including air and full kitchens. There are also studios sans cooking facilities. A pretty pool and two tennis courts are on-site, but no restaurant or bar.

George Town Villas $165–$420   ★

Seven Mile Beach, West Bay, ☎ *(809) 949-5172, FAX (809) 947-0256.*
Single: $165–$405. Double: $165–$420.
A condominium community with two-bedroom units that come equipped with two baths, full kitchens, air conditioning, living and dining areas and washer/dryers. There's a pool and tennis court, and shopping and restaurants are nearby.

Grand Bay Club $120–$310   ★★★

Seven Mile Beach, West Bay, ☎ *(809) 947-4728, FAX (809) 947-5681.*
Single: $120–$195. Double: $120–$310.
All units at this modern complex are suites, ranging from studios that lack kitchens to one- and two-bedroom units with cooking facilities. Maids keep things tidy. The site includes a large pool, Jacuzzi and tennis. No restaurant, but there are many within a walk.

Grapetree/Cocoplum Condos $135–$280   ★★

Georgetown, ☎ *(800) 635-4824, (809) 949-5640.*

Single: $135–$280. Double: $135–$280.

Situated in a secluded area of Seven Mile Beach—-though the beach here is not the greatest—-this condo complex includes one- to three-bedroom units with all the usual amenities, as well as daily maid service. Watersports are available nearby, and the grounds include a tennis court and two pools. No restaurant, though.

Harbour Heights　　　　　　　$190–$295　　　　　★ ★ ★

Seven Mile Beach, West Bay, ☎ *(800) 327-8777, (809) 947-4295, FAX (809) 947-4522.*

Single: $190–$280. Double: $190–$295.

This three-story condominium overlooks the pool and seafront along Seven Mile Beach. Two-bedroom suites are attractive, with living/dining areas, complete kitchens, air conditioning and balconies. The grounds are nicely landscaped, and the beach is good for swimmers. Restaurants are nearby.

Indies Suites　　　　　　　　$160–$290　　　　　★ ★ ★

West Bay Road, West Bay, ☎ *(800) 654-3130, (809) 947-5025, FAX (809) 947-5024.*
Single: $160–$290. Double: $160–$290.

This very comfortable and attractive hotel houses guests in nicely furnished suites with full-size kitchens. The complimentary Continental breakfast is a nice touch. There's no restaurant, but guests can grab snacks at the pool bar. The beach is across the street, a liability when so many similar properties lie directly on the sand. Nevertheless, this is a good choice.

Island Pine Villas　　　　　　$110–$225　　　　　★

Seven Mile Beach, West Bay, ☎ *(800) 223-9815, (809) 949-6586, FAX (809) 949-0428.*
Single: $110–$220. Double: $110–$225.

This two-story condo complex is within walking distance of shops and restaurants. Units are quite comfortable, with one or two bedrooms, air conditioning, kitchenettes and patios or balconies. No pool or restaurant, but a good value nonetheless.

Lacovia Condominiums　　　　$200–$285　　　　　★ ★ ★

Seven Mile Beach, West Bay, ☎ *(800) 223-9815, (809) 949-7599, FAX (809) 949-0172.*
Single: $200–$285. Double: $200–$285.

Stylish and tasteful, this condo complex surrounds a free-form pool and clubhouse with sauna and games. Units have one to three bedrooms with separate living/dining areas, full kitchens and Spanish-style balconies; most also boast oversized tubs. Maids tidy up daily. The grounds include nice landscaping, and there's a tennis court for working up a sweat.

London House　　　　　　　$235–$750　　　　　★ ★ ★

West Bay Beach, West Bay, ☎ *(800) 423-4095, (809) 947-4060, FAX (809) 947-4087.*
Single: $235–$290. Double: $235–$750.

This mission-style complex has well-maintained accommodations and a pool, watersports and maid service to round out the picture. Units have one or two bedrooms and kitchenettes. Ceiling fans supplement the air conditioning. The beach is nice and quiet, happily not frequented by cruise ship passengers.

Morrit's Tortuga Club $145–$440 ★★★

East End, ☎ (800) 447-0309, (809) 947-7449, FAX (809) 947-7669.
Single: $145–$380. Double: $130–$440.

This plantation-style condo complex is situated on eight beachfront acres near some of Grand Cayman's best diving sites. Three-story buildings house comfortable one- and two-bedroom units with full kitchens. Built on the site of the former Tortuga Club, today's resort is a far cry from that hideaway spot, but it remains popular with divers. In addition to a pool, there's a decent restaurant and both windsurfing and 'diving schools.

Pan-Cayman House $150–$370 ★★★

Seven Mile Beach, West Bay, ☎ (800) 248-5115, (809) 947-4002, FAX (809) 947-4002.
Single: $150–$370. Double: $150–$370.

A popular apartment complex with 10 units ranging from two to three bedrooms, all with two baths, air conditioning, full kitchens and maid service. Great views from the private balconies or patios.

Plantana $180–$425 ★★

Seven Mile Beach, West Bay, ☎ (809) 947-4430, FAX (809) 947-5076.
Single: $180–$425. Double: $180–$425.

One- and two-bedroom condominiums are arranged on three floors, with the ones higher up offering the best views. All are individually decorated and have full kitchens and screened balconies or patios; most also have washer/dryers. A pool supplements the sea for splashing about. One of the nicer condo complexes on the island.

Plantation Village Resort $145–$405 ★

Seven Mile Beach, West Bay, ☎ (800) 822-8903, (809) 949-4199, FAX (809) 949-0646.
Single: $145–$405. Double: $145–$405.

Set on four acres of Seven Mile Beach, this condo complex has individually deco- rated two- and three-bedroom units with two baths, complete kitchens, central air and screened lanais. Maids pick up daily. There are two pools, a Jacuzzi, a tennis court and a playground for the kids. Lots of families here.

Silver Sands $200–$235 ★★

West Bay Road, Seven Mile Beach, West Bay, ☎ (800) 327-8777, (809) 949-3343, FAX (809) 949-1223.
Single: $200–$235. Double: $200–$235.

Set amid tropical gardens, this casual complex has air-conditioned two-bedroom units with all the modern amenities. There's a nice resort feel to this place with its extra-large pool, gazebo, two tennis courts and nearby watersports.

Tarquynn Manor $143–$395 ★★

Seven Mile Beach, West Bay, ☎ (800) 223-9815, (809) 947-5060, FAX (809) 947-5060.
Single: $143–$395. Double: $230–$395.

At least one bedroom in these two- or three-bedroom units fronts the beach. The modern units have air conditioning, kitchens and patios or balconies. A concierge handles special requests. There's an outdoor pool and games room to keep kids occupied.

Victoria House $165–$395   ★★

Seven Mile Beach, West Bay, ☎ *(800) 327-8777, (809) 947-4233, FAX (809) 947-5320.*

Single: $165–$380. Double: $175–$395.

These Caribbean-style apartments front the ocean and are far from the madding tourist crowds. Units are air-conditioned and come in a variety of configurations, from studios to penthouses. All are comfortable with tropical styling and have full kitchens. There's no pool on-site, but watersports are available nearby, and there is one tennis court. Sea turtles frequent the quiet beach in the mornings.

Villas Pappagallo $160–$284   ★★

Seven Mile Beach, West Bay, ☎ *(800) 232-1034, (809) 949-8098, FAX (809) 947-7054.*

Single: $160–$284. Double: $180–$284.

Located on a private, secluded beach on the northwest shore, this complex consists of Mediterranean-style villas, all with air conditioning, kitchenettes and balconies. Lots to do here, including two tennis courts, a pool and noshing at the Italian restaurant. You'll have to travel a half-mile for watersports.

Villas of the Galleon $200–$430   ★★

West Bay Beach, West Bay, ☎ *(809) 947-4433.*

Single: $200–$430. Double: $200–$430.

Facing a private beach, this condo complex offers units with one or two bedrooms, all with air conditioning, modern kitchen, small baths and balconies; maids tidy up daily but take Sundays off. Most folks here are staying for a long time. Request an upper floor unit for the best sea views.

West Indian Club $130–$365   ★★★★★

West Bay Beach, West Bay, ☎ *(809) 947-5255.*

Single: $130–$365. Double: $130–$365.

These two-story beachfront apartments are situated near the center of famed Seven Mile Beach. The well-appointed one- and two-bedroom units have full kitchens, terraces and air conditioning only in the bedrooms. A maid keeps things looking fresh, and you can hire a cook for a custom-made meal.

Inns

These are basically scuba-devoted inns, low on luxury, but high on congeniality. Seaview hotels attracts a very young crowd.

Grand Cayman

Island Hill Resort $60–$80   ★★★

Church Street, West Bay, ☎ *(809) 949-4242, FAX (809) 949-3347.*

Single: $60–$80. Double: $60–$80.

Discover the real Caymans at this friendly, intimate inn near Seven Mile Beach. The large guest rooms are air conditioned and come with welcome extras like hammocks and portable ice chests to take to the beach. Locals hang at the open-air bar, and there's live reggae music each Wednesday, Friday and Saturday night. The food's good, too.

Seaview Hotel $65–$105 ★★

Near GeorgeTown, ☎ *(809) 949-8804, FAX (809) 949-8507.*
Single: $65–$105. Double: $65–$105.

Opened in 1952, this is the oldest operating hotel on the island. Rooms are air-conditioned and have private baths. Guests can splash in the outdoor pool or head for the beach, where a dive center and watersports are offered. The piano lounge is a pleasant spot by night.

Little Cayman

Pirates Point Resort $140–$405 ★

Pirates Point, ☎ *(809) 948-1010, FAX (809) 948-1011.*
Single: $140–$200. Double: $255–$405.

Most accommodations at this pleasant inn are in air-conditioned rooms with private baths; there are also four cottages overlooking the sea. The best reason to come, however, is mealtime: owner Gladys Howard is a graduate of Paris' Cordon Bleu, and judging from the food, she passed with flying colors. A friendly, peaceful spot.

Sam McCoy's Lodge $105–$185 ★★

Crawl Bay, ☎ *(800) 626-0496, (809) 948-4526.*
Single: $105–$185. Double: $105–$185.

Only some rooms at this very informal spot have their own bath. The food's great though, with casual meals taken with Sam, his family and fellow guests. The rates include three squares a day and transportation to and from the airport.

Low Cost Lodging

One way to save money in the Caymans is to cram a lot of people into a multi-bedroom apartment. But individuals can find single rooms for rent in guest houses (don't hesitate to ask the tourist board). The nightclub keeps things hopping at **Windjammer Hotel**, where rooms are also air-conditioned and come with kitchenettes. Diving is the main topic of conversation at these lodgings, especially at the **Ambassadors Inn**, which attracts the diehards.

Grand Cayman

Ambassadors Inn $60–$80 ★★★

South Church Street, ☎ *(800) 648-7748, (809) 949-7577, FAX (809) 949-7050.*
Single: $60–$70. Double: $70–$80.

Located a mile from George Town and some 200 yards and across the street from the beach, this casual spot appeals to divers on a budget. Rooms are basic but do offer air conditioning and private baths. There's a pool on site.

Windjammer Hotel $100–$155 ★

West Bay Road, West Bay, ☎ *(809) 947-4608, FAX (809) 947-4391.*
Single: $100–$155. Double: $100–$155.

Located at the Cayman Falls Shopping Plaza, across from Seven Mile Beach, this small hotel offers air-conditioned rooms with kitchenettes. There are two restaurants, a bar and a nightclub, and this place does do a good after-dark trade.

Where to Eat

Fielding's Highest Rated Restaurants in Cayman Islands

★★★★★	Hemingway's	$17–$23
★★★★★	Lantana's	$20–$34
★★★★★	Ottmar's Restaurant	$12–$25
★★★	Crow's Nest	$5–$19

Fielding's Special Restaurants in Cayman Islands

★★★★★	Lantana's	$20–$34
★★★	Crow's Nest	$5–$19
★★	Grand Old House	$13–$34
★★	Ristorante Pappagallo	$14–$25

Fielding's Budget Restaurants in Cayman Islands

★★★	Crow's Nest	$5–$19
★★	Hog Sty Bay Cafe	$5–$19
★★	Corita's Copper Kettle II	$10–$15
★★	Cracked Conch	$6–$25
★★	Edd's Place	$6–$25

Although most of the food is imported on this dry, scrubby island, the Caymans took top honors in the first annual Caribbean Culinary Competition in 1993. However, prices, in general, tend to be highly inflated in regards to quality (one plus is that portions tend to be enormous). Of course, fresh fish is the basis of most menus; the biggest Caymanian specialty is turtle in all its varied forms (turtles on the Cayman Islands are specifically bred for food). The best time to eat lobster is from August through January. Chef Tell, the TV cooking celeb, has his own restaurant on Church Street called **Chef Tell's Grand House**, which specializes in both German delicacies as well as

tropical delights such as spicy fried coconut shrimp and deep-fried grouper
in a minted yogurt-and-curry sauce. (Reservations are required and be prepared to spend between $15–$31 for a main course). **Hemingway's** in the
Hyatt Regency on West Bay Road is considered to serve the best seafood
around. For ambiance, try the **Ristorante Pappagallo**, set on a 14-acre bird
sanctuary and housed in an elegant thatch and reed Polynesian tribal lodge—
the Italian chefs work wonder with tropical products. Risk-takers should try
the blackened alligator tail at **Benjamin's Roof** at Coconut Place, off West Bay
Road. The best bargain bet is to splurge at lunch at the better restaurants
and save almost 50 percent off dinner prices. Reservations are usually necessary. Supermarkets are more expensive than in the U.S. but now feature salad
bars and prepared salads for about $4 per pound—perfect for picnics or eat-
ing in. Try **Kirks**, **Foster's Food Fair** and **Hurley's**, all located along Seven Mile
Beach. Or make breakfast your main meal at the enormous all-you-can-eat
buffet at the Holiday Inn for under $10. Also, don't miss the all-you-can-eat
buffets of fajitas and seafood as listed in the Friday *Cayman Compass* publications, available everywhere.

Cayman Brac

Edd's Place $$$ ★★
West End, ☎ *(809) 948-1208.*
Asian cuisine.
Lunch: 7 a.m.–4 p.m., entrees $6–$15.
Dinner: 4-11 p.m., entrees $10–$25.
A nice change from resort cookery on Cayman Brac is this restaurant and bar that's
open early for breakfast and later on serves Chinese food and local favorites. If you
phone the management, they'll arrange to pick you up, as there is no bus service,
and taxis are expensive.

Little Cayman

Pirate's Point Resort $$$ ★★★
☎ *(809) 948-4210.*
International cuisine.
Lunch: entrees $25–$35.
Dinner: entrees $25–$35.
Owner Gladys Howard, trained at Paris' Cordon Bleu, whips up wonderful seafood
dishes supplemented by lots of local fruits and vegetables. You can try to recreate
some of her dishes back home by buying one of her cookbooks.

Grand Cayman

Almond Tree, The $$$ ★★★
North Church Street, ☎ *(809) 949-2893.*
Seafood cuisine. Specialties: Callaloo, conch, turtle steak.
Dinner: 5:30-10 p.m., entrees $14–$22.
An informal and reliable restaurant located just north of George Town, the Almond
Tree is a good place to try turtle steak, which is unavailable stateside. More sensitive
diners will find all types of seafood, including conch, lobster, filets and a popular all-

you-can-eat main course extravaganza for under $15 on Wednesdays and Fridays. It's lit up dramatically at night with tiki torches.

Benjamin's Roof $$$ ★★

Coconut Place, ☎ *(809) 947-4080.*
International cuisine. Specialties: Lobster bisque, cajun shrimp.
Dinner: 3-10 p.m., entrees $12–$30.

Greenery abounds in this cool spot in the Coconut Place retail center with a bar dispensing strong libations, a pianist in the corner and spicy blackened-cajun style fish and seafood, with barbecued ribs, lamb and pastas to round out the menu. Desserts are also notable for their richness.

Corita's Copper Kettle II $$ ★★

Eastern Avenue, ☎ *(809) 949-5475.*
Latin American cuisine. Specialties: Conch, callaloo.
Lunch: entrees $10–$15.

Busy office workers grab a Jamaican-style breakfast and come back for lunch at this spic-and-span diner located in George Town. Simple, island-style fare includes conch and lobster burgers and local spinach soup. Hot peppers are sprinkled liberally here and there, so beware.

Cracked Conch $$$ ★★★

Selkirk's Street Plaza, ☎ *(809) 947-5217.*
Seafood cuisine. Specialties: Cracked conch, conch fritters, key lime pie.
Lunch: 11:30 a.m.–3 p.m., entrees $6–$15.
Dinner: 6-10 p.m., entrees $10–$25.

Not a place for intimate conversation, the noisy Cracked Conch serves lots of seafood in dim, rather stark surroundings. But the food, especially conch, served lightly fried, is smashing. Burgers, soups and other fast meals are also available, and all meals are prepared for takeout.

Crow's Nest $$$ ★★★

South Sound, ☎ *(809) 949-9366.*
Latin American cuisine. Specialties: Lobster, conch.
Lunch: 11:30 a.m.–2 p.m., entrees $5–$8.
Dinner: 5:30-10 p.m., entrees $12–$19.

Romance is in the air at this exquisite little eatery on the south point of the island, where diners eat with the ocean waves lapping behind them. Wonderful for a star-filled evening meal or view lunch, the Crow's Nest offers tasty, usually spicy dishes like chicken with hot pepper sauce, coconut fried shrimp and key lime pie. It's hard to believe that George Town is only four miles away.

Garden Loggia Cafe $$$ ★★

West Bay Road, ☎ *(809) 949-1234.*
International cuisine. Specialties: Roast suckling pig, lobster.
Lunch: entrees $9–$16.
Dinner: entrees $16–$34.

This top-rated indoor-outdoor cafe facing an elegant expanse of greenery is noted for Sunday buffets replete with champagne and roast suckling pig, and a Friday night all-you-can-eat seafood spread. Otherwise, the bill of fare usually includes jerk chicken and seafood.

Grand Old House $$$

Petra Plantation, ☎ *(809) 949-9333.*
International cuisine. Specialties: Grouper.
Lunch: 11:45 a.m.–2:30 p.m., entrees $13–$32.
Dinner: 6-10:30 p.m., entrees $20–$34.
This lovely gingerbread house in George Town is owned by jolly, red-cheeked TV celebrity Chef Tell Erhardt, who also labors in the kitchen. Cuisine is savory and often deep-fried, but good for a splurge. Erhardt uses herbs, curries and sauces liberally, but with a sure hand, as befits the island's No. 1 caterer. German specialties are also offered from time to time, reflecting the chef's heritage. Expect spaetzle and sauerkraut interspersed with local delicacies. Closed May through October.

Hemingway's $$$ ★★★★★

West Bay Road, ☎ *(809) 949-1234.*
International cuisine. Specialties: Jerk chicken, lobster.
Lunch: 11:30 a.m.–2:30 p.m., entrees $17–$23.
Dinner: 6-10 p.m., entrees $17–$23.
Spectacular Seven Mile Beach looms blue in front of diners supping at this, the Hyatt Regency Grand Cayman's luxury dining room. The chefs here create nouvelle Caribbean dishes utilizing local fish, turtle steak and chicken, accompanied by lightly zingy herb and citrus sauces. Cocktails are creative and service is attentive.

Hog Sty Bay Cafe $$$

North Church Street, ☎ *(809) 949-6163.*
English cuisine.
Lunch: 11:30 a.m.–5:30 p.m., entrees $5–$12.
Dinner: 6-10 p.m., entrees $12–$19.
A good, casual American-English style pub, the Hog Sty Bay Cafe in George Town Harbor is a relaxing perch for burgers and sandwiches or fish and chips. It's hard to miss the brightly painted bungalow that hums inside with a crowd of regulars who also like to come for the romantic sunset views and happy hour drinks. Breakfast is also served, with all the usual offerings plus Mexican-style eggs for added zing.

Lantana's $$$ ★★★★★

West Bay Road, ☎ *(809) 947-5595.*
Mexican cuisine. Specialties: Conch fritters with ancho chile mayonnaise.
Dinner: 5:30-10 p.m., entrees $20–$34.
Lantana's is one of the island's most prestigious dining establishments due to its creative New Mexican-style food. Most dishes are prepared with flair by an Austrian chef, Alfred Schrock, who understands how well West Indian culinary treats blend with dessert hot sauces and condiments. Witness his lightly fried conch fritters with ancho chile mayonnaise and Santa Fe cilantro pesto pasta with seafood. A Viennese tarte tatin is scrumptious. Surroundings recall Santa Fe's Coyote Cafe.

Lobster Pot $$$ ★★

North Church Street, ☎ *(809) 949-2736.*
Seafood cuisine. Specialties: Lobster, turtle soup.

Lunch: 11:30 a.m.–2:30 p.m., entrees $10–$25.
Dinner: 5-10 p.m., entrees $15–$28.

When the Hog Sty Bay Cafe is busy, this upper-level pub facing West Bay fits the bill. The Lobster Pot manages an intimate atmosphere despite its popularity and the tendency of servers to rush diners through their meals. Nevertheless, the food is good, encompassing lobster, salads and frozen tropical drinks. There's a dart board, natch, for diversion.

Ottmar's Restaurant $$$ ★★★★★

West Bay Road,
International cuisine. Specialties: Fresh fish, rijstaffel.
Dinner: 6-10 p.m., entrees $12–$25.

Another excellent dining room run by an Austrian expatriate, Ottmar's in the Clarion Grand Hotel proffers classical-French cuisine like bouillabaisse and then turns around and offers a Dutch-Javanese rijstaffel (a spicy feast of 16 courses surrounded by steamed rice). The room is elegant and spacious, and conversations are carried on unheard by diners at neighboring tables.

Ristorante Pappagallo $$$ ★★

Palmetto Drive, ☎ (809) 949-1119.
Italian cuisine.
Dinner: 6-10:30 p.m., entrees $14–$25.

Northern Italian cuisine is served in a series of thatched-roof huts facing a lagoon, surrounded by palm trees and wooden bridges. Despite the overwhelming atmosphere and chattering macaws in cages for background music, the food is reasonably good, with veal and seafood predominating. Even if you don't come to eat, it's a good spot for a cocktail.

The Wharf $$$ ★★

West Bay Road, ☎ (809) 949-2231.
Latin American cuisine. Specialties: Seafood.
Lunch: Noon-2:30 p.m., entrees $21–$30.
Dinner: 6-10 p.m., entrees $21–$30.

The ultimate West Indian dining experience is a seafood supper on a huge deck overlooking the waterfront at the Wharf, which is justly famous for its sublime conch chowder and great service. Chef Tony Egger likes to pair fresh local seafare with Caribbean touches, including a seafood medley baked with a papaya sauce. Harp players rove from table to table, taking requests, and calypso bands play in the attached popular bar. Come at 9 p.m. to see them feed giant tarpon off the rear dock.

Verandah Restaurant, The $$$ ★

West Bay Road, ☎ (809) 947-4444.
American cuisine. Specialties: Breakfast buffet.
Lunch: 6 a.m.–4 p.m., entrees $6–$15.
Dinner: 6-9 p.m., entrees $18–$32.

The only reason this restaurant in the Holiday Inn is mentioned is because it serves up a bountiful all-you-can-eat breakfast for $10, a great buy in bargain-starved Grand Cayman. This morning feast could easily get you through the rest of the day.

Where to Shop

You wouldn't go to Grand Cayman just to shop, but George Town does boast charming shops that offer the high-end designer luxury items; the bait is the duty-free status that makes imported crystal, china, French perfumes and British woolen goods seem a sometime-bargain. Casual resort wear in stylish designs can be found at **Mango Mames**, in Coconut Place on West Bay Road. For an unusual buy, take home some genuine gold pieces-of-eight and other ancient coins and artifacts recovered from pirate ships and turned into jewelry. The **Jewelry Centre** on Fort Street stocks the most complete collection of loose and set diamonds, as well as black coral (imported) and caymanite.

Cayman Islands Directory

ARRIVAL AND DEPARTURE

Grand Cayman is serviced by **Cayman Airways** ☎ *(800) 422-9626)* from Miami, Tampa, Atlanta and Houston; by **American Airlines** ☎ *(800) 433-7300* from Miami and Raleigh-Durham, by **USAir** ☎ *(800) 428-4322* from Baltimore-Washington, and by **Northwest Airlines** ☎ *(800) 447-4747* from Detroit, Minneapolis and Memphis via Miami. Cayman Airways is also the only airline that services Little Cayman and Cayman Brac.

A taxi from the airport to central Seven Mile Beach is $8–$12, Seven Mile Beach to George Town is about $8, taxi rates are set by law.

BUSINESS HOURS

Shops open Monday–Saturday 9 a.m.–5 p.m. Banks open Monday–Thursday 9 a.m.–2:30 p.m. and on Friday 9 a.m.–1 p.m. and 2:30–4:30 p.m.

CLIMATE

With an average temperature of 79 degrees, the Caymans are pleasant year-round. High season runs from mid-December to mid-April, but July and August, when waters are clearest, are the prime times for diving.

DOCUMENTS

U.S. and Canadian citizens may show either a valid passport or proof of citizenship (voter registration or birth certificate with photo ID) and an ongoing or return ticket.

ELECTRICITY

The current runs 110 volt, 60-cycles, as in the United States.

GETTING AROUND

Taxis are omnipresent whenever a plane arrives, and rates are officially fixed. Since the islands are small and flat, bicycling and walking are pleasant alternatives to walking. Autos, are nevertheless, easy to rent. Major U.S. firms are here as well as local ones, such as **Just Jeeps** ☎ *(809) 949-7263*. Motorcycles and motorscooters are for hire at **Soto's** ☎ *(809) 947-4652*.

Driving is on the left side of the street.

LANGUAGE

English is the main tongue, though the accent is a highly musical melange of Irish, Welsh, Scottish and West Indian lilts.

MEDICAL EMERGENCIES

George Town Hospital ☎ *949-8600* is the only facility on Grand Cayman, located on Hospital Road. Cayman Brac has an 18-bed facility called **Faith Hospital** ☎ *948-2243*.

MONEY

The official currency is the Cayman Islands dollar, unique to the islands. Most tourist establishments accept U.S. dollars and credit cards. Local banks will cash traveler's checks. Keep track which dollars (American or Cayman) are being quoted on menus, etc. If quoted in Cayman dollars, the price will look a lot cheaper than it actually is.

TELEPHONE

Area code is 809. International calls can be made 24 hours a day. Local calls now use 7 digits (as opposed to 5 digits in the past).

TIME

Eastern Standard Time all year long, with no change during the northern shift to Daylight Savings.

TIPPING AND TAXES

Service charges are not standardized among hotel establishments and can range from 5 percent at condos to 15 percent at top hotels. Always check your bill before adding your own tips. Taxi drivers generally don't expect tips unless you've exhausted them with huge trunks. Bellboys expect 50 cents per bag.

TOURIST INFORMATION

The **Cayman Islands Department of Tourism** is located in the Harbour Centre in George Town ☎ *(809) 49-0623*. Tourist information booths can also be found at the pier and at the airport. In the U.S. call ☎ *(213) 738-1968* or *(212) 682-5582*.

TOURS

Half-day guided sightseeing tours (Turtle Farm, Hell, Governor's Residence, George Town) average $30 per person a half-day; a tour to the caves and blowhole sites on the eastern end is $45 per person; full-day tours including lunch and stops at all island sites average $65 per person. None include swimstops. An all-day snorkel trip with lunch averages $50 per person; a one-tank offshore dive is $30–$35, with all equipment, $35–40. **Evco Tours** ☎ *(809) 949-2118* offers six-hour tours around the island, as does **Greyline** ☎ *(809) 949-2791* and **Reids** ☎ *(809) 949-6311*.

WHEN TO GO

Pirates Week Festival in October is celebrated with parades, songs, contests and games; even businessmen arrive at the office dressed in costume. Million Dollar Month brings anglers from all over the world to compete in one of the world's biggest big-fish contests. Batabano, the weekend before Easter, is the island's cultural carnival weekend. Queen Elizabeth's birthday in mid-June is celebrated with a full-dress uniform parade, marching band and 21-gun salute.

CAYMAN ISLANDS HOTELS		RMS	RATES	PHONE	CR. CARDS
Cayman Brac					
West End Point					
★★	Divi Tiara Beach Resort	58	$95–$200	(800) 948-1553	A, D, MC, V
★	Brac Reef Beach Resort	40	$106–$147	(800) 327-3835	A, MC, V
Grand Cayman					
George Town					
★★★★★	Clarion Grand Pavilion	90	$155–$455	(809) 947-5656	A, D, DC, MC, V
★★★★★	West Indian Club	6	$130–$365	(809) 947-5255	A, MC, V
★★★★	Beach Club Hotel	41	$125–$265	(800) 223-6510	A, DC, MC, V
★★★★	Hyatt Regency Grand Cayman	236	$180–$500	(800) 233-1234	A, MC, V
★★★★	Radisson Resort	315	$165–$390	(800) 333-3333	A, DC, MC, V
★★★★	Spanish Bay Reef North Wall	50	$160–$218	(800) 223-6510	A, D, DC, MC, V
★★★★	Treasure Island Resort	280	$160–$275	(800) 327-8777	A, MC, V
★★★	Ambassadors Inn	18	$60–$80	(800) 648-7748	A, MC, V
★★★	Caribbean Club	18	$160–$425	(800) 327-8777	A, MC, V
★★★	Grand Bay Club	21	$120–$310	(809) 947-4728	A, MC, V
★★★	Harbour Heights	46	$190–$295	(800) 327-8777	A, MC, V
★★★	Holiday Inn Grand Cayman	212	$238–$832	(800) 465-4329	A, DC, MC, V

CAYMAN ISLANDS HOTELS		RMS	RATES	PHONE	CR. CARDS
★★★	Indies Suites	40	$160–$290	(800) 654-3130	A, MC, V
★★★	Island Hill Resort		$60–$80	(809) 949-4242	
★★★	Lacovia Condominiums	45	$200–$285	(800) 223-9815	A
★★★	London House	21	$235–$750	(800) 423-4095	A, MC, V
★★★	Morrit's Tortuga Club	85	$145–$440	(800) 447-0309	A, D, MC, V
★★★	Pan-Cayman House	10	$150–$370	(800) 248-5115	MC, V
★★	Cayman Kai Resort	20	$140–$220	(800) 223-5427	A, MC, V
★★	Christopher Columbus Apts	28	$190–$390	(809) 947-4354	A, MC, V
★★	Discovery Point Club	45	$145–$315	(809) 947-4724	A, MC, V
★★	Grapetree/Cocoplum Condos	50	$135–$280	(800) 635-4824	A, MC, V
★★	Plantana	49	$180–$425	(809) 947-4430	A, MC, V
★★	Seaview Hotel	15	$65–$105	(809) 949-8804	A, D, MC, V
★★	Silver Sands	42	$200–$235	(800) 327-8777	A, MC, V
★★	Sleep Inn	116	$90	(800) 627-5337	A, CB, D, DC, MC, V
★★	Sunset House	59	$90–$190	(800) 854-4767	A, D, MC, V
★★	Tarquynn Manor	20	$143–$395	(800) 223-9815	MC, V
★★	Victoria House	26	$165–$395	(800) 327-8777	A, MC, V
★★	Villas Pappagallo	40	$160–$284	(800) 232-1034	A, MC, V
★★	Villas of the Galleon	75	$200–$430	(809) 947-4433	A, MC, V
★★	Westin Casuarina Resort		$180–$385	(800) 228-3000	A, MC, V
★	Beachcomber Condos	19	$190–$395	(800) 327-8777	MC, V
★	Colonial Club	15	$230–$500	(809) 947-4660	A, MC, V
★	George Town Villas	54	$165–$420	(809) 949-5172	A, MC, V
★	Island Pine Villas	40	$110–$225	(800) 223-9815	A, D, DC, MC, V
★	Plantation Village Resort	70	$145–$405	(800) 822-8903	A, MC, V
★	Windjammer Hotel	12	$100–$155	(809) 947-4608	A, MC, V

Little Cayman

Crawl Bay

★★★★	Little Cayman Beach	32	$118–$137	(809) 948-1033	A, MC, V

CAYMAN ISLANDS HOTELS	RMS	RATES	PHONE	CR. CARDS
★★ Sam McCoy's Lodge	6	$105–$185	(800) 626-0496	None
★★ Southern Cross Club	10	$125–$285	(800) 899-2582	None
★ Pirates Point Resort	10	$140–$405	(809) 948-1010	MC, V

CAYMAN ISLANDS RESTAURANTS	PHONE	ENTREE	CR. CARDS

Cayman Brac

West End Point

Asian

★★ Edd's Place	(809) 948-1208	$6–$25	MC, V

Grand Cayman

George Town

American

★ Verandah Restaurant, The	(809) 947-4444	$6–$32	A, MC, V

English

★★ Hog Sty Bay Cafe	(809) 949-6163	$5–$19	A, MC, V

International

★★★★★ Hemingway's	(809) 949-1234	$17–$23	A, MC, V
★★★★★ Ottmar's Restaurant		$12–$25••	A, MC, V
★★ Garden Loggia Cafe	(809) 949-1234	$9–$34	A, MC, V
★★ Grand Old House	(809) 949-9333	$13–$34	A, MC, V
★ Benjamin's Roof	(809) 947-4080	$12–$30••	A, MC, V

Italian

★★ Ristorante Pappagallo	(809) 949-1119	$14–$25••	A, MC, V

Latin American

★★★ Crow's Nest	(809) 949-9366	$5–$19	A, MC, V
★★ Corita's Copper Kettle II	(809) 949-5475	$10–$15•	A, MC, V
★★ The Wharf	(809) 949-2231	$21–$30	D, MC, V

Mexican

★★★★★ Lantana's	(809) 947-5595	$20–$34••	A, D, MC, V

CAYMAN ISLANDS RESTAURANTS	PHONE	ENTREE	CR. CARDS
Seafood			
★★ **Almond Tree, The**	(809) 949-2893	$14–$22••	A, MC, V
★★ **Cracked Conch**	(809) 947-5217	$6–$25	A, MC, V
★★ **Lobster Pot**	(809) 949-2736	$10–$28	A, D, MC, V

Little Cayman

Crawl Bay

International			
★★ **Pirate's Point Resort**	(809) 948-4210	$25–$35	None

Note: • Lunch Only

•• Dinner Only

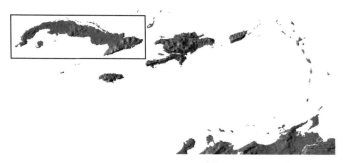

CUBA

Palm thatched huts are a common sight in Cuba's rural areas.

Pearl of the Caribbean, "Forbidden Paradise," Hemingway's hideaway, defiant David to Uncle Sam's Goliath...Cuba. The very name conjures up images of sensuality and beauty, and the traveler to Castro's island will find that the home of the world's best cigars and rum, strongest coffee and most passionate music is every bit as sensual and beautiful as he or she has imagined. Developing rapidly as a tourism destination, the largest island in the Caribbean is filled with natural splendors, bacchanalian pleasures, and warm, friendly people who have managed to come through centuries of often painful history with a smile.

Cuba's cities are old, in a number of senses. **La Habana**, the capital, and **Trinidad**, on the central south coast, are two of the finest examples of Spanish colonial cities to be found anywhere in the Caribbean. Walking through their narrow, winding streets past cavernous doorways leading mysteriously into big, square apartment buildings with peeling pastel paint jobs, from which the omnipresent strains of salsa music can be faintly heard, you lose all sense of time. Look around and you're unsure if you've been transported back to the days of Spanish rule, or are about to come face to face with a stumbling, daiquiri-charged Ernest Hemingway around the next corner. A moment later you're certain you're trapped in the '50s, as you find that the few cars on the road are pink and yellow Buick Roadmasters and Cadillac DeVilles, their bodywork rusty and their emission controls nonexistent. Indeed, Cuba is a country frozen in time, or rather several times. The colonial period is still going on, manifested in the unchanged architecture and the age-old trades plied on every corner (including the oldest of them all). The pre-Revolutionary period, when the U.S., at just 90 miles away, was far and away the island's foremost trading partner in both commerce and culture, lives on as if by cryogenics. And the bombastic, nationalistic period of the '70s, when Fidel's bushy mug was plastered on billboards everywhere and rah-rah slogans covered every available space, has never been displaced by the new pragmatism born out of the collapse of Cuba's more recent patron, the USSR. Urban Cuba is a feast for the senses—at every turn there's an outdoor cafe serving tiny shots of scalding, venomous coffee, the atmosphere rife with the pungent odor of puros, or a restaurant dishing up generous portions of simple but unbelievably tasty seafood, rice and fried plantains, or a museum or art gallery showcasing Cuba's rich heritage of poets, sculptors, painters and musicians.

Cuba's beauty is not wrought by artists' hands alone, however. Venture into the countryside and you will find one of the most unspoiled areas in the world. Cuba is home to more native species than any other island in the Caribbean, and a network of biospheres and nature preserves throughout the island allow the visitor to drink in the scent and color of a thousand tropical flowers, dive beneath the waves in warm, azure waters among technicolor displays of coral construction, or get up close and personal with 40,000 crocodiles at a breeding farm off Treasure Lake. Cuba's beaches are magnificent—from the legendary **Varadero**, once the playground of Yankee millionaires, then a workers' retreat, to any of the 300 beaches around the island's 3600-mile coastline, sun worshippers, watersports lovers and regular old lovers are sure to find a perfect slice of paradise.

Not to be outdone by its flora and fauna are Cuba's people; gracious and welcoming, although a bit entrepreneurial in the cities, Cubanos make excellent hosts. They are lively and friendly, always ready to teach a quick cha-cha-cha, give directions, or talk animatedly about the Revolution and how it has changed their lives. Indeed, in spite of all its other offerings, one friend who

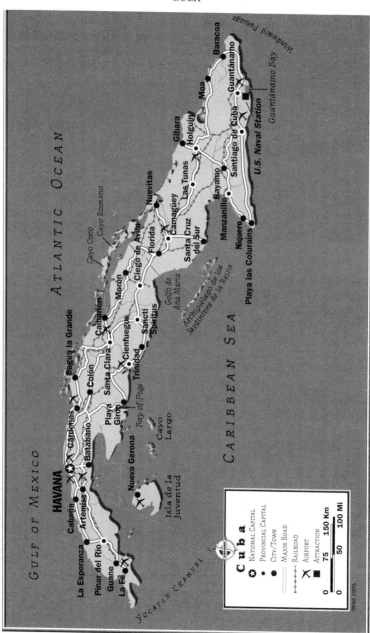

Cuba

✪ National Capital
● Provincial Capital
● City/Town
Major Road
╪╪╪ Railroad
✕ Airport
■ Attraction

0   75   150 Km
0   50   100 Mi

©RWI 1995

recently returned from Cuba told me her most vivid memory was the intelligent conversation on a number of topics with a Cuban student—an elementary school student. Open your mind, as well as your eyes, ears and taste buds, and you'll return from the Pearl of the Caribbean educated like that boy, as well as renewed in your soul.

Bird's Eye View

Often described as shaped like a crocodile, Cuba, although the largest of the Caribbean islands, is only 120 miles across at its widest point, but, stretching 775 miles from northwest to southeast, covers 44,218 square miles. Just 90 miles south of Florida's Key West, Cuba is separated from Mexico's Yucatan Peninsula to the west by the 85-mile wide Yucatan Channel, from Haiti to the east by the 48-mile wide Windward Passage, and from Jamaica to the south, by a 90-mile wide expanse of the open Caribbean Sea. The main island's coastline is 3600 miles in circumference, pockmarked by more than 200 bays and boasting almost 300 separate beaches. The large island of Isla de Juventud and the smaller Cayo Largo in the Los Canarreos archipelago off the southern coast, and the islands of Cayo Coco and Cayo Romano off the northeastern coast in the Camaguey archipelago, are the only heavily developed ones among some 4000 offshore cays and islets in Cuba. Some 75 percent of the country's land area is flat plains, largely cultivated with sugar and other crops; three mountain ranges crisscross the country—the Cordillera de los Organos in the west, the Escambray Mountains in the central region, and the Sierra Maestra in the southeast. The island's highest point, Pico Turquino, rises to 6470 feet in the Sierra Maestra, a range created by persistent seismic activity over the ages that also hewed the 23,000-foot deep Cayman Trench just 20 miles off the southeastern coast. Cuba is divided into 14 provinces. The capital city, La Habana, situated on the extreme northern coast in the west of the island, is home to about 3 million of the island's 11 million inhabitants. The U.S. naval base at Guantánamo Bay is located on the southeastern tip of the island.

History

Archaeological artifacts have been found in Cuba dating to 4000 B.C., when the island was inhabited by Siboney and Guanahacaibe peoples. These tribes were supplanted by the more advanced Tainos by about the 10th century A.D. The Tainos introduced collective farming, bringing maize and tobacco to the island from the South American mainland, and their civilization was flourishing when Christopher Columbus set foot on Cuba in 1492, exclaiming, "This is the most beautiful land man has set eyes upon!" (The name Cuba is believed to originate from the Taino word *cubanacan*, meaning center, or central [the word is now used as the name for one of the state transportation companies], or alternatively from the name given to the island by the Tainos, rendered in Spanish by Columbus' recorders as "Colba.")

Spain began its military conquest of Cuba under Diego de Velásquez in 1512, and by 1515 he had founded settlements at Baracoa, Bayamo, Santiago de Cuba (established as the capital from 1523 to 1552), Trinidad and San Cristobal de la Habana. La Habana quickly became an important trading port for Spain's colonial empire, although there was little economic development of the interior of the island since the Spaniards were preoccupied with looting the Aztec civilization in Mexico. The next two centuries saw the Spanish presence in Cuba develop slowly, even as the colonizers wiped out the native population through violence, disease and forced labor. Subsistence farming, timber felling and tobacco cultivation constituted the basis of the island's economy during this period, as nearby Haiti and Jamaica developed into centers of sugar production. During the Spanish-British conflict of the late 18th century, Britain took control of Cuba from 1762 until 1763, when the Spaniards reoccupied the island in exchange for giving London possession of Florida. Anxious to strengthen its hold on the island, Spain invested heavily in sugarcane farming (it is estimated that 50 percent of the native forest was cleared for sugarcane production in the following 20 years), and slaves were brought from Africa en masse to work the fields. A census taken by the Spaniards in 1774 recorded 44,000 slaves on the island; by the 1840s they numbered half a million.

During the middle part of the 19th century, native Spanish Cubans began to chafe at the rule of Madrid, and this, coupled with a growing desire on the part of the U.S. to gain influence over the island (the U.S. consumed 40 percent of Cuba's sugar production by 1850), provided the impetus for Cuba's first revolution. Led by Carlos Manuel de Céspedes and Máximo Gómez, the rebellion against Spain began in 1868 and lasted for a decade, earning it the somewhat exaggerated name of the Ten Years' War. The only real concession granted to the independistas under the terms of the armistice signed in 1878 was the abolition of slavery, which took effect in 1886. The lot of the slaves changed little if at all, however, and even the white landowners and mixed-race freemen felt that Cuba was still unreasonably controlled by Spain. The U.S., too, became increasingly anxious to evict the European colonial power, since over the next 20 years U.S. concerns poured tens of millions of dollars into modernization of the sugar industry, construction, railroads and roads.

In 1895, José Martí, still Cuba's greatest revolutionary hero, led a second armed uprising against the Spanish, this time with barely tacit U.S. support (even though Martí himself spoke often against the danger of one colonial power—Spain—being simply supplanted by another—the U.S.). Martí was killed in battle in 1895, but others continued the struggle, and in 1897 Spain formally recognized Cuban independence, although it did not remove any of the trappings of its power. Cuba for the next year and a half was in a state of political flux, as the various factions in the nationalist movement struggled for power among themselves and with the vestiges of the Spanish rulers. In 1898 a U.S. battleship moored in Havana harbor, ostensibly to protect U.S. citizens in Cuba, was blown up by still unidentified persons. Even though there is evidence to suggest that the explosion was the work of Cuban nationalists, the U.S. blamed Spain and used the incident as a pretext to declare war on Madrid. U.S. forces overran the island at once, and Cuba was under U.S. control for the next three years.

Independence finally came to Cuba on May 20, 1902. The U.S. still retained some political power over the island, however, reserving the right to intervene in its affairs to "preserve stability" (this proviso was repealed by the U.S. Congress in 1934, although a 1903 treaty leasing the Guantánamo Bay to the U.S. for a naval base remains in effect), as well as great, and greatly increasing, economic power. Almost immediately after independence, U.S. companies invested another $100 million in Cuba (a gargantuan amount for the time), and by the 1920s almost the entire sugar industry in Cuba was owned by U.S. concerns. In 1924, thanks in large part to political intervention by the U.S., Gerardo Machado, a general in the Cuban army, was elected president. Machado was the nation's first native dictator, using intimidation, imprisonment and firing squads to quash any dissention against his regime. In 1933 Machado was deposed in a coup d'etat led by Army sergeant Fulgencio Batista, who ruled Cuba for the next 26 years with the same strongman tactics as Machado.

Fidel Castro was a leader of the popular opposition to Batista's dictatorship, and led an armed uprising against it in July 1953. Castro's forces were routed in a July 26 attack on the army barracks in Santiago de Cuba, and he, along with the other survivors, was imprisoned on Isla de Juventud. In 1955 Batista granted an amnesty, and Castro was exiled to Mexico. There, Castro joined forces with the Argentinian-born revolutionary Che Guevara, forming the July 26th Movement. In 1956 Castro and 80 men landed in Cuba to stage a guerilla campaign against Batista, but his forces were again defeated and most of the men killed. Castro went into hiding in the Sierra Maestra mountains, his guerilla reduced to just 12 men, but in what is recognized as the greatest revolutionary campaign the world has ever seen, he steadily built support for his clandestine July 26th Movement, and in 1959 Batista fled to Florida and the revolutionaries took control of the country.

Castro's government began to institute socialist reforms immediately upon taking power; the first of these included land reforms in which much privately held land was confiscated and all beaches were made public, with a state-mandated 50 percent cut in rents. The U.S. at once began to resist the new government, concerned for its estimated $1 billion in investments in the country. Che Guevara, as minister for industry, established trading partnerships with other socialist and nonaligned nations including Egypt, India and the Soviet Union. U.S.-owned oil refineries in Cuba refused to refine Soviet crude oil, but in 1960 Castro established full diplomatic relations with the Soviets, further angering the U.S., which imposed the first of a series of economic and political sanctions on Cuba. Cuba responded by nationalizing all U.S. property and assets in the country, following which Washington broke off diplomatic relations with La Habana in January 1961. Immediately after the deposition of Batista, many thousands of Cuba's wealthy elite had fled to the U.S., most settling in and around Miami. They became emboldened by the U.S.'s increasingly hard line against Castro, and in April 1961, 1500 mercenaries and disgruntled Cuban expatriates, trained and supported by the C.I.A., launched a calamitous failed invasion of Cuba, landing at the Bay of Pigs. Following the fiasco, the U.S. established a full-scale trade embargo against Cuba, which naturally drove the nation into even further cooperation with the Soviet Union. In 1962 the Soviets stationed missiles believed to be equipped with nuclear warheads on the island, and the two superpowers engaged in a face-off that brought the world closer than ever before or since to a bilateral nuclear conflict, ending peacefully only when the Soviets removed the missiles. The same year, U.S. citizens were banned from travelling to Cuba (see "Traveling to Cuba"). Later in 1962, Castro publicly declared himself a Marxist-Leninist and Cuba a communist nation.

Throughout the remainder of the 1960s, Cuba, economically healthy despite the U.S. embargo thanks to its close partnership with the Soviet Union, was able to focus on exporting revolution around the world, particularly to other South American countries. Attempts to aid in the overthrow of dictators in many of these nations were foiled, however, by massive U.S. support for the regimes—the most serious failure coming in 1967 when Che Guevara, who had been sent by Castro to Bolivia to coordinate an insurgency there, was killed and the revolution fizzled out. In the 1970s and 1980s Cuban troops were deployed in numerous countries around the world, notably in Ethiopia, Mozambique, Angola and other African nations, in support of popular insurgencies. As the Soviet subsidy began to falter in step with the communist bloc's own economic difficulties, however, Cuba's foreign involvement was eliminated. Nevertheless, and despite the establishment of mutual "interest sections" under the auspices of the Swiss Embassy, Cuban-U.S. relations remained chilly. Responding to a barrage of propaganda from Washington about alleged restrictions on Cubans' freedom to travel, Castro responded by authorizing the Mariel boatlift of 1980, in which tens of thousands of Cubans wishing to emigrate arrived in South Florida—the U.S. was shocked to discover later that Castro had included several thousand criminals and mental patients among the emigres. In 1983 relations improved slightly when Castro agreed to repatriate the "excludables" he had foisted upon the U.S. in the Mariel boatlift, but continued U.S. anti-Castro intervention, culminating in the inception of "Radio Martí" Voice of America radio propaganda broadcasting to Cuba, chilled relations once again.

Despite some evidence that Castro's was a totalitarian regime that brooked no dissent, living conditions in Cuba continued to improve during these years. Illiteracy was eradicated, the index of infant mortality fell to 11.1 per 1000 live births in 1989 from 19.6 in 1980 and over 30.0 during the Batista regime, over 400 free colleges and technical schools were created in rural areas, and Cubans enjoyed the most successful system of socialized health care outside Scandinavia, according to the United Nations. Nevertheless the nation's economy remained heavily dependent on subsidies from the Soviet Union, and when the USSR collapsed in 1989–90, the Cuban economy was plunged into turmoil. In 1990 the government announced the beginning of a "special period," under which the nation was run on a wartime footing—basic goods and foodstuffs were rationed, and radical changes were made in the law to stimulate the economy (the U.S. dollar was made legal tender, and foreign ownership of some property was permitted). The U.S., however, believing that Castro was weakened, decided to tighten the economic blockade against the island. The so-called Cuban Democracy Act of 1992 forbade foreign subsidiaries of U.S.-owned companies from trading with Cuba (although most other nations refused to adhere to the restriction and the United Nations General Assembly approved a resolution condemning the U.S. law), and in 1995 draft legislation was being debated in the U.S. Congress that would prohibit U.S. banks from loaning money to foreign-owned companies trading with the island.

Despite 35 years of attempts by Washington to strangle Castro and the revolution in Cuba, however, the people of the island have only become more fiercely nationalistic and loyal to their leader, and despite economic difficulties that have become quite severe since the demise of the Soviet Union, the Cuban people remain one of the best educated, most healthy and most vivacious in the world. Most other Western nations besides the U.S., including European countries, Mexico and Canada, meanwhile, have taken the severing of Cuba's relationship with Moscow as an opportunity, and trade with these nations is gradually increasing, while a modern tourism infrastructure and burgeoning tourism industry are springing up in the wake of Castro's new pragmatism.

People

Cuba is a very ethnically mixed society. The gradual merging of the Spaniards with the African slaves (indigenous people were almost completely exterminated by the Spanish) has led to a community that runs the gamut from very black to very white. Cubans as a people have inherited the *joie de vivre* and rich expressiveness of both of these cultures, and the island is a feast for the senses with its music, dance and art.

Slavery persisted in Cuba until almost the end of the 19th century, much longer than in other Caribbean countries, so the African traditions have survived much more strongly than elsewhere. This is most evident in *santería*, the popular faith practiced by more Cubans than any other. Based on ancient African beliefs similar to Yoruba that hold that everything—man, woman, tree, rock, river—is inhabited by a sensate spirit or spirits, the religion also incorporates elements of Catholicism (ironically, orthodox Catholicism almost died out after the Revolution), and is a sort of an all-encompassing mix of icon worship and animal sacrifice.

The music of Cuba, too, traces its roots very clearly to Africa. The prevalence of percussion instruments, including congas, maracas, tambores and batá drums, comes straight from the African tribes from which the first slaves were snatched. The *rumba*, Cuba's most exported and copied music and dance, was originally a religious tribal chant with dancing. In Cuba it originated in the slave communities on the sugar plantations, migrated to the poor *barrios* of the cities, and finally won widespread acceptance. Its complex, syncopated rhythms, supported only by percussion and solo voice, were supplemented by horns and even a full orchestra, as the rumba became popular in New York and eventually all over the world. The real thing is still practiced in Cuba, however, and after listening to a recording or, if you're extremely fortunate, a performance of the incomparable Israel López "Cachao" y Su Descarga, Desi Arnaz seems like just another lounge lizard.

The other main Cuban musical form is *salsa*. (There is not room here to discuss the *cha-cha-cha*, *tango* [which originated in Cuba before migrating to Argentina], *conga*, *guajira*, and others.) This most sensual of dancing music derives from the traditional song, a very tropical form of love song that began in eastern Cuba. Again, the modern *salsa* band has trumpets, trombones and saxophones as well as several percussionists, but in this case the evolution is definitely an improvement. Celia Cruz, known around the world as the Queen of Salsa, is from Cuba, as are many other popular performers now living in the U.S. (mostly in Miami), including Eddie Santiago, Willy Chirino, Gilberto Santarosa and others. These performers have evidently chosen to leave the country for the love of filthy lucre, however, and not because of repression of their music—the government of Cuba actively promotes *salsa* and other art forms; there are *Casas de Cultura* in every town where free performances of music, dance, theater, films and poetry readings are given regularly.

The Revolution encouraged the participation in the arts of the masses, where hitherto they had been the domain of the patronized elite. Included in the free education every Cuban can enjoy through university is film school and art school, and Cuban painters, sculptors, and cinematographers have produced exceptional work since then. Some is very political, for example the *nueva trova* folk songs of performers such as Silvio Rodríguez and Pablo Milanés, or movies like 1994's *Fresas y Chocolate (Strawberries and Chocolate)*, which enjoyed considerable international success.

Eco-tours

A burgeoning branch of the travel industry in general and throughout the Caribbean in particular, eco-tours are especially popular and widely available in Cuba. The reasons for this are simple. First, along with the infectious vivaciousness of its people, Cuba's main asset in attracting tourism has always been its breathtaking natural beauty. Second, and perhaps more immediately, the economic difficulties Cuba has faced in recent years due to the U.S. blockade and the collapse of its main trading partner, the Soviet Union, have obliged it to undertake a concerted program of developing sustainability in all sectors.

Even prior to the "special period," Cuba's car culture was anachronistic, consisting mostly of lovingly maintained and sparingly used 1940s and '50s monsters from Detroit. These gas guzzlers can still be seen throughout the island, but the limited availability of petroleum products has reduced the use of the private automobile to almost nil. From 1990–1992 the number of cars on the roads of La Habana decreased by two-thirds, and even the bus traffic fell by half, while the number of bicycles jumped from an estimated 30,000 to more than 800,000. Cuba is still pressing ahead with its bicycle revolution, having ordered a further 1.2 million bicycles from China, and designated bicycle lanes on almost all roads have been established (some roads have been closed to cars altogether). An urgent need to shift agricultural production from export crops to food has led to dramatic changes in farming practices in Cuba. Coupled with the sudden elimination of the island's source of pesticides (the Soviet Union), the need for food crops has forced farmers to implement more environmentally friendly techniques, including crop rotation in place of monocropping and the use of biological agents such as fungi and insects to control pests. Small vegetable gardens have sprung up throughout the country—an estimated one million since 1990—including some 30,000 in La Habana where previously there were none, giving the city a decidedly greener look. Alternative energy sources are being used more and more—massive public investment in solar, wind and photovoltaic power is beginning to pay off in practical applications, and more than 100 of the island's 160 sugar mills are now powered entirely by the mill's own waste.

Besides the advances in sustainability, Cuba has preserved its natural resources remarkably well; in fact, a reforestation effort has left the island with more woodland than at any time since the Spanish conquest in the 16th century. And with 4000 species of shellfish, 900 species of fish, and more than 300 different birds, Cuba is truly a natural paradise waiting to be explored. The National Committee for the Protection and Conservation of National Treasures and the Environment, created in 1978, administers the island's six national parks.

The Freedom to Travel Campaign and Global Exchange (see "Traveling to Cuba") offer well-planned eco-tours of the island. Global Exchange's research trips include tours of the incredibly diverse Pinar del Rio eco-preserve and a weeklong study of organic farming in Cuba, with visits to small and large farms that are pursuing sustainable development. Freedom to Travel's

"Challenge" trips also visit Piñar del Rio, with an itinerary that includes nat ural wonders such as the province's limestone caves and underground rivers teeming lakes and beautiful, lush valleys with native vegetation undisturbed by man, as well as the Cuban people's ecological projects, including organic farms, alternative energy generating plants, a bicycle factory and meetings with urban planning officials.

Even the mainstream tour operators are getting into the eco-tourism act **Horizontes Hoteles** (☎ *(53) 7-33-4042*), one of the major hotel chains in Cuba, has a special division for "Close to Nature" destinations, with facilities in Pinar del Rio, Matanzas, Villa Clara, Sancti Spiritus, Cienfuegos, Holguin and Granma. **Delta Cuba** (☎ *(800) 268-1133*) offers even more specialized tours, including stays at their El Colibri Lodge in the northeastern rainforest (named after a small humming bird native to the region), La Gran Piedra Lodge outside Santiago de Cuba, El Saltón Lodge in the Sierra Maestra mountains and Piñares de Mayari Lodge near Holguín. Each of these lodge provide comfortable if simple accommodations in cottages and small houses and activities including horseback riding, trekking and visits to botanical gar dens, nature preserves and ecological research stations.

For more information on Cuba's natural resources see the individual sec tions on each of the island's regions.

Underwater

Cuba is one of the most attractive destinations for scuba diving and snor keling in all the Caribbean, yet it remains undiscovered—or at least unvisit ed—by most practitioners of the sport. With 900 species of fish and 4000 species of shellfish in its waters, which hover around 75°F, Cuba's underwa ter scenery is just as lovely as that on land.

Most of the bigger hotel chains have on-site dive facilities at all their beach front hotels, including **Cubanacán** (☎ *(416) 601-0343*), **Gran Caribe** (☎ *(53, 7-33-0238*), and **Horizontes** (☎ *(53) 7-33-3722*). Check with your tour oper ator for specific hotel information. The diving operation at Superclub Vara dero is the island's most complete, with a well-stocked dive shop, three boats, six instructors, and two certified divemasters. Despite the U.S. trade blockade, equipment here and throughout the island is all brand name stuff including Sherwood, Dacor, Cressi Sub and U.S. Divers. The Superclub op eration charges about $20 for a 20–30 minute dive; unfortunately there' not too much to see as the Atlantic seabed is very flat-bottomed and the constant swell kicks up sand and reduces visibility to just 50 or 60 feet.

Better diving is to be had on the Caribbean coast, where the ocean is calmer. Marina Aqua and Náutico are two diving operations located in the Varadero area that offer trips to the south coast—the bus ride takes about two hours each way; with two dives included expect to pay about $60. There are also diving shops in the south coast resorts, where serious divers normally prefer to stay. The **Bay of Pigs** is one of the best areas for viewing and photographing marine life, with 20-foot coral at 50 or 60 feet about 100 yards out, before the ocean bed drops into the bottomless Cayman Trench. **Playa Girón** comes highly recommended, as does **Cayo Largo del Sur**. **Guardalavaca** is a favorite of snorkelers, for its coral reefs that almost reach the surface, but there are underwater caves and schools of rays and other fish to be seen at 60 or 70 feet.

The **Zapata Peninsula**, while not as easily accessible as, say, Varadero, offers some of the best diving in all of Cuba in terms of wildlife, as might be expected from the country's primary beachside ecological preserve. Contact the dive center at your hotel for availability of trips to the area.

Sports

Not only scuba divers and snorkelers will get their fill of water sports in Cuba. As to be expected from a country with magnificent beaches, and one that is actively promoting its tourism industry, the island offers a full range of beach recreation. Most of the major hotels have parasailing and water-skiing available behind nifty little speedboats; the water at some of the exposed northern Atlantic beaches is often too choppy for skiing. Windsurfing is also widely available through independent operators on the beaches, or ask in your hotel. Deep-sea fishing is very popular in Cuba, and compared to almost anywhere else in the world, it's amazingly inexpensive. A charter boat with crew and bait can be had for around $250 a day. The premier spot for this is off **La Habana's Hemingway Marina** (☎ *(53) 7-225590)* where international marlin fishing contests are held; Varadero also has a good outfit at the **Marina Gaviota** (☎ *(53) 66269)*. Catch can include marlin, yellowfin tuna and sailfish, so it's very good sport.

Hunting of the land-based variety is available throughout the island; there are a number of game reserves where you can shoot quail and snipe as well as wild boar. Ask in your hotel or contact Cubatur for information on open season dates, locations, etc. Remember, do *not* bring your own gun; rent one from the operator! Freshwater fishing is especially good at Zaza Lake and the Masopotón Fishing and Hunting Center in Piñar del Rio. Tennis is widely available throughout Cuba; even the medium-sized hotels usually have an outdoor court.

All spectator sports are free to attend, and there are plenty of them. Cuba is justifiably proud of its sporting achievements, especially in the areas of track and field and boxing; in the 1992 Olympic Games, the small nation placed fifth in the overall medal count. Amateur boxing as well as track meets are held regularly in all the provincial capitals and are great fun. An even better time is to be had watching a *beisbol* game; the Cubans play excellent ball and there are leagues at every level all around the island. Pickup games go on in all the parks and even in the streets, too, so if you think you can hang, join in and contribute to cultural exchange through sports!

La Habana

Founded in 1514 as a tiny settlement of *bohíos* (the palm-thatched huts that are still common in some of Cuba's most rural areas), **San Cristobal de la Habana** soon assumed strategic importance thanks to its natural harbor, and now, besides the capital of Cuba, the most populated city in the Caribbean. With such a storied history the city unsurprisingly has multiple personalities, and it will take you a few days to experience all of them properly, from the magnificent colonial buildings to the opulent temples to wealth and decadence of the 1930s, '40s, and '50s, and the ugly, squat Soviet-built concrete towers of the post-revolution. **Habana la Vieja**, the old part of the city, has been designated a World Heritage Site by UNESCO, and it is the most charming square mile among all the Caribbean's urban areas. The **Plaza de Armas** area houses the oldest buildings in the city, including the Castillo de la Fuerza, an ancient fort that is now a museum, and the Templete, a 240-year-old church built on the site of where the first Mass was said in Cuba. At the north end of the park the old merges with the new, as flat-bed trucks carrying dozens of cyclists emerge from the tunnel under the Bahía de la Habana that links the old city with the newer, residential areas in Habana del Este.

The **Malecón**, the seawall that rings the oceanfront of the city for five miles west from the Plaza de Armas, is a delightful paseo dotted with palm trees, strolling lovers and ice cream vendors. There are parks everywhere in La Habana, but one definitely not to be missed is the giant **Parque Central**, filled with lush trees and plants, open-air cafes and men of all ages playing chess. There are so many museums and public art galleries in La Habana your biggest problem will be deciding which to visit. Highly recommended are the **Museo de la Ciudad** (City Museum), housed in the **Palacio de los Capitanes Generales** (the 18th century palace that was once the seat of the Spanish colonial government) in the Plaza de Armas; the Museo de la Revolución in the former Presidential Palace in La Habana Central, providing the most comprehensive historical record of the island and the capital; the **Museo Nacional de Bellas Artes** (the National Museum of Fine Arts), housed in an ugly modern building but offering a broad collection of Old Masters and modern Cuban artists; and the **Museo Nacional de la Música** (the National Museum of Music), which houses interesting displays of Cuban musical instruments used from the days of slavery to the present.

Hemingway

If you're interested in author Ernest Hemingway, there are plenty shrines to him in La Habana. The **Hotel Ambos Mundos** in Habana la Vie keeps a room in which he occasionally stayed in the exact condition in whi he left it for the last time, although the more interesting time capsule is h house, **La Vigia**, in San Francisco, on the outskirts of the city. The walls a covered with hunting and fishing trophies, his typewriter still stands on t cabinet in front of which he wrote standing up, and the especially morb can view the piece of paper he kept in his bathroom during his last days do umenting his weight loss due to liver cirrhosis. The suburb of Cojimar w once a separate fishing village in which Hemingway set *The Old Man and t Sea;* it is one of many areas and institutions in the city that attempt to make living off his name. These include the Bodeguita del Medio on Calle Emp drado and the Floridita by Parque Central on Calle Obispo, two of a numb of bars that claim to have been Hemingway's favorite haunts (although it not unreasonable to assume that he may have had several).

Beaches around La Habana

There are two main beaches in the city itself, **Miramar** and **Playa de Ma anao**. They are usually very crowded with city residents and much of the area is enclosed in private beach clubs belonging to labor unions (althoug sometimes visitors are allowed in these). El Mégano, Santa María del M and Bacuranao beaches stretch away from the city to the east, and are mu less heavily used as well as less rocky and generally closer to the Caribbe ideal. To the west a short drive or bus ride away are **Arena Blanca** and **Bah Honda**, both of which offer deep sea fishing as well as scuba diving equipme rental and instruction. These activities can generally be arranged in advan at your hotel.

What to See

Historical Sites

Capitolio

Calle Prado, La Habana.
Hours open: 10:15 a.m.–5:45 p.m.
Built in 1929, this building is an exact replica (on a smaller scale) of the U.S. Capitol building in Washington, DC. Now housing the National Museum of Natural History, it was formerly the legislative assembly building. Set in the center of the floor under the rotunda dome is a huge 24-carat diamond, the point from which distances to and from La Habana are measured.

Castillo de la Fuerza

Avenida de Céspedes, La Habana.
Hours open: 10 a.m.–6 p.m.
El Castillo de la Fuerza is Cuba's oldest standing building and second oldest fort in the Americas. Built in 1538, it is now a museum with an excellent display on weapons through the ages. Art shows are on display in the lower floors.

Castillo de la Punta

Habana la Vieja, La Habana.
Hours open: 10 a.m.–6 p.m.
Sitting on the opposite side of the harbor mouth from the Castillo del Morro, this fort provided the second half of the defenses of the city in its early days. The fort is now a historical museum with interesting exhibits on the city's history.

Castillo del Moro

Casablanca, La Habana.
Hours open: 10 a.m.–6 p.m.
Built in the 16th Century to protect the entrance to La Habana harbor from pirates and the British navy, the castle has a 20-yard wide moat and imposing battlements that look out to sea as well as over the Old City across the harbor mouth. There is now a museum housed in the fort, with good exhibits on Cuba's early history.

Cathedral

Calle Oficios, La Habana.
Hours open: 9 a.m.–11:30 a.m.
Built in 1704, La Habana's cathedral is one of the most impressive in the Caribbean. Christopher Columbus' remains were buried here for a time (they are now in Santa Domingo). The view over the old city from the twin bell towers is one of the city's best. An arts and crafts fair is held on Saturdays outside the cathedral.

Cementerio Cristóbal Cólon ★★★

Vedado, La Habana.
This huge cemetery contains the mausoleums of several revolutionary heroes, including Céspedes, José Martí, and others. It is worth a visit for the impressive marble monuments and funerary sculpture.

El Presidio Modelo ★★★

Isla de la Juventud.

Hours open: 9 a.m.–5 p.m.

The Presidio Modelo is an ancient fort on Cuba's largest offshore island, located in the major town of Nueva Gerona. When the fort was used as a high security prison during the Batista regime, Fidel Castro was among the dissidents incarcerated in one of the five round cell-blocks. The building is now a school but parts of it can be toured.

La Vigia ★★★

San Francisco de Paula, La Habana.

Hours open: 9 a.m.–noon

Ernest Hemingway's house has been kept as it was when he died. His typewriter still stands on the chest where he wrote standing up; the notepad on which he recorded his precipitously declining weight in the final days of his battle with liver cirrhosis is still in the bathroom; his dogs' grave markers still stand in the garden. Visitors are not allowed inside the house but may walk around the gardens and view the interior of the house through open windows and doors.

Museums and Exhibits

Guam· Indian Village ★★★

Playa Larga, Zapata Peninsula.

Hours open: 10 a.m.–5 p.m.

Beside the Villa Guam· Hotel in the Zapata Peninsula National Park, there is a reconstructed Indian Village, replete with bohio palm-thatched huts, displays of indigenous civilization and art. There is also a crocodile farm nearby on Treasure Lake.

Hotel Ambos Mundos ★★★

Calle Obispo, 153, La Habana.

Hours open: 9 a.m.–5 p.m.

Besides being a working hotel, the Ambos Mundos has as its claim to fame the fact that Ernest Hemingway lived here for 10 years before moving to Cojimar. His room has been preserved exactly as he left it (according to the brochure), and may be visited but not photographed.

Museo Farmacético ★★★

Parque Central, Matanzas.

Hours open: 2 p.m.–9 p.m.

The pharmaceutical museum in Matanzas is interesting for its displays of traditional remedies, once derisively referred to as "old wives' remedies" but now accepted as alternative medicine. Cuba has long been at the forefront among western nations in the use of traditional healing in conjunction with modern medicine, in which it is also a leader.

Museo José Echevarría ★★★

Calle José Echevarría, Cardenas.

Hours open: 9:30 a.m.–6 p.m.

This small museum to the sugar industry is housed in the home of José Echevarría, a revolutionary leader executed by the Batista regime in 1957. The town is also believed to be the first place the Cuban flag was raised in the fight for independence from Spain.

Museo Municipal ★★★

Calle 57 y Avenida de la Playa, Varadero Beach.
Hours open: 10 a.m.–5 p.m.
The small museum in the center of Varadero is dedicated mostly to exhibits on the Taino Indians who were indigenous to the island before the arrival of the Spanish. Worth a look, and the highest culture in Varadero!

Museo Nacional Palacio de Bellas Artes ★★★★★

Agramonte y Montserrat, La Habana.
Hours open: 10:30 a.m.–6:30 p.m.
The National Museum of Fine Arts is the best collection of art in the Caribbean. A huge number of old masters, including works by Goya, Velázquez, Gainsborough and Turner, as well as permanent displays and scheduled exhibits of art by modern Cubans. There are also galleries with Greek, Roman, and Egyptian artifacts.

Museo Nacional de la Música ★★★★

Calle Capdevilla, 1, La Habana.
Hours open: 10 a.m.–6 p.m.
The National Museum of Music is a fascinating repository of instruments and artifacts documenting the evolution of Cuban music, including son and rumba, from ancient African rhythms to the present. Not to be missed.

Museo Romántico ★★★

Plaza , Trinidad.
Hours open: 10 a.m.–5 p.m.
The Museum of Romance refers to the Romantic period in arts and culture, not the amore kind (although the colonial mansion in which it is housed, with its lush, old gardens, is a romantic place all of its own). There are excellent collections of porcelain, glassware, and furniture from the period. The views from the upstairs windows and balconies over the old city are magnificent.

Museo de Historia ★★

Calle José Martí, Piòar del Rio.
Hours open: 10 a.m.–6 p.m.
This is Piòar del Rio's major historical museum, and has displays on Cuban history and culture from the time of the Tainos to the present, but the displays are rather dingy and poorly documented. In a country so rich with museums, you can miss this one.

Museo de la Bahía de Cochinos ★★★

Bahía de los Cochinos, Playa Girón.
Hours open: 10 a.m.–5 p.m.
This museum to what the Cubans proudly call "the first major defeat of Imperialism in Latin America" is a comprehensive monument to the invasion of 1961 Cuba by CIA-supported Cuban exiles and mercenaries. There are tanks and airplanes on dis-

play, as well as a memorial to those who died, and photographs of the battle, which
Castro himself led.

Museo de la Ciudad   ★ ★ ★ ★

Plaza de Armas, La Habana.
Hours open: 11:30 a.m.–5:30 p.m.
Formerly the Palacio de los Capitanes Generales, site of the signing of the treaty
between Spain and the United States in 1899 and official residence of governors
and presidents as well as the City Hall for a time this century, the building was constructed in 1780. Now the City Historical Museum, this is one of the best historical
exhibits in the capital. There is a large collection of furnishings and clothes from the
Spanish colonial period. Poor explanations identifying the exhibits.

Museo de la Revolución   ★ ★ ★

Avenida de la Misiones La Habana.
Hours open: 10 a.m.–5 p.m.

The building was constructed in 1922 as the Presidential Palace in a most opulent
style; it has ornate facades and a dome on top. It has been converted into a museum
of the Revolution, providing a detailed history of the struggle for independence
from Spain as well as the Revolution itself and U.S. harassment since then, including
the Bay of Pigs attack. The yacht *Granma*, on which Castro arrived in Cuba from
Mexico, is on display in the grounds.

Museo del Tabaco   ★ ★ ★ ★ ★

Calle Ajete, Piòar del Rio.
Hours open: 2 p.m.–10 p.m.
The Museo del Tabaco in the Piòar del Rio, the country's main cigar producing
region, is more of a shrine to the great Cuban cigar than to tobacco in general. It's
a fascinating look at the industry from planting to production, as well as at the history of cigar making. You can get a good deal on a box of Montecristos here, too!

Tren Blindado   ★ ★ ★

Villa Clara, Trinidad.
Hours open: 8 a.m.–6 p.m.
One of the most interesting museums of all Cuba's hundreds of them is the
Armored Train against which Che Guevara and a handful of men led one of the final
attacks of the Revolution. There are exhibits from the Revolution on display inside
the train carriages.

Music

Casa de la Trova

Plaza Martí, Trinidad.
Hours open: Noon–midnight
Of all the Casas de Trova (troubadour houses) in Cuba, the one in Trinidad is one
of the best to visit. It's open from lunchtime til late on the weekends, and the audience is almost all Cuban residents of the city, so you really feel like you're joining in
with the locals. Musical and theater groups give free performances, there are also art
displays.

Nightlife

opicana Cabaret ★ ★ ★ ★ ★

Vedado.
Hours open: 7 p.m.–dawn

The Tropicana is the most famous of all Cuba's cabarets, and rightfully so. From the 1950s to the present day, in size, spectacle, and glamor it is unsurpassed. The dancing girls number in the hundreds, bedecked with huge headdresses, brown bodies shimmering and shaking in the lights as the salsa music and African drumbeats work them—and the audience—into a frenzy. Not to be missed. Most hotels in the La Habana area offer all-inclusive excursions to the club, including taxi, entrance, and the first two drinks, for about US$60 a couple—less expensive than it was in the 1950s!

Parks and Gardens

oroa Botanical Gardens ★ ★ ★ ★ ★

Carretera de Caelaria, Soroa.
Hours open: 8:30 a.m.–4 p.m.

This botanical garden, built on the site of a spa and hot springs, is the best collection of Cuba's abundant trees and plants. There are also many species of birds, insects, and butterflies. The orchidarium is one of the best in the world, with more than 700 different species on display. The best time for viewing the orchids is in November and December.

Sports/Recreation

tadio Latinoamericano ★ ★ ★

Cerro, La Habana.

The main sporting stadium in La Habana is, like all sport venues in the country, free admission. This is a great place to watch Cuba's excellent athletes compete in track meets, and the baseball played regularly here is major league level.

Tours

ueva del Indio ★ ★ ★

Carretera de Viòales, Viòales.
Hours open: 10 a.m.–5 p.m.

On the road west out of Viòales in the Cueva del Indio, the best of the many cave systems in Piòar del Rio province. There is a separate entrance and exit, and you can either walk the length of the cavern or travel by boat on the underground river. There are petroglyphs from the Taino Indian culture here.

Where to Stay

Fielding's Highest Rated Hotels in Cuba

★★★★★	El Saltón Ecolodge	$28–$44
★★★★★	Hotel Faro Luna	$37–$54
★★★★★	Hotel Los Galeones	$75–$100
★★★★★	Melia Varadero	$86–$198
★★★★★	Superclub Varadero	$118–$101
★★★★★	Villa Capricho	$66–$120
★★★★	Casas Villa Paraíso	$140–$200
★★★★	Hotel Bella Costa	$104–$161
★★★★	Hotel El Viejo y El Mar	$123–$143
★★★★	Sol Palmeras	$78–$192

Fielding's Most Romantic Hotels in Cuba

★★★★★	El Saltón Ecolodge	$28–$44
★★★★	Hostal Valencia	$22–$34
★★★★★	Hotel Faro Luna	$37–$54
★★★★★	Hotel Los Galeones	$75–$100
★★★★★	Superclub Varadero	$118–$101

Fielding's Budget Hotels in Cuba

★★	Camaguey Hotel	$20–$35
★★★	Bacuranao Villa Resort	$22–$35
★★★	Pasacaballos Hotel	$22–$35
★★★	Villa Tropico Resort	$22–$35
★★★	Hotel Mariposa	$27–$40

Hotels and Resorts

Bacuranao Villa Resort   **$22–$35**   ★★★

Carretera Via Blanca y Celimar, ☎ *(53) 4431.*
Single: $22–$28. Double: $29–$35.
With a total of only 50 units, divided among studios and single/double rooms, this small resort 10 miles outside La Habana is situated on 10 acres of beachfront property. Every unit has a private balcony facing the ocean, as well as air conditioning. There is a pleasant open-air bar by the pool, a tourism information office on site, and water sports are offered just yards from the hotel's beach frontage.

Capri Hotel   **$47–$78**   ★★★

Calle 21 Esquina Norte Vedado, ☎ *(53) 32-0511.*
Single: $47–$59. Double: $63–$78.
Centrally located just four miles from the central Nacional railway station, this 40 year-old high rise hotel wears the years well. Its rooms are spacious and well appointed with air conditioning and television (try to get one of the 17 corner rooms that have views of the ocean and over Old Habana). The rooftop swimming pool with its cabana-style bar offers spectacular views over the whole city. There are two restaurants, two bars, and one of La Habana's best cabarets in the hotel nightclub. Ample meeting facilities make this a popular lodging for businesspeople as well as tourists.

Chateau Miramar   **$92–$120**   ★★★

Calle 1ª entre Calles 62 y 64, ☎ *(53) 7-331952.*
Single: $92. Double: $120.
The rooms in this light, airy hotel are comfortable, clean, and well equipped with air conditioning (nine are suites with their own terrace), minibar, and color television with VCR. There is a scuba diving center with equipment rental and instruction, and other water sports, but the pool is disappointing, being salt water—for that you can go to the beach nearby.

Comodoro Hotel & Bungalows   **$67–$110**   ★★★★

Avenida Primera y Calle 84, Miramar, ☎ *(53) 225551.*
Single: $67–$83. Double: $90–$110.
This resort rates a special recommendation as being the best value in or around the capital. Just 15 minutes from downtown La Habana, it features 164 self-contained bungalows with kitchen and living room (rates from $100–$176 for a one-bedroom; $125–$220 for a three bedroom), in addition to 124 rooms and suites, all with air conditioning, television, radio, phone, and ocean-facing balcony. The amenities are excellent, including three restaurants, three bars, a discotheque, bowling alley, and two swimming pools (one salt water, one fresh), as well as shops and a small supermarket for the self-caterers. Situated right on the beach; there are ample water sport facilities including a dive center with equipment rental and instruction.

Deauville Hotel   **$38–$60**   ★★★

Calle Galiano, 1, ☎ *(53) 616901.*
Single: $38–$45. Double: $50–$60.

This is a really average hotel except for one thing—its superconvenient location right between the old city and the downtown commercial area. Add to that the inexpensive rates and the Deauville is an excellent choice for a few days in La Habana if you're touring the country on a budget.

Habana Riviera　　　　　　　　**$66–$117**　　　　　　　★★

Paseo y Malecon, ☎ *(53) 306051, FAX (53) 304385.*
Single: $66–$82. Double: $94–$117.
Although it was built in 1959, this high rise hotel across the street from the beach on the Malecon has a very modern, continental flavor. The rooms are spacious with twin single or double beds, and each has a full bath—not just a shower! There are three restaurants, two bars, a cafeteria by the pool, car rental facilities, and even a post office. The hotel is a favorite of the tour groups, though, so book early if you are traveling independently.

Hotel Biocaribe　　　　　　　　**$43–$77**　　　　　　　★★★

Calle 158 y Avenida 31, ☎ *(53) 7-217379.*
Single: $43–$54. Double: $61–$77.
Against a backdrop of towering palms, this fairly modern hotel definitely lets you know you're in the Caribbean, but the name Biocaribe is a bit of a misnomer. In fact, only minutes from the Palacio de Congresos, this is a popular destination for business travelers. It's well appointed, however; there's a hairdresser, store, post office, a game room, child care services, a nightclub with live music every night, and room service from 6 a.m. to 9 p.m. The rooms are clean and comfortable, all with air conditioning and television, almost all with balcony.

Hotel El Viejo y El Mar　　　　　**$123–$143**　　　　　★★★★

Qunita Avenida y Calle 248, Marina Hemingway, ☎ *(57) 7-219457.*
Single: $123. Double: $143.
This tall hotel stands like a watchtower overlooking the Hemingway Marina, extremely modern and well appointed. There is 24-hour room service, a good restaurant, separate grill, lobby bar, swimming pool bar, nightclub, two tennis courts, and abundant beach recreation opportunities. Sailing boat and windsurf board rentals, deep sea fishing from the marina, and scuba diving and snorkeling are all on offer.

Hotel Mariposa　　　　　　　　**$27–$40**　　　　　　　★★★

Autopista del Mediodía, Km 6.5, ☎ *(53) 7-204913.*
Single: $27–$30. Double: $34–$40.
A good budget choice just outside town, this is an ugly modern, but functional place. All the rooms have air conditioning but no television. There's room service and a decent restaurant; the brochure boasts "taped music" (!) Set breakfast is just US$4. Only a few of the rooms have a balcony, so be sure to request one when you make your reservations, then insist on it when you check in.

Hotel Nacional de Cuba　　　　　**$114–$204**　　　　　★★★

Calle 21 y Vedado, ☎ *(53) 78981.*
Single: $114–$143. Double: $163–$204.

La Habana's Nacional de Cuba Hotel has a storied history. Built in 1927, it was at one time thought of as the finest hotel in all the Caribbean. After the revolution it was nationalized and became a worker's retreat where workers from the rural areas of the island could stay for free when visiting the capital. In recent years it has been completely renovated and is once again an elegant, if pricey, tourist hotel. The main restaurant has a fabulous view of La Habana harbor; facilities are generous, including several shops, a post office, car rental facilities, cabanas by the pool, and a nightclub popular with locals and tourists alike. The rooms are spacious and well-equipped except for the fact that they lack a television—residents of all 480 rooms must share a single lobby television!

Hotel Victoria $60–$107   ★★★

Calle 19 Esquina M, ☎ *(53) 326531.*
Single: $60–$75. Double: $86–$107.
The Victoria is another standard big city hotel—all you need, but no frills. There's a television in every room, a decent sized swimming pool, and a good restaurant, but the main advantage of staying here is its location in the old city.

Presidente Hotel $51–$92   ★★

Calle Calzada y Avenida de los Presidentes, ☎ *(53) 327521.*
Single: $51–$64. Double: $73–$92.
The Presidente does its job—provides a good, clean room with television, phone, and air conditioning, has a restaurant, bar, ho-hum nightclub with a fairly decent cabaret, shops and a beauty salon…good spot to spend a couple of nights in the capital before you head to the beaches or the countryside.

Vedado Hotel $33–$53   ★★

Calle 0, Numero 244, ☎ *(53) 326501.*
Single: $33–$40. Double: $44–$53.
Just your basic downtown hotel, the Vedado offers competitive rates for being in the heart of old La Habana, but it's nothing to write home about. There's a post office in case you want to, and car rental facilities if you want to get out and about (you will). Rooms are comfortable but a little cramped, and while each has air conditioning, they lack a television.

Villa Daiquiri $38–$64   ★★★★

Carretera de Baconao, Km 25, ☎ *(53) 24849.*
Single: $38–$42. Double: $56–$64.
The 150 cabins look out over the sea or up to the mountains from their perch atop an S-shaped cliff above the beach, surrounded by green coastal vegetation. In spite of its situation in one of the island's least developed areas, the resort is well equipped with both a fresh water and salt water pool, game room, scuba diving center with equipment rental and instruction, horse, bike and motorcycle rentals, and there's even a post office.

Villa Tropico Resort $22–$35   ★★★

Villa Blanca Limite de Santa Cruz, Habana del Este, ☎ *(53) 64180.*
Single: $22–$26. Double: $29–$35.

This is one of the typical hotel/resorts constructed after the revolution, consisting of rather ugly concrete units in a pleasant setting on the beach. The gardens are actually quite nice, and there is a nice pool surrounded by a lawn on one side and an open air bar on the other. The units are well-equipped with air conditioning, television, and phone; and there are car rental facilities on site along with a tourist information bureau and a modest shop.

Apartments and Condominiums

Casas Villa Paraíso   **$140–$200**   ★ ★ ★ ★

Quinta Avenida y Calle 248, Marina Hemingway, ☎ (53) 7-336006.
Double: $140–$200.

Forty-two villas and 36 bungalows make up this resort—the prices quoted here sound rather steep, but they are per unit. A three bedroom townhouse is only US$274 in high season, so six people could stay here for just US$45 a night. That's a great deal for what is really a luxury resort. There are four restaurants, five bars, on-site medical services and child care, and the airy accommodations are set in charming tropical gardens right on the beach by the Marina. Of the many, many hotels named Paradise, this one comes close to deserving the name!

Low Cost Lodging

Hostal Valencia   **$22–$34**   ★ ★ ★ ★

Calle Oficios, 53, ☎ (53) 623801.
Double: $22–$34.

Set right in the heart of Old La Habana, this tiny hostel is exquisitely romantic. The rooms—each named after a Spanish province and each decorated in a unique style—face onto a central courtyard crowded with plants and birds in cages. The floors are tiled, not carpeted, and the walls far from perpendicular, but if you're like me, this will enhance, not detract from, the appeal of the place. Very limited dining to be had here, although the cafeteria serves up a good breakfast in the mornings.

Where to Eat

Fielding's Highest Rated Restaurants in Cuba

★★★★★	El Tocoroco	$12–$35
★★★★★	Floridita	$10–$25
★★★★	Bodeguita del Medio	$8–$22
★★★★	El Oasis	$5–$10
★★★★	La Cecilia	$12–$28
★★★★	La Cueva del Cameron	$8–$24
★★★★	Rancho King	$8–$15
★★★	A la Cubana	$10–$18
★★★	El Barracun	$10–$15
★★★	Papa's	$8–$20

Fielding's Special Restaurants in Cuba

★★★★★	El Tocoroco	$12–$35
★★★★	El Oasis	$5–$10
★★★	El Bodegón Criollo	$8–$15
★★★	Mi Casita	$8–$15

Fielding's Budget Restaurants in Cuba

★★★	Cafetería Cuba Centro	$5–$10
★★	Mesón el Palatino	$5–$10
★★	Mesón del Regidor	$5–$12
★★★	Dante	$8–$15
★★★	El Bodegón Criollo	$8–$15

Bodeguita del Medio $$$ ★★★★

Calle Empedrado, 207.
Latin American cuisine. Specialties: mojito (rum, crushed ice, mint, lemon juice, carbonated water).
Lunch: Noon–3 p.m, entrees $8–$15.
Dinner: 5-11 p.m., entrees $10–$22.

This restaurant was one of Ernest Hemingway's favorites, and still serves the best mojito in La Habana. The atmosphere is exuberant; patrons are encouraged to sign their names on the wall. The roof terrace is a beautiful setting for a meal, and the food here is excellent. For some reason there's an unusually wide selection of vegetarian dishes.

El Barracun $$ ★★★

Calle La Rampa.
Latin American cuisine.
Lunch: from noon, entrees $10–$15.
Dinner: until midnight, entrees $10–$15.

This is an excellent traditional Cuban restaurant set in one of the most elegant hotels in the city, specializing in seafood and fish dishes.

El Oasis $ ★★★★

Paseo Martí, 256.
African cuisine. Specialties: hummus and lamb.

Housed in the Arab Cultural Institute, this unusual restaurant offers tasty Arabic food. Traditional lamb and couscous dishes, as well as the hummus, are recommended. The air conditioning is extremely cold, to the point that you'll want to take a sweater or jacket.

El Tocoroco $$$ ★★★★★

Calle 18 Esquina 3ª, ☎ (53) 7-334530.
Latin American cuisine. Specialties: Seafood.
Lunch: from 12:30 p.m., entrees $12–$25.
Dinner: until midnight, entrees $12–$35.

Named after the national bird of Cuba, El Tocoroco is regularly rated as the best restaurant in La Habana. It is set in an elegant colonial mansion in the old city, with a beautiful terrace. The food is exquisite, especially the fresh seafood caught each day locally.

Floridita $$$ ★★★★★

Calle Obispo y Calle Montserrat.
Latin American cuisine. Specialties: Seafood; lobster, fish and shrimp in garlic sauce.
Lunch: Noon to 3 p.m., entrees $10–$16.
Dinner: 5:30 p.m.–11 p.m., entrees $12–$25.

The Floridita was another favorite of Hemingway's, a place where he consumed innumerable daiquiris. They are excellent here, but expensive, about $5 a drink. The restaurant is one of the best spots for seafood in all of La Habana. Decor is swanky, velvet, low lights, a "Bogart atmosphere."

La Cecilia $$$ ★★★★

Quinta Avenida entre Calles 110 y 111, ☎ (53) 7-331562.
Latin American cuisine. Specialties: Traditional Cuban food.

Lunch: from noon, entrees $12–$18.
Dinner: until midnight, entrees $12–$28.

One of the nicest restaurants in the capital, La Cecilia is a bright, airy place with bamboo-covered walls and potted palms all over the place. The food is good traditional Cuban cuisine, a little expensive, but the fresh seafood is outstanding. There is a lovely but small terrace with a few tables outside, and a piano bar.

La Cova $ ★★

Calle 248 y Quinta Avenida, Marina Hemingway, ☎ (53) 7-331150.
Italian cuisine. Specialties: Pasta dishes.

Set in the rather touristy Hemingway Marina, this is one of the La Habana area's best Italian restaurants (the second most popular brand of restaurant after native Cuban food).

La Torre $$ ★★★

Edificio Fosca, Calle 35, Vedado.
Latin American cuisine. Specialties: Traditional Cuban food.
Lunch: entrees $8–$15.
Dinner: entrees $8–$15.

One of the most pleasant restaurants in the Vedado area, La Torre serves up good traditional Cuban dishes with plenty of black beans and rice, as well as fish and seafood. The view from the eighth floor is quite spectacular.

Papa's $$ ★★★

Calle 258 y Quinta Avenida, Marina Hemingway, ☎ (53) 7-331150.
Latin American cuisine. Specialties: Seafood and fish.
Lunch: from noon, entrees $8–$15.
Dinner: until midnight, entrees $8–$20.

Another restaurant in the modern Hemingway Marina, Papa's specializes in seafood and fish dishes. There is also a grill, serving hamburgers and quick snacks, open from 9 a.m. to 1 a.m. There are interesting murals of marine life on the walls of the restaurant.

The West

Piñar del Rio

Piñar del Rio is the name of the province that occupies Cuba's western tip, as well as the capital city of the province. Thanks to abundant rainfall from the rain clouds drawn to the Sierra de los Organos, this is one of the most fertile and biodiverse regions on the island. The Soroa region in the hills north of San Cristobal is prized for its mineral waters; there is a spa/resort with spring baths and massages available, also a splendid botanical garden that has a wide selection of Cuba's 8000 plant species, including more than 250 species of orchids, as well as hummingbirds, dragonflies, and other tropical insects (all the literature assures the visitor that Cuba has no poisonous animals).

A couple of hours further west is the stunning **Viñales valley**, a verdant pancake-flat plain dotted with palms and unusual haystack-shaped limestone hills called *mogotes*. The hills are riddled with caves and underground streams; many can be explored and there are guided tours of some. The **Cueva del Indio** four miles outside the town of Viñales offers boat tours for $2. The floor of the valley is actually green with tobacco plants; Piñar del Rio is the main tobacco-farming province. Throughout the area you will see *vegas*, the steep-roofed barns in which the tobacco leaves are dried. In the city of Piñar del Rio there are numerous cigar factories that can be visited and even a **Museo del Tabaco**.

Zapata Peninsula

The entire **Zapata Peninsula** on the southeastern coast is a national park, a 1600 square-mile reserve consisting mostly of dense mangrove swamps teeming with tropical life of all kinds. The rare freshwater manatee is to be found here in the wild, while a crocodile farm on Laguna de Tesoro (Treasure Lake) breeds 40,000 of the toothy critters at any one time. The bee hummingbird, the smallest bird in the world, as well as the colorful tocororo, the national bird, and countless other species nest in this area. The network of cenotes, or flooded sinkholes and caves, is the most developed in the Caribbean, although most of the caverns are inaccessible except to serious spelunkers. Nature lovers can even stay in the park; the Villa Guamá hotel provides accommodations on the shore of the lake in individual cabins constructed in the style of the native bohios.

Varadero

Varadero Beach, one of the most spectacular in the entire Caribbean, is Cuba's premier resort area. The narrow strip of land, formally known as the Hicacos Peninsula, has an uninterrupted 12-mile-long golden beach on each side; a desert island paradise that is the beginning, middle and end of many visitors' Cuban itinerary. The beach was originally developed in the 1920s as a playground for wealthy Americans. The delightfully inane travel book from the time by Basil Woon, *When It's Cocktail Time in Cuba*, describes the project this way: "Varadero Beach, or part of it, has lately been purchased by a group headed by Irenée Du Pont and work is progressing toward making the place into a costly private club for executives of General Motors and other Du Pont interests. When finished this will probably be the largest private club in the world. It will have its own port of entry for yachts, its own private casino, a large clubhouse, and a number of homes will be built there by American executives who will make the place their winter home." And indeed Varadero became the standard for opulence of the time, its magnificent art deco hotel and the Du Pont mansion the scene of idle rich frivolity without any peer ever. After the revolution the entire resort was nationalized, turned into a worker's resort, and opened to all Cubans. Now it is again an exclusive temple to hedonism of a slightly lower tone, as tourists from all over the world come to bask in the golden sunshine and splash in the warm, azure water. There are golf courses, horseback riding excursions, hunting and fishing, as well as every water sport known to man available here, and accommodations ranging from simple high-rise hotels to all-inclusive resorts.

Off the northeastern tip of the peninsula is the **Archpiélago de Sabana**, a string of uninhabited small islands and islets that are a favorite venue for sailors, windsurfers and divers. A few miles due south of the Varadero area is **Cárdenas**, a small sugar town that is far off the beaten tourist path and a nice respite from the holiday scene. There is a museum of the sugar industry in the former home of Jose Echevarría, a student revolutionary leader who was killed by Batista's regime in 1957. **Matanzas**, the nearest large city, has attractive colonial architecture and a network of bridges spanning the two rivers that bisect the town. Popular with writers and poets in the late 19th century (the city was once known as "the Athens of Cuba"), Matanzas has numerous libraries and art galleries and is a feast for those in search of Cuban culture.

What to See

Theme/Amusement Parks

Parque Josone　　　　　　　　　　　　　　　　★ ★ ★ ★

　　Calle 56 y Calle 1, Varadero Beach.
　　Hours open: Dawn–midnight

Josone Park is an ideal spot for a walk under the shady trees beside the lake that is crowded with ducks, swans and flamingos. But there are also five restaurants, a couple of bars, bowling, mini-golf, billiards, pleasure boats, bikes, and musical performances in this Cuban version of an amusement park.

Tours

Neptune's Cave   ★★★

Carretera de Matanzas, Varadero Beach.
Hours open: 10 a.m.–5 p.m.

This underground cave system, renamed to make it more attractive to visitors, is actually very interesting. There is a lagoon inside, excellent examples of stalagmites and stalactites, some Indian petroglyphs, and a display commemorating its use as a clandestine hospital during the revolution.

Where to Stay

Hotels and Resorts

Atabey Hotel   **$47–$76**   ★★★

Calle 61 y Tercera Avenida, ☎ (53) 63013.
Single: $47–$57. Double: $63–$76.

With its sister hotel, the Siboney, the Atabey represents the best value on Varadero Beach. It's modern and functional, and the facilities are definitely on the luxurious side, but, hey, you're on Varadero... you won't be spending much time in the hotel. The pool/games room/shopping center complex is shared with the Siboney. There are car, bicycle, and moped rental facilities on site.

Club Tropical   **$81–$125**   ★★★

Avenida Primera y Calle 22, ☎ (53) 663915.
Single: $81–$94. Double: $108–$125.

One of the best values on Varadero Beach (yes, it's still quite expensive, but all things are relative), this hotel is situated on the beach right in the center of the oldest part of Varadero itself, so it's a great spot if you enjoy walking out in the not so touristy part of town in the cool evenings after a raucous day at the beach. Accommodations are simple but comfortable; each room has a phone and television, and they are quite spacious. Many residents of La Habana stay here when they get away to Varadero for a break.

Hotel Bella Costa   **$104–$161**   ★★★★

Avenida las Americas, ☎ (53) 7-216936.
Single: $104–$115. Double: $138–$161.

A modern hotel with all the luxury qualities you'd expect from a resort on the finest beach in the Caribbean, the Bella Costa has marble floors throughout, an enormous (clean!) swimming pool, and a very good restaurant. All manner of water sports and recreational activities, as well as a children's entertainment program. As good as the other resorts on the strip, and a little less expensive.

Hotel LTI-Tuxpan   **$80–$150**   ★★★★

Avenida de las Americas, km 3.5, ☎ (53) 66200, FAX (53) 66219.
Single: $80–$100. Double: $130–$150.

An extremely modern resort right on Varadero Beach, with every room equipped with air conditioning, satellite television, and a sea-view balcony. The large swimming pool has a swim-up bar, there is a snack bar and two restaurants, room service, a well-stocked gift shop, car, bicycle and motorcycle rental; in short, a full service holiday resort.

nternacional Hotel	$64–$122	★ ★ ★ ★

Carretera Dupont, ☎ *(53) 66180.*
Single: $64–$86. Double: $98–$122.

This is one of the grand hotels built in the 1950s when Varadero Beach was the playground of American millionaires, and it still retains its elegance. Nowadays it's also a full-service tourist resort of that rare kind, with class. Excellent amenities including rooms with a balcony overlooking the ocean are supplemented by comprehensive recreational opportunities including scuba diving, horseback riding, hunting, fishing, moped and bicycle rental. Very good cabaret in the nightclub, decent food in the restaurant, and generous drinks in the bar make this a good choice for a stay at Varadero.

Melia Varadero	$86–$198	★ ★ ★ ★ ★

Autopista Sur, ☎ *(53) 7-337162, FAX (53) 7-337012.*
Single: $86–$125. Double: $120–$198.

A true luxury resort with lush gardens, glass elevators, interior fountains and plants, aquariums with multicolored fish in the lobby. All rooms have air conditioning, telephone, satellite television, music center, minibar, safe, and terrace with sea view. Complete offering of recreational opportunities, including sailing, windsurfing, scuba diving, horseback riding, as well as child care and children's entertainment program. Spanish operator Melia is expert at luxury beach resorts around the world and they have not failed here.

Paraiso-Puntarenas Resort	$84–$140	★ ★ ★

Avenida Kawama Final, ☎ *(53) 62993.*
Single: $84–$105. Double: $112–$140.

A thoroughly modern complex built just 10 miles from Varadero Beach in 1990, this complex is not quite an all-inclusive, but it does offer everything on site that the vacationer could wish for, including a supervised children's program, scuba diving equipment rental and instruction, and all manner of recreational activities. There are four restaurants and six bars on site, as well as a lavish cabaret in the nightclub each evening. The rooms are well-appointed, including a television, and the availability of nonsmoking rooms is a welcome rarity in Cuba.

Sol Palmeras	$78–$192	★ ★ ★ ★

Autopista Sur, ☎ *(53) 66110, FAX (53) 66353.*
Single: $78–$116. Double: $114–$192.

Managed jointly by Cubatur and the Spanish hotel giant Melia Sol, this is a large modern resort-type hotel on a par with any beach resort in the world. The rooms are spacious and airy, most with beach views, and the recreational facilities are endless. Sailing, windsurfing, scuba diving, beach volleyball, and lying around the pool clutching a cuba libre are all on offer, in a somewhat busy environment, but clean and professional. A good place for a hard core beach vacation.

Superclub Varadero   **$118–$101**   ★★★★★

Avenida las Americas km 3, ☎ *(53) 66180, (905) 771-8664.*
Single: $118. Double: $101.

The monster of them all on Varadero Beach, the Superclub sprawls over 100 acres of glorious beachfront. An all-inclusive resort (note that prices quoted are per person), Superclub offers suites-only accommodations, each with its own kitchen, fridge, satellite television, and balcony overlooking the ocean. A safety deposit box is also provided in the lobby. The amenities are fantastic—the best scuba diving center on the island is here, there are classes and rentals in windsurfing, parasailing, and water-skiing, horseback treks, motorcycle and bicycle rentals, and a huge swimming pool to cool off in after a long day. The food served in the restaurant and three barbecue bars is great—lots of fresh seafood—and the nightlife in the resort's disco and nightclub is jumping!

Apartments and Condominiums

Hotel Atlantico   **$54–$97**   ★★★

Avenida de las Terrazas, ☎ *(53) 2551.*
Single: $54–$68. Double: $78–$97.

This is a good spot to stay if you want to be close to the golden sands of Varadero Beach without the madding crowds of the main resort area. Called an "Aparthotel," the rooms are self-catering, although a clean and simple cafeteria serves a good breakfast in the mornings. There is a store owned by the hotel across the street where you can by basic foodstuffs.

Where to Eat

Dante   **$$**   ★★★

Calle 56 y 1ª, Josone Park, ☎ *(53) 566204.*
Italian cuisine. Specialties: Pasta dishes.
Lunch: from noon, entrees $8–$15.
Dinner: until midnight, entrees $8–$15.

A nice place to relax after a hard day or evening's playtime in the amusement park. Dante serves up generous portions of spaghetti and meat sauce and other pasta dishes.

El Anzuelo   **$**   ★★

Calle 56 y 1ª, Josone Park, ☎ *(53) 663647.*
Latin American cuisine.

Open very late, serving good grilled meats and fish and cold beers. A great place for a casual but very tasty meal. Try the Parillada la Campana—the most expensive item on the menu but so much grilled meat, beans, and vegetables that you probably will need to take some home.

El Bodegón Criollo   **$$**   ★★★

Avenida la Playa y Calle 40.
Latin American cuisine. Specialties: Grilled meats, Cuban traditional cooking.
Lunch: entrees $8–$15.

Dinner: entrees $8–$15.

A charming restaurant much patronized by the locals, El Bodegún Criollo is set in a coral rock house, the interior walls of which have been covered with graffiti in something of a Cuban tradition. Try the *bistec a la parilla* or *picadillo a la criollo*, for some good down home Cuban red meat dishes. There is no vegetarian item on the menu at this establishment.

El Palacete $$ ★★

Calle 56 y 1ª , Parque Josone, ☎ (53) 562933.
Latin American cuisine. Specialties: Traditional Cuban food.
Lunch: from noon, entrees $8–$15.
Dinner: until 2 a.m., entrees $8–$15.

A pleasant restaurant in a rather touristy environment—the Josone amusement park—this is actually one of the better places to eat in Varadero. Try the *chicharrones de viento* (similar to the pork rinds to which former President George Bush was partial) before ordering an entree of meat or fish.

Mi Casita $$ ★★★

Avenida la Playa entre Calles 11 y 12,
Latin American cuisine. Specialties: Seafood.
Lunch: prix fixe $8–$15.
Dinner: prix fixe $8–$15.

A very quaint locale to this inexpensive restaurant, set in a large coral rock house that used to be the vacation home of a rich American, with charming decor, antique furniture and artwork on the walls. Good simple food, usually fish or lobster.

Isla de Juventud

Sixty-five miles off the mainland and reachable by air or ferry, the **Isle of Youth** is home to some 60,000 people, and Cuba's major citrus producing region. Called Isla de Piños until 1978, the island takes its name now from the youth work-study programs run there by the government. Many students from all over the world, especially Africa, come stay on the island, so it has a character matching its name. The main town of **Nueva Gerona** has a number of hotels and resorts, and a couple of museums including El Presidio Modelo, the former high security prison where, at various times, José Martí and Fidel Castro were both imprisoned. **Playa Bibijagua** beach, east of Nueva Gerona, is one of the few black sand beaches in Cuba. There are several other excellent beaches on the island's east and west coasts, including **Punta del Este** in the east and **Punta Francés** in the southwest. Most of the south coast is inaccessible, covered by dense swamps. The **Cueva de Punta del Este** and the **Cueva de Caleta Grande** are two huge caves in the east of the island that offer some of the most prolific Indian petroglyphs anywhere in the Caribbean.

Where to Stay

Hotels and Resorts

Colony Hotel $36–$66   ★ ★ ★ ★

Carretera de la Siguanea, Km 41, ☎ *(53) 8181/8282.*

Single: $36–$44. Double: $52–$66.

A piece of history on Isla de Juventud, the Colony was built in 1958 and renovated from top to bottom in 1986. The grounds are spacious and lush, and the hotel is on the waterfront with its own private beach, offering a complete array of water sports, as well as horseback riding on the island and even hunting expeditions. Every room has a balcony facing the ocean as well as air conditioning. One of the best spots on the island.

Where to Eat

El Corderito $$ ★ ★ ★

Calle 39, Nueva Gerona.

Latin American cuisine. Specialties: Lamb.

Lunch: from 11 a.m., entrees $8–$15.

Dinner: until midnight, entrees $8–$15.

As its name suggests (El Corderito means "the little lamb") this restaurant specializes in rack of lamb, grilled to perfection, roast lamb, lamb chops...well, you get the picture. It's also the only dollar restaurant on the island outside the hotels.

Beaches

The beaches on the extreme western tip of the island along the **Bahía de Corrientes** and the **Península de Guanahacabibes** are among the most desolate and lovely, but swimming can be dangerous here due to strong ocean currents as the Atlantic and Caribbean come together. Besides the dense jungle nature reserves, there are also beautiful beaches on the Zapata Peninsula, among which the **Playa Larga** and **Playa Girón** beaches on the eastern end near the Bay of Pigs stand out, ringed as they are with sea-grape trees and palms. Offshore there is the tiny undeveloped cay of **Cayo Ernst Thálmann**, reached by ferry boat, with pristine sands and shallow, clear blue waters.

The Central Region

Cienfuegos

On the shore of the enormous Bahía Jagua in the south central part of the island is the city of **Cienfuegos**, sacked and looted countless times over the years by colonists from various nations as well as pirates and buccaneers. The plain behind the town and the Sierra de Trinidad mountains off to the southeast give the city a beautiful natural setting. Many of the street names are in French, a leftover of the French settlers that arrived here from Louisiana en masse in the 19th century. The Spanish-style Cathedral, topped with a rare octagonal cupola, is but one example of the charming colonial architecture here.

What to See

Palacio del Valle   ★★★
Calle Jagua, Cienfuegos.
Hours open: 9:30 a.m.–6 p.m.
The Palacio del Valle, built in 1917, is an extremely ornate building both inside and out, constructed in Moorish style. It now houses the Museo de Arte Decorativa (Museum of Decorative Art), with interesting displays of fabrics, murals, and furniture from the 18th and 19th centuries.

Theatre

Teatro Terry   ★★★
Parque Martí, Cienfuegos.
The Teatro Terry, named after American playwright Thomas Terry, who once lived in Cuba, is one of the most attractive theaters on the island. Originally built in 1895, the 900-seat theater was completely renovated in 1965, and offers an excellent modern venue for plays while retaining all its original colonial beauty.

Where to Stay

Hotel Faro Luna   **$37–$54**   ★★★★★
Carretera Pasacaballos, Km 18, ☎ *(53) 65582.*
Single: $37–$46. Double: $44–$54.
Pleasantly situated atop a wooded hill overlooking a horseshoe-shaped bay, this small hotel is a nice intimate setting much favored by honeymooners. The rooms are all air-conditioned, all have a balcony overlooking the ocean, the pool is big and clean, and there is a good selection of activities for the energetic, including scuba diving instruction, moped rental, and occasional dancing to live music in the restaurant.

Pasacaballos Hotel   **$22–$35**   ★★★
Pasacaballos, ☎ *(53) 8545.*
Single: $22–$26. Double: $29–$35.

Built in 1976, this modern hotel lies about 15 miles outside the southern city of Cienfuegos on the bay, overlooking the historic Fort Jagua. The rooms are small but comfortable, each with air conditioning, television and phone. There is a bar and nightclub as well as an inexpensive cafeteria and dining room. The swimming pool is salt water. Nice views out over the bay, excellent beach access.

Where to Eat

La Cueva del Camerón   **$$$**   ★★★★

Calle 37, 4, ☎ (53) 338238.
Latin American cuisine. Specialties: Fish and seafood.
Lunch: from noon, entrees $8–$15.
Dinner: until 2 a.m., entrees $12–$24.
As its name (Cueva del Camerón means "Cave of the Shrimp") would suggest, this restaurant specializes in food of the mollusk variety. The shrimp *al mojo de ajo, a la parilla*, and in ranchera sauce, are all excellent, and the lobster is sublime. The building in which the restaurant is housed is a former colonial mansion, all tall windows, tiled floors, and elegant artwork.

Mesûn el Palatino   **$**   ★★

Avenida 54, 2514,
Latin American cuisine. Specialties: Snacks and juices.
Lunch: from 9 a.m., entrees $5–$10.
Dinner: until 7 p.m., entrees $5–$10.
Well situated right downtown, this is a good spot to drop in for a light lunch, snack or a cool drink. The tavern itself is over 150 years old, a low, flat-roofed building with charming colonades on all sides.

Trinidad

Fifty miles farther east lies the spectacular city of **Trinidad**, one of two Cuban cities (La Habana is the other) declared World Heritage Sites by the United Nations. The entire city was declared a national monument by the government in the 1950s, and restoration efforts have restored it to its old world glory. The **Plaza Mayor** is the central square in the town, surrounded by imposing town houses, most of which are now museums. The **Museo de Arquitectura** has displays explaining the development of Spanish-style architecture; the **Museo Humboldt**, named after a German scientist who once resided in the town, is a repository of natural history artifacts; the 18th century **Palacio Brunet** houses artwork and everyday objects from Cuban society in the 18th and 19th centuries; and the **Museo de Archaeología** has exhibits detailing the various pre-Columbian Cuban cultures.

North of the city are the **Escambray mountains**, a picturesque range rich in Cuba's omnipresent flora and fauna, atop which sits the small spa town of **Topes de Collantes**, long a destination of those seeking to benefit from its rejuvenating natural springs. In the mountains are also a number of hunting

eserves—check with your hotel in Trinidad for trips. About 40 miles to the
ortheast is another beautiful colonial town, **Sancti Spiritus**, the provincial
apital, which is the site of the **Museo de Esclavitud** (Slave Museum) and the
ldest church in Cuba. Outside Sancti Spiritus is **Zaza Lake**, a man-made res-
rvoir that offers excellent large-mouth bass fishing.

Street Names in Trinidad

When asking for directions in Trinidad, you need to be aware that the lo-
als still use prerevolutionary names, while the maps and addresses in the
our guide material you pick up—as well as the streets themselves—will have
he new names. Here is a chart converting the principal streets.

Old Name	New Name
Calle de la Gloria	Calle Gustavo Izquierdo
Calle Desengaño	Calle Simón Bolivar
Calle Gutiérrez	Calle Antonio Maceo
Calle Rosario	Calle Francisco J. Zerquera
Calle Encarnación	Calle Vicente Suyama
Calle Guaurabo	Calle Pablo Pichs Girón
Calle del Cristo	Calle Fernando Hernández Echerri
Calle Jesús María	Calle José Martí
Calle Real de Jigüe	Calle Rubén Martínez Villena
Calle de la Media Luna	Calle Ernesto Valdés Muñoz
Calle San Procopio	Calle Lino Pérez
Calle Reforma	Calle Anastacio Cárdenas
Calle Boca	Calle Prio Ginart
Calle San José	Calle Ciro Redondo
Calle Alameda	Calle Jesús Menéndez
Calle Santa Ana	Calle José Mendoza
Calle Santo Domingo	Calle Camilo Cienfuegos
Calle Lirio	Calle Abel Santamaría
Calle Guásima	Calle Julio A. Mella

Where to Stay

Hotels and Resorts

otel La Granjita   **$40–$52**   ★ ★ ★

Carretera Maleza, Km 2.5, ☎ *(53) 26059.*
Single: $40. Double: $52.

Off the beaten path in the interior, this small hotel is surrounded by lush tropical vegetation, mango and orange trees, and is built in the Cuban rustic style—the buildings have palm-thatched roofs and wooden walls that facilitate keeping cool. There is also air conditioning in each of the rooms, a swimming pool that is usually green, and good recreational activities including squash, bowling and horseback treks.

Rancho Hatuey   **$40–$52**   ★ ★ ★

Carretera Central, Km 383, ☎ *(53) 626015.*
Single: $40. Double: $52.
Attractive mainly for its location just outside Sancti Spiritus atop a thickly wooded hill, this hotel offers double rooms or bungalows with living room; all have air conditioning and television. There is a fresh water pool but it's not well kept. There's a squash court and baby sitting services, as well as on-site car rental and a very inexpensive restaurant.

Where to Eat

Mesûn del Regidor   **$**   ★ ★

Calle SimÚn Bolivar.
Latin American cuisine. Specialties: Chicken, fish.
Lunch: from 9 a.m., entrees $5–$12.
Dinner: until 9 p.m., entrees $5–$12.
A very limited selection, but good wholesome Cuban food—chicken, fish, pork, beans, and rice—at economical prices. Also some Spanish dishes, including a pseudo paella.

Restaurante Trinidad   **$$**   ★ ★ ★

Calle Maceo.
Latin American cuisine. Specialties: Traditional Cuban cuisine.
Lunch: from 11 a.m., entrees $8–$15.
Dinner: until 10 p.m., entrees $8–$15.
A charming setting in an old colonial house and robust creole cooking make this a good choice for a meal in the beautiful eponymous city of Trinidad.

Camagüey

The agricultural city of **Camagüey** is the largest in Cuba's interior. There are numerous museums and historic plazas here, among the most noteworthy of which are the **Iglesia de la Soledad church**, built in 1775; the cathedral, begun in 1530 but displaying architecture of every period since then; and the **Casa Natal de Ignacio Agramonte**. This, the birthplace of one of Cuba's national heroes who led the war of liberation from Spain, is an excellent example of Spanish colonial architecture, now housing a museum with many exhibits on the war as well as on Camagüey's storied past, which includes several Indian and slave rebellions. The **Museo Ignacio Agramonte** is one of the largest and most comprehensive historical records in Cuba. The **Parque Agramonte** (almost every major feature of the town bears the rebel leader's name) is studded with giant earthenware jars used to cool water before the advent of electricity, but looking as though Ali Baba and his 40 thieves might jump out at any moment.

Off the northern Atlantic coast of Camagüey province is the archipelago of the same name, a string of cays that provides unparalleled diving and snorkeling—the Cuban tourist board claims the area is home to the largest coral reef in the world, although the Australians would probably dispute that. **Cayo Coco**, the most developed of these, is a true tropical paradise, surrounded by crystal clear blue waters and ringed with towering palm trees. Most of the cayes are undeveloped, however, and their beaches are among the most beautiful and uncrowded on the island.

What to See

Museums and Exhibits

Casa Natal de Ignacio Agramonte ★★★
Avenida Ignacio Agramonte, Camagüey.
Hours open: 10 a.m.–5 p.m.
The famed rebel leader's home is now a museum, and offers an excellent look at not only the life of the man, but also a good example of a simple, 19th century Cuban home (as opposed to so many of the museums, which are in stately colonial palaces and mansions).

Museo Ignacio Agramonte ★★★★
Avenida de los M·rtires, Camagüey.
Hours open: 10 a.m.–5 p.m.
This is one of the biggest and best museums in Cuba. Named after one of the nation's great revolutionary heroes who was born in the city, the museum is housed in a 19th century building that was formerly a military garrison. It has excellent displays on modern Cuban history and archaeology, and an excellent collection of Cuban art.

Where to Stay

Hotels and Resorts

Camaguey Hotel $20–$35 ★★
Carretera Central Este km 4.5, ☎ *(53) 72015.*
Single: $20–$26. Double: $26–$35.
A fairly modern hotel built in the 1970s, the Camaguey Hotel is simple to the point of almost being rudimentary—rooms all have private bathroom, phone and radio, but most lack a television. There are two bars and a nightclub that offers a so-so cabaret, and a gift shop with basic goods. Situated two miles outside Camaguey on a main road, this hotel's biggest selling point is its inexpensive rates.

Club Caracol $53–$72 ★★★★
Playa Santa Lucía, Nuevitas, ☎ *(53) 48302.*
Single: $53. Double: $72.
The 150 rooms are divided into bungalows of four rooms each in this moderately priced hotel on the beach. There's a nice sized swimming pool with a swim-up bar,

scuba diving center, horseback riding and bicycle rental. The restaurant is quite elegant, and there's a nightclub with a modest cabaret show. A great getaway spot.

Club Coral   **$45–$65**   ★★★

Playa Santa Lucía, Nuevitas, ☎ *(53) 48130.*
Single: $45. Double: $65.
Set in a huge estate covered in lush vegetation and palm trees, the Club Coral is a good bargain resort on the Atlantic coast. There's plenty to do—waterskiing, scuba diving, windsurfing and sailing, fishing expeditions, moped and bike rental, a discotheque and live music in the nightclub. The rooms, including 12 bungalows and eight suites are comfortable if not luxurious, with oversized beds and color television in each.

Villa Tararaco   **$31–$48**   ★★★★

Playa Santa Lucía, Nuevitas, ☎ *(53) 36222.*
Single: $31–$38. Double: $41–$48.
This hotel only rates two stars from the Cuban tourist board, but that's because it doesn't have some of the frills—beauty shop, post office, etc.—that other resorts have. Nevertheless it's a very comfortable hotel with a scuba diving and snorkeling center and water sports on the impossibly beautiful beach. You won't believe the whiteness of the fine sand and the clarity of the water, as you lounge under the palm umbrellas. The restaurant is simple but adequate, and the set breakfast is just US$3.

Where to Eat

Las Brisas   **$$**   ★★★

Playa Santa Lucía, ☎ *(53) 336187.*
Latin American cuisine.
Lunch: from 10 a.m., entrees $8–$15.
Dinner: until 9 p.m., entrees $8–$20.
As its name (Las Brisas means "the breezes,") this restaurant is extremely airy, in fact it is better suited for lunch than dinner in the winter months. Still, even with the chill there's something magical about eating freshly caught snapper or lobster right on the beach, the sound of the surf just yards away.

Rancho King   **$$**   ★★★★

Calle San Miguel.
Latin American cuisine. Specialties: Traditional Cuban cuisine.
Lunch: from noon, entrees $8–$15.
Dinner: until midnight, entrees $8–$15.
Don't be put off by the hokey-sounding name; this is a great spot to eat. Traditional Cuban dishes par excellence, try the *lonjas de cerdo al jugo* (roast pork chops) or the *pollo en salsa* (chicken in a spicy sauce with black beans). Strolling guitar players singing traditional trova folk songs add to the ambience.

Via Appia   **$**   ★★

Playa Santa Lucía, ☎ *(53) 336101.*
Italian cuisine.
Situated just outside Camagüey, on the beach, this Italian restaurant serves up generous portions of decent pasta, though it's not great and will remind you once again

that the safest thing is to do as the Romans when in Rome (i.e., wait to eat spaghetti until you're in Italy!)

Cayo Largo

This small island is exclusively used for tourism; there are five resort hotels that all share swimming pool, restaurants and bars and water sports facilities. The island, reached by air from La Habana (round trip fare U.S.$75) is very relaxing, but there's not much to do other than play on the beach. A day trip to nearby **Cayo Rico** can be arranged through your hotel for U.S.$37, where tame iguanas roam unworried by human visitors.

Where to Stay

Villa Capricho	**$66–$120**	★ ★ ★ ★ ★

Cayo Largo, ☎ (53) 513033, FAX (53) 332108.
Single: $66–$120.

The Villa Capricho on Cayo Largo has to be one of the most romantic resorts in the entire caribbean. The islet is reached by air from La Habana (US$75 round trip) and there's nothing there except for this and a couple of other hotels. The rooms are actually small bungalows dotted through lush tropical gardens, complete with thatched roof and hammock outside the door. The hotel is situated on the beach, and there is an abundance of watersports for those who find soaking up the sun not quite energetic enough. The low price quoted here is for independent reservations; the $120 figure is per person for an all-inclusive (three meals and air transpot from the mainland) package offered by **Turcimex** (☎ *228230*).

Beaches

Rancho Luna beach just outside the city of Cienfuegos is one of the best on the south coast, the seabed sloping gently out to sea for several hundred feet. The **Playa Ancón** beach, which stretches away to the south from Trinidad, is a gorgeous strand of golden palm tree-lined sand that has so far escaped the modern development that plagues so many beaches in the Caribbean. The Camagüey archipelago's cayes are an uninterrupted string of golden beaches; many are quite developed, but the more intrepid traveler who is willing to hire a boat can reach the uninhabited ones. **Playa Santa Lucía** is almost 10 miles long, with palms all along it to provide shade, and is usually frequented only by divers exploring the coral reefs there. **Cayo Guajaba** and **Cayo Sabinal**

are two small islets that can be reached for a day trip from Santa Lucía. In the otherwise uninspiring province of Ciego de Avila (loosely translated as The Blind Guy from Avila), **La Tinaja beach** and **XI Festival** are two lovely beaches that are well off the beaten path, near the small town of Morón.

The East

Santiago de Cuba

The second largest and third oldest community in Cuba, **Santiago** was its first capital and in many ways is the most important city in the island. Considered the birthplace of the movement for independence from Spain, it is also the site of Castro's first attack on the Moncada army barracks in 1953. Touring Santiago means making something of a pilgrimage to the revolution and Cuban nationalism in general. *De rigeur* is a trip to the **Santa Efigenia** cemetery, where Céspedes and Martí are buried, and to the **Moncada barracks** themselves—like many military installations of the Batista days it is now a school, but has a display chronicling Castro's attack, having preserved even the bullet holes from it. The **Museo de Clandestinidad** (Museum of Clandestine Activity) is an unusual exhibit of subversive and guerilla tactics, and the **Museo Hermanos País**, an exhibit on the lives of the País brothers who organized the resistance to Batista in the city prior to Castro's return from Mexico, is another interesting monument to the resistance.

The main square in town, the **Parque Céspedes**, is the site of the original home of Diego de Velásquez, built in 1516. It is now the **Museo Colonial** (Colonial Museum), with comprehensive displays on every era of Cuban history. Another very good museum is the **Museo Bacardí**, founded by the godfather of the rum clan. The **Fortaleza del Morro** fortress, built in 1643, is an impressive sight and offers impressive views south along the coast. It now houses the **Museo de la Piratería** (Piracy Museum), with displays of ancient cannons, cutlasses and muskets. Known in Cuba as the most Caribbean of its cities, Santiago is definitely the most multiethnic, thanks to waves of immigration of African slaves, French Haitians, in addition to the Spaniards. The cuisine reflects this, as you will find dishes cooked with red beans and garlic more typical of other islands than of the rest of Cuba.

What to See

City Celebrations

Festival del Caribe ★★★★★

Citywide, Santiago de Cuba.
Open: April 16–19
More enjoyable even than Carnaval (in this city or anywhere else in Cuba), the Festival del Caribe is a citywide celebration of Santiago's African roots. There is music and dancing everywhere, and the local young men and women dress up in traditional costumes. Much rum is consumed at this event.

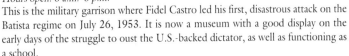

Moncada Barracks   ★★★

Avenida de los Libertadores, Santiago de Cuba.

Hours open: 8 a.m.–6 p.m.

This is the military garrison where Fidel Castro led his first, disastrous attack on the Batista regime on July 26, 1953. It is now a museum with a good display on the early days of the struggle to oust the U.S.-backed dictator, as well as functioning as a school.

Museums and Exhibits

Fortaleza Matachín   ★★★

Carretera de Baracoa, Baracoa.

Hours open: 10 a.m.–5 p.m.

One of the forts guarding the isolated city of Baracoa, the Matachín has been turned in to a museum with displays of the region's history. The views from the battlements over the Atlantic Ocean are spectacular, and the breeze up there will blow your cobwebs away. One of the better sites in a generally quite dull town.

Museo Barcardí   ★★★

Calle Aguilera, Santiago de Cuba.

Hours open: 8 a.m.–10 p.m.

Formerly a home of the rum giant, this colonial house is now a museum featuring exhibits on Cuban art and culture from pre-Columbian times to the Revolution. There are several interesting displays of Cuban art from the 19th century.

Museo Colonial   ★★★★

Parque Céspedes, Santiago de Cuba.

Hours open: 8 a.m.–6 p.m.

This museum is housed in the original home of the conqueror Diego de Vel·squez, built in 1516 and the oldest building on the island. After the Revolution the house was used as office space but has since been restored and houses interesting exhibits on life in Cuba in the 16th, 17th, and 18th centuries.

Museo de la Clandestinidad   ★★★

Calle Padre Pico, Santiago de Cuba.

Hours open: 9 a.m–6 p.m.

The Museum of Clandestine Activity, besides having the most intriguing name of any museum anywhere, is a great exhibit on the citizens' underground struggle against Batista in the early days of the Revolution. Fittingly, the building housing the museum is a former headquarters of the feared and hated secret police of the Batista regime. The museum is at the top of an ancient flight of steps, from the top of which there are great views of the whole city.

Museo de la Piratería   ★★★

Carretera L. Dacnesse, Santiago de Cuba.

Hours open: 9 a.m.–6 p.m.

This ancient fortress, built on the cliffs overlooking the entrance to the Bahía de Santiago, was built in 1643. It survived many attacks over the years, including one in 1662 by the notorious pirate Henry Morgan, who is one of the buccaneers commemorated inside in the Museum of Piracy. this is a good display with cutlasses, flintlock muskets, and old maps. The fortress is a few miles south of the city itself.

Music

Casa de la Trova ★★★

Calle Heredia, 206, Santiago de Cuba.
Hours open: Noon–midnight
This is, with the Casa de Trova in Trinidad, one of the most interesting venues for traditional Cuban music, dance, and theater. You can watch a performance of *son* or *nueva trova*, a play, or hear poetry readings almost every day. Admission is free.

Parks and Gardens

Gran Piedra ★★★

Carretera de Pujol, Santiago de Cuba.
Atop the mountain of the same name is the Gran Piedra (Great Rock), a lava boulder estimated to weigh 63,000 tons. From the 4000-foot summit you can see all the way to Jamaica and Haiti. The rock itself is ascended by means of a flight of more than 400 steps carved into the stone.

Tours

Carretera la Farola ★★★

Baracoa.
The city of Baracoa, the oldest on the island, having been founded in 1510, was until a few years ago inaccessible by land—visitors had to enter by sea or by air (this explains why Santiago, La Habana, and others quickly eclipsed Baracoa in importance). In the 1960s the government built La Farola, an incredible feat of engineering that is a 20-mile stretch of road hung on the side of the cliffs by concrete pillars and columns.

Where to Stay

Hotels and Resorts

Hotel Los Galeones $75–$100   ★★★★★

Carretera a Chivirico, ☎ *(53) 26160.*
Single: $75–$85. Double: $90–$100.
This delightful if rather pricey little hotel sits atop a mountain that plunges into the ocean below, affording its handful of guests what is in effect a private beach. Lying around the small pool under the endless blue sky is a very idyllic experience. The hotel is one Cuba's International Scuba Diving Centers, and has extensive facilities for that sport, including a separate swimming pool for training. The bright, airy rooms all have balconies, tiled floors, but little in the way of modern conveniences, such as telephones and televisions. For some, that may be the most attractive feature of the place.

Hotel Santiago de Cuba $69–$121   ★★★★

Carretera Las Americas y Cuarta, ☎ *(53) 42656.*
Single: $69–$84. Double: $89–$121.
This is a great hotel to stay in if you plan to travel around the Santiago area, rather than just lay on the beach, as it's a good 10 minutes from the ocean but conveniently located for other things right in the center of town. The 15-story hotel has

all the modern conveniences, including an excellent gym/sauna/pool facility, mini-bar and music center in each room, dry cleaning service, car and bicycle rental, shops, a quick-service (not quite fast food but close) grill/snack bar, and a charming piano bar for relaxing after a busy day sightseeing.

Hotel Versalles   **$48–$77**   ★★

Alturas de Versalles, Carretera del Morro, ☎ *(53) 91016.*
Single: $48–$53. Double: $66–$77.

The only thing this hotel has going for it is the magnificent view over the city from its lofty perch in the Alturas on the outskirts of town. The rooms all have air conditioning and a balcony, but they are spartan, with old furniture and bare walls. The pool is a disconcerting shade of green, and overall the place is overpriced and not at all great.

LTI Los Corales   **$30–$60**   ★★★

Carretera de Baconao, Playa Cazonal, ☎ *(53) 7191.*
Single: $30–$39. Double: $48–$60.

A nice mid-range hotel on the beach outside Santiago, the Los Corales has clean, airy rooms, most looking out on the dense coastal vegetation that surrounds the hotel, all with air conditioning and terrace. There are abundant recreational opportunities, including scuba diving instruction and equipment rental, a games room, and bike and motorcycle rental.

Lodge

Villa la Gran Piedra   **$28–$44**   ★★★★

Carretera de la Gran Piedra, Km 14, ☎ *(53) 5913.*
Single: $28–$37. Double: $37–$44.

Set in Gran Piedra National Park almost 4000 feet above sea level, this resort is a breathtakingly beautiful and peaceful getaway. The cabins are squat and not that pretty themselves, but the view from the resort as well as the rock itself is the best on the island. The interior accommodations are comfortable, but there's no pool, television, or in-room phones. Unless you're a real fan of nature, you'll probably be satisfied with two or three days here.

Where to Eat

A la Cubana   **$$**   ★★★

Avenida las Américas, 10 con Calle M.
Latin American cuisine. Specialties: Traditional Cuban food, Italian.
Lunch: 10 a.m., entrees $10–$18.
Dinner: until 9 p.m., entrees $10–$18.

Excellent service and good food at this restaurant. The hotel in which it is situated also permits nonresidents to use the swimming pool.

Cafetería Cuba Centro   **$**   ★★★

Carretera del Aeropuerto, Km 1, ☎ *(53) 691476.*
Latin American cuisine. Specialties: Snacks, juices.
Lunch: 8:00 a.m., entrees $5–$10.
Dinner: until 7 p.m., entrees $5–$10.

Closed Sundays in the afternoons after brunch. Serving juices, beer and wine, light meals and snacks. A good place to stop in for a quick bite before setting out on one of the many excursions in the Santiago area.

El Tocoroco   **$$$**   ★ ★ ★
Avenida Manduley, 159, ☎ (53) 7-43761.
Latin American cuisine. Specialties: International cuisine.
Lunch: from noon, entrees $8–$15.
Dinner: until midnight, entrees $8–$24.
Named after the national bird of Cuba, this restaurant is a twin of El Tocoroco in La Habana. The fish and seafood dishes are excellent, and the kitchen puts out a decent hamburger and spaghetti sauce too, in keeping with its claim to specialize in international cuisine.

La Cecilia   **$$**   ★ ★
Carretera de Ciudamar, Entronque, ☎ (53) 91889.
Latin American cuisine. Specialties: Cuban traditional cuisine.
Lunch: from noon, entrees $8–$15.
Dinner: until midnight, entrees $8–$15.
Nice patio in this sister restaurant of La Cecilia in La Habana. Good traditonal meat and fish dishes with black and red beans and rice.

Around Santiago

Siboney, a small farming village about 10 miles east of Santiago, is another place of pilgrimage for Cubans. It is here, from the Garjita Siboney, that Castro and his men set out to attack the Moncada barracks, some taking taxis there. Further east of Siboney is the **Valle de la Prehistoria** (Prehistoric Valley), an unusual park filled with giant sculptures of dinosaurs created by various Cuban artists. A few miles to the north is the **Gran Piedra National Park**, a nature reserve crowned by the mountain of the same name. Atop the mountain is a huge volcanic rock estimated to weigh 63,000 tons that can be climbed by means of 465 steps cut into the stone. The views from here on a clear day reach all the way to Jamaica and Haiti. There is excellent hiking to be had in the **Sierra Maestra** mountains to the north, which are home to Baconao Park and Pico Turquino, the island's highest point.

Where to Stay

Hotels and Resorts

Sierra Maestra Hotel   **$26–$41**   ★ ★ ★
Ruta Central, ☎ (53) 45013.
Single: $26–$31. Double: $34–$41.
The largest hotel in the Bayamo area north of Santiago Cuba, the Sierra Maestra is well equipped with air conditioning, television, refrigerator, radio, and phone in every room. There is a horse-drawn carriage and taxi service from the hotel until 10 p.m., as well as well-stocked shops, three bars, and a quite good cabaret in the nightclub.

Lodge

El Saltûn Ecolodge   **$28–$44**   ★ ★ ★ ★ ★

Carretera Filé, ☎ *(800) 268-1133.*
Single: $28–$37. Double: $37–$44.
Nestled in the Sierra Maestra mountains about 40 miles from Santiago de Cuba,
this tiny lodge is adjacent to El Saltûn, a picturesque waterfall. The dining area is
outdoors, surounded by jungle vegetation, converting to a small music/dance floor
in the evenings; the relaxation facilities are excellent (the lodge was constructed in
the 1970s as an anti-stress center for the Cuban elite); you can swim in the lodge
pool or at the base of the waterfall…paradise!

Baracoa

The oldest town in Cuba, having been founded in 1510, **Baracoa** is in the
extreme eastern end of Guantánamo province. Isolated from the rest of the
country by near impassable mountains, the town has kept a separate culture
and is home to the last significant numbers of native Cubans. Until recently
Baracoa could only be reached by air or sea, but in the 1960s the government built one of the most impressive roads in the world, **La Farola**, a 20-
mile road hung on the side of the mountains on concrete pillars and pylons.
Matachín fort, on the outskirts of town, houses a museum of the region's history. The new cathedral, built in the 19th century to replace the original, is
noteworthy for its Cruz de Parra, a venerated Catholic relic that survived the
revolution's period of official atheism.

Holguín

The city of **Holguín** itself is rather uninteresting: a small provincial capital
that became a center for planned industrialization in the early days of the
revolution, it is quite ugly and dirty. The beaches of the province, however,
are stunning (see below).

Where to Stay

Hotel Atlantico   **$50–$92**   ★ ★ ★ ★

Playa Guardalavaca, Banes, ☎ *(53) 630280.*
Single: $50–$56. Double: $81–$92.
A nice modern hotel with expansive lobby, pool area, and game room, and spacious
rooms with balcony and air conditioning, this is probably the best bet for the
Guardalavaca area. The recreational opportunities are very comprehensive, ranging
from scuba diving to horseback riding; the restaurant is very good, and the entertainment schedule is one of the best in any hotel reviewed here.

Villa Turey   **$54–$101**   ★ ★ ★

Playa Guardalavaca, Banes, ☎ *(53) 630195.*
Single: $54–$61. Double: $87–$101.

A relaxing hotel near the Guardalavaca Beach, this is a hastily constructed collection of concrete quadplexes that offer clean and comfortable, if inelegant accommodations. All rooms have air conditioning and televsion, there's a nice pool and extensive water sports organized by the hotel on the beach, which is just 100 yards away through a strip of fruit and palm trees. Residents are allowed to use all the recreational facilities at the Atlantico.

Lodge

Villa Pióares de Mayari   **$28–$44**   ★ ★ ★ ★

Mensura, Pióares de Mayari, ☎ *(53) 64008.*
Single: $28–$37. Double: $37–$44.

Located about 80 miles outside Holguín in the Sierra de Nipe mountains, this ecolodge is ideally situated for those wishing to explore and understand Cuba's vast natural resources. There are more than 130 native plant species within easy trekking distance of the lodge, and the government Integral Mountain Research Station is just a short drive away. There are swaths of true rain forest, and orchids blooming abundantly. The hotel accommodations are very charming, most in log cabins that were built for the Cuban elite and consequently have all the modern amenities. There's a good swimming pool, horseback trekking, and live music in the evenings.

Where to Eat

Miramar   **$$**   ★ ★ ★

Calle Donato M·rmol, 13, ☎ *(53) 434466.*
Latin American cuisine. Specialties: Fish and seafood.
Lunch: from 11:30 a.m., entrees $8–$15.
Dinner: until 9 p.m., entrees $8–$15.

A nice basic restaurant, seafood and fish caught fresh locally, try the catch of the day and lobster special (price varies, around US$15).

Restaurante Pernik   **$$**   ★ ★ ★

Avenida Jorge Dimitrov y Avenida XXAniversario, ☎ *(53) 481663.*
Latin American cuisine. Specialties: Cuban traditional cuisine.
Lunch: 11:30 a.m.–2 p. m., prix fixe $8–$12.
Dinner: 5:30-9 p.m., entrees $8–$18.

A little touristy, this restaurant has good seafood but its attempts at what it thinks are American food are best left untasted (soggy French Fries, greasy hamburgers). The buffet for lunch is a great deal, sample everything.

Beaches

Playa Siboney outside the village of Siboney is the nicest beach in the Santiago area. North of the lost town of Baracoa the beaches are desolate and beautiful, if extremely hard to reach. Near Holguín, **Playa Don Lino** is well sheltered and very quiet; supposedly this is the spot where Columbus first landed (lost as usual, he thought he was in Japan) and praised the unprecedented beauty of the island. Further north is Cuba's most beautiful beach of all, Playa **Guardalavaca**. Unfortunately this area is being developed rapidly, but it remains, with its powdery white sand, lush tropical backdrop, crystal clear blue water and spectacular coral reef just offshore, a must-see destination.

Where to Eat

Eating out in Cuba is not as a simple a proposition as you will find elsewhere in the Caribbean, or in most of the world, for that matter. The economic crisis caused by the twin pressures of the U.S. economic blockade and the collapse of the Soviet Union has left Cuba extremely short of food. Foreigners are only able to eat in special "dollar restaurants," of which there are precious few, besides the built-in restaurants and cafés in the hotels. If you go to a restaurant that is not authorized to accept payment in dollars you will likely be turned away.

In some parts of the country, notably in Piñar del Rio province in the west and the extreme east of the country, there are almost no "dollar restaurants" outside the hotels. We have listed the best ones around the country—the food in Cuba is generally excellent; simple but good. The prices here are accurate as far as we know, but be aware that the fluctuating exchange rate, as well as the volatile availability of even the most basic foodstuffs, renders these prices subject to frequent change.

Shopping

Shopping in Cuba is a mixed bag, if you'll pardon the pun. By and large, the stores are extremely poorly stocked, due to the economic crisis, and most basic goods as well as food are rationed. Foreigners are not welcomed in most regular stores. On the other hand, Cuba wants your foreign currency, so stores catering only to those bearing dollars are everywhere in the tourist areas. These shops are mostly stocked with imported goods, and duty-free prices make liquor a good deal, but there's a limited selection of other items—musical instruments and typical cheesy souvenirs are most easy to find. The big exception, of course, are cigars—a box of 25 full-size Monte

Cristos, Davidoffs or Romeo y Julittas will cost between US$35 and US$50, depending where you buy them (they are generally cheaper in the factories in Piñar del Rio than in the stores in the big cities), which is a good deal better than the US$500 you would pay in the U.S. (where it would be illegal to buy them anyway). Most stores, even those catering to tourists, are only open from 12:20–7:30 p.m., although some open in the morning one day a week.

Cuba Directory

TRAVELING TO CUBA

Cuba, once a pariah among many western nations, has recently been welcomed back into the fold by all but the U.S. European countries and Canada, especially, now maintain full diplomatic relations and extensive trading partnerships with the island. Tourism from these nations to Cuba is simple and well-developed; no visa is needed for entry (a tourist card must be obtained from the Cuban embassy—see below).

The situation for travelers from the U.S., however, is quite different and deserves special attention here. Under the Cuban Assets Control Regulations of the U.S. Treasury Department, any person subject to U.S. jurisdiction must be licensed to engage in "transactions" with Cuba, including any that involve travel to and from the island. A license is required by law even when the travel contemplated originates in a third country, such as Canada or Mexico. Tourism and business-related travel are not licensed by the U.S. government under any circumstances. Licenses are routinely granted to government officials on official business, working accredited journalists on assignment and representatives of international organizations of which the U.S. is a member. Applications for a license considered on a case-by-case basis include those by persons wishing to travel to Cuba for humanitarian reasons, including hardship visits to close relatives, for telecommunications projects and for scholars engaging in research.

Thus, the prospective U.S. tourist to Cuba must engage in some creative travel plans in order to reach the "Forbidden Paradise." The most common method of traveling to Cuba from the U.S. is simply to flout the law and travel through a third country. The most popular gateways for American travelers are Montreal, Mexico City, Cancún, Mexico, Nassau in the Bahamas and Jamaica. U.S. travelers are welcomed into Cuba from these departure points either as independent visitors or as part of a package tour group. In either case the visitor will need a tourist card, as mentioned above; these are available from the Cuban embassies in Canada, Mexico and other nations, and in theory, may be purchased upon arrival at José Martí International Airport in La Habana, but a far simpler method is to purchase the card from an authorized wholesaler, such as **Cuban Holidays** in Montreal *(☎ (514) 382-9785)*. The card costs about $15. Since 1990, the passports of visitors to Cuba are not stamped by Cuban immigration officials on entry or exit so there should be no problems reentering the U.S. from the third country as there will be no record of the traveler having been in Cuba. The Cuban authorities do, however, require at least three nights' confirmed hotel reservations for admittance to the country, so make your reservations before you leave. Good agencies that assist independent travelers are **Cuban Holidays** in Montreal or **Viñales Tours** *(☎ (52) 208-37-04)* in Mexico.

A number of U.S. organizations arrange group trips to Cuba. **Global Exchange** in San Francisco *(☎ (800) 497-1994)* offers special interest trips to Cuba as well as other nontraditional destinations, focusing on the education or health care systems, for example. The trips include seminars and meetings with Cuban officials, as well as all accommodations and meals, and Global Exchange assists participants in obtaining a license from the U.S. Government under the researcher category. Travelers must submit a copy of their resume and a signed statement indicating they have an established interest in studying Cuba at least two months prior to departure. Partial scholarships are even available for low-income persons wishing to join the trips.

A more defiant approach is taken by the **Freedom to Travel Campaign**, also based in San Francisco *(☎ (415) 558-9490)*, which to date has organized five "Freedom to Travel Challenge" trips to Cuba. A philosophical descendent of the Venceremos Brigades of the 1970s, the organization's purpose is to draw attention to what it believes are unfair and unjust restrictions on U.S. citizens' freedom to travel, and it thus takes pains to publicize its trips as much as possible, recommending that participants "form support groups and seek sponsorship from church, community, union, peace and justice, and other local groups as well as high profile people in your community." In June 1994 the U.S. Treasury Department froze the group's bank account just prior to that month's trip, but its members were able to raise an equivalent $50,000 in just a few days and the trip went ahead as planned. Soon after the group returned, the government released the funds. Some members of Freedom to Travel, as well as bold individual travelers, request an entry and/or exit stamp on their passports in Cuba, in order to challenge the government regulations when returning to the U.S. The government has backed down in most instances, only prosecuting one individual for violating the prohibition against visiting Cuba. Freedom to Travel tours include ecotours (described in "Ecotours" above), focusing on Cuba's development of a sustainable economy.

ARRIVAL AND DEPARTURE

Cubana flies to La Habana from Montreal, Madrid, Berlin, Brussels, Paris, Sao Paolo, Buenas Aires and even Miami (but if you are subject to U.S. jurisdiction you'll need a license to travel to Cuba from the Treasury department to board this flight—see "Traveling to Cuba" above). There are direct connections from Madrid, on Iberia, Cologne and Dusseldorf on **LTU** and Condor, Mexico City and Cancún on **Aeroméxico** and **Mexicana**, Amsterdam on **KLM**, and from Russia on **Aeroflot**. **Air Canada** and at least four other airlines offer charter service to La Habana, Santiago de Cuba, Holguín, Varadero, Manzanillo, Cienfuegos, Ciego de Avila, Cayo Largo and Camagüey as part of package tours. There are also flights from Venezuela on **Aeropostal** and **Viasa**, from San José on **LACSA**, and from Angola on **Taag**. If you have arranged your trip with a tour operator, you'll probably have shuttle service from the airport to your hotel included; if not, count on taking a taxi since bus service is pretty patchy. Negotiate your fare before setting out, and be prepared to pay in dollars, as for everything in Cuba. There is a $11 departure tax when you leave the island.

BUSINESS HOURS

Stores open from 12:30–7:30 p.m. Monday–Saturday. Banks open 8:30 a.m.–noon and 1:30–3 p.m. weekdays and 8:30 a.m.–10:30 p.m. on Saturdays.

CLIMATE

Cuba's climate is tropical, with a rainy season from May to October and a dry season from November to April. There is a fairly constant east breeze; bring a sweater as it can get quite cool in the evenings, even by the beaches. The average temperature is 80°F. Highs in La Habana in summer are up to 90°F, daytime lows to 66°F in winter. There are quite frequent hurricanes between June and October, so check weather reports before your trip.

ELECTRICITY

110 volts is standard throughout the island, although some of the new hotels offer 220 volts. Plugs are of the two-pronged American type; adaptors are on sale in most hotels for European travelers.

GETTING AROUND

It's almost vital to rent a car if you want to get around Cuba—the bus service is in a real shambles because of the petroleum shortage. Buses either don't run, only run for 30 miles before turning back, or refuse to let foreigners aboard. If you do get on, be prepared, as usual, to pay in dollars. Internal air service, on the other hand, is quite good, and fairly inexpensive. **Cubana de Aviación** (☎ *(53) 7-709391*) charges about $52 each way from La Habana to Camagüey, US$68 to Santiago, for example. If you can plan your flights in advance it's advisable to book tickets from your home country. Train travel is fun and scenic and pretty inexpensive, but the trains are always breaking down and services are often cancelled with no notice. Book tickets in La Habana through **Ferrotur** *(☎ (53) 7-621770)*.

Cars can be rented for about $55 per day with the first 100 km included, plus optional CDW insurance for $5 per day. Fill up with gas wherever and whenever you can—you never know when the next gas station with gas/electricity to pump the gas will be available. **Havanautos Rent-a-Car** *(☎ (53) 7-332369, FAX: (53) 7-331416)* offers models from Nissans to Mercedes Benzes; **Cubanacán** has a car rental division that can get you a car at most of their hotels, *(☎ (53) 202188 or 204410)*.

LANGUAGE

The language in Cuba is Spanish. Many people in the cities speak English, as do those working in the tourist industry, and Russian and French are also quite widely spoken.

MEDICAL EMERGENCIES

Cuba's health care system is free to all citizens and is the best in Latin America. Visitors, however, had better have plenty of greenbacks if they fall sick. In La Habana and Varadero Beach there are separate clinics for visitors. The Gira García Clinic in La Habana sells prescription drugs that you may not be able to find in pharmacies. Alternative medicine is widely practiced in Cuba, so if you get mildly ill in the countryside, ask around, you may find a cure from a plant you'd never thought of.

MONEY

The Cuban peso is the national currency, except for you! Visitors are expected to pay for everything in dollars—there are, as mentioned, special clinics, shops and hotels for visitors, for example, that only trade in dollars, but the economic situation is so desperate that almost no one, not even the peddlers of cigars on the Malecón, will take pesos from a foreigner. The government has set up a system of "B" currency for visitors, so you don't have to change your cash into pesos, but most vendors scoff at these certificates since they have to change them back into pesos, while the government keeps the foreign currency. Naturally there is a thriving black market in currency exchange; you can get much better rates from the hustlers than from the Bank of Cuba (the nation's only bank) or official money exchange centers, but again, why would you want to get pesos? You won't be able to spend them. Credit cards, including Visa, MasterCard, Access, Diner's Club, and Eurocard are quite widely accepted, but not if they are issued from a U.S. bank—the bank won't honor the receipt, so the Cuban establishment understandably won't take the card. Traveler's Checks from Visa and Thomas Cook are fine.

SECURITY

The crime rate is very low in Cuba, although attacks on foreigners have escalated from nonexistent to plausible in recent years as the economic crisis has worsened. Prostitution is rampant in the major cities, especially La Habana, but still illegal. The gravest problem is the legions of would-be money changers. Other than these minor irritants, things will be fine if you just obey common sense—lock up your valuables, don't leave your stuff unattended, etc. Many of the newer hotels have safes in the rooms or safety deposit boxes in the lobby.

TELEPHONE

Phone service in Cuba is patchy at best. You can call a number there five consecutive times and get five different error messages, never once connecting. It's a trial and error thing—U.S. giant AT&T recently established direct service to the island (the country code is 53), and the connection is good and clear once you get one, but there aren't enough lines and anywhere outside La Habana you'll probably need an operator to dial into or out of. The international code for dialing out of Cuba is 8. Operator assistance is available by dialing ☎ *113* in the daytime and ☎ *607110* in the evening.

TIME

Cuba adheres to U.S. Eastern Standard Time (five hours behind GMT) and Daylight Savings Time (five hours behind GMT).

TIPPING

Service charge is not included anywhere but in the fanciest hotels. It's expected, however, at the usual rates—10 to 15 percent in restaurants, 10 percent in taxis, a dollar a day for room maids in hotels and at least a dollar for porters at the airports. It's up to you but you may want to bear in mind that some of the self-employed (for example taxi drivers) are already making money off you by insisting on dollar payment; those working for hotels or restaurants are not.

TOURIST INFORMATION

Cuba depends on tourism, especially these days, so they go out of their way to see that you have all you need. There are tourist bureaus and offices of Cubanacán and Cubatur in almost every hotel; the main Cubatur office is in **La Habana** *(☎ (53) 7-324521)*. Bear in mind that Cubatur is a booking agency, so the staff is sometimes less willing to dispense advice than to sell you an excursion, but it is their job to do so.

WHEN TO GO

December to March is the cooler season, but even then Cuba is a tropical paradise. Go any time! Carnaval in La Habana and Santiago de Cuba is in July, climaxing on July 26. Every city in Cuba, large and small, has a carnaval during the summer months.

CUBA HOTELS	RMS	RATES	PHONE	CR. CARDS
Around Santiago				
★★★★★ **El Saltón Ecolodge**	22	$28–$44	(800) 268-1133	
★★★ **Sierra Maestra Hotel**	188	$26–$41	(53) 45013	
Camagüey				
★★★★ **Club Caracol**	150	$53–$72	(53) 48302	
★★★★ **Villa Tararaco**	30	$31–$48	(53) 36222	
★★★ **Club Coral**	298	$45–$65	(53) 48130	
★★ **Camaguey Hotel**	136	$20–$35	(53) 72015	A, MC, V
Cayo Largo				
★★★★★ **Villa Capricho**	60	$66–$120	(53) 513033	
Cienfuegos				
★★★★★ **Hotel Faro Luna**	14	$37–$54	(53) 65582	
★★★ **Pasacaballos Hotel**	188	$22–$35	(53) 8545	
Holguín				
★★★★ **Hotel Atlßntico**	232	$50–$92	(53) 630280	
★★★★ **Villa Pi±ares de Mayari**	25	$28–$44	(53) 64008	
★★★ **Villa Turey**	136	$54–$101	(53) 630195	
Isla de la Juventud				
★★★★ **Colony Hotel**	77	$36–$66	(53) 8181/8282	DC, MC, V
La Habana				
★★★★ **Casas Villa Paraíso**	78	$140–$200	(53) 7-336006	DC, MC, V
★★★★ **Comodoro Hotel & Bungalows**	288	$67–$110	(53) 225551	
★★★★ **Hostal Valencia**	11	$22–$34	(53) 623801	
★★★★ **Hotel El Viejo y El Mar**	186	$123–$143	(57) 7-219457	DC, MC, V
★★★★ **Villa Daiquiri**	150	$38–$64	(53) 24849	
★★★ **Bacuranao Villa Resort**	50	$22–$35	(53) 4431	
★★★ **Capri Hotel**	318	$47–$78	(53) 32-0511	
★★★ **Chateau Miramar**	50	$92–$120	(53) 7-331952	DC, MC, V
★★★ **Deauville Hotel**	150	$38–$60	(53) 616901	
★★★ **Hotel Biocaribe**	105	$43–$77	(53) 7-217379	

CUBA HOTELS	RMS	RATES	PHONE	CR. CARDS
★★★ Hotel Mariposa		$27–$40	(53) 7-204913	
★★★ Hotel Nacional de Cuba	480	$114–$204	(53) 78981	
★★★ Hotel Victoria		$60–$107	(53) 326531	
★★★ Villa Tropico Resort	51	$22–$35	(53) 64180	
★★ Habana Riviera	360	$66–$117	(53) 306051	MC
★★ Presidente Hotel	140	$51–$92	(53) 327521	
★★ Vedado Hotel	185	$33–$53	(53) 326501	

Santiago de Cuba

	RMS	RATES	PHONE	CR. CARDS
★★★★★ Hotel Los Galeones	32	$75–$100	(53) 26160	
★★★★ Hotel Santiago de Cuba	302	$69–$121	(53) 42656	DC, MC, V
★★★★ Villa la Gran Piedra	22	$28–$44	(53) 5913	
★★★ LTI Los Corales	144	$30–$60	(53) 7191	DC, MC
★★ Hotel Versalles	61	$48–$77	(53) 91016	

Trinidad

	RMS	RATES	PHONE	CR. CARDS
★★★ Hotel La Granjita		$40–$52	(53) 26059	
★★★ Rancho Hatuey	22	$40–$52	(53) 626015	

Varadero Beach

	RMS	RATES	PHONE	CR. CARDS
★★★★★ Melia Varadero	490	$86–$198	(53) 7-337162	DC, MC, V
★★★★★ Superclub Varadero	160	$118–$101	(53) 66180	
★★★★ Hotel Bella Costa	307	$104–$161	(53) 7-216936	DC, MC, V
★★★★ Hotel LTI-Tuxpan	218	$80–$150	(53) 66200	
★★★★ Internacional Hotel	155	$64–$122	(53) 66180	
★★★★ Sol Palmeras	402	$78–$192	(53) 66110	
★★★ Atabey Hotel	175	$47–$76	(53) 63013	
★★★ Club Tropical	142	$81–$125	(53) 663915	
★★★ Hotel Atlantico	20	$54–$97	(53) 2551	
★★★ Paraiso-Puntarenas Resort	510	$84–$140	(53) 62993	

CUBA RESTAURANTS	PHONE	ENTREE	CR. CARDS

Camagüey

Italian			
★★ Via Appia	(53) 336101	$5–$10	

Latin			
★★★★ Rancho King		$8–$15	
★★★ Las Brisas	(53) 336187	$8–$20	

Cienfuegos

Latin			
★★★★ La Cueva del Camarón	(53) 338238	$8–$24	
★★ Mesón el Palatino		$5–$10	

Holguín

Latin			
★★★ Miramar	(53) 434466	$8–$15	
★★★ Restaurante Pernik	(53) 481663	$8–$18	

Isla de la Juventud

★★★ El Corderito		$8–$15	

La Habana

African			
★★★★ El Oasis		$5–$10	

Italian			
★★ La Cova	(53) 7-331150	$5–$10	

Latin			
★★★★★ El Tocoroco	(53) 7-334530	$12–$35	MC, V
★★★★★ Floridita		$10–$25	DC, MC, V
★★★★ Bodeguita del Medio		$8–$22	DC, MC, V
★★★★ La Cecilia	(53) 7-331562	$12–$28	
★★★ El Barracón		$10–$15	MC, V
★★★ La Torre		$8–$15	
★★★ Papa's	(53) 7-331150	$8–$20	

CUBA RESTAURANTS	PHONE	ENTREE	CR. CARDS

Santiago de Cuba

Latin

★★★ A la Cubana		$10–$18	
★★★ Cafetería Cuba Centro	(53) 691476	$5–$10	
★★★ El Tocoroco	(53) 7-43761	$8–$24	
★★ La Cecilia	(53) 91889	$8–$15	

Trinidad

Latin

| ★★★ Restaurante Trinidad | | $8–$15 | |
| ★★ Mesón del Regidor | | $5–$12 | |

Varadero Beach

Italian

| ★★★ Dante | (53) 566204 | $8–$15 | |

Latin

★★★ El Bodegón Criollo		$8–$15	
★★★ Mi Casita		$8–$15	
★★ El Anzuelo	(53) 663647	$5–$12	
★★ El Palacete	(53) 562933	$8–$15	

Note: • Lunch Only

•• Dinner Only

CURAÇAO

uraçao offers great beaches, diving, excellent restaurants, shops and casinos.

The "C" in the ABC Islands (part of the five-island Netherlands Antilles deration), Curaçao is an excellent choice when one-half of the traveling ouple dives and the other one doesn't. Beaches here are small and intimate; ou can get cable TV, and the bustling harbor, expensive stores, excellent staurants and lively casinos of the Dutch-inspired capital of Willemstad ould tempt even a devoted diver to take off his wet suit.

The fact that Curaçao is such an excellent dive spot is one of the Caribbe- n's deepest guarded secrets. Because most hard-core divers naturally gravi- te toward the diving mecca of Bonaire, Curaçao has become a poor lation when it comes to enticing divers from the U.S., but in truth, uraçao attracts many Dutch recreational divers who might spend up to

three weeks underwater. In fact, these Dutch scubaniks are rough-and-read
divers who love to wear "Sea Hunt" suits and go where no diver has gor
before. With visibility from 60–150 feet and water temps 70-85 degrees
the island offers a wide range of sites at every skill; and eco-sensitive diver
especially, will appreciate the permanent moorings of the 12-mile long **Na
tional Underwater Park**, where spearfishing is prohibited and the fish are ju
beginning to get used to the divers. No one should leave Curaçao, howeve
without a vigorous trek through **Christoffel Park**, where cacti grow over 1
feet tall and iguanas scurry underfoot before they are made into a delicio
soup the whole island adores.

Bird's Eye View

At 171 square miles, Curaçao rates as the largest of the five islands in th
Netherlands Antilles. Shaped like the arched wings of a great heron, it is l
cated 35 miles north of the coast of Venezuela (which explains why it w
long a tourist haven for Venezuelans before the rest of the world discover
it). The entrance of the harbor splits the main downtown area of Willemst
into two. Downtown, which is well developed and recently renovated, is th
hub of Curaçao shopping and its vibrant colors and pastel-house facades a
true picture ops. The contrast between the bustling Dutch-cobbled past
fronts of Willemstad and the countryside is stark; once you leave the capit
the landscape takes on the color of brown and russet, studded with thre
pronged cactuses, spiny-leafed aloes, and divi-divi trees. You can still s
Dutch windmills pumping water to irrigate the arid fields. Since the islar
receives very little rainfall, much of its landscape looks like the Sonor
Deserts of the American Southwest. Continuing past East Point of Curaç
you will get to the tiny island of Klein Curaçao ("Klein" is little in Dutch
There are two sides to the island: windward and leeward.

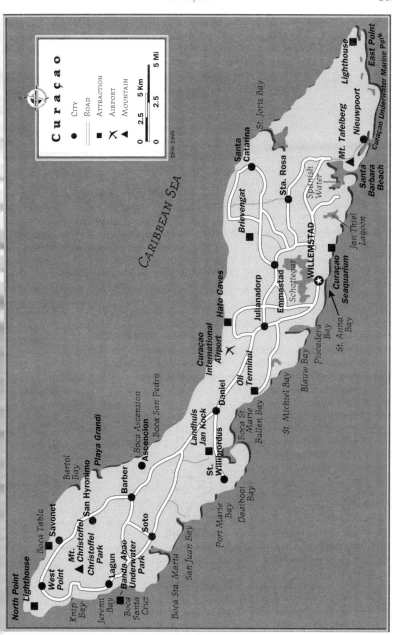

Curaçao

- CITY
- ROAD
- ATTRACTION
- AIRPORT
- MOUNTAIN

0 2.5 5 Km
0 2.5 5 Mi

©HW 1995

North Point
Lighthouse
Boca Tabla
Savonet
West Point
Mt. Christoffel
Christoffel Park
Banda-Abao Underwater Park
Knip Bay
Jeremi Bay
Boca Santa Cruz
Lagun
Soto
Boca Sta. Marta
San Juan Bay
Port Marie Bay
Daaibooi Bay
Bartol Bay
San Hyronimo
Playa Grandi
Barber
Boca Ascension
Ascencion
Boca San Pedro
St. Willibrordus
Landhuis Jan Kock
Daniel
Oil Terminal
Boca Sta Marie
Buiten Bay
St. Michiel Bay
CARIBBEAN SEA
Curaçao International Airport
Hato Caves
Julianadorp
Emmastad
Schottegat
Blauw Bay
Piscadera Bay
St. Anna Bay
Brievengat
Santa Catarina
St. Joris Bay
Sta. Rosa
WILLEMSTAD
Spanish Water
Curaçao Seaquarium
Jan Thiel Lagoon
Mt. Tafelberg
Santa Barbara Beach
Nieuwpoort
Lighthouse
East Point
Curaçao Underwater Marine Park

History

Long before Alonso de Ojeda set foot on the island in 1499, Arawak tribes—from the clan of the Caquetios called Curaçaos—were inhabiting the island. After Ojeda marked his claim, a Spanish settlement followed in 1527. A hundred years later, the Spanish unceremoniously left the island, leaving it in the hands of Holland, which deemed it a possession of the Dutch West Indies Company. The island's natural harbors and strategic location in the Caribbean inspired predatory interest among the French and British, who continually tried to send the Dutch packing, with little success. In 1642, a young Dutchman named Peter Stuyvesant became governor of the island, a mere three years before he took over governorship of the Dutch colony of New Amsterdam, today known as New York. During Dutch rule, the island was divided up into plantations. Not all were devoted to agriculture; some of the estates were utilized for salt mining. In 1863 emancipation freed the slaves. The island made waves on the international scene until oil was discovered in Venezuela, and the Royal Dutch Shell Company, impressed with Curaçao's fine harbor potential, erected the world's largest oil refinery there. The industry lasted well into this century, attracting laborers from many nations who have created the melting pot that makes up Curaçao's population today.

Today Curaçao is part of the kingdom of the Netherlands. The other Dutch territories—Bonaire, Saba, St. Eustatius and St. Martin—are administered through Willemstad, the capital of the Netherlands Antilles.

People

Curaçao is one of the few islands in the Caribbean where the annual income averages $5000 or more (most people on other islands scrape by on $1500 or less). The Shell refinery remains an important element in the island's economy. In addition, Curaçao has obtained the reputation as an international banking center, with hundreds of millions of dollars passing through businesses that only have a phone and P.O. box number. Today there are 79 nationalities represented on the island, from Dutch, English, Spanish and Portuguese, to Chinese, East Indian and Venezuelan. About 80 percent of the population are Roman Catholics; the Jewish population totals today about 600. Rabbi Aaron L. Peller remains the head of the Mikve Israel-Synagogue, which is thought to be the oldest in continuance in the Western Hemisphere, since Jews from Spain and Portugal, via Brazil, were among the earliest settlers on the island.

Beaches

Good beaches are hard to come by in Curaçao. The northwestern coast should be avoided by swimmers since it is too rough, though the west has some calm bays good for swimming and snorkeling. Many of the beaches are private and charge a fee, but in return you get changing facilities, clean stretches and snack bars. Public beaches are notoriously unkempt. Avoid the beach near Willemstad (at the Avila Beach Hotel); it's artificial, gritty and too dense for good snorkeling. **Santa Barbara**, located at the mouth of Spanish Water Bay, is popular with locals and has full services. The Curaçao Yacht Club is close by. On the northwest side, **Boca St. Martha**, where the Coral Cliff Resort is located, exudes a certain peacefulness and the bay is gorgeous. **Knip**, farther up the coast, rates as one of the best on the island, with its large, sandy stretch; on weekends it can get crowded and noisy with music. **Playa Forti**, on the western tip, has dark sand and is good for swimming.

Klein Curaçao, a small, uninhabited island off East Point, makes a nifty day excursion; many charter boats and dive operators offer packages with lunch included.

Underwater

The independent spirit will be well-served on Curaçao, where shore diving from rugged cliffs is a chief attraction. The island is encircled by a fringing reef which features several dozen excellent sites along its southern (leeward) side; there are over 40 permanent mooring buoys established. Typically, the shallow reef drops gently to 50 feet followed by a second slope 200 to 300 feet from shore; the terrain in between is frequently undulating and surreal. Because diving did not become established here until the 1980s, the reefs are in good shape and new sites await discovery. Local marine biologists claim that Curaçao actually possesses a greater diversity of hard and soft corals and sponge life than the reefs of famed Bonaire. However, heavily populated Curaçao has depleted much of the fish life existing on the reefs. Otherwise, while not always as convenient or accessible as the diving available on its sibling to the east, many of Curaçao's sites are genuinely comparable to the best dives on Bonaire. The main drawback in comparing the two destinations is that Curaçao is a more developed island, and little of its coastline remains untouched.

Curaçao's underwater attractions are just beginning to generate press in the U.S., though American divers are still substantially outnumbered by their European counterparts, who have been coming here for years. The newly created **Banda Abao Underwater Park** is home to some of Curaçao's most adventurous diving and occupies much of the island's northern half; the **Central Underwater Park** lies north of Willemstad. The island's original marine reserve, the **Curaçao Underwater Park**, situated along the 12.5 mile shoreline east from the Princess Beach Hotel to the tip of the island, offers good diving and a snorkeling trail (in front of the Jan Thiel Lagoon). The south coast, from Newport east to the lighthouse, is private property and diving must be accessed by boat; at press time a plan to develop this coastline was generating considerable controversy. A locally available *Guide to the Curaçao Underwater Park* by Jeffrey Sybesma and Tom van't Hos, provides additional information about dive sites, and the *Complete Guide to Landside Diving and Snorkeling Locations in Curaçao* by Jeffrey Sybesma and Suzanne Koelega, features maps and road directions to shore sites. Among a number of good snorkeling areas are **Playa Lagoon**, a beach tucked between two outsized rocks formations, and the **Jan Thiel Reef**, located just outside the bay and snorkeling trail. A decompression tank is available at the island's St. Elizabeth Hospital.

Mushroom Forest

As the name implies, this is a trip to Alice's wonderland, highlighted by a swim through a forest of mountainous star coral, 10 to 12 feet high, which are shaped like giant mushrooms. The access is either by boat or shore (although the latter requires negotiating a rocky entry), and the mushrooms are set on a gently sloping terrace 50 feet down; don't miss the surprisingly diverse selection of colorful anemones nestling in the cracks of the coral. A nearby underwater cave against the shoreline cliffs provides shelter for tiger groupers and vast schools of glassy sweepers. An ideal second dive.

Maya Kalki

A sheltered cove, just south of Curaçao's western tip, provides entry to a rolling landscape covered in a dense blanket of coral (40 to 60 feet). Green morays slither through mountainous star coral, while spotted eagle rays and even an occasional hammerhead explore the deeper waters.

Vata Mula

At the western tip of the island is a niche in the cliffs which provides an idyllic beach entry leading to soft coral growth over a sandy plain. Schools of rainbow runners, jackknife fish, green razorfish and spotted snake eels inhabit the reef, and the slope descends moderately to 50 or 60 feet and a steep drop-off. Seas here can be rough, and an experienced dive guide is recommended.

Wreck of the *Superior Producer*

A 100-foot freighter, the Superior Producer sunk unexpectedly in 1977, settling upright on a sandy floor (110 feet) at the base of a drop-off. The ship has become beautifully encrusted with yellow, red, purple and green corals, and the cargo hold and captain's quarters can be entered, which lead to a staircase and the wheelhouse where schools of silversides reside. Usually done as a boat dive, but calm seas invite strong swimmers to access the site from shore; discovering the ship in the distance is an eerie, unforgettable experience.

Dive Shops

Landhuis Daniel

Daniel; ☎ *(599) 9-648400.*
Based out of a 350-year-old plantation house in the center of the island, this informal operation encourages a "do your own thing" approach. Although a boat is available for groups, virtually all site access is done by car. $13 for a single-tank shore dive, or $17 buys unlimited tank fills for a day. Accompanying instructor is $5 per dive, transportation an additional $5 (or provide your own). $35 per day to rent equipment. PADI-affiliated, and an instructor training center for PDIC. Mostly European clientele.

Princess Divers/Peter Hughes Diving

Willemstad; ☎ *(599) 9-658991.*
A full PADI five-star facility with courses to assistant instructor. Resort course $55, taught in the nearby lagoon. Two-tank boat dive, $55; one-tank night boat dive, $38.50, including taxes (Tuesdays and Thursdays). Unlimited boat and/or shore dive packages available. Snorkeling trips.

Toucan Diving

Willemstad; ☎ *(599) 9-612500.*
Boat dives on Monday and Tuesday only (two tanks, $65, including a barbecue and open bar). Shore dive, $18, or $67 buys four dive package ($90 for six, $125 for 10). Not PADI or NAUI-affiliated, but an Instructor Dive Development training center; six-year-old facility.

Underwater

Curaçao. Willemstad; ☎ *(599) 9-618100.*

One of the island's larger operations, established in 1987 and part of the Lion Dive Hotel. PADI five-star facility, with courses to assistant instructor. Two-tank boat dive, $60. Single-tank boat dives, $33. Shore dive, $11 for tank rental; $3 for refills.

On Foot

Although most of Curaçao's arid interior is comprised of rocky hills or flat scrublands, as one heads northwest on the island's two main roads, a bumpier topography of chalky mountains and relatively greener valleys emerge. The terrain, including a flat-topped mesa, will remind some visitors of the rugged beauty found in the American Southwest. **Mount Christoffel National Park** occupies 4500-acres, much of Curaçao's northern tip, and is home to four tracks, each color-coded for easy identification, including a path which ascends 1238-foot Christoffel itself, the highest point on the island. The remaining three tracks are named after the three plantations which once tenanted this land—Savonet, Zevenbergen and Zorgvlied—and are usually driven, although each is suitable for (exposed) on-foot exploration. The crawl through a varied and interesting landscape, between century plant (which bloom only once every hundred years), wind-shaped divi divi trees and fields of oversize cactus; keen eyes will also spot the several species of orchids growing on the hillsides. There are roughly 150 species of birds, as well as the tiny, indigenous Curaçao deer, a subspecies of the more common white-tailed deer. Two small slitherers inhabit the park, whipsnakes and silver snakes, but neither are poisonous. The park administration office can provide you with detailed maps, or you can purchase the in-depth *Excursion Guide to the Christoffel Park*, by Peer Reijns. Christoffel's summit is an ideal location to enjoy the sunrise or sunset, but the park is open only between 8 a.m.–5 p.m. (6 a.m.–3 p.m. on Sundays). There are, however, occasional guided walks at dawn or dusk; additional information may be obtained by calling the park at ☎ *(599) 9-640363*.

Mount Christoffel

Birdwatching is a highlight of this fine hike, which ascends the highest point in the ABCs. Begin your trek at the visitor's center, following the path marked in red; a half-hour walk along the road will lead to the base of the peak. From here, it is a hot one-hour climb to the top, first through thorned vegetation, then through broader leafed plants and trees, including ferns and epiphytes. The push to the summit involves both hands and feet, but is not really difficult. Views across Curaçao and excellent and, if the weather is clear, you'll spot Aruba, Bonaire and even Venezuela, 80 miles away.

> ### FIELDING'S CHOICE:
>
> *With more than 150–200 deer on the island, Christoffel National Park now offers a new deer-watching program. Sessions are held in the afternoon 4-6:30 p.m., with small groups led by guides (maximum of eight people) on a ten-minute walk to the observation tower for a presentation and to await the deer. Call for reservations. Located on the highest point of the island, the park also offers unusual walking trails that take you past fascinating flora, Indian caves and wildlife. A museum on the grounds features an exhibit on the geology of the island.*

What Else to See

Willemstad, capital of Curaçao, features Dutch-inspired architecture.

Willemstad is a port ready-made for cruise passengers. Shopping is the best in the Caribbean and most of the sightseeing can be seen within a six-block radius. The city is cut in half by Santa Anna Bay. On one side is the Punda, and the other side the Otrabanda (literally, "the other side"). The Punda is the touristic side, with its numerous boutiques, restaurants and marketplaces. The Otrabanda is more residential, the heart of the local Curaçao life.

To cross from one side to the other, you can either 1) ride the free ferry; 2) drive or take a taxi over the Juliana Bridge; or 3) walk across the Queen Emma Pontoon bridge.

One of the most fantastic views of Willemstad can be had standing on the Otrabanda side, looking back at the pastel-colored face of the other side, where spiffy rows of townhouses and gabled roofs attest to the Dutch heritage. The **Queen Emma Bridge**, beloved by the natives and affectionately called the Lady, is a 700-ft. floating bridge, the creation on the American consul Leonard Burlington Smoth, who made a small fortune off the tolls. Today there's no fee. Farther north is the 1625-foot-long **Queen Juliana Bridge**; the view from here is terrific, especially at sunset when the various colors of the dying sun turn the sea into a colorful palette.

The **floating market on the Punda side** is a must first stop. Early mornings Venezuela schooners park and unload their dazzling loads of fresh fruits, vegetables and freshly caught fish. The best time to see the arrivals is 6:30 a.m., but traffic bears up all day.

The **Mikveh Israel Emmanuel Synagogue** is the oldest temple still in use in the Western Hemisphere, founded in 1651. Twenty thousand visitors a year come to see the special floor of brilliant white sand, which signifies Moses' deliverance of his people to the Promised Land. Visit the museum, which displays Jewish artifacts from the centuries.

At the foot of the Pontoon Bridge is **Fort Amsterdam**, an 18th-century citadel that was once the center of the city. On the far side of the plaza stands the **Waterfort**, a 17th-century bastion that now houses, under the Waterfort Arches, one of the most delightful shopping malls on the Caribbean.

 It will take a car to reach, but a visit to the **Curaçao Museum** will be worth it. On display are numerous Indian artifacts, as well as colonial and historical antiques. On the same road trip you can visit the **Landhuis Jan Rock**, a supposedly haunted house from the 17th century. Sunday mornings are the best time to come when the proprietor serves pancakes in the restaurant nearby.

A quick pass through the village of Soto in the northwest tip of the island is warranted. Past Soto a dry Arizona-type landscape is in evidence, with cacti and flamboyant dry bushes. The road continues out to Westpunt Highway, curving back south to Boca Tabla, where the sea has carved a fine grotto. It's a lovely place just to lie back and listen to the waves crashing against the rocks.

On the eastern side of the island, the **Curaçao Seaquarium** is as fun as it is informative. Forty-six freshwater fish hold more than 400 species of fish; nearby a man-made beach of white sand is good for young swimmers.

The **Senio Liqueur Factory** is the center of local production and distribution for the island's original Curaçao liqueur. The small open-air showroom is situated in a handsome landhouse. You can take a self-guided tour and read the story of the distillation process. Samples are offered and there is ample opportunity to stock up on your favorite flavors. A free tour of the Amstel Brewery is offered in nearby Salina—it's the only beer made from distilled seawater.

Craft demonstrations and folklore shows are held at **Landhuis Brivengat** on the last Sunday of each month. An Indonesian smorgasbord is served at the adjacent restaurant on Wednesdays. Dance bands play every Friday night for a party held on the veranda.

Historical Sites

Landhuis Brievengat   ★ ★ ★

Brievengat, Willemstad.

This restored 18th-century plantation house has 18-inch-thick walls, watchtowers (where long-ago lovers met), and antiques of the era. The last Sunday of each month sees crafts demonstrations and folkloric shows, and there's live music on Wednesdays and Fridays. Located about 10 minutes out of Willemstad.

Museums and Exhibits

Curacao Museum   ★ ★ ★

Van Leeuwenhoekstraat, Willemstad.

Housed in a former military quarantine hospital for those with yellow fever, this 1853 building displays art and Indian artifacts of historical significance. There's also a garden with specimens of all the plants and trees of Curacao, and the small Children's Museum of Science, where kids are asked to please touch.

Curacao Seaquarium   ★ ★ ★ ★ ★

Bapur Kibra, Willemstad.

More than 400 species of fish and marine life—in fact, EVERY species native to the area—is on display at this excellent aquarium. You can touch some of the creatures and take a glass-bottom boat ride—the truly daring can enjoy the "Animal Encounters" in which divers and snorkelers feed sharks by hand through a thick (let's hope so) mesh fence. You can also swim with sting rays, angelfish and grouper—or just watch the fun from a 46-foot-deep underwater observatory.

Jewish Cultural Historical Museum   ★ ★ ★

Kuiperstraat, Willemstad.

Located in two buildings constructed in 1728, this fine museum exhibits ceremonial and cultural objects from the 17th and 18th centuries used by one of the oldest Jewish communities in this hemisphere.

Octagon House   ★ ★

Penstraat, Willemstad.

This small museum houses antiques and personal items of Venezuelan liberator Simon Bolivar.

Parks and Gardens

Christoffel National Park

Savonet, West Point.

Hours open: 8 a.m.–4 p.m.

This 4500-acre nature preserve is located on the island's highest point, crowned by 1230-foot-high St. Christoffelberg, the highest point in all the Dutch Leewards. Well worth a visit, but come early to avoid the overwhelming late-afternoon heat. The park includes 20 miles of one-way roads, hiking trails, a small museum, rare orchids, cacti, divi-divi trees, palms, lots of birds and wild goats, Curacao deer and donkeys.

Curacao Underwater Marine Park ★★★★★

Princess Hotel, East Point.

A wonderful spot for divers and snorkelers, this 12.5-mile unspoiled reef is a protected national park. Sights include two well-preserved shipwrecks and an 875-foot underwater nature trail. On a clear day, you can see almost forever—or up to 150 feet, anyway.

Tours

Curacao Liqueur Distillery ★★

Salinja, Willemstad.

The orange-flavored liquor chobolobo is produced here in a 17th-century landhuis (land house). Witness the process and sample the results. While in the area, head over to the Amstel Brewery, where beer is made from distilled seawater. Tours are conducted only on Tuesdays and Thursdays at 10:00 a.m., after which you can drink all you want for free (designate a driver!). ☎ *612944* for information.

Hato Caves ★★★★★

F.D. Rooseveltweg, Willemstad.

Hours open: 10 a.m.–5 p.m.

Just recently opened to the public, these limestone caves are imbedded with fossil coral formations. An hour-long guided tour takes you into several caverns and past Indian petroglyphs, active stalagmites and stalactites, and underwater pools. Neat!

Old City Tours ★★★

De Ruyterkade 53, Willemstad.

Interesting walking tours of Willemstad and its wonderful architecture are sometimes led by owner Anko van der Woude, a local expert on the island's history. The two- to three-tour trek costs $15. Old City also conducts harbor tours on a small fishing bark. Prices range from $10–$17.00.

BEST VIEW:

A spectacular view of the sunset is available at Fort Nassau, on one of the highest hills in the city.

Sports

Windsurfing is one of the most popular sports here, given a tremendous boost by the constant trade winds that cool the island and blow the divi-divi trees into shape. The Curaçao Open international Pro-Am Windsurfing Championship, attracting masters from around the world, is held annually here. The best windsurfing spot is on the southeast coast between Jan Thiel and Princess beaches, the site of the annual competitions. Novices should begin at the more protected lagoon Spanish Water. Sports fishing has become extremely fashionable in Curaçao, with anglers hoping to catch tuna, dolphin, marlin, wahoo, sailfish and others. Boats may be chartered, with half- or full-day trips, and can be arranged through most hotels, or at the marinas in Spanish Water. Only hook-and-line fishing is permitted in the Curaçao Underwater Park. Yachting is popular, and regattas are held frequently, but little sailing is commercially developed for visitors. Small crafts such as Sunfish are available through hotels.

Sports/Recreation

Cruises

Various locations, Willemstad.

Tabor Tours (☎ *376637)* offers sunset cruises with wine and munchies, snorkel trips to Point Marine, and excursions aboard the Seaworld Explorer, a "semi-submarine" that cruises five feet below the water's surface. The 120-foot **Insulinde** (☎ *601340)*, a rigged sail logger, offers sunset and afternoon sails. Finally, **Sail Curacao** (☎ *676003)* has day and evening sails and snorkel trips. Bon voyage!

Curacao Golf & Squash Club

Wilhelminalaan, Willemstad.

Tourists and other nonmembers can golf on this nine-hole course only from 8 a.m.–noon Fri.–Wed., and Thur. from 10 a.m. to dusk. Greens fees are $15.

Watersports

Various locations, Willemstad.

Try one of the following: **Coral Cliff Diving** (☎ *642822)* for dive and snorkel excursions and one-week courses on scuba, sailing and windsurfing; **Underwater Curacao** (☎ *618131)*, a PADI-accredited dive shop; **Seascape Dive and Watersports** (☎ *625000)* for snorkel and scuba trips and lessons, deep-sea fishing, water-skiing and glass-bottom boat rides; **Peter Hughes Diving** (☎ *367888)* for diving, snorkeling and deep-sea fishing; and **Curacao High Wind Center** (☎ *614944)* at the Princess Beach Hotel for windsurfing lessons and rentals.

Where to Stay

Fielding's Highest Rated Hotels in Curaçao

★★★★★	Avila Beach Hotel	$90–$415
★★★★★	Lions Dive Hotel & Marina	$105–$120
★★★★	Curacao Caribbean Hotel	$140–$210
★★★★	Holland Hotel	$70–$130
★★★★	Princess Beach Resort	$140–$185
★★★★	Sonesta Beach Hotel	$160–$220
★★★★	Van der Valk Plaza Hotel	$105–$210
★★★	Ortabanda Hotel & Casino	$80–$140

Fielding's Most Romantic Hotels in Curaçao

★★★★★	Avila Beach Hotel	$90–$415
★★	Porto Paseo Hotel	$95–$125
★★★★	Sonesta Beach Hotel	$160–$220

Fielding's Budget Hotels in Curaçao

★★	Trupial Inn Hotel	$65–$100
★★★★	Holland Hotel	$70–$130
★★	Holiday Beach Hotel	$95–$115
★★★	Ortabanda Hotel & Casino	$80–$140
★★	Porto Paseo Hotel	$95–$125

Curaçao has a variety of accommodations that range from sprawling hotels with casinos to small, family-style inns. Many of the hotels have been renovated and expanded in recent years. You can choose to stay either in the suburbs (10 minutes from the shopping center) or in Willemstad Unfortunately, none of the hotels are situated on notable beaches. The Hilton and Holiday Inn chains are now owned by the government, as is the Intercontinental and a number of other hotels, and the seeming indifference of some of the staff may be attributed to the fact that they are civil servants. Hotels charge a five percent government tax and at least a 10 percent service charge. There are a number of self-catering possibilities and a couple of inns.

Hotels and Resorts

Resorts in Curaçao run from the intimate, cliff-hugging kind (**Coral Cliff Resort**) to the deluxe beachfront extravaganza (**Curaçao Caribbean Hotel & Casino**), where there's no lack of nighttime entertainment. Serious divers tend to head for the **Lions Dive Hotel & Marina**. One of the best locations is the **Van der Calk Plaza Hotel & Casino**, which is tucked into an ancient fort at the mouth of Willemstad's harbor. Nearby the ancient arches have been renovated into a charming enclave of shops.

Avila Beach Hotel   **$90–$415**   ★ ★ ★ ★ ★

Netherlands, Penstraat 130-134, Willemstad, ☎ *(599) 9-614377, FAX (599) 9-614493. Single: $90–$135. Double: $145–$415.*

History buffs revel in this hotel, which comprises the former Governor's Mansion dating back to 1780; a modern extension was added in 1991. This is Willemstad's only beachfront hotel and the spot where the royal family of Holland stays when in town. Guest rooms in the original mansion are small and simple, though individually decorated and rather charming. Those seeking more luxurious digs—and dependable hot water—should book the newer section, which has modern amenities and 18 spacious one- and two-bedroom apartments, some with kitchenette. All units are air conditioned and have cable TV and phones. The two small cove beachs are private and quite pretty, while the three European-style restaurants are grand. There's also one tennis court lit for night play. A lovely spot.

Coral Cliff Hotel   **$85–$150**   ★

Santa Marta Bay, Willemstad, ☎ *(599) 9-641610, FAX (599) 9-641781. Single: $85–$130. Double: $90–$150.*

Lots of Europeans stay at this beachfront enclave of bungalows situated on a bluff overlooking Spain Main. Guest rooms are quite spartan and could use an overhaul, but the rates are reasonable and the beach is gorgeous. There's lots to do here, including tennis, watersports, a slot casino and miniature golf. A daily shuttle transports guests to the restaurants and shopping of Willemstad, some 25 minutes away.

Curaçao Caribbean Hotel   **$140–$210**   ★ ★ ★ ★

John F. Kennedy Boulevard, ☎ *(599) 9-625000, FAX (599) 9-625846. Single: $140. Double: $150–$210.*

Located at the site of historic Fort Piscadera, just outside of Willemstad, this five-story hotel overlooks a tiny beach. Guest rooms are adequate but cry out for renovation; even the nicest rooms, on the top Executive Floor have seen better days. Nonetheless, there's a lot happening here, with organized parties, theme nights and dance lessons. A free bus takes you into town. Facilities include a dive shop, two tennis courts, pool and casino.

Holiday Beach Hotel   **$95–$115**   ★ ★

Nether Angelus, Pater Euwensweg, ☎ *(599) 9-625400, FAX (599) 9-624973.*
Single: $95–$105. Double: $110–$115.

Though it's located on one of the island's better beaches and has a large, happening casino, this former Holiday Inn still brings to mind, well, a Holiday Inn. Still, this is a good middle-market property for those seeking all the amenities without sacrificing a year's salary. Recently renovated guest rooms are decent but only a few have ocean views. There's lots to do here: two tennis courts, watersports and scuba, supervised children's activities, a lively beach bar, organized tours and a large pool.

Holland Hotel   **$70–$130**   ★ ★ ★ ★

Roosevelt Weg, FDR weg 524, Willemstad, ☎ *(599) 9-688044, FAX (599) 9-688114.*
Single: $70. Double: $80–$130.

The air-conditioned guest rooms are basic but comfortable at this small hotel near the airport. Though it's not on the beach, they do offer scuba packages, and have a pool and small casino to keep guests busy.

Las Palmas Hotel   **$93–$140**   ★ ★

Piscadera Bay.
Single: $93–$140. Double: $93–$140.

Located two miles out of Willemstad on a hillside near a private beach, this sprawling complex—-its full name is Las Palmas Hotel Villas Casino Beach Club—-is a decent choice for those watching the purse strings. Accommodations are in air-conditioned guest rooms and two-bedroom villas with kitchens. All the expected recreational facilities, from watersports to pool to tennis to casino.

Lions Dive Hotel & Marina   **$105–$120**   ★ ★ ★ ★ ★

Bapor Kibra Street, Willemstad, ☎ *(599) 9-618100, FAX (599) 9-618200.*
Single: $105–$115. Double: $115–$120.

Located next to Willemstad's Seaquarium on the island's largest beach, this spot specializes in the scuba diving trade. Their PADI dive center is superb, and offers everything from resort courses to excursions to sunset sails. There's also an excellent fitness center with all the latest equipment for whipping that body into shape. The air-conditioned guest rooms are standard but fine. Guests get to visit the aquarium for free; the shuttle that runs back and forth to town is also complimentary.

Ortabanda Hotel & Casino   **$80–$140**   ★ ★ ★

Hoek Breedesstraat, Willemstad, ☎ *(599) 9-627400, FAX (599) 9-627299.*
Single: $80–$90. Double: $95–$140.

Located in the heart of Willemstad's business and shopping district next to Queen Emma Bridge, some air-conditioned guest rooms have great harbor views. There's a restaurant and casino on site, but little else in the way of extras. Reasonable rates make this a good value.

Porto Paseo Hotel   **$95–$125**   ★ ★

De Rouvilleweg 47 Street, Willemstad, ☎ *(599) 9-627878, FAX (599) 9-627969.*
Single: $95. Double: $95–$125.

A peaceful oasis right in city center, this newer (1993) hotel has basic but comfortable air-conditioned rooms. The ubiquitous pool, casino and restaurant cater to recreational needs, and the gardens are splendid. A good in-town choice.

Princess Beach Resort   **$140–$185**   ★ ★ ★
Dr. Martin Luther King Blvd., Willemstad, ☎ *(800) 327-3286, (599) 9-367888, FAX (599) 9-617205.*
Single: $140–$145. Double: $180–$185.
Despite the name, this hotel is a Holiday Inn Crowne Plaza property, and is not affiliated with the cruise line. Located directly in front of Curacao's Underwater Park on a lovely but small beach, the hotel offers spacious guest rooms with all the modern comforts. The grounds are nicely landscaped and include two restaurants, four bars, a happening casino, pool and tennis court and all watersports. This lively spot leaves visitors satisfied.

Sonesta Beach Hotel   **$160–$220**   ★ ★ ★
Piscadera Bay, ☎ *(800) 766-3782, (599) 9-368800.*
Single: $160–$220. Double: $160–$220.
Set on the beach and built in Dutch Colonial style, this newer (1992) resort receives raves for its luxurious appointments, beautiful landscaping and attractive guest rooms, all with a patio or balcony and at least a partial ocean view. Parents like the fact that two of their kids (up to age 12) can stay with them free, and that complimentary activities keep the little ones busy. Lots of nice artwork scattered about—a Sonesta trademark—and gracious service help make this place tops. Health club, full casino, pool, tennis and watersports as well.

Van der Valk Plaza Hotel   **$105–$210**   ★ ★ ★
Plaza Piar, Willemstad, ☎ *(599) 9-612500, FAX (599) 9-618347.*
Single: $105–$180. Double: $105–$210.
Its 12-story tower sticks out like a sore thumb in quaint Willemstad, and the nearest beach is a 15-minute drive away. But nice harbor views make this hotel, built in the walls of a 17th-century fort, a pleasant choice. The central city location attracts lots of working travelers who are catered to with secretarial and business services. Guestrooms are merely adequate, but the great views of passing ships make a lot forgivable. There's a full casino and pool on site.

Apartments and Condominiums

Options range from the elegant at **La Belle Alliance** and **Las Palmas** to uninspiring apartment buildings that have basic kitchenettes.

Inns

One of the most atmospheric of all Curaçao's accommodations is the **Landhuis Hotel**. If you can get one of its few charming bedrooms, you'll feel as if you've been transported back 100 years ☎ *(599) 9-648-400.* Porta Paseo is more run-of-the-mill, though the restaurant attracts a lot of movement.

Low Cost Lodging

Best bet is to arrive in town and ask around for rooms in private homes. The tourist office can direct you to possibilities. In the off-season, Coral Cliff Resort's rooms drop down to 450, and a free shuttle bus will take you to Willemstad. Cheap rooms with kitchen privileges are also available, though they take a young, adventurous constitution to enjoy them.

Trupial Inn Hotel $65–$100   ★ ★

5, Groot Davelaarweg, Willemstad.
Single: $65–$100. Double: $75–$100.

This bungalow-style motel is located in a residential neighborhood and has no beach, though a free shuttle will take you to the sea. Rooms are basic but comfortable and have air conditioning; there are also eight suites with kitchenettes. There's a restaurant, pool and tennis court, with additional eateries and shops within walking distance.

Where to Eat

Fielding's Highest Rated Restaurants in Curaçao

★★★★★	De Taveerne	$18–$32
★★★★★	L'Alouette	$18–$40
★★★★	Bistro Le Clochard	$20–$30
★★★★	Fort Nassau	$20–$28
★★★★	Rijstaffel Restaurant	$9–$20
★★★★	Seaview	$15–$30
★★★	Belle Terrace	$10–$24
★★★	La Pergola	$25–$35
★★★	Pirates	$15–$35
★★★	Wine Cellar	$20–$35

Fielding's Special Restaurants in Curaçao

★★★★	Fort Nassau	$20–$28
★★★★	Rijstaffel Restaurant	$9–$20
★★★	Belle Terrace	$10–$24
★★★	Golden Star	$8–$26
★★★	Wine Cellar	$20–$35

Fielding's Budget Restaurants in Curaçao

★★	Cactus Club	$4–$15
★★	Playa Forti	$5–$16
★★★★	Rijstaffel Restaurant	$9–$20
★★★	Belle Terrace	$10–$24
★★★	Golden Star	$8–$26

Dining in Curaçao is an international smorgasbord of delights, from French, Swiss and Italian, to Danish, Dutch, Indonesian, Creole, South American and junk-food American-style. Excellent food isn't cheap here, but when combined with some of the most romantic atmospheres in the islands, you'll feel the bill was worth it. Ensconced in a wine cellar in one of the old landhouse estates, **De Taveerne** is a must for anyone on a honeymoon who wants the soap-opera-dinner-by-candlelight-on-a-tropical-isle experience. **Bistro Le Clochard** also rates high for romance, with its cozy, candlelit rooms tucked into an old fort overlooking the sea. For local dishes at bargain prices, prepare to trek a bit to **Golden Star**, on the coast road leading southeast from St. Anna Bay. Surroundings are humble, but such Curaçao delicacies as *kiwa* (criollo shrimp), *bestia chiki* (goat-meat stew) and *bakijauw* (salted cod) are superb. One of the best views of the island is at **Playa Forti**, in the extreme northwest of the island. Snorkel before lunch or dinner, then order a brimming plate of *ayaca*, a chicken-beef combo, stuffed with nuts, raisins, spices and olives, rolled up in a corn dough tortilla. *Funchi*, the local cornmeal staple, comes with everything.

'T Kokkeltje $$$ ★★

F.D. Rooseveltweg 524.
International cuisine. Specialties: Split-pea soup, herring, Caribbean chicken.
Lunch: entrees $12–$27.
Dinner: entrees $12–$27.

Sample Dutch fare by the pool at the Hotel Holland located on the highway to the airport. The hard-to-pronounce name means cockles and this cozy restaurant serves marinated mussels when available. Other specialties to savor are split-pea soup, pickled herring and salads. There is also a dimly lit dining room for those who prefer it. Food is served from 7 a.m. to 10:30 p.m.

Belle Terrace $$$ ★★★

Penstraat 130, ☎ *(599) 961-4377.*
Scandinavian cuisine. Specialties: Danish smorgasbord, keshi yena, barracuda.
Lunch: Noon–3 p.m., entrees $10–$15.
Dinner: 7–10 p.m., entrees $14–$24.

Eating out in Willemstad is very often a historic experience—one day it's breakfast high above the sea (never far away here) on a hilltop in a converted 18th-century fort, or, in the case of the Belle Terrace, right on the beach (albeit a rocky one) in a 200-year-old mansion, the former home of the island's governor. Sometimes the cuisine, which includes a smorgasbord at lunch, featuring salmon and other fish smoked on the premises, can be less than stellar, but with a setting like this, who cares? Breads and ice creams are homemade.

Bistro Le Clochard $$$ ★★★★

Rif Fort, ☎ *(599) 962-5666.*
French cuisine. Specialties: Bouillabaisse, raclette, fondue.
Lunch: Noon–2 p.m., entrees $20–$30.
Dinner: 6:30–11 p.m., entrees $20–$30.

Dine in this traditional French/Swiss bistro, one of a number of restaurants built in the vaults of what is left of the old (early 19th century) Rif Fort near the harbor. As with many Willemstad restaurants, you may dine indoors or on the open-air Harborside Terrace. Various fondues reflect the tastes of the owner's wife (who is Swiss), and they include raclette with potatoes, pickles and onions, and bourguignone. There's also fresh fish, veal and lobster. The outdoor terrace is only open for dinner, and there's no lunch served on weekends.

Cactus Club $$ ★★

6 van Staverenweg, ☎ *(599) 937-1600.*
American cuisine. Specialties: Fajitas, buffalo wings, cajun snapper.
Lunch: 11:30 a.m.–3 p.m., entrees $4–$15.
Dinner: 5–11:30 p.m., entrees $7–$15.
A transplanted, stateside-style after-work restaurant and bar, the Cactus Club doles out tasty burgers, shakes, nachos, pastas and fajitas to homesick Americans and locals who love the place, which is always full. Decor is Southwest-desert, but it's nice and cool inside.

De Taveerne $$$ ★★★★★

Landhuis Groot Davelaar, Salina, ☎ *(599) 937-0669.*
French cuisine. Specialties: Salmon carpaccio, chateaubriand stroganoff for two.
Lunch: Noon–2 p.m., entrees $18–$32.
Dinner: 7–11 p.m., entrees $18–$32.

The owners of this innovative and highly regarded French restaurant in the Salina residential area have renovated a traditional old octagonal country mansion—the Landhuis Groot Davelaar, built in the early 18th century by a South American revolutionary—into an antique-filled mini-museum. Once the main house of a cattle-producing estate, it is one of many scattered throughout the arid countryside. Prime beef shows up on its tables in the form of platter-size steaks and chateaubriand for two. Closed for lunch on Saturdays.

Fort Nassau $$$ ★★★★

Fort Nassau, ☎ *(599) 961-3086.*
International cuisine. Specialties: Smoked salmon, shrimp with red linguine in a spicy sauce.
Lunch: Noon–3 p.m., entrees $20–$28.
Dinner: 7–10 p.m., entrees $20–$28.
If you never dine anywhere else in Curacao, don't miss Fort Nassau, which sings with history even though some dishes may be overambitious and miss the mark at times. Perched like an eagle's nest above Willemstad and overlooking Santa Anna Bay, diners can see forever from here. Used as a fort by the Dutch in the late 18th century and by Americans in World War II, it became a restaurant in the 1950s. Cuisine runs the gamut from Asian to Italian, utilizing fresh fish, pasta and game in combination with local tropical fruits. No lunch served on weekends.

Fort Waakzaamheid Bistro $$$ ★★

Seru di Domi, ☎ *(599) 962-3633.*
Seafood cuisine. Specialties: Veal curry, barbecued steaks.
Dinner: 5–11 p.m., entrees $17–$26.

An alternative to the often-crowded Fort Nassau, which gets inundated with cruise-ship passengers, this hilltop aerie in the Otrabanda was held captive many moons ago by the notorious Captain Bligh, probably in part because he was spellbound by the view. There is no need to dress up for this American-style tavern and bar, which is open for dinner only. There is a fresh fish and salad special daily, as well as barbecued steaks, scampi and veal curry.

Golden Star $$$ ★★★

Socratesstraat 2, ☎ (599) 965-4795.
Latin American cuisine. Specialties: Carni stoba, stoba de Carco, grilled conch.
Lunch: 11 a.m.–1 p.m., entrees $8–$26.
Dinner: 11 p.m.–1 a.m., entrees $8–$26.

Go local in this deliberately tacky restaurant dive, which has the best authentic Antillean food in town. There may be no better place for carni stoba (meat stew), conch served lightly grilled or with vegetables, goat and criollo shrimp, accompanied with plenty of starchy and filling (and good) rice, fried bananas and funchi (cornmeal pancakes). Beer, especially locally brewed Amstel, is the preferred beverage with this food. Golden Star is open until 1:00 a.m.

L'Alouette $$$ ★★★★★

Orionweig 12, Salina, ☎ (599) 961-8222.
International cuisine. Specialties: Cheese flan, seafood sausage.
Lunch: Noon–2:30 p.m., entrees $18–$30.
Dinner: 6–9 p.m., entrees $30–$40.

Amid beautiful, sleek surroundings, you can eat creative French cuisine and still keep your weight down at this sophisticated eatery specializing in the best ingredients available, embellished with light and springlike herbs and spices. Chef Maria Eugenia Saban pays close attention to detail in this restored house in a residential area on the east side of the harbor. Specials that never change are her cheese flan duet with mushroom and basil sauces. Cuisine may be light, but portions are substantial and worth the high tariff.

La Pergola $$$ ★★★

Waterfort Arches, ☎ (599) 961-3482.
Italian cuisine. Specialties: Smoked salmon with olive oil and cloves, grouper siciliana.
Lunch: Noon–2 p.m., entrees $25–$35.
Dinner: 6:30–10:30 p.m., entrees $30–$35.

A seaside Italian eatery in the trendy Waterfort Arches shopping center, La Pergola serves pizzas, fresh fish and desserts with a light hand—no heavy tomato or gloppy cream sauces here. Take your seat on the lovely terrace facing wraparound windows and watch the wavy action below, and feast on the likes of grouper Sicilian-style with a puttanesca sauce and conclude with an airy, angelic Zuppa Inglese. Closed for Sunday lunch.

Pirates $$$ ★★★

Piscadera Bay, ☎ (599) 962-5000.
Latin American cuisine. Specialties: Paella, red snapper almendrado, ceviche.
Lunch: entrees $15–$35.
Dinner: entrees $15–$35.

In addition to an Indonesian restaurant, La Garuda, and bountiful buffets served on the Pisca Terrace bar facing a spectacular swimming pool, this newcomer to the Curacao Caribbean Hotel and Casino's dining scene might assure that its guests needn't leave this minicity-within-a-city resort on Piscadera Bay. Famous for theme-night parties, the hotel's latest successful scheme is Pirates, specializing in tasty Latin-style seafood, including paella and ceviche, served by a charming waitstaff in nautical garb.

Playa Forti $$ ★★

Westpunt, ☎ *(599) 964-0273.*
Latin American cuisine. Specialties: Cabrito, fish soup, keshi yena.
Lunch: entrees $5–$16.
Dinner: entrees $6–$16.
If you find yourself in the northwest point of the island, dine at this clifftop retreat overlooking Playa Forti beach. It's a hangout for tasty criollo food, and a good place to try keshi yena, an island specialty of meats cooked with Creole sauce and covered with Edam or Gouda cheese. Other specialties to try are cabrito or goat stew, and funchi, or local cornbread. Sunsets are gorgeous here as well. Meals are served from 10 a.m. to 6 p.m.

Rijstaffel Restaurant $$$ ★★★★

Mercuriusstraat 13, Salina, ☎ *(599) 961-2999.*
Asian cuisine. Specialties: Rijstaffel, bami goreng, jumbo shrimp in garlic sauce.
Lunch: Noon–2 p.m., prix fixe $9–$17.
Dinner: 6–9:30 p.m., prix fixe $13–$20.
A carryover of Dutch colonial days, rijstaffel is a banquet of up to 25 spicy and savory Indonesian-Javanese dishes surrounded by a mound of steaming rice. A delightful change from the usual steaks and surf and turf awaits at this restaurant in the Salina area, known for its nightlife. To eat here, get a group together and book a table several days ahead for a 16-to-25 dish feast that includes bami goreng (fried noodles, shrimp, meat and vegetables) and krupuk (gigantic shrimp chips). Vegetarian and a la carte dishes are also available.

Seaview $$$ ★★★★

Waterfort Arches, ☎ *(599) 961-6688.*
Seafood cuisine. Specialties: Salpicon de mariscos, pepper filet.
Lunch: Noon–2 p.m., entrees $15–$30.
Dinner: 6–10 p.m., entrees $15–$30.
An amiable surfside spot located right in the heart of the Waterfort Arches, one of Willemstad's many converted old army posts and now a busy retail, nightlife and culinary bazaar, Seaview offers up spectacular ocean and sunset vistas from a breezy terrace or air-conditioned dining room. Its forte, naturally, is fresh-from-the-briny fish and shellfish, as well as prime meats, fresh vegetables and international dishes.

Wine Cellar $$$ ★★★

Concordiastraat, ☎ *(599) 961-2178.*
International cuisine. Specialties: Roast goose, lobster salad, red snapper.
Lunch: Noon–2 p.m., entrees $20–$35.
Dinner: 5–11 p.m., entrees $20–$35.

Connoisseurs of fine wines repair here to master sommelier and rotisseur Nico Cornelisse's lair, a traditional, small (about eight tables) and comfortable Dutch home near the cathedral in downtown Willemstad. The voluminous wine list consists of vintages from the Alsace region of France, as well as Germany and Italy. To complement these refined labels are some hearty dishes to warm the blood, including filet of beef with goat cheese sauce, venison and roast goose. More delicate appetites will appreciate light seafood salads and red snapper. Service is attentive and personable.

Where to Shop

Curaçao is famed for its shopping, some of the best in the Caribbean, with more than 200 shops. Three of the main shopping streets are pedestrian malls with no traffic or exhaust, making strolling a joy. Cruise ships dock at the downside terminal, which is a short walk to the shopping center; when ships dock, stores stay open on Sunday and holidays. Right in the heart of Willemstad is the Punda shopping district in a five-block square. Since everyone speaks three or four languages, you won't have any trouble understanding shop clerks. Best of all, Curaçao has a very low duty (3 percent) on imported tourist items and no sales tax. No import duty is charged on locally made jewelry, handcrafts, art and antiques. Good bargains can be found on German and Japanese cameras, Swiss watches, Dutch Delft blue souvenirs and Curaçao liqueur. **Little Switzerland** is the premier watch store in the Caribbean. Designer clothes can be found at **Penha 7 Sons**. The **Yellow House** handles the best stock of perfume on the island.

The most charming shopping center is the **Waterfront Arches**, an historic waterfront remodeled into a cove of quaint boutiques with exotic imports from Paris, Indonesia and South America.

Curaçao Directory

ARRIVAL

American Airlines provides daily nonstop flights to Curaçao from Miami. American also offers flights to Aruba from New York, Miami, and San Juan, Puerto Rico, where you can make an easy transfer to Curaçao. American also offers discounts if their agent makes your hotel reservation at the same time as your air passage. **ALM**, the national carrier of Curaçao, also flies 13 times a week from Miami to Curaçao (three nonstop) and four times a week from Atlanta. **Air Aruba** also flies seven times a week to Aruba from Newark; easy transfers can be made to Curaçao.

BUSINESS HOURS

Shops open Monday–Saturday 8 a.m.–noon and 2–6 p.m. Banks open Monday–Friday 8:30 a.m.–noon and 1:30–4:30 p.m.

CLIMATE

Like Bonaire and Aruba, its neighbors, Curaçao is to the south of the Hurricane Belt, making storms an extremely unusual occurrence. The island is constantly refreshed by trade winds blowing from 10–20 miles per hour and the temperature stays constant all year round, seldom fluctuating out of the mid-80s. Summer can be a few degrees hotter and winter a little cooler. Light, casual clothing is the rule. Hotels and casinos are air-conditioned so you may wish to bring fancier clothes, or a sweater.

DOCUMENTS

U.S. and Canadian citizens need to show proof of citizenship (passport, birth certificate, or voter's registration) plus a photo ID, and an ongoing or return ticket beyond the Netherlands Antilles.

ELECTRICITY

Current is 110–130 volts AC, 50 cycles. Outlets are American-style. Converters are not necessarily needed for American appliances, but hotels have supplies.

GETTING AROUND

Inquire whether your hotel has a free shuttle service to the shopping district of Willemstad. If not, yellow city buses stop at Wilhelmina Plein, near the shopping center, and travel to most parts of the city. Buses stop when you hail them.

Taxi rates are regulated by the government. Don't tip a driver unless he carries your luggage. Charges after 11 p.m. go up by 25 percent. You'll find lots of taxis waiting for passengers on the Otrabanda side of the floating bridge. If you want to make a tour by taxi, expect to pay about $20 per hour (up to four passengers allowed).

Rental cars are represented by **Avis** toll-free ☎ *(800) 31-2112*, **Budget** toll free ☎ *(800) 527-0700* and **Hertz** toll-free ☎ *(800) 654-3001*. Check your credit card to see if you can obtain insurance just by charging. To save money, reserve the car from the States before you arrive. Do note that all driving is on the right.

LANGUAGE

The native language is Papiamento, the official language Dutch, but most everybody speaks some form of English, as well as Spanish.

MEDICAL EMERGENCIES

The 550-bed St. Elizabeth Hospital is the main facility of the island.

MONEY

Official currency is guilder (Netherlands Antilles florin), noted as NAf. U.S. dollars and credit cards are accepted unilaterally.

TELEPHONE

Country code is *5999*. From the States, dial *011* (international access code), *5999* (country code) + local number. If you are calling from another Caribbean island, check to see if the same code applies. Within Curaçao itself, use only the six-digit number.

TIME

Atlantic Standard Time all year long.

TIPPING AND TAXES

Ten percent service charge is added to restaurant bills, but waiters appreciate an extra five percent.

TOURIST INFORMATION

The **Curaçao Tourist Board** has offices in *Willemstad at the Waterfront Arches* ☎ *613397, closed weekends, and 19 Pietermaai* ☎ *661600.* At all offices you can obtain brochures, maps and have questions answered by English-speaking staff. An office is also at the airport ☎ *668678* (open daily till last flight arrives). In the U.S. call ☎ *(800) 270-3350.*

WATER

Tap water, distilled seawater, is safe to drink.

WHEN TO GO

Carnival takes place in January, an unrestrained revel complete with costumes, parades and street parties. Best time is the weekend right before Ash Wednesday. The International Sailing Regatta is held in March.

CURAÇAO HOTELS		RMS	RATES	PHONE	CR. CARDS
Willemstad					
★★★★★	**Avila Beach Hotel**	90	$90–$415	(599) 9-614377	A, DC, MC, V
★★★★★	**Lions Dive Hotel & Marina**	72	$105–$120	(599) 9-618100	A, DC, MC, V
★★★★	**Curaçao Caribbean Hotel**	200	$140–$210	(599) 9-625000	A, DC, MC, V
★★★★	**Holland Hotel**	40	$70–$130	(599) 9-688044	A, DC, MC, V
★★★★	**Princess Beach Resort**	341	$140–$185	(800) 327-3286	A, D, DC, MC, V
★★★★	**Sonesta Beach Hotel**	248	$160–$220	(800) 766-3782	A, DC, MC, V
★★★★	**Van der Valk Plaza Hotel**	350	$105–$210	(599) 9-612500	A, MC, V
★★★	**Ortabanda Hotel & Casino**	45	$80–$140	(599) 9-627400	A, D, DC, MC, V
★★	**Holiday Beach Hotel**	200	$95–$115	(599) 9-625400	A, D, DC, MC, V
★★	**Las Palmas Hotel**	184	$93–$140		A, DC, MC, V

CURAÇAO HOTELS	RMS	RATES	PHONE	CR. CARDS
★★ Porto Paseo Hotel	44	$95–$125	(599) 9-627878	A, DC, MC, V
★★ Trupial Inn Hotel	74	$65–$100		A, DC, MC, V
★ Coral Cliff Hotel	35	$85–$150	(599) 9-641610	A, DC, MC, V

CURAÇAO RESTAURANTS	PHONE	ENTREE	CR. CARDS

Willemstad

American			
★★ Cactus Club	(599) 937-1600	$4–$15	DC, MC, V
Asian			
★★★★ Rijstaffel Restaurant	(599) 961-2999	$9–$20	A, DC, MC, V
French			
★★★★★ De Taveerne	(599) 937-0669	$18–$32	A, DC, MC, V
★★★★ Bistro Le Clochard	(599) 962-5666	$20–$30	A, DC, MC, V
International			
★★★★★ L'Alouette	(599) 961-8222	$18–$40	A, DC, MC, V
★★★★ Fort Nassau	(599) 961-3086	$20–$28	A, DC, MC, V
★★★ Wine Cellar	(599) 961-2178	$20–$35	A, MC, V
★★ 'T Kokkeltje		$12–$27	A, MC, V
Italian			
★★★ La Pergola	(599) 961-3482	$25–$35	A, D, DC, MC, V
Latin American			
★★★ Golden Star	(599) 965-4795	$8–$26	A, DC, MC, V
★★★ Pirates	(599) 962-5000	$15–$35	A, DC, MC, V
★★ Playa Forti	(599) 964-0273	$5–$16	A, MC, V
Scandinavian			
★★★ Belle Terrace	(599) 961-4377	$10–$24	A, DC, MC, V
Seafood			
★★★★ Seaview	(599) 961-6688	$15–$30	A
★★ Fort Waakzaamheid Bistro	(599) 962-3633	$17–$26••	A, MC, V

Note: • Lunch Only

•• Dinner Only

DOMINICAN REPUBLIC

The best place to tee off in Santo Domingo is the course at Casa de Campo.

The Dominican Republic is the granddaddy of the Caribbean. It can claim age rank over any other island in the region in nearly every category. It has the oldest city, Santo Domingo, in the New World; the oldest street, the oldest cathedral, the oldest university, and even the remains of the oldest hospital. Despite its intense historical interest, the country has lagged behind in tourism for decades due to the negative influence of Generalissimo Rafael Leónidas Trujillo, the former ruthless dictator who controlled the government for more than 30 years till 1961. His regime and the purposes of tourism were at cross-purposes, despite the building of several casinos; the presence of paramilitary troops on the streets didn't attract tourists in any case. Not until the mid-'70s did interest in the island return, as the government poured millions into renovating and building a viable touristic infrastructure. The American firm, Gulf & Western, also contributed to the building of a famous resort in the south as well as other hotels, expanding the number of available rooms and offering new luxury accommodations. These days annual tourists have swelled to more than 2 million, seeking many of the comforts of other islands—and at a fraction of the cost. The island is being heavily promoted today by tourist officials under the fantasy name "Dominicana," suggesting a calmer, less frantic paradise—not exactly the picture of bustling Santo Domingo where the crime rate has risen and tourists must travel with a big eye to caution. Electricity failures are common, which might be why many people head straight for outdoor treks—considered to be spectacular here. What the Dominican Republic excels in are beaches, a thousand miles' worth, anywhere from mountainous backdrops to powdery coves.

Bird's Eye View

The Dominican Republic, which shares the island of Hispaniola with Haiti, is situated between Cuba and Puerto Rico in the Caribbean Sea. An ecological wonder, the island harbors 14 national parks and seven reserves. Beyond the beaches are tropical forests and mountains sprinkled with more than 300 varieties of orchids, and 5600 other plant species, 36 percent of which are endemic. The highest peak is **Pico Duarte** at 10,400 feet, which ranks as the highest mountain in the Caribbean. **Lago Enriquillo**, an unusual saltwater lake 144 feet below sea-level, is home to a large reserve of American crocodiles. *Isla Cabrito*, **Goat Island**, which lies in the lake, has a research center where scientists collaborate with the National Zoo to increase the crocodile population. The capital and chief seaport is **Santo Domingo**, whose 12-block historical center, brings great charm to the island. The road from Santo Domingo leads through lush banana plantations and rice and tobacco fields to the groves of royal poinciana trees in the Cibao Valley, where the island's oldest settlement, **La Vega**, is located. A hundred miles north of the capital is the industrial city of **Santiago los Caballeros**, a center for tobacco leaf production. Once a dynamic town now turned sleepy, **Puerto Plata** in the northern coast is home to many of the island's most luxurious resorts.

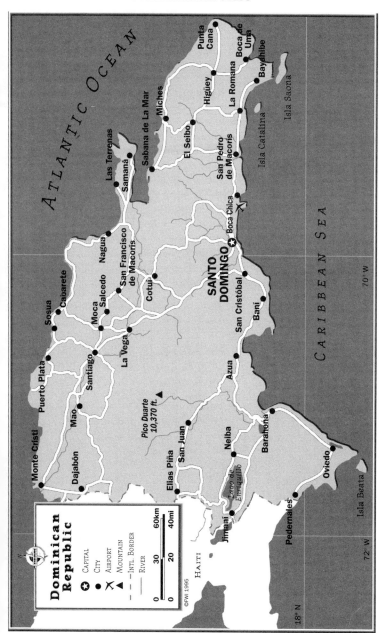

History

One could say that the Dominican Republic is really a family affair. The great Christopher Columbus dropped anchor in the Dominican Republic on his first voyage in 1492; four years later, his brother Bartolomeo founded the colony of Santo Domingo; 13 years after that, Christopher's son became the colony's governor, serving as viceroy when the Dominican Republic, then the colony of Santo Domingo, was the provisioning port and jump-off place for some of Spain's greatest expeditions to the New World. The list of explorers who sailed from this port is as impressive as a Hollywood A-list: Juan Ponce de Léon to Puerto Rico, Velasquez to Cuba, Cortés to Mexico. Even Sir Francis Drake put his mark on the port, attacking it, ransacking it, and then setting fire to it in 1586.

Over the next 300 years, the island changed hands between France, Spain and Cuba, and for a time it was even self-ruled in a phase called "Ephemeral Independence." Since winning its independence from Spain in 1821 and from Haiti in 1844, the Dominican Republic has been plagued by recurrent domestic conflicts and foreign intervention; between 1916 and 1924 it was occupied by American forces. In 1930 the country entered into a 30-year dictatorship led by General Rafael Leónidas Trujillo Molina, who ruled personally until 1947 and indirectly thereafter until his assassination in 1961. His death gave rise to renewed political turmoil, and an election in December 1962 led to the inauguration of Juan Bosch Gaviño, a left-of-center democrat, as president in February 1963. In the same year, Bosch was overthrown by a military coup; subsequently the military installed a civilian triumvirate which ruled until April 1965, when civil war erupted. Military forces intervened on April 28, 1965, and imposed a truce while arrangements were made to establish a provisional government and prepare for new elections. For the next 12 years the country was run by a moderate, Dr. Joaquin Balaguer, who then returned after one term for another two consecutive ones. Presently there are at least 10 different political parties representing diverse ideological viewpoints, including the Social Christian Reformed Party of 80-year-old Dr. Balaguer to the Dominican Revolutionary Party, a left-democratic grouping, to the right-wing Quisqueyan Democratic Party, the Dominican Communist Party (a traditionally pro-Moscow party), and the Dominican Popular Movement, which is pro-Peking.

People

The population of the island (more than 3 million) is a mixture of black, white and mestizo, but each of those terms come with a special island definition. *Blanco* (or white) refers to anybody who is white, white/Indian mestizo, or substantially white with either or both Indian and African mixture. *Indio claro* is anybody who is white/black mixed mulatto or a mestizo; *indio oscuro* is anyone who is not 100 percent black; *negro* is 100 percent African. The African and Afro-Cuban influence is deeply present in the song and dance of the island, with merengue the dominant beat, typically played by a three-man group. There are festivals throughout the year, and international merengue celebrations that attract music lovers from all over. Due to political unrest and an unstable economy (not to mention high unemployment) there is, sad to say, a level of violence that underscores society here; in the past few years, unruly demonstrations and strikes have marred the island's equilibrium. Because of the hard economic conditions, great care should be taken with one's valuables (from luggage to camera to purse) at all times. Crime is quite prevalent, and tourists are often conned into various compromising situations (big and small). About a quarter of the population is employed in agriculture, and the farther you go from the main city, the more simple and less harried will be the people you meet. Almost all profess Christianity and 80 percent are Roman Catholics. There are small Protestant and Jewish communities.

Beaches

A whopping 1000 miles of beaches await visitors, who often have a hard time just deciding which beach to pick for the day. Unfortunately, the beach closest to the city—**Boca Chica** (about 21 miles from the capital)—is also the most crowded, a veritable zoo on the weekends as locals and tourists alike invade the vanilla-white strands. In the past five years the fine white sands have gone from nearly deserted to a clutter of pizza huts, plastic beach tables and lounge chairs, and rental cottages full of screaming babies. The one thing that has remained protected here are the coral reefs, which serve to keep dangerous marine life from getting too close. As such, feel free to walk out in to the sea. Twenty minutes east of Boca Chica is **Juan Dolio**, with its powdery white beach. Here you'll find the Villas del Mar Hotel and the Punta Garza Beach Club. Other excellent beaches are the thumbprint-sized **Minitas** beach and lagoon, and the palm-fringed **Bayahibe**, only accessible by boat. This area, called **La Romana**, also houses the Casa de Campo Resort, which means it is usually crowded. The island's pride and joy is **Punta Cana**, a 20-mile sprawl (though it seems longer for its beauty), lined with shady trees and coconut palms. Here is located **Club Med**, the **Melia Punta Cara**, and the **Bavaro Beach Resort**. Primitive is the only description for **Las Terrenas**, tucked into the north coast of the Samaná peninsula. You'll be hard-pressed to find anything here other than tall palms, sea, mountains and sand. **Sosuá** could be pleasant since the waves are gentle and the sand white and soft, but the scene is marred by camping tents and hawkers selling cheap trinkets. The beach of the future is **Puerto Plata**, on the north Amber Coast, where there are excellent reefs for snorkeling and the horizon hasn't yet been marred by too much civilization. Windsurfers and waterskiers particularly love the conditions, and many fishing expeditions take off from here. Windsurfing conditions on **Cabarete Beach** are excellent; between June and October wind speeds at 20–25 knots and 3- to 15-foot waves attract some of the best windsurfers in the Caribbean.

The Dominican Republic is known for its beautiful beaches.

Underwater

Diving in the Dominican Republic is an activity undergoing a slow evolution. There have always been a number of good diving possibilities off the island's extensive coastline. Unfortunately, with few exceptions, the island's fish population is substantially depleted, even in the so-called marine parks which have been set up to counteract the shortage of fish life. Extensive spear fishing has also hurt the reefs themselves along the coastline; they are battered and trashed within swimming distance from many shores. Reportedly, most of the coral off **Barahona** is dead; even the reefs ringing remote **Monte Cristi** are said to be largely destroyed. Artificial wrecks (see below) are slowly helping to boost the marine creatures, but the entire island, sadly, will never be the first-class dive destination it might have been a few decades ago.

Perhaps the island's best diving lies off the **Pedernales Coast**, near the southern border with Haiti, but access to this part of the island is through a distant, forbidding frontier, requiring a sort of mini-expedition to reach. The seclusion is the key to its beauty and serious dive visitors will want to inquire about a multi-day trip. A number of the Dominican Republic's better sites are located off the **Boca Chica Lagoon**, where two small islands within **La Caleta Marine Park**, provide some diversion. Visibility is limited, by Caribbean standards, to an average of 50 to 60 feet, though it can hit 75 feet on good days. There is a wall (15 to 100 feet) and reef on the north side of **Catalina Island**, an outpost just off the coast from Romana—"real Caribbean-style diving," says one local diver—but plans for a cruise ship pier may wreck havoc. Further east, at **Bayahibe**, a small fishing village approaching tourism with a cautious eye, there is also good diving. At the eastern tip of the island, off **Punta Cana**, the Atlantic Ocean and Caribbean Sea meet; there is reported to be nice reefs and several interesting wrecks, but dive shops appear to be based only out of the all-inclusive resorts for now. At **Las Terrenas**, on the Samana Peninsula, dive shops have started springing up, but visibility here can be hampered by freshwater runoff from the lush forests. Those who enjoy wrecks can be occupied by several sites. Among the major finds are two 17th-century Spanish galleons, the *Tolosa* and the *Guadeloupe*, both located near the entrance to Samana Bay. La Caleta Marine Park has two artificial reefs for diving; the wreck of the 140-foot steel-hulled *Hickory* sits on a slope which drops to 60 feet, while the wooden 90-foot patrol boat *Capitan Alcina* is wedged in a canyon, 126 feet down. The north coast reefs off Monte Cristi, near the Haitian border, are a graveyard for a number of pirate ships, although the wooden hulls are long gone.

Outside the major resorts, Dominican dive shops have mixed reputations and tend to change hands with alarming frequency. Although most of the Dominican Republic's visitors are European, the outfit listed below caters to Americans. It's also possible to contact the major coastal resorts and arrange a day or two of diving with them. There is a recompression chamber located in Santo Domingo.

Dive Shops

Treasure Divers

> *Boca Chica;* ☎ *(809) 523-5320.*
> Walter and Peter are the owners of this seven-year-old PADI and CMAS facility, offering courses to assistant instructor. Single tank dive, $40 including all equipment (or $37 if you bring your own); packages also available. Night dives, $55. Resort course (in pool), $75. Arranges multi-day trips to the Pedernales coastline off Cabo Rojo, as well as whale-watching in season.

On Foot

Supporting one of the most diverse eco-systems in the Caribbean basin, the Dominican Republic is an explorer's paradise. Cresting at a majestic 10,370 feet, **Pico Duarte** represents the highest point in the Caribbean basin, high enough to attract a delicate mantle of snow a few times each winter. Physically, the island's major summits—almost a dozen rising higher than 8000 feet—do not look anything like the craggy Sierras or Rockies, but actually more resemble the gentle terrain found in the Adirondacks of New York. The country features 5500 species of flowering plants and ferns. The **Armando Bermudez National Park**, which encompasses most of the island's highest points, is a prime destination for visitors inclined toward outdoor activities.

Pico Duarte

> Perhaps the grandest trek available in the Caribbean, the ascent of Pico Duarte requires a solid three days from the tiny hamlet of Boca de Rios, located in a stunning valley above Jarabacoa. A small National Park office (La Cienaga) serves as the starting point at an elevation of 3300 feet. From here, it is 14 miles to the top, ascending the Rio Yaque del Norte river valley through broadleaf forest to steeper slopes supporting a montane forest environment of orchids, epiphytes and tree ferns. Higher, one enters the pine forest and, at the nine-mile point, there is a spring

and mountain shelter, La Comparticion (elevation 7900 feet), for overnighting before the final summit assault. About 2500 people climb Pico Duarte each year, about 80% of them are Dominicans, many of whom make the ascent in the cold winter months to savor an alpine experience (if you want the trail to yourself, avoid the periods surrounding Christmas and Easter). Summer months bring little or no rainfall, but you'll still need to dress properly; even in August, nighttime temperatures on the upper slopes can drop to 40°F! Late fall brings particularly wet weather, and muddy trails. Guides are not absolutely essential, but they can help with transportation, food and sleeping logistics and ensure a smoother venture; you can check around in Boca de Rios for a local guide, or arrange your trip in advance with an outfit like Iguana Mama (see By Pedal, below). It's possible to complete the hike in two long days, but before locking down establishing provisions and equipment for such a trip, remember that you will be undergoing a healthy 7000-foot elevation change on the 28-mile round-trip.

FIELDING'S CHOICE:

From January to late February, whales can be seen at the mouth of the Samaná Bay. There are no organized excursions, but local boatmen will arrange trips, though permission must be obtained from the Naval Station in advance. From late December to early March, 3000 migrating humpback whales come to mate in Silver Bank, a marine sanctuary located 50 miles off the coast, directly north of Cabrera. Occasional expeditions by scientists are taken to the site, which run about 7-12 hours. To join an expedition, contact the National Parks Office in Santo Domingo.

BEST VIEW:

The panoramic sweep of the island, seen from the top of the Pico Duarte mountain, is spectacular. At almost 11,000 feet, it's a climb only the truly fit should attempt. It's best to go with a guide. Beginning in late fall 1994, Ecoturisa, in partnership with Occidental Hotels, began offering five-day packages, blankets, flashlights, guides, mules and meals. Part of the climb is covered on muleback, the rest on foot. During December and January, frost glazes the tropical landscape and intensifies the grandeur of the view.

By Pedal

The Dominican Republic is an old-fashioned country in many ways, but is slowly building a network of cyclists. Many locals still wonder why anyone would want to bike through their country on a vacation, but will receive you openly. One of the best areas to ride is in the **Bermudez National Park**, which features virtually no paved access, but offers a surfeit of single track roads and donkey trails through the dense forests.

Bike Rental Shops

Iguana Mama

Cabarete; ☎ *(809) 571-0908.*

Mountain bike rental shop run by an enthusiastic American woman determined to make the Dominican Republic the mountain bike capital of the Caribbean. Also assembles adventure tours that combine elements of cycling, hiking, rafting and more. The outfit is an excellent resource on nonresort exploration.

What Else to See

The 12-block area known as the **Colonial Zone** is a must-see on any itinerary. The area today bristles with feverish activity, as people and cars jostle their way through the narrow cobbled streets, home to some of the finest restaurants, shops and galleries on the island. Strange how all the noise and confusion of the modern cityscape takes one immediately back centuries, when the city was yet a colony and a home port for pirates, colonists and great explorers. Most recently, the island has invested millions of dollars to renovate this area, and numerous sights are well worth the time to visit. Top on the list should be the **Alcázar de Cólon**, an imposing Renaissance castle, once the home of Don Diego Colon (aka Columbus). The antiques and tapestries did not all belong to Columbus, who lived here with his bride (some are even of the wrong century), but the total effect gives the feeling of life with the great explorers. Built in 1514, it was reconstructed and restored in 1957.

Across the street is the **La Ataranza**, the Royal Mooring Docks, once the colonial commercial district, and now home to several crafts stores, restaurants, and galleries. The **Museu de las Casas Reales** (Museum of the Royal House) presents exhibits that include replicas of Columbus' famous three ships, ancient maps, coats of arms, coaches and a royal courtroom, as well as Indian artifacts. The **Casa de Bastidas** (south on Calle Las Damas and cross Calle El Conde) boasts a beautiful courtyard full of tropical plants and temporary art exhibits that show unusually excellent pieces.

Make time to step inside the most wondrous **Catedral Santa Maria la Meno, Primada de America**, the first cathedral in America. In the nave are four baroque columns, carved to resemble royal palms, which for more than four centuries guarded the magnificent bronze and marble sarcophagus containing (some Dominican historians claim) the final remains of Christopher Columbus. Started in 1514, the church was finally finished in 1540, its facade a heady mixture of late Gothic to Plateresque styles. The sarcophagus has been moved of late to the **Columbus Memorial Lighthouse**. (Actually, it was Columbus' last wish that he be buried in Santo Domingo.) After the French occupation, the Spaniards stole his remains from the cathedral and sent them to Cuba. Later, both Spain and Cuba claimed to have confiscated the bones of someone named Columbus, but nobody really knows whether it was Christopher (or even *the* Christopher) or one of his grandsons.

If you have time, stop by the Columbus Lighthouse, a newly constructed memorial that includes six museums, a laser-beam lighthouse, and a chapel (one more place that claims to hold the dear old bones of Columbus) and the **Parque Zoological Nacional**, a lake for water-bound birds and an open plains park where animals roam freely. Children particularly love the children's section and the caves that are perfect for prowling and hooting up a storm. One of the most romantic things to do on the island is to take the horse carriage ride through the **Jardin Botanico Nacional Dr. Rafael M. Moscoso**. Other excellent museums are the Museum of Fine Arts, the Museum of Natural History, and the Public Library. The Museu del Hombre Dominicano is an excellent way to absorb the main points of Caribbean history, but a working knowledge of Spanish would seriously help. On the fourth floor is a fantastic exhibit of masks and costumes that feature the various carnivals around the country.

Historical Sites

Alcazar de Colon ★★★

Calle Las Damas, Santo Domingo, *(809) 687-5361.*
Hours open: 9 a.m.–5 p.m.
Situated on the bluffs of the Ozama River, this is the castle of Don Diego Colon, Christopher Columbus' son, who was the colony's governor in 1509. Built in 1514 and reconstructed, after decades of neglect, in 1957, the 22-room house has 40-inch-thick limestone walls and 22 rooms filled with antiques from the 16th century.

Capilla de los Remedios ★★

Calle Las Damas, Santo Domingo.
Hours open: 9 a.m.–6 p.m.
The Chapel of Our Lady of Remedies was built in the 17th century in the Castilian-Romanesque style. Sunday masses begin at 6 a.m.

Cathedral Santa Maria la Menor ★★★

Calle Arzobispo Merino, Santo Domingo.
Hours open: 9 a.m.–4 p.m.
This is the first cathedral built in the Americas, begun in 1514 and completed three decades later. The Spanish Renaissance-style building has a gold coral limestone facade and houses an impressive art collection and a high altar of beaten silver. Sunday masses begin at 6 a.m.

El Faro a Colon ★★★★★

Av Espana, Santo Domingo.

Hours open: 9 a.m.–4 p.m.

The Columbus Memorial Lighthouse was completed in 1992 to celebrate the 500th anniversary of his "discovery" of the Dominican Republic. The impressive pyramid cross-shaped monument houses six museums on the explorer and the early days of the New World. It also reportedly contains the remains of Columbus. Several institutions around the world make similar claims. At night, the monument projects a huge cross on the clouds above that can be seen as far away as Puerto Rico.

Fort San Felipe ★★★

Puerto Plata.

This, the oldest fort in the New World, dates back to 1564. You can explore its small rooms and eight-inch-thick walls and be glad you weren't a prisoner here during Trujillo's rule. Lots of sidewalk vendors lend a tawdry air.

National Pantheon ★★★

Calle Las Damas, Santo Domingo.
Hours open: 10 a.m.–5 p.m.

This Spanish-American colonial-style building dates back to 1714 and was once a Jesuit monastery. A mural of Trujillo's assassination is on the ceiling above the altar, and the ashes of martyrs who tried to oust him in 1959 are preserved here.

Santa Barbara Church ★★

Av Mella, Santo Domingo.
Hours open: 8 a.m.–12 p.m.

This combination church and fortress, unique to the city, was built in 1562 and is worth a gander if you're in the neighborhood. Sunday masses begin at 6 a.m.

Torre del Homenaje ★★★

Paseo Presidente Belini, Santo Domingo.
Hours open: 8 a.m.–7 p.m.

The Tower of Homage in Fort Ozama was built in 1503, and was the place where condemned prisoners awaited execution.

Museums and Exhibits

Museo de la Familia Dominicana

Calle Padre Bellini, Santo Domingo, ☎ *(809) 689-5057.*

See how the other (richer) half lived during the 19th century at this Museum of the Dominican Family.

Museo de las Casas Reales

Calle Las Damas, Santo Domingo, ☎ *(809) 682-4202.*
Hours open: 9 a.m.–5 p.m.

Two 16th-century palaces house the Museum of the Royal Houses, which spotlights Dominican history from 1492-1821. Exhibits include antiques and artwork, Indian artifacts, relics from two galleons sunk in 1724, pre-Columbian artwork, and replicas of Columbus' ships.

Museum of Dominican Amber

Calle Duante 61, Puerto Plata, ☎ *(809) 586-2848.*
Hours open: 9 a.m.–5 p.m.

A beautiful mansion houses exhibits on amber, the country's national stone, which is found only in the Dominican Republic, Germany and the former Soviet Union. You can buy amber pieces and jewelry at the gift shop. Guided tours are conducted in English daily.

Plaza de la Cultura

Av Maximo Gomez, Santo Domingo.
This large, modern complex includes a theater, the national library and museums of Dominican man, natural history and modern art—each well worth a look. Guided tours of the complex are offered in English on Tuesday and Saturday afternoons at 2:30 p.m.

Parks and Gardens

Jardin Botanico Nacional ★★★

Arroyo Hondo, Santo Domingo.
Hours open: 10 a.m.–6 p.m.
This is the largest botanical garden in the entire Caribbean, with 445 acres of orchids, Japanese plants and trees, colorful flowers and 200 varieties of palms. You can tour it via foot, boat, train or horse-drawn carriage.

Los Haitises National Park

Samana, Santo Domingo.
A natural rainforest, pristine and primitive, with mangrove swamps, lakes and caves with Indian petroglyphs.

Tours

Acuario Nacional

Av de las Americas, Santo Domingo.
Hours open: 10 a.m.–6 p.m.
This is the Caribbean's largest aquarium, with lots of tropical fishes and dolphins swimming about.

Parque Zoologico Nacional ★★★

Av Maximo Gomez, Santo Domingo, ☎ *(809) 562-2080.*
Hours open: 10 a.m.–6 p.m.
Lions and tigers and bears roam in relative freedom at this 320-acre national zoo. There's also an aquatic bird lake, a pond teeming with crocodiles, a snake pit and a large aviary.

Sports

Although there is a plethora of sports activities on the island, most of the island's resorts have monopolized the organized programs. Even if you aren't staying at these resorts, you can still make use of their services, although some hotels offer their all-inclusive activities only to their own guests. Tennis is omnipresent (nets almost seem to be a national symbol); if your hotel is lacking one, make a reservation at one of the big hotels. Windsurfing between June and October is delightful, particularly on Cabarete Beach. Bicycling is a passion on the island, and you can choose your destination according to your own skill and endurance—from pancake-flat beaches to steep hill and mountain roads. Small-boat sailing is limited, though most resorts can hunt up at least one ragtag vessel for rent. The golf courses on the island are among the best on the Caribbean, especially the 18-hole Peter Dye wonders at **Casa De Campo**. Two new 18-holers are being planned for the Punta Cana Beach Resort and the Bávaro Beach. The Playa Dorada hotels also boast their own 18-hole courses designed by Robert Trent Jones. If you're staying in Santo Domingo, you'll be allowed to use the Santo Domingo Country Club course on weekdays—after members have teed off.

Canodromo el Coco

Av Monumental, Santo Domingo, ☎ *(809) 560-6968.*

Greyhounds race at this track about 15 minutes from Santo Domingo. Post times are Monday, Wednesday and Friday at 7:30 p.m. and Sunday at 4:00 p.m.

Golf

Various locations, Santo Domingo.

The best place to tee off is at one of the courses at Casa de Campo in La Romana; ☎ *(809) 523-3333* for details. Over at Puerto Plata, the Robert Trent Jones, Jr.-designed links are also good; ☎ *(809) 320-4340.* Santo Domingo's only course is private, but if you're staying at one of the better hotels, they can arrange to get you in on weekdays.

Hipodromo Perla Antillana

Av San Cristobel, Santo Domingo, ☎ *(809) 565-2353.*

You can wager on a horse year-round at this racetrack. Post times are Tuesday, Thursday and Saturday at 3:00 p.m.

Watersports

Various locations, Santo Domingo.

Your hotel will probably offer all you need in the way of aqua activity. If not, try one of these: Deep-sea fishing: **Andres Boca Chica Club** *(Boca Chica,* ☎ *(809) 685-4950),* and **Casa de Campo** *(La Romana,* ☎ *(809) 682-2111).* Scuba diving: **Mundo Submarino** *(Santo Domingo,* ☎ *(809) 566-0344).* Boat rentals: **Heavens** *(Playa Dorada,* ☎ *(809) 568-5250),* and **Casa de Campo** *(La Romana,* ☎ *(809) 682-2111).* Windsurfing: **CaribBIC Windsurfing Center** *(Caberete Beach,* ☎ *(809) 635-1155).*

Where to Stay

★★★★★ Fort Young Hotel	$105–$135
★★★★ Evergreen Hotel	$75–$165
★★★★ Lauro Club	$73–$140

| ★★★★ Casa de Campo | $180–$240 |
| ★★★★★ Hotel Gran Bahia | $105–$155 |

Fielding's Budget Hotels in Dominican Republic

★ San Geronimo Hotel	$35–$40
★★ Hotel Sousa	$35–$65
★ Yaroa Hotel	$45–$55
★ Hostal Nicolas de Ovando	$45–$75
★ Naco Hotel and Casino	$40–$80

The Dominican Republic has—flat out—more available lodging rooms than any other island in the Caribbean—6000 units. Most of the luxury resorts are located on the finest beaches on the island. One enclave is centered at Punta Cana on the east coast; another at Playa Juan Dolloa, Boca Chica, and La Romana on the south coast, and Puerto Plata on the far north coast. As such, most of these hotels offer fine watersports packages that will serve your every need. More European-style hotels with first-class amenities can be found in the city of Santo Domingo, complete with tennis courts and casinos. Most hotels are high-rises and extremely modern but with a Spanish/Dominican flair. Sometimes visitors stay in several hotels to vary the landscape of their vacation, from city to beach to forest to mountain, but it's just as easy to hunker down into an all-inclusive and not miss a thing. Resorts have found a way to link their walls to each other so that finding your way home may require a map and some creative signposts. Though charming decor is not a national attribute here, the low prices more than make up for any deficiencies. Even the larger resorts and all-inclusive hotels offer programs that won't break the budget. Since few restaurants are not within walking distance of most hotels, an easy way to save time and money is to buy the MAP or all-inclusive plan, where you take your meals at the hotel. (Most visitors tend to end up doing that anyway.)

Hotels and Resorts

The trend among resorts today is toward the all-inclusive program. Always check your contract to make sure what your particular program includes, but most include all meals and sports activities. The hotels in Santo Domingo, at least 30 minutes by car from any acceptable beach for swimming, often provide excellent views of the sea. (In contrast, hotels in Playa Dorado that are not situated on a beach offer a shuttle bus service that takes you to a suitable strand.) Among the top hotels in Santo Domingo are the **Ramada Renaissance Jaragua** resort, with its splashy Vegas-type casino, luxurious bedrooms and bathrooms that belong on a Hollywood set. **Gran Hotel Lima** is known island-wide for its excellent restaurant and the nearby casino, which can be happening if you pick the right day (depends on the traffic). Hotel Santo Domingo retains both the elegance and the tropical feel of the island, and its views of the sea from many of the rooms are stellar.

Puerto Plata

Bayside Hill Resort   **$180–$350**   ★★

Costambar, Puerto Plata, ☎ *(800) 877-3648, (809) 523-3333, FAX (809) 523-8548.*
Single: $180–$185. Double: $180–$350.

Leave the kids at home—only adults are welcome at this resort set on a hill, with nice views of the Caribbean. All watersports are available, and there are also two pools, a gym, tennis and a handfull of bars and restaurants.

Boca Chica Resort   **$150–$390**   ★★

Juan Bautista Vicini, Puerto Plata, ☎ *(809) 523-4522, FAX (809) 523-4438.*
Single: $150. Double: $240–$390.

Located near but not on the beach, this property offers decent accommodations and resort amenities like watersports and tennis. The all-inclusive rates cover all activities, meals and drinks.

Caribbean Village Club   **$120–$330**   ★★

Playa Dorada, Puerto Plata, ☎ *(809) 320-1111.*
Single: $120. Double: $190–$330.

What is it with swim-up bars? Does anyone really use them? In any event, you'll find another one at this all-inclusive resort with accommodations in two-story buildings in a landscaped garden setting. The health club is excellent, and there are 18 holes of golf and seven tennis courts for the active set. Guests can choose from three restaurants, and there's nightly entertainment. The beach is a good 10-minute walk, or you can catch the free shuttle.

Club Mediterranee   **$110–$230**   ★★★★★

Alta Gracia, Puerto Plata, ☎ *(800) 258-2633, (809) 687-2606.*
Single: $110–$230. Double: $110–$230.

This all-inclusive vacation village appeals to singles and fun lovers who spend beads in lieu of cash. Accommodations are in bungalows clustered above the beach; nothing fancy, but the idea is to spend lots of time out and about among your fellow guests. There's tons going on at all hours—-tennis, watersports, circus workshops—-and the disco is lively. Nice, if you like Club Meds. Note that the company charges a one-time $30 initiation fee plus a $50 per year membership fee, on top of the rates.

Flamengo Beach Resort $110–$150 ★★

Playa Dorada, Puerto Plata, ☎ *(809) 320-5084, FAX (809) 320-6319.*
Single: $110. Double: $110–$150.
Spanish-style in appearance, this resort is on a nice stretch of beach and has lushly landscaped grounds and a pretty lagoon. Accommodations, scattered about the property, are spacious and nicely decorated. All the standard resort diversions, including a pool, two tennis courts, watersports and nightly entertainment. Not bad.

Heavens $65–$150 ★★

Playa Dorada, Puerto Plata, ☎ *(809) 586-5250, FAX (809) 320-4733.*
Single: $65–$120. Double: $75–$150.
This all-inclusive resort has a casual environment and tons of activities to keep guests busy. Rooms are pleasant and all have air conditioning, but the ones closest to the disco—-which hops—-can be noisy. You can choose to eat at a few restaurants, and for an added fee, dine at a steak house.

Hotel Confresi $100–$120 ★

Puerto Plata, ☎ *(809) 586-2898, FAX (809) 658-6806.*
Single: $100–$120. Double: $100–$120.
Situated on a rocky promontory over the Caribbean Sea, this all-inclusive resort appeals to those who crave a casual getaway. Rooms are air-conditioned, though you probably won't be spending much time in them, as the rates include tennis, watersports, scuba and the gym. There are also two pools, and for nightlife, live shows and a disco.

Hotel Rio Taino $80–$305 ★★★★

Playa de Arena Gorda, Puerto Plata, ☎ *(809) 221-2290, FAX (809) 685-9537.*
Single: $80–$305. Double: $115–$305.
Sitting right on a lovely beach, this newer (1991) hotel has pretty tropical gardens surrounding Dominican-style white two-story bungalows; inside are pleasant, air-conditioned rooms. The usual pool, tennis courts and watersports are on hand; those looking to dance head to the disco at sister property Riu Naiboa next door. If you're torn between the two, choose this one—it's nicer all around.

Hotel Rui Naiboa $101–$277 ★★★★

Playa de Arena Gorda, Puerto Plata, ☎ *(809) 221-7515, FAX (809) 658-6806.*
Single: $101–$277. Double: $101–$277.
It's a five-minute walk to the beach—-no big deal, but all the other hotels in the area are right on the sand. This newer (1992) property has pretty guest rooms done up in pink and gray. The lagoon-style pool has a sandy area for those who don't feel

like hoofing it to the real thing. There's also tennis and a disco, and lots of activities for children, making this primarily a family resort.

Hotel Sousa $35–$65 ★★

El Batey, Puerto Plata, ☎ *(809) 571-2683, FAX (809) 571-2180.*
Single: $35–$50. Double: $50–$65.
Set five minutes from the beach in a suburban neighborhood, this budget, three-story hotel has basic but clean rooms that rely on ceiling fans to keep things cool. Three apartments offer kitchenettes. There's a pool and restaurant, but not much else in the way of extras. Good value for the money, though.

Jack Tar Village $90–$160 ★★★

Playa Dorada, Puerto Plata, ☎ *(800) 999-9182, (809) 586-3800, FAX (809) 809-4161.*
Single: $90–$110. Double: $150–$160.
Situated on extensive grounds, this all-inclusive resort offers accommodations in Mediterranean-style villas with one to three bedrooms. Rates include all meals and most activities, but you'll pay extra for golf. Those into organized activity love this place; you get points for joining the fun, then redeem them for prizes at the end. Corny perhaps, but no one's complaining. All the usual amenities: tennis, pool, watersports, horseback riding and 18 holes of golf.

La Esplanada $90–$225 ★★

Pedro Clisante Street, Puerto Plata, ☎ *(809) 571-3333, FAX (809) 571-3922.*
Single: $90. Double: $150–$225.
Located 10 minutes from downtown Sousa, as well as the beach, this newer (1991) resort has light and airy air-conditioned guest rooms, some with minibar and balcony. There are also 12 apartments for those who like to spread out. The grounds include a few restaurants and bars, a pool and two tennis courts. Decent.

Melia Bavaro Resort $90–$225 ★★★★

Playas de Bavaro, Puerto Plata, ☎ *(800) 336-3542, (809) 221-2311, FAX (809) 686-5427.*
Single: $90–$200. Double: $150–$225.
This resort houses guests in split-level suites with high-quality furnishings and impressive touches or bungalows with kitchenettes and platform beds. Fountains and ponds dotted throughout the grounds lend a nice touch. A shuttle takes guests back and forth to the beach, where there is also a large free-form pool with that inescapable swim-up bar. Tennis, horseback riding and watersports keep the doldrums away.

Paradise Beach Club $110–$330 ★★

Playa Dorada, Puerto Plata, ☎ *(800) 752-9236, (809) 586-3663, FAX (809) 320-4858.*
Single: $110–$150. Double: $220–$330.
Another of the area's many all-inclusive resorts, Paradise is stylish, with pretty architecture lending an elegant touch. Accommodations run the gamut from standard rooms to two-bedroom suites on two levels; all are pleasant and comfortable. Guests can dine in five restaurants and toss some back in another five bars. The lushly landscaped grounds include a cute artificial river, large pool, two tennis courts, watersports and a disco. Nice

Playa Dorada Hotel　　　　　**$95–$155**　　　　　★★

Playa Dorada, Puerto Plata, ☎ *(800) 423-6902.*
Single: $95–$155. Double: $95–$155.
This contemporary beach resort, located two minutes out of Puerto Plata, has nice
accommodations, most with balconies. Like many of the other properties in the
area, the pool has a swim-up bar, and there are three tennis courts for working up a
sweat. Watersports and 18 holes of golf complete the scene.

Puerto Plata Beach Resort　　　　　**$130–$210**　　　　　★★★

Malecon Avenue, Puerto Plata, ☎ *(809) 586-4243, FAX (809) 568-4377.*
Single: $130–$175. Double: $210.
Victorian-style in design, all accommodations are in suites with limited kitchenettes.
All the typical resort amenities, including a pool, three tennis courts, sauna and
watersports. The tiny beach is across the road and not especially good for swim-
ming, but the restaurants and casino are nice. Generally a good choice.

Punta Cana Beach Resort　　　　　**$105–$200**　　　　　★★★

Punta Cana, Puerto Plata, ☎ *(809) 686-0084, FAX (809) 687-8745.*
Single: $105–$195. Double: $160–$200.
Located on a long, sandy beach, this well-run resort has nicely landscaped grounds.
Accommodations are in studios, suites and villas, all with air conditioning, kitchen-
ettes and balconies. The grounds include five restaurants, eight bars, a pool, four
tennis courts, watersports, horseback riding and, for kids, supervised activities.
Guests are mainly from Europe.

Victoria Resort　　　　　**$100–$120**　　　　　★★★★

Playa Dorada, Puerto Plata, ☎ *(809) 586-1200, FAX (809) 320-4862.*
Single: $100–$120. Double: $100–$120.
Surrounded by a golf course on two sides, this family-run hotel has nice country and
mountain views. The large guest rooms are well furnished. The beach is a bit of a
stroll; if you're feeling lazy they'll shuttle you there, or you can hang by the pool.
All watersports, tennis and even horseback riding is complimentary. Peaceful and
elegant.

Villas Doradas Beach　　　　　**$115–$270**　　　　　★★★

Playa Dorada, Puerto Plata, ☎ *(809) 320-3000, FAX (809) 320-4790.*
Single: $115–$185. Double: $180–$270.
Situated in a lush tropical setting, all accommodations at this resort have kitchenettes. A short walk leads to the private beach, which provides plenty of shade and
has 24-hour security, a nice touch. Eighteen holes of golf, three tennis courts,
horseback riding and organized tours keep folks active. An inviting spot.

Santo Domingo

Bavaro Beach Resort　　　　　**$80–$220**　　　　　★★★★

Playa Bavaro, Santo Domingo, ☎ *(809) 221-2222.*
Single: $80–$220. Double: $105–$220.
Located on its own private beach, this sprawling resort consists of several low-rise
properties. Accommodations vary from standard guest rooms to apartments; all are
air-conditioned and pleasant. The facilities are varied and ample, with nine restau-

rants, 16 bars, a disco, live entertainment, 18 holes of golf, six tennis courts, horseback riding, watersports and organized tours. Supervised programs keep kids out of harm's way. Tight security, too. A fun and very busy complex.

Casa de Campo $180–$240   ★★★★

La Romana Street, Santo Domingo, ☎ *(800) 773-6437, (809) 523-3333, FAX (809) 523-8541.*

Single: $180–$240. Double: $180–$240.

A true mega-resort, set on 7000 acres, this is the country's best resort—in fact, it's one of the best in the entire Caribbean. The resort is essentially its own town—you can even fly directly into their own airstrip—with 16 bars and restaurants, seven pools, 13 tennis courts, 36 holes of golf, beaches, etc., etc. Guests get around on electric carts. Despite its sheer size, they do everything right here. The accommodations, designed by Oscar de la Renta, are in two-story villas with plush furnishings and kitchenettes. You'll hate to leave.

Decameron Super Club $100–$300   ★★

Juan Dolio Beach, Santo Domingo, ☎ *(809) 526-2009, FAX (809) 526-1430.*

Single: $100–$200. Double: $200–$300.

The name makes it sound like a restaurant, but in fact this is an all-inclusive resort with one- and two-bedroom suites. There's lots happening, from horseback riding to disco dancing to tennis to bike rides to the casino, and this place appeals mostly to a young crowd. Those with refined tastes will be put off by the gaudy decor, and the service is nothing to brag about.

Dominican Fiesta Hotel $100–$200   ★★★★

Avna Anacaona, Santo Domingo, ☎ *(809) 562-8222, FAX (809) 562-8938.*

Single: $100–$200. Double: $110–$200.

Located opposite Paseo de los Indios Park, this full-service resort and convention hotel has nice guest rooms with original artwork, refrigerators and balconies. The extensive grounds include a huge pool with swim-up bar, eight tennis courts, basketball, volleyball, a gym and casino. A great spot for those seeking all the bells and whistles of a large resort, as long as they don't mind sharing the facilities with a bunch of name tag-wearing business travelers.

El Embajador Hotel $105–$115   ★★★★

Ave Sarasota 65, Santo Domingo, ☎ *(800) 457-0067, (809) 221-2131, FAX (809) 532-9444.*

Single: $105–$115. Double: $105–$115.

One of the island's original resorts, dating back to 1956, this hotel was built as dictator Rafael Trujillo's showplace. Guest rooms are oversized and done in French provincial style; each has a large balcony with sea or city views but could use an overhaul. There are all kinds of things to keep you busy here: Olympic-size pool, four tennis courts, wonderful restaurants (especially the Chinese one), casino, even a Turkish bath.

El Portillo Beach Club $95–$145   ★

Las Terrenas Beach, Santo Domingo, ☎ *(809) 688-5715.*

Single: $95. Double: $145.

Set on a lovely beach, this all-inclusive resort houses guests in cottages or standard hotel rooms. A pool, two tennis courts, watersports and horseback riding supply recreation at this fairly isolated property. Nice, if you don't mind being far from other attractions.

Gran Hotel Lina $105–$135 ★ ★ ★

Maximo Gomez Avenue, Santo Domingo, ☎ *(800) 942-2461, (809) 563-5000, FAX (809) 686-5521.*
Single: $105–$110. Double: $110–$135.
This Spanish-style high-rise is stylish, though guest rooms are disappointingly basic and only some have terraces. The public spaces are grand, though, with lots of colorful modern art and elegant touches. The gym is well equipped, and there's a large pool, boutiques, a casino and several restaurants and bars. Frequented by both tourists and business travelers.

Hotel Cayacoa Beach $105–$0 ★ ★ ★

Samana Bay, Santo Domingo, ☎ *(809) 538-3131, FAX (809) 538-2985.*
Single: $105. Double: $155.
Surrounded by a park and near the National Park of the Haitises, this all-inclusive resort has attractive, air-conditioned accommodations. All the typical recreational pursuits, including tennis and watersports. All meals are served in a single restaurant; two bars provide a little more variety.

Hotel Cayo Levantado $125–$200 ★

Cayo Vigia, Santo Domingo, ☎ *(800) 423-6902, (809) 538-3426.*
Single: $125. Double: $200.
This all-inclusive hotel reopened in 1993 after extensive renovations. The grounds are lush and green, with wonderful beaches—one that remains secluded and one that is popular with locals and vendors. Accommodations are in standard guest rooms or cabanas of two or three bedrooms; all have air conditioning and bright artwork. No pool, but ample watersports on the beach.

Hotel Gran Bahia $105–$155 ★ ★ ★ ★ ★

Samana Bay, Santo Domingo, ☎ *(809) 562-6971.*
Single: $105–$120. Double: $130–$155.
Set on a bluff near a mountainside rain forest, this Victorian-style hotel appeals to lovers of all ages. Wonderful views abound everywhere. Guest rooms are spacious and comfortably done. The rocky shore below has sandy inlets for sunbathing, and there's also a pool. A good spot for whalewatching.

Hotel Hispaniola $80–$125 ★ ★

Avenida Independencia, Santo Domingo, ☎ *(800) 877-3643, (809) 221-1511, FAX (809) 535-4050.*
Single: $80–$90. Double: $90–$125.
Located in the heart of the city and certainly one of its better bargains, this older (1956) hotel has nicely appointed guest rooms with hand-crafted pine furniture, large walk-in closets and tiled balconies. There's a restaurant, bar, elegant casino and disco on-site, and guests can use the tennis courts at sister property Hotel Santo Domingo. The rates make this one worth a look.

Hotel Santo Domingo   **$150–$150**   ★★★★

Av Independencia, Santa Domingo, ☎ *(809) 221-1511, FAX (809) 535-4050.*
Single: $150. Double: $150.
This elegant resort is appreciated especially by business travelers—-the true jet set
can land right on their helipad and then check in. Accommodations are beautifully
done with handsome furnishings, large modern baths, and good views. Three tennis
courts and a pool offer recreational diversion. Located some 15 minutes from
downtown, tourists may be happier in the historic district, but either way, this place
is a winner.

Hotel V Centenario Global   **$195–$255**   ★★★★

Avenue George Washington, Santo Domingo, ☎ *(800) 221-0000, (809) 221-0000,*
FAX (809) 221-2020.
Single: $195–$255. Double: $210–$255.
This highrise, opened in 1992, has spacious guestrooms with marble accents, orig-
inal art and minibars; only the suites, alas, have balconies. Facilities include four res-
taurants, four bars, a casino, pool, tennis, squash, racquetball and a health club.
Locals like the cellar tapas bar; you will too.

Jaragua   **$80–$125**   ★★★★★

367 George Washington Avenue, Santo Domingo, ☎ *(800) 327-0200, (809) 221-*
2222, FAX (809) 535-4050.
Single: $80–$125. Double: $90–$125.
This elaborate resort complex, situated on 14 garden acres facing the Caribbean, is
a Ramada Renaissance property. The glittering resort includes a large and happening casino, a large pool, four tennis courts and very nice guest rooms with all kinds
of amenities, like three phones. Six restaurants and five bars give you lots of evening
options, and the upscale spa and health club will help you burn it back off. Resort
lovers need look no further.

Metro Hotel & Marina   **$75–$115**   ★★

Juan Dolio Beach, Santo Domingo, ☎ *(809) 526-2811, FAX (809) 526-1808.*
Single: $75–$115. Double: $75–$115.
Situated on a nice, palm-studded beach, this modern hotel houses guests in adequate, if unexciting, standard rooms. Two restaurants and two bars keep people
sated, and the activities range from watersports to a lively disco. There's also two
pools and a pair of tennis courts.

Naco Hotel and Casino   **$40–$80**   ★

Av Tiradentes 22, Santo Domingo, ☎ *(809) 562-3100, FAX (809) 544-0957.*
Single: $40–$80. Double: $45–$80.
Near a large shopping mall in a mixed commercial and residential area, this budget
property is 10 minutes from downtown. Rooms are clean and comfortable and
come with kitchenettes. Reflecting the rates, the casino draws mainly low-rollers.
The pool, set in a pleasant garden, is small. Nothing too exciting, but rates are
extremely reasonable.

Punta Goleta Beach Resort   **$85–$100**   ★★

Punta Goleta, Santo Domingo, ☎ *(809) 571-0700, FAX (809) 571-0707.*
Single: $85–$90. Double: $85–$100.

Set on 100 acres across the street from a beach known for good windsurfing, this resort has large rooms with air conditioning and Victorian-style balconies. All the typical amenities, including a pool and tennis, at this all-inclusive resort, as well as three restaurants and four bars to keep things interesting.

Renaissance Capella Beach Resort $120–$160 ★★★★

Villas del Mar Beach, Santo Domingo, ☎ *(800) 228-9898, (809) 562-4010.*
Single: $120–$160. Double: $120–$160.
This new beachfront resort, opened in spring 1994, offers all the luxury amenities resort guests expect, including an excellent health club. Spread out over several buildings in eclectic architectural styles, the grounds include three restaurants, a picturesque beach, two free-from pools, a watersports center and a disco. Guestrooms are nicely done; those opting to spend extra for the "Renaissance Club" units get VIP treatment, special amenities and complimentary Continental breakfast. Ocean-view penthouse suites feature Jacuzzis and wraparound decks.The 17-acre site is lushly landscaped; city center is 45 minutes away.

Sand Castle Beach Resort $80–$125 ★★★★

Puerto Chiquito, Santo Domingo, ☎ *(809) 571-2420.*
Single: $80–$120. Double: $85–$125.
Set on a bluff between the ocean and a saltwater pond, this isolated spot offers dramatic views and prettily furnished rooms; 80 suites offer up kitchenettes and very large baths as well. Everything is really nicely done here, with lots of marble, stained glass and finished stone. The beach below, reached via a stairway, is decent. Five restaurants, another five bars, two tennis courts and two pools keep folks busy.

Sheraton Santo Domingo $110–$130 ★★★★

Av George Washington, Santo Domingo, ☎ *(800) 325-3535, (809) 221-6666, FAX (809) 687-8150.*
Single: $110–$130. Double: $120–$130.
This highrise, overlooking the sea, offers stylish rooms with the typical extras. A casino, two restaurants, disco and a few bars provide nightlife. By day, there's a large pool and two tennis courts. Nice, but not terribly noteworthy.

Talanquera $70–$130 ★★

Juan Dolio Beach, Santo Domingo, ☎ *(809) 541-1166.*
Single: $70–$130. Double: $70–$130.
The well-landscaped grounds here lead to a nice beach, where all the usual watersports take place. There are also three pools and atypical activities like shooting and archery. Accommodations run the gamut from standard rooms to junior suites in cabanas; only some have balconies. Four bars and a disco keep things interesting once the sun goes down.

Tropics Club $115–$165 ★★

Juan Dolio Beach, Santo Domingo, ☎ *(809) 529-8531.*
Single: $115–$165. Double: $145–$165.
This small resort offers all-inclusive packages, but lacks many of the facilities you'll find at its larger competitors. Rooms are air-conditioned, and those wishing to cook in can rent a suite with kitchen. There's the standard handful of restaurants and

bars, but you'll have to indulge in watersports and gambling next door at the Decameron Super Club.

Yaroa Hotel　　　　　　　　**$45–$55**　　　　　　　　★

El Batey, Santo Domingo, ☎ *(809) 571-2651, FAX (809) 571-2651.*
Single: $45–$55. Double: $45–$55.
Located on a quiet street five minutes from the beach, the comfortable hotel is in a U shape surrounding a small pool. Guest rooms are nicely appointed, with air conditioning and screened balconies. Pleasant.

Apartments and Condominiums

In general, few of the self-catering units available in the Dominican Republic are anything to write home about, except for the luxury villas at Casa de Campo. If you don't speak good English, you will have a real adventure trying to communicate your needs to the management. Boca Chica and Juan Dolio boast more modern apartments; kitchens are usually fully furnished. For units in the cityscape, contact **ARAH** (*194 Avenida 27 de Febrero, Santo Domingo, R.D.* Another source is the **Villa, Condo and Apartment Rental Service**, *Box 30076, Pedro Henriques Urena 37, Santo Domingo, R.D.,* ☎ *(809) 686-0608.*

Puerto Plata

Dorado Naco Suite Resort　　　　　**$80–$145**　　　　★★★★

Playa Dorada, Puerto Plata, ☎ *(800) 322-2388, (809) 586-2019.*
Single: $80–$145. Double: $80–$145.
All accommodations are in one- and two-bedroom suites with full kitchens and balconies at this Spanish Caribbean-style hotel. The beach is a short stroll away. There's live entertainment nightly around the pool and two restaurants and three bars for after-dark diversions. Kids are kept occupied in supervised programs year-round. Guests can also use the facilities at the adjacent Playa Naco.

Plaza Nico Hotel　　　　　　　　**$85–$85**　　　　　　　★

Plaza Nico Mall, Puerto Plata, ☎ *(809) 541-6226, FAX (809) 541-7251.*
Single: $85. Double: $85.
Every room at this 12-story twin tower is a suite with kitchenette. Handy, but could use a redo. There's a disco, fitness center and cafe on-site, as well as lots of shopping and eating options in the adjacent shopping center, but this spot doesn't offer much of a resort feel for tourists. Decent for business travelers, though.

Inns

Inns have not found their identity in the Dominican Republic, but the following property comes closest to that old congenial feel, tucked into the historical section of the old city.

Low Cost Lodging

In a country where hotel rates start low (comparatively for the Caribbean), the cheapest rooms are not going to be impressive, or even acceptable according to some Western standards of cleanliness. However, deals can be found, especially among hotels geared to Dominican businessmen and Dominican tourists, which are always lower than the European and American-owned hotels and resorts. Figure out beforehand if you are really saving any money, since you will no doubt have to rent a car to get around. Also be careful you have not stumbled upon a front for a brothel or pay-by-the-hour-room rate.

Puerto Plata

Hotel Montemar   **$45–$120**   ★ ★

Av Hermanas Mirabel, Puerto Plata, ☎ *(809) 586-2800, FAX (809) 586-2009. Single: $45. Double: $90–$120.*

This is the nation's hotel-training school, so you can be assured of perky, attentive service. Guest rooms are decent but lack balconies. There's no beach at this in-town spot, but guests can use the one at sister property Villas Doradas in Playa Dorada. Two tennis courts and a pool help make up for the off-sea location. Good value.

Santo Domingo

Continental Hotel   **$60–$65**   ★ ★

Maximo Gomex 16, Santo Domingo, ☎ *(809) 689-1151, FAX (809) 687-8397. Single: $60–$65. Double: $65.*

Located opposite the Palace of Fine Arts, this modern hotel is a block from the beach. Guest rooms are adequate; don't bother upgrading to a "deluxe" unless you really want that refrigerator. There's a disco, restaurant and small pool, but not much else to justify the rates. You can do better elsewhere in the same price range.

El Napolitano   **$50–$75**   ★

51 George Washington Avenue, Santo Domingo, ☎ *(809) 687-1131, FAX (809) 387-6814. Single: $50. Double: $55–$75.*

It's bare bones here, but the rates appeal to those on a tight budget. Rooms are air-conditioned and have sea views. There's a pool and restaurant, but not much else, though plenty to do within an easy walk. This hotel does big business with Dominicans, and the atmosphere can be lively.

Hostal Nicolas de Ovando   **$45–$75**   ★

53 Calle las Damas, Santo Domingo. Single: $45–$75. Double: $45–$75.

Originally the palace of the first Spanish governor, dating from the 16th century, this hotel has old-fashioned, Spanish-style guest rooms with antique or reproduction furniture but little else of note. One courtyard houses a pool; the other three have patios and fountains. A restaurant and two bars round out the facilities. History buffs will like it here, but it has a way to go to reach its true potential.

San Geronimo Hotel   **$35–$40**   ★

1067 Av Independencia, Santo Domingo, ☎ *(809) 533-1000. Single: $35. Double: $40.*

Located near the sea and five minutes from downtown, this budget choice has small, air-conditioned rooms, some with kitchenettes. There's a restaurant, two bars, a pool and the inescapable casino.

South Coast Resorts

The majority of the beach resorts on the southern coast are located along a strip that includes Boca Chica, near the Las Américas International Airport, Playa Juan Dolio, a little farther east on the south coast, and La Romana, even farther east. Most of these resorts have all-inclusive plans and a full line of watersports activities. **Hamaca Beach Hotel**, only three years old, is the hub of Euro trash and jetsetters who adore the health club and sauna as well as the wonderfully air-conditioned bedrooms. **Don Juan Resort** is located near a wonderful beach with talcum-smooth sand that can now be truly appreciated since the hawking vendors have been evicted.

Playa Juan Dolio

About 20 minutes east of Boca Chica is the beach of Juan Dolio—dazzling white. Euro babes and dudes have found their way to this strand, joining the well-to-do Dominicans who openly ogle the gal (and guy sometimes!). You won't have any trouble finding a place to stay here—there are many. Some of the best include the **Ramada Capella Beach** resort, a fully modern low-rise with two pools and two tennis courts and spa; **Talanquera**, with three pools (who needs so many with the beach?) as well as horseback riding facilities; and **Decameron Resort**, whose casino and disco attracts a wild scene at night.

Where to Eat

	Fielding's Highest Rated Restaurants in Dominican Republic	
★★★★★	**Casa del Rio**	$14–$26
★★★★★	**De Armando**	$10–$22
★★★★★	**Lina Restaurant**	$15–$30
★★★★	**Chopin**	$5–$25
★★★★	**La Bahia**	$10–$20
★★★★	**Restaurant Montparnasse**	$5–$20
★★★	**El Alcazar**	$9–$25
★★★	**El Conuco**	$8–$15
★★★	**Pez Dorado**	$18–$30

	Fielding's Special Restaurants in Dominican Republic	
★★★★★	**Casa del Rio**	$14–$26
★★★★★	**De Armando**	$10–$22
★★★★	**La Bahia**	$10–$20
★★★★	**Restaurant Montparnasse**	$5–$20
★★★	**El Conuco**	$8–$15

	Fielding's Budget Restaurants in Dominican Republic	
★★★★	**Evergreen**	$17–$20
★★★	**Coconut Beach**	$10–$25
★★★	**De Bouille**	$5–$30
★★★★★	**La Robe Creole**	$7–$27
★★★	**Balisier**	$9–$22

Dining out is a special event in the Dominican Republic—best done in elegant clothes (at the very least, don't go out dressed like a beach bum, unless you're on the beach); the rule is smart casual at lunch and dressier at dinner. The normal local time for dinner (Spanish style) is about 9 or 10 o'clock, but most American-style visitors cave in much earlier; luckily, restaurants usually open around 6 p.m. (as such, it will be easier to get a table in a popular restaurant if you eat early). Local dishes are spiked with Latin zest, especially the omnipresent paella, which is uniformly excellent. *Sancocho* is one of the most filling dishes, a thick stew made from five to seven different meats; if you eat it for lunch, you may be inclined to take a very long siesta. *Arroz con pollo* (chicken with rice) is a staple on every menu. *Plátanos*, or plantains, are cooked in a million different ways. A light delicious lunch might be a *tortilla de jamón* (spicy ham omelet). One of the most favored desserts is a heart cornmeal custard called *majarete*. For to-die-for snacks that will ruin your diet and your cholesterol for many weeks, try *chicharrones* (fried pork rinds) or the less dangerous *galletas* (flat, biscuit crackers). The local beers are Bohemia, Quisqueya and Presidente, and the local rums are Brugal and Bermúdez. It's always a Dominican delight to salute the end of a good meal with dark brown aged rum over ice, called *añejo*.

Among the resort hotels, the best chefs are at Dominican Fiesta (La Casa) the Sheraton (Antoine) and Embajador (Manhattan Grill). After 10 p.m. is when the night owls, dressed to kill, turn out for the post-supper stroll down the Malecón. Another delicious tidbit is the *bollito de yucca*, a postage stamp-sized hors d'oeuvre made of ground yucca root and cheese—much tastier than it sounds. If you get homesick for American-style fixings, head for the hotel coffee shops, where a steak sandwich, hamburger, or simple fruit salad will soothe the aching palate. Remember to peel and/or wash any fruit you may pick up in the local markets.

Puerto Plata

Chopin   **$**   ★★★★

Playas de Bavaro, ☎ *(809) 221-2311.*
cuisine.

This wonderfully romantic open-air restaurant at the equally romantic Melia Bavaro resort is reached via a short stroll through the rainforest. The restaurant offers a different buffet each night; Tuesday, for example, features Italian fare. Other nights you may find smoked salmon, paella or Spanish ham. After dinner, you're serenaded by a quartet from the Symphony Orchestra of Belgrade playing classical tunes. Lovely! Hotel guests on the meal plan pay $5.00, while the fee for non-guests is $25.00.

De Armando   **$$$**   ★★★★★

Avenida Antera Mota 23, Puerto Plata, ☎ *(809) 586-3418.*
International cuisine. Specialties: Fresh fish, lamb in wine sauce.
Lunch: 11 a.m.–3 p.m., entrees $10–$22.

Dinner: 3–11 p.m., entrees $10–$22.

The pride of North Coast dining is this top-rated restaurant in a Victorian building, where guests are served international cuisine serenaded by a guitar and string trio. Specialties have included fresh sea bass prepared with shellfish or mushroom sauces, lamb marinated in red wine, steaks and lobster. The menu also features Dominican specialties like lentils and rice and green plantains.

Roma II **$$** ★★

Calle Beller, Puerto Plata, ☎ (809) 586-3904.
International cuisine. Specialties: Pizza, octopus.
Lunch: 11 a.m.–2 p.m., entrees $6–$15.
Dinner: 2 p.m.–midnight, entrees $6–$15.

This plain but comfortably air-conditioned bistro with charming service serves an excellent array of pizzas, plain or fancy—cheese or perhaps shrimp, made on dough baked fresh daily. More challenging appetites might go for the octopus, a specialty here, served with a vinaigrette sauce, or with fresh tomatoes, or on pasta. Steaks and filets are also on the menu.

Santo Domingo

Cafe del Sol **$** ★★

Altos de Chavon Village, Altos de Chavon, ☎ (809) 523-3333.
Italian cuisine.
Lunch: 11 a.m.–4 p.m., entrees $8–$10.
Dinner: 6–11 p.m., entrees $8–$10.

This pretty rooftop cafe in the artists' colony of Altos de Chavon is a perfect stop for a light repast of pizza or salad.

Caribae **$$$** ★★

Camino Libre 70, Sosua.
International cuisine.
Dinner: entrees $20–$30.

Pick your own lobster or shrimp from myriad tanks in this unpretentious little restaurant in the gorgeous beach resort town of Sosua. The crustaceans you choose are all raised at the restaurant's private shrimp farm nearby. For accompaniment, a plate of organic vegetables from the same farm round out a healthy meal.

Casa del Rio **$$$** ★★★★★

Altos de Chavon Village, Altos de Chavon, ☎ (809) 523-3333.
French cuisine.
Lunch: 11 a.m.–4 p.m., entrees $14.
Dinner: 6:30–11 p.m., entrees $18–$26.

Possibly the most expensive restaurant in the Dominican Republic (and the chicest), Casa del Rio is just the place for resort dwellers at the nearby Casa de Campo to go for a night on the town, but many fans have no compunction about driving the 100 miles from Santo Domingo to eat here. Any why not—it's hard to resist dining in a tower room glowing with candlelight, overlooking the Chavon River. French chef Philippe Mongereau likes a challenge, and constantly experiments with Asian and Caribbean spices to dress up shellfish, meats and poultry.

Che Bandoneon   **$$$**   ★★

El Conde, ☎ *(809) 687-0023.*
Latin American cuisine. Specialties: Argentinian churrasco.
Dinner: 6 p.m.–midnight, entrees $15–$30.

Tango to this Argentinian charmer that nests in a restored home in the Old City area of Santo Domingo. Specialties include huge, choice cuts of ranch-style beef fillets or steaks. Seating is indoors or out on a pretty terrace, serenaded by troubadours playing the *bandoneon* (Argentinian accordion) for you. Desserts are rich and very French.

El Alcazar   **$$$**   ★★★

Avenida Independencia, ☎ *(809) 221-1511.*
International cuisine.
Lunch: Noon–3 p.m., prix fixe $9.
Dinner: 6–11 p.m., entrees $10–$25.

The noonday lunch buffet at the El Alcazar is an exotic and very reasonable dining adventure, with a bevy of international dishes and succulent seafood items available daily. World-renowned couturier (and local hero) Oscar de la Renta designed the interiors of the chic hotel-restaurant on a grand North African theme, with gorgeous fabrics, shells and mirrors for accents.

El Conuco   **$$**   ★★★

Calle Casimiro de Moya, ☎ *(809) 686-0129.*
Latin American cuisine. Specialties: Sancocho, chicharrones de pollo.
Lunch: 11 a.m.–4 p.m., entrees $8–$15.
Dinner: 6–11 p.m., entrees $8–$15.

This comically hokey but fun restaurant is situated in an ersatz thatched-roof house, where hanging artifacts from former diners provide a running commentary along with the hearty country cooking (*conuco*). Fill up on rice and kidney beans, stews, cod and crunchy fried chicken bits while hammy waiters turn into musicians and/or dancers at the drop of a sombrero.

Fonda La Aterazana   **$$**   ★★

Calle Aterazana 5, ☎ *(809) 689-2900.*
Latin American cuisine. Specialties: Chicharrones de pollo.
Lunch: 10 a.m.–4 p.m., entrees $5–$20.
Dinner: 4 p.m.–1 a.m., entrees $5–$20.

Feel like a Spanish grandee in this whitewashed-stone building in the Aterazana section of the Colonial Zone, sharing seafood or crunchy fried Dominican chicken strips (more delicious than it sounds) with someone special. This bright and festive spot is often jumping with musical groups and dancers performing to a merengue beat.

Jade Garden   **$$$**   ★★

Avenida Sarasota 65, ☎ *(809) 221-2131.*
Chinese cuisine. Specialties: Peking chicken and duck.
Lunch: Noon–3 p.m., entrees $12–$22.
Dinner: 7:30–11:30 p.m., entrees $12–$30.

Considered one of the best Chinese restaurants in town, Jade Garden boasts Hong-Kong trained chefs who prepare Peking duck or chicken in a beautifully decorated room in the imposing Hotel Embajador.

La Bahia $$$ ★★★★

Avenida George Washington, ☎ (809) 682-4022.
Seafood cuisine. Specialties: Kingfish in coconut sauce, conch.
Lunch: 9 a.m.–2:30 p.m., entrees $10–$18.
Dinner: 2:30–11:30 p.m., entrees $12–$20.

Completely unpretentious and a very popular local hangout, La Bahia sits quietly on Santo Domingo's wide seafront and park, surrounded by towering luxury hotels and convivial cafes. It's very difficult to choose from a huge variety of luscious sea creatures served here, but you can't go wrong with a fish and shellfish soup loaded with shrimp and lobster, or kingfish with a tropical coconut sauce. The prices are so reasonable for what you're served, it's almost beyond belief.

Lago Grill $$ ★★

Casa de Campo, La Romana, ☎ (809) 523-3333.
American cuisine.
Lunch: Noon–4 p.m., entrees $5–$15.

Terrific breakfasts and lunches are served at this view spot on the golf course of the Casa de Campo resort. Happily for the many top stateside executives who stay here, they (and you) can have cooked-to-order eggs and omelets any style or an array of freshly squeezed juices from an exotic fruit bar. Dominican and Caribbean entrees, delicious burgers and sandwiches, and a copious salad bar are top choices for lunch.

Lina Restaurant $$$ ★★★★★

Avenida Maximo Gomez, ☎ (809) 685-5000.
Spanish cuisine. Specialties: Zarzuela de mariscos, paella.
Lunch: 11 a.m.–4:30 p.m., entrees $15–$24.
Dinner: 6 p.m.–midnight, entrees $15–$30.

Before the Dominican Republic became a popular tourist destination, Chef Lina Aguado was already a legend; after serving as personal chef to long-reigning president Rafael Trujillo, she opened a small eatery which grew like Topsy into a hotel/restaurant that bears her name. Today, others with equal skill and passion have inherited the great cucinera's recipes for paella valenciana or cazuela de mariscos with Pernod, and interpret them with aplomb.

Meson de la Cava $$$ ★★

Avenida Mirador del Sur, ☎ (809) 533-2818.
International cuisine.
Lunch: 11 a.m.–3:30 p.m., entrees $25–$30.
Dinner: 6 p.m.–midnight, entrees $25–$40.

In order to eat here, diners must descend to a cavern way below ground (some 50 feet), reached via a scary staircase. What's down under is some rollicking entertainment from a live band (contemporary and merengue) and simply prepared, unsurprising, but delicious food. Some people might find this sort of thing silly, but kudos must be given to whomever thought up this clever idea, which seems to be working. Reserve way in advance, and dress fashionably.

Neptuno's Club   **$$$**   ★ ★

Boca Chica Beach, Boca Chica, ☎ *(809) 523-4703.*
Seafood cuisine.
Lunch: 9 a.m.–2 p.m., entrees $10–$20.
Dinner: 2–10 p.m., entrees $10–$25.

Calm and warm waters and a short (about 45 minute) drive from the capital make
Boca Chica Beach, where this little hut is located, popular with daytrippers. Nep-
tuno's has a good reputation for fish stews and sauteed kingfish, although interna-
tional meals are served as well.

Pez Dorado   **$$$**   ★ ★ ★

43 Calle el Sol, Santiago Caballeros, ☎ *(809) 582-2518.*
Chinese cuisine. Specialties: Chinese seafood.
Lunch: 11 a.m.–3 p.m., entrees $18–$30.
Dinner: 6–11:30 p.m., entrees $18–$30.

If you find yourself visiting the historical city of Santiago de los Caballeros, about
two hours away from Santo Domingo, this restaurant serving seafood Chinese-style
in a posh, comfortable room is one of the best dining choices in town. Perhaps
afterwards, you can wend your way to a local dance club—after all, this is the birthplace of the merengue.

Reina de Espana   **$$**   ★ ★

Avenida Cervantes 103, ☎ *(809) 685-2588.*
Spanish cuisine.
Lunch: Noon–4 p.m., entrees $8–$20.
Dinner: 4–11 p.m., entrees $8–$20.

In a city where Spanish food is treated with respect, Reina de Espana, located in a
restored home not far from the sea, manages to present more than just the average
paella or seafood stew for discriminating diners. The menu traverses each region of
Spain, with roast quail or suckling pig prepared as specials from time to time. But
the old favorites like gazpacho are all represented and rarely disappoint.

Restaurant Montparnasse   **$$$**   ★ ★ ★ ★

Avenida Lope de Vega 24, ☎ *(809) 562-4141.*
Latin American cuisine.
Lunch: Noon–2 p.m., entrees $5–$18.
Dinner: 2 p.m.–midnight, entrees $11–$20.

Prominent local folk like to eat here, especially for lunch, making this creative
Franco-Caribbean bistro a good place to observe them. But those not inclined to
eavesdropping or voyeurism will still enjoy the unusual combinations of native vegetables like pumpkin and plantain pureed into creamy bisques or a vichyssoise. Dec-
adent desserts like chocolate souffle are served all day and night—in true Dominican
fashion, the place stays open late.

Vesuvio I   **$$**   ★ ★

Avenida G. Washington, ☎ *(809) 221-3333.*
Italian cuisine.
Lunch: 11 a.m.–2 p.m., entrees $8–$18.
Dinner: 2 p.m.–midnight, entrees $8–$20.

The Bonarelli family from Naples has been running this boisterous family restaurant on the Malecon since the 1950s. As they are not content to rest on past laurels, every visit brings a new specialty or improvements on old favorites. The voluminous menu features seafood and plenty of it, including crayfish with garlic, although veal scallopine with fresh herbs is worth noting. Decor is contemporary, with plenty of colorful marine life painted on the walls.

Where to Shop

Bargaining is as second nature as breathing in the Dominican Republic. If you don't bargain, you aren't respected; shopkeepers enjoy the cat-and-mouse game and even look forward to it. Don't disappoint them. At the same time, don't give in to a vendor's first, second, or third price—they can be hard-nosed because they know your time is precious and your wallet is on vacation. Before you go, bone up on a few choice phrases in Spanish, including the well-understood "Non!"

Everyone comes to the Dominican Republic hot on the trail of jewelry made from amber. The island boasts one of the world's largest deposits, and the prices for this translucent, semiprecious stone will make your jaw drop. (Don't succumb to the tourist disease called "souvenir overkill" when you see too many displays of them; they are lovely and will look special by the time you get your piece home.) A type of petrified resin taken from coniferous forests that disappeared from the Earth more than 50 million years ago, amber comes in many colors ranging from pale lemon to dark brown. Best buys are those which have a tiny insect or small leaves embedded inside. (Remember that childhood novel *Bug in Amber*?)

Santo Domingo's main covered market is called **El Mercado Modelo**. Located in the Colonial Zone bordering Calle Mella, it has lots of shops, eateries, bars and boutiques located in the restored buildings of La Ataranza, across from the Alcázar. It's lovely to walk down the Calle El Conde, Santo Domingo's main shopping street in the Colonial Zone, now sectioned off for pedestrians only. Some of the best shops here are far north of the Colonial Zone between Calle Mella and Av. Las Américas. Fine art galleries are located in the **Altos de Chavón**, with stores grouped around the main square. The **Tourist Bazaar** *(Calle Duarte 61)* in Puerto Plata boasts seven showrooms in a finely renovated old mansion. For good souvenirs and local jewelry, try **Calle Beller** (in the Plaza Shopping Center *at Calle Duarte and Av. 30 de Marzo.*)

Avoid buying a tortoise shell since a U.S. customs official will confiscate it if he finds it in your bag.

Fine art galleries are located in the Altos de Chavón, with stores grouped around the main square. Among the best names are **Arawak Gallery** and **Novo Atarazana**. Other great home-crafted buys are hand-carved wood rocking chairs; they are sold unassembled and boxed for transport, so make sure you are handy with a screwdriver. For other woodcrafts, check out the stalls at the El Mercado Modelo. Macrame, baskets and pottery figurines are all reminiscent of the island's crafts.

Dominican Republic Directory

ARRIVAL AND DEPARTURE

Travelers to the Dominican Republic use two major international airports: Las Américas International Airport, about 20 miles outside Santo Domingo, and La Unión International Airport, about 25 miles east of Puérto Plata on the north coast. (Both airports have been undergoing extensive renovation; a major fire in the old terminal at Las Americas has caused congestion in a new terminal that was meant to solve the problem.) **American Airlines** offers the most flights to the island, with nonstops from New York to Santo Domingo. **American**, **Continental**, and **Dominica** also fly nonstop from New York to Puerto Plata. Continental Airlines offers connecting service to both Santo Domingo and Puerto Plata from San Juan, Puerto Rico; and **American Eagle** has two flights a day from San Juan to La Romana.

For inter-island service, ALM flies from Santo Domingo to St. Maarten and Curaçao. There is also limited domestic service available from La Herrera Airport in Santo Domingo to smaller airfields in La Romana, Samana and Santiago.

Be cautious in both airports with regard to your luggage and personal valuables. Luggage theft is a common occurrence, and the general confusion can often lead to "lost" luggage. Try to carry your own luggage as you will be royally hassled for service by porters. The island is famous for *buscones*, who offer you assistance and then disappear with your belongings. If you have arranged for transport by your hotel, the representative should be awaiting you in the immigration hall.

BUSINESS HOURS

Stores open weekdays 8 a.m.–12:30 p.m. and 2:30–5 p.m. and Saturday 8 a.m.–noon. Banks open weekdays 8:30 a.m.–4:30 p.m.

CLIMATE

The climate is subtropical; with an average annual temperature of 80 degrees in Santo Domingo, temperatures are generally between 66 and

88 degrees F. The west and southwest of the country are arid. Hispaniola lis in the path of tropical cyclones.

DOCUMENTS

In order to purchase a $10 tourist card, good for 90 days, visitors must present a valid passport or other proof of citizenship (birth certificate, voter's registration card, with an official photo ID such as driver's license). Cards may be purchased upon arrival, or through the consulate.

ELECTRICITY

Current is 100 volts, 60 cycles, as in the United States.

GETTING AROUND

Taxis are available at the airports, and the 25-minute ride into Santo Domingo averages about U.S.$20. There is no bus service, but fellow travelers are usually open to sharing a taxi.

Buses in Santo Domingo are called *públicos*, small blue-and-white or blue-and-red cars that run regular routes, stopping to let passengers on and off. The fare is two pesos. There are also *conchos* or *coléctivos* (privately owned buses) whose drivers tool around the major thoroughfares, leaning out the window and trying to seduce passengers onboard. (For this inconvenience you get to pay a peso less.) Privately owned air-conditioned buses make regular runs to Santiago, Puerto Plata and other destinations. Avoid night travel because the country is rife with potholes. Reservations can be made by calling **Metro Buses** *(Av. Winston Churchill;* ☎ *(809) 586-6063* in Puerto Plata).

Cars can be rented in the airports and at many hotels. The top names are **Budget** ☎ *(809) 562-6812*; and **Hertz** ☎ *(809) 688-2277*. Driving is on the right side of the street, but drivers here are maniacs, often driving down the middle of the road and passing dangerously whenever they feel like it. They are nice enough, however, to flash their light-on when they know the highway patrol is lurking about—the 50 mph. (80 kph) limit is strictly enforced. (Police have been known to stop drivers on the pretext of some violation and insinuate the need for a bribe. If you must drive around the unilluminated mountain roads at night, drive with utmost caution since many cars do not have headlights or taillights, cows stand in the middle of the road, and bicycles are rarely well lit. Gas stations are few and far between.

Motorbikes, called *motoconchos*, are a popular and inexpensive way to tool around the island, especially in such places as Puerto Plata, Sasúa and Jarabacoa. Bikes can be flagged down in road and town.

LANGUAGE

The official language is Spanish, so do as much as you can to bone up on Spanish before you go. Officially, nearly everyone involved in tourism speaks English, but it is sometimes a quizzical version and many people have trouble understanding English. Waitresses in coffee shops may simply drop their jaws when you speak to them in English. In the outlying areas, it is absolutely necessary to speak Spanish. Bring along a phrase book and keep it handy in your purse.

MEDICAL EMERGENCIES

The island has numerous hospitals and clinics; that is not say that you should pursue any medical attention with enthusiasm. The biggest and most revered is **José Maria Cabral y Baez**; ☎ *(809) 583-4311* on Central, near the church in the town of Santiago. You'll find a number of American medical students working here since the national medical school uses the facilities. Hospitals in Santiago tend to be crowded and harassed. Hospital Marion in Santo Domingo is known for its cardiovascular center. Bring your Spanish phrase book, particularly if you get stuck in a hospital for any length of time. Do your best to fly home to the States. Remember to bring any medications you need from home, with a copy of the prescription and a letter from your doctor that you have been medically directed to take them.

MONEY

Official currency is the Dominican peso. Most hotels and shops welcome American dollars as well as major credit cards and traveler's checks. Try to spend your pesos rather than having to exchange them back into dollars before you leave.

TELEPHONE

The country code is *809*. To call the Dominican Republic from the United States, dial *011* (international access), the country code *(809)* and the local number. Connections from the U.S. are generally made with ease and are clear. Calling from the Dominican Republic can become a headache—fast. There is a direct-dial system, but you should feel extraordinarily blessed to have it work right. Try dialing 1, then the area code, followed by the number.

TIME

Atlantic Standard Time year-round.

TIPPING

Hotels and restaurants add a whopping 21 percent government tax (which includes a 10 percent service charge) to all bills. It is customary to leave a dollar per day for the maid; if you balk, just imagine her income status in such a poor country. In restaurants and nightclubs, an extra 5–10 percent above the service charge included on the bill will be greatly appreciated by the waiters and waitresses. Taxi drivers expect a 10 percent tip; tip more if you arrive alive. Skycaps and hotel porters expect at least five pesos per bag.

TOURIST INFORMATION

The **Dominican Tourist Information Center** is located at the corner of *Avs. México an d30 de Marzo;* ☎ *221-4660* or *00-752-1151*. There are also information booths in Santiago (City Hall Av. Duarte; ☎ *582-*

5885 and in Puerto Plata Av. Hermanas Mirabel ☎ *586-3676*. You can also find a booth at the airport open daily. In the U.S. call ☎ *(212) 768-2481*.

WHEN TO GO

Merengue Week explodes in late July, the island's biggest rum-filled festival dedicated to the national dance. Carnival is held on February 27.

DOMINICAN REPUBLIC HOTELS		RMS	RATES	PHONE	CR. CARDS
Puerto Plata					
★★★★★	Club Mediterranee	339	$110–$230	(800) 258-2633	A, V
★★★★	Dorado Naco Suite Resort	150	$80–$145	(800) 322-2388	A, DC, MC, V
★★★★	Hotel Rio Taino	360	$80–$305	(809) 221-2290	A, DC, MC, V
★★★★	Hotel Rui Naiboa	372	$101–$277	(809) 221-7515	A, DC, MC, V
★★★★	Melia Bavaro Resort	776	$90–$225	(800) 336-3542	A, DC, MC, V
★★★★	Victoria Resort	120	$100–$120	(809) 586-1200	A, MC, V
★★★	Jack Tar Village	283	$90–$160	(800) 999-9182	A, DC, MC, V
★★★	Puerto Plata Beach Resort	216	$130–$210	(809) 586-4243	A, DC, MC, V
★★★	Punta Cana Beach Resort	340	$105–$200	(809) 686-0084	A, DC, MC, V
★★★	Villas Doradas Beach	207	$115–$270	(809) 320-3000	A, MC, V
★★	Bayside Hill Resort	150	$180–$350	(800) 877-3648	A, MC, V
★★	Boca Chica Resort	273	$150–$390	(809) 523-4522	A, MC, V
★★	Caribbean Village Club	336	$120–$330	(809) 320-1111	A, MC, V
★★	Flamengo Beach Resort	310	$110–$150	(809) 320-5084	A, DC, MC
★★	Heavens	150	$65–$150	(809) 586-5250	A, MC, V
★★	Hotel Montemar	95	$45–$120	(809) 586-2800	A, MC, V
★★	Hotel Sousa	39	$35–$65	(809) 571-2683	A, MC, V
★★	La Esplanada	210	$90–$225	(809) 571-3333	A, DC, MC, V
★★	Paradise Beach Club	436	$110–$330	(800) 752-9236	A, MC, V
★★	Playa Dorada Hotel	254	$95–$155	(800) 423-6902	MC, V
★	Hotel Confresi	200	$100–$120	(809) 586-2898	A, MC, V
★	Plaza Nico Hotel	220	$85	(809) 541-6226	A, CB, DC, MC, V
Santo Domingo					
★★★★★	Hotel Gran Bahia	96	$105–$155	(809) 562-6971	MC, V

DOMINICAN REPUBLIC HOTELS		RMS	RATES	PHONE	CR. CARDS
★★★★★	Hotel Santo Domingo	220	$150	(809) 221-1511	A, DC, MC, V
★★★★★	Hotel V Centenario Global	200	$195–$255	(800) 221-0000	A, DC, MC, V
★★★★★	Jaragua	310	$80–$125	(800) 327-0200	A, MC, V
★★★★	Bavaro Beach Resort	1295	$80–$220	(809) 221-2222	A, MC, V
★★★★	Casa de Campo	750	$180–$240	(800) 773-6437	A, MC, V
★★★★	Dominican Fiesta Hotel	337	$100–$200	(809) 562-8222	A, DC, MC, V
★★★★	El Embajador Hotel	300	$105–$115	(800) 457-0067	A, DC, MC, V
★★★★	Renaissance Capella Beach Resort	283	$120–$160	(800) 228-9898	A, DC, MC, V
★★★★	Sand Castle Beach Resort	240	$80–$125	(809) 571-2420	A, DC, MC, V
★★★★	Sheraton Santo Domingo	258	$110–$130	(800) 325-3535	A, DC, MC, V
★★★	Gran Hotel Lina	217	$105–$135	(800) 942-2461	A, DC, MC, V
★★★	Hotel Cayacoa Beach	70	$105	(809) 538-3131	A, DC, MC, V
★★	Continental Hotel	100	$60–$65	(809) 689-1151	A, DC, MC, V
★★	Decameron Super Club	292	$100–$300	(809) 526-2009	A, MC, V
★★	Hotel Hispaniola	165	$80–$125	(800) 877-3643	A, MC, V
★★	Metro Hotel & Marina	180	$75–$115	(809) 526-2811	A, DC, MC, V
★★	Punta Goleta Beach Resort	130	$85–$100	(809) 571-0700	A, DC, MC, V
★★	Talanquera	250	$70–$130	(809) 541-1166	A, MC, V
★★	Tropics Club	77	$115–$165	(809) 529-8531	A
★	El Napolitano	73	$50–$75	(809) 687-1131	A, DC, MC, V
★	El Portillo Beach Club	159	$95–$145	(809) 688-5715	A, MC, V
★	Hostal Nicolas de Ovando	107	$45–$75	(809) 688-9220	A, DC, MC, V
★	Hotel Cayo Levantado	37	$125–$200	(800) 423-6902	A, MC, V
★	Naco Hotel and Casino	107	$40–$80	(809) 562-3100	A, DC, MC, V
★	San Geronimo Hotel	72	$35–$40	(809) 533-1000	A, DC, MC, V
★	Yaroa Hotel	24	$45–$55	(809) 571-2651	A, MC, V

DOMINICAN REPUBLIC RESTAURANTS	PHONE	ENTREE	CR. CARDS
Puerto Plata			
Continental			
★★★★ Chopin	(809) 221-2311	$5–$25	A, DC, MC, V
International			
★★★★★ De Armando	(809) 586-3418	$10–$22	A, DC, MC, V
★★ Roma II	(809) 586-3904	$6–$15	A, MC, V
Santo Domingo			
American			
★★ Lago Grill	(809) 523-3333	$5–$15•	A, DC, MC, V
Chinese			
★★★ Pez Dorado	(809) 582-2518	$18–$30	MC, V
★★ Jade Garden	(809) 221-2131	$12–$30	A, DC, MC, V
French			
★★★★★ Casa del Rio	(809) 523-3333	$14–$26	A, MC, V
International			
★★★ El Alcazar	(809) 221-1511	$9–$25	A, DC, MC, V
★★ Caribae		$20–$30••	MC, V
★★ Meson de la Cava	(809) 533-2818	$25–$40	A, DC, MC, V
Italian			
★★ Cafe del Sol	(809) 523-3333	$8–$10	A, MC, V
★★ Vesuvio I	(809) 221-3333	$8–$20	A, DC, MC, V
Latin American			
★★★★ Restaurant Montparnasse	(809) 562-4141	$5–$20	A, DC, MC, V
★★★ El Conuco	(809) 686-0129	$8–$15	MC, V
★★ Che Bandoneon	(809) 687-0023	$15–$30••	MC, V
★★ Fonda La Aterazana	(809) 689-2900	$5–$20	A, DC, MC, V
Seafood			
★★★★ La Bahia	(809) 682-4022	$10–$20	A, MC, V
★★ Neptuno's Club	(809) 523-4703	$10–$25	MC, V
Spanish			
★★★★★ Lina Restaurant	(809) 685-5000	$15–$30	A, DC, MC, V

DOMINICAN REPUBLIC RESTAURANTS	PHONE	ENTREE	CR. CARDS
★★ Reina de Espana	(809) 685-2588	$8–$20	A, MC, V

Note: • Lunch Only

•• Dinner Only

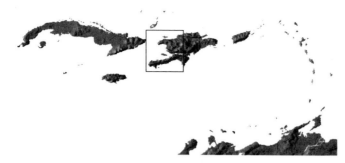

HAITI

Haitians celebrate sunset on the beach.

American troops ironically referred to their 1994 occupation of this island as their "Haitian Vacation." Judging from their comments, it's hard to recommend the same experience at the moment to anyone looking for a Caribbean thrill, although the troops are now gone. The survivor of one of the strangest dramas of American intervention since Grenada, Haiti at the forefront of international news in summer 1994, awaiting a future that no one can see quite clearly yet. Even in the best of times (which hasn't happened in Haiti for a long time), it takes a certain kind of traveler to enjoy this country which is so poor (one of the hemisphere's poorest) that peasants have been known to steal across the border to the Dominican Republic just to filch away some topsoil. If you make an excursion in the interior, you sometimes

313

won't be able to find even a scrap of food, even in a private home. It says something about the condition of Haiti that three American soldiers on assignment committed suicide. Simply, many American-born soldiers raised in suburbia were not at all prepared for the squalor, ramshackle poverty, and unsanitary conditions that they found when they arrived. One Georgian corporal was quoted in *Newsweek* as saying that the entire country, because of the homeless, looked like one big ghetto. The smell alone (caused by the lack of toilets) caused one female private, driving through the city of Port-au-Prince, to gag. Many of the troops, especially black ones, said their first look at Haiti was like being transported to the poor rural South of the '60s, with poor-quality roads, small houses with tin roofs, and kids playing in the street without underwear.

What's in Haiti's future as it stands poised to be led by the recently reinstated President Jean-Bertrand Aristide? The nation held free elections in June 1995; while they were fraught with chaos and fraud, it still was a baby step toward democracy. "Whether it is a step forward or sideways remains to be seen," says the Council of Freely Elected Heads of Government, an international group that observed the elections. Throughout the Caribbean, tourism has been the engine of growth, and it's quite possible that a stabilized Haiti could be a lot more interesting and friendlier destination than say, the Dominican Republic or even Jamaica.

When military thugs are not around, soldiers reported, the sheer joy of the people over the arrival of U.S. troops was a wonderful sight to behold, with little kids walking hand in hand with tough soldiers wearing flak jackets and carrying assault rifles. Despite the poverty, the culture and music and spirituality of Haitians are quite rich and stimulating, and when Club Med finds enough reason and resources to reopen (the property now is locally run and not sold through the corporation), the movement might warrant new interest. In the meantime, visitors should be severely cautioned that they are visiting an ultra-poor nation with limited medical care, shoddy domestic airlines and indifferent law enforcement agencies.

Bird's Eye View

Haiti and the Dominican Republic together make up the island known as Hispaniola (from the Spanish word "Isla Española"—the Spanish island). The entire island is mountainous and covered with forests, plains and pla-

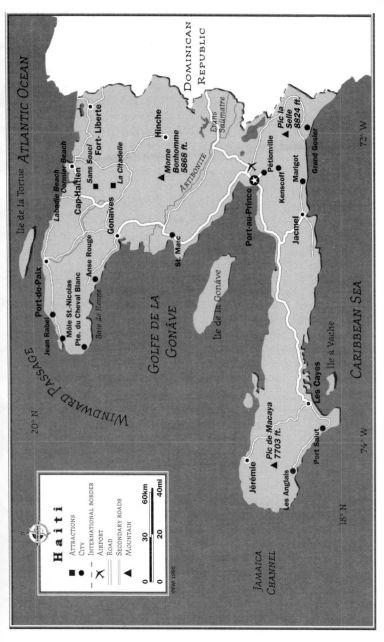

teaus. The Republic of Haiti, which occupies the western third of the island sprawls over 27,400 square kilometers; the Dominican Republic is abou twice as big. The shape is quite unusual; it could be described as the face of a woman (facing east) with a top knot and a long flowing neck scarf behind her. The highest peak is **La Selle**, at 2674 meters, lying southeast of **Port-au-Prince**, the capital. Most of the natural forests have been cleared for farming or fuel; in fact the island is considered an ecological tragedy. The southwes peninsula and the eastern two-thirds of the northern coast receive the mos rainfall. Port-au-Prince lies on the Gulf of Gonâve in the western crook. A small island called **Ile de la Gonave** lies in the bay to the northwest of Port-au Prince.

History

Haiti's history is best described as turmoil, right from the very beginning Columbus left the first Europeans there in 1492 and all ended up dying within a year. In 1617 the French were given control of the western part o Hispaniola (called Saint Domingue then by the Spanish) and turned it into an extremely wealthy colony, exporting sugar, coffee and indigo. Years o torture and subjugation followed for the imported African slaves who tilled the lands for rich European gentry. Finally, at the end of the 18th centur the slaves conducted a massive rebellion, led by Youssaint l'Ouverture. (A that time, U.S. plantation owners were terrified that the Caribbean revolu tionary wave would inspire their slave population.) In 1804, the country o Haiti declared itself independent and Jean Jacques Dessalines emerged as th world's first black emperor. He was assassinated in 1806 and the country be came divided again. Ever since then, strife has marked the country's nature the mulattos of the south waged fierce civil war against the blacks in th north, only to be followed by a succession of tyrannical dictators and a American invasion in 1915. (The 1915 U.S. takeover of Haiti was led by Virginian-born commander who boasted that he knew all about handlin black people, and during their 19 years the "blans" (foreigners, literall "whites" in Creole) smashed an insurgency, imposed Jim Crow rules in Hai ti's best clubs, and set up a Haitian army whose brutality, greed and incom petence decades later set the stage for a new intervention. By 1934 th Americans had returned. In 1957, the country was taken over by Franco Duvalier, known as Papa Doc, who wielded a reign of terror through th

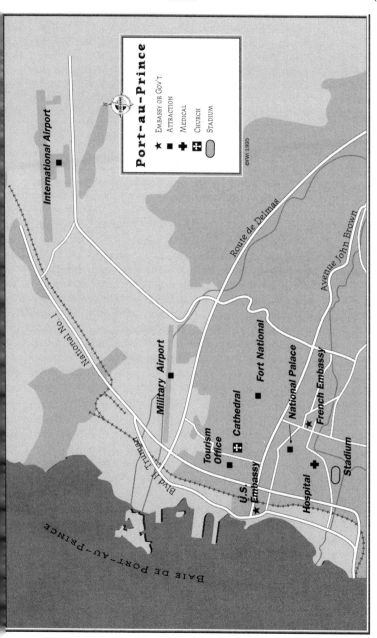

help of sadistic secret police. Until the mid-1980s his son Baby Doc (Jean-Claude) continued in his father's bloody footsteps, until a political movement called Operation Deschoukay drove him out of the country. Elections were held, but coup after coup shook the stability of the country. In the last eight years, there have been three coups.

In 1990, in the first genuinely public elections, a black charismatic priest, Father Jean-Bertrand Aristide, won the presidency to about 67 percent of the vote, only to be overthrown in a military coup led by Lt. General Raul Cédras. For the next three years, Cédras and his "attaches" (a Haitian term for what amounts to paramilitary thugs), introduced a new reign of terror, killing over 3000 people and committing untold human rights abuses from the killing of children to the raping of women. Since 1991, the country has been faced with great economic and social crisis largely due to the trade embargoes (enforced by the U.S. out of protest) and a lack of viable opportunities that have always plagued Haiti. In the fall of 1994, the sparring of threats between the Clinton administration and the military junta escalated beyond endurance for both side's pride. Cédras, who is white and sports a Jay Leno chin, held onto a diplomacy-of-defiance as the U.S. began threats to invade. The U.S. goal was to reinstate Aristide as president, whose power over the masses was singular in Haiti's history. Many poor Haitians (though considered fanatics) considered Aristide as some sort of prophet, or messiah, who could create miracles that would instantly solve the people's problems (Aristide himself advised against such ideology). Nevertheless, even before his ousting, Aristide was used to making strong impressions without bearing much responsibility for the political consequences, with his sermons often bringing the people out to the streets, only to be gunned down by the army.

The final denouement of the conflict became dramatic. On the eve of an American invasion, former President Jimmy Carter with General Colin Powell and Senator Sam Nunn flew to Haiti to negotiate a surrender among the ruling dictatorship. The last-minute drama was complicated by Cédras's wife who claimed she would rather die with her children than leave the country. Cédras refused to sign a surrender, on risk of court-martial, without the permission of the incumbent president Jonaissant, whom the U.S. did not recognize. At the last minute, Jonaissant finally signed the agreement at the very moment that planes were on the way, forcing Clinton to stop the invasion midair.

Nevertheless, what started out as an invasion was diplomatically renamed "intervasion" and American soldiers were instructed to come ashore and "cooperate" with Haitian police as long as they refrained from violence and abuse. The Haitian army looked on sullenly as over 20,000 American troops fanned through the country in full combat gear, dismantling their only arsenal of heavy weapons and their few armored cars. American tanks turned their tanks on FRAPH, the paramilitary thugs who did the regime's dirty work, built barbed wire around the airport, and locked up 75 of the worst attaches. Americans also took control of the state-controlled radio, TV station, and gave the city its first dependable electricity in years. Casualties were incurred, however, when Marines engaged Haitieds in a firefight in Cap Hatien, in which nine were killed. The irony is that the agreement provided for a general amnesty and honorable retirement for dictators. As November 1994 rolled towards Thanksgiving, the American troops continued to witness Haitian-style brutality; one American military policeman, when he needed to make a phone call, was told by a Haitian cop just to break into a private home and commandeer the phone.

The future: the reinstated Aristide faces a daunting task in trying to govern a country that has been sharply divided between a tiny, light-skinned French-speaking elite and the desperately poor, black Creole-speaking masses. Haiti's history has left it virtually without a civil polity; the elite, the army, and the allied gunmen outside any law have long pillaged the country for their own benefit. Since being reinstated, Father Aristide has thrown out his simple peasant shirt and trousers, and replaced it with the conservative dark suit and tie that he wore in exile.The elite of Pétitionville, in the words of one businessman, look at Aristide as their cook, maid, or gardener. The rich have stepped up private patrols of their flower-fringed villas and sleep with pistols beneath their beds. An atmosphere of fear surrounds them, and the president of the Chamber of Commerce believes Aristide's people could destroy things in a matter of hours. Haiti's other elite, the families of Lebanese and Palestinian immigrants who grew rich enough during the years of junta rule, also curse Aristide and his American patrons.

Aristide's view of modern society stands well to the left of mainstream America, and ultimately may require a lot of blood-pressure medication among Washington officials. The international trade embargo has been lifted, and the United Nations plans to give $555 million, while the U.S. is setting up a jobs program. Aristide's character, his long journey from poverty to church prodigy to returning president, bespeaks a man of depth and conviction and courage, but putting Haiti back on its feet will require an uncommon flair and delicacy. Aristide must not only instill a sense of realism among his followers but also carve out a detente with Haiti's new business elite, the only group with the capital he needs for the economic progress of his followers. Expectations among the masses for Aristide are so great that disappointment may be inevitable, particularly for a leader who is not used to working with parliament. His domestic problems are daunting; as one recent unclassified report described it, Haiti is not on the way to becoming a basket case—it already is one. It remains to be seen how the June 1995 free elections alter the country's course.

WARNING:

Looting has increased since Aristide's return and the possibility of crime against the elite is enormous. The U.S. State Department states that although crime remains a problem in Port-au-Prince and the provinces, there have been few reported incidents involving American citizens (though the number of Americans in Haiti at the present is probably extremely low). Rioting breaks out all the time. Food distribution centers are systematically looted. Crowds have even looted the police station. As such, rich-looking tourists travel at great risk.

All American citizens in Haiti should register with the Consular Section of the U.S. Embassy, located at Harry Truman Blvd., P.O. Box 1761, Port-au-Prince; ☎ (509) 22-0200, 22-0354, or 22-0612; FAX (509) 23-1641. The Consular Section is located on Rue Oswald Durand, Port-au-Prince; ☎ (509) 23-7011, FAX (509) 23-9665.

People

The people of Haiti have obviously been under great strain in recent years, but a strong spirituality underlies their tenacity to survive. (In fact, even Haitian analysts have said that whatever the instigators of the coup d'etat may have said, religion is the basis of all Haitian social, cultural, political, and economic structure.) That kind of passion is necessary to survive conditions, such as the lowest per capita income in the world—$250, about the same as Rwanda, a life expectancy of 55-years-old, a 35 percent adult literacy rate, and safe drinking water for only 41 percent of the population. The country has been so black, so isolated, and so racially polarized that the cheering throngs welcoming the American troops addressed black Americans as "blans," a Creole term (meaning white) that signifies any foreigner. Though they are said to make poor guerillas (there are 7000 in the army of a 7 million people), they are unilaterally considered hard workers. Haitians have survived their misery through a well-honed humor and they are quite prone to direct eye contact; like Brazilians or other Latin Americans, they tend to familiarize even relationships of acquaintance with much light touching and flirting. It is a matter of course to greet anyone you meet in passing with a nod or a hello. In most business encounters, and many social settings, depending on the economic status of the host, a visitor will usually be offered a cup of coffee; drinking it together is considered a social custom. The practice of Haitian voodoo finds an enormous number of adherents in the country, and many leaf doctors, sorcerers and voodoo priests hold a profound knowledge of the medicinal use of plants, for both good and adverse effects. (More information about the nefarious side of this work can be found in the book *The Serpent and the Rainbow*, by Harvard ethnobiologist Wade Davis.) Interest in elaborate Carnival productions withered after the military coup took over, but now with the return of democracy, enthusiasm might return. If there is a parade, it is usually filled with *bandes-a-pieds*, roving bands on foot who attract large crowds with their chanting and circular dancing. Most of the lyrics are highly satirical and often erotic. (Do avoid being crushed by crowds since fights tend to break out easily; you might find the safest perch near the Holiday Inn.) During the three or four weekends prior to Carnival, there may be open-air concerts. Most of the upper-class head for Jacmel for Carnival, where you will find a more sophisticated costume party; the downside is that the music tends to be less than thrilling. More fascinating is the peasant carnival called Rara, which follows on its heels, a ritual of voodoo societies. During every weekend of Lent (including the Easter weekend), flamboyantly dressed bands wander the countryside, asking for donations while singing and dancing. Some bands have up to a thousand members. One of the most important voodoo festivals is the Gede on November 1 and 2 (All Saints Days and the Day of the Dead), where spirit-filled participants dress up as dead people and prowl through cemeteries as a reminder that eros is the source of life. During this celebration, the dance movements become quite vulgarized, and hangers-on are pulled in to participate.

Insider Tip:

To attend a voodoo ritual is not easy for a foreign visitor. They are not publicized and you will have to have an introduction from an insider. Most of the worship happens in lower-class neighborhoods. Most of the time an enormous sum of money is asked for the privilege of attending; don't be bribed but understand that your income level is probably heads beyond that of the average Haitian. Some offering should be made, at the very least a bottle or two of local whiskey or rum. On the western side of Port-au-Prince is a voodoo dancehall run by Max Baeuvoir ☎ 34-2818/3723, who can provide you introductions into the cult.

Beaches and Underwater

Snorkelers in Haiti set out for Sand Cay from Port-au-Prince or Petionville.

Don't go looking for good beaches near Port-au-Prince; most of them are located along the Caribbean and Atlantic coasts. Those at resorts at St. Marc, about an hour's drive from the capital, are adequate, though not spectacular. Beaches west of the capital are to be avoided. The best are in the north coast of **Cap Haitien**, although the sand is not powdery, tending toward grit and pebbles. Excellent views of the mountainsides can be seen from here, however. Calm, shallow waters make for good swimming. A small white beach can be found near Km 30 of the Route Nationale 1. Take the painted turnoff sign four kilometers after the flour mill. A simple restaurant serves inexpensive but hearty fare. The stretch of beach resorts starts at **Côte des Aradins** 60 kilometers north of the capital. If you are not a guest at one of these hotels, there is a small fee charged for use of the beach, about $2 per person. There are three uninhabited sandy cays in the sea about three kilometers from the shore with excellent reefs. A small but highly fetching beach called **Amani-Y Beach** lies about five kilometers before St. Marc, where there is a restaurant and bar that has been closed for many years. A hurricane in past years destroyed the beach at Jacmel in the south coast, but there are few lovely white strands found along a dirt road running east of the city. At km 15, just before Cayes Jacmel, there is Raymond-les-Baions, alongside the road without facilities and a slight undertow. There are two beaches right after Cayes Jacmel, at **Ti Mouilliage**. Small beach homes can be rented along the second one, and the first one has an okay restaurant. At **Cap Haitien**, the second largest city in Haiti, the beaches are polluted and decidedly unappetizing. The finest beaches are reachable by a 20-minute ride by car. **Cormier Plage**, where the Hotel Cormier is situated, offers good food, its own generator, and scuba facilities. You'll find good wreck and reef diving. Traveling five minutes further west (30 minutes on foot) is **Labadie Beach**, an enclosed sandy peninsula used by Royal Caribbean Lines as a private beach for its visiting cruise ships. If you are not a guest of the cruise line you can use the facilities for about a $3 charge ($20 when a cruiseship is in port). Further along is **Belli Beach**, a small sandy cove with basic lodging rumored to be a brothel for visiting cruise personnel. Boats are available for rent here to visit Labadie village, situated on the foot of a cliff. About 10 kilometers west you will find **Club Roche Sauvage**, a newly built all-inclusive 144-bed resort with its own 300-meter beach. Spa and scuba facilities are not included. Beyond Roche Sauvage is **Labadie Shore**, which Crown Cruise Line uses as a private beach. The best beach in the north is at **Pointe Saline**, at the western tip. Do take extra precautions here since there is no shade and it is the driest part of the island. A fine excursion to take is the **La Grotte at Bassin**, east of Palmist, where there is an immense cave with a 10-meter high pre-Columbian rock carving of a goddess, as well as two other caves. On the peninsula's south side, from Baie de Henne to Anse Rouge, you'll only find barren rock and desert-like terrain, few inhabitants, and salt pans on either side.

On Foot

There are no marked hiking trails or organized excursions, but walking is a way of life in this country, and you may be forced to do so anyway, especially if your car breaks down or you run out of gas when all the stations are closed or empty. (Despite the lifting of the embargo, all supplies are still in short supply.) The interior is laced with footpaths and donkey tracks that hikers can make use of, but the island is poor in flora and fauna due to deforestation and soil erosion. Do not hesitate to ask directions or advice from locals, but don't count on directions always being correct. (Depending on the way the political flow is going, you may be given the wrong instructions simply because of your nationality.) Educated Haitians speak French and some English; rural unschooled folk speak neither and their patois is nearly unintelligible.

One of the most delightful hikes is located 30 miles from Pétitionville at the hill resort called **Kenscoff**, where elite Haitians retire to their country homes in July and August to escape the heat. Hire a guide in the village of **Godet** for the 2–3 hour hike to the summit above Kenscoff where there is a large radio mast; another good hike is to the summit to the west called **Morne Zombi**. The best views are found on the trail just to the east of the radio, accessed by a poor road. From here, you can see the entire south over a rugged, dark massif.

About a five-mile hike from the hill resort of Kenscoff behind Port-au-Prince is **Morne La Visite National Park**, a 1000-acre reserve full of Haitian pineforest and montane broadleaf forest. Few streams cross the park, but there are about 80 species of birds (some rare and unique to Haiti) in abundance. Permission is needed from the ISPAN office in Port-au-Prince to visit.

The highest peak in Haiti is **Pic La Selle** at 8824 feet near the border with the Dominican Republic. No road goes to the summit, but very advanced hikers can climb to the top, provided they carry a compass and altimeter— make sure you have a topographical map as well. Do bring all your own supplies (food and water), and although you can camp on the flat land, there will be no facilities of electricity of any kind. The office of ISPAN will know whether the park cabin near Seguin can be used for temporary shelter.

On the southwestern tip of the peninsula, is the **Macaya National Park**, much harder to reach, though it is the last of the island's virgin cloud forest, and there are numerous species of orchids, moss, reptiles, birds and bats. The endangered peregrine falcon also takes its winters here. There is a basic camping area, maintained by the University of Florida, which takes a half day to reach at the edge of the park. To reach the 2347-meter **Pic de Macaya**, you'll need another two days on foot.

The **Ville Bonheur Waterfall** is a beloved destination for Catholic devotees in Haiti, who make pilgrimages to it. The stream-fed falls drop about 100 feet to create a pool at the base. Usually, visitors park their cars at the top and descend carefully down the trail. Bring your own picnic lunch, but there are also cold drink and beer stands.

The Northwest Peninsula remains the most virgin land of Haiti, but the going is so rough that it can only be traversed in a four-wheel drive jeep or pickup. Avoid going after a heavy rainfall since potholes and ditches will be obscured by water puddles. The best views, possibly on the whole island, are seen on the ascent to **Bombardopolis** and the descent into **Môle St. Nicholas**. From Môle St. Nicholas you can hike a trail leading to the ruins of a fortress and onto the **Presqui'ile Môle St. Nicholas**, which is entirely uninhabited. A dry dwarf forest covers the terrain here. If you venture forth into this wilderness, you must take all food and water supplies and plenty of refills of gas. In most places there are no restaurants or lodgings, and even locals have very little food.

What Else to See

Port-au-Prince is a poor city and its shantytowns are growing, but what it lacks in architectural excellence is made up by the stunning mountainous backdrop towering over the city to the south. The business district commences near the harbor and covers about a 10-block area moving inland. The most interesting section of it was remodelled for the 1949 bicentennial. Here you'll find the American embassy, the French Institute, parliament, foreign ministry and the post office.

The presidential palace is located on the northwestern corner of the **Champs de Mer**, a large park which starts east of the commercial quarter. You can still see evidence of gunshots that were fired when President Aristide tried to resist the coup in 1991. To the northeast are the white and gold walls of the army high command building, where Aristide was practically hung by soldiers.

At the southwest corner of the Champs de Mars, you'll find the **Musée d'art Haitien**, which houses a fine naive collection; there's also a craft store and a restaurant. The **Hotel Oloffson**, a quaint gingerbread-style inn, is about one kilometer from the Champs de Mars. About four blocks away is the **Cathédrale de la Sainte Trinité**, where some exquisite sacred art can be seen. A small crafts shops is next to the exit run by Episcopal nuns.

A fine museum, the **Musée du Panthéon National** (MUPANAH) located on Place des Héros de Independence, has interesting artifacts from Columbus' journeys, as well as some fine art and an odd assortment of personal artifacts from various freedom fighters and politicians, as well as native Indians.

Excursions can be made to two small communities, Pétitionville and Kenscoff. Situated in the hills about 15 minutes from Port-au-Prince, Pétitionville has some of the best restaurants in the country, having evolved into a middle-to-upper-class suburb. Take the Panaméricaine Road, rather than the dirty Delmas Road, which is traversed by camionettes. The best views are seen from Route Canapé Vert.

Kenscoff is about 30 minutes from Pétitionville, some 1500 meters above sea level. (For more information about what to do, see under "Treks" above.)

Once called the "Paris of Antilles," **Cap Haitien**, Haiti's second largest city, is perched dramatically on the sheltered southeast side of an 824-meter-high cape. Today it's often called "Cap" or "Okap," in Creole. It's been destroyed by fire three times during the 18th and 19th centuries, as well as by an 1842 earthquake that decimated half of its residents. What remains in the city today is Spanish-style architecture, with fascinating arcades, grand porches and garden courtyards. (For information about beaches, see the section "Beaches" above.) Several excursions can be made from Cap Haitien, especially to the **La Citadelle fortress**, built by King Henri Christophe between 1805 and 1820 to deter any French reinvasion. Much work has gone into restoring the massive walls; about a kilometer and a half behind are four more forts worth visiting for the stupendous views. An easy way to get to the Citadelle is by a taptap (open-air truck) which leaves from the Hotel Bon Dieu Bon. Make sure you wear substantial shoes and take shade and water. At the nearby village of **Milto**, you can horseback ride as well as visit Christophe's royal palace, **Sans Souci**, begun in 1810 and inaugurated in 1813. Do try to avoid this area when cruise ships are in port. After 5 p.m. it's impossible to catch a taptap going back to Cap. Eight kilometers southwest of Cap is **Morne Rouge**, where you'll find the Habitation Le Normand de Mexy, a sugar plantation famous for its slave rebellions. Voodoo ceremonies are reportedly held under a tree in the village. Twelve kilometers southwest of Cap is the town of **Plaine du Nord**, where voodoo groups from all over the country, camp out and spend July 24-25 dancing and drumming nonstop. Many are possessed by voodoo spirits and wallow in a mud pool.

Probably Haiti's most charming city is **Jacmel**, about a two-hour drive from Port-au-Prince. The name itself comes from the Indian word for "rich land." It has stayed suspended in time since its late 19th century heyday when it became a bustling port for the export of coffee. It is filled with creole-style mansions with French balconies. The Victorian architecture is still apparent along the horseshoe bay and three small hills. The beach contains black sand and is fringed with palms; unfortunately it is not clean. (For beaches close by, see the section "Beaches" above.) Along rue Commerce there are many antique stores, crafts stores and art galleries; the American-owned **Salubria** has an intriguing collection. Several fine family mansions have been turned into guest houses, one of the loveliest being **Manoir Alexandre**. Two blocks to the east is the iron market built in 1895. Most restaurants in the area can be found in the dining rooms of inns, usually situated on open-air porches, or in private homes along the narrow streets leading to the interior of the city. About 12 kilometers into the southwest hills leads to a group of natural pools and waterfalls cascading over a multitiered limestone gorge, **Bassin Bleu**. You can hire horses in Jacmel to make the trek the 2–3 hour way or you can trek on foot, though you should hire a guide.

Historical Sites

Cathedrale de la Sainte Trinit ★★★★

Rue Pavee, Port-au-Prince.

Biblical murals by Haiti's best-known painters cover the walls of this cathedral. Created in 1949 by Castera Bazile, Philome Obin and other great painters, the colorful murals depict the last supper, Christ's baptism and other Biblical tales. All the figures are black, while Judas is white.

La Citadelle la Ferriere ★★★★

Pic le Ferriere, Milot.

It's rough going—up an incredibly steep road, then a 20-minute walk, or reached via horse or mule—but well worth the trouble. The massive fortress, ordered by King Christophe in 1805, took 15 years and 200,000 men to build; some 20,000 died in the pursuit. Built to withstand an invasion by Napoleon (which never happened), it was designed to shelter 10,000 people for up to a year. You can inspect the room that holds 45,000 iron cannonballs, marvel at the thickness of the walls (anywhere from 12 to 20 feet, depending on the source), or just drink in the spectacular views from 3000 feet up. Haitians call the Citadelle the eighth wonder of the world; they may be right.

Sans Souci ★★★

Milot.

The impressive ruins of King Henri Christophe's palace make for an interesting day trip. The palace, completed in 1813, covered 20 acres and was a monument to excessive consumption, done throughout in marble, mosaics, crystal chandeliers and priceless tapestries. It fell into disrepair after Christophe's suicide in 1820, and was completely ruined by an earthquake in 1842. Try to schedule your visit when no cruise ships are in port, or you'll be overrun with fellow tourists.

Museums and Exhibits

Le Centre d'Art ★★★

56 Rue de 22 Septembre, Port-au-Prince.
Hours open: 9 a.m.–5 p.m.

The city's main art center pioneered the selling of colorful Haitian art. The site includes a museum, displays of crafts and lots of modern art. An essential stop if you're interested in Haitian art.

Musee National ★★

Turgeau, Port-au-Prince.
Hours open: 8:30 a.m.–12:30 p.m.

Housed in a former presidential palace, the national museum is chock-full of interesting items relating to Haiti's past, including Indian artifacts, slave bells, Haitian dolls and portraits of political figures. Don't miss the anchor from Columbus' flagship, the Santa Maria, and the pistol King Christophe used to kill himself (with a silver bullet).

Musee d'Art Haitien   ★

Rues Capois and Legitime, Port-au-Prince.
This art museum boasts a wonderful native art collection and a good craft shop.

Tours

Marche de Fer   ★ ★ ★

Grand Rue, Port-au-Prince.
One of the Caribbean's biggest tourist attractions, the Iron Market is a teeming mass of humanity selling and buying everything from food—tropical fruits, rice, maize, yams, fish, even livestock—to local handicrafts and native art to baskets and wood carvings. The red and green iron building dates back to 1889. Be prepared to bargain, and to ward off aggressive hucksters.

Sports

There is a modicum of sports activities for the tourist; most will be available from a resort, but don't count on facilities to be high-class. You're best off bringing your own equipment rather than relying on a country which barely has the means to maintain itself properly. The conditions of tennis courts will be no way comparable to others in the Caribbean. Interesting horseback riding trails can be found at various spots, especially at Cap Haitien, and Kyona and Kaliko Beach. Golfers won't find the conditions at the nine-hole Pétitionville Gulf Club very inspiring, but in the absence of other entertainment it could prove endurable.

Where to Stay

☆	Fielding's Highest Rated Hotels in Haiti	
★★★★	Christopher Hotel	$50–$74
★★★★	Coconut Villa Hotel	$35–$49
★★★★	Hotel Caraibe	$39–$73
★★★★	Hotel Oloffson	$70–$130
★★★★	Le Xaragua Hotel	$124–$245
★★★★	Mont-Joli Hotel	$57–$65
★★★★	Montana Hotel	$68–$98
★★★★	Moulin sur Mer	$55–$115
★★★★	Prince Hotel	$50–$65
★★★★	Villa St. Louis	$60–$75

♡	Fielding's Most Romantic Hotels in Haiti	
★★★★	Christopher Hotel	$50–$74
★★★★	Hotel Oloffson	$70–$130

	Fielding's Budget Hotels in Haiti	
★★★★	Coconut Villa Hotel	$35–$49
★★★★	Roi Christophe Hotel	$41–$67
★★★★	Ibo Beach Club	$40–$70
★★★★	Hotel Caraibe	$39–$73
★★★★	Prince Hotel	$50–$65

Hotels are available in Port-au-Prince, but if you want any sort of beach experience, you should head for the resorts on the western and southern coasts. (The beaches in Port-au-Prince are highly unfavorable.) Most elite

Haitians head for summer vacation in the area around Jacmel, in the south. Most of the better restaurants are near Pétitionville, though there are no beaches there. Although official discounts were not available in the past for off-season, the situation may change as more tourists flood into the country.

Hotels and Resorts

Years of short supplies have permitted the condition of some accommodations to deteriorate; much patience will need to be exerted by any tourist. **Le Plaza Holiday Inn**, of the American chain, has valiantly survived throughout the political dramas, housing most of the international journalists who covered the tumultuous scene. **Prince Hotel**, ensconced in a former mansion, provides an intimate artistic appeal. The air-conditioning at the **Grand Hotel Oloffson's** cottages will be greatly appreciated, and the three-story Victorian edifice is alive with passersby who know what the latest events are—an important base in an unpredictable country.

Christopher Hotel $50–$74 ★★★★

John Brown Road, Port-au-Prince, ☎ *(590) 45-6124.*
Single: $50–$63. Double: $63–$74.
Located on a hillside with spectacular views, this basic hotel has comfortable guest rooms with air conditioning and locally crafted furniture. Lots of Haitian artwork in the public spaces adds a striking touch. There's a pool on-site and a few restaurants and bars, but active folks will probably be happier at a full-fledged resort.

Cormier Plage Resort $65–$95 ★★★

Jacmel, Cap Haitien.
Single: $65–$75. Double: $85–$95.
Set on a secluded site occupied by wild peacocks and exotic birds, this beach resort houses guests in two-story bungalows with tropical styling, but no air conditioning. Ground-floor units open right onto the beach. There's a tennis court and watersports, but no pool. Nice and relaxing, and popular with divers.

El Rancho Hotel $55–$155 ★

Petionville, Petionville.
Single: $55–$155. Double: $70–$155.
Set in a residential area high up on a hillside, this resort hotel is one of Haiti's best bets. Accommodations vary from small and simple rooms to larger units, all nicely furnished and cooled by air conditioning. The suites are especially nice, filled with antiques and Oriental rugs. For nightlife, there are three bars, a disco and casino; by day, two pools (one with a waterfall and swim-up bar), gym and tennis. Wonderful views abound.

Hotel Caraibe $39–$73 ★★★★

13 Rue Leon Nerette, Petionville.
Single: $39–$58. Double: $51–$73.
This older hotel dates back to 1946 and has lots of Haitian atmosphere, but not much in the way of plush accommodations, though rooms are air-conditioned. There's a restaurant, bar and pool, with nightlife within walking distance.

Hotel Oloffson $70–$130   ★ ★ ★ ★

Ave. Christophe 60, Port-au-Prince, ☎ *(509) 13-0919.*
Single: $70–$130. Double: $100–$130.

Dating back to 1890 and reopening in 1987 after extensive renovations, this giant Victorian is set on a hill with fine views. Guest rooms are simply decorated in antique mahogany and wicker, and are individually named after famous people who have stayed there over the years. Colorful local art abounds. There's a pool and restaurant serving French-Creole fare. Popular with artist types.

Ibo Beach Club $40–$70   ★ ★ ★ ★

Cacique Island, Cap Haitien, ☎ *(509) 17-1200.*
Single: $40–$55. Double: $55–$70.

Located on rustic and peaceful Cacique Island, three minutes from the mainland via boat, this beach property has seen better days and could really use a complete renovation. But it offers a lot for a little money—if you don't mind the general run-down look of the place. Rooms are air-conditioned but quite basic. There are three saltwater pools, tennis courts and all watersports, but this spot may be best appreciated as a day trip rather than a destination in itself.

Jacmelienne Beach Hotel $69–$137   ★ ★ ★

Rue Ste. Anne, Jacmel, ☎ *(509) 22-4899.*
Single: $69–$137. Double: $103–$137.

Located on Jacmel's beautiful black sand beach, this charming hotel is family run. Accommodations are spacious with hand-crafted local furnishings, native art and ceiling fans in lieu of air-conditioners. There are two restaurants and bars, but besides the pool and watersports, little else in the way of resort amenities.

Le Plaza Holiday Inn $58–$84   ★ ★ ★

Rue Capois Champ de Mars, Port-au-Prince, ☎ *(800) 465-4329, (509) 23-9800, FAX (590) 238697.*
Single: $58–$74. Double: $68–$84.

Located near the President's Palace and Central Park area, this standard Holiday Inn offers dependable, if not exactly exotic, lodging. Accommodations are among the city's best, with air conditioning, modern baths, local art and small patios. A casino and pool are on site. Popular with business travelers and foreign journalists.

Le Xaragua Hotel $124–$245   ★ ★ ★ ★

Deluge, Port-au-Prince, ☎ *(509) 22-5000.*
Single: $124–$245. Double: $185–$245.

Located 50 miles north of Port-au-Prince, on the beach, this hotel has extra-large guest rooms with all the usual amenities, including air conditioning. There's a tennis court and swimming pool, and watersports are nearby. Nice Haitian decor and artwork lends a Caribbean touch.

Mont-Joli Hotel $57–$65   ★ ★ ★ ★

Cap Haitien, Cap Haitien, ☎ *(509) 32-0300.*
Single: $57–$65. Double: $57–$65.

Set high on a hill with appealing views, this family-run operation has colorful, air-conditioned guest rooms, some filled with antiques. A pool, tennis court and small library keep the doldrums away, and the restaurant and bars are nicely done. The beach is some 20 minutes away via auto.

Montana Hotel   **$68–$98**   ★★★★

Rte F Cardozo, Petionville, ☎ (509) 57-1921.
Single: $68–$98. Double: $74–$98.
Situated on a hillside overlooking the city, this colonial-style hotel is peaceful and family run. Guest rooms are nicely done with air conditioning and Haitian art; most also have cable TV and balconies. There's a pool and tennis court, and they'll help arrange babysitting. A comfortable, friendly spot.

Moulin sur Mer   **$55–$115**   ★★★★

Rte. Nationale No. 1, Montrouis, ☎ (509) 22-1844.
Single: $55–$115. Double: $80–$115.
Set on the beach and incorporating a sugar mill that dates back to 1750, this resort is popular with honeymooners. Accommodations are in bungalows and wings with wicker furnishings and Haitian art; not all are air-conditioned but rely on ceiling fans to keep things cool. There's tons to do here, including a pool, miniature golf, watersports, racquetball and volleyball. Especially charming is the small museum that focuses on colonial times. Nice.

Prince Hotel   **$50–$65**   ★★★★

30 Rue 3, Port-au-Prince.
Single: $50–$60. Double: $60–$65.
Located in a residential area on a wooded hillside, this small hotel is housed in a converted colonial mansion. Accommodations vary, but all are air-conditioned and include antiques and handcrafted Haitian furnishings. There's a pool and a restaurant that serves Creole fare. A shuttle runs guests to the beach and downtown.

Roi Christophe Hotel   **$41–$67**   ★★★★

Rue 24, Cap Haitien, ☎ (509) 32-0414.
Single: $41–$57. Double: $51–$67.
This historic villa hotel is set in a former governor's mansion dating back to 1724 and once occupied by Pauline Bonaparte, Napoleon's sister. The hotel retains much French colonial detail, as well as local charm. Rooms have antique furnishings and most are air-conditioned; local art abounds everywhere. The lushly landscaped grounds include a free-from pool and restaurant serving regional fare.

Royal Haitian Hotel   **$45–$305**   ★★★★

Rte. de Carrefour, Port-au-Prince.
Single: $45–$305. Double: $55–$305.
Set on 15 acres of tropical gardens, this hotel is across the road from the marina and beach. The European-style casino is the big draw. Guest rooms are spacious and nicely done with Haitian furniture and artwork; all are air-conditioned. The hotel has fallen on hard times in recent years, so buyer beware.

Villa St. Louis   **$60–$75**   ★★★★

95 Bourdon, Petionville, ☎ (509) 45-6241.
Single: $60. Double: $75.

Located in a residential area, this small hotel provides just the basics: air-conditioned rooms, a restaurant and pool.

Hotels on Beaches

Beach resorts, in general, are disappointments in Haiti, since the beaches themselves are hardly favorable. Do avoid beach resorts during national holidays since they become packed with elite Haitians trying to avoid the bustle of the city. Few of the beaches on which the hotels are located are large; Ibo Beach even had to create its own. Club Med north of Port-au-Prince is not yet open, but do check with the tourist board. It has the best beach and has been waiting for the democracy to take hold before recharging its resources.

Hotels in Cap Haitien

There's not much to choose from in Cap Haitien, and most are small inn-type lodgings. Some close and open according to the political situation, like the Labadee resort. One of the most charming is the **Cormier Plage**, while not air-conditioned, it was intelligently designed for cross-tradewind ventilation.

Hotels in Jacmel

Inns are the prime style of accommodations in Jacmel. Do avoid national holidays since most of Haiti's elite head for this area for vacation. Visitors should be aware that at the print time, due to political conditions, the elite may be targets of violence.

Inns

Inns tend to have better luck in Haiti since the upkeep is smaller relative to larger hotels. The **Grand Hotel Oloffson**, listed under hotels/resorts can actually count as inn, if you judge by coziness and amiability. **Hotel Montana** exudes a personality that only owner-operated inns can., reflecting the family's Creole background. **Moulin sur Mer** is one of the atmospheric accommodations, ensconced in an old sugarcane farm, reflecting the style of plantation owners.

Low Cost Lodging

Conditions should always be checked in advance at the following options; economic reversals or sudden improvements could make all the difference. In general, most accommodations in Haiti are cheaper than other Caribbean islands; the trick is to find a price with a condition that you're comfortable with. Self-catering, and in some cases, air-conditioning, are available at the Coconut Villa, where you can even enjoy a pool, sometimes a great relief to have in the heat.

Coconut Villa Hotel $35–$49   ★★★★

Delmas, Petionville.

Single: $35–$39. Double: $45–$49.

Located in a quiet garden setting with nice views of the surrounding area, this simple hotel offers good value for the bucks. All rooms are air-conditioned and most (but not all) have a private bath; seven apartments with kitchen facilities are also available. There's a restaurant, pool and racquetball on site; you'll have to venture elsewhere for other diversions.

Where to Eat

Fielding's Highest Rated Restaurants in Haiti

★★★	Chez Gerard	$16–$25
★★★	Cormier Plage Hotel	$8–$30
★★★	La Belle Epoque	$15–$25
★★★	La Plantation	$15–$25
★★★	Les Cascades	$8–$25
★★★	Souvenance	$15–$25

Fielding's Special Restaurants in Haiti

★★★	La Plantation	$15–$25
★★★	Les Cascades	$8–$25
★★	Hotel Kinam	$8–$10

Fielding's Budget Restaurants in Haiti

★★	Musee d'Art Haitien	$5–$8
★★	Hotel Kinam	$8–$10
★★★	Les Cascades	$8–$25
★★★	Cormier Plage Hotel	$8–$30
★★★	La Belle Epoque	$15–$25

As to be expected, Haiti is no culinary oasis. Shortage of supplies, lack of training, and poor capital has led to few good restaurants. In Port-au-Prince; eateries serving dinner include the restaurants at Holiday Inn and the Oloffson hotels. On the southeast corner of the Champs de Mars, there are also several outdoor cafés selling barbecue chicken. Better to go to Pétitionville, where you can find some spicy Creole specialities and environments with a touch of tropical romance. **La Belle Epoque** remains the country's best French restaurant. Sunday buffet dinner at the **Holiday Inn** on Rue Capois serves not only the best food, but also the best gossip. Do check with the tourist board or your hotel upon arrival. Some real gems may have sprung up in the meantime.

Chez Gerard $$$ ★★★

17 Rue Pinchinat, Petionville.
French cuisine.
Lunch: entrees $16–$25.
Dinner: entrees $16–$25.

This French-run, first-class establishment, boasting a dining room set in a patio surrounded by lush gardens, was formerly a private residence. A perfect location for an intimate dining experience, visitors can eat extremely well for a reasonable price, given the current exchange rate. Sauces are the chef's metier, and the well-prepared meals of fresh local seafood and poultry can be capped off with sinful chocolate desserts. Visit the clubby bar before dinner.

Cormier Plage Hotel $$$ ★★★

La Badie Beach, Cap Haitien, ☎ (590) 62-1000.
Seafood cuisine.
Lunch: entrees $8–$15.
Dinner: entrees $8–$30.

Just minutes away from the port city of Cap Haitien is this charmingly rustic cottage-resort set on a stretch of white sand beach on the north coast. The French owners run a tight operation here, and the oceanfront restaurant draws seafood enthusiasts who stroll in for the fresh catch of the day—often prawns or lobster.

Hotel Kinam $ ★★

Place St. Pierre, Petionville, ☎ (590) 57-0462.
Latin American cuisine.
Lunch: entrees $8–$10.
Dinner: entrees $8–$10.

This lovingly restored, gingerbread-trimmed old Creole townhouse is one of the most pleasant dining and lodging bargains in town. The interior gleams with spiffy white wicker, and the food is a showcase of Haitian cuisine. The delights that appear on your plate could be griot (savory and crisp pork cutlets), peas and rice with djondjon (little local mushrooms) or barbecued goat. The location is a few minutes walk from the area's finer shops and galleries.

La Belle Epoque $$$ ★★★

21 Rue Gregoire, Petionville, ☎ (590) 57-0897.
French cuisine.
Dinner: entrees $15–$25.

The times are always good at this traditional Creole homestead in Petionville's choicest area. Diners enjoy French and Haitian specialties with an emphasis on nicely spiced (not too hot) seafood, chicken and pork. Tables are set on the patio, and it's also a great place for rum concoctions in the adjoining bar. La Belle Epoque has traditionally been one of the better eateries in the country.

La Plantation $$$ ★★★

Impasse Fouchard, Petionville, ☎ (590) 57-0979.

French cuisine.

Dinner: entrees $15–$25.

La Plantation has one of the best wine lists in town, which accentuates the imaginative cuisine prepared by a French chef. Surroundings are Haitian-homey. Figure on a bill of $25 for two.

Les Cascades $$$ ★★★

73 Rue Clervaux, Petionville, ☎ *(590) 57-5704.*

French cuisine.

Dinner: entrees $8–$25.

After the original structure, known as La Cascade, was destroyed in a fire a few years ago, the owners rebuilt in its place this aerie of hanging plants and splashing pools that provide a serene outpost in the heart of this hillside suburb. Many choose Les Cascades for a grand splurge, although the prices are very moderate. The evening begins with cool drinks on the second floor before guests sit down to dine on classic French cuisine. Seafood is the best choice, but the menu also features pork, veal and chicken.

Musee d'Art Haitien $ ★★

Rue Capois and Legitime, ☎ *(590) 22-2510.*

International cuisine.

Dinner: 3:30–1:30 a.m., entrees $5–$8.

Light meals, pastries and coffees are served in the garden of what is considered to be the premier showcase for naif Haitian art. Although it is only open for a few hours a day, this is the chance for visitors to rub shoulders with Port-au-Prince's cultural cognoscenti and other colorful characters.

Souvenance $$$ ★★★

8 rue Gabart, Petionville,

French cuisine.

Dinner: entrees $15–$25.

Another French-owned charmer, this restaurant has been deemed le restaurant un moment by Haiti's fickle elite. Service is polished, the atmosphere serene and gracious. Souvenance is most often recommended by seasoned travelers.

Where to Shop

The few items available in tourist stores can be found in the marketplaces, but vendors there have a tendency to raise prices when they see a foreigner coming by. You will have to use all your bargaining savvy to get a more common price if you are so inclined. The Iron Markets in Jacmel and Cap Haitien are a bit safer than in Port-au-Prince, but you should always keep a sure eye on your belongings. It's best, in fact, to carry little money, and avoid carrying expensive-looking cameras and camera bags, unless absolutely necessary for professional work. Backpacks should be carried in front of you, and any extra money tucked in a money belt inside your clothes. It's customary to ask for a discount in boutiques and shops; with the exception of groceries or food markets. Buy film for your camera before you come since the price is invariably higher.

Among the most desired craft items are voodoo flags, papier-maché statues and horn carvings. You can buy good voodoo flags outside the **Musée d'Art Haitien**. There is also a brisk business done in copies of Haitian naive master painters, usually sold near the post office. Art galleries specialize in various artists; one of the biggest dealers is the Nader family with two galleries. Check out the paintings hung in the Oloffson hotel, which are usually for sale. A good stop for jewelry is **Ambiance** on *17 rue M. Pacot.*

Haiti Directory

ARRIVAL AND DEPARTURE

There are direct flights from Miami to Cap Haitien Monday to Friday on **Gulfstream International**. **American Airlines** and **Haiti Trans Air** fly from New York. American Airlines, Haiti Trans Air and **ALM** fly direct from Miami. Fort-Lauderdale-Cap Haitien link is provided by **Lynx Air**. **ALM** flies from Curaçao to Cap Haitien. Once a week **Air France** flies from Santo Domingo to Cap Haitien. **Cairbintaxi**, a Haitian air taxi service, flies three times a week from Santo Domingo. Do check your reservation several times from Miami since they tend to be overbooked. Sometimes credit vouchers are given if you want to give up your confirmed seat to someone else.

The airport at Port-au-Prince is located at the northern edge of Delmas, 13 kilometers outside the capital. It would help facilitate you through customs if you have a working knowledge of French; the scene can get crazy, crowded and hot if more than one flight has landed. Baggage inspection is rigorous and thorough, with a strict drug law enforcement (whatever you do, don't carry drugs—life in a Haitian prison is the definition of hell). It's best just to keep your head about you, your eye on your luggage and documents, and your goal fixed on getting to your hotel. Once you get outside, you are pushed into another mass of humanity waiting for taxis and families to pick them up. You can either take a taxi to town (about U.S.$10 or sit in the back of a tap-tap, an open-backed truck, which costs about 10 cents (probably the cheapest transportation in the Caribbean, if not the most colorful); throw in another ten cents per bag.

There is a US$25 departure tax and a US$2 security fee, payable in U.S. currency.

CLIMATE

In coastal areas temperatures range from 68 degrees F to 95 degrees F. Further inland, it is generally hot, but offshore trade winds keep the air endurable. It is hotter between April and September. The drier months are December-March. As you go further up the hill, where several resorts are situated, you will find the air gets cooler.

DOCUMENTS

U.S. and Canadian citizens need a tourist card to enter Haiti (about US$10) purchased from consulates, tourist offices, airlines on departure or at the airport on arrival. Do not wait to buy it in Haiti because the airport is usually a vision of pandemonium and you will be needlessly tied up for hours. The limit time on tourist cards is two months; extensions may be obtained from the Immigration Department. All visitors should have an ongoing or return ticket.

ELECTRICITY

The current runs 110 volts, 60 cycles, AC. Power cuts are regular occurrences in Port-au-Prince for half a day at a time, although American troops have tried to solve the problem. One reason to stay at the best hotels is that they have their own private generators. Do take a flashlight for emergency blackouts.

GETTING AROUND

Taxis in Port-au-Prince are usually shared vehicles, called *Publiques*, which you flag down in the street. There is usually a standard fare (about 20 American cents) which is multiplied according to the length of the destination. There is also a minibus called a camionette and open-backed pickup trucks, called taptaps which run fixed routes and charge about 15 American cents. They do not carry luggage well and rarely travel after 10:30 p.m. There are few radio taxis at present, although democracy may have changed all that. Sometimes you may have to wait an hour for one to arrive. Try **Nick's Taxis** (☎ *57-7777*). Sometimes a Publique that has no customers can sometimes be persuaded to act as a private taxi, with the right monetary incentive.

Chauffeurs-guides cater to the foreign trade, usually waiting outside the finest hotels or at the airport; you can hire them as regular taxis or for a portion of the day. To make a reservation, call ☎ *22-0330.*, or go to the office of the Association des Chauffeurs-Guides at *18 Blvd. Harry Truman.* This is a more expensive, but more comfortable way to go to outlying beaches.

To reach other cities, take buses or colorful converted pickup trucks, leaving from what is called a station, most of them somewhere along the Blvd. Jean-Jacques Dessalines and the waterfront. There is no regular schedule, and buses depart when they have enough passengers (usually they are required to be full). You may, therefore, have a long wait. The trip can be torturous, since roads are incredibly poor and the conditions hot and dirty. You will be safer to pay a little extra to sit closer to the driver, especially if you have any valuables. (Do your best to carry only essential goods with you. It goes without saying that you should not wear any jewelry, watches should be kept out of sight, and it's best to carry your money, credit cards, etc., inside your clothes in a body pouch. Simply, whatever you do, do not call attention to any personal wealth.)

Car rentals are available, though gas supplies are so iffy that you probably should think twice about renting one. Avis, Budget, and Hertz all have offices. Airplane flights are sometimes available to Jeremie, Cap, and Hinche, but schedules are not reliable, since fuel has been a problem. Only time will tell as the democratic regime take what supplies are available.

LANGUAGE

All Haitians understand Creole and speak it part of the time. Only the elite and middle-class use French. Eighty-five percent of the population can't even understand French. The 1987 constitution, however, gave Creole equal status with French, and popular music is increasingly being written in Creole as a sign of national identity. It's been said that Aristide's charisma with the masses was his ability to speak Creole.

MEDICAL EMERGENCIES

Community sanitation is very poor. You should never drink the tap water in Haiti, and you should carefully choose your food. Avoid eating food that has not been properly washed or cooked; do not eat food cooked on the streets, and avoid anything raw or unpeeled. Stomach troubles are best soothed by a local herb tea. Prophylaxis against malaria is essential; ask your family physician for the proper medication, which he can receive by calling the Centers for Disease Control in Atlanta, Georgia. You can call yourself and listen to the latest up-to-date reports on Haitian conditions (☎ *(404) 332-4557)*. You will need a push-button phone to proceed through the menu.

Take all medicines and prescriptions that you will need. Shortages frequently occur, although pharmacists/chemists can fill prescriptions if they have supplies. Always bring a letter from your doctor explaining your need for certain medication and also several copies of the prescription itself.

The best hospitals are **Canapé Vert**, *on rue Canapé Vert;* ☎ *(404) 45-1052/3/0984*, and **Adventistse de Diquini** *on Carrefour Road;* ☎ *(404) 34-2000/0521*. However medical care is not up to U.S. standards and you will be expected to pay doctors and hospitals in cash.

Strong warning: Prostitution is not illegal in Haiti, but foreigners are targeted. All precautions should be taken as the country suffers from a very high AIDS epidemic, among both sexes and sexual orientations.

MONEY

The official currency unit is the gourde, divided into 100 centimes. What makes things confusing is that, at least in the past, Haitians have referred to some of their own money as the dollar, so be dead-sure when exchanging money, that you know which dollars—American or Haitian—is being quoted. The best exchange rate is obtained from money changers. American dollars get the best rate of all currencies. Credits cards, such as American Express, Visa and Mastercard are all widely accepted. However, do call your car d company before going since conditions in Haiti are ever-changing.

TELEPHONE

The telephone system is a nightmare in Haiti. It's been said that fewer than 33 percent ever make their connection. The international operators in Haiti seem to be sleeping, or else they don't like to answer—you can give a hero's try by dialing the number 09. If you are staying at the Holiday Inn, Montana, El Rancho and Oloffson hotels, you will have AT&T, USA Direct telephones for easy collect calls to the USA or anywhere else in the world with an AT&T credit card.

TIME

Eastern Standard Time, five hours behind GMT, same as New York.

TIPPING AND TAXES

All hotels charge 10 percent government tax, and many add a 10 percent service charge. American money is always welcome for extra services; do feel free to be generous.

TOURIST INFORMATION

The tourist office in Cap Haitien is located at Ruse, 24, Esplanade ☎ *57-4647* or in the U.S. ☎ *(212) 697-9767.*

WHEN TO GO

New Year and Ancestors Day on January 1–2. Mardi Gras is three day before Ash Wednesday. Americans Day is April 4. Assumption Day i. August 16. Deaths of Henri Christophe and Sessalines is October 6 and 17. United Nations Day is October 24. All Saints Day is November 1 Armed Forces Day is November 18. Discovery of Haiti is in December Christmas is December 25. Corpus Christi and Ascension are also public holidays.

HAITI HOTELS	RMS	RATES	PHONE	CR. CARDS
Port-au-Prince				
★★★★ **El Rancho Hotel**	100	$55–$155		A, MC, V
★★ **Christopher Hotel**	83	$50–$74	509-45-6124	A, DC, MC, V
★★ **Coconut Villa Hotel**	50	$35–$49		A, MC, V
★★ **Cormier Plage Resort**	32	$65–$95		A, DC, MC, V
★★ **Jacmelienne Beach Hotel**	31	$69–$137	509-22-4899	A, DC, MC, V
★★ **Le Plaza Holiday Inn**	82	$58–$84	(800) 465-4329	A, DC, MC, V
★ **Hotel Caraibe**	12	$39–$73		A, MC, V
★ **Hotel Oloffson**	22	$70–$130	509-13-0919	A, MC, V
★ **Ibo Beach Club**	70	$40–$70	509-17-1200	A, CB, DC, MC, V
★ **Le Xaragua Hotel**	51	$124–$245	509-22-5000	A, V
★ **Mont-Joli Hotel**	45	$57–$65	509-32-0300	A, MC, V
★ **Montana Hotel**	73	$68–$98	509-57-1921	A, MC, V
★ **Moulin sur Mer**	45	$55–$115	509-22-1844	A, MC, V
★ **Prince Hotel**	32	$50–$65		A, CB, DC, MC, V
★ **Roi Christophe Hotel**	16	$41–$67	509-32-0414	A, DC, MC, V
★ **Royal Haitian Hotel**	75	$45–$305		A, MC, V
★ **Villa St. Louis**	43	$60–$75	509-45-6241	A, MC, V

HAITI RESTAURANTS	PHONE	ENTREE	CR. CARDS
Port-au-Prince			
French			
★★★ **Chez Gerard**		$16–$25	A, MC, V
★★★ **La Belle Epoque**	509-57-0897	$15–$25••	A, MC, V
★★★ **La Plantation**	509-57-0979	$15–$25••	A, MC, V
★★★ **Les Cascades**	509-57-5704	$8–$25••	A, MC, V
★★★ **Souvenance**		$15–$25••	A, MC, V
International			
★★ **Musee d'Art Haitien**	509-22-2510	$5–$8••	None
Latin American			
★★ **Hotel Kinam**	509-57-0462	$8–$10	A, DC, MC, V

HAITI RESTAURANTS	PHONE	ENTREE	CR. CARDS
Seafood			
★★★ **Cormier Plage Hotel**	509-62-1000	$8–$30	A

Note: • Lunch Only

•• Dinner Only

JAMAICA

Jamaica is famous for its magnificent waterfalls.

Rastas and reggae, jerk pork and ginger beer, cool mountains, hot beaches, damp jungles and the cold refreshing water of streams and rivers—Jamaica is a continuous dance of the senses. The island can be so stimulating, in fact, that when Ian Fleming created his immortal character James Bond here in 1952, he insisted on facing a white wall in order to avoid the distracting beauty of both women and landscape. Midwife to the great all-inclusive resorts that have given immediate pleasure a new definition, Jamaica today is fostering the growth of a new, less-traditional style of resort—small, private places away from the beaches that allow intimate glimpses of island life and culture. In a back-to-the-future gesture, many of the great houses of century-old sugar plantations are being renovated today with artistic aplomb, and a pioneer in this work is Chris Blackwell, the rock entrepreneur who made Bob Marley an international superstar; his luxurious 10-room Good Hope Great House, a 45-minute drive from Montego Bay high in Jamaica's lush green hills, gives you the opportunity to relax in the gentile atmosphere of a British country home, six miles from the beach. Ecologically, Jamaica is still a treasurehouse—rain forests, rivers, waterfalls, wetlands, coral reefs and caves are found in every corner of the island, and hundreds of miles of well-marked trails can run from the easy to the daredevilish. From Montego Bay to Ocho Rios, around the perimeter of the island, excellent conditions for all watersports make for exciting adventures, though one of the best is still the rafting sojourn down the Rio Grande River on a banana boat (a favorite pastime of Errol Flynn).These days, with a rising crime rate, you do need to take precautions in Jamaica, but once you sit down to a cold local brew and a big plate of Jamaican-style barbecue, shaded by a palm and served with the most gracious smile you can imagine, every care you've ever had will disappear in a wink.

Bird's Eye View

Located 700 miles southeast of Miami, 110 miles west of Haiti, and 90 miles south of Cuba, Jamaica sprawls over 4400 square miles, making it the third-largest island in the Caribbean. Like other West Indian islands, it was formed from the outcropping of a submerged mountain range. A mountain range, reaching 7402 feet at the Blue Mountain Peak, crosses the island in the east and descends westward; a series of gullies and spurs cross north to south. The north and west coasts harbor the majority of beaches, though a few good ones can be found in the south. The cultural and social pulse of the island, Kingston, the capital, is located in the southeast coast—one of the largest and best natural harbors in the world. Montego Bay, another landmark name in Jamaican tourism, lies in the northwest part of the island.

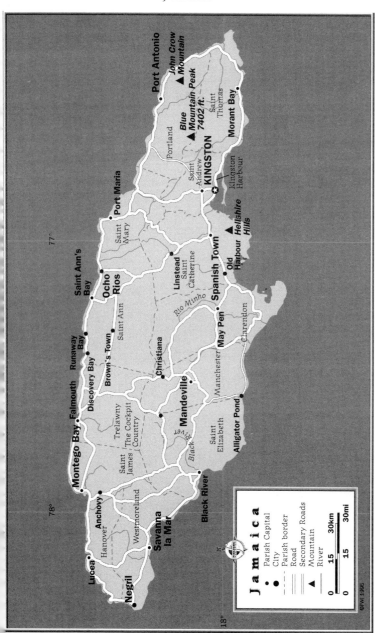

Jamaica

• Parish Capital
● City
- - - Parish border
═══ Road
═══ Secondary Roads
▲ Mountain
River

| 0 | 15 | 30km |
| 0 | 15 | 30mi |

©IPW 1996

Port Antonio
John Crow Mountain
Blue Mountain Peak 7402 ft.
Saint Thomas
Morant Bay
Portland
Saint Andrew
KINGSTON
Kingston Harbour
Port Maria
Hellshire Hills
Saint Mary
Spanish Town
Old Harbour
Saint Ann's Bay
Ocho Rios
Linstead
Saint Catherine
Rio Minho
Runaway Bay
Brown's Town
Saint Ann
May Pen
Clarendon
Falmouth
Discovery Bay
Christiana
Mandeville
Montego Bay
Trelawny
The Cockpit Country
Manchester
Alligator Pond
Saint James
Black River
Saint Elizabeth
Anchovy
Hanover
Westmoreland
Savanna la Mar
Lucea
Negril

77°
78°
18°

History

Columbus first glimpsed the north coast of the island in May 1494, land
ing in Montego Bay before he went back to Cuba. When he returned nine
years later, stormy weather crippled two of his ships and he was forced to an
chor at St. Ann's Bay, where he and his men were shipwrecked until the gov
ernor of Hispaniola retrieved them. In 1510, a permanent Spanish
settlement was finally established under the orders of Don Diego, the son o
Columbus, who was then governor of the West Indies, based in Santo Do
mingo. A new capital was erected in 1935 at Villa de la Vega (the Town o
the Plain), now known as Spanish Town. In 1655, Britain, under Olive
Cromwell, challenged Spain's claim on the island, ultimately triumphing and
establishing a head base at Port Royal, across the harbor from what is now
Kingston. (The Spaniards fled to Windsor Cave, the home even today o
many of their descendants.) The new headquarters at Port Royal became the
hub of some of the most nefarious activities on the high seas, under the di
rection of the buccaneer Henry Morgan, whose sacking of the Spanish colo
ny in Panama clinched England's claim to Jamaica. A massive earthquake i
1692 actually shook half the town—like Sodom and Gomorrah—into the
sea. The multi-ethnic, though black-based, population of Jamaica began to
be born in the next centuries as sugarcane farming took root, and the nee
for imported labor in the form of black slaves became imperative. After Ja
maica's slave population rose to 300,000 at the end of the 18th century, th
ratio of blacks to whites was a staggering 15 to one. Included in the mi
were free coloureds, the offspring of white men and slave women, and Ma
roons, descendants of free slaves. (For more information about the Maroons
see below under "People.") Slave revolts became a common occurrence i
Jamaica, the largest, bloodiest conflict led by "Daddy" Sam Sharpe, a Baptis
preacher whose oratory and convictions led the way to the abolishment o
slavery in Jamaica in 1838. Emancipation, however, led directly to the fall c
the sugarcane industry since there was a decided lack of labor. The conditio
of the freed blacks was further worsened by drought and unsteady economi
conditions, leading to another revolt in 1865, which resulted in the murde
of a government official. As a result, the island was designated a Britis
Crown Colony in 1866, which it remained until 1944, when full adult suf
frage was granted.

A British colony from 1655–1962, Jamaica developed a two-part system before World War II. A considerable measure of self-government was introduced in 1944, but full independence was delayed by attempts to set up a wider federation embracing all or most of the Caribbean Commonwealth territories. Jamaica joined the now-defunct West Indies Federation in 1958 but withdrew in 1961 because of disagreements over taxation, voting rights, and location of the federal capital. Sir Alexander Bustaments, one of the original founders of the two-party system, became the nation's first prime minister at independence in 1962. Under the 1962 constitution the queen is the titular head of state. Her representative, a governor general, is advised in areas bearing on the royal perogative, by a six-member privy council. Jamaica is divided into 13 parishes and the Kingston and St. Andrew Corporation, a special administrative entity encompassing the principal urban areas.

People

Like Brazil, Jamaica is a wonderful place to visit—if you don't get robbed. Jamaicans are a cheerful, generous bunch, full of an earthy humor and deeply inspired by the natural beauty of their island. As a society, they are inherently musical, with great artistic gifts—some of the finest craftwork in the Caribbean is done by untrained Jamaican artisans. And Jamaican people are deeply spiritual—it's said there are more churches per square mile than anywhere else in the world. Most are Protestant, though there are some Roman Catholics, Jews, Seventh Day Adventists, and Pentecostals, but the most apparent are the dreadlocked **Rastafarians**, a local minority cult best recognized by their long braided hair that resembles a rat's nest (Rastas take a religious vow not to wash their hair). Though they can often look a bit intimidating (their hairdos can look voluminous when they pull off their caps), they are nonviolent and do not eat pork; they believe the late Emperor Haile Selassie was a divine being, whose call for the end of racial superiority was connected to the belief that God would lead the blacks out of oppression and back to the Promised Land. Marcus Garvey, the ideologist born in St. Anne's Bay in 1887, is considered a prophet by the Rastas and is today a national hero.

The soul of Rastafarianism lives in the musical genre called reggae, Jamaica's most popular export known throughout the world. Over the years, such musical greats as Bob Marley, Peter Tosh, Jimmy Cliff and others have used reggae as political and spiritual inspiration through strong lyrics often disguised in meaning. Recently in Jamaica reggae has been supplanted by a newer genre called Dance Hall, which sports a heavier beat, and like American rap, tends to focus on urban violence and sex. Both musical forms can be heard throughout the island; beaches cannot be considered Jamaican if there isn't at least one jam session going on close by.

In the heart of the mysterious and rugged Cockpit country live the Maroons, descendants of escaped slaves who through incredible courage and cunning managed to evade capture for a century. The attitude toward this community is diverse—they have been called anything from the world's most successful revolutionaries to desperate villains and rogues. The peace treaty they eventually signed with the British still exists, like their culture 250 years later. Hidden deeply inside the hills along a barely passable road their isolated, self-governing enclaves are only slightly more accessible today. In the past there have been stories reported by travelers of being stopped along the road to Moore Town by Maroons armed with machetes demanding a payment of a road tax. (Being self-ruled, the Maroons can do anything—only in the event of murder are they subject to Jamaican jurisdiction). Their resistance has been buoyed by strong African religious beliefs and rites, and modern Maroon leaders are thought to be imbued with supernatural powers aligned not only to religion but to military prowess. Obeah, the ashanti-inspired system of belief, plays a major part in the Maroon tradition in Jamaica. The January Accompong Festival celebrates the victory of the Maroons over the English. To get to their enclaves is difficult and can often end in a futile search. (For more information, see below under the section "Porto Antonio—Treks")

There are many excellent Jamaican novelists whose fiction gives an excellent glimpse into the heart and soul of the people. *Abeng*, a novel by Michelle Cliff, explores the sensitive issues of race and class as seen through the eyes of a young girl. *Jamaica Farewell*, by Morris Cargill, is an honest portrait of the country and its people by a native newspaper columnist. Other fine writers include Olive Senior, H. Orlando Patterson and the poets Mervynn Morris and Dennis Scott.

INSIDER TIP

Note:. Illegal under Jamaican law, the "herb" locally called ganja (marihuana) is known to be a major source of income in the highlands. Officials, however, claim that ganja does not grow anywhere in the residential areas, adding that if it grows "anywhere," it is in the wilderness.

Beaches

The best way to acquaint yourself with the beaches of Jamaica—before even buying a ticket—is to rent a video of the first James Bond film, *Dr. No*—it's practically a travel promotional for the island's most beautiful strands. Then look for more specific information under the individual areas—Kingston, Montego Bay, Port Antonio—below.

Underwater

Although the deep Cayman Trench lies off Jamaica's north coast, one unfortunate tradeoff on a densely populated Caribbean island is that every shoreline is a potential fishing area. As such, divers will find most of Jamaica's touristy north coast overfished and barren, despite having attractive reef architecture and well-developed sponge life. The island's main exception is **Negril**, situated on the smallish west coast, and more protected from the wind and currents which sometimes play havoc with the rest of the island. Negril's 10-mile reef parallels the beach and encircles nearby Booby Cay, and features more than 40 known dive sites at all levels of ability. **Montego Bay** is the location of Jamaica's first marine park, but virtually all sites close to shore are well-trammelled and contain few fish. The **Falmouth/Runaway Bay** area represents probably the best of the north coast diving; fish life is a little better developed, and the reef structure features good wall and canyon diving. The name Ocho Rios translates to eight rivers, each of which come pouring down from the mountains and can create less-than-stellar visibility after wet weather. Otherwise, north coast visibility averages 60 to 100 feet, with occasional summer days soaring to 150 feet.

The true dive frontier of Jamaica lies on the largely unvisited south coast, where offshore cays, wrecks and walls, await more extensive exploration. One of the Caribbean's most unusual underwater locations is a veritable sunken Pompeii lying in Kingston Harbor, **Port Royal**. The current (above-ground) fishing village of the same name bears little resemblance to its former self: a pirate lair that was once referred to as "the wickedest city in Christendom," and which succumbed to a devastating earthquake in 1692 by sinking, literally, into the bay. Old Port Royal has since been frozen in time over 300 years, collecting silt and rust from the harbor; unfortunately, the government has closed the site to sport diving while it contemplates how best to salvage it. There are other locations to enjoy, including **Wreck Reef**, a shallow bank of coral off the Hellshire Hills which has proven a magnet for many ships. Visibility off Kingston is limited by harbor traffic and turbulent waters, but averages 50 to 70 feet. A fledgling operation has recently sprung up at tiny **Alligator Pond**, and is exploring the southern offshore reefs with some success. In addition to the dive shops listed below, there are a number based out of the all-inclusive resorts. There is a recompression chamber in Discovery Bay.

The Arches

A large coral arch decorates this site, located off Negril, that also features a series of ledges, caverns and swimthroughs, graced by healthy invertebrate life. As part of the same dive, a nearby Cessna sits on a shelf at 55 feet and has begun to develop a nice blanket of sponges and soft corals.

Devil's Reef

A popular Ocho Rios site, Devil's Reef has the best accumulation of fish life, which swarms enthusiastically around an extended pinnacle formation. The sea mount rises from 200 feet below the surface to 60 feet, and its corrugated structure provides caverns and tunnels, with healthy sponge life and forests of black coral.

Throne Room

A split in the Negril reef invites divers into a sloping canyon that drops to 65 feet, and through a "picture frame" colorfully adorned with black coral and sponges, which opens onto a sandy level. An undercut ledge supporting a large orange elephant ear sponge in the shape of a throne provides the name.

Wreck of the *Kathryn*

A 110-foot Canadian mine sweeper was sunk in 1991 as an artificial reef to help boost the fish population east of Ocho Rios. The ship sits on a bank about 50 feet down and can be penetrated by novice wreck divers. A series of intriguing caverns are found just off the Kathryn's stern and can be visited as part of the same dive.

Wreck of the *S.S. Texas*

Jamaica's best wreck, a 301-ton U.S. Navy vessel built in 1919, lies behind Lime Cay, just outside Kingston Harbour. The 125-foot ship was sold to the British Navy in 1940 and was turned into an anti-sub corvette; it sunk in 1944 and has become a fascinating dive. The Texas sits upright and intact, but lists slightly to the starboard, the bow of the ship sitting in 88 feet of water, with the aft 110 feet down. Although the Texas is not penetrable, the antiaircraft guns and depth charges are poised at the ready; enormous stands of black coral forest the site.

Dive Shops

Buccaneer Scuba Club

Port Royal; ☎ *(809) 967-8061.*

One-year-old shop visits Wreck Reef, the cays off Kingston Harbor and a site known as the Edge. PADI affiliated. Two-tank dive, $50; resort course, $80 (in pool at Morgan's Harbour Hotel). Mostly local clientele.

Negril Scuba Center

Negril; ☎ *(800) 818-2963 or (809) 957-4425.*

Situated near the harbor, this is the only Negril shop not directly tied to a resort and boasts a multilingual staff. Open since 1983, a PADI and SSI facility, with courses through assistant instructor. Two tank dive, $55; night dives scheduled regularly, $40.

Resort Divers

Ocho Rios; ☎ *(809) 974-5338.*

Probably Jamaica's largest dive operation (since 1986), with shops set up in Ocho Rios, Runaway Bay, Falmouth and Montego Bay. PADI five-star outfit with training to assistant instructor. Two-tank dive, $65, all equipment included; night dives, $60, but this price seems negotiable based on group size. Free hotel transfer from nearby resorts included in dive price.

Sea Riv Resort

Alligator Pond; ☎ *(800) 772-0727 or (809) 962-7265.*

Two-year-old 18-room lodge in tiny south coast village, wants to showcase the adventurous Jamaica. Dives unexplored south coast reefs, snorkels spring-fed rivers with manatees and crocodiles, cave exploration, etc. Not set up for individual dives, but all-inclusive packages (including airfare from Atlanta) start at $1025. NASDS affiliated.

Sundivers of Jamaica

Negril; ☎ *(809) 957-4069.*

Two Negril Beach locations, plus a Runaway Bay branch; an Instructor Development Center and PADI five-star facility. Two tank dive, $60; resort course, $75. Free "discover scuba" program.

On Foot

A local saying has it that "you can walk anywhere in Jamaica." Maybe so, but hiking in Jamaica is no small adventure. The 14- or 27-mile trek to the 7402-foot summit of the **Blue Mountains** takes the better part of two days. Nighttime temperatures can drop to freezing in this magnificent mountain range, the second-highest in the Caribbean. Several areas of the country are rarely traveled, and at least one range, the **John Crow Mountains** above Port Antonio, have been uncharted since a major British expedition explored in 1819. Shorter trails are few and far between, although there are plenty of goat and unmarked foot paths that will appeal to intrepid walkers. In sum, the wilds of Jamaica are truly spectacular, but are best ventured through in the company of a qualified guide.

The island features a great diversity of flowering plants—about 3000 of which 827 are not known elsewhere—and over 550 types of fern, most of which are found in lovely **Fern Gully** near Ocho Rios. Jamaica's wildlife is also a chief asset in the island's first tentative steps toward developing eco-tourism. An endemic lizard, the Jamaican iguana, was thought to be extinct for several decades, but a family made an appearance in 1990 in the **Hellshire Hills** southwest of Kingston, an uninhabited area local conservationists are now trying to protect. The Jamaican boa grows to eight feet and also lives in these gentle hills of dry scrub and cactus (there are several species of snake on the island; none are poisonous). A very rare native butterfly, papillio homerus—one of the world's largest—can sometimes be spotted in the foothills of the John Crow Mountains. Several places outside the rugged Blue Mountains invite birdwatching: the Kingston foothills and nearby Clydesdale National Park (near Hardwar Gap), Marshall's Pen (a nature reserve three miles outside Mandeville), the Black River area, the mangrove swamps of Falmouth Lagoon, and on the trails surrounding the Rockland Bird Sanctuary, west of Montego Bay. A 1990 book, *Birds of Jamaica: a Photographic Field Guide* by Audrey Downer and Robert Sutton, can be located in some stores and will aid in identifying the island's many species.

In addition to the popular Blue Mountain Peak hike, a classic 25-mile trading route between Kingston and Port Antonio, the **Vinegar Hill Trail**, is available for those excited by a true, jungle backpacking adventure (allow two-to-three days). Another ambitious hike is one which traverses the mysterious **Cockpit Country**, from the village of Cockpit to Windsor Caves (nine miles each way); the muggy area can only be visited on foot, but reveals a strange landscape of limestone karst formations and a reclusive community of ex-slaves, the Maroons. Both of these rewarding treks should be undertaken only with a guide. A simpler excursion for those wanting to experience the Blue Mountains without the commitment of an overnight adventure are the paths which climb above Jack's Hill to Peter's Rock (two hours) and nearby points. **Catherine's Peak** (5060 feet) can be attained via a short military track out of Newcastle; this and other nearby trails are maintained by the forestry department, which has an office in Hollywell. An area that may eventually develop into a hiking destination is the **Montego Bay River Valley**, a surprising respite from the pace and intensity of Montego Bay, but trails are not yet marked or mapped, leaving this a somewhat spunky option without a guide. Although the vast majority of Jamaicans are friendly and helpful, and are proud to show off their verdant backcountry, it's worth noting that some innocent-looking paths may wind up in the middle of an otherwise secluded ganja field. Those who till these fields are understandably protective of their illegal crop; these are not places to hang out should you stumble onto one. When hiking below 3000 feet and near cow pastures, you'll need to be prepared for ticks, particularly during February and March; in swampy areas, mosquitoes are generally combated by repellent. The topographical map is the best resource for heading off the beaten track, and is available at the Land and Survey department in Kingston on Charles Street; unfortunately, black and white reproductions are all that are available at this writing.

Blue Mountain Peak

One of the Caribbean's premiere treks ascends the lush, stream-carved slopes of the Blue Mountains, which represent the majestic eastern spine of the island between Kingston and Port Antonio. Although there are several summits in the range, the main crest (Blue Mountain Peak), is a lofty goal and requires most of two days to accomplish, one night spent halfway up in a hostel. The 27-mile trail (a shorter option is explained below) begins in the town of Mavis Bank, elevation 2500 feet, where a coffee plantation processes the famed Blue Mountain coffee grown on the slopes above you. From here, the track drops into a valley, crossing two rivers and then ascends an exposed hillside to village of Penlyne Castle (elevation 3900 feet), and continues for a mile through fields of banana, coffee and vegetable gardens. Typically, this seven-mile section of the hike is done in the afternoon, reaching accommodations before dusk (either Whitfield Hall Hostel, a rustic plantation house, or Wildflower Lodge, a newer facility with views; both have showers available, but no electricity or meal service, $12.50 per person at either location). The next morning, you'll climb Jacob's Ladder, the steepest part of the trek, and then ascend a series of switchbacks through tree ferns and elfin forest which lead to the summit, 7502 feet above sea level. The top is usually shrouded in clouds and can actually be quite chilly; you'll need to come prepared with a windbreaker, sweater and long pants, particularly in the winter months. If you are lucky to have reached the summit on a cloudless day, you'll see Kingston and Port Antonio, and possibly Cuba, 90 miles to the north. One popular plan is to depart the hostel about 2 a.m. and reach the summit just prior to sunrise, which is the most likely time for clear skies; you'll need to carry a flashlight, even if traveling under the light of a full moon. A shorter option is available by driving a four-wheel vehicle on a difficult road to Penlyne Castle, reducing the trek to 13 miles round-trip. Although the trail is long and requires some stamina, it is well-marked and not technically difficult; a guide is a good idea if you are new to hiking in the region, but not necessary for those comfortable in the rugged rainforest environment.

Trekking Shops

Sense Adventures

Jack's Hill; ☎ *(809) 927-2097.*

President of the Jamaican Alternative Tourism, Camping and Hiking Association, Peter Bentley's guide company specializes in two-day treks to Blue Mountain Peak, $125 per person including ground transportation to the Penlyne Castle hostels (or $75 per person if hiking from Mavis Bank), as well as day-trips in the Newcastle area. Also arranges iguana tours, raft and canoe trips and "clothes optional recreation." Bentley's operation is based out of the Maya Lodge overlooking Kingston.

By Pedal

Perhaps wisely intimidated by the bristling pace of minibus (and other) drivers, cyclists have yet to find their niche in Jamaica. As overwhelming as vehicular traffic can be, it's heavily concentrated along the north coast drag, between Negril and Ocho Rios, and in the vicinity of Kingston. Surprisingly, visiting riders tell us that even north coast drivers are actually respectful of cyclists, providing they spot you as they careen around those hairpin turns. Although there aren't many east-west alternates to this well-traveled corridor, heading into the hills along some of the dirt or so-called "inoperable" roads will transport you to the real Jamaica, the one which exists outside the purview of most tourists. Distances can be deceiving on this big island; plot your general route in advance, carry a good road map and don't be shy about requesting directions from villagers (you'll be at least as curious a sight to them as vice versa). If you're determined to tour the north coast, consider the beautiful stretch between Port Maria (20 miles east of Ocho Rios) and Port Antonio. This magnificent, 40-mile ride (one way) visits breezy bays, cool forests and rolling coastline, with friendly locals vastly outnumbering tourists en route to east coast resorts (the ill-maintained road past Port Antonio around the eastern tip of the island is known for bad drivers). Out of Montego Bay, one attractive 40-mile loop heads east out of town on route B15 (not the coastal road) up the lush Montego River Valley to Wakefield. From here, rough, potholed roads head south toward Maroon Town, skirting the northwest side of the Cockpit Country, and then descend back into Montego Bay using the other side of the valley you came up. Both of these rides, and virtually any others heading off the busy road between Negril and Ocho Rios, are best-suited for mountain bikes. A circuit of the entire island is roughly 435 miles, though there are a number of possibilities to shorten or extend that figure; plan to maintain a flexible itinerary and allow at least 10 days. For those bringing their own bikes onto the island, there are repair shops in Montego Bay, Ocho Rios and Kingston. It may be overstating the obvious, but always wear a helmet, and do not ride after dark; Jamaican traffic accidents result in hundreds of deaths annually.

Bike Tours & Rental Shops

Blue Mountain Tours

Ocho Rios; ☎ *(809) 974-7075.*
Six-hour, 18-mile guided rides in the Blue Mountains, $78; includes transportation, brunch and lunch and 18-speed mountain bike.

Montego Bike Rentals

Walter Fletcher Beach, Montego Bay; ☎ *(809) 952-4984.*
Rents Diamond Back and other mountain bikes; $10 per day, weekly rentals, $65. 15 bikes on hand.

Sports (Island-Wide)

Every imaginable water sport is available in Jamaica; the all-inclusive resorts are masters at accommodating guests to arrange any and all levels of expertise. With such luxurious countryside, however, the latest trends are to pursue challenging treks (see the "Treks" section, above)—from floating lazily down the White River (near Ocho Rios) or tooling down the Martha Brae River on an inflatable raft.

Kingston

For many tourists, Kingston on first sight is everything they don't want in a Caribbean isle—grimy, traffic-clogged, polluted, noisy, crime-ridden and ir-respressibly raucous, but it is, nevertheless, the soul and spirit of most native islanders whose eyes wax over when they remember their childhood memories. This is where the ethnic melting pot first produced the crossbreeding that makes up the present heady spice called Jamaican society. What Kingston truly is today is Bob Marley turf, the undisputed (albeit deceased) king of reggae whose 1974 song "Lively Up Yourself" became the cry of the masses. Today you can't go anywhere in Kingston without making homage to his name; indeed, some travelers come to Kingston *only* for that. His dreadlocked statue stands in the middle of the square across from the National Arena and his records can be found in every store on the island. The **Bob Marley Museum**, ensconced into a 19th-century home on Hope Road, is a visual testimony to his life, struggles and musical influence.

To see the full variety of sights in Kingston, you will probably need to rent a car, or hire a taxi for the day. At the top of the itinerary should be the **Devon House**, a restored 19th-century mansion that first belonged to one of the Caribbean's first black millionaires, George Steibel. The **National Gallery of Jamaica** is a fine place to appreciate the island's art, from 17th-century portraits to impressionist paintings and sculptures. **Hope Botanical Gardens** is a lovely pace to stroll and enjoy the exotic flora of the island; Sundays are crowded but give you a chance to see Jamaican families in action. Across the harbor is **Port Royal**, or what is left of Port Royal, once the island's premier city in the 17th century when buccaneers ruled the waves. Henry Morgan, the British pirate, called the city his home, before it toppled, in 1692, into the harbor by an earthquake and subsequent tidal wave. There's still quite a lot left to see, including the cockeyed **Giddy House**, which has been tilting off-center since a 1907 earthquake, as well as **St. Peter's Church**, **Fort Charles** and the old **Naval Hospital**. At **Morgan's Harbor** marina you'll find a few restaurants, bar and small hotel.

West of Kingston is **Spanish Town,** Jamaica's old capital, with a few historical sites still standing. On the south coast, **Madeville** represents a quieter, calmer Jamaica. Bird-watchers will enjoy **Marshal's Pen**, an 18th-century greathouse set on a 300-acre wildlife sanctuary. Two of the best places to see the sunset are **Yardley Chase** and **South St. Elizabeth**. For touring the area as an ecologist, contact **South Coast Safaris** (on the Black Rover); ☎ *(809) 965-2513* for a 1.5 hour excursion covering 10 miles round-trip where you can photograph a variety of birds, crocodile and other wildlife. Special fishing tours can also be arranged.

Beaches in Kingston

Gunboat Beach is one of the most popular beaches around Kingston. A rare black sand beach is found at **Fort Clarence**, tucked into the Hellshire Hills southwest of the city. There you'll find changing facilities and live entertainment. Locals think nothing of driving the 30-odd miles for the special surroundings at **Lyssons Beach** at Morant Bay, whose golden sands gleam in the sun.

A delightful excursion is to hire a boat at the Morgan's Harbor Marina at Port Royal to cruise to **Lime Cay**, an island just beyond Kingston Harbor. Here is an ideal place to picnic, swim and sunbathe.

What Else to See

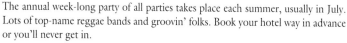

City Celebrations

Reggae Sunsplash ★★★★★

Jam World, Kingston.

The annual week-long party of all parties takes place each summer, usually in July. Lots of top-name reggae bands and groovin' folks. Book your hotel way in advance or you'll never get in.

Historical Sites

Devon House ★★★★

26 Hope Road, Kingston, ☎ (809) 929-7029.
Hours open: 10 a.m.–5 p.m.

This 1881 mansion is filled with period furnishings but the best reason to come is for the excellent crafts shops on the grounds. There are two restaurants and a great ice cream shop.

Museums and Exhibits

Bob Marley Museum ★★★

56 Hope Road, Kingston, ☎ (809) 927-9152.
Hours open: 9:30 a.m.–4:30 p.m.

The national hero's clapboard house was his home and recording studio for many years. Reggae fans will appreciate the collection of Marley memorabilia and consider this a five-star attraction. Those not into Marley's brand of music can pass.

Institute of Jamaica

12 East Street, Kingston, ☎ (809) 922-0620.
Hours open: 8:30 a.m.–5 p.m.
This museum has excellent exhibits on the island's history, with some impressive old charts and almanacs. It also houses the National Library.

National Gallery

12 Ocean Blvd., Kingston, ☎ (809) 922-1561.
This waterfront gallery displays paintings, sculpture and other works of art by Jamaica's most famous artist, Kapo. Other artists' works include Edna Manley, Alvin Marriott, Isaac Belisari and Augustin Brunias.

Parks and Gardens

Royal Botanical Gardens

Hope Road, Kingston, ☎ (809) 927-1257.
A peaceful refuge from city life, these gardens encompass 50 acres. Most plants and trees are marked for identification.

Theatre

Little Theatre

4 Tom Redcam Road, Kingston, ☎ (809) 926-6129.
This theater presents a variety of dramas, musical and special performances. Each December 26-April they produce the LTM Pantomime, a variety show with song, dance and stories.

Theme/Amusement Parks

Anancy Family Fun ★★★

Negril, Kingston, ☎ (809) 957-4100.
This newer attraction consists of three acres of miniature golf, a fishing pond, go-carts and a nature trail. Geared toward kids.

Tours

Cruises

Various locations, Kingston.
Lots of choices for cruising the ocean blue. Montego Bay: **Paco Rabanne** *(☎ (809) 951-5020)*, the **Mary-Ann** *(☎ (809) 953-2231)*, the **Calico** *(☎ (809) 952-5860)*, and the **Rhapsody** *(☎ (809) 979-0104)*. Port Antonio: **Lady Jamaica** *(☎ (809) 993-3318)*. Ocho Rios: **Heave-Ho Charters** *(☎ (809) 974-5367)* and **Red Stripe** *(☎ (809) 974-2446)*. Negril: **Aqua Nova Water Sports** *(☎ (809) 957-4323)* and the **Lollypop** *(☎ (809) 952-4121)*. Excursions range from snorkel trips to catamaran sails to booze cruises with live bands.

Port Royal

Near Kingston, Kingston, ☎ (809) 924-8706.
Hours open: 9 a.m.–5 p.m.

Now it's more touristy than anything, but this port used to be known as the "wickedest city in the world" because of its buccaneering past and frequent visits by Blackbeard. That all changed in 1692, when it was destroyed by an earthquake. There's lots to see in the complex, including St. Peter's Church, which dates back to 1725; the Archaeological and Historical Museum; a small maritime museum housed in the former British navel headquarters; Fort Charles, which dates back to 1656 and is the port's only remaining fort; and the Giddy House, permanently tilted after an earthquake.

River Rafting ★★★★★

Various locations, Kingston.

Jamaica's many rivers make for great float trips, usually in a bamboo raft that holds just two and is piloted by a character who spins tales of local lore. Several outfits offer trips that last an hour or so and cost about $40 per couple. Highly recommended! In the Montego Bay area, try **Martha Brae's Rafting Village** (☎ *(809) 952-0889)* or **Mountain Valley Rafting** (☎ *(809) 952-0527)*. Near Port Antonio, try the **Rio Grande** (☎ *(809) 993-2778)*. In Ocho Rios, call **Calypso Rafting** (☎ *(809) 974-2527)*. "An Evening on the Great River" is a touristy but fun boat ride down the river lined with torchlights, followed by dinner and a folkloric show.

Sports in Kingston

Yachting is one of the major activities in Kingston since there are so many attractive offshore islets in the area. A well-attended regatta is sponsored in August by the Morgans Harbor Hotel. If you belong to a yacht club at home, inquire whether you have privileges to participate. Ask at the Morgans Harbour Hotel regarding cruises around the harbor.

Many resorts have tennis courts. Public courts are available at the Ligunea Club across the road from the hotels in New Kingston. Squash can also be played at the Ligunea Club. Eighteen-hole golf courses can be found at the Caymanas Golf Club and the Constant Spring Golf Club.

Jamaica has a passion for **polo**. In the Kingston area, the Kingston Polo Club on the Caymanas Estates holds regular matches. For more information about activities at Chukka Cove, see "North Coast" below.

Golf

Various locations, Kingston.

Jamaica has lots of golf courses. The best by far are the links at Tryall, a PGA tour-approved, par-71 course that is considered one of the world's best. Call ☎ *(809) 952-5110.* Also in the Montego Bay area are the **Half Moon Golf Club** (☎ *(809)*

953-2280), a spacious, par-72 course designed by Robert Trent Jones; **Ironshore Golf and Country Club** *(☎ (809) 953-2800)*, par 72 and known for its many blind holes; and **Wyndham Rose Hall Country Club** *(☎ (809) 953-2650)*, a par-72 course on the historic Rose Hall estate with an imaginative layout. In Kingston, try **Caymanas Golf Club**, *(☎ (809) 926-8144)*, a par 72 known for its very challenging 12th hole; and **Constant Springs** *(☎ (809) 924-1610)*, a par-70 course.

Horseback Riding

Various locations, Kingston.

Several operations offer horseback riding. Ocho Rios: **Chukka Cove Farm** *(☎ (809) 972-2506)*, $20 per hour; and **Prospect Plantation** *(☎ (809) 974-2373)*, $18 per hour. Montego Bay: **Rocky Point Stables** *(☎ (809) 953-2212)*, where 1.5-hour rides start at $38. Negril: **Horseman Riding Sables** *(☎ (809) 957-4474)*, $25 for two hours.

Watersports

Various locations, Kingston.

Most hotels offer a variety of watersports, or check out one of the following operations. For scuba and snorkel, try **Fisherman's Inn** *(Falmouth, ☎ (809) 247-0475)*. Runaway Bay: **Jamaqua Watersports** *(☎ (809) 973-4845)* and **Sun Divers Jamaica** *(☎ (809) 973-2346)*. Negril: **Negril Scuba Centre** *(☎ (809) 957-4425)* and **Sun Divers Jamaica** *(☎ (809) 957-4069)*. Ocho Rios: **Sea and Dive Jamaica** *(☎ (809) 947-5762)*. Montego Bay: **Seaworld** *(☎ (809) 953-2180)* and **Sandals Beach Watersports** *(☎ (809) 949-0104)*. Port Antonio: **Lady Godiva** *(☎ (809) 993-3281)* and **Aqua Action** *(☎ (809) 993-3318)*. In addition to the above, **Resort Divers** *(☎ (809) 974-0577)* has six locations around the island. For deep-sea fishing, check out **Seaworld Resorts** *(☎ (809) 993-3086)* and **Sans Souci** *(☎ (809) 974-2353)*.

Bamboo rafts on the Rio Grande River take tourists past magnificent scenery.

Where to Stay

Fielding's Highest Rated Hotels in Jamaica

★★★★★	Grand Lido	$350–$290
★★★★★	Half Moon Beach Club	$255–$805
★★★★★	Round Hill Hotel & Villas	$305–$454
★★★★★	Sans Souci Lido	$465–$945
★★★★★	Trident Villas & Hotel	$255–$755
★★★★	Boscobel Beach Hotel	$415–$995
★★★★	Jamaica Pegasus Hotel	$180–$564
★★★★	Plantation Inn	$300–$999
★★★★	Sandals Ocho Rios	$355–$455
★★★★	Tryall Resort	$235–$465

Fielding's Most Romantic Hotels in Jamaica

★★★★	Ciboney Ocho Rios	$175–$690
★★★★★	Half Moon Beach Club	$255–$805
★★★★★	Round Hill Hotel & Villas	$305–$454
★★★★★	Trident Villas & Hotel	$255–$755
★★★★	Tryall Resort	$235–$465

Fielding's Budget Hotels in Jamaica

★★	Negril Cabins	$40–$55
★	Indies Hotel	$35–$62
★★	Coral Cliff Hotel	$54–$64
★	Caribbean Isle Hotel	$55–$65
★★	Toby Inn	$45–$80

Hotels and Resorts

Courtleigh House & Hotel $79–$195 ★ ★

31 Trafalgar Road, ☎ *(800) 526-2400, (809) 926-8174, FAX (809) 926-7801.*
Single: $79–$195. Double: $83–$195.

This traditional garden-style property accommodates guests in large hotel rooms and suites and apartments with one to three bedrooms and kitchens. There are two pools, a few restaurants and a very popular disco on-site. Friendly service, but this spot could really use a renovation. Still, this is good value for the rates.

Four Seasons $71–$83 ★

18 Ruthven Road, ☎ *(809) 929-7655, FAX (809) 929-5964.*
Single: $71–$83. Double: $71–$83.

Obviously (if you noticed the rates) not affiliated with the luxury hotel chain of the same name, this small hotel in New Kingston is housed in an old mansion. Guest rooms are simple but adequate. No pool, but you can use the one at the very nice Pegasus, a five-minute stroll away.

Jamaica Pegasus Hotel $180–$564 ★ ★ ★ ★

81 Knutsford Blvd., ☎ *(809) 926-3690, FAX (809) 929-5850.*
Single: $180–$564. Double: $185–$564.

Located in New Kingston, three miles north of downtown, this high-rise hotel offers a sophisticated atmosphere that attracts lots of business travelers and conventioneers. Guest rooms are nice, with extras like coffeemakers and large balconies. There's a large pool, two tennis courts, and a jogging track, and guests can work out at a nearby fitness club. The top five floors of the 17-story building, the Executive Club, have added amenities. An excellent choice for the business traveler, though tourists may feel out of place.

Medallion Hall Hotel $79–$83 ★ ★

53 Hope Road, ☎ *(809) 927-5721.*
Single: $79–$83. Double: $79–$83.

This small hotel, a former private residence, has an inn-like feel. Accommodations are simple but pleasant with traditional decor and dark woods. There's a small restaurant and bar, but nothing else in the way of diversions; you'll have to venture out for excitement. Good value, though.

Morgan's Harbour Hotel $98–$255 ★ ★ ★

Port Royal, ☎ *(809) 924-8464, FAX (809) 967-8030.*
Single: $98–$255. Double: $216–$255.

Downtown Kingston is 20 minutes away from this colonial-style hotel. Completely rebuilt after devastating Hurricane Gilbert, it houses guests in extra-nice rooms with luxurious furnishings, good artwork, and wet bars. The pleasantly landscaped grounds include a saltwater pool, a marina that attracts lots of yachters, a disco and watersports. Perfect for those who need to be near Kingston but want the resort feel of a waterfront property.

Terra Nova Hotel $120–$150 ★ ★ ★

17 Waterloo Road, ☎ *(809) 926-2211, FAX (809) 929-4933.*
Single: $120–$150. Double: $120–$150.

Set on five acres near a commercial area, this motel-style property has an excellent restaurant, and recently redone, but rather drab, guestrooms. Still, this is a popular spot for business travelers not looking to spend an arm or leg on a room. Resort amenities are in short supply, save for the pool, oddly set out front in full view of passersby.

Wyndham Kingston **$165–$505**

77 Knutsford Blvd., ☎ *(800) 322-4200, (809) 926-5511, FAX (809) 929-7439.*
Single: $165–$505. Double: $165–$505.
Situated in the business center on 7.5 acres, this towering hotel was recently redone, with good results. Primarily appealing to business travelers and conventioneers, it offers modern accommodations in the 16-story tower or older and funkier cabana units. There are two tennis courts, a pool and a fully equipped health club, as well as several bars and restaurants. Quite decent, but the Pegasus remains superior.

Low Cost Lodging
Indies Hotel **$35–$62**

5 Holborn Road, ☎ *(809) 926-2952, FAX (809) 926-2879.*
Single: $35–$58. Double: $58–$62.
This small guesthouse offers incredible rates, but not much else besides a popular restaurant.

Where to Eat

Fielding's Highest Rated Restaurants in Jamaica

★★★★★	Evita's	$7–$19
★★★★★	Reading Reef Club	$10–$24
★★★★★	Temple Hall	$25–$25
★★★★★	Trident Hotel Restaurant	$25–$50
★★★★	Almond Tree	$12–$26
★★★★	Blue Mountain Inn	$12–$24
★★★★	Norma's at the Wharfhouse	$26–$34
★★★★	Sugar Mill	$14–$31
★★	De Montevin Lodge	$11–$18
★★	Pork Pit	$2–$9

Fielding's Special Restaurants in Jamaica

★★★★★	Temple Hall	$25–$25
★★★★	Almond Tree	$12–$26
★★★★	Blue Mountain Inn	$12–$24
★★★★	Norma's at the Wharfhouse	$26–$34
★★★★	Sugar Mill	$14–$31

Fielding's Budget Restaurants in Jamaica

★	Chelsea Jerk Centre	$3–$5
★★	Chicken Lavish	$3–$5
★★	Hot Pot, The	$3–$4
★★★	Pork Pit	$2–$9
★★	Front Line, The	$5–$8

Blue Mountain Inn $$$ ★★★★

Gordon Town Road, ☎ *(809) 927-1700.*
International cuisine.
Dinner: 7–9 p.m., entrees $12–$24.

This is probably one of Jamaica's most elegant dining experiences, set in an old coffee plantation house overlooking the Mamee River, located about half an hour from Kingston. It's a good excuse for women to air out a little black dress and men a jacket (ties are not required) while sampling continental cuisine that's impeccably prepared and served by a gracious staff. Steak and lobster thermidor and flambeed desserts are some of the old fashioned but delicious choices frequently on the menu.

Chelsea Jerk Centre $ ★

9 Chelsea Avenue, ☎ *(809) 926-6322.*
Latin American cuisine. Specialties: Jerk Chicken and Pork.
Lunch: Noon–3:30 p.m., entrees $3–$5.
Dinner: 3:30–10 p.m., entrees $3–$5.

No, this isn't a self-improvement workshop for nerds on Chelsea Avenue - the Jerk Centre proffers blazingly hot barbecued chicken or pork that's been marinating for hours in a medley of incendiary spices that are a closely-guarded secret. Most dishes here are under $5 and come with sides of rice and peas (white rice with red beans). A half-chicken or pork slab can be packaged to go.

Devon House Restaurants $$ ★★

Devon House, ☎ *(809) 929-6602.*
Latin American cuisine.
Lunch: 10 a.m.–4 p.m., entrees $6–$16.
Dinner: 4 p.m.–midnight, entrees $6–$16.

This former colonial mansion turned restaurant/coffee house/craft emporium is one of Kingston's most visited tourist sites. An incredible Jamaican breakfast is served on the breezy Coffee Terrace every day except Sunday. Diners saunter to a long table topped with red-checked country cloths for a buffet of beautifully carved fresh fruit, ackee and saltfish, cod fish balls and breads. Blue Mountain coffee and exotic juices are included. If you have room, pop into the adjoining I-Scream for a frozen concoction of soursop or mango.

El Dorado Room $$ ★

17 Waterloo Road, ☎ *(809) 926-9334.*
International cuisine.
Lunch: Noon–2:30 p.m., entrees $7–$20.
Dinner: 7:30–11 p.m., entrees $7–$20.

The main dining room of the Terra Nova Hotel, a boutique style hostelry, provides a gracious ambience for local residents taking a breather from the vibrant Kingston restaurant scene. Picture windows look out onto the spacious grounds of the former private estate built in the early 20s. Seafood shines here, whether it's freshly-caught grilled lobster or red snapper in ginger sauce.

Gap Cafe, The $$$ ★★

Hardwar Gap, Blue Mountain, ☎ *(809) 923-7055.*
International cuisine.

Lunch: entrees $12–$15.
Dinner: entrees $17–$22.

A visit to the Gap Cafe is a journey to another Jamaica—one where a fireplace may be glowing all year round, understandable at a height of 4200 feet. Gloria Palomino welcomes guests to sip Blue Mountain coffee and savor some of the best pastries on the island, served all day and at high tea on Sundays. Native guavas are used in the cheesecake, as well as soursop and passion fruit for the cakes and mousses. The Cafe, once an old fixer-upper, is now a cozy, flower-filled charmer decked out in tones of maroon and blue. There's a gift shop on the premises.

Hot Pot, The $ ★★

2 Altamont Terrace, ☎ *(809) 929-3906.*
Latin American cuisine. Specialties: Fricassee Chicken, Saltfish and Ackee.
Lunch: 8 a.m.–4 p.m., entrees $3–$4.
Dinner: 4–10 p.m., entrees $3–$4.

A dandy place to try Jamaican specialties is this informal joint behind the Wyndham Hotel. The decor isn't much, but the authentic dishes are cheap and filling. The Hot Pot serves three meals a day, including the legendary saltfish and ackee (a vegetable brought over by Captain Bligh of Bounty fame) for breakfast.

Indies Pub and Grill $ ★

8 Holborn Road, ☎ *(809) 926-5050.*
Latin American cuisine.
Lunch: entrees $4–$12.
Dinner: entrees $4–$12.

This is the Jamaican version of a local pub, roosting companionably in a New Kingston neighborhood. The fare is nothing fancy: just burgers, fish and chips or pizza, but sometimes there's nothing better than rubbing elbows with office workers on a comfortable alfresco terrace. The Indies is a popular late night spot as well, it serves food and drink until 1:30 a.m. on weekends and until midnight the rest of the week.

Ivor Guest House $$$ ★

Jack's Hill, ☎ *(809) 977-0033.*
International cuisine.
Lunch: entrees $18–$22.
Dinner: entrees $22–$30.

This cozy guest house/dining room on a hill high above Kingston boasts a million dollar view (at 2000 feet) and the chef prepares reasonably-priced lunches and dinners with a Jamaican flair. The terrace of this small colonial inn is a popular spot for high tea and cocktails on the open terrace. On a clear night, the lights of the city in the distance make strong men (and women) swoon.

Le Pavilion $$$ ★★

81 Knutsford Boulevard, ☎ *(809) 926-3690.*
International cuisine.
Lunch: 12:30–3 p.m., prix fixe $16.
Dinner: 7–11 p.m., entrees $16–$26.

As hotel dining rooms go, Le Pavilion just might be the most popular downtown meeting spot. Sophisticated city dwellers flock here for high tea on weekdays while others like the seafood buffets on Fridays and the reasonably-priced three-course lunches with a variety of Caribbean and Continental meat and fish concoctions. No lunch is served on Saturday.

Minnie's Ethiopian $$ ★

176 Old Hope Road, ☎ *(809) 927-9207.*
Latin American cuisine. Specialties: Gungo-Pea Stew, Festival Bread, Juices.
Lunch: entrees $10–$20.
Dinner: entrees $10–$20.
After a pilgrimage to reggae icon Bob Marley's Museum and Tuff Gong Recording Studio nearby, fans can repair to his former chef's eating establishment for some Rasta Ital food (mostly vegetarian, utilizing local bounty) prepared by Chef Minnie. The full name of this round wooden restaurant is Minnie's Ethiopian Herbal Health Food, and after a few freshly-squeezed juices and her signature gungo (pigeon pea stew, you'll feel truly cleansed.

Norma's at the Wharfhouse $$$ ★★★★

Reading Road, Reading, ☎ *(809) 979-2745.*
Latin American cuisine.
Lunch: Noon–2:30 p.m., entrees $26–$34.
Dinner: 7:30–10:30 p.m., entrees $26–$34.
The finest restaurant on the island may be this historical dockside beauty created by Norma Shirley, Jamaica's most famous chef. Dine with influential Jamaicans and visiting celebrities while watching the action at a table set on the wharf of this 300-year-old warehouse, or in an antique-filled salon. Shirley, who owned a restaurant in New York, utilizes the rich bounty of the region to spectacular effect; the menu, which changes daily, often includes succulent smoked marlin with papaya or grilled deviled crab backs. The elegantly-dressed plates are a treat.

Temple Hall $$$ ★★★★★

Temple Hall Estate, ☎ *(809) 942-2340.*
Latin American cuisine. Specialties: Fettucine Boston Jerk.
Dinner: 6:30–11:30 p.m., entrees $25.
Of the handful of gracious plantation homes on the outskirts of Kingston, The Restaurant at Temple Hall Estate is probably on most gourmet lists of "don't miss" experiences. For the most part the vast property is self-sustaining, growing most of the herbs and vegetables and raising the livestock for the scrumptious meals. Guests are provided with complimentary transportation by the owners, who like to put on a light show at night by illuminating the long driveway with torches. Reservations required.

Montego Bay

Known to locals as Mo' Bay, Montego Bay is the primary port of entry by air for Jamaica. It's here, along the shoreline, where Jamaican tourism was born. Once a sleepy town, it's burgeoned into the apotheosis of what some tourists feel is the Caribbean nightmare, but for others it's a town that epitomizes the bustling, sweaty, crowded charm of a Third-World port. Downtown is a joggerhead of traffic, people, vendors and markets, and if you want to stay in the middle of all that, you'll be able to find some small (but noisy, count on it) hotels. The Montego Bay experience starts even on arrival, at the Donald Sangster International Airport, where you will have to jostle your way past crowds, walk long hot distances to your luggage, and nearly kill your fellow travelers to get a porter's attention. In order to minimize the discomfort, arrange for your hotel to pick you up (many allinclusives include airport transfer in the package). There's nothing like seeing a sign with your name on it and a helpful assistant when you are hot, tired and cranky after an international flight. (For more taxi information, see the directory under "Getting Around" at the end of the chapter.)

Beaches in Montego Bay

Cornwall Beach is a man-made phenomenon to provide tourists with an alternative to the postage-stamp patch called Doctor's Cave Beach—once the hub of Montego Bay's social scene during its heyday in the '60s. The scene is still happening at Cornwall, but with so many locals and tourists, that if you're the kind of person who needs to see the color of the sand beneath your feet, stay away. These days Doctor's Cave itself is just too reminiscent of Florida to get our vote for exotica, but the five-mile stretch of vanilla-colored sand still has its charm, though its overexposure in the press has brought every loud obnoxious tourist out of the woodwork. On the plus side, the changing facilities can be useful and there is a large variety of junk food to choose from. **Walter Fletch Beach**, on the bay near the center of town, is very good for swimming, since it is well protected from the strong winds.

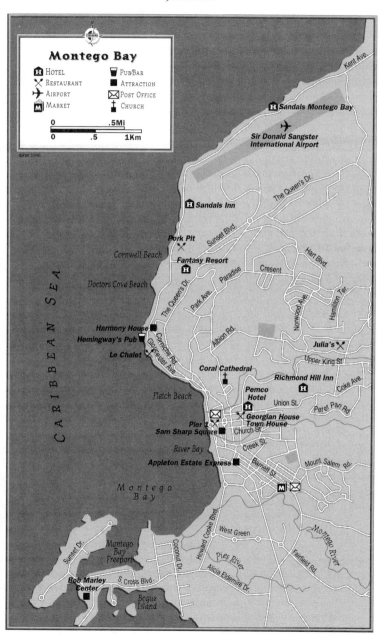

Montego Bay

- 🏠 Hotel
- ✕ Restaurant
- ✈ Airport
- Ⓜ Market
- 🍺 Pub/Bar
- ■ Attraction
- ✉ Post Office
- ✝ Church

0   .5Mi
0   .5   1Km

©FWI 1996

Sandals Montego Bay

Sir Donald Sangster
International Airport

Kent Ave.

The Queen's Dr.

Sandals Inn

Sunset Blvd.

Hart Blvd.

Pork Pit

Cornwell Beach

Fantasy Resort

Cresent

Paradise

Norwood Ave.

Hamilton Ter.

Doctors Cove Beach

Park Ave.

The Queen's Dr.

Albion Rd.

Julia's

Harmony House

Cornelia Rd.

Hemingway's Pub

Gloucester Ave.

Le Chalet

Coral Cathedral

Upper King St.

Richmond Hill Inn

Coke Ave.

Pemco Hotel

Fletch Beach

Union St.

Peter Pan Rd

Georgian House
Town House

Pier 1

Sam Sharp Square

Church St.

River Bay

Creek St.

Appleton Estate Express

Barnett St.

Mount Salem Rd.

Montego Bay

Montego River

Howard Cooke Blvd.

West Green

Sunset Dr.

Montego Bay Freeport

Coconut Dr.

Pies River

Fairfield Rd.

Bob Marley Center

S Cross Blvd

Alicia Eldemire Dr.

Bogue Island

CARIBBEAN SEA

What Else to See

Historical Sites

Greenwood Great House   ★★★★

Highway A1, Montego Bay.
Hours open: 9 a.m.–6 p.m.

One of Jamaica's greatest great houses, this one belonged to the Barrett family, of which Elizabeth Barrett Browning is a descendant. The early 19th-century mansion is nice to tour, filled with antiques, unusual musical instruments, rare books, custom-made china and portraits of the family.

Rose Hall Great House   ★★★★

Rose Hall Highway, Montego Bay, ☎ *(809) 953-2323.*
Hours open: 9 a.m.–6 p.m.

Not as architecturally impressive as Greenwood, but this great house from the 1700s is filled with tales of murder and intrigue. It seems that mistress Annie Palmer seduced slaves and then killed them, as well as murdering three husbands. Her story has been fictionalized in several books, which you'll find in the gift shop. There's also a neat pub in the basement.

Parks and Gardens

Columbus Park Museum   ★★★

Queens Highway, Discovery Bay, ☎ *(809) 973-2135.*
Hours open: 9 a.m.–5 p.m.

This outdoor park, studded with pimento trees, has some interesting and eclectic exhibits. There are 18th-century cannons, a stone cross, a large mural of Columbus' landing in 1494, and displays on the history of sugarcane. Stop by if you're in the area, but don't bother making a special trip.

Rocklands Wildlife Station   ★★★

Anchovy, St. James, ☎ *(809) 952-2009.*
Hours open: 2 p.m.–5 p.m.

This privately owned reserve is a must for birders (the rest can probably live without it). Doves, finches and other feathered creatures eat right off your hands.

Tours

Appelton Estate Express   ★★★★

Appelton Estate Station, Montego Bay, ☎ *(809) 952-3692.*

All aboard the Appelton Express, an air-conditioned diesel railcar that chugs some 40 miles into the mountains. Along the way you'll pass Jamaican villages, coffee and fruit plantations, and wonderful scenery. You'll also tour a rum factory and get to taste the goods. The fee includes transportation from your hotel, continental breakfast, buffet lunch, and an open bar. The train departs at 8:50 a.m. on Monday, Thursday and Friday, and returns about 5:00 p.m.

JUTA Tour Company ★★★★
Claude Clarke Avenue, Montego Bay, ☎ (809) 952-0813.
This well-established tour company has offices all over Jamaica. They'll take you river rafting, on sea cruises, through great houses, and into Kingston.

Where to Stay

Hotels and Resorts

Coral Cliff Hotel **$54–$64** ★★
Gloucester Avenue, ☎ (809) 952-4130, FAX (809) 952-6532.
Single: $54–$63. Double: $58–$64.
This older hotel consists of a former mansion and a newer addition, perched on a hillside about five minutes from Doctor's Cave Beach. Rooms are pleasant and comfortable, but lack extras like TV. There's a bar and restaurant, pool, and entertainment during high season. A good budget hotel.

Doctor's Cave Beach Hotel **$85–$135** ★★★
Gloucester Avenue, ☎ (800) 223-6510, (809) 952-4355, FAX (809) 952-5204.
Single: $85–$135. Double: $105–$135.
Set on four acres of tropical gardens in the heart of the resort district, this informal hotel is across the street from Doctor's Cave Beach. Guest rooms, decorated in rattan and air-conditioned, are comfortable. Facilities include a pool, two restaurants, watersports across the street and a small gym. The atmosphere is lively, with lots of special events like crab races and rum parties.

Fantasy Resort **$55–$85** ★★
2 Kent Avenue, ☎ (800) 237-3421, (809) 952-4150.
Single: $55–$85. Double: $55–$85.
Located across the street from Doctor's Cave Beach, this high-rise property is only the fantasy of someone with low self-esteem. Everything is quite dated here and in real need of renovation. There's tennis on two courts, a fitness center, pool and Jacuzzi. Guest rooms are small but do have nice ocean views. Decent value, but not too exciting.

Gloucestershire, The **$60–$80** ★★
Gloucester Avenue, ☎ (800) 423-4095, (809) 952-4420, FAX (809) 952-4420.
Single: $60–$80. Double: $60–$80.
Doctor's Cave Beach is across the street from this modern hotel. Guest rooms are adequate with cable TV and air conditioning. Besides the Jacuzzi, there's not much in the way of resort amenities.

Half Moon Beach Club **$255–$805** ★★★★★
Rose Hall, ☎ (800) 626-0592, (809) 953-2211, FAX (809) 953-2731.
Single: $255–$505. Double: $305–$805.
Located on 400 acres with its own one-mile private beach, this resort is simply outstanding in every way. Accommodations are in standard rooms, cottages and villas.

All are luxurious, with tropical furnishings, antique reproductions, sitting areas, and patios or balconies with sea views. One-bedroom suites have full kitchens and spacious living areas, while the villas offer lots of space on two levels. There are two main swimming pools, plus 17 other pools shared among the villas, an equestrian center, 13 tennis courts, four squash courts, all kinds of watersports, and a children's center. There's also 18 holes of golf on a Robert Trent Jones-designed course. Aerobics classes are available in the fitness center, as well as sauna and massage for working out the kinks. Eating choices are varied and fine. This is one of Jamaica's best resorts, well worth the high rates.

Holiday Inn Montego Bay $160–$205

Rosehall, ☎ *(800) 465-4329, (809) 953-2485, FAX (809) 953-2840.*
Single: $160–$205. Double: $160–$205.

Located on a private beach and part of the historic Rosehall Sugar Plantation Estate, this large resort complex lives up to the dependable, if unexciting, Holiday Inn name. Accommodations are acceptable but many lack water views. There's lots going on, from organized activities and entertainment (crab races, anyone?) to a large pool, health club, four tennis courts, watersports and supervised activities for the kids. Good security keeps non-guests at bay. Decent, and a recent $13-million renovation has kept things looking nice.

Jack Tar Village $155–$205

Gloucester Avenue, ☎ *(809) 952-9504, FAX (809) 952-6633.*
Single: $155–$205. Double: $134–$205.

Located a mile from downtown Montego Bay, this all-inclusive resort is perched right on the beach, albeit, a narrow one. Guest rooms are comfortable and modern. The rates include all meals, drinks and activities, and there's lots to do, including four tennis courts, volleyball, watersports, and nightly entertainment. (You'll pay extra for scuba and jet skiing.) Those who book far in advance are rewarded with lower rates.

Montego Bay Racquet Club $50–$155   ★★

Sewell Avenue, ☎ *(809) 952-0200, FAX (809) 979-7210.*
Single: $50–$155. Double: $55–$155.

Located in the Red Hills area overlooking the harbor, three minutes from Doctor's Cave Beach (they'll shuttle you over for free), this informal resort lures tennis lovers with excellent facilities, including seven courts and two pros on hand to offer tips. Choose from simple and not especially pleasing villas or traditional guest rooms, which are a bit nicer. Besides the restaurant and pool, not much happens here other than tennis, tennis and tennis. Unless you're into that racquet, stay elsewhere.

Reading Reef Club $65–$370

Bogue Lagoon, ☎ *(800) 223-6510, (809) 952-5909, FAX (809) 952-5204.*
Single: $65–$370. Double: $80–$370.

Located some 15 minutes west of Montego Bay, this small resort sets on 2.5 acres with its own small beach. Air-conditioned accommodations include rooms and suites. There's a few restaurants, a pool, and watersports, and, best of all, a lack of hustlers on the beach. A nice, quiet spot.

Round Hill Hotel & Villas   **$305–$454**   ★★★★★

Highway A1, ☎ (800) 223-6510, (809) 952-2505, FAX (809) 952-2505.
Single: $305–$615. Double: $285–$454.

Set on a lush green peninsula with a private beach eight miles from Montego Bay, this exclusive resort encompasses nearly 100 acres. Accommodations are in the main building (most with twin beds) or luxurious villas, some with their own private pools and all with the pampering of a maid, gardener and cook. Lots of rich and famous types stay here; keep your gawking to a minimum, please. Activities include five tennis courts, morning exercise classes, a pool, watersports, and glass-bottom boat rides. Tres chic—if you can afford it.

Royal Court Hotel   **$45–$85**   ★

Sewell Avenue, ☎ (809) 952-4531.
Single: $45–$100. Double: $55–$85.

Located on a hillside with nice views, this simple hotel is a half-mile from the beach (they'll shuttle you there). Rooms are nicely done, and some sport kitchenettes. Two restaurants, a pool and disco complete the scene. Decent for the rates.

Sandals Inn   **$290–$348**   ★★★

Kent Avenue, ☎ (800) 726-3257, (809) 952-4140, FAX (809) 952-6913.
Single: $290–$348. Double: $290–$348.

Open only to heterosexual couples, this small all-inclusive resort is hampered by its location across from, not on, the beach. Guest rooms are colonial-themed and large, but the sea is only visible from the more expensive units. There's lots to keep busy couples happy, including a pool, tennis, a gym and watersports. Guests can hop a free shuttle to the area's other two larger Sandals. This is the most inexpensive one of the trio.

Sandals Montego Bay   **$2375–$2835 per wk.**   ★★★★

Kent Avenue, ☎ (800) 726-3257, (809) 952-5510, FAX (809) 952-0816.
The largest of the area's three Sandals couples-only resorts, this one sits right on its own private beach. Guest rooms are quite nice, but avoid the few over the dining room if you can help it. The all-inclusive rates cover all meals, drinks, entertainment and facilities. Diversions include two pools, two tennis courts, a gym, all watersports, exercise classes, and several Jacuzzis. Dining options range from Jamaican to Asian to Continental. Decent, but the noise from the nearby airport can be a drag. $2375 to $2835 per couple per week.

Sandals Royal Caribbean   **$2465–$2920 per wk.**   ★★★★

Kent Avenue, ☎ (800) 726-3257, (809) 953-2231, FAX (809) 953-2788.
The most expensive of the three Sandals in the area, this couples-only (heterosexual please) resort operates on an all-inclusive plan. Many guest rooms open right onto the beach. All the bells and whistles associated with the chain are here, including four restaurants and four bars, three pools, three tennis courts, a good health club, all watersports, and lots of organized activities and entertainment. Those wanting to tan sans suits have their own private island. A bit more sophisticated than its siblings. $2465 to $2920 per couple per week.

Sea Garden Beach Hotel   **$297–$357**   ★★

Kent Avenue, ☎ *(800) 545-9001, (809) 952-4780, FAX (809) 952-7543.*
Single: $297–$357. Double: $297–$357.

Located across the street from the beach, this all-inclusive resort suffers from some airport noise. Guest rooms are dated and could use spiffing up. The rates include all meals, drinks and activities, including tennis, volleyball and watersports. There's nightly entertainment and a disco. Service is not the greatest, and Sandals remains a superior choice.

Seawind Beach Resort   **$75–$120**   ★★★

Montego Freeport, ☎ *(800) 526-2422, (809) 979-8070, FAX (809) 979-8660.*
Single: $75–$120. Double: $90–$120.

Situated on a private 100-acre peninsula, this complex includes two 10-story towers and two two-story wings. The towers house most of the guest rooms and are local landmarks with their colorful bands. There are also studios and one-bedroom apartments with kitchen facilities. Lots going on at this lively spot, including four tennis courts, two pools, watersports and horseback riding. Several restaurants and five bars, including a popular disco. The locale, near the busy port, is a bit removed from the action.

Tryall Resort   **$235–$465**   ★★★★

Sandy Bay, ☎ *(800) 742-0498, (809) 965-5660, FAX (809) 956-5673.*
Single: $235–$415. Double: $285–$465.

Set on 2200 acres of a former sugar plantation estate some 30 minutes out of Montego Bay, this deluxe resort has a true country club feel. Guest rooms are located in the 1834 Great House and are beautifully done; luxurious villas with maid and cook service are also available. The resort's centerpiece is the 18-hole PGA championship golf course, but there are also nine tennis courts, a pool, a private beach, and all watersports. Lovely and grand.

Wexford, The   **$85–$130**   ★★

Gloucester Avenue, ☎ *(800) 237-3421, (809) 952-3679.*
Single: $85–$120. Double: $95–$130.

This small hotel is across the street from Doctor's Cave Beach, and it's a bit of a walk to the sand. Accommodations are simple but adequate, and one-bedroom apartments with kitchenettes are available. The pool is small and uninspired. You can do better at comparable rates elsewhere.

Winged Victory   **$95–$230**   ★★

5 Queens Drive, ☎ *(809) 952-3892.*
Single: $95–$230. Double: $95–$230.

Situated on a hill overlooking the bay, five minutes from Doctor's Cave Beach, this is a peaceful, off-the-beaten-track spot. Guest rooms are comfortable and most face the ocean. There's a small pool and the restaurant is good.

Wyndham Rose Hall Resort   **$165–$705**   ★★★

Rose Hall, ☎ *(809) 953-2650, FAX (809) 953-3266.*
Single: $165–$705. Double: $165–$705.

Set on 400 acres fronting a beach, this stylish property has large guestrooms accented by nice artwork and quality furnishings. Guests can choose from 18 holes of golf, six tennis courts with a pro on hand, a fitness center, three interconnected swimming pools and all watersports. Lots in the way of dining options, too. Parents can stash the little ones in the supervised Kid's Klub, and there are also lots of organized activities for adults. Very nice, but lacks any Jamaican mood.

Apartments and Condominiums

Seacastles   **$75–$155**   ★★★

Rose Hall, ☎ *(800) 526-2422, (809) 953-3259, FAX (809) 953-3062.*
Single: $75–$155. Double: $75–$155.
Located on a 14-acre estate, this modern complex has one- to three-bedroom apartments, all with nice tropical furnishings and kitchenettes. Combining the convenience of apartment living with the amenities of a hotel, it offers turndown service and limited room service. There's a pool, two tennis courts, a playground for the kids, watersports, and a private, though small, beach. Nice, especially for families who don't mind the somewhat remote location.

Inns

Richmond Hill Inn   **$78–$112**   ★★

Union Street, ☎ *(809) 952-3859, FAX (809) 952-6106.*
Single: $78. Double: $112.
Set high on a hill with stunning views, the main building of this casual inn dates from the 1700s. Guest rooms are simple but comfortable, and a few suites with kitchenettes are available for those who prefer to cook in. A pool and games room offer daytime diversions; the piano bar and open-air restaurant help fill evening hours. Not the greatest, especially since lots of tour groups troop through to check out the view. The beach is a 10-minute drive.

Toby Inn   **$45–$80**   ★★

1 Kent Avenue, ☎ *(809) 952-4370, FAX (809) 952-6591.*
Single: $45–$55. Double: $70–$80.
Located in a few acres of tropical gardens one block from Doctor's Cave Beach, this relatively peaceful inn houses guests in simple but attractive rooms that lack telephones and TV. There are two pools, one with a waterfall, a restaurant, and two bars, one built to resemble a treehouse. Shopping, restaurants and nightlife are within an easy walk. Excellent value.

Low Cost Lodging

Belvedere Beach Hotel   **$50–$80**   ★

33 Gloucester Avenue, ☎ *(809) 952-0593, FAX (809) 979-0498.*
Single: $50–$75. Double: $55–$80.
This small hotel is across the street from Walter Fletcher Beach and within walking distance of city center. There's a pool, restaurant and bar, but not much else, and it gets noisy here. Not especially recommended.

Blue Harbour Hotel   **$35–$105**   ★★

Sewell Avenue, ☎ *(809) 952-5445, FAX (809) 952-8930.*
Single: $35–$105. Double: $47–$105.

Set on a hill on the site of an old Spanish fort, this small hotel has adequate accommodations for the rates. Besides the pool, there's not much here to keep visitors occupied.

Buccaneer Beach Hotel   **$83–$175**   ★

7 Kent Avenue, ☎ (809) 952-6489, FAX (809) 952-7658.
Single: $83–$175. Double: $83–$175.

Located near the airport and across the street from a public beach, this budget choice offers bland but functional rooms. Appealing mainly to college students hellbent on having a good time, it is best avoided by anyone over 25 during spring break. Typical hotel amenities include a restaurant, bar, nightclub and pool.

Where to Eat

Georgian House   **$$$**   ★

2 Orange Street, ☎ (809) 952-3353.
International cuisine. Specialties: Pan-Barbecued Shrimp, Coconut Pie.
Lunch: Noon–2:30 p.m., entrees $22–$32.
Dinner: 6–10:30 p.m., entrees $22–$32.

This restaurant's private van will pick you up from your hotel to dine in an 18th century townhouse and art gallery. Once there, you can eat outdoors on the patio if you prefer a more casual atmosphere—in any case feel free to dress resort-casual. Specialties are from the sea; usually shrimp or spiny lobster, barbecued, or sauteed with vegetables, or in a wine sauce. Steaks and filets are also marvelous, the coconut pie is deadly, and the wine list is well-chosen.

Julia's   **$$$**   ★

Bogue Hill, ☎ (809) 952-632.
International cuisine.
Dinner: 6–10:30 p.m., prix fixe $35.

It's highly advisable to take this mountaintop restaurant's offer of a private van to pick you up at your door. Negotiating the steep road that leads to this estate above MoBay (800 feet or thereabouts) can be hazardous. Once ensconced in your seat, relax and enjoy a four-course dinner served by an attentive staff, while the lights of the bay and the city glow below. The mostly-Italian entrees of veal (usually Parmesan), chicken, or fish will include a salad, pasta, dessert and choice of beverage.

Pier I   **$$$**   ★

Howard Cooke Boulevard, ☎ (809) 952-2452.
Seafood cuisine.
Lunch: 11 a.m.–4 p.m., entrees $16–$25.
Dinner: 4 p.m.–midnight, entrees $16–$25.

The cocktails and punches are fruity and potent, and the burgers are juicy; but even if kibble was served, the view from the waterfront bar would still be stellar. There's a tony dining room within where you can dine on well-prepared seafood and some hearty soups, chicken and steaks.

Pork Pit   **$**   ★★★

Gloucester Avenue, corner, ☎ (809) 952-1046.

Latin American cuisine.

Lunch: 11 a.m.–4:30 p.m., entrees $2–$9.

Dinner: 4:30–11:30 p.m., entrees $2–$9.

Eat fiery jerk pork, chicken or spare ribs picnic-style on benches or tables open to the sea breeze. Common accompaniments include local cornbread (called festival) and Red Stripe beer. Location is close to Cornwall Beach and the airport.

Reading Reef Club $$$ ★★★★★

Bogue Lagoon, ☎ *(809) 952-5909.*

Italian cuisine.

Lunch: Noon–3 p.m., entrees $10–$24.

Dinner: 7–10 p.m., entrees $10–$24.

Located in a discreet, small (21-room) hotel situated halfway between Montego Bay and the Round Hill Resort, this Caribbean-influenced Italian restaurant reflects the tastes of the hotel's owner, JoAnne Rowe, a New York-born expatriate. These include a strange combination of pasta served with ginger that works quite well, judging by its popularity. Crayfish, seafood and steaks are other standards paired with local produce.

Sugar Mill $$$ ★★★★

Rose Hall, ☎ *(809) 953-2228.*

International cuisine. Specialties: Bouillabaise, Smoked Marlin.

Lunch: Noon–2:30 p.m., entrees $14–$31.

Dinner: 7–10 p.m., entrees $14–$31.

Swiss chef Hans Schenck creates Jamaican-Continental specialties at this restaurant in a historical house with a terrace that overlooks the ocean and the golf course of the Half Moon Club. Marlin, a specialty catch of the area, is often smoked and served with pasta; bouillabaisse is spiced with local pepper and citrus sauces. Even if you're just passing through, come for a look at the remains of the old sugar plantation that have been incorporated into the grounds of this sleek resort.

Town House $$$ ★★

16 Church Street, ☎ *(809) 952-2660.*

Latin American cuisine. Specialties: Red Snapper Baked in Parchment.

Lunch: 11:30 a.m.–2:30 p.m., entrees $13–$30.

Dinner: 6–10 p.m., entrees $13–$30.

This grand, 300-year-old Georgian building is a fun place to eat, especially in an art-filled, brick-walled cellar room, which is a novel change from the favored practice of dining alfresco. But that can also be achieved here on an outdoor terrace. Specialties include a signature fresh red snapper baked in parchment with a cheese and seafood sauce.

Negril

Negril became known to the world at large in the early '70s when it was a mecca for hippies, escapists, artists and visionaries who spent most of the day bonged out on the local weed. Located on the extreme northwestern point of the island, it has grown from a sleepy bohemian town to one of Jamaica's finest resort areas—some of the best allinclusives are situated right on the beach here. There are also campsites at the **Negril Lighthouse Park** and at **Roots Bamboo** (both off West End). The seven-mile stretch of pure-white, powder-fine beach dotted with sea grape and coconut palms has inspired many a fantasy, and numerous fashion shoots have been conducted here. For some unexplained reason, the sunsets here are extraordinarily spectacular, bursts of neon color across the horizon. Although there's little sight-seeing available, most visitors are just happy to relax and soak in the atmosphere. For the active, there are numerous watersports, superb scuba diving (see below), and fine snorkeling.

If you get to Negril, you must make an extra excursion to **Booby Cay**, a small island across from Rutland Point that attracts an inordinate number of nude bathers. Also spectacular is the sunset cruise on the *Sunsplash*, a 155-foot catamaran that can be booked through Sandals Negril. After you pass through town and head west to Negril Point, the resorts tend to get smaller and more quaint. Here the beach gives way to high limestone cliffs. At **Xtabi**, the sea caves cut into the cliffs to create a romantic setting that is ideal for sunset viewing. Everyone heads for **Rick's Cafe** —a terrific place to watch divers jump off from the cliff below and a perfect place to celebrate the glorious sunset, but if you don't like crowds, you won't love Rick's. If you're a night prowler, you'll find some of the biggest reggae stars in Jamaica performing throughout Negril until the wee hours. Recently, Negril, through the efforts of the Coral Reef Preservation Society, has instituted a very active mooring and education program. At present, 35 separate moorings virtually eliminate the need for anchoring.

Beaches in Negril

Negril Beach is seven long miles of heaven—everyone's idea of Eden. Unfortunately, much of it is fenced off today, especially the nude area. Fortunately, some resorts have had the foresight to build their properties overlooking the nude areas. The famous (infamous) singles-only club **Hedonism II** is located on this beach. If you saw the movie *Exit to Eden* and fantasized about being at a resort like *that*, you will probably love Hedonism II.

Divers enjoy the beautiful cliffs and caves at the west end of Negril.

Where to Stay

Chuckles $75–$260   ★★

Negril Square, ☎ *(809) 957-4277.*
Single: $75–$260. Double: $90–$260.
Located on a hill above the commercial center, this Mediterranean-style resort is
peaceful and quiet. Guest rooms are nicely done and very clean; two-bedroom villas
have kitchens. On-site facilities include two tennis courts, a large pool, volleyball
and a disco. The public beach is down the hill.

Drumville Cove Resort $40–$100   ★★

West End, ☎ *(800) 423-4095, (809) 957-4369, FAX (809) 929-7291.*
Single: $40–$100. Double: $45–$100.
Set on the side of a cliff overlooking the sea, this complex is 2.5 miles from town.
Accommodations are in cottages, some with kitchenettes. There's nightly entertain-
ment, a weekly barbecue, restaurant and bar.

Foote Prints on the Sands $55–$105   ★★★

Norman Manley Blvd., ☎ *(809) 957-4300, FAX (809) 957-4301.*
Single: $55–$105. Double: $55–$105.
This family-run hotel sits right on Seven Mile Beach. Guest rooms are nice and
comfortable, and a few have whirlpool tubs. Four kitchenette suites are also available. There's no TV in the rooms, though you can watch the tube in the lounge. No
pool.

Grand Lido $350–$290   ★★★★★

Norman Manley Blvd., ☎ *(800) 423-4095, (809) 957-4010, FAX (809) 957-4317.*
Single: $350–$390. Double: $250–$290.

Very glamorous and elegant, this all-inclusive resort is open only to adults, though
it's a lot less of a meat market than its neighbor, Hedonism II. Set on 22 acres, the
Mediterranean-style property wows guests with a dramatic entrance, personalized
check-in, and the M.Y. Zein, a yacht given by Ari Onassis as a wedding gift to Princess Grace and Prince Rainier. Accommodations are in wings that run parallel to the
beach, all with sea views. They are beautifully done with tasteful decor, large baths,
sitting areas, and such niceties as stereos. Four restaurants, six bars, two pools, four
tennis courts, a full health club, cruises aboard the yacht, a beauty salon, and on and
on and on. The large beach is divided in two for those who wear suits and those who
don't. Service, of course, is superb. This place, part of the SuperClubs group, is
really special for those who like to splurge and be in the company of equally monied
people.

Hedonism II $205–$376   ★★★

Norman Manley Blvd., ☎ *(800) 423-4095, (809) 957-4200, FAX (809) 957-4289.*
Single: $205–$260. Double: $305–$376.
This all-inclusive resort, open only to those over 18, is aptly named, as it is dedicated
to the pursuit of pleasure—and partying. Lots of singles are mixed in with the couples, and depending on the clientele, this can be a bit of a meat market. Set on 22

acres at the northern end of Seven Mile Beach, it houses guests in comfortable though uninspired rooms; the whole point is to be out frolicking, anyway. The rates include all meals, drinks (drinking is a big pastime), and activities, and tips are forbidden. Two restaurants, five bars, a pool and two Jacuzzis, six tennis courts, all watersports, a gym, and nightly entertainment in the disco. The beach is divided for "prudes" and "nudes." Not for the conservative by any stretch, but lively and fun for young partyers.

Negril Beach Club Hotel $77–$185   ★★

Negril Main Road, ☎ (800) 526-2422, (809) 957-4220, FAX (809) 957-4364.
Single: $77–$185. Double: $65–$185.
Very, very casual and informal, this complex includes traditional rooms, studios, and one-bedroom suites with kitchens. There's a small pool, health club and two tennis courts, but most activity centers around the beach, where watersports await and most bathers are topless.

Negril Cabins $40–$55   ★★

Bloody Bay, ☎ (809) 957-4350, FAX (809) 957-4381.
Single: $40–$55. Double: $40–$55.
Set in a forest across from Bloody Bay beach, this complex of log cabins offers true bargain rates and rustic accommodations. Each unit has a balcony and simple furnishings, but only some are air-conditioned. There's a restaurant and occasional live entertainment, but not much else in the way of amenities. A nice alternative to the cookie-cutter beach hotels.

Negril Inn $115–$145   ★★

Negril Beach, ☎ (800) 634-7456, (809) 957-4209, FAX (809) 957-4074.
Single: $115–$145. Double: $115–$145.
A nice alternative to the larger and livelier all-inclusives, this small resort offers everything for one price in a more peaceful setting. Guest-rooms are simple but pleasant. Most meals are served buffet style, and there are two bars and nightly entertainment for dessert. Recreational facilities include two tennis courts, bicycles, horseshoes, a pool and gym. No kids under 16.

Negril Tree House $85–$275   ★★★★

Norman Manley Blvd., ☎ (800) 423-4095, (809) 957-4288, FAX (809) 957-4366.
Single: $85–$275. Double: $85–$275.
Set right on Seven Mile Beach, this unusual spot accommodates guests in two-story octagonal "tree house" cottages and oceanfront villas. They are generally nicely done with rattan furniture, but some could use repairs. Ask for a room on the second floor; they have better views and more atmosphere. Twelve suites offer one or two bedrooms, full kitchens and wide verandas. There's a pool, watersports, a handful of bars and restaurants where locals hang out, a Monday night beach party and twice-weekly island picnics. Very nice, if you don't mind rustic. The elevated bar and restaurant, perched in a mango tree, attract lots of locals.

Paradise View $75–$135   ★★

Norman Manley Blvd., ☎ (809) 957-4375, FAX (809) 957-4074.
Single: $75–$95. Double: $100–$135.

Modest in most ways, this hotel's real asset is its location on a gorgeous beach. Guest rooms are comfortable but on the small side. Watersports on the beach, but no pool.

Poinciana Beach Hotel   **$249–$294**   ★ ★ ★

Norman Manley Blvd., ☎ *(800) 468-6728, (809) 957-4100.*
Single: $249–$499. Double: $165–$294.

Set on six tropical acres fronting Seven Mile Beach, this resort went all-inclusive in late 1994, making it Negril's only one-price property. Guests are housed in a varied mix of standard rooms, studios, and one- and two-bedroom apartments in villas. All are nicely done, with Murphy beds in the studios and kitchens, as well as cooks in the apartments. All kinds of watersports await, including PADI certification for divers. There's also two tennis courts, miniature golf, a weight room, rental bikes, two pools and a disco. Good for the active set.

Sandals Negril   **$2890–$3995 per wk.**   ★ ★ ★ ★

Rutland Point, ☎ *(800) 726-3257, (809) 957-4216, FAX (809) 957-4336.*

Another of the chain's couples-only resorts, this operation is set on a narrow beach, with a boat shuttling guests to a small island where they can tan in the buff. Rooms are comfortable, but only the more expensive units have balconies and sea views. All kinds of activities (plus meals and drinks) are covered in the rate, including three tennis courts, watersports, a gym, two pools, and the usual resort diversions. A few bars and a disco provide nighttime fun. Appeals mainly to the young and in love, and a bit more subdued than Hedonism II. Rates are $2890 to $3995 per couple per week. Partying couples may be happier at Hedonism II, which is cheaper.

Swept Away Resort   **$2770–$3785 per wk.**   ★ ★ ★ ★

Long Bay, ☎ *(800) 545-7937, (809) 957-4040.*

Yet another all-inclusive resort open only to couples, this special spot puts an emphasis on sports and fitness. Accommodations are in two-story villas near the beach and are beautifully decorated with large verandas. The centerpiece is the fitness center, an excellent facility with a gym, lap pool, ten tennis courts, and squash and racquetball. There's also all the usual watersports and a lagoon-style pool. You're welcome to booze, but the emphasis is on juice and veggie bars. Dedicated partyers look elsewhere! $2770 to $3785 per couple per week.

T-Water Beach Hotel   **$125–$155**   ★ ★

Norman Manley Blvd., ☎ *(800) 654-1592, (809) 957-4270.*
Single: $125–$155. Double: $125–$155.

Set on Seven Mile Beach, this resort accommodates guests in a varied mix of traditional rooms, studios with kitchens and suites. Popular with families (kids under 12 stay free), it offers a pool, watersports, and constant volleyball games. Not too exciting, but the rates are relatively reasonable.

Apartments and Condominiums

Beachcomber Club   **$105–$185**   ★ ★ ★

Norman Manley Blvd., ☎ *(800) 423-4095, (809) 957-4171, FAX (809) 957-4097.*
Single: $105–$135. Double: $155–$185.

Set right on Seven Mile Beach, this Georgian-style condominium complex has one-and two-bedroom units with attractive furnishings, large verandas and full kitchens. Some also sport four-poster beds. Hotel-like touches include room service and nightly turndowns. Two restaurants, tennis, watersports, a pool and supervised programs for children year-round.

Crystal Waters Villas **$85–$110** ★ ★

Negril, ☎ *(809) 957-4284, FAX (809) 957-4889.*
Single: $85–$110. Double: $85–$110.
Located right on the beach, this complex offers villas with full kitchens, porches, one to three bedrooms, and the services of a personal maid and cook. No restaurant on-site, but many are nearby. Reasonable rates.

Point Village **$100–$155** ★ ★ ★

Rutland Point, ☎ *(809) 957-4351.*
Single: $100–$145. Double: $115–$155.
Set on Rutland Point on the northern coastline among lush foliage, this village-style resort has tropically decorated studios and suites with kitchens and one to three bedrooms. A house band entertains six nights a week, and there are also theme parties and a few bars for nighttime recreation. By day, there's a pool, private beach with watersports, and tennis. Parents can stash the kids in supervised programs.

Xtabi Club Resort **$50–$145** ★ ★ ★

West End, ☎ *(809) 957-4336, FAX (809) 957-0121.*
Single: $50–$145. Double: $50–$145.
Perfect for nature lovers and just plain lovers, this resort houses guests in octagonal cottages set on rugged cliffs or across the road in a garden setting. All are simply furnished and have small kitchens and enclosed outdoor showers, but no air conditioning. The grounds are lovely and natural, with dense foliage, sea caves and nice views—the sunsets are especially dramatic. Spiral stairs lead down though a cave to a tiny beach, where great snorkeling awaits; there's also is a pool for cooling off. Lots of nude sunbathers here.

Inns

Charela Inn **$55–$165** ★ ★ ★

Norman Manley Blvd., ☎ *(800) 423-4095, (809) 957-4648, FAX (809) 957-4414.*
Single: $55–$165. Double: $55–$165.
This small Spanish hacienda-style inn has lush inner gardens and is set right on Seven Mile Beach. Guest rooms have plenty of character with four-poster beds and balconies. Request one on the upper floor for the best views. There's a pool and free watersports, and a decent restaurant. Peaceful and friendly.

Low Cost Lodging

Hotel Samsara **$40–$115** ★ ★

Light House Road, ☎ *(809) 957-4395, FAX (809) 957-4073.*
Single: $40–$115. Double: $40–$115.
Perched on low cliffs overlooking the sea, this small hotel has no beach, but a waterslide will dunk you right into the ocean, if you so desire. Accommodations are in cottages and quite spacious, but decorated with a minimal of fuss. Only some are

air-conditioned. Relaxed and informal, the place hops during the Monday night reggae concerts. There's also a pool and tennis court.

Negril Gardens $105–$140   ★★

Norman Manley Blvd., ☎ *(800) 423-4095, (809) 957-4408, FAX (809) 957-4374.*
Single: $105–$140. Double: $105–$140.

Located on Seven Mile Beach, this two-story hotel puts up guests on the beach or across the road near the pool. There's entertainment four nights a week, and by day, a pool, tennis and watersports on the public beach. Informal and friendly.

Rock Cliff Resort $55–$100   ★★★

Light House Road, ☎ *(809) 957-4331.*
Single: $55–$100. Double: $55–$100.

This complex of two-story colonial-style buildings appeals mainly to divers with its excellent PADI center. There's no beach, but a free shuttle will take you to one. Guest rooms are modestly decorated but of good size. There's a pool, volleyball, basketball, and two restaurants. Unless you're into diving, you'll probably be happier at a beach property.

Where to Eat

Cafe au Lait $$$ ★★

Lighthouse Road, ☎ *(809) 957-4471.*
French cuisine.
Lunch: Noon–3 p.m., entrees $9–$29.
Dinner: 5–10 p.m., entrees $9–$29.

Located in a cottage resort on the West End, this authentic bistro (for Jamaica) features island-influenced, light French meals, including pizza and crepes (some made with callaloo), French bread, local seafood and French wines.

Chicken Lavish $ ★★

West End Road, ☎ *(809) 957-4410.*
Latin American cuisine.
Lunch: 9 a.m.–4 p.m., entrees $3–$5.
Dinner: 4–10 p.m., entrees $3–$5.

Super informal, super cheap, and super delicious—with a juicy name like that what else can you expect? Once a local hangout jealously guarded by those in the know, the word is out about this unpretentious little spot on the beach renowned for toothsome fried chicken and curried goat.

Cosmo's $ ★★

Norman Manley Boulevard, ☎ *(809) 957-4330.*
Seafood cuisine. Specialties: Curried Conch.
Lunch: 11 a.m.–4 p.m., entrees $5–$12.
Dinner: 4–10 p.m., entrees $5–$12.

Seafood is pretty much IT here, but what seafood! Owner-character Cosmo Brown specializes in conch, either stewed, curried or in a generous vat of soup. Since this chewy gastropod appears more often in other Caribbean islands, this is a good spot to try it. Otherwise, a grilled or baked escovitch (well-marinated in spices) whole fish is a popular choice. Cosmo's is situated in an informal, thatched-roof hut on a sparsely-populated East End beach.

Hungry Lion   **$$$**   ★★

West End Road.
Latin American cuisine.
Lunch: entrees $18–$30.
Dinner: entrees $18–$30.

The setting at this small and popular restaurant is as verdant and colorful as the Rastafarian Ital cuisine served here. Ital, which is based on local vegetarian ingredients, often features foods that display the Rasta colors of green, red and gold. At the Hungry Lion, if you dine outside by a fountain, you'll be surrounded by a greenhouse of flowering plants. Inside, the dining room is a living canvas of sophisticated tie-dye hues. A plate consisting of a marinated whole fish will be dressed with a hibiscus flower. It's that kind of place.

Paradise Yard   **$$**   ★★

Gas Station Road, ☎ *(809) 957-4006.*
Latin American cuisine. Specialties: Rasta Pasta.
Lunch: 8 a.m.–4 p.m., entrees $6–$15.
Dinner: 4–10 p.m., entrees $6–$15.

Life is fine at this relaxing open-air restaurant with a tin roof situated on the road to the port city of Savannah-del-Mar. You can get here early for a full-on Jamaican breakfast of saltfish and ackee, juicy local fruits and bammies (cassava bread). At lunch and dinner, ackee appears again in the Rasta Pasta—the golden vegetable (which tastes like scrambled eggs) is teamed with a thick tomato sauce and green peppers over fettuccine. There's also curried goat, pumpkin soup and enchiladas. This is a very authentic experience.

Rick's Cafe   **$$$**

West End Road, ☎ *(809) 957-4335.*
Seafood cuisine. Specialties: Grilled Lobster, Fresh-Fruit Daiquiris.
Lunch: Noon–4 p.m., entrees $11–$28.
Dinner: 4–10 p.m., entrees $11–$28.

This famous (circa 1974) bar-restaurant-hangout is a scene and a place to be seen. One of the many draws here is a concept imitated from the La Quebrada divers in Acapulco—locals and visitors plunge some 25 feet into the sea from the cliffs at Rick's before emerging (it's hoped) for a papaya daiquiri. A tamer ritual takes place just before sunset when crowds of tanned and buffed young people pack the rock-encrusted, palm-fronded terrace for fun and frolic and a last glimpse of old sol. You can also come here for lunch or brunch, but for that you can go anywhere.

Tan-ya's   **$$$**

Norman Manley Boulevard, ☎ *(809) 957-4041.*
Latin American cuisine.
Lunch: 11 a.m.–3 p.m., entrees $5–$8.
Dinner: 6:30–10 p.m., entrees $8–$25.

This restaurant at the quietly elegant Seasplash Resort is where guests and others go to dress up (just a little) for French-inspired seafood and a creative way with lobster.

North Coast

About 30 miles east from Montego Bay, **Falmouth** gives you the feeling of being a fairly quiet area while still maintaining proximity to the cities of Mo' Bay or Ocho Rios. This small 18th-century port town takes about a half-hour to explore on foot. There are a number of historical buildings that are interesting to see, such as the courthouse, a reconstruction of the 19th-century building, the customs office, the William Knubb Memorial Church, at George and King Street, and the 1796 parish church. Nearby is the **Good Hope** great house (leaving town, turn south), the 18th-century estate of John Thorpe, one of the richest Jamaican planters. The restoration of the main house and several outbuildings is exquisite, and it now stands as a fine hotel. Save time for a magnificent horseback ride through the countryside, over the estate's 6000 acres. (Make reservations in advance; ☎ *(809) 954-3289*). Near here, you will find the turnoff to **Rafter's Village**, where you can take a bamboo raft down the Martha Brae River (for information about river rafting and other river treks, see the section "On Foot" above). Two miles east of Falmouth is the **Caribatik factory**, which is the artwork of a fine Jamaican artist, Muriel Chandler. At **Glistening Waters Marina**, east of Caribatik, you'll discover Oyster Bay, which glows with bioluminescence caused by microorganisms in the water.

Where to Stay

Hotels and Resorts

Ambiance Jamaica $70–$215   ★★
Runaway Bay, ☎ *(800) 523-6504, (809) 973-4606, FAX (809) 973-2067.*
Single: $70–$215. Double: $70–$215.
Set on a small private beach, this casual hotel offers adequate accommodations and services. There's a pool, gym and two restaurants, but not much else to write home about. In 1995, the hotel began offering reasonably priced all-inclusive packages.

Caribbean Isle Hotel $55–$65   ★
Runaway Bay, ☎ *(809) 973-2364.*
Single: $55–$60. Double: $60–$65.
This small, casual hotel offers budget accommodations and not much else, though there is a pool. The beach comes and goes, depending on the tides.

Club Caribbean $125–$295   ★★
Runaway Bay, ☎ *(800) 647-2740, (809) 973-4702.*
Single: $125–$395. Double: $215–$295.
This resort offers all-inclusive resort amenities with self-serve accommodations. Guests are put up in octagonal cottages with ceiling fans (no air conditioning) and kitchenettes. There's lots happening in the activities department, with organized crab races, volleyball games and the like. Watersports, two tennis courts, a swim-up bar in the pool, and a disco. Just about everything but lunch is included in the rates.

Eaton Hall Beach Hotel **$135–$299** ★★★
Runaway Bay, ☎ *(809) 973-3503, FAX (809) 973-2432.*
Single: $135–$299. Double: $185–$299.
This former 18th-century Georgian-style slave station is an all-inclusive resort that caters to a predominantly young crowd. Guests stay in standard rooms, suites, or villas with kitchenettes; all comfortable, but showing their age. No beach to speak of, but there are two pools, as well as tennis, watersports, glass-bottom boat rides, and organized activities.

H.E.A.R.T. Country Club **$55–$75** ★★★
Runaway Bay, ☎ *(809) 973-2671.*
Single: $55. Double: $75.
This plantation-style country club is staffed by people learning the hotel business (it stands for Human Employment and Resource Training), so you can count on enthusiastic service. Set on a hillside with nice views, guest rooms are nice and bright. There's a decent restaurant and pool, golf next door, and they'll shuttle you to a small private beach. Really good for the rates.

Jamaica Jamaica **$167–$240** ★★★★
Runaway Bay, ☎ *(800) 423-4095, (809) 973-2436, FAX (809) 973-2352.*
Single: $167–$240. Double: $167–$240.
Encompassing 214 acres opening onto a wide, sandy beach, this all-inclusive resort does just about everything right. Not only do the rates include all meals, drinks and activities, they even throw in free cigarettes! Accommodations are bare-bones, but everyone's too busy with organized activities to notice. There's an excellent golf course, four tennis courts, classes in Jamaican handicrafts, all watersports, horseback riding, and a full health club with aerobics classes. The disco hops and the snorkeling offshore is great. No kids under 16 at this generally singles resort.

Apartments and Condominiums

Franklyn D. Resort **$3205–$7205 per wk.** ★★★★
Runaway Bay, ☎ *(800) 423-4095, (809) 973-4591, FAX (809) 973-3071.*
This Georgian-style resort is especially suited to families. Accommodations are in suites with one to three bedrooms, kitchens, and a "Girl Friday" to cook clean and look after the kids by day (there's an extra charge for nighttime babysitting). There's only one television set per unit, and air conditioners only in the bedrooms. Kids under 16 stay free, so you'll see a lot of them here; romantic couples will be happier elsewhere. The beach is small but quite nice, but there are two pools (one for kids), tennis, exercise room, and tons of organized activities for both kids and their parents. Rates are $3205 to $7205 weekly per couple.

Portside Villas & Condos **$85–$280** ★★
Highway A-1, ☎ *(809) 973-2007.*
Single: $85–$280. Double: $85–$280.
Located 20 minutes outside of Ocho Rios at Discovery Bay, this complex has studios and suites of one to three bedrooms, all with kitchens and cooks for an extra fee. The beach is small, and there are also two pools and nonmotorized watersports. You're on your own for meals.

Ocho Rios

Over the past 15 years, Ocho Rios has become one of the busiest, if most elite, tourism sites in Jamaica. Cruise ships dock nearly daily and a number of fine resorts are located here. Five outstanding beaches, excellent restaurants, abundant nightlife and lots of sports make the area ideal for those who want to escape the Third-World chaos of Kingston and Montego Bay. The town has fiercely hung onto its charm despite the massive development. The most exciting natural phenomenon near here is **Dunn's River Falls**, the internationally renowned stair-stepped falls that rush under the road and reappear to join the sea on the white beach to the left. Even if you don't throw yourself to the wetness in a fun tour of the falls, you must come to see its dramatic descent over the mountainside. Other natural attractions are plenty, from the Shaw Park Botanical Garden, where you can wile away a few hours studying the exotic tropical plants of the island.

If you're still feeling athletic, a terrific horseback riding jaunt can be arranged at the **Prospect Plantation**, which will take you through trails of citrus groves and coffee trees, and down by the banks of the White River. Jitney tours of the estate are free of charge. Rafting tours on the nearby White River are also available (see the section under "Treks.") Out on Annotto Bay, you'll find the 250-acre **Crystal Springs**, a natural garden replete with hundreds of birds, a myriad of tropical orchids, fierce waterfalls, rivers and restaurant.

Beaches in Ocho Rios

Ocho Rios beach is giving Mo Bay a run for its money these days in terms of traffic. Mallard's attracts the most crowds, somewhat due to the presence of the Jamaica Grande hotel, which caters to the convention crowd. (Don't write us if you find yourself on the beach sitting next to someone with elk ears.) Turtle Beach is the adjacent strand, which has a very good reputation for swimming.

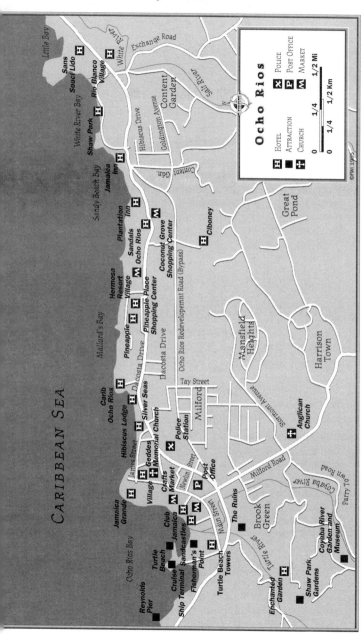

CARIBBEAN SEA

Ocho Rios

- 🏨 HOTEL
- ■ ATTRACTION
- ✝ CHURCH
- ✗ POLICE
- 🄿 POST OFFICE
- 🅼 MARKET

0   1/4   1/2 Mi
0   1/4   1/2 Km

©FWI 1995

Little Bay
Sans Souci/Lido
White
Exchange Road
Rio Blanco Village
White River Bay
Shaw Park
White River
Content Garden
Hibiscus Drive
Goldington Avenue
Salt River
Jamaica Inn
Sandy Beach Bay
Content Gdn
Plantation Inn
Hermosa Resort
Sandals Ocho Rios
Coconut Grove Shopping Center
Ciboney
Pineapple Place Shopping Center
Pineapple Village
Dacosta Drive
Ocho Rios Redevelopemnt Road (Bypass)
Mansfield Heights
Great Pond
Harrison Town
Mallard's Bay
Carib Ocho Rios
Silver Seas
Memorial Church
Tay Street
Milford
Stormont Avenue
Anglican Church
Hibiscus Lodge
James Street
Geddes
Police Station
Clafts
Market
Village
Jamaica Grande
Newlin Street
Post Office
Milford Road
Parry Town Road
Coyaba River
Ocho Rios Bay
Club Jamaica
Cruise Terminal
Sandcastles
Fisherman's Point
Main Street
The Ruins
Brook Green
Turtle River
Coyaba River Garden and Museum
Reynolds Pier
Turtle Beach
Ship Terminal
Turtle Beach Towers
Shaw Park Gardens
Enchanted Garden

What Else to See

Historical Sites

Firefly   ★ ★ ★

Grants Pen, St. Mary.

Hours open: 9 a.m.–5 p.m.

This is the home of Sir Noel Coward, who spent the last 25 years of his life in Jamaica. Donated to the Jamaican government upon his death in 1973, the mansion remains unchanged since the actor and author lived there. Guided tours take you through the house to gawk at his bedroom, closets filled with clothes, antique furnishings and paintings by the man himself. His grave is also on the site, as well as a cafe and gift shop. Continue your literary tour at **Goldeneye** ☎ *(809-974-5833)* located on the outskirts of Oracabessa, 20 miles east of Ocho Rios. This 15-acre beachfront estate was the winter home of Ian Fleming, creator of the James Bond books. He penned 14 of the popular novels here, five set in Jamaica. The house is much more modest than Firefly, but the grounds are gorgeous.

Museums and Exhibits

Harmony Hall   ★ ★ ★

Highway A3, Tower Isle, ☎ (809) 460-4120.

Hours open: 10 a.m.–6 p.m.

This late 19th-century great house is now a gallery displaying high-quality paintings and arts and crafts by Jamaican artists.

Parks and Gardens

Coyaba River Garden and Museum   ★ ★

Shaw Park, Ocho Rios, ☎ (809) 974-6235.

This former plantation is now a private estate with lovely gardens, waterfalls, a river and fish ponds. The small museum displays relics from pre-Columbian days. *Coyaba* is the Arawak word for paradise and this spot is certainly a small slice of it.

Tours

Dunn's River Falls   ★ ★ ★

Highway A3, Ocho Rios, ☎ (809) 974-2857.

Hours open: 9 a.m.–5 p.m.

These much-photographed falls cascade down some 600 feet into the sea. The best way to experience them is to hire a guide and make a human chain that climbs right up the slippery rocks. Wear sneakers, and don't forget to tip your guide. You can stop along the way to dip in pools and be massaged by the tumbling water. There's a path on dry land for the less daring.

Prospect Plantation   ★ ★ ★
Highway A3, St. Ann, ☎ *(809) 974-2058.*
Located just east of Ocho Rios, this working plantation can be toured via jitney.
Among the highlights are sweeping views, gorgeous scenery, and lots of trees
planted by famous folks, including Noel Coward and Charlie Chaplin.

Where to Stay

Hotels and Resorts

Boscobel Beach Hotel   **$415–$995**   ★ ★ ★ ★
Ocho Rios, ☎ *(800) 423-4095, (809) 975-3330.*
Double: $415–$995.
Set on the beach, this all-inclusive resort, part of the SuperClubs group, caters to
families. Accommodations range from spacious guestrooms to suites, all nicely done
and some with sunken tubs. The grounds include a large playground, two theaters
showing films, a disco and two pools, one in the adults-only section. Four tennis
courts, watersports and a health club round out the action. Kids are kept busy with
supervised programs, and for additional fee, will be minded by their own private
nanny. Great for families (and superior to the Franklyn D. Resort for those with
more than one kid), but those without kids should look elsewhere.

Braco Village Resort   **$235–$260**   ★ ★ ★
Rio Bueno, ☎ *(800) 654-1337, (809) 973-4882, FAX (809) 954-0020.*
Single: $235–$335. Double: $160–$260.
Just opened in spring 1995, this new all-inclusive village is located 38 miles east of
Montego Bay and 30 miles west of Ocho Rios. The village reflects Jamaica's various
architectural styles, from Georgian to gingerbread. The centerpiece is the Town
Square, with several restaurants, bars, and artists in residence creating and exhibiting their work. The idea is to make the village as authentically Jamaican as possible,
while still spoiling guests with the amenities of a resort. Recreational facilities
include an Olympic-size pool, a nine-hole golf course, four tennis courts, a soccer
field, 85 acres of jogging and hiking trails, a fitness center, and all watersports,
including scuba and kayaking. Each guestroom will have a unique feature such as a
gazebo, balcony, or love seat. The 2000-foot beach has a clothing-optional section.

Ciboney Ocho Rios   **$175–$690**   ★ ★ ★ ★
Main Street, ☎ *(800) 777-7800, (809) 974-1036, FAX (809) 974-7148.*
Single: $175–$345. Double: $350–$690.
Set just outside of town on 45 hillside acres, this all-inclusive resort is impressive and
stylish. Most accommodations are in villas with full kitchens, semiprivate pools, and
personal attendants. You can work out and be pampered in the European-style spa,
play golf on six courts, swim in two pools, and partake in all watersports. Very nice.

Club Jamaica Beach Resort   **$180–$235**   ★ ★
Main Street, ☎ *(800) 423-4095, (809) 974-6642, FAX (809) 974-6644.*
Single: $180–$235. Double: $115–$235.

Located on Turtle Beach near the crafts market, the all-inclusive property has comfortable guestrooms. As with other all-inclusives, there's lots to do, including themed buffets at poolside, nightly entertainment, a disco, and organized activities. No kids under 12.

Couples Jamaica $365–$520

Autoroute 3, ☎ (800) 423-4095, (809) 975-4271, FAX (809) 975-4439.
Double: $365–$520.

Like the name applies, this all-inclusive resort is open to couples only—their logo is two lions copulating, in case you don't get the message. Guestrooms are modern and comfortable, with king beds, cable TV and CD players (pack your own discs)—though sometimes run out of hot water. The beach is small but great and there's always something happening, from nightly entertainment to five tennis courts with pros and free lessons to all watersports (there's even a windsurfing school). Guests can dine at any of the three restaurants, which all have live entertainment at mealtime. There's also ferry service to the small nude island just off the coast and sunset sails, scuba lessons, and optional day trips.

If you get carried away by romance, they'll marry you for free. You'll be making like lions in no time.

Enchanted Garden $95–$555

Main Road, ☎ (800) 323-5655, (809) 974-1400.
Single: $95–$555. Double: $95–$555.

It really is rather enchanting at this all-inclusive resort set in the foothills and surrounded by jungle greenery. The many gardens and waterfalls lend a truly exotic feel. Accommodations range from standard rooms to villas with kitchens and one to three bedrooms, all nicely done. You can swim in the pool or natural ponds with waterfalls. Dining is quite varied, with lots of ethnic choices. Two tennis courts, a fully equipped health spa, and an aviary. They'll take you to the beach or into town for free.

Jamaica Grande $135–$195

Ocho Rios, ☎ (800) 228-9898, (809) 974-2201, FAX (809) 974-2289.
Single: $135–$195. Double: $135–$195.

Ocho Rios' largest hotel is a modern high-rise known for its fantasy pool, a large and fanciful body of water with grottos, waterfalls, a swinging bridge, and a swim-up bar. Accommodations are found in two towers and are generally nicely done. Facilities include a fitness center, four tennis courts, all watersports, activities for children, and a large and happening disco. Nightly entertainment and lots of theme parties. Nice, but the sheer size can be a bit overwhelming, and there's not much in the way of authentic Jamaican style.

Jamaica Inn $225–$250

Ocho Rios, ☎ (809) 974-2516, FAX (809) 974-2449.
Single: $225–$250. Double: $225–$250.

Located in a tropical setting on a private beach, this intimate resort requires guests to dress up in the evening. Most accommodations are in junior or full suites beautifully decorated with antiques, local artwork and large lanais. There's a pool and watersports, and guests can play tennis for free at a nearby resort. No kids under 14 at this very affluent and rather conservative property. If you're looking for riotous action, look elsewhere.

Plantation Inn $300–$999   ★ ★ ★ ★ ★

Ocho Rios, ☎ *(800) 423-4095, (809) 974-5601, FAX (809) 974-5912.*
Double: $300–$999.
Located on a lush hillside, this colonial-style hotel has a country club atmosphere that draws a predominantly conservative (and rich) crowd. Rooms are quite nicely done with pampering amenities. The grounds include two beaches (reached via a steep walk down the hill), two tennis courts, a small pool, watersports, a gym and massage services. Not as nice as its neighbor, the Jamaica Inn, but a bit more casual, though you're still required to dress up at night.

Sandals Dunn's River $2295–$4200 per wk.   ★ ★ ★ ★

Main Street, ☎ *(800) 726-3257, (809) 972-1610, FAX (809) 972-1611.*
Set on 10 tropical acres fronting a beach, this couples-only resort is among the chain's best. Guest rooms come in a variety of configurations and are generally pleasant and comfortable. There's lots happening at all hours: 18 holes of golf (included in the rates), four restaurants and seven bars, frequent live entertainment, a huge pool and another smaller one, four tennis courts, a gym, all watersports, a free trip to Dunn's River Falls, and a 20-minute massage. A bit more sophisticated than its siblings. $2295 to $4200 per couple per week.

Sandals Ocho Rios $355–$455   ★ ★ ★ ★

Main Street, ☎ *(800) 726-3257, (809) 974-5691, FAX (809) 974-5700.*
Double: $355–$455.
Set among lush beachfront gardens, this couples-only resort boasts immaculate grounds and excellent service. The all-inclusive rates cover all meals, drinks and activities, including nightly entertainment, all watersports, a gym with exercise classes, two tennis courts and nearby golf on 18 holes. Accommodations are nice and open onto furnished balconies, most with sea views. Dining is varied with three restaurants; afterwards, there are four bars and a disco in which to unwind. Very professional and well run.

Sans Souci Lido $465–$945   ★ ★ ★ ★ ★

Ocho Rios, ☎ *(800) 203-7450, (809) 974-2353.*
Single: $465–$945. Double: $465–$945.
This elegant all-inclusive resort, part of the SuperClubs group, is tops in any book.
It is best known for its rejuvenating Charlie's Spa, where guests are pampered and treated like royalty. Accommodations are quite smashing and range from standard rooms to suites with one or two bedrooms, some with Jacuzzis and kitchens. Set on a lush, steep hillside overlooking the sea, the small beach is reached via elevator or steep walkways. There are three tennis courts, two outdoor pools, mineral baths, and watersports. The Terrace restaurant is a lovely outdoor spot where you dine to the light of candles and stars; afterwards, there's live entertainment with local cabaret artists and cultural shows. Really special.

Shaw Park Beach Hotel   **$165–$436**   ★★★

Cutlass Bay, ☎ (800) 243-9420, (809) 974-2552.
Single: $165–$436. Double: $179–$436.

Set on a private though narrow beach, this Georgian-style resort has adequate but
quite simple guest rooms; the two-bedroom suites with kitchens are much nicer,
but also much pricier. Standard recreational activities include two tennis courts, a
pool, watersports, and exercise classes. Nights are kept busy with three bars, a lively
disco and organized entertainment. Decent, but aging in a not particularly graceful
fashion.

Apartments and Condominiums

Comfort Suites   **$105–$205**   ★★★

17 DeCosta Drive, ☎ (800) 423-4095, (809) 974-7084, FAX (809) 974-8070.
Single: $105–$180. Double: $125–$205.

Brand-new in March 1994, this downtown hotel accommodates guests in suites
with kitchenettes and patios. There's a pool, tennis and year-round supervised kids'
programs, as well as maid service and a restaurant. Beaches are found within walking
distance.

Sea Palms   **$145–$145**   ★★★

61 Main Street, ☎ (800) 423-4095, (809) 974-4400.
Single: $145. Double: $145.

A casual complex of apartments with a pool, but no other facilities. Units are comfortable and range from one to three bedrooms, all with patios or balconies and
kitchens.

Inns

Hibiscus Lodge   **$65–$93**   ★★★

Main Street, ☎ (800) 526-2422, (809) 974-2676, FAX (809) 974-1874.
Single: $65–$93. Double: $65–$93.

Situated in a quiet topical garden fronting the sea, this intimate Jamaican-style inn
has no beach, but there is a pool for cooling off. Guest rooms are spacious and comfortable, but only a few have air conditioning. There's tennis and a well-regarded
restaurant on site, as well as a bar built into the cliffs. Lots of atmosphere here.

Low Cost Lodging

Fisherman's Point   **$95–$135**   ★★

Turtle Beach, ☎ (800) 423-4095, (809) 974-5317, FAX (809) 974-2894.
Single: $95–$103. Double: $125–$135.

This complex on Turtle Beach has one-, two-, and three-bedroom apartments with
kitchenettes and maid and cook services. There's also a bar and restaurant if you
can't face your own cooking. The modest grounds include a pool. The Ocean Village Shopping Centre is within walking distance.

Turtle Beach Towers   **$87–$225**   ★★

Ocean Village, ☎ (809) 974-2801, FAX (809) 974-5014.
Single: $87–$225. Double: $93–$225.

Their modern high-rises are on the beach and next to the Ocean Village Shopping
Centre. Units are nicely done and run the gamut from studios to apartments with

one to three bedrooms. Most have balconies and all have maid service. The grounds include a coffee shop, pool, two tennis courts, and watersports.

Where to Eat

lmond Tree $$$ ★ ★ ★ ★

87 Main Street, ☎ (809) 974-2813.
Latin American cuisine. Specialties: Roast Suckling Pig, Pumpkin Soup.
Lunch: Noon–2:30 p.m., entrees $12–$26.
Dinner: 6-9:30 p.m., entrees $12–$26.

If you can stop swinging in the unique chairs suspended from the ceiling in the bar of this small inn on a cliff overlooking the sea, you'll find the food in the restaurant to be quite good. The Almond Tree has a real tree growing through its roof, a diverse clientele (famous rock stars have been known to swing in) and roast suckling pig on the menu. Soups are divine, especially the pumpkin. Drop in at the piano bar on the hotel grounds for some good tunes to accompany after-dinner drinks in a more subdued atmosphere.

vita's $$ ★ ★ ★ ★ ★

Eden Bower Road, ☎ (809) 974-2333.
Italian cuisine. Specialties: Homemade Pasta.
Lunch: 11 a.m.–4 p.m., entrees $7–$19.
Dinner: 4-11 p.m., entrees $7–$19.

Don't cry for Evita—in this instance, restaurateur Eva Myers - who has no trouble drawing in pasta lovers and others to this 1860s-era gingerbread house perched over Ocho Rios Bay. Many guests prefer eating on the terrace as the sun sets over the deep blue Caribbean waters. Some of the seemingly endless parade of pastas include a lasagne rastafari with bell peppers, tomatoes and ackee - the Rastafarian (and Italian) colors. Fresh and delicious fish, especially red snapper, steaks and ribs are also available.

arkway Restaurant $$$ ★ ★

60 Da Costa Drive, ☎ (809) 974-2667.
Latin American cuisine.
Lunch: 7:30 a.m.–4 p.m., entrees $6–$25.
Dinner: 4-11 p.m., entrees $6–$25.

This tropical diner-roadhouse in downtown Ocho Rios serves up some very reasonably priced and tasty Jamaican specialties to simple folk as well as prime movers and shakers. You can join them too, while watching local programming from the ever-present TV. Spicy Jamaican chicken or curries and banana cake or pie are popular choices.

uins Restaurant $$$ ★

Da Costa Drive, ☎ (809) 974-2442.
Chinese cuisine.
Lunch: Noon–2:30 p.m., entrees $12–$33.
Dinner: 6-9:30 p.m., entrees $12–$33.

The cuisine is mostly American-Chinese (chop suey, chow mein, etc.), but the scene is the thing at this refreshing alfresco restaurant named after the ruins of an old sugar mill that once occupied the site. Expect a lot of fellow revelers marveling at the surrounding waterfalls and pools that are softly lit at night. Dress is casual, and there is a cocktail lounge in an adjoining building. Specialties include shellfish and lobster; but you can also order a steak. No lunch is served on Sunday.

Port Antonio

Port Antonio is a miniature island port built around two **picturesque harbors** that could have served well as a Hollywood set. Indeed, Port Antonio *was* nearly a Hollywood set, at least the winter stomping ground, for such luminaries as Ginger Rogers, Bette Davis, Clara Bow and such financial magnates as J.P. Morgan and William Randolph Hearst, who in the'20s,'30s, and'40s were drawn to the tropical exoticism and serene beauty of the bay. Port Antonio's biggest fan was actor Errol Flynn, who often could be seen prowling the bars at night. Strange architectural fantasies took shape in this town: the dream castle of architect Earl Levy, complete with turrets, over the shoreline east of the Trident Hotel, and the sprawling concrete mansion built by a Connecticut tycoon, now in crumbling remains. Ecologists won't want to miss the 282-foot deep lagoon called **Blue Hole** off Route 44, or **Somerset Falls**, in the gorge of the Daniel River, above Hope Bay (you can't find a more romantic trip than the gondola ride under the falls). Hiking up to the **Blue Mountains** is spectacular and offers a terrific vista (for more information, see under "Treks"). Only the hardiest climbers will make it to the top of **Reach Falls** at Machioneal (no wonder the name!), but the effort will be worth it since the falls are considered to be the most beautiful in Jamaica. Nonsuch Cave is a few miles to the southeast where there are fossils and other hieroglypic signs of the Arawak tribes. There is no public transportation available so you will have to take a taxi and ask the driver to wait (about $10 round trip). The entrance fee is $5.

Beaches in Port Antonio

The best beaches in Port Antonio are **Boston Bay** and **San San Beach**. A delicacy of the area is the eye-watering peppery jerk pork, which will drive you to down a beer as quickly as possible. Just follow your nose and eyes to the smoke-spewing shacks, where local chefs cook them right on the beach. Cave Beach is a notable place to plop east of the town. **Navy Island** is located in the harbor and boasts two nude beaches—take the jetty on West Street near Musgrave Market. The island, once owned by Errol Flynn, has a memorial gallery to his life and career, where you can view movie stills and screenings of his old films. Snorkeling is available for a small fee, but the currents are strong and the fish are few. A complete wedding ceremony can be conducted in the chapel (for more information contact ☎ *(809) 993-2667*).

What Else to See

Parks and Gardens

Athenry Gardens and Cave of Nu   ★★★

Portland, Port Antonio, ☎ *(809) 993-3740.*
Hours open: 9 a.m.–5:30 p.m.
The Nonsuch Cave dates back some 1.5 million years give or take a century or two, and can be toured to see its stalagmites and stalactites. Back on ground level there are great views at the pretty flowering gardens. Port Antonio is about 20 minutes away.

Crystal Springs   ★★★

Highway A2, Port Antonio, ☎ *(809) 993-2609.*
This former sugar plantation is a privately owned estate that covers 158 acres. A peaceful spot to while away the hours, it has more than 15,000 orchids and lots of hummingbirds and other feathered friends. Bring binoculars.

Where to Stay

Hotels and Resorts

Bonnie View Plantation   **$49–$83**   ★★

Port Antonio, ☎ *(800) 448-5398, (809) 993-2752.*
Single: $49–$63. Double: $71–$83.
Sweeping views from this small hotel perched atop a hill and set on a farm. Guest rooms are quite simple, fitting in with the bargain rates. There's a pool, restaurant and bar, but not much else in the way of extras. They'll shuttle you down to the beach.

Dragon Bay   **$101–$161**   ★★

Port Antonio, ☎ *(800) 423-4095, (809) 993-3281, FAX (809) 993-3284.*
Single: $101–$161. Double: $101–$161.
Set on 55 acres with its own private cove, this villa-style resort is adjacent to Blue Lagoon. Accommodations are pleasant and run the gamut from single rooms to two-bedroom villas. Two restaurants and bars, weekly reggae concerts, a pair of pools and tennis courts, and all the usual resort amenities. A bit off the beaten track, so you'll want a rental car.

Fern Hill Club   **$215–$385**   ★★★

Port Antonio, ☎ *(800) 263-4354, (809) 993-3222.*

Double: $215–$385.
Set on a hillside and encompassing 40 acres, this is an all-inclusive resort with wonderful views and a predominantly Canadian clientele. Accommodations vary from standard guest rooms to villas with kitchens; none are air-conditioned. The grounds include four pools, a restaurant and two bars, tennis, and an exercise room. The beach is down a steep hill; a shuttle bus will take you there if you're not up to the hike. Lots of honeymooners.

Jamaica Palace Hotel $115–$285 ★★★
Port Antonio, ☎ (800) 423-4095, (809) 993-2020, FAX (809) 993-3459.
Single: $115–$285. Double: $115–$285.
Set on five well-manicured acres, this colonial-style mansion draws mainly European guests. The elegant Guest rooms are quite nice with antiques, Oriental rugs, and marble floors. There's no beach nearby, but you can dip in the 114-foot pool, which is shaped like Jamaica. Elegant and refined, but a bit too out of the way for some folks.

Navy Island Resort/Marina $75–$185 ★★
Port Antonio Harbour, ☎ (809) 993-2667.
Single: $75–$185. Double: $135–$185.
Comprising 64 acres on a 17th-century British naval station, this secluded resort later acted as Errol Flynn's personal hideaway. Like the name implies, it is located on its own small island a quarter-mile off the coast. Accommodations are in oceanfront villas with sun decks and kitchens, but no air conditioning.

One of the three beaches is clothes optional. There's also a pool, tennis and watersports.

Trident Villas & Hotel $255–$755 ★★★★★
Port Antonio, ☎ (800) 237-3237, (809) 993-2705.
Single: $255–$480. Double: $305–$755.
This is one of Jamaica's most luxurious resorts, set on 14 lush acres fronting the sea, two miles east of town. Guest rooms and villa suites are exquisitely furnished with antiques, plush decor and ocean views. Only some are air-conditioned, but constant breezes keep everything cool. The lovely grounds include a small private beach, flowering gardens, pretty walkways, and two pools. Dinner is a formal affair that includes white-glove service; you'll have to dress up for the occasion. Service, of course, is outstanding. Truly elegant.

Apartments and Condominiums
Goblin Hill Villas $1760–$2135 per wk. ★★★
Port Antonio, ☎ (800) 423-4095, (809) 925-8108, FAX (809) 993-6248.
Situated on 12 tropical acres of a hill above San San Beach, this complex has Georgian-style villas perfect for families. All are very nicely done, with locally made furniture and artwork, kitchens, and air-conditioned bedrooms. Each comes with a maid and cook. There are two lighted tennis courts, the beach down the hill, a pool and watersports. There's also a bar and restaurant, but besides occasional entertainment, not much of a nightlife. Rates, which range from $1760 to $2135 per couple weekly, include a rental car.

Where to Eat

De Montevin Lodge $$ ★★★

21 Fort George Street, ☎ (809) 993-2604.
Latin American cuisine.
Lunch: 12:30–2 p.m., prix fixe $11–$18.
Dinner: 7–9 p.m., prix fixe $11–$18.

Errol Flynn's chef used to rule the kitchen at this veddy British Victorian-style inn on Titchfield Hill (I don't think he paid much attention to what he was eating) but the food served here now is unadulterated Jamaican, prepared home-style; the number of courses that arrive depends on what you paid—the cheaper menus are just a tad over $10. Dishes include pumpkin soup, fricassee chicken, dessert and coffee.

Front Line, The $ ★★

Boston Bay.
Latin American cuisine.
Lunch: entrees $5–$8.
Dinner: entrees $5–$8.

After leaving the chic resorts of Port Antonio (a town bereft of inexpensive eateries) travelers eagerly stop at Boston Bay beach for a soak and the best jerk barbecue on the islands. Of course, nothing is fancy, just a series of roadside stands vying for your attention—but the best one may be The Front Line, with the grills presided over by colorful pit men. Marinated chicken, pork or sausage swathed with a top secret sauce (lots of hot pepper and cayenne) is perfect with Red Stripe beer or rum.

Trident Hotel Restaurant $$$

Route A4, ☎ (809) 993-2602.
International cuisine.
Lunch: Noon–2:30 p.m., entrees $25–$35.
Dinner: 8–10 p.m., prix fixe $50.

Even if you aren't staying at this bastion of subdued luxury, it's a memorable experience to dine in the high-ceilinged restaurant of this 14-acre hotel. Here five course dinners are served on the terrace or in the main dining room by white-gloved waiters; the only sounds you hear are gentle murmurings from fellow guests and the softly-whirring ceiling fans above. Once in a while the stillness is broken by the shrill cries of the tame peacocks that live on the property.

South Coast

The south coast is Jamaica's ecological haven—the place where Jamaicans long to visit when they go on holiday. Here you'll find some truly "undiscovered" beaches, though you'll have to do a bit of driving to get there. The South Coast is also known as the best place for **deep-sea fishing**, and boat trips sail out from Belmont to the offshore banks and reefs. The bay is so calm here that **snorkeling** is often an exciting experience. Southeast of Bluefield are simply some of the most pristine, unspoiled strands in all Jamaica, but unfortunately, a new Sandals resort is moving in soon. Transport from Montego Bay is easily arranged. If you take the A2 road past Scotts Cove, proceed to the town of **Black River**, one of the oldest on the island, once a thriving port during the 18th century for logwood dyes. Along the coast are some handsome colonial mansions presently being restored. The longest river in Jamaica, the Black River is perfect for canoe and **rafting** trips. If you stay on A2 instead of turning off at Black River, proceed past Middle Quarters to the left turn that takes you to the **Y.S. Falls**, a glorious unspoiled area in the middle of a plantation—be prepared for a 15-minute hike from where you park your car. (For more information on Black River and Y.S. Falls excursions, see above under "Treks").

Mandeville is a lovely, peaceful upland town with what locals feel is the best climate on the island. For some reason, there are no slums among the population of 50,000—its present prosperity is due to the production of bauxite/alumina. The village green is reminiscent of New England, with its Georgian courthouse and parish church; visit on Mondays, Wednesdays and Friday, if you want to see the market in full swing. Horseback riding, tennis, and golf on an 18-hole course are available. The Seventh Day Adventists run the Westici Health Foods store and also a vegetarian restaurant behind the church in the center of town. A craft center is located on Manchester Road.

Beaches

Bluefield Beach, near Savanna-la-Mer south of Negril, is the easiest to get to. Farther out, another gem is Crane Beach at Black River. Most secluded is **Treasure Beach** (a strand that truly lives up to its name), 20 miles along the coast beyond Crane. To the east of Treasure Beach is **Lovers Leap**, a gorgeous view, where legend has it that a plantation owner's daughter and her love, a slave, leaped to their death.

What Else to See

Museums and Exhibits

Arawak Museum ★★★

White Marl, Spanish Town, ☎ *(809) 922-0620.*
Hours open: 10 a.m.–5 p.m.
Located on the site of a large Arawak settlement, this small museum houses relics and artifacts from that era.

Jamaica People's Museum ★★★

Constitution Square, Spanish Town, ☎ *(809) 922- 620.*
Hours open: 9 a.m.–5 p.m.
This museum of native craft and technology houses farm implements, a sugar mill, an old fire engine and a hearse, as well as vintage prints, models and maps.

Tours

Milk River Mineral Baths ★★★

Milk River, Clarendon, ☎ *(809) 924-9544.*
Arthritis acting up? Rheumatism got you down? Liver ailing? Come for a half-hour soak in what is reportedly the world's most radioactive mineral waters, said to help all those conditions—and more. The baths are private and tepid at 90 degrees.

Somerset Falls ★★★

Highway A4, Hope Bay, ☎ *(809) 926-2950.*
Hours open: 9 a.m.–5 p.m.
Ride in a gondola to these scenic falls, located in a deep grove and surrounded by tropical rainforest. Wear your swimsuit so you can take a dip in the refreshing pools.

Where to Stay

The tourism infrastructure is so well-developed that there are many housing options in Jamaica. Many hotels are dedicated on-the-property dive services, from villas (Villa Draybar at Ocho Rios) to smaller dive resorts such a Fisherman's Inn in Falmouth to small hotels such as Seaworld's Cariblue (Montego Bay) and Rock Cliff (Negril), the larger all-inclusive resorts. The all-inclusive has become one of Jamaica's most popular resort options—in fact, winter occupancies have risen back to the 80–90 percent range because of their popularity. One prepaid fee covers everything from food to alcohol to water and land sports and some island excursions. Resorts can be luxurious with long beaches, superb dining, sports facilities and entertainment, etc., such as Hedonism in Negril (though it is a dedicated singles resort). Others are geared for couples or families, and some have an open policy. The focus of activities at these all-inclusive resorts vary. Some including Swept Away in Negril or Jamaica, Jamaica in Runaway Bay, are very sports- and health-oriented. While some resorts have dedicated dive operations, others will offer only a single tank per day. Do research and contact the resort to ask questions before you go. Many a misunderstanding that might have been diverted with some careful questioning has resulted in near-disaster vacations. (For more information, see "Where to Stay" under the individual sections.)

Apartments and Condominiums

Not too long ago you'd see flights to Jamaica filled with tourists toting their own food and staples. Not any more, not with the rise in quality imported foods, but you will find the cost of such "necessities" of life back home quite high, but not higher than at any other island.

Inns

If you are not athletic, don't care about a big social scene, and are adventurous enough to experience come what may, you'll save a lot of money staying in smaller inns—the majority have beachfront locations, or at the very least, provide a free shuttle to the nearest strand.

Astra Country Inn $60–$115   ★★

62 Ward Avenue, Mandeville, ☎ *(809) 962-3265.*
Single: $60–$115. Double: $60–$115.
Set high up, some 2000 feet above sea level in the mid-island hills, this informal hotel is in a former home. Guest rooms are comfortable though not air-conditioned. There's a pool and sauna on site, as well as horseback riding. Great for birders and nature lovers.

Mandeville Hotel $60–$200   ★

4 Hotel Street, Mandeville, ☎ *(809) 962-2460.*
Single: $60–$200. Double: $60–$200.
This mountain hotel has traditional guest rooms, some with air conditioning, as well as apartments with kitchen facilities. Two restaurants, three bars, a disco, and, for recreation, a pool and horseback riding. Guests can golf at the nearby Manchester Club.

Low Cost Lodging

If you're going to Jamaica for the wild outdoors, camping may be your best bet for saving money. There are extensive camping facilities in attractive locations that allow you immediate access to the wilderness. Because of the variety of fine local restaurants, you won't be losing any taste buds by not eating in the big fancy hotel restaurants; in fact you're more likely to find delightful surprises—including at "jerk centers" on the beach—that will whet your palate for years to come.

Where to Eat

The motto "Out of many, one people" goes as much for politics as it does for cuisine in Jamaica—for the influences that have gone into the dutchie, or cast-iron cooking pot, to create Jamaican menus, are many—the barbecuing techniques of the Arawaks, the African meat-preserving techniques in the country's best known dish, jerk pork; Spanish marinades meet New World vegetables in twice-cooked escovitched fish. British **cornish pastries**, which are meat-and-potato-filled pastries, have become Jamaican spicy beef patties. And the spices of Asia and the Levant come together in dishes such as curried goat. Today nouvelle cuisine is also dressing up traditional ingredients in trendy resort restaurants along the North Coast. Rastafarianism—Jamaica's contribution to 20th-century religion—has created a cuisine all its own, one that places the accent on nature's bounty. Rastas don't drink alcohol or eat meat, but their vegetarian cooking is delicious, including hearty vegetable stews with ingredients such as *calllallo* (a spinach-like vegetable), *chocho* (a pear-shaped squash), pumpkin and yams. Johnnycakes—flat, dense, unleavened breads—were a slave adaptation of British breads, while *bammie* was the Amerindian cassava bread that Columbus wrote about in his journals. Another newer addition is the popular Rasta Pasta, which features the Rastafarian colors in the red of tomatoes, the green of bell peppers, and the gold of ackee, all served over pasta. One of the bases of Jamaican cooking is "poor folk's food," like codfish, stew peas and roast breadfruit. It takes some experience to learn to like boiled green bananas as a breakfast dish.

Other Jamaican delicacies include: *bun* (a dark fruitcake served with cheese usually at Easter time); *cowfoot soup* (spicy soup of cow trotters and vegetables, claimed by Jamaican men to be an aphrodisiac); *dunkanoo* (a dessert of grated corn, flavored with sugar, cinnamon, ginger, and coconut milk, and steamed in a banana leaf); *pepper rum* (a mixture of fiery Scotch bonnet chiles and dark rum, used as a seasoning); *matrimony* (a dessert that blends orange segments with star apple pulp in cream); *mannish water* (a heavy goatmeat and vegetable soup, flavored with white rum and hot peppers, and reputed to be an aphrodisiac); *rundown* (mackerel or codfish boiled in coconut milk and eaten with ashed onions and peppers); *Solomon gundy* (pungent spiced pickled herring); and *stamp-and-go* (batter-fried saltfish fritters, usually eaten as a finger snack).

In Kingston, Sunday brunch is special at Devon House, a restored historic home dear to many Jamaicans for its food and ice cream. Seated on the wide veranda of mansions such as The Coffee Terrace, with whirling fans overhead, you can indulge in fluffy yellow ackee, a Jamaican-grown tree vegetable, whose custardy flesh tastes and looks somewhat like scrambled eggs.

This mixture of the savory ackee and salt fish harks back to the days of slavery when feeding the slaves was a major concern for plantation owners. **Jerked cooking** is a method of barbecue using well-seasoned meat, said to have originated with the Maroons, the fierce escaped slaves who retreated to the mountains of Cockpit Country and kept the British at bay for more than a century. They would roast pork over hot coals in earthen pits that were covered with branches of green pimento, or allspice, wood. The smoking wood is what provides the unique seasoning. At Boston Beach today, pit men such as Vasco "Kojak" Allen at Front Line #1, are famous for their grillwork, which includes jerked chicken, (pork, the classic dish), jerked sausage, and jerked fish.

In Ocho Rios, the **Ciboney Beach Resort** has some of the best options for dining: head for Orchid's, for pork chops filled with bread and chutney, or the alfresco **Casa Nina**, for ackee and callalloo. The **Ciboney Grill and Market Place** is designed like a Jamaican outdoor market with colorful food stalls.

In Montego Bay, the restaurant at the four-bedroom hostelry called **Norma's** at the Warehouse is a treasurehouse of delicacies, from smoked marlin with papaya salsa to roast loin pork with prunes. Desserts run the course between plantain turnover with brandied whipped cream or a vine-ripened papaya, with a drizzle of island grown ortanique (cross between an orange and a tangerine). Less fancy digs on the North Coast include the **Rite Stuff Café** and Caterers in Montego Bay's Westgate Plaza, where you can dig into curried goat, stew bee, or a steaming bowl of pumpkin soup. Meat patties, flaky turnovers stuffed with a savory chopped meat and herb mixture, are a favorite snack on this island of nibblers.

You won't know the cuisine of Jamaica until you make a stop at the island's hub of hedonism, Negril. Head for the **Hungry Lion**, one of the best spots on the North Coast to try Italian food, and at **Paradise Yard**, where you can indulge in a special Jamaican breakfast feast.

FIELDING'S CHOICE:

Want a home-cooked meal while you're in Jamaica? Sign up with the "Meet the People" program and one of some 400 volunteer Jamaican families will spend the day showing you their island and taking you back to their house for dinner. Call the Jamaican Tourist Board at ☎ (800) 233-4582 before you leave home and contact their local office when you arrive.

Where to Shop

Jamaica has some wonderful opportunities for committed shoppers; you may find yourself wishing you had brought an extra piece of luggage to handle the overflow. Duty-free shopping is available in the cosmopolitan areas, with good buys on perfumes, crystals and china. Stop at the crafts markets or roadside stands for more authentic goods. Excellent wood carvings sell generally for a modest sum.

Kingston is the New York City of Jamaica—nearly anything you can buy in Jamaica can be found here. You can choose from a luxury list of duty-free items or concentrate on local crafts made by well-skilled artisans. Despite a 10 percent General Consumption tax that has been added to all goods and services, **duty-free bargains** will generally reap you significant savings from back home in the States. (Of course, if you are vulnerable to such bargains, you should figure in the cost of buying things you probably wouldn't buy at home.) This duty-free wish-list in Kingston includes: Swiss watches, gold jewelry, camera, electronic equipment, liquor, cigarettes, fine European crystal, china, French perfume and British woolens. You must carry proof of identity with you to receive the duty-free discount. Best liquors to pick up include the Jamaican rums, Rumona (a rum liqueur), and the coffee-flavored Tia Maria. Royal Jamaican **cigars** are a connoisseur's delight, available at the airport as well as the pier. **Blue Mountain coffee** is the native brew, and will make one of the finest cups you have ever drunk. If you plan to do serious duty-free shopping, bring a list of comparative prices in the States, so that you don't go home and want to shoot yourself.

Local artists do excellent work in various media, but especially wood carvings, usually using *lignum vitae*, a rosy native hardwood. All kinds of objects are carved—from bookends to statues of saints (and Bob Marley) to furniture. You can pick up the best pieces in the crafts markets as well as at roadside stands on the north shore between Montego Bay and Falmouth. Straw work is also native to Jamaica, and good finds can also be found in basketry and batiks. Some of the best crafts at the best prices can be found at **Things Jamaica** at the Devon House (as well as at the airport); special buys are carved wood bowls and trays to reproduction of silver and brass historical pieces. Jamaican designers have quite a flair with resort wear, particularly using colorful fabrics silk-screened on the island. Silk batiks, sold by the yard, and so beautiful they can be used as wall art, can be found at **Caribatik**, the studio of the late Muriel Chandler, two miles east of Falmouth. Search through the shopping malls for fashionable clothes, such as at the New Kingston Shopping Mall, not far from the Pegasus hotel. If you need a new pair of sandals, try Lee's New Kingston in this mall.

You can't—don't even think about—leave Jamaica without buying a few reggae tapes. Records by some of reggae's greats including Bob Marley, his son Ziggy Marley, Peter Tosh and Burning Spear can be found at **Randy's Record Mart** at *17 N. Parade*—a legendary store where you can be directed to records by some of the new crop of up-and-coming stars.

Another shopping center for more mundane necessities is Lane's Shopping Mall (just one of half a dozen along Constant Spring Road). Hotel boutiques may have some cosmetics and toiletries, but they will be highly overpriced. Discover the pleasure of aloe-based Jamaican skin creams. They also make excellent gifts.

Jamaica Directory

ARRIVAL AND DEPARTURE

American Airlines and **Air Jamaica** both fly nonstop from New York; **Air Jamaica** also flies nonstop from Miami and has service from Atlanta, Baltimore, Orlando and Philadelphia. **BWIA** flies from San Juan. **Continental** flies in daily from Newark. **Northwest Airlines** flies in daily from Minneapolis and Tampa and **Aeroflot** flies in from Havana. **Air Canada** offers service from Toronto and Montreal in conjunction with **Air Jamaica**, and both **British Airways** and **Air Jamaica** fly to London.

Donald Sangester International Airport in Montego Bay is the best place to arrive if you are headed for Montego Bay, Round Hill-Tyrall, Ocho Rios, Runaway Bay and Negril. If you are staying in Port Antonio or Kingston, the capital, it's best to land at Norman Manley Airport in Kingston. **Trans-Jamaican Airlines** ☎ *(809) 923-8680* offers a shuttle service.

In general, there is no public transportation to and from the airports. Taxi rates are not fixed, but sample fares to popular destinations are usually posted in public places. Negotiate beforehand. All-inclusive resorts provide free transfers from the airport, as do many small hotels when you are using their package. Sometimes a hotel will throw it in for free if you ask in advance. If transfers are included in your package, you will normally be given a voucher with the name of the operator, and a company representative will meet you at the airport. If not, it's a good idea to ask your travel agent to reserve space in advance. **JUTA** (Jamaica Union of Travellers Association) offers taxis that hold up to five people and (total price $80) run from the nearest airports to hotels in Negril,

Ocho Rios and Port Antonio. Runs to Montego Bay and Kingston, which are much closer, are much cheaper. If you are heading beyond Montego Bay (and you have time to spare), you'll save lots of money if you book one of Tropical Tours' air-conditioned minibuses at their desk just outside the luggage area of Sangster Airport ☎ *(809) 953-1111*. They run to Ocho Rios and Negril and charge a per-person fare. Unfortunately, you won't be able to leave right away until the bus is at least half full.

BUSINESS HOURS

Stores open weekdays 9 a.m.–5 p.m. and Saturday 9 a.m.–6 p.m. Banks open weekdays 9 a.m.–5 p.m.

CLIMATE

Jamaica has a tropical climate with considerable variation. High temperatures on the coast are usually mitigated by sea breezes, while upland areas enjoy cooler and less-humid conditions. Jamaica lies in the hurricane zone, so always check weather reports before you come (even before you book). Rainfall falls plentifully throughout Jamaica; the heaviest season is in May and from August-November. In Kingston temperatures range from 6 degrees F in January to 81 degrees F in July.

DOCUMENTS

U.S. citizens need either a passport or other proof of citizenship (birth certificate, voter's registration) and a photo ID. All others need a passport. Departure tax is U.S.$5.

ELECTRICITY

Current is not consistent throughout the island. Some hotels feature 110, some 220. Adapters and converters are supplied by hotels who need them for foreign visitors.

GETTING AROUND

Taxis are best taken for short trips in Jamaica. At the airport you can always find a JUTA taxi and coach, as well as at most resorts. If you are planning an out-of-the-way excursion, particularly for dinner, arrange for the driver to pick you up afterwards and negotiate a good round-trip fare. Most taxis are unmetered; if you seem to be having trouble with the driver, enlist the help of your hotel's concierge or doorman, though you can never be sure if they are in cahoots with each other. When in doubt, ask to see the rate sheet, which all cabs are supposed to carry. After midnight, a 25 percent surcharge is added, though that is often negotiable, particularly if you have negotiated a round-trip deal or if your destination is especially far away.

Buses prove to be a cheap way to toot around the Kingston and Montego Bay areas; they run often but they are often unbearably overcrowded, hot and dirty. (Moreover, a tourist on a crowded local bus is often a sitting duck for crime; if you are wearing your camera and an "I Love Jamaica" T-shirt, you might as well just hand over your valuables before being asked for them.) Kingston bus fares range from $3 JDS to $7.50 JDS (about 15 cents to 35 cents in American currency) at press time. The fee depends on the distance traveled. You can tour the island on a bus, but here you will have to share aisle space with the local riffraff—meaning chickens on their way to getting their heads chopped off at market. Minibus jitneys also travel around the island, but they are unscheduled and you may have to flag them down in the street—not a reliable way to get somewhere on time. As a result, most people cave in and rent cars or hire a cab.

Car rentals are a good idea on Jamaica since the roads are well-paved and your own car will allow you to conduct your sightseeing at your own pace. You must be able, however, to handle that "British thing" of driving on the left; it takes getting used to, so be careful the first few days (the moment you "space out," a common occurrence on long trips or in new lands, you may find yourself veering to the right, which will be disastrous in the face of oncoming traffic. If you're driving with a companion, let them be a front-seat driver for a while and spot for you.) About a dozen agencies on the island offer rentals; among the best are **Avis** ☎ *(809) 926-1560*; **Budget** ☎ *952-1943*; and **National** ☎ *(809) 924-8344*. In Ocho Rios you'll find **Sunshine Car Rental** ☎ *(809) 974-2980*. In Port Antonio try **Eastern Car Rental** ☎ *(809) 993-3624*. Major international chains accept bookings through stateside toll-free *(800)* numbers. Always ask for a written confirmation (a fax will do) and be sure you bring it along. There have been numerous cases of lost reservations, and supply often runs low, despite the presence of 2800 rental cars on the island. Also remember to add the cost of gas to your expenses (no free gas) and a 10 percent government tax. Valid U.S. and Canadian licenses are acceptable, but many agencies have a 25-and-over age limit (ask before you book). Beware of Jamaican drivers who suddenly and unexpectedly turn macho and wipe the road with the tar of their tires. In such cases, it is always best to yield. **Vacation Network**, an agency in Chicago ☎ *(800) 423-4095* offers a special "Fly Drive Jamaica/The Great Escape Package," which combines a rental car with air transportation and overnight accommodations. Vouchers that come with the package allow you to use them at 45 participating small hotels and inns; the package comes with a guidebook geared for drivers as well as road maps.

LANGUAGE

The official language is English. The unique Jamaican dialect, used by natives, is English with African and native words and a British inflection and tropical rhythm.

MEDICAL EMERGENCIES

The most efficient and advanced medical facilities are in Kingston, where you will find the country's largest hospital.

MONEY

The official currency is the Jamaican dollar, which has proven to be quite unstable in relation to the American dollar. American dollars are accepted in most establishments, but exchange rates will vary (also make sure when you are quoted a price, that you know which "dollar" is being used). All airports have exchange houses; best rates are found at banks. Major credit cards are accepted by most hotels and many restaurants, as are traveler's checks. When changing money, be sure you keep the receipt so you can change the money back before you leave.

SECURITY

Crime in Jamaica is lower per capita than in most large U.S. cities, but the city of Kingston is rife with incidents. Downtown Kingston is particularly bad, and you should never walk in the street after dark. Don't even think about going to West Kingston, even in a car with the doors locked. Don't ever leave money, wallets, purses or valuables such as cameras unattended at the beach. Police foot patrols are present in all the major tourist areas, so head directly for one if you sense trouble approaching. Also avoid standing in the middle of a street to hail a taxi; it's best to head for a shopping center or ask your hotel to arrange one ahead of time.

TELEPHONE

The area code is *809*. Direct telephone, telegraph, telefax and telex services are all available.

TIME

Eastern Standard Time throughout the year.

TIPPING

Most Jamaican hotels and restaurants add a service charge of 10 percent; always check first to see if it's included. If not, tip waiters 10–15 percent (depending on the service). Hotel maids should receive about $1–2 per person per day. Airport porters and hotel bellhops should be tipped 50 cents per bag (but not less than a $1). It's not necessary to tip taxi drivers, although 10 percent of the fare is usually appreciated.

TOURIST INFORMATION

The main office of the Jamaica Tourist Board is in Kingston *(Tourism Centre Building, New Kingston, Box 360, Kingston 5;* ☎ *(809) 929-9200)*. There are also JTB desks at both Montego Bay and Kingston airports and in all resort areas. In the U.S. ☎ *(213) 384-1123.*

WHEN TO GO

Carnival is a recent addition to Jamaica, held oddly at Easter time. The annual reggae festival called Sun Splash is usually held in the middle of August, in Montego Bay, at the Bob Marley Centre. The Independence celebrations, also held for a week in August, are colorful blowout bashes (usually on Independence Day, Aug. 1). In October the annual International Marlin Tournament at Port Antonio attracts fishermen from all over the world and includes festivals other than fishing. Contact the Tourist Board for a twice-yearly calendar of events covering a wide spectrum of sports and arts festivals.

JAMAICA HOTELS		RMS	RATES	PHONE	CR. CARDS
Kingston					
★★★★	Jamaica Pegasus Hotel	350	$180–$564	(809) 926-3690	A, DC, MC, V
★★★	Braco Village Resort	180	$235–$260	(800) 654-1337	A, MC, V
★★★	Morgan's Harbour Hotel	45	$98–$255	(809) 924-8464	A, MC, V
★★★	Terra Nova Hotel	33	$120–$150	(809) 926-2211	A, DC, MC, V
★★★	Wyndham Kingston	384	$165–$505	(800) 322-4200	A, DC, MC, V
★★	Courtleigh House & Hotel	80	$79–$195	(800) 526-2400	A, MC
★★	Medallion Hall Hotel	16	$79–$83	(809) 927-5721	A, DC, MC, V
★	Four Seasons	39	$71–$83	(809) 929-7655	A, DC, MC, V
★	Indies Hotel	15	$35–$62	(809) 926-2952	A, MC, V
Montego Bay					
★★★★★	Half Moon Beach Club	213	$255–$805	(800) 626-0592	A, MC
★★★★★	Round Hill Hotel & Villas	110	$305–$454	(800) 223-6510	A, MC, V
★★★★	Sandals Montego Bay	243	$2375–$2835	(800) 726-3257	A, MC
★★★★	Sandals Royal Caribbean	190	$2465–$2920	(800) 726-3257	A, MC
★★★★	Tryall Resort	52	$235–$465	(800) 742-0498	A, MC, V
★★★	Doctor's Cave Beach Hotel	90	$85–$135	(800) 223-6510	A, MC, V
★★★	Reading Reef Club	26	$65–$370	(800) 223-6510	A, MC
★★★	Sandals Inn	52	$290–$348	(800) 726-3257	A, MC
★★★	Seacastles	198	$75–$155	(800) 526-2422	A, MC, V
★★★	Seawind Beach Resort	468	$75–$120	(800) 526-2422	A, D, MC, V
★★★	Wyndham Rose Hall Resort	500	$165–$705	(809) 953-2650	A, MC, V
★★	Blue Harbour Hotel	24	$35–$105	(809) 952-5445	A, MC, V
★★	Coral Cliff Hotel	32	$54–$64	(809) 952-4130	A, MC
★★	Fantasy Resort	119	$55–$85	(800) 237-3421	A, MC
★★	Gloucestershire, The	88	$60–$80	(800) 423-4095	A, MC
★★	Holiday Inn Montego Bay	516	$160–$205	(800) 465-4329	A, MC, V

JAMAICA HOTELS	RMS	RATES	PHONE	CR. CARDS
★★ Jack Tar Village	128	$155–$205	(809) 952-9504	A, MC
★★ Montego Bay Racquet Club	51	$50–$155	(809) 952-0200	A, MC, V
★★ Richmond Hill Inn	20	$78–$112	(809) 952-3859	A, MC
★★ Sea Garden Beach Hotel	104	$297–$357	(800) 545-9001	A, MC
★★ Toby Inn	60	$45–$80	(809) 952-4370	A, MC
★★ Wexford, The	61	$85–$130	(800) 237-3421	A, MC
★★ Winged Victory	27	$95–$230	(809) 952-3892	A, MC
★ Belvedere Beach Hotel	27	$50–$80	(809) 952-0593	A, CB, MC, V
★ Buccaneer Beach Hotel	72	$83–$175	(809) 952-6489	A, MC
★ Royal Court Hotel	25	$45–$85	(809) 952-4531	A, MC

Negril

	RMS	RATES	PHONE	CR. CARDS
★★★★★ Grand Lido	200	$350	(800) 423-4095	A, MC
★★★★ Negril Tree House	70	$85–$275	(800) 423-4095	A, MC
★★★★ Sandals Negril	199	$2890–$3995	(800) 726-3257	A, MC
★★★★ Swept Away Resort	134	$2770–$3785	(800) 545-7937	A, MC, V
★★★ Beachcomber Club	46	$105–$185	(800) 423-4095	A, MC
★★★ Charela Inn	39	$55–$165	(800) 423-4095	A, MC
★★★ Foote Prints on the Sands	33	$55–$105	(809) 957-4300	A, MC
★★★ Hedonism II	280	$205–$376	(800) 423-4095	A, MC
★★★ Poinciana Beach Hotel	130	$168–$281	(800) 468-6728	A, MC
★★★ Point Village	130	$100–$155	(809) 957-4351	A, MC
★★★ Rock Cliff Resort	33	$55–$100	(809) 957-4331	A, MC
★★★ Xtabi Club Resort	16	$50–$145	(809) 957-4336	A, MC
★★ Chuckles	78	$75–$260	(809) 957-4277	A, MC
★★ Crystal Waters Villas	10	$85–$110	(809) 957-4284	A, MC
★★ Drumville Cove Resort	20	$40–$100	(800) 423-4095	A, MC, V
★★ Hotel Samsara	50	$40–$115	(809) 957-4395	A, MC
★★ Negril Beach Club Hotel	85	$77–$185	(800) 526-2422	A, MC
★★ Negril Cabins	50	$40–$55	(809) 957-4350	A, MC
★★ Negril Gardens	54	$105–$140	(800) 423-4095	A, MC
★★ Negril Inn	46	$115–$145	(800) 634-7456	A, MC

JAMAICA HOTELS		RMS	RATES	PHONE	CR. CARDS
★★	Paradise View	17	$75–$135	(809) 957-4375	A, MC
★★	T-Water Beach Hotel	70	$125–$155	(800) 654-1592	A, MC

Ocho Rios

		RMS	RATES	PHONE	CR. CARDS
★★★★★	Sans Souci Lido	111	$465–$945	(800) 203-7450	A, MC, V
★★★★	Boscobel Beach Hotel	228	$415–$995	(800) 423-4095	A, MC
★★★★	Ciboney Ocho Rios	300	$175–$690	(800) 777-7800	A, MC
★★★★	Couples Jamaica	172	$365–$520	(800) 423-4095	A, MC
★★★★	Jamaica Grande	720	$135–$195	(800) 228-9898	A, CB, MC, V
★★★★	Jamaica Inn	45	$225–$250	(809) 974-2516	A, MC
★★★★	Plantation Inn	78	$300–$999	(800) 423-4095	A, MC, V
★★★★	Sandals Dunn's River	256	$2295–$4200	(800) 726-3257	A, MC
★★★★	Sandals Ocho Rios	237	$355–$455	(800) 726-3257	A, MC
★★★	Comfort Suites	137	$105–$205	(800) 423-4095	A, CB, MC, V
★★★	Enchanted Garden	112	$95–$555	(800) 323-5655	A, MC, V
★★★	Hibiscus Lodge	26	$65–$93	(800) 526-2422	A, CB, MC, V
★★★	Sea Palms	45	$145	(800) 423-4095	A, MC
★★★	Shaw Park Beach Hotel	118	$165–$436	(800) 243-9420	A, MC, V
★★	Club Jamaica Beach Resort	95	$180–$235	(800) 423-4095	A, MC, V
★★	Fisherman's Point	64	$95–$135	(800) 423-4095	A, MC
★★	Turtle Beach Towers	218	$87–$225	(809) 974-2801	A, MC

Port Antonio

		RMS	RATES	PHONE	CR. CARDS
★★★★★	Trident Villas & Hotel	28	$255–$755	(800) 237-3237	A, MC
★★★	Fern Hill Club	36	$215–$385	(800) 263-4354	A, MC
★★★	Goblin Hill Villas	28	$1760–$2135	(800) 423-4095	A, MC
★★★	Jamaica Palace Hotel	80	$115–$285	(800) 423-4095	A, MC
★★	Bonnie View Plantation	20	$49–$83	(800) 448-5398	A, MC, V
★★	Dragon Bay	86	$101–$161	(800) 423-4095	A, MC
★★	Navy Island Resort/ Marina	21	$75–$185	(809) 993-2667	A, MC

North Coast

		RMS	RATES	PHONE	CR. CARDS
★★★★	Franklyn D. Resort	76	$3205–$7205	(800) 423-4095	A, MC
★★★★	Jamaica Jamaica	242	$167–$240	(800) 423-4095	A, MC

JAMAICA HOTELS		RMS	RATES	PHONE	CR. CARDS
★★★	Eaton Hall Beach Hotel	52	$135–$299	(809) 973-3503	A, CB, MC, V
★★★	H.E.A.R.T. Country Club	20	$55–$75	(809) 973-2671	A, MC
★★	Ambiance Jamaica	80	$90–$215	(800) 523-6504	A, MC
★★	Club Caribbean	128	$125–$295	(800) 647-2740	A, MC, V
★★	Portside Villas & Condos	15	$85–$280	(809) 973-2007	A, MC
★	Caribbean Isle Hotel	24	$55–$65	(809) 973-2364	A, MC

South Coast

★★	Astra Country Inn	22	$60–$115	(809) 962-3265	A, MC
★	Mandeville Hotel	60	$60–$200	(809) 962-2460	A, MC

JAMAICA RESTAURANTS		PHONE	ENTREE	CR. CARDS
Kingston				
International				
★★★★	Blue Mountain Inn	(809) 927-1700	$12–$24••	A, DC, MC, V
★★	Gap Cafe, The	(809) 923-7055	$12–$22	A, MC, V
★★	Port Royal	(809) 926-3690	$16–$26	A, DC, MC, V
★	El Dorado Room	(809) 926-9334	$7–$20	A, DC, MC, V
★	Ivor Guest House	(809) 977-33	$18–$30	A, MC, V
Latin American				
★★★★★	Temple Hall	(809) 942-2340	$25–$25••	A, DC, MC
★★★★	Norma's at the Wharfhouse	(809) 979-2745	$26–$34	MC, V
★★	Devon House Restaurants	(809) 929-6602	$6–$16	A, MC, V
★★	Hot Pot, The	(809) 929-3906	$3–$4	V
★	Chelsea Jerk Centre	(809) 926-6322	$3–$5	A, MC, V
★	Indies Pub and Grill	(809) 926-5050	$4–$12	A, MC, V
★	Minnie's Ethiopian	(809) 927-9207	$10–$20	None
Montego Bay				
International				
★★★★	Sugar Mill	(809) 953-2228	$14–$31	A, MC, V
★	Georgian House	(809) 952-3353	$22–$32	A, DC, MC, V
★	Julia's	(809) 952-632	$35–$35••	A, DC, MC, V

JAMAICA RESTAURANTS	PHONE	ENTREE	CR. CARDS
Italian			
★★★★★ **Reading Reef Club**	(809) 952-5909	$10–$24	A, DC, MC, V
Latin American			
★★★ **Pork Pit**	(809) 952-1046	$2–$9	None
★★ **Town House**	(809) 952-2660	$13–$30	A, DC, MC, V
Seafood			
★ **Pier I**	(809) 952-2452	$16–$25	A, MC, V

Negril

	PHONE	ENTREE	CR. CARDS
French			
★★ **Cafe au Lait**	(809) 957-4471	$9–$29	MC, V
Latin American			
★★ **Chicken Lavish**	(809) 957-4410	$3–$5	MC, V
★★ **Hungry Lion**		$18–$30	MC, V
★★ **Paradise Yard**	(809) 957-4006	$6–$15	None
★ **Tan-ya's**	(809) 957-4041	$5–$25	A, MC, V
Seafood			
★★ **Cosmo's**	(809) 957-4330	$5–$12	MC, V
★ **Rick's Cafe**	(809) 957-4335	$11–$28	None

Ocho Rios

	PHONE	ENTREE	CR. CARDS
Chinese			
★ **Ruins Restaurant**	(809) 974-2442	$12–$33	A, DC, MC, V
Italian			
★★★★★ **Evita's**	(809) 974-2333	$7–$19	A, MC, V
Latin American			
★★★★ **Almond Tree**	(809) 974-2813	$12–$26	A, DC, MC, V
★★ **Parkway Restaurant**	(809) 974-2667	$6–$25	A, MC, V

Port Antonio

	PHONE	ENTREE	CR. CARDS
International			
★★★★★ **Trident Hotel Restaurant**	(809) 993-2602	$25–$50	A, MC, V
Latin American			
★★★ **De Montevin Lodge**	(809) 993-2604	$11–$18	None
★★ **Front Line, The**		$5–$8	None

JAMAICA RESTAURANTS	PHONE	ENTREE	CR. CARDS

Note: • Lunch Only

        •• Dinner Only

PUERTO RICO

Watersports of all kinds are available at Sun Bay.

Puerto Rico is probably the best kept secret in the Caribbean. Few people are aware that visitors from the U.S., Asia and South America reached a record four million for 1993–94, registering a 12.2 percent increase in hotel bookings. More than half of that four million were from the U.S.

The year 1994 was key for other reasons. A wet September enabled Puerto Rico officials to lift the drought restrictions in key tourist areas of the island following four months of such barriers. The surrounding areas of Old San Juan, Isla Verde and Condado—where many of the largest hotels are located—have returned to normal water service. Old San Juan, refurbished with a $41 million budget and another $41 million waterfront renewal project, is on a roll, though still a bit reeling from the 500th anniversary of Columbus' first sighting of Puerto Rico on Nov. 19, 1493. There are 16 historic blocks that compose this World Heritage site. Known as El Viejo, San Juan, embodies the spiritual heart of the island's nearly four million inhabitants. With centuries-old architecture, it symbolizes Puerto Rico's fight for identity in the face of 400 years of foreign assault and occupation.

A lovely way to visit Puerto Rico is to take a week to travel down the **Ruta Panorâmica** (the island's Panoramic Route), which twists and turns from one end of the island to another across the Cordilleria Central—staying at a different parador, or country inn, every night.

Bird's Eye View

The farthest east of the four major islands that form the Greater Antilles, Puerto Rico is 110 miles by 35 miles in size. To the north lies the Atlantic Ocean, to the south the Caribbean. Three islands are situated off the coast of Puerto Rico: Vieques and Culebra to the east and Mona to the west. The island's terrain ranges from palm-lined beaches on four coastlines to rugged mountain ranges, gently rolling hills and dry desertlike areas. The island boasts 20 designated forest reserves and an additional six are in proposal. The most notable are the 28,000-acre El Yunque rain forest near San Juan, part of the Caribbean National Forest and the only tropical rain forest in the U.S. Forest Service; the Guajataca Forest, with 25 miles of trails through karst reserves; and the Guanica Forest Reserve, a dry forest with the largest number of bird species on the island. There are also two Phosphorescent Bays, one off the southwest coast and the other off the island of Vieques.

History

In 1493, Columbus arrived on the island of Puerto Rico in the company of one Ponce de León, who named the island for his patron saint, San Juan. The island, however, already had a name—Borinquen—a Taino Indian nomenclature and one that is still lovingly used today by native Puerto Ricans. Caparra, inland and across the bay, was the first choice for a capital in 1508

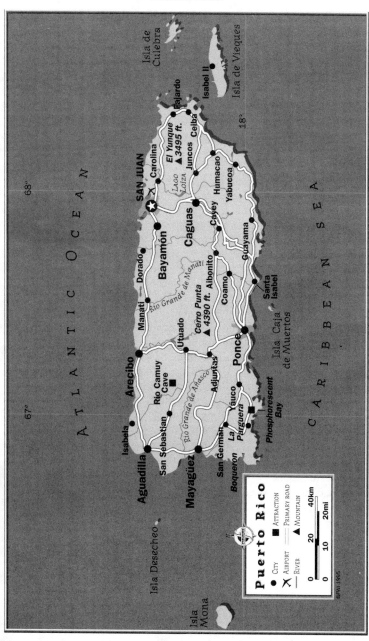

when Juan Ponce de León (the island's first governor) and his men with the permission of supreme cacique Agueybana, first scouted the island of San Juan Bautista. Eventually de León set off on his journey to discover eternal youth and never actually resided in the handsome home, Casa Blanca, that had been built for him. Thirteen years later, settlers decamped for the drier, windier islet fronting the Atlantic, where they permanently settled. During early years of colonization, the city repelled the British, French and Dutch corsairs. La Fortaleza, now the governor's mansion, and El Morro and San Cristóbal forts were built during those times with the specific aim of keeping marauders at bay.

By the early 1800s, the era of Caribbean piracy was finally brought to a halt. At the same time, Spain threw open her doors to immigration; subsequent increase in economic prosperity coupled with new aesthetic influences from abroad were soon reflected in the island's architectural styles. It was during this period that Old San Juan developed the colonial/neoclassic look that predominates today—all within the urban grid pattern envisioned by the original Spanish planners. In 1897 the island gained independence from Spanish rule in 1897. On July 25, 1898, however, Spanish troops landed in Guánica, in the middle of the Spanish-American War, and disturbed whatever modicum of peace had been achieved. The Treaty of Paris of 1899 handed the island over to the U.S. In 1917, Puerto Ricans were granted American citizenship; in 1952, the island achieved unique status by becoming the only member of the commonwealth to receive its own constitution and government. Although there have been several movements geared toward achieving complete independence, the 1993 vote to remain a U.S. possession has ensured a long-standing and stable future with the mother country.

During the early 20th century a burgeoning population brought growth beyond the Old City gates and soon after, the destruction of substantial sections of its massive walls. Today Old San Juan boasts only 5000 *residents*, no longer the financial hub, it still pulls 5000 *workers* to offices and government buildings, eateries and shops. A seven-block enclave that boasts a large number of art studios, florists, doctor's offices, galleries, etc., is considered one of the more desirable spots to live in island.

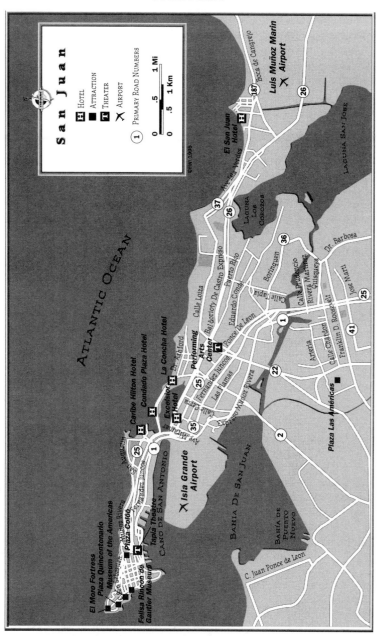

San Juan

H HOTEL
■ ATTRACTION
T THEATER
✕ AIRPORT
① PRIMARY ROAD NUMBERS

0   .5   1 Mi
0 .5 1 Km

©PW 1995

Luis Muñoz Marin Airport

El San Juan Hotel

ATLANTIC OCEAN

El Moro Fortress
Plaza Quincentenario
Museum of the Americas
Felisa Rincon de
Gautier Museum
Plaza Colón
Tapia Theatre
CAÑO DE SAN ANTONIO

Caribe Hilton Hotel
Condado Plaza Hotel
La Concha Hotel
Excelsior Hotel
Performing Arts Center

Isla Grande Airport

BAHÍA DE SAN JUAN

BAHÍA DE PUERTO NUEVO

C. Juan Ponce de Leon

Plaza Las Américas

LAGUNA SAN JOSÉ

LAGUNA LOS CORZOS

People

Puerto Ricans consider themselves American but have a fierce pride about their island and their special Caribbean identity. American products are ubiquitous; in fact, Puerto Rico is considered among the top 10 overseas markets for American goods manufactured on the mainland. Through such media as American cable TV, music, dance and fashion from the mainland have also invaded the culture, though tempered for tropical climes. Salsa, the music, is the biggest dance bet on the island, although it is often mixed with American rock'n' roll. Immense precautions, however, should be taken in regards to crime and petty thievery. Don't walk around with an ostentatious show of valuables, keep cameras tucked away in inexpensive-looking bags, and avoid wearing jewelry in the streets. Take special care when strolling through large cities such as San Juan, and in targeted tourist areas, such as Old San Juan.

Beaches

All the beaches on the island are public with one exception—the artificial beach at the Caribe Hilton in San Juan. Many hotels are situated right on the beach; if they aren't, they are but a short walk away. Hotels that do not enjoy such proximity usually provide a shuttle to the beach free of charge. **Luquillo Beach** is probably the best beach on the island for swimming. The waters are calm, and the coral reefs protect the pristine lagoon from the stronger waves of the Atlantic. Picnic tables are available as well as camp facilities. Also suitable for swimming is **Seven Seas**, a long strand with compacted sand. Trailers may be parked nearby as well as tents pitched. Water sports of all kinds can be arranged at **Sun Bay**, a sugar-white beach on Vieques. Vessels for sailing may be rented here. One of the most famous beaches is **Condado Beach**, along Ashford Avenue in San Juan. It's a beauty-watcher's delight, especially for those who want to see the latest trend in swimwear and the prettiest island girls. Within walking distance are the long beaches of **Rincón**, **Cabo Rojo** and **Paguera**. Surfers claim that the best waves are along the Atlantic coastline from Borinquén Point south to Rincón. The surf is best from October through April. In summer, La Concha and Aviones have the best curls. All these beaches have board rentals nearby.

The best beaches near San Juan, are at Isla Verde in front of the major hotels.

Underwater

Many knowledgeable divers regard the 51st state as little more than a hub for changing planes en route to Bonaire. The undersea reality is quite different. Some of the Caribbean's best and least exploited diving can be found in Puerto Rico. Why isn't it more famous? One reason may be that San Juan and the island's biggest resort area lie on the long northern coast, which offers none of Puerto Rico's prime diving. You have to venture away from the tourist mecca—to **Fajardo**, tiny **Parguera**, or the offshore islands—to experience the most succulent reefs and walls. Additionally, as happens on some other regional islands with a substantial variety of top-side activities, diving frequently takes a back-seat to a diversified vacation. So, to whet your appetite, pack up the car for a front-row tour of Puerto Rico's coastline.

When combined with **Culebra**, the east coast offers the island's greatest concentration of dive sites. Mini-walls, spur-and-groove formations, and solid marine life are standouts, but there is a wide variety of reef topographies to sample; at **Red Hog**, for instance, the abrupt wall drops 1000 feet. Day trips from San Juan are possible (it's less than an hour drive to Fajardo or Humacao) while offshore Culebra, in particular, has several outstanding dives. Diving on the sprawling south coast is found on the stretch between Ponce and tiny **La Parguera** where hotels are low-key and swamps of mangrove replace beaches, deterring a number of would-be visitors. But the dive shops overlooking the patch reefs of La Parguera will proudly stack their precipitate wall—which is 22 miles long and plunges 3000 feet—against any other in the Caribbean. Throw in a stunning phosphorescent bay (you'll swim, not dive) and you have a sparkling marine experience. Circling around to Puerto Rico's choppy west coast, there are lightly visited patch reef sites between Boqueron and Aguadilla, and attractive underwater caves near Isabela. But the best is found around two offshore destinations, **Desecheo** and **Mona Islands**, which yield a spectacular glimpse of what Caribbean diving might have been like a few decades ago, before overfishing and coral destruction began to take their toll. These two islands (and Culebra) illustrate one local problem: many of the best sites are an hour or more away from a dock. If you want convenient diving, stick to the reefs off **Humacao** or quiet La Parguera, where great sites are closer to shore. Visibility varies more than wildly, but averages 75 feet or more, and can extend to 150 feet on the really good days; the east coast sites can be impacted by freshwater runoff more than the other areas.

Long ignored, environmental concerns have finally become a front burner issue for local divers. The government has not instituted a permanent mooring system, which means a number of reefs in heavily traveled cruising locations are anchor-damaged; the busy Fajardo area is one abused spot. The dive operations will apparently have to undertake this project on their own. Although there are more than two dozen dive shops encircling the island, the three listed below are the standouts. Some of the other operations are not environmentally-oriented and others have shown inconsistent ownership. Watch for this to shake out in coming years, as dedicated divers focus more attention on Puerto Rico as a legitimate underwater destination. Dive style is friendly and casual, and it's not uncommon to be diving with the actual owners of the shops, which are generally smaller outfits than typically found in the Caribbean.

The Cracks

An earthquake faultline beneath a cliff creates a spectacular swim-through fissure immediately off the coast from Humacao. The resulting maze of cracks and caves is mostly rock, with coral buttresses dropping to a sand floor, 80 feet down. Gobies man the cleaning stations, while the area's channels serve as veritable freeways for the reef fish and lobster to scoot about.

Desecheo Island

Roughly 30 different sites surround this tiny, uninhabited outpost, ringed by fringing reefs which lead to an immense drop-off. Turtles, stingrays and eels are common, as are large schools of jacks, but Desecheo is famous for cracks and caverns sliced into the island below sea level. Huge barrel sponges, red rope sponges and a whole field of immense lavender sea fans color the depths. The island is a one-hour boat ride from either Aguadilla or Rincon; access across the channel can sometimes be rough, making most of the island's sites for intermediate or better divers.

Fallen Rock

A staggering wall dive, suitable for nearly all abilities, the titular item is a house-sized limestone boulder which separated from the site's spur-and-groove system, leaving a deep gash in the wall after falling to a shelf 120 feet down. Locals refer to an adjacent trench as the L.A. Highway due to the breathtaking quantity of colorful tropicals converging on the busy throughway, which is paved with rare orange ball corallimophs, plume worms, black gorgonians, bluebell tunicates and more.

Mona Island

Forty-five miles off Puerto Rico's western coast, midway across the bumpy channel leading to the Dominican Republic, lies breathtaking Mona Island, which the government tourism office refers to as the "Galapagos of the Caribbean." In addition to sheltering at least five marine species found nowhere else, Mona's isolation guarantees spectacular diving through pristine spur-and-groove reef structures, patch reefs, dead vertical walls and an underwater cave system, La Carmelitas. At least 11 shipwrecks, including several Spanish galleons, adorn Mona's reefs, and the island has been nominated as a national marine sanctuary. It's a rough ride to the island—four to five hours, depending on sea conditions—and visitors will be foregoing all the usual amenities (there's no electricity, for starters), but Mona is a unique destination and represents some of the last true virgin diving in the Caribbean.

The Pinnacles

One of the reef locations close to Parguera, the Pinnacles is a popular dive due to its delightful architecture, but can only be visited mornings, or when currents allow. A series of ancient coral structures shaped like immense mushrooms decorate this fantasy landscape, like a warped Disney dream out of the deep. Plenty of invertebrates to peruse, and delightful red-lipped blennies filtering through the dense forests of elkhorn coral.

The Reserve

Four miles off the Humacao docks, the Reserve boasts a well-defined spur-and-groove reef structure featuring large star and brain coral heads (50 to 80 feet). A few bigger pelagics visit the site, as well as good-sized green moray eels and hunky hogfish, but a colorful assortment of smaller tropicals are always guaranteed.

Dive Shops

Aquatica Underwater Adventures

Aguadilla; ☎ *(809) 890-6071.*

Small, but full service PADI dive center, opened in 1985. Specializes in underwater photo/video training. Two tank dive, $65 in immediate area, or $85 to Desecheo; shore diving possible. Can arrange charters to Mona.

Coral Head Divers

Palmas del Mar Resort, Humacao; ☎ *(800) 635-4529 or (809) 850-7208.*

One of the island's more firmly established operations (since 1978), a PADI and NAUI outfit with training to assistant instructor. Requires computers on all dives (included in price if you don't have your own); two tank dive, $75. Resort course, $45. All sites within 30 minutes from dock.

Parguera Divers

La Parguera; ☎ *(809) 899-4015.*

Smaller operation, but owner Efra Figueroa is respected islandwide and pioneered most of the Parguera sites. PADI and NAUI affiliated. Two-tank dive, $65, including lunch ($80 if you didn't bring your equipment). All Parguera dives within 30 minutes.

On Foot

It speaks well of Puerto Rico and its visitors that **El Yunque National Forest** is probably the single most popular day trip outside San Juan, drawing upward of a million visitors annually. Thirteen trails of varying length cover 23 miles of the park's verdant terrain, though it may surprise you to discover that most of these paths are paved. In theory, this helps prevent erosion (the summits receive up to 240 inches of rain a year), but the pavement may also be a slight concession to taming the wilds for city dwellers and tourists. With the exception of the longer **El Toro** and **El Yunque** trails, most of these hikes will take no more than an hour or two. The 28,000-acre El Yunque preserve covers four different types of forest, and is home to 240 species of tropical trees, flowers and wildlife, including 20 varieties of orchids and 50 types of ferns. A quarter-sized tree frog, the *coqui*, exists only on Puerto Rico and has become a local mascot, while the island's extremely rare Puerto Rican parrot—only a couple dozen in the mid-70s—is making a gradual comeback in the El Yunque forests.

Trails are not limited to those found in El Yunque; it's worth investigating some of the 19 other existing forest preserves sprinkled around the island.

The bat-filled **Rio Camuy Cave** features the third-largest subterranean river in the world. **Pinones Forest**, just east of San Juan, contains the island's biggest thicket of mangroves, and several other preserves line the island's scenic **Panoramic Route**. There are a few snake species on the island, but none are poisonous; one, the Puerto Rican boa constrictor is large enough to be intimidating—as long as seven feet—but it's considered harmless to humans.

The Big Tree/La Mina Trail

El Yunque's popular Big Tree trail starts at kilometer mark 10.4 on Route 191, and tours the rainforest on its way to La Mina Falls. En route, you'll pass through the dense tabonuco forest, which includes a variety of ferns, draping vines and the endemic laurel sabino. The falls of La Mina (the mine) are about a half-hour walk; from here, you may continue on to another, larger waterfall, and to the gold mine which gave the area its name. Allow two-to-three hours, round-trip.

El Toro Trail

Also called the Tradewinds Trail, El Toro is El Yunque's highest point, (3524 feet), and commands spectacular views, although it is frequently shrouded in clouds. Still, the walk is the island's longest maintained trail, and it doesn't travel via pavement, meaning the rainy season can bring muddy sections and washouts. The six-mile trail begins on Route 191, just beyond the El Yunque Trail, and passes through all four types of forest found within the park: the rain forest of the lower elevations, the palo colorado forest (where the Puerto Rican parrot lives), the more open sierra palm forest, and the dwarf or elfin forest, where stunted and windblown trees are draped with moss near the summit ridges. Allow the whole day for a round-trip, or, arrange for a pickup and connect with Route 186 on the other side of El Toro.

El Yunque/Bano De Oro/Mount Britton Trail

Beginning in the Caimitillo Picnic Area, the main trail ascends the slopes which lead to the summits of El Yunque and Mount Britton (3495 and 3088 feet, respectively). You'll pass through a bounty of pink impatiens which carpet much of the forest floor, while the lush sierra palm forest offers exotic bromeliads and other epiphytes. This is the easiest way into the unusual dwarf forest which blankets the upper ridges and requires three-to-four hours of moderate hiking to fully explore the various side trails.

Trekking Tour Groups

Encantos Ecotours

San Juan; ☎ *(800) 272-7241 or (809) 272-0005.*
Diversified outdoor touring organization, visiting a different part of the island each day of the week, including manatee encounters, El Yunque walks, biking excursions, river swims, Culebra trips, kayaking, etc. Groups limited to 20 people; $89–149, including lunch and transportation costs; percentage of fee goes to local conservation foundations. Three day Mona Island trips scheduled once a month, $599. Whale watching trips in winter. Stump Jumper mountain bike rentals, $30 per day; $100 per week.

By Pedal

Puerto Ricans are devoted to touring their island. They also adore driving and positively love their cars. Bicycles are regrettably few and far between. This is not to say that you won't be welcome on the island's roads. One visiting rider noted that, although locals drive everywhere and quickly, they respected his right-of-way, at least out of curiosity, he mused. The intricate network of paved roads provides stirring challenges, from coastal highways to meandering mountain byways. One obvious route is to circumnavigate the island's perimeter—almost 300 miles, plus side-trips—which would make for an excellent one week biking vacation, but don't discount the island's lush interior which is more interesting than many parts of the developed coastline. One area which invites exploration by mountain bike is **El Yunque National Forest**. Route 191 used to connect the north and south entrances of the park for cars, but a huge landslides closed the road and there are currently no plans to reopen it; tooling through this lightly traveled section of the park on a mountain bike would be quite enjoyable (the landslide area can be traversed on a path). This ride can be done as a moderate day trip out of San Juan. Another attractive area for off-roading are the trails of the **Bosque de Susua**, a forest reserve located between Mayaguez and Ponce; the entire southwest offers excellent riding, but carry a path kit for thorns. A pair of associations covering both mountain and road bikers exist on the island, and we may see cycling activities develop in coming years. Bike rentals are available from Encantos Ecotours in San Juan (see "One Foot" above); their staff is an excellent resource for visitors interested in adventurous excursions.

What Else to See Around the Island

The world's largest rum distillery is the famed **Bacardi Distillery**, a short hop across the San Juan Bay by ferry. Daily tours are offered through its 127 acres and plant, where 100,000 gallons can be distilled daily. Complimentary rum drinks are offered at the beginning of the tour, so by the time you've finished, you're bonkered enough to want to stock up at the gift shop. The prices of Bacardi rums are better here than in the U.S. and some rums not sold on the mainland are excellent presents for the "exclusive" sort.

The **Arecibo Observatory** (two hours west of San Juan) is the site of the world's largest radar/radio telescope, operated by Cornell University and the National Science Foundation. Here scientists monitor radio emissions from distant galaxies, pulsars, mysterious quasars and, perhaps, even more mysterious sources. This is also home base for **SETI**, the Search for Extraterrestrial Intelligence, and rumor has it that great strides has been made in that direction, although the results of research still remains difficult to obtain. A 600-ton suspended platform hovers over a 20-acre dish set in a sinkhole 565 feet below.

After 30 years of silence, the **Hacienda Buena Vista**, an early 19th-century coffee plantation, has been reopened to the public following a massive restoration. Located along the Canas River just north of Ponce, the hacienda is a step back in time, and visitors are invited to explore the plantation's mills and two-story estate house, observe original machinery in action, and enjoy a sensory feast—coffee drying in the trays, and pineapples and bananas growing on the hillsides. The ground floor of the manor estate, now a museum, contains old maps, photographs, bills of sale and other memorabilia of hacienda life. The rooms have been furnished with authentic period pieces from the 1850s, right down to the chamber pots, armoires, bathtubs and family portraits. Experts have considered the machinery—dating from the early days of the industrial revolution—of international importance because such machines rarely survived on the U.S. mainland. The entire estate resembles a hamlet of bygone days, including the manor house, the coffee and corn mills, a masonry storage shed that doubles as a hurricane shelter, and the former slave quarters that became a coffee storage and drying shed. Feel free to take a leisurely stroll on paths over which wagons once traveled carrying sacks of just harvested coffee beans or newly milled cornmeal. The hills surrounding Buena Vista (aptly named "beautiful view") are rich with gurgling streams, cascading waterfalls and a variety of plant and animal life. Ducks wander freely over the grounds. Also available for sighting are the Puerto Rican screech owl, the mangrove cuckoo and the hummingbird.

Historical Sites

Capilla de Cristo ★★★

Calle del Cristo, Old San Juan, *(809) 721-2400.*

The Christ Chapel was built in 1753 after a horse rider's life was supposedly spared after a tragic accident. (Supposedly, because historical records say the youth did, indeed, die.) In any event, the small silver altar is dedicated to the Christ of Miracles.

Casa de los Contrafuertes   ★★★★

Calle San Sebastian 101, Old San Juan, ☎ *(809) 724-5477.*
Hours open: 9 a.m.–4:30 p.m.

Called the House of Buttresses (for obvious reasons once you see it), this is believed to be the oldest residence left in Old San Juan, dating back to the early 18th century. Inside are two museums, one devoted to graphic arts, the other displaying a 19th-century pharmacy.

Cathedral de San Juan   ★★★

Calle del Cristo 151, Old San Juan, ☎ *(809) 722-0861.*
Hours open: 8:30 a.m.–4:30 p.m.

The San Juan Cathedral was built in 1540, destroyed by hurricane in 1529, looted in 1598, and damaged by another hurricane in 1615. Today it holds the remains of Ponce de Leon and the relic of San Pio, a Roman martyr. Sunday masses begin at 9:00 a.m.

Convento de los Dominicos   ★★★

Plaza de San Jose, Old San Juan, ☎ *(809) 724-5949.*

This was Puerto Rico's first convent, started in 1523. It was home to Dominican friars until 1838, when it became barracks for the United States Army. Today, it is headquarters for the Institute of Puerto Rican Culture. Inside you'll find the old chapel, art exhibits and a fine gift shop.

Fort San Cristobel   ★★★★

Calle Norzagaray, Old San Juan, ☎ *(809) 729-6960.*
Hours open: 9 a.m.–5 p.m.

This massive fort dates back to 1634. Its walls rise 150 feet above sea level, and it covers 27 acres. Now run under the auspices of the National Park Service, the site includes a replica of 18th-century Spanish troop barracks. Free tours are given daily from 10:00 a.m.–4:00 p.m.

Fort San Jeronimo   ★★★

Next to the Caribe Hilton, Cordado Bay, ☎ *(809) 724-5949.*

This tiny fort was attacked by the British in 1797, 11 years after it was built. Now run by the Institute of Puerto Rican Culture, it houses a small military museum.

Fuerte San Felipe del Morro   ★★★★

Calle Norzagaray, Old San Juan, ☎ *(809) 729-6960.*
Hours open: 9 a.m.–5 p.m.

This fort, commonly known as El Morro, guards the entrance to San Juan Bay. The Spaniards started construction in 1540, but it wasn't until 1787 that the fort was deemed complete. Now run under the auspices of the National Park Service, the six-level fort can be explored via guided tours (free, from 10 a.m. to 4 p.m.) or on your own. The dramatic fort contains dungeons, lookouts, barracks and vaults, as well as a small museum on its history.

Governor Mansion

Recito Oeste Street, Old San Juan, ☎ *(809) 721-2400.*
Hours open: 9 a.m.–4 p.m.

Puerto Rico boasts a lot of "oldest in the Western Hemisphere" —here's the oldest executive mansion in continuous use. It started as a fortress in 1553 and is the office and residence of Puerto Rico's governor. Now a U.S. National Historic Site, the mansion can be toured in the mornings, with tours of the gardens running all day.

Inglesia de San Jose ★★★

Plaza de San Jose, Old San Juan, ☎ *(809) 725-7501.*
Hours open: 8:30 a.m.–4 p.m.

The San Jose Church is the second-oldest in the Western Hemisphere, dating back to 1532. It was originally a Dominican chapel and was the family church of Ponce de Leon's descendants, many of whom are buried here. Among the highlights are a crucifix that belonged to the explorer, oil paintings by Jose Campeche and Francisco Oller, and ornate processional floats. Sunday mass is at 12:15 p.m.

Museums and Exhibits

Casa Blanca ★★★

Calle San Sebastian 1, San Juan, ☎ *(809) 724-4102.*

The land on which the "White House" sits was given to explorer Ponce de Leon by the Spanish Crown. He died before the house was built in 1521, but his descendants lived there for some 250 years. In 1779, it was taken over by the Spanish military, then used later by the United States as a residence for military commanders. Today the mansion is restored to its former glory and is a National Historic Monument. It houses two museums, one on the Taino Indians (believed to be Puerto Rico's first inhabitants) and one on the house's history, with emphasis on life in the 16th and 18th centuries. Casa Blanca is the oldest continuously occupied residence in the Western Hemisphere.

La Casa del Libro ★★★

Calle del Cristo, Old San Juan, ☎ *(809) 723-0354.*
Hours open: 11 a.m.–4:30 p.m.

Exhibits on printing and bookmaking are displayed at this 19th-century house. Noteworthy are pages from the Gutenberg Bible, a decree signed by Ferdinand and Isabella concerning Columbus' second voyage, and other pre-16th century examples of the art.

Museo de Arte y Historia ★★★

Calle Norzagaray, Old San Juan, ☎ *(809) 724-1875.*

This center for Puerto Rican arts and crafts displays works by local artists. It was a marketplace in the 1850s in a previous incarnation. Audiovisual shows in English on the city's history are shown daily at 11 a.m. and 1:15 p.m.

Museo de Pablo Casals ★★★

Calle San Sebastian 101, Old San Juan, ☎ *(809) 723-9185.*
Hours open: 9:30 a.m.–5:30 p.m.

The famed Spanish cellist spent his last years in Puerto Rico, leaving behind a collection of memorabilia from his long and distinguished career. The 18th-century house displays his cello, manuscripts and photos from his life, as well as videotaped performances, shown on request.

Parks and Gardens

Cabezas de San Juan Nature Res   ★ ★ ★ ★

Route 987, Fajardo, ☎ *(809) 722-5882.*

Located on a peninsula, this nature reserve encompasses 316 acres and 124 acres of lagoons. It contains all of Puerto Rico's ecosystems except for the rainforest. A two-hour guided tour (reservations essential) will take you through a half-mile-long coral reef, mangrove swamps, beaches, a dry forest, and beds of turtle grass (thalassia). A highlight is El Faro, a lighthouse built in 1880 and still used by the U.S. Coast Guard. The small nature center in the lighthouse, which is a designated National Historic Place, has touch tanks, aquariums, and an observation deck. Bilingual tours are at 9:30 a.m., 10 a.m., 10:30 a.m.; the one at 2 p.m. is in English only. Well worth a visit.

Theatre

Centro de Ballas Artes   ★ ★ ★ ★

De Diego and Ponce de Leon avs, San Juan, ☎ *(809) 724-4747.*

This fine arts center is the largest in the Caribbean. Call the box office or inquire at your hotel about events—from operas to plays—while you're in town

Teatro Tapia   ★ ★ ★ ★

Ave. Ponce de Leon, San Juan, ☎ *(809) 722-0470.*

Dating back to 1832, this is one of the Western Hemisphere's oldest theaters. It is named after Puerto Rican playwright Alejandro Tapia y Rivera. Check with the box office for a schedule for upcoming plays and cultural events.

Tours

Bacardi Rum Plant   ★ ★ ★

Poute 888, Catano, ☎ *(809) 788-1500.*

Located across the bay from San Juan (a short hop ferry), this plant offers 45-minute tours at 9 a.m., 10:30 a.m., noon, and 4 p.m. You'll see the distillery and bottling plant, and get to judge the results yourself.

Caribbean National Forest   ★ ★ ★ ★ ★

Near Luquillo Beach, Puerto Rico, ☎ *(809) 887-2875.*

Known simply as El Yunque, this pristine spot encompasses 28,000 acres of virgin rainforest, with some 240 species of tropical trees, flowers and wildlife. It is home to rare creatures like the Puerto Rican boa, which grows to seven feet, the colorful Puerto Rican parrot, and 26 other species found nowhere else. There are more than 20 kinds of orchids, 50 varieties of ferns, and millions of tiny tree frogs, who serenade visitors with their tiny croaks. Stop at the Sierra Palm Visitor Center on Route 191 to peruse the interesting exhibits and pick up a map. Numerous trails traverse the park, leading to waterfalls, natural pools and the peak of El Toro.

Rio Camuy Cave Park   ★ ★ ★ ★

Route 129, near Arecibo, ☎ *(809) 898-3100.*
Hours open: 8 a.m.–4 p.m.

Located in Northwest Puerto Rico, 2.5 hours from San Juan, is one of the world's largest cave networks. Sixteen entrances have been found and seven miles of passages explored so far. A tram takes you to the cave, where you get out and walk through, passing sinkholes, one of the world's largest underground rivers, and giant stalagmites and stalactites. The Taino Indians, believed to be Puerto Rico's first inhabitants, also explored the cave. Reservations are essential, as this place is understandably popular.

Sports

Every water sport imaginable is played on Puerto Rico's 272 miles of beachfront. *Balnearios* (public beaches) offer lockers, showers and parking at nominal rates, though they are closed on Mondays, Election Day and Good Friday. For information about overnight stays call ☎ *(809) 722-1551* or *721-2800*. The Puerto Rico Water Sport Federation sets standards and guidelines for members specializing in scuba diving, snorkeling, sailing, deep-sea fishing, windsurfing and other aquatic activities. Members, including the Caribbean School of Aquatics, Coral Head Divers, and many others, can make arrangements for surfing (the 1988 World Cup Surfing Championship was held in Aguadilla), scuba diving, sailing, etc. Arrangements can also be made at the island's many resort hotels.

Puerto Rico hosts many deep-sea fishing tournaments, in which 30 world records have been broken. The **Annual Billfish Tournament** is the world's largest consecutively held tournament of its kind. Deep-sea fishing boats can be chartered in San Juan, Fajardo, Humaco, Mayaguez and other towns. Lake fishing for largemouth bass, peacock bass, sunfish, catfish and tilapia is also popular. For more details, contact the **Department of Natural Resources** ☎ *(809) 722-5938*.

Horseback riding is tremendous on Puerto Rico—the island's palm-lined beaches are romantic settings. Riding and/or trail riding can be arranged through the Palmas del Mar Equestrian Center or the Hacienda Carabali.

Tennis is omnipresent here—there are over 100 tennis courts throughout the island, including 17 in San Juan's Central Park. A total of nine **golf championships** take place on Puerto Rico (public as well as at major resorts). The Hyatt Regency Cerromar and the Hyatt Dorado Beach resorts have two 18-hole Robert Trent Jones courses each. The newest 18-hole course is east of San Juan at the Bahia Beach Plantation. The Berwind Country Club near Rio Grande has an 18-hole course open to the public on Tuesdays, Thursdays and Fridays (except holidays). Ramey Golf Club, an 18-hole course, is located on the former Ramey Air Force Base in Aguadilla, in the northwestern part of the island. Greens fees and prices of equipment rentals vary with the season.

Cockfighting is a popular native spectator sport in Puerto Rico, particularly in the Cordillera Central.

Boating and Cruising

Various locations, Puerto Rico.

Lots of firms will take you out on the high seas for a simple sail or snorkel trip. Most charge about $45 per person. Try: **Fondo de Cristal** *(☎ (809) 889-5891)*, **Island Safari** *(☎ (809) 728-6606)*, **Spread Eagle** *(☎ (809) 863-1905)*, **Erin Go Braugh** *(☎ (809) 860-4401)*, **East Wind Catamaran** *(☎ (809) 863-2821)*, **Captain Jack Becker** *(☎ (809) 860-0861)*, and **Land and Sea Excursions** *(☎ (809) 382-4877)*.

Golf

Various locations, Puerto Rico.

Unlike most of the Caribbean islands, which have just one or two golf courses (if any), Puerto Rico has a wealth of greens. All are 18-hole courses unless otherwise noted. Rio Grande: **Bahia Beach Plantation** *(☎ (809) 256-5600)*, **Berwind Country Club** *(☎ (809) 876-3056)*, **Club Riomar** *(☎ (809) 887-3964)*. Fajardo: **Conquistador Resort** *(☎ (809) 863-1000)*. Dorado: **Dorado del Mar Country Club** (nine holes, *☎ (809) 796-2030)*, **Hyatts Dorado and Cerromar** (38 holes, *☎ (809) 796-1234)*. Humacao: **Palmas del Mar Resort** *(☎ 852-6000)* Aguadilla: **Punta Borinquen** *(☎ (809) 890-2987)*. Check at your hotel or call **Luiz Ortiz** *(☎ (809) 786-3859)* for access to courses in metropolitan San Juan.

Horseback Riding

Various locations, Puerto Rico.

Just hop on a horse and ride off into the sunset (or along the beach or through the rainforest) at **Hacienda Carabali** *(☎ (809) 889-5820)* or **Palmas del Mar's** Equestrian Center *(☎ (809) 852-6000)*.

Watersports

Various locations, Puerto Rico.

If your hotel doesn't offer watersports, try one of these. For general watersport equipment rentals, **Carib Aquatic Adventures in Miramar** *(☎ (809) 724-1882)*, does everything from boat rentals to deep-sea fishing excursions. For scuba diving, call: **Adventure by the Sea** *(Cerro Gordo, ☎ (809) 251-4923)*, **Caribbean Divers** *(☎ (809) 722-7393)*, **Caribbean School of Aquatics** *(Condado, ☎ (809) 728-6606)*, **Coral Head Divers** *(Humacao, ☎ (809) 850-7208)*, **Dorado Marine Center** *(☎ (809) 796-4645)*, and **Mundo Submarino** *(Isla Verde, ☎ (809) 791-5764)*. For deep-sea fishing, try: **Benitez** *(San Juan, ☎ (809) 723-2292)*, **Makaira Hunter** *(Miramar, ☎ (809) 397-8028)*, **Southern Witch** *(Miramar, ☎ (809) 731-9252)*, **Western Tourist Services** *(☎ (809) 834-4008)*.

Where to Stay

Fielding's Highest Rated Hotels in Puerto Rico

★★★★★	El Conquistador Resort	$170–$420
★★★★★	Horned Dorset Primavera	$150–$440
★★★★★	Hyatt Dorado Beach	$160–$490
★★★★★	Hyatt Regency Cerromar	$165–$420
★★★★★	Sands Hotel & Casino	$290–$305
★★★★	Caribe Hilton & Casino	$200
★★★★	Condado Plaza Hotel	$195–$355
★★★★	El San Juan Hotel/Casino	$250–$995
★★★★	Palmas del Mar Humacao	$145–$715
★★★★	Radisson Ambassador Plaza	$170–$320

Fielding's Most Romantic Hotels in Puerto Rico

★★★★	Caribe Hilton & Casino	$200–$1200
★★★★	El San Juan Hotel/Casino	$250–$995
★★★★★	Horned Dorset Primavera	$150–$440
★★★★	Palmas del Mar Humacao	$145–$715

Fielding's Budget Hotels in Puerto Rico

★	Green Isle Inn	$43–$73
★★	Parador Banos de Coamo	$55–$65
★	Parador La Familia	$50–$70
★★	Sea Gate Guest House	$40–$85
★	Arcade Inn	$40–$90

Accommodations in Puerto Rico rank among the finest in the world for th value. The top-class resorts and hotels offer all the amenities of sophistica tion, from casinos to spas, to some of the most glorious pool complexes i the world. Hotel spas on Puerto Rico have simply raised the facility to an ar The **Caribe Spa** at the Caribe Hilton offers both Universal and Nautilu weight machines, aerobic and yoga classes, aerobicycles, massages, herb. wraps, loofah body polish and facials. The **Penthouse Spa** at the El San Jua Hotel & Casino offers fitness evaluations, supervised weight-loss progran aerobics classes, sauna, steam room and massage. The fitness center at th **Palmas del Mar Resort** in Humacao features hydrafitness exercise equipmen exercise program, free-weight training and computerized evaluations. Th **Plaza Spa** at the Condado Plaza Hotel & Casino features universal weigh training machines, video exercycles, sauna, whirlpool, facials and massage In contrast, moderate-priced hotels are rather anonymous and make tempting either to splurge or economize. But budget accommodations ca offer some wonderful treasures, especially if you look among the goverr ment-sponsored inns called *paradores*, which can turn a tropical vacatio into a most memorable and intimate experience.

In San Juan and Condado Area

Today the Condado area, which runs around the Atlantic between Ocean Park an Miramar, is one of the main areas for hotels and resorts, now returning to its glitzy rep c years gone by. The **Condado Plaza Hotel & Casino** is practically a planet unto itself, wit a full range of eateries, casinos, Vegas-type shows, its own shopping mall and top Amer can furnishings. One of the closest to the airport is **El San Juan Hotel & Casino**, also a lux ury property of top proportions, including an enormous pool that inspires a lot of soci climbing. A good moderate option is **Carib Inn**, near the airport, but a mere short wa to the beach. In Isla Verde, east of San Juan/ Santurce, is the U.S.-run **TraveLodge**, wit comfortably large beds, modernized bathrooms and an acceptable pool.

Hotels and Resorts

Best Western Pierre	**$97–$145**	★ ★ ★

105 de Diego Avenue, ☎ *(800) 528-1234, (809) 721-1200, FAX (809) 721-3118. Single: $97–$135. Double: $107–$145.*

Located in the heart of the Santurce business district, four blocks from Condade this Best Western appeals to business travelers on a budget. Facilities are limited t a restaurant, bar, and pool.

Carib Inn Tennis Club	**$105–$320**	★

Isla Verde, ☎ *(800) 548-8217, (809) 791-3535, FAX (809) 791-0104. Single: $105–$120. Double: $110–$320.*

Located near the airport and a few minutes from the beach, this resort caters to ten nis players, with eight courts, a ball machine, and video playback. Oddly enough guests must pay extra to use the courts, and even more still for night play, whic gives the feeling of being nickeled and dimed. The tennis theme continues with pool shaped like a racquet. Accommodations are adequate but cry out for renov.

tion. There are a few restaurants and bars on-site, and the salsa bands on Friday and Saturday nights are popular.

aribe Hilton & Casino $200–$1200   ★ ★ ★ ★

Fort San Jeronimo, ☎ *(800) 468-8585, (809) 721-0303, FAX (809) 724-6992.*
Single: $200–$755. Double: $225–$1200.

This behemoth does a huge business with meetings and conventions, so you'll be sharing facilities with lots of folks wearing name tags. Nevertheless, this is a smashing resort, with lots going on all the time. There's a putting green, six tennis courts, a health club with air-conditioned racquetball and squash courts, supervised programs for kids, six restaurants, and several bars, one with live entertainment. Snorkel and scuba equipment can be found on the small beach. Guest rooms are housed in two towers, one 10 stories, the other 20. All are quite decent, and most have ocean views. Business travelers are catered to on three executive levels. Fort San Jeronimo, which dates back to the 16th century, is footsteps away. The $40 million that Hilton poured into the resort a few years back really shows, but individual travelers may be happier at a smaller property, away from conventioneers.

ondado Beach Trio $140–$195   ★ ★ ★

Ashford Avenue, ☎ *(800) 468-2775, (809) 721-6090.*
Single: $140–$195. Double: $140–$195.

This government-owned complex consists of two hotels and the El Centro Convention Center, all greatly renovated with great results. The Spanish Colonial-style Hotel Condado Beach dates back to 1919. Guestrooms are elegant and tastefully done with nice furnishings and original art. The grounds include a few restaurants and bars, a casino and a pool. The nearby La Concha Hotel is oriented more toward families, with facilities like two tennis courts and a pool. Guest rooms there are not as nice as at Condado Beach, but they are cheaper. There's also a disco, two restaurants, and live entertainment in one of the two bars. The disco is quite upscale and shaped like a conch shell. Guests can use the facilities at both hotels; Condado Beach has better service. The "beach" in the title is quite narrow. Lots of conventioneers meet and stay at this complex.

ondado Plaza Hotel $195–$355   ★ ★ ★ ★

999 Ashford Avenue, ☎ *(800) 468-8588, (809) 721-1000, FAX (809) 722-4613.*
Single: $195–$335. Double: $225–$355.

This full-service resort has a small beach, but most guests hang out at one of the five pools. The five-acre property was renovated in 1993, with good results. Accommodations are housed in two towers and are quite nice, though only some have sea views. Those shelling out extra for a Plaza Club room enjoy added amenities and the use of a lounge. The grounds include two tennis courts, a fitness center, air-conditioned squash and racquetball courts, a business center, and Puerto Rico's largest casino. There's also several eateries, bars and a hopping disco.

Canario by the Lagoon $65–$110   ★ ★

4 Calle Clemenceau, ☎ *(809) 722-5058, FAX (809) 723-8590.*
Single: $65–$85. Double: $75–$110.

Located in the heart of Condado, this small European-style hotel is just a bloc
from the beach. Rooms are basic but comfortable. Besides a tour desk, there are fe
facilities on-site, but many within walking distance. Not bad for the rates.

El Canario by the Sea $80–$125

4 Condado Avenue, ☎ (800) 533-2649, (809) 722-8640, FAX (809) 725-4921.
Single: $80. Double: $95–$125.

Located just off the beach, this small hotel is family-run. Rooms are modest bu
comfortable and air-conditioned. Each morning, a complimentary continent.
breakfast is served in the courtyard. There's a bar and tour desk, but little else in th
way of extras. Good value, though.

El San Juan Hotel/Casino $250–$995   ★★★★

Isla Verde Avenue, ☎ (800) 468-2818, (809) 791-1000, FAX (809) 263-0178.
Single: $250–$430. Double: $305–$995.

Opulence dominates at this well-known resort, one of the Caribbean's best and ce
tainly among the most lavish. Accommodations are luxurious, with VCRs, stereo
TVs in the bathroom, minibars and modern art. Some have lanais and sitting area
while others have sunken baths, whirlpools, or private garden spas. Facilities a
quite extensive, and the service is excellent. The grounds include seven restauran
ranging from the formal Dar Tiffany to casual snackbars, eight bars, a disco,
casino, and three lighted tennis courts. There's also a Chinese restaurant housed
a pavilion from the 1964 New York World's Fair, all watersports including divir
and waterskiing, a modern health club, and a pool for the kiddies. Staying here is a
experience you won't soon forget.

Grande Hotel El Convento $85–$200   ★

*55 Condado Avenue, Cristo Street, ☎ (800) 468-2779, (809) 721-0810, FAX (80
725-7895.*
Single: $85–$175. Double: $95–$200.

This highrise hotel consists of two linked towers. Accommodations range fro
standard guest rooms to suites with kitchenettes. The modest grounds include
casino, two restaurants, a bar and two pools, one for kids. Decent for the rates, b
nothing special.

Holiday Inn Crowne Plaza $185–$390   ★★

Highway 187, ☎ (800) 468-4578, (809) 253-2929, FAX (809) 253-0079.
Single: $185. Double: $205–$390.

Located on Isla Verde Beach, close to the airport, this highrise is just a few years ol
Accommodations are modern and comfortable, and most have sea views off the ba
cony. Facilities include a pretty casino, business center, gym, a pool, and two resta
rants and three bars. All quite acceptable, but this hotel is so generic you'd hard
know you're in the Caribbean, and airport noise, particularly low-flying jets, can
obnoxious.

Hotel Portal Del Condado $95–$125   ★

76 Condado Avenue, ☎ (809) 721-9010, FAX (809) 724-3714.
Single: $95. Double: $115–$125.

Located in Condado within walking distance of the beach, this modest hotel offers clean and comfortable rooms for reasonable rates. There's no pool but guests can work on their tans on a rooftop deck.

Radisson Ambassador Plaza $170–$320 ★★★★

1369 Ashford Avenue, ☎ (800) 333-3333, (809) 721-7300, FAX (809) 723-6151.
Single: $170–$310. Double: $180–$320.
Set in the heart of the Condado district, this glitzy hotel consists of an older hotel and an all-suite tower. Accommodations vary, but all are pleasant, though only some have ocean views. As expected, the suites offer the plushest digs and are well-suited to business travelers. Facilities include a rooftop swimming pool, business services center, health club, supervised children's programs, casino, and several restaurants and bars, one with entertainment nightly. This place has come a long way from its Howard Johnson roots.

Radisson Normandie $160–$240 ★★★

Munoz Rivera Avenue, ☎ (800) 333-3333, (809) 729-2929, FAX (809) 729-3083.
Single: $160–$200. Double: $240.
Housed in a landmark art deco building that dates back to 1940, this hotel is on the outskirts of Old San Juan. The hotel is shaped like a ship, and the staff wears nautical garb. Guest rooms are spacious and nicely decorated with art deco touches. Those on the Concierge Level enjoy extra amenities. Facilities include a few bars and restaurants and a pool. There's also a small beach.

Ramada Hotel Condado $130–$300 ★★

1045 Ashford Avenue, ☎ (800) 468-2040, (809) 723-8000, FAX (809) 722-8230.
Single: $130–$160. Double: $160–$300.
Located adjacent to the San Juan Convention Center and on the beach, this high-rise offers adequate yet uninspired guest rooms and public areas. Facilities are limited to a bar, restaurant and pool. You can do better at these rates.

Regency Hotel $140–$225 ★★

1005 Ashford Avenue, ☎ (800) 468-2823, (809) 721-0505, FAX (809) 722-2909.
Single: $140–$225. Double: $140–$225.
This modest operation offers spacious guest rooms, studios with kitchenettes, and suites with full kitchens. All have balconies but not necessarily ocean views. Facilities are limited to a restaurant, pool and Jacuzzi. The beach is reached through an underground parking garage, an odd arrangement. Continental breakfast is included in the rates, and while this is nothing to write home about, it offers comfortable housing at a decent price.

San Juan Travelodge $125–$175 ★★

1313 Isla Verde Avenue, ☎ (800) 428-2028, (809) 728-1300, FAX (809) 268-0637.
Single: $125. Double: $140–$175.
Located near the airport, this budget choice offers acceptable rooms, some with balconies. There's a restaurant, deli and lounge on-site, as well as limited room service and a pool.

Sands Hotel & Casino $290–$305 ★★★★★

Isla Verde Road, ☎ (809) 791-6100, FAX (809) 791-8525.

Single: $290. Double: $305.

Situated on five acres fronting three miles of sandy beach, this luxurious property is next door to the splashier El San Juan. Accommodations are generally plush with extras like minibars and floor to ceiling windows. All have balconies but not all have an ocean view. The extensive grounds include five restaurants, three lounges, a huge casino, daily activities, and a large free-form pool with a waterfall and swim-up bar. Nice, but the El San Juan is better, and the rates are comparable.

Apartments and Condominiums

Local Puerto Ricans with luxury apartments or villas often rent their homes during high season, especially those located near the Hyatt Dorado Beach resort. Condominiums in high-rise buildings are also popular for tourist rentals; even rooms in hotels that have kitchenettes can be rented. Among the latter are ESJ Towers, the Regency, and the Excelsior. Shopping is easy because supermarkets tend to boast traditional mainland products along with more Latin-flavored spices, vegetables and fruits, etc.

Inns

Puerto Rico is famous for its network of charming country inns called *paradores puertorriqueños* (established in 1973), which offer superb accommodations and the ideal location for exploring the island's diverse attractions. Several privately owned and operated guest houses also serve as quiet and quaint accommodations far from the maddening crowds. What makes the paradores so special is they are each situated in a historic place or site of unusual scenic beauty. Prices range from $38–$96 per night, double occupancy, and are located from mountains to sea. Most have swimming pools and all offer the island's tantalizing cuisine. Many are even within driving distance from San Juan. Perhaps one of the most special sites is that of the **Parador Baõs de Coamo**, situated on the site of America's oldest thermal springs, once believed to be Ponce de Leon's "fountain of youth." Even FDR took advantage of the medicinal waters, praised by the Indians for more than three centuries. Just a half-hour away is Ponce, the island's second largest city and home to the Caribbean's most extensive art museum.

Casa San Jose $205–$315 ★★★

159 San Jose Street, Old San Juan, ☎ *(800) 223-6510, (809) 723-1212, FAX (809) 723-7620.*

Single: $205–$225. Double: $245–$315.

Set in Old San Juan, this charmer is housed in a converted 17th-century mansion. Each room and suite in the four-story Spanish Colonial house is decorated differently, and all are lovely, furnished with antiques, Persian rugs, Roman tubs, exquisite artworks, and ceiling fans. Suites have one or two bedrooms and even more opulent trappings. The rates include continental breakfast, afternoon tea and evening cocktails. The interior courtyard is accented by a fountain; its pleasant trickling can be heard in every room. Marvelous!

El Canario Inn $80–$125 ★★

1317 Ashford Avenue, Condado, ☎ *(809) 722-3861, FAX (809) 722-0391.*

Single: $80. Double: $95–$125.

This modest inn is located a block from the beach. Rooms are air-conditioned and also have ceiling fans and private baths. They'll feed you breakfast, and there's a communal kitchen for self caterers, as well as lots within walking distance. The very reasonable rates make this a real bargain.

Parador Hacienda Gripinas $64–$107

6a Ocean Drive, Jayuya, ☎ *(800) 443-0266, (809) 721-2884, FAX (809) 889-4520. Single: $64–$74. Double: $64–$107.*

Located on a 20-acre plantation that in the 18th century produced coffee, this small country inn in the mountains is loaded with character. Guest rooms are simple but attractive; most have ceiling fans in lieu of air conditioning. There's little in the way of recreational facilities save a pool and basketball court; note that this area gets a lot of rain. The dining room serves up three tasty squares a day; Sunday brunch is especially popular. Not for those seeking a partying holiday, but perfect for relaxing and enjoying the scenery.

Low Cost Lodging

During low season, mid-April through December, expect to find the most expensive hotels dropping their rates down to a moderate range. Other hotels give special packages for low season. It doesn't hurt to sniff out the possibility of bargaining; just do it tactfully. The Puerto Rico Tourism Company currently recognizes 35 camping areas throughout the island, from El Yunque National Forest to Luquillo Beach and many of the public beaches around the island. Camping facilities in Puerto Rico come with a broad definition, including cottages, pup tents, huts, lean-tos and even trailer homes. Fees range from $5–$12. Don't always count on finding hot water or toilets. Be prepared to go rustic, if necessary.

Arcade Inn $40–$90   ★

8 Taft Street, ☎ *(809) 728-7524. Single: $40–$90. Double: $50–$90.*

This guesthouse is within walking distance to the beach. Rooms are modest but air-conditioned and with private baths; a few efficiencies are also available. There's a bar on the premises, but you'll have to venture out for meals. That's easily done, as there is much within an easy walk.

Atlantic Beach Hotel $60–$140   ★★

1 Calle Vendig, ☎ *(809) 721-6900, FAX (809) 721-6917. Single: $60–$110. Double: $75–$140.*

This modest hotel caters mostly to gays, though anyone is welcome (except for children)—but check your homophobia at the door. Rooms are spartan but comfortable and air-conditioned; not all have private baths, so be sure to request one if that's important to you. The beach is footsteps away. There's no pool but the Jacuzzi offers pleasant soaking. The restaurant serves only breakfast and lunch, with lots of dinner options within walking distance. A complimentary Continental breakfast is served daily on the new roof sundeck.

Green Isle Inn $43–$73   ★

Villamar Street, ☎ *(800) 677-8860, (809) 726-4330, FAX (809) 268-2415. Single: $43–$73. Double: $43–$73.*

This small hotel has basic air-conditioned rooms, many with kitchenettes. There's a bar and restaurant, and two pools. Limited room service is available. The beach is an easy walk.

International Airport   **$80–$90**   ★ ★

Isla Verde, ☎ *(809) 791-1700, FAX (809) 291-4050.*
Single: $80. Double: $90.

Located right in the airport, on the third floor of the terminal building, this budget choice is adequate, but unless you're between flights, there's really no reason to stay here. More atmospheric lodging can be found at similar rates.

Where to Eat

Fielding's Highest Rated Restaurants in Puerto Rico

★★★★★	Horned Dorset Primavera	$15–$45
★★★★★	La Compostela	$15–$29
★★★★★	Ramiro's	$24–$33
★★★★	Amadeus	$8–$16
★★★★	La Chaumiere	$22–$37
★★★	Ajilli-Mojili	$15–$25
★★★	Back Street Hong Kong	$15–$32
★★★	La Casona de Serafin	$10–$31
★★★	La Mallorquina	$14–$30
★★★	Parador Villa Parguera	$5–$20

Fielding's Special Restaurants in Puerto Rico

★★★★★	Horned Dorset Primavera	$15–$45
★★★★★	La Compostela	$15–$29
★★★★★	Ramiro's	$24–$33
★★★★	La Chaumiere	$22–$37
★★★	AjilliMojili	$15–$25

Fielding's Budget Restaurants in Puerto Rico

★★	Butterfly People	$5–$9
★★★	La Bombonera	$5–$8
★★★★	Amadeus	$8–$16
★★	Al Dente	$10–$15
★★★	Parador Villa Parguera	$5–$20

The first thing you must learn before sitting down to dinner in Puerto Ric is the lively island equivalent to "bon appetit"—*Ibuen provecho!* The phras becomes easily prophetic here where traditional island fare as well as contem porary cuisine is lovingly and expertly prepared. Puerto Rican cuisine is a de licious blend of Spanish, African and Taíno Indian cooking. Each of thes traditions have contributed in terms of seasonings, cooking methods an basic ingredients. *Cocina criolla* or creole cuisine, began with the Taínos, th indigenous tribe of the island. The Taínos cultivated many crops, notab *yuca* (yucca), corn, yam and *yautía* (taniers). Yuca was used to prepare *casc be*, a flatbread that was eaten daily and is still enjoyed today. Taínos also use yuca to make vinegar, which was an important seasoning since salt was n used in cooking. Foods introduced by the Spaniards include wheat, chick peas, cilantro, eggplant, onions, coconut, garlic and rum. The African slav trade also brought important foods and techniques to the island, includir pidgin peas, plantains and okra. The African population is also credited wit developing many coconut dishes that remain popular today. Their favori technique was frying, which quickly became the most common way of coo ing on the island. The blending of flavors and ingredients evolved from ge eration to generation, combining to form the Puerto Rican cuisine today.

As for noshing, the island has no lack of things on which to while aw your calories. Fritters are the favorite finger food, and are sold at fritt stands and even incorporated into the daily menus in most homes. The mo famous fritters are *tostones* (fried green plantains), which are used as well as side dish with rice and beans, onion steak or fried pork chops. Other favo ites include *alcapurrias*, made from grated yautia, and green bananas, stuffe with *picadillo* (cooked ground meat), crabmeat or chicken, *empanadilla* small deep-fried flour turnovers with cheddar or swiss cheese, ground me or shredded chicken; *bacalaítos*, flour fritters made from salt codfish; *surru los de maíz* or *surrullitos*, made of cornmeal, shaped like a cigar and serv with a sauce made of mayonnaise and ketchup; and *rellenos de papa*, mashe potato balls stuffed with almost any filling and deep-fried to a crispy textur Other traditional appetizers are chicken nuggets and marinated green b nanas. The latter are now combined with the new ingredients such as f vored vinegars to create interesting variations found even in elega restaurants.

Get used to the fact that side dishes are often as hearty as the main dish Puerto Rico. In fact, if you are dieting and/or trying to save money, eati side dishes can be your vacation saver. Nearly standard for every meal in P erto Rico is *arroz blanco* (white rice boiled in water and oil), and *habichuel* (beans stewed in sofrito (piré of onions, peppers, cilantro, garlic, and s pork), and a tomato and coriander sauce. *Mofongo* is also popular—frie green plantains mashed with garlic, salt and fried pork rinds and rolled int ball. It's usually served with beef or chicken broth or *carne frita* (pork meat, diced and fried).

The national soup of Puerto Rico is *asopao*, a hearty chicken and rice gumbo-like soup which can serve as an entree. Sometimes it's made with lobster and shrimp. Roast suckling pig is a national dish, especially for holidays. Steak and onions is an everyday dish, as are pork ribs stewed or prepared with yellow rice and green pigeon peas. With such exquisite access to the sea, fish dishes are supremely fresh and display the island's Spanish heritage, as they are mostly prepared in a sofrito-based sauce or *escabeche* (marinated) style. Escabeche is a combination of olive oil, white vinegar and spices. *Bacalho* (salt cod) has been a menu staple for centuries; other seafood to look for are red snapper, shrimp, langostinos (saltwater crayfish), mussels, and the spiny lobster characteristic of the Caribbean. The national dessert is flan, a condensed milk and vanilla custard, variations of which can be made by adding any one of the following ingredients: cream cheese, coconut milk, mashed pumpkin, or breadfruit. Puerto Ricans also prepare bread pudding: *tembleqque*, a gelatin-like coconut milk and cornstarch custard often eaten sprinkled with cinnamon, *arroz con dulce*, rice pudding cooked with condensed coconut milk, ginger and raisins, and fruit sherbets made with tamarins and soursop. Other favorite desserts are green papaya or guava shells simmered in heavy syrup and served with white or cottage cheese.

Puerto Rican coffee is exquisitely aromatic, served either black or with frothy boiled milk. Since Puerto Rico is the leading producer of rum, you'll find the piña coladas on the island some of the tastiest you've ever had.

Ajilli-Mojili $$$ ★ ★ ★

Calle Clemenceau.
Latin American cuisine. Specialties: Mofongo.
Lunch: entrees $15–$25.
Dinner: entrees $15–$25.
This is probably one of the most popular eateries for tipico Puerto Rican food. A specialty is Mofongo, fried plantain stuffed with seafood, beef or chicken (here it's usually shrimp), a dish you probably won't find outside of these isles. Although it's located in a Condado hotel, many local families make this a regular gathering spot, so the ambience is cheerful and festive.

Al Dente $$ ★ ★

Calle Recinto Sur, Old San Juan, ☎ (809) 723-7303.
Italian cuisine. Specialties: Fresh Pasta.
Lunch: Noon–4 p.m., entrees $10–$15.
Dinner: 4–10 p.m., entrees $10–$15.
This restaurant is a touch of old Palermo in Old San Juan. Located in a historical building in the heart of the colonial city, the dining room features fresh pasta, chicken and fish in light sauces, utilizing fresh herbs and spices. The atmosphere is as unstuffy as the food.

Amadeus $$ ★★★★

Calle San Sebastian, Old San Juan, ☎ *(809) 722-8635.*
Latin American cuisine.
Lunch: entrees $8–$16.
Dinner: entrees $8–$16.

A name like Amadeus connotes glittering candelabra, spinets and powdered wigs. Contrary to that idea, this restaurant and cafe is as modern as can be—the clever chef adds a dash of French flair to native dishes; for example, a combination of caviar and sour cream with green plantain. A version of cassoulet is made here with chorizo and black beans. Some people could make a whole meal from a plate of some very creative appetizers that a group of four or more can share; a sort of Puerto Rican dim sum. Call in advance to reserve space in the back room. It's open from noon to midnight.

Anchor's Inn $$$ ★★

Route 987, Km. 2.7, Fajardo, ☎ *(809) 863-7200.*
Latin American cuisine.
Lunch: 11 a.m.–4 p.m., entrees $8–$15.
Dinner: 4–11 p.m., entrees $15–$20.

This unpretentious spot by the sea offers a scrumptious plate of paella and an equally appealing vista of the Fajardo harbor. It's an ideal stopping point for people driving around the island, with a location near one of Puerto Rico's prime boating and watersports areas. If you tire of the nine restaurants at the posh El Conquistador resort nearby, give this place a try; it stays open late.

Back Street Hong Kong $$$ ★★★

Avenida de Isla Verde, Isla Verde, ☎ *(809) 791-1000.*
Chinese cuisine.
Dinner: 6 p.m.–midnight, entrees $15–$32.

This isn't your typical greasy spoon chop-suey, in fact, people like to dress up a bit to eat the savory Chinese food in a restaurant that recreates a Hong Kong back alley. The eclectic dining room was transported piecemeal from a Seattle World's Fair exhibition; it also contains a tropical aquarium that delights young children.

Butterfly People $ ★★

152 Calle Fortaleza, Old San Juan, ☎ *(809) 723-2432.*
International cuisine.
Lunch: 10 a.m.–6 p.m., entrees $5–$9.

Notice to lepidopterists—you will be dazzled at this restaurant and gallery that sells butterflies under glass from one of the most extensive private collections in the world. While the prices for these winged beauties range from moderate to stratospheric, the mostly-Puerto Rican dishes here are fairly reasonable. You can also have a soup (gazpacho is good), or salad in a plant-filled patio.

El Patio de Sam $$$ ★★★

102 Calle San Sebastian, Old San Juan, ☎ *(809) 723-1149.*
International cuisine.
Lunch: entrees $9–$25.
Dinner: entrees $9–$25.

This oft-visited eatery is remarkable for serving the juiciest burgers in town in the oldest building in town. Of course, there's a well-balanced menu of lobster tail, soups, desserts and tropical fruit libations. The late-night crowd likes to party here; it stays open till the wee hours on weekends.

La Bombonera $ ★★★

Calle San Francisco, Old San Juan, ☎ *(809) 722-0658.*
Latin American cuisine.
Lunch: entrees $5–$8.
Dinner: entrees $5–$8.

Like its name says, this old-fashioned eatery proffers a plethora of bonbons both sweet and savory. You can have a plate of *calamares en su tinta* (squid in its own ink served with rice), while your youngster sips hot chocolate. This place serves as the corner malt shop and tryst spot for locals who have been flocking to it since 1902. It's great for breakfast, very crowded at lunch, and ideal for tea and snacks. Take-out available. It's open from 7:30 am to 8:30 p.m.

La Casona de Serafin $$$ ★★★

Hwy 102, Km. 9, Cabo Rojo, ☎ *(809) 851-0066.*
Latin American cuisine. Specialties: Lobster.
Lunch: entrees $10–$20.
Dinner: entrees $21–$31.

Some people think the best seafood in Puerto Rico is served in this area of Joyuda Beach. Certainly the atmosphere at La Casona is great for eating peel-it-yourself shrimp or its specialty, lobster. Steaks and Puerto Rican dishes are also available, and there's a full bar and lounge. This restaurant is popular with local families who flock here on weekends, when the sleepy town wakes up to a noisy string of craft shops and oyster bars along the beach.

La Chaumiere $$$ ★★★★

367 Tetuan Street, Old San Juan, ☎ *(809) 722-3330.*
French cuisine.
Dinner: 6 p.m.–midnight, entrees $22–$37.

This restaurant serves classic French cuisine to a faithful clientele in surroundings that transport guests to the Gallic countryside. It's the kind of place where you can order rarely-found specialties like floating island (merengues in a sauce of creme anglaise) or oysters Rockefeller. Perfect for a pre-show supper; it's located behind the famous Tapia Theater.

La Compostela $$$ ★★★★★

Avenida Condado, Santurce, ☎ *(809) 724-6088.*
Spanish cuisine.
Lunch: Noon–3 p.m., entrees $15–$29.
Dinner: 6:30–10:30 p.m., entrees $15–$29.

Many repeat visitors recommend this Spanish restaurant with a French touch in a commercial suburb of San Juan. The owner has spent time laboring in the kitchens in both countries; he blends the styles effortlessly. The wine cellar is amazing: close to 10,000 bottles!

La Mallorquina $$$ ★★★

Calle San Justo 207, Old San Juan, ☎ *(809) 722-3261.*

Latin American cuisine.

Lunch: 11:30 a.m.–3 p.m., entrees $14–$30.

Dinner: 4–10 p.m., entrees $14–$30.

This restaurant may be a bit of a tourist trap, but it's still worth visiting for the house special asopao, the Puerto Rican version of risotto, served with a choice of seafood or chicken. It's one of the oldest restaurants in town, founded in 1848. Service is gracious and attentive.

Parador Villa Parguera $$ ★★★

Route 307, Lajas, ☎ *(809) 899-7777.*

Latin American cuisine. Specialties: Red Snapper Stuffed with Seafood.

Lunch: 7:30 a.m.–4 p.m., entrees $5–$20.

Dinner: 4–9:30 p.m., entrees $5–$20.

Simply prepared but very fresh seafood is a specialty at this seaside inn (one of the island's touted "paradores") surrounded by coconut palms on Phosphorescent Bay, on the West Coast. The Parador is an excellent base for viewing the local phenomenon—on moonlit nights, the bay is "lit" by thousands of tiny organisms called dinoflagellates. Come during the week, as hordes of families crowd the area on weekends.

Ramiro's $$$ ★★★★★

Avenida Magdalena 1106, Condado, ☎ *(809) 721-9049.*

Spanish cuisine. Specialties: Lamb, Homemade Desserts.

Lunch: Noon–3 p.m., entrees $24–$33.

Dinner: 6:30–10:30 p.m., prix fixe $22–$33.

Patrons dress up to dine at this plush salon of cocina fantastica; owner Jesus Ramiro may be the island's most creative chef. Although he uses local produce and ingredients, his technique is distinctly French, especially in the elaborate constructions of his sinful desserts. Lamb is one of his favorite meats to work with, on the menu you will find it in ravioli or paired with buffalo or venison in a spicy sauce, or a perfectly roasted rack.

The Chart House $$$ ★★

1214 Ashford Avenue, Condado, ☎ *(809) 728-0110.*

American cuisine. Specialties: Prime Rib, Mud Pie.

Dinner: 6–11 p.m., entrees $16–$25.

If the food here seems familiar to mainland guests, it is. The Chart House is a local link in the California-based steak and lobster chain, but what a link! The setting is in a historic turn-of-the-century homestead, which belonged to the Rauschenplat family. The property is surrounded by well-tended gardens and a treehouse. The all-American food is very popular with locals as well.

Where to Shop

Puerto Rico has duty-free shopping at the Luis Munoz Marin International Airport and several factory outlets in Old San Juan. Both traditional and contemporary items can be bought in Old San Juan and out on the island, and you shouldn't go home without at least some representative of local craft. A day's excursion in a car could be spent touring the island to visit various craftsmen in their studios. (When you meet an artist and then buy his work, his personality and your memory of him or her always become indelibly entwined with the object itself—one of the true meanings of art.) The **Puerto Rico Tourism Company** ☎ *(809) 721-2400* offers a researched list of studios to visit along with a map to help you get there. Some studios are only open to the public at specific times, so make sure your itinerary fits the schedules. Possible workshops range from wood carvers to hammock-makers, to jewelry and furniture makers. It is always fascinating to visit the studio of an artisan who makes *santos* (saints); they are usually very spiritual people and the atmosphere of the saints themselves often pervades the workshop.

Even without the Biennial, Old San Juan has a remarkably lively arts scene. Walking along Cristo and San Jose Streets, you could lose count of the galleries. One of the best known is the **Galeria Botello** at *208 Cristo* with works by local artists as well as the Spanish artist Angel Botello and a fine collection of santos (small carved wooden figures of saints).

You'll find modern santos, carnival masks, pottery and the like at **Puerto Rican Arts and Crafts** at *204 Fortaleza*, old San Juan. And you can still get a Panama hat ($30–$50) at the **Casa Mendez Suarez**, which has been at *251 San Justo* since 1886, and elaborate flowered Spanish fans ($3.95 and up) at **La Nueva Opera**, *254 Fortaleza*. Another good place to check out is **La Piazoleta**, a Puerto Rican Craft Center, at *Pier 3, at the Customs House in Old San Juan.*

Old San Juan is also thick with antiques stores, including **El Alcazar** at *103 San Jose* and *109 Sol*. Both locations concentrate on 17th- and 18th-century Spanish art and 19th- and 20th-century French bibelots and brocante, and can ship home anything you buy.

The Book Store at *255 San Jose, Old San Juan*, has a good selection of English-language books as well as books on Puerto Rico, and CDs of Puerto Rican danza and salsa music.

Calle Fortaleza in Old San Juan is a treasurehouse of boutiques and stores. If you're in need of brightly colored resort wear made of special batiks and tie-dyes, stop by **La Casita**. On **Calle San Francisco**, the finest of the island's handmade lace can be found at **Aguadilla en San Juan**, including tablecloths and dresses.

The Northwest Coast

Dorado

Dorado, about 20 miles from San Juan off Route 693, is the closest town to the Hyatt Regency Cerromar Beach and the Hyatt Dorado Beach hotels. (If you're cruising the area, these are two fine resorts to plunk yourself down for a lunch or a drink.) The town has remained stuck in time despite the construction of the hotels. A few distracting hours can be whiled away at the shopping center and the handful of arts and crafts stores on the main streets. If you are staying at the resorts, a limousine will be sent to pick you up at San Juan's International Airport, about a three-quarters-of-an-hour drive. The hotels also use a small airstrip a few minutes away from their front doors.

There are numerous mountain treks that can be taken in this area, especially through the **Parque de las Cavernas del Rio Camuy**, a 268-acre reserve featuring caves with an amazing array of stalactites and stalagmites. (For more information, see the section called "Treks" above.) The **Arecibo Observatory** also makes a fascinating excursion. (For more information see "What Else to See on the Island," above.) Excursions from Dorado can easily be made to see the historic center of Old San Juan (45 minutes by car), as well as day trips down the southern coast at La Parguera and Cabo Rojo.

Where to Stay

The **Hyatt Dorado** is a no-holds-barred resort set on lushly landscaped grounds that caters to families as well as conventioneers. That might mean you forsake a bit of honeymoon-type privacy for the all-inclusive touch that makes some vacationers feel at home and others overwhelmed by overenthusiastic social directors. The **Hyatt Regency Cerromar Beach** is a bit less tropical, ensconced in a tall high-rise, with an absolutely spectacular pool that includes a waterfall, hydromassage and other playtoys.

Hotels and Resorts

Days Inn $80–$140   ★★

Route 1, Mercedita, ☎ *(800) 325-2525, (809) 841-1000, FAX (809) 841-2560.*
Single: $80. Double: $90–$140.

Located near the Intra-American University, this budget choice offers typical Days Inn accommodations and facilities. Rooms are on the basic side, but provide modern conveniences like TV and air conditioning. The premises include a pool, Jacuzzi, restaurant, nightclub and a games room.

Hyatt Dorado Beach $160–$490   ★★★★★

Dorado, ☎ *(800) 233-1234, (809) 796-1234.*
Single: $160–$490. Double: $160–$490.

Located on a 1000-acre estate shared with its sister property, the Hyatt Regency Cerromar, this deluxe operation aims to please—and succeeds. Superior to its sibling, it has extensive facilities, all of the highest quality. Accommodations are in 14 two-story buildings and quite plush, with lots of room in which to move, rattan furnishings, balconies or terraces, minibars, and marble baths. There are also cottages of two or three bedrooms that line the fairway. Recreational options are the best on the island, with two 18-hole golf courses designed by Robert Trent Jones, a club house, two pools (one Olympic sized), a health club with aerobics classes, eight tennis courts, a windsurfing school and a private beach with watersports. Dining options range from formal restaurants to the casual beach bar to theme night dinners; the food is high priced, but if you can afford the rates, you probably can afford the meals, too. A shuttle bus takes you to the casino and other facilities at the Hyatt Regency Cerromar. If you're torn between the two, keep in mind that the Dorado has nicer rooms, a better beach and appeals to an older crowd, while the Cerromar has a better pool and a younger clientele (including children).

Hyatt Regency Cerromar $165–$420   ★ ★ ★ ★ ★

Dorado, ☎ (800) 233-1234, (809) 796-1234.
Single: $165–$420. Double: $165–$420.

Sister property to the above-mentioned Hyatt Dorado and sharing its 1000 acres, this plush resort centers around a seven-story Y-shaped hotel. Guest rooms are decorated in an island theme and have minibars, spacious baths and balconies. The hotel boasts of having the world's largest pool, which comes in at 1776 feet, complete with whirlpools, a Jacuzzi grotto, a swim-up bar, 14 waterfalls, five separate swimming areas and an impressive water slide. There's also an Olympic-size pool for the more sedate crowd. There's also a health club, 14 tennis courts, a fine beach, supervised children's activities, all watersports, bicycle and jogging trails, and 36 holes of golf on Robert Trent Jones-designed courses. Guests can choose from four restaurants—one serving sushi, a rarity in Puerto Rico—or hop the shuttle to try the food at the Hyatt Dorado. For nightlife, try the casino disco, or several bars. Excellent all the way, though expect to see a fair amount of business travelers and families.

Parador El Guajataca $77–$95   ★ ★

Route 2, Quebradjlas, Quebradillas, ☎ (800) 964-3065, (809) 895-3070, FAX (809) 895-3589.
Single: $77–$83. Double: $83–$95.

Set on a bluff overlooking the beach, this small hotel has many resort amenities at an unbeatable price. Accommodations are comfortable and modern. Guests can enjoy the nice beach, play tennis on two courts, or swim in the Olympic-size pool. The restaurant serves creole cuisine, and there's entertainment in the bar on weekends.

Inns

Puerto Rico is famous for its network of charming country inns called *paradores puertorriqueños* (established in 1973), which offer superb accommodations and the ideal location for exploring the island's diverse attractions. Several privately owned and operated guest houses also serve as quiet and quaint accommodations far from the madding crowds. What makes the paradores so special is they are each situated in a historic place or site of unusual scenic beauty. Prices range from $38–$96 per night, double occupancy, and are located from mountains to sea. Most have swimming pools and all offer the island's tantalizing cuisine. Many are even within driving distance from San Juan.

Parador Vistamar $60–$75 ★★

Highway 113, Quebradillas, ☎ *(800) 443-0266, (809) 895-2065, FAX (809) 895-2294.*

Single: $60–$75. Double: $60–$75.

Fine views of the sea from this hilltop inn, which offers air-conditioned rooms that are comfortable but on the plain side. There's a large pool, Jacuzzi, tennis court, and game room on-site, as well as a few dining outlets and three bars, one with music and dancing on the weekends.

Low Cost Lodging

Ask the Tourist Board about the possibility of renting rooms in the houses of local families. Also locals tend to know out-of-way places that do not appear in more established publications. Do note that you may not find standards of cleanliness at the level to which you are accustomed.

Where to Eat

Best international cuisine is found at the two Hyatt resorts, where you can be assured of cleanliness and safety. True Puerto Rican delicacies, with a Spanish twist, can be found at **Los Naborias**. You will probably run into a strong local family scene at **La Famillia**, a warm, inviting, if simple place, particularly lively on Sundays.

East and Southeast Coast

Fajardo and Humacao

Full of small-town spirit, the seaport of Fajardo lies but five miles south of Las Cabezas on Route 3. The lifestyle is slower-paced than in San Juan, and you can take morning and afternoon ferries to Culebra and Vieques. Treks can be made to the **Caribbean National Forest**, of which El Yunque Mountain is a part (see "Treks" above) and Losquillo Beach. Special expeditions can be arranged through Las Cabezas Nature Reserve (see "Trek" above) which could last all day, especially if you are interested in bird-watching. Native sloops set sail for Iacos where you will find fine snorkeling and swimming conditions. Deep-sea fishing and other watersports can be arranged at the **Puerto del Rey Marina**. The region has a fine 18-hole golf course and myriads of opportunities for scuba (see "Dive Sites" above.) Also see "Sports" above for more information.

This part of the island can be reached by taxis (expensive from the international airport), by small planes that land at the airport of Palmas del Mar, near Humacao; or by ferry boat (the cheapest at $2.50).

Where to Stay

Two hotels/resorts command the region with their enormous facilities. The patron saint of resorts, **El Conquistador**, has an amazing 16 restaurants and lounges—if you want to avoid the conventioneer crush, you should probably stay elsewhere. **Candelero**, near the beach at Palmas in the south, is more intimate, and less demanding socially, with activities geared for the athletic, including fine horseback riding, golf, tennis and artistic performances. Also in this area are the Puerto Rican paradores, intimate inns that reflect the congeniality of the owner/host, and cheaper guest houses.

Hotels and Resorts

El Conquistador Resort $170–$420   ★ ★ ★ ★ ★

Las Crobas, ☎ (800) 468-8365, (809) 863-1000, FAX (809) 253-4387.
Single: $170–$420. Double: $170–$420.
This is the mega-resort of mega-resorts, a huge enclave perched atop a cliff, overlooking the Caribbean on one side and the Atlantic on the other. The complex consists of five hotels. Guest rooms are quite spiffy, with three phones, two TVs, VCRs, stereos, and refrigerators. There are also 88 suites and 176 casitas with more room and special amenities. The resort's 500 acres include a casino, six pools, eight tennis courts, pro shops, a health spa, 16 restaurants and bars, and watersports. There's also an 18-hole golf course, with another one planned at a future date. It's easy to see that the owners plucked down a cool $250 million to create this resort, which

just opened in 1993. Among the gee-whiz attractions is an art collection worth a million dollars, a private island where you can spend the day, a 55-slip marina, and tons of shops. Despite its sheer size, service is efficient and cheerful.

Palmas del Mar Humacao $145–$715   ★ ★ ★ ★
Palmas del Mar, Humacao, ☎ *(800) 468-3331, (809) 852-6000, FAX (809) 852-6320.*
Single: $145–$715. Double: $145–$715.

This resort community, still under development in some areas, encompasses 2750 acres and fronts three miles of beach. Guests have a number of lodging options. The 100-room Candelero Hotel has spacious rooms with high ceilings and tropical decor, and offers the most affordable accommodations. The Palmas Inn has 23 suites with large living rooms, combination baths with bidets, and opulent furnishings. You can also book a two- or three-bedroom villa complete with kitchen. The well-tended grounds include an equestrian center, casino, marina, watersports, seven pools, 20 tennis courts (six lighted), 18 holes of golf, a fitness center with exercise classes, and supervised children's programs year-round. Dining outlets include a formal French restaurant, a casual Oriental eatery, and lots more. There's nightly entertainment at the Candelero. A free shuttle takes you to and from the action. Inquire about golf and tennis packages that can save you bucks.

Apartments and Condominiums
Accommodations with fully equipped kitchens are available in any range of luxury, from the bareback simple near the seashore to the more luxurious privately owned condo rented in the owner's absence, usually during high season.

Inns
Paradores, or small inns, are for the more adventurous-minded who like to take chances on quality and ambiance. The best are true gems, and usually come complete with a very congenial host.

Parador La Familia $50–$70   ★
Route 987, Las Croabas, ☎ *(800) 443-0266, (809) 869-5345.*
Single: $50–$61. Double: $61–$70.

Located near Las Cabezas de San Juan Nature Preserve, this guesthouse is three miles from town; you'll definitely want a car for mobility. Rooms are basic but air-conditioned and comfortable. There's a good restaurant and pool on the premises.

Parador Martorell $50–$85   ★
Ocean Drive 6-A, Luquillo, ☎ *(800) 443-0266, (809) 889-2710.*
Single: $50–$85. Double: $70–$85.

This small family-run inn is located in Puerto Rico's northeast section. Rooms are small but comfortable; three share a bath and rely on ceiling fans to keep cool. The other seven have private baths and air conditioning, well worth the small bump in rates. There's a restaurant and pool on-site, and the beach is just two minutes away.

Where to Eat

Best cuisine is found at the resorts; with so many facilities at **El Conquistador**, you may never have to leave the premises (that's their goal). Snacks can be found beachside (a cheap way to get through lunch on your way to a more expensive dinner). The best Italian food (if the most expensive) is at the **Azzuro** at the Palamas Mar Marriott hotel.

The South Coast

Ponce

Ponce is Puerto Rico's second-largest city, located about 70 miles south and west of San Juan. It dates back to 1692 when Ponce de Léon's great-grandson founded the small community. A high-speed road connects the two cities, which takes only about 90 minutes to traverse; you can also reach the area by plane from San Juan's International Airport. Many historical buildings, such as the stunning Cathedral of Our Lady of Guadeloupe, are masterpieces of construction, as are some one thousand colonial houses designated national historic sites in a 40-by-80-block area. Nineteenth-century gas lamps illuminate the marble-edged streets glimmering with a pink glow; at night the stroll is extremely romantic. A fine collection of Latin American artists and international masters can be found in the **Museu de Arte de Ponce**, a light, airy place to stroll and relax out of the sun. Particularly fine are the works by Rubens and Rodin as well as many pre-Raphaelite paintings and sculptures. Anyone interested in sugarcane production and plantations will find an interesting exhibit at the **Castillo Serralles**, a restored 19th-century mansion, which has been refurbished to its 1930s furnishings. On Route 10, you'll discover the **Hacienda Buena Vista**, a restored coffee plantation which is open to visitors. (For more information, see under "What Else to See on the Island" above.)

Trekkers should head straightaway to the **Toro State Forest**, a 7000-acre preserve with waterfalls, the island's tallest peak, and an observation tour. (For more information, see under "Treks" above).

BEST VIEW:

A terrific perspective of the surrounding countryside and town can be seen from the 100-foot-tall El Vigia, an observatory tower, next to Castillo Serrallés.

What Else to See

Historical Sites

Hacienda Buena Vista ★★★
Route 10, near Ponce, ☎ *(809) 848-7020.*
From 1833 to the 1950s, this thriving plantation produced corn, citrus fruits and coffee. Today, under the auspices of Puerto Rico's Conservation Trust, it is a reconstructed farm from the late 19th century. Reservations are required for 1.5-hour tours, which are conducted Friday through Sunday; call ☎ *722-5882.* The grounds include the estate house, former slave quarters, a 60-foot water slide, and working corn and coffee mills.

Tibes Indian Ceremonial Center

Route 503, near Ponce, ☎ *(809) 840-2255.*
Hours open: 9 a.m.–4:30 p.m.
This is the oldest cemetery in the Antilles, with some 200 skeletons unearthed from A.D. 300 and ballcourts and dance grounds from A.D. 700. The site also includes a recreated Taino village and a museum.

Museums and Exhibits

El Museo Castillo Serralles

El Virgia 17, Ponce, ☎ *(809) 259-1774.*
Hours open: 10 a.m.–5 p.m.
This Spanish-Revival mansion, Ponce's largest building, dates back to the 1930s. It is the former home of the Serralles family, producers of Don Q rum. Today it is a museum exhibiting elegant furnishings, the history of the local rum industry and a cafe. The lavishly landscaped grounds are a treat, and the views up here are breathtaking.

Museo de Arte de Ponce

Ave. las Americas 25, Ponce, ☎ *(809) 848-0505.*
Designed by Edward Durell Stone, this fanciful museum exhibits traditional and modern art from the Americas and Europe, as well as contemporary works by Puerto Ricans.

Ponce History Museum

Calle Isabel, Ponce, ☎ *(809) 844-7071.*
Hours open: 10 a.m.–5 p.m.
The name says it all: the history of Ponce detailed in two wooden houses dating back to the turn of the century. Closed Tuesday.

Where to Stay

On the south shore of Ponce, the Hilton is making waves among southern resorts, but it's high-rise modernity takes a bit away from the tropical feel. It does have, however, an extensive water sports program and can make any arrangement for treks, etc. Other hotels in the middle of town give you easy access to the historic part of the city, especially at night when it is most atmospheric.

Hotels and Resorts

Melia Hotel $70–$90   ★★

2 Cristina Street, Ponce, ☎ *(800) 742-4276, (809) 842-0260, FAX (809) 841-3602.*
Single: $70–$80. Double: $75–$90.
This hotel in the historic district is pretty historic itself, dating back to 1914. The Spanish-colonial building includes interesting touches such as antiques and old chandeliers. Guest rooms are small and the furnishings dated—not antiques, just old. There's a decent restaurant on-site, but no other extras. Not a top choice by any means, but those who like historic hotels will be satisfied. Light sleepers should request a room in the back, as street noises can be loud. Note that this hotel is not affiliated with the upscale Melia chain.

Parador Boquemar $65–$70

Route 101, Cabo Rojo, Boquemar, ☎ *(800) 443-0266, (809) 851-2158, FAX (809) 851-7600.*

Single: $65–$70. Double: $65–$70.

This three-story hotel is near the beach. All the guest rooms, which are quite basic, have air conditioning, but some share baths. There's a restaurant and bar on-site, as well as a pool.

Parador Villa Parguera $80–$90

Route 304, Lajas, La Parguera, ☎ *(800) 443-0266, (809) 899-3975, FAX (809) 899-6040.*

Single: $80–$90. Double: $80–$90.

Located near the beach on the southwestern shore, this parador offers rooms in an older guest house and in more modern wings, all with air conditioning, private baths, and balconies or patios. They have a restaurant and nightclub on the premises. The pool is filled with saltwater.

Ponce Hilton and Casino $170–$375

P.R. 14 Avenue, Santiado de los Caballeros, Ponce, ☎ *(800) 445-8667, (809) 259-7676, FAX (809) 259-7674.*

Single: $170–$190. Double: $190–$375.

By far the area's nicest hotel, this Hilton sits on 80 acres of beachfront. Accommodations are stylish, with high-quality furniture, minibars, bidets, and balconies or patios. Nice public spaces and lots of recreational facilities, including a large lagoon-style pool, Jacuzzi, four tennis courts, gym, games room, and watersports on the private beach. There are also five restaurants, several watering holes and a casino. This well-run property does a lot of business with the meetings and convention markets.

Ponce Holiday Inn $97–$145

Highway 2, Ponce, ☎ *(800) 465-4329, (809) 844-1200, FAX (809) 841-8683.*
Single: $97–$120. Double: $99–$145.

Perched on a hillside one mile from the ocean, this commercial hotel has wonderful views of the surrounding area. Guest rooms are comfortable and pleasant; all have balconies with nice views. For an extra charge, they'll throw in a refrigerator. There's nightly entertainment in the lounge, as well as a disco, games room, pool and restaurant. You can count on the reliability that comes with a Holiday Inn, but you won't be writing home about it. Good especially for business travelers.

Inns

Some of the nicest paradores, or government-sponsored inns, are located in this area; the **Parador Baõs de Coamo** is famous for its hot springs, and its most celebrated guest, Franklin Delano Roosevelt, who came to be healed. Many locals flock to the spring even today, which are rumored to cure a lot of illnesses. Find a map of the panoramic route of this area; many of the paradores make good stops for atmospheric lunch or dinner.

Parador Banos de Coamo $55–$65

Route 546, Coamo, ☎ *(809) 825-2239, FAX (809) 825-4739.*
Single: $55. Double: $65.

Situated on the south coast on plains at the base of the mountains, this guest house dates back to 1847 and was once visited by Franklin Roosevelt. Guests can soak in natural hot springs that are said to be the most radioactive in the world—a dubious claim to fame. Guest rooms are large and comfortable, though minimally furnished. Besides the hot springs, there's a regular swimming pool and a tennis court.

Parador Posada Porlamar $45–$90   ★

La Parguera Road, La Parguera, ☎ *(800) 443-0266, (809) 899-4015, FAX (809) 899-6082.*
Single: $45. Double: $60–$90.
This modest inn is right in the heart of this picturesque fishing village. Rooms are simple but comfortable and air-conditioned; all have private baths. There's no restaurant on-site, but guests have free use of a common kitchen, or can walk to nearby eateries. No pool, either.

Where to Eat

The Hilton has fine dining facilities, and you can always be assured of safe cooking techniques. Seafood is a specialty along the south coast. As you head west, along route 2, you'll run across several possibilities.

El Ancla $$$ ★ ★ ★

9 Hostos Avenue, Ponce, ☎ *(809) 840-2450.*
Seafood cuisine.
Lunch: 11 a.m.–4 p.m., entrees $3–$28.
Dinner: 4 p.m.–midnight, entrees $3–$28.
This is an established family-owned restaurant perched over the water in Ponce Beach. Although it's long been popular with Poncenos and visitors, the welcome is always warm. That's probably what sets it apart from other restaurants serving seafood, which is the specialty of this eatery. Enjoy red snapper stuffed with lobster and shrimp served on a plate heaped with plenty of starchy side dishes.

Lupita's Mexican $$$ ★ ★

Calle Isabel 60, Ponce, ☎ *(809) 848-8808.*
Mexican cuisine.
Lunch: 11 a.m.–4 p.m., entrees $7–$26.
Dinner: 4–11 p.m., entrees $7–$26.
The better-than-average Mexican fare served here is blended with local specialties—lobster is grilled and served with green plantain, but you can also have tacos and nachos. Entertainment is provided several times a week by mariachis. It's located in a historic building near Plaza las Delicias, Ponce's main square. Lupita's stays open until 2 a.m. on Saturdays and until midnight on Sundays.

The West Coast

Mayaguez

Mayaguez is the island's third-largest town, located about 10 miles from Rinceon on Route 2. Baroque and Victorian buildings make this pretty, bustling port even more charming. It's the launching pad for treks into the western and southwestern interior; routes into the mountains lead to some spectacular climbs (see "Treks") and can be easily reached by car. Long a center of fine needlepoint, intrepid shoppers can still find some wonderful samples of fine island artistry in some of the older shops downtown. The island's only zoo is located behind the University of Puerto Rico's campus. The city itself is centered around the impressive Spanish-style **Plaza Colón**, a tribute to Christopher Columbus, whose statue stands in the middle of the square. The **Cathédrale de la Virgen de la Candelaria** is also a fine structure, dating back four centuries.

About 50 miles west of Mayaguez, stands Mona Island, a rugged uninhabited island whose only residents are large colonies of seabirds and enormous iguanas. The stunning cliffs make excellent photo ops; years ago it was said they held the booty of pirates who combed these waters. Rustic adventurers can find perfect places for camping overlooking the sea. Permission to visit must be granted by the tourist office. Twenty miles south of Malagues is **Boqueón Beach**, a stunning mile-long beach that boasts balneario facilities and excellent low prices for lodging. The small cottages are owned by the government and must be applied for four months in advance through the **Recreation and Sports Department**, *Box 2923, San Juan, PR 00903;* ☎ *(809) 722-1551.* Avoid weekends when local families with noisy teenagers carrying boom boxes disrupt the peacefulness of the area. Excellent seafood restaurants can be found a bit farther north at **Joyuda Beach**. Along Route 301 can be found the **Cabo Rojo Wildlife Refuge** (see "Treks"). If you would like a guide, check at the visitor's desk, where you can also get maps and individual assistance. At the southwesternmost top of the island, the best place to watch sunsets is at the **Cabo Rojo Lighthouse** at El Faro. The lighthouse is not open to the public, but the promontory overlooking red cliffs and ocean make for a spectacular lookout.

What Else to See

Parks and Gardens

Puerto Rico Zoological Gardens ★★★

Route 108, Mayaguez, ☎ *(809) 834-8110.*
Hours open: 9 a.m.–5 p.m.

Check out the birds and beasts—500 in all—at this tropical zoo spread over 45 acres.

Where to Stay

Hotels and Resorts

Holiday Inn Mayaguez					**$120–$240**					★★★

2701 Highway 2, Mayaguez, ☎ (800) 465-4329, (809) 833-1100, FAX (809) 833-1300.
Single: $120–$130. Double: $130–$240.

The beach is eight miles away from this typical Holiday Inn. Guest rooms fit the standard HI formula, which means clean, comfortable, air-conditioned, and on the bland side. One nice touch is a signal alert system for the hearing impaired. The hotel has a restaurant, lounge with live music, gym, sauna, and pool. Not exactly bursting with local flavor, but a safe choice.

Horned Dorset Primavera					**$150–$440**					★★★★★

Route 429, Rincon, ☎ (809) 823-4030, FAX (809) 823-5580.
Single: $150–$245. Double: $325–$440.

The name may be odd, but everything else is nearly perfect at this small and exclusive enclave. Guests are housed in plush suites with Persian rugs, armoires, four-poster beds, sitting areas, furnished balconies, and large baths. There are not a lot of facilities on-site, as the idea is to rest, relax and be pampered by the excellent staff. There is a pool and library, but that's about it. The grounds are exquisitely landscaped and open onto the sea, but there's really no beach to speak of. Dinner is a memorable affair with six courses nightly. No kids under 12 permitted.

Mayaguez Hilton					**$135–$180**					★★★

Route 104, Mayaguez, ☎ (800) 445-8667, (809) 831-7575, FAX (809) 834-3475.
Single: $135–$170. Double: $155–$180.

Set on 20 landscaped acres overlooking the harbor, this Hilton has a country club feel. Rooms are very comfortable and nicely furnished with all the amenities expected from Hilton. The grounds include a casino, nightclub, Olympic-size pool, three tennis courts, and a putting green. Children's activities are scheduled during high season. Very nice, but as the beach is 20 minutes away, this hotel caters mainly to a business clientele.

Inns

The paradores system works well in this region; however, there is no real standard of quality and there may be big differences in service and surroundings. **Parador Hacienda Gripinas** is perhaps one of the most natural, replete with the sounds of nature. The **Parador Villa Antonio** tends to caters to the older; younger travelers might enjoy the **Parador Perichi** more. Businessmen tend to tuck in at the **El Sol**.

Parador Oasis					**$107–$107**					★★

72 Luna Street, San German, ☎ (800) 223-9815, (809) 892-1175, FAX (809) 892-1175.
Single: $107. Double: $107.

This Spanish-style mansion, which dates back to 1896, is three blocks from the Inter-American University. Rooms are in the mansion (the least desirable ones, in fact) and a newer annex; all are air-conditioned and most are comfortable, though on the basic side. Facilities include a pool in a pretty courtyard, gym, sauna, restaurant, and bar.

Where to Eat

Horned Dorset Primavera   **$$$**   ★ ★ ★ ★ ★
Route 429, Km. 3, Rincon, ☎ *(809) 823-4030.*
cuisine.
Lunch: Noon–2:30 p.m., entrees $15–$25.
Dinner: 7–9 p.m., prix fixe $45.
This plush, whitewashed hotel/restaurant stands quite alone in its glory in a frontier location catering to surfers and daytrippers. That isn't to say the area isn't sublimely beautiful; it is. Many visitors make a special trip to eat here; it's quiet, it's right on the beach and the $40 fixed-price, six-course dinner is served with great ceremony. Although it's named after a breed of English sheep, seafood is a specialty. Location is six miles northwest of Mayaguez. Lunch hours vary, call for information.

San Germán

About 25 miles beyond the Cabo Rojo Lighthouse is San Germán, the island's second-oldest city.

It takes about three hours to drive from San Juan, and one hour from Mayaguez. The colonial atmosphere still pervades, despite the presence of a new highway; small-town customs still linger. A stroll around the town should reveal fine architecture including shops with gingerbread trim and turrets. The **Porta Coeli** Cathedral is considered to be the New World's oldest, dating back to 1606. Today the old church houses a fine museum with impressive sacred and secular art that dates back even a hundred years earlier than the building itself. The restoration of the former monastery and church is a model of perfection, and is considered one of the island's finest possessions.

Puerto Rico's Islands
Culebra

Culebra is one of several islands located off the east coast between Puerto Rico and the U.S. Virgin Islands, and is rich in natural resources but not yet developed for tourism. The five-mile-long island of Culebra is actually an archipelago of one main island and 20 surrounding cays. Most of the cays are part of the Culebra National Wildlife Refuge, which offers fine opportunities for bird-watching. More than 86 bird species are represented, including several nearly extinct ones. Four endangered sea turtles are also protected—green, loggerhead, hawksbill and leatherback. From April to July, the ecological organization Earthwatch sends teams of volunteers to the island for scientific studies, particularly along the beaches of Resaca and Brava.

Families run watersports businesses here, and boats can be chartered for a day-sailing around the islands. Windsurfing and limited deep-sea fishing can also be arranged from Dewey, the island's sole community. There are also excellent snorkeling sites here, especially at Punta Molines and Punta del Soldado.

To get to Culebra, you have two options. Ferryboats sail from Fajardo, which takes about one hour (the fee is extremely cheap). Getting to Fajardo, though, will tax your imagination, as taxi drivers charge exorbitant amounts for the ride. A small plane can be taken from Isla Grande airport aboard Flamenco Airways (though other local airlines also fly). The landing on the tiny strip can cause fibrillation, but it's best just to shut your eyes and keep breathing.

Where to Stay

Accommodations in this region run toward the simple, unpretentious and cheap.

Hotels and Resorts

Club Seabourne $65–$125 ★★

Culebra Island, ☎ (809) 742-3169, FAX (809) 742-3176.
Single: $65–$115. Double: $70–$125.
Overlooking Fullodosa Bay, this small complex consists of air-conditioned rooms, villas and cottages, with refrigerators in the larger accommodations. Morning coffee and juice are on the house. The grounds include a pool, bar and restaurant that is closed on Mondays.

Apartments and Condominiums

Harbour View Villas $50–$95 ★★

Culebra Island, ☎ (809) 742-3855.
Single: $50–$75. Double: $75–$95.

This small enclave of villas is on the island of Culebra, reached via a 10-minute ferry ride from Fajardo. The town and beach are a quarter-mile stroll. All units are air-conditioned, have kitchens for do-it-yourselfers, and sleep up to six. French doors open onto large balconies overlooking the town and the Vieques Sound. You'll want a car to get around, as there's not much on-site.

Self-catering

Several options are available for self-catering, the best being the **Culebra Island Villas**, situated near enough to sea to make sports activities a cinch. Six people can pile into one of two houses that make up the **Harbor View Villas**, a perfect option for a small group of friends or a family who want to do their own thing.

Budget Bunks

You get what you pay for, and anything cheap in this region tends to run toward the dilapidated and unclean. An exception is the **Coral Island Guest House,** which is mostly used by divers.

Vieques

Vieques is larger and a bit more cosmopolitan than Culebra, though the difference may be negligible. The port, **Isabel Segunda**, holds the distinction of having the last fort built by the Spaniards in the New World. Indian settlements date back to 200 B.C., a source of great interest to archaeologists who are presently studying them with passion. Two-thirds of the present land of Vieques is used by the U.S. Navy, some for military maneuvers, and some for the grazing of livestock. Some of the greatest primitive, unspoiled beaches are located on Navy land, which you can enter when there are no military maneuvers taking place. A fine beach is Sun Bay, which has bathing facilities and camping grounds. From Esperanza, you can make a nightly visit on a boat to the nearby bioluminescent bay, more spectacular than the better-known Phosphorescent Bay near La Parguera. With three protected sites called "hurricane holes," diving options can be arranged, along with other watersports, including windsurfing, at **Vieques Divers** at Esperanza. Certification courses are also available. There are also opportunities for horseback riding.

As a shopping hub, Isabel Segunda is best described as lethargic until tourists arrive in the ferry. Taxis and rental cars (Suzuki jeeps are best), available though local agencies, are the way to get around the island. To get to the island, you can either take a small plane from San Juan's Isla Grande airport, or a ferry boat from Fajardo—a two-hour sojourn. (As said above, getting to Fajardo is the difficulty here, since taxi rides from San Juan and its airports can be enormously expensive.)

Where to Stay

Don't expect any fancy resort here; most accommodations run the gamut from simple to simpler. The most atmospheric is La Casa del Frances, a restored Victorian house that gives off the ambience of a country inn.

Apartments and Condominiums

Kitchen facilities can be found at the **Sea Gate** ☎ *(809) 741-4661* and **La Lanchita** ☎ *(809) 741-8449.*

Inns

Sea Gate Guest House	**$40–$85**	★ ★

Vieques Island, ☎ *(809) 741-4661.*
Single: $40–$85. Double: $45–$85.
This small property is up on a hill overlooking the harbor town of Isabel Segunda and the sea beyond. Most rooms are efficiencies with kitchenettes. There's a very small pool on the premises, and the friendly owners will take you to the beach and arrange watersports.

Low Cost Lodging

Very cheap accommodations can be found in guest houses and a few apartment blocks. You'll be lucky if the furnishings are anything but basic.

Where to Eat

Fresh seafood is the way to go on this island. Anything else is probably shipped in. The best local cooking can be found at **Cerromar** in Puerto Real; you can tell it's good because most of the locals congregate there and you can enjoy watching how they interact. A plate of land crabs at the **Cayo Blanco** in Isabella Segunda is considered a must-do before you leave. In Esperanza, most of the local traffic ends up at the casual, laid-back **La Central Café**— ask anybody where it is.

Puerto Rico Directory

ARRIVAL

There are three airports in Puerto Rico, all undergoing extensive and expensive renovation. The Luis Munoz Marin in San Juan is the major hub for international travel. Since 1988 **American Airlines** has spent $260 million tripling the size of its San Juan hub, including the reservation center. The Mercedita Airport is located in Ponce, and the Rafael Hernandez is in Aguadilla. Major airlines including **American**, **Delta**, **TWA**, **Tower**, **United** and **USAir** fly into San Juan from most major U.S. cities. **Carnival Airlines** operates service to Aguadilla and Ponce from New York and Newark. American has made San Juan its hub for all flights from Puerto Rico to other Caribbean destinations, the U.S., Europe and Latin America. American Airlines also operates nonstop service from Miami and New York's JFK to Aguadilla and from Miami to

Ponce. International carriers include **British Airways**, **Iberia** and **Lufthansa**. **Continental Airlines** will begin nonstop service to San Juan. Starting Dec. 15, the airline will offer three flights a day from Newark. Packages start at $468 per person for four days including air fare and hotel accommodations.

The airport departure tax is included in the price of the airline ticket.

BUSINESS HOURS

Shops open 9 a.m.–6 p.m. Banks open weekdays 8:30 a.m.–2:30 p.m. and Saturday 9:45 a.m.–noon.

CLIMATE

Coastal weather in Puerto Rico is warm and sunny year-round. During the summer, temperatures average in the mid 80s; during the winter, they hover in the low 70s to the low 80s. The rainiest months are May to December, generally heavier on the north than the south coast. Temperatures in the mountains tend to be 5–10 degrees cooler.

DOCUMENTS

Since Puerto Rico is a commonwealth of the United States, no passports are required for U.S. citizens. Visitors do need a valid driver's license to rent a car. If you are a citizen of any other country, a visa is required. Vaccinations are not necessary. U.S. citizens do not need to clear customs or immigration (other citizens do). On departure, luggage must be inspected by the U.S. Agriculture Department, as law prohibits the taking of certain fruits and plants in the U.S. Dogs and cats may be brought to Puerto Rico from the U.S. with two documents: a health certificate dated not more than 10 days prior to departure showing that the animal is certified disease-free by an official or registered veterinarian, and a certificate of rabies vaccination, dated not more than 30 days prior to departure, authenticated by the proper authorities.

ELECTRICITY

Current runs A.C. 60 cycles, 100 volts, single phase or 220 volts, three phase.

GETTING AROUND

Taxis, buses and rental cars are available at the airport and major hotels. All taxicabs are metered, but they may be rented unmetered for an hourly rate. There's an additional charge of 50 cents for every suitcase. *Publicos* (public cars) run on frequent schedules to all island towns (usually during daytime hours) and depart from main squares. They run on fixed rates. The *Ruta Panoramica* is a scenic road meandering across the island offering stunning vistas.

San Juan is the largest home-based cruise port in the world. Twenty-eight vessels use San Juan as their home port and each year new cruise ships either originate or call at the port.

Ferries shuttle passengers to and from Culebra and Vieques at reasonable rates. Car transport is also available. San Juan's harbor can also be crossed by the Catana ferry (50 cents) to the Bacardi Rum plant's free tours.

LANGUAGE

Spanish and English are both official languages of Puerto Rico. Many speak English—and many people don't, especially older people in outlying rural areas. In San Juan however, English is taught from kindergarten to high school as part of the school curriculum.

MEDICAL EMERGENCIES

Officially, the medical community of Puerto Rico meets the same standards as those required on the U.S. mainland (just explain why most rich Puerto Ricans come to the States for medical attention). Most physicians on the island are based in San Juan with almost all medical specializations represented. San Juan has 14 hospitals, most districts have at least one. Ask your hotel to recommend a physician on call.

MONEY

The official currency is the U.S. dollar and credit cards are widely accepted by hotels, restaurants and shops. Several foreign exchange offices are available in San Juan and at the airport.

TELEPHONE

The area code is *809*. Postage stamps are equivalent to those in the U.S. as are mail costs. You can dial direct to the mainland.

TIME

Atlantic Standard Time, year-round, which is one hour earlier than New York. During Daylight Saving Time, it is the same.

TIPPING AND TAXES

All hotels include a 6 percent government tax on the bill. Gratuities on restaurant bills are not included, but a usual 15 percent tip is expected.

TOURIST INFORMATION

For more information about the island, contact the **Puerto Rico Tourism Company**, *La Princesa Building, Old San Juan, PR 00901;* ☎ *(809) 721-2400*. There are offices in New York, Los Angeles, Coral Gables, London, Madrid, Mexico City, Milan, Paris, Stockholm, Toronto and Weisbaden, Germany. In the U.S. ☎ *(213) 874-5991*.

WHEN TO GO

January-May the Puerto Rico Symphony Orchestra conducts its season with performances through May. January 6 is traditional gift-giving day in Puerto Rico, celebrated by island-wide festivals with music, dance, parades, puppet shows and caroling troubadours. Jan. 1–19 is the International Folklore Festival, featuring dance groups from around the world. February (usually 3rd weekend) is the Coffee Harvest Festival. Carnival usually happens the second week in February. The Sugar Harvest Festival takes place in May. The Festival Casals takes place in early June, honoring the late cellist. San Juan Bautista Day is June 23, celebrating the island's patron saint, as sanjuaneros walk backward into the sea three times at midnight for good luck. The Albonito Flower Festival takes place in July. The Barranquitas Artisans Fair is held July 16–18, the island's oldest crafts fair with 130 local artisans. The 42nd International Billfish Tournament takes place in September. The Inter-American Festival of the Arts takes place in September. The National Plantain Festival occurs in late October. The baseball season begins in October. The Festival of Typical Dishes lasts from November-December. Old San Juan's White Christmas Festival takes place December-January. Island-wide Christmas festivities with life-size nativity scenes are held December–January. The Bacardi Arts Festival featuring more than 200 craftsmen is in December. Lighting of the Town of Bethlehem occurs for three days in mid-December.

In general, spring is always a good time to visit San Juan. Old San Juan is less crowded with cruise ship day trippers than during the winter, hotels rates begin to drop, and many hotels offer inexpensive summer packages to lure visitors during the slowest months. Puerto Rico doesn't have extreme seasonal changes so you may see that quintessential Christmas flower, the poinsettia blooming and mangoes ripening in the same gardens. San Juan shuts down for much of Holy Week, but there are Easter celebrations. An annual sunrise Easter service is usually held at **El Morro**. For more information call Rev. Martha McCracken ☎ *(809) 722-5372.*

PUERTO RICO HOTELS	RMS	RATES	PHONE	FAX
Culebra				
★★ **Club Seabourne**	10	$65–$125	(809) 742-3169	A, MC, V
★★ **Harbor View Villas**	10	$50–$95	(809) 742-3855	MC, V
Puerto Rico				
East and Southeast Coast				
★★★★★ **El Conquistador Resort**	926	$170–$420	(800) 468-8365	A, CB, D, MC, V
★★★★ **Palmas del Mar Humacao**	298	$145–$715	(800) 468-3331	A, MC, V
★ **Parador La Familia**	28	$50–$70	(800) 443-0266	A, D, MC, V
★ **Parador Martorell**	10	$50–$85	(800) 443-0266	A, MC
Northwest Coast				
★★ **Days Inn**	121	$80–$140	(800) 325-2525	A, CB, D, DC, MC, V
★★ **Parador El Guajataca**	38	$77–$95	(800) 964-3065	A, CB, D, DC, MC

PUERTO RICO HOTELS	RMS	RATES	PHONE	FAX
★★ **Parador Vistamar**	55	$60–$75	(800) 443-0266	A, CB, D, MC, V
San Juan				
★★★★★ **El San Juan Hotel/Casino**	390	$250–$995	(800) 468-2818	A, CB, MC, V
★★★★★ **Hyatt Dorado Beach**	298	$160–$490	(800) 233-1234	A, CB, D, MC, V
★★★★★ **Hyatt Regency Cerromar**	504	$165–$420	(800) 233-1234	A, CB, D, MC, V
★★★★★ **Sands Hotel & Casino**	410	$290–$305	(809) 791-6100	A, CB, D, DC, MC, V
★★★★ **Caribe Hilton & Casino**	670	$200–$1200	(800) 468-8585	A, CB, D, MC, V
★★★★ **Condado Plaza Hotel**	575	$195–$355	(800) 468-8588	A, CB, D, MC, V
★★★★ **Radisson Ambassador Plaza**	233	$170–$320	(800) 333-3333	A, CB, D, MC, V
★★★ **Best Western Pierre**	184	$97–$145	(800) 528-1234	A, CB, D, DC, MC, V
★★★ **Casa San Jose**	10	$205–$315	(800) 223-6510	A, DC, MC, V
★★★ **Condado Beach Trio**	481	$140–$195	(800) 468-2775	A, CB, D, DC, MC, V
★★★ **Holiday Inn Crowne Plaza**	254	$185–$390	(800) 468-4578	A, CB, D, DC, MC, V
★★★ **Radisson Normandie**	177	$160–$240	(800) 333-3333	A, CB, D, DC, MC, V
★★ **Atlantic Beach Hotel**	37	$60–$140	(809) 721-6900	A, D, MC, V
★★ **Carib Inn Tennis Club**	225	$105–$320	(800) 548-8217	A, CB, D, DC, MC, V
★★ **El Canario Inn**	25	$80–$125	(809) 722-3861	A, CB, D, DC, MC, V
★★ **El Canario by the Lagoon**	40	$65–$110	(809) 722-5058	A, D, MC, V
★★ **Grande Hotel El Convento**	150	$85–$200	(800) 468-2779	A, CB, D, DC, MC, V
★★ **Hotel Portal Del Condado**	48	$95–$125	(809) 721-9010	A, CB, D, DC, MC, V
★★ **International Airport**	57	$80–$90	(809) 791-1700	A, CB, MC, V
★★ **Parador Hacienda Gripinas**	11	$64–$107	(800) 443-0266	MC, V
★★ **Ramada Hotel Condado**	96	$130–$300	(800) 468-2040	A, D, DC, MC, V
★★ **Regency Hotel**	127	$140–$225	(800) 468-2823	A, CB, D, MC, V
★★ **San Juan Travelodge**	88	$125–$175	(800) 428-2028	A, CB, D, MC, V
★ **Arcade Inn**	19	$40–$90	(809) 728-7524	A, MC

PUERTO RICO HOTELS	RMS	RATES	PHONE	FAX
★ El Canario by the Sea	25	$80–$125	(800) 533-2649	A, DC, MC, V
★ Green Isle Inn	44	$43–$73	(800) 677-8860	A, MC, V

South Coast

★★★ Ponce Hilton and Casino	153	$170–$375	(800) 445-8667	A, CB, D, DC, MC, V
★★ Harbour View Villas	8	$50–$95	(809) 742-3855	A, MC, V
★★ Melia Hotel	77	$70–$90	(800) 742-4276	A, CB, D, DC, MC, V
★★ Parador Banos de Coamo	48	$55–$65	(809) 825-2239	A, CB, D, DC, MC, V
★★ Ponce Holiday Inn	119	$97–$145	(800) 465-4329	A, CB, D, DC, MC, V
★ Parador Boquemar	63	$65–$70	(800) 443-0266	A, CB, DC, MC, V
★ Parador Posada Porlamar	18	$45–$90	(800) 443-0266	A, MC, V
★ Parador Villa Parguera	63	$80–$90	(800) 443-0266	A, CB, D, DC, MC, V

West Coast

★★★★★ Horned Dorset Primavera	30	$150–$440	(809) 823-4030	A, MC, V
★★★ Holiday Inn Mayaguez	152	$120–$240	(800) 465-4329	A, D, MC
★★★ Mayaguez Hilton	141	$135–$180	(800) 445-8667	A, MC
★★ Parador Oasis	53	$107	(800) 223-9815	A, CB, D, MC, V

Vieques

★★ Sea Gate Guest House	17	$40–$85	(809) 741-4661	None

PUERTO RICO RESTAURANTS	PHONE	ENTREE	CR. CARDS

San Juan

American			
★★ The Chart House	(809) 728-0110	$16–$25••	A, DC, MC, V
Chinese			
★★★ Back Street Hong Kong	(809) 791-1000	$15–$32••	A, MC, V
French			
★★★★ La Chaumiere	(809) 722-3330	$22–$37••	A, DC, MC, V

PUERTO RICO RESTAURANTS	PHONE	ENTREE	CR. CARDS
International			
★★★ **El Patio de Sam**	(809) 723-1149	$9–$25	A, DC, MC, V
★★ **Butterfly People**	(809) 723-2432	•$5–$9	A, DC, MC, V
Italian			
★★ **Al Dente**	(809) 723-7303	$10–$15	A, MC, V
Latin American			
★★★★ **Amadeus**	(809) 722-8635	$8–$16	A, MC, V
★★★ **Ajilli-Mojili**		$15–$25	A, MC, V
★★★ **La Bombonera**	(809) 722-0658	$5–$8	A, MC, V
★★★ **La Casona de Serafin**	(809) 851-0066	$10–$31	A, MC, V
★★★ **La Mallorquina**	(809) 722-3261	$14–$30	A, DC, MC, V
★★★ **Parador Villa Parguera**	(809) 899-7777	$5–$20	A, CB, D, DC, MC, V
★★ **Anchor's Inn**	(809) 863-7200	$8–$20	A, MC, V
Spanish			
★★★★★ **La Compostela**	(809) 724-6088	$15–$29	A, DC, MC, V
★★★★★ **Ramiro's**	(809) 721-9049	$24–$33	A, DC, MC, V

South Coast

Mexican			
★★ **Lupita's Mexican**	(809) 848-8808	$7–$26	A, DC, MC, V
Seafood			
★★★ **El Ancla**	(809) 840-2450	$3–$28	A, DC, MC, V

West Coast

Seafood			
★★★★★ **Horned Dorset Primavera**	(809) 823-4030	$15–$45	A, MC, V
Note: • Lunch Only			
•• Dinner Only			

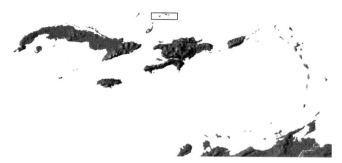

TURKS & CAICOS ISLANDS

The Caicos feature extensive caverns and caves.

Turks & Caicos sound like something out of an Arabian fantasy, and indeed, most Americans have never heard of this archipelago of arid and rough-hewn islands lying 575 miles southeast of Miami. The beauty of this region is simply the pure interplay of earth and water, the contrast of sculpted limestone formations interspersed with sprawling, unspoiled beaches, groves of cactus and thickly entwined scrub bush, and acres of spreading mangroves and wetlands. As a result, these islands offer plenty of opportunities for the observation of natural behavior, particularly in the deserted cays etched along the shoreline. The entire chain of the large Caicos islands, from

473

uninhabited East Caicos to North Caicos, is cut through with extensive caverns and cave systems, many of which have offered up artifacts traced back to the Taino Indians. Besides excellent diving, the wetlands offer serious exploration to the intrepid, graced by the flaming pinks of flamingos that inhabit the islands of South Caicos, North Caicos and Grand Turk. Other great bird-watching is found along the shores of Lake Catherine on West Caicos.

Providencials (familiarly known as Provo), is one of the most popular roosting grounds for visitors, having led the Turks and Caicos into the modern age of tourism. Just 25 years ago, Provo had no roads other than foot or donkey paths connecting its three settlements; there was not even a single motorized vehicle, and most locals made their living by fishing, farming or bartering. Today one of Provo's greatest assets is a broad, unbroken extent of beach stretching 12 miles along the shore of Grace Bay. Accommodations here can run from the small- to the medium-sized hotel to luxury condos to resorts. There's a modern telecommunications system, and access to items generally unavailable elsewhere. There is also fine dining, nightclubs, casinos, a bit of shopping, tennis courts and an 18-hole golf course. Virtually every type of watersports toy is available. But the best thing about the Turks & Caicos is that nobody cares who or what you are, as long as you pay the bill.

Bird's Eye View

Located 575 miles southeast of Miami and about 100 miles north of Hispaniola (the Dominican Republic and Haiti), the Turks and Caicos are an extension of the same geological structures that make up The Bahamas. In fact, they were part of the same country until 1874, when the two countries were divided by Great Britain to make governing them easier.

The 50-plus islands of the Turks and Caicos are arrayed around the edges of two large, limestone platforms. These platforms are not unlike the great mesas of the American southwest, huge, flat-topped structures surrounded by cliffs. The big difference is that the limestone platforms of the Turks and Caicos are awash in water that seldom exceeds a depth of 20 feet. The westernmost bank, Caicos, is the largest of the two by far. It serves as the base for six primary islands—West Caicos, Providenciales (Provo), North Caicos, Middle Caicos, East Caicos and South Caicos—along with some 30 smaller

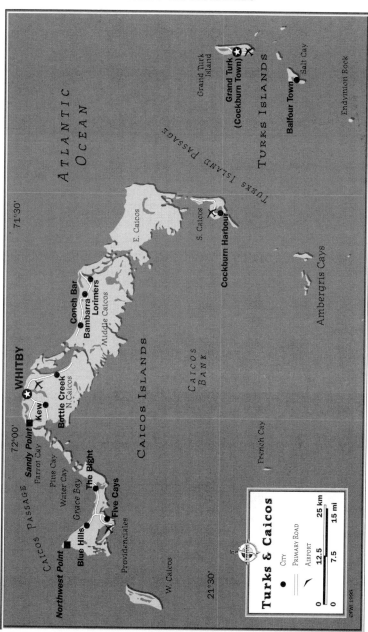

Turks & Caicos

● CITY

═══ PRIMARY ROAD

✈ AIRPORT

0   12.5   25 km

0   7.5   15 mi

©PMI 1998

cays. The bulk of this land mass is clustered across the north of the bank, with just a few small (but significant) islands elsewhere.

The Caicos are encircled by a barrier reef lying from one to two miles offshore. Between the reef and the islands are scattered coral in calm, clear waters. The two groups of islands are separated by a deep channel between the Caribbean and the Atlantic.

History

Serious evidence suggests that Grand Turk was the first landfall made by Columbus in 1492. Since the islands had no riches, however, the fleet quickly moved on. For 900 years prior, the Taino and Lucayan Amerindians had occupied these islands, having originated in the Orinocco region in South America—peace-loving tribes who had survived by fishing, farming and trading dried conch meat and conch pearls in Hispaniola to the south. Only 40 years after their first European contact, the native tribes were totally wiped out by enslavement, disease and abuse. With the exception of an odd shipwrecked sailor, the islands remained uninhabited for more than 200 years.

In the mid-1600s, Bermudian salt rakers arrived and their influence is still felt. They divided the tidal lakes on Salt Cay, Grand Turk and South Caicos into salt pans (called *slainas*), controlled the flooding and evaporating of the sea water and raked out the salt, creating an industry that was the mainstay of the economy for the next 275 years. Even today, broken windmills stand, ghostly sentinels over the salinas. Simultaneously, buccaneers hiding out in the Caicos preyed on treasure vessels passing through the Caicos Passage. Colorful legends still abound about Calico Jack Rackman and the two women pirates Bonnie Anne and Mary Reid. In the late 1700s, British patriots departing from the newly formed United States arrived, taking up the role in the growing plantocracy of sisal and cotton—a valiant but frustrating attempt doomed to failure. The most extensive ruins of plantations may be seen at Yankeetown on West Caicos and Wade's Green on North Caicos.

Today with the exception of Provo, time stands still here. History is found in every cove on the Turks and Caicos. The outlines of wrecked vessels in the shallow sand, the Loyalist plantation homes and workhouses abandoned to weather lie rusting and in ruins. The history is peppered with tales of explorers and adventurers, indentured servants, slaves, fishermen, pirates, salt rakers and shipbuilders.

Underwater

Divers in the Turks/Caicos Islands may run into the Spanish hogfish.

Providenciales

Although its walls are comparable in many ways to those of the world re-nown Cayman Islands, diving amid the Turks and Caicos Islands still feels a little like an insider's secret. But the reality is that one dive shop has been es-tablished for over a quarter-century now, and the number of divers visiting the islands has skyrocketed over the past decade. You may not be touring vir-gin reefs and walls, but the undersea display is still quite wild and pristine, with magnificent visibility (almost always exceeding 100 feet, and approach-ing 200 feet during the summer months), and you won't have to deal with the crowds who pack the Caymans year-round.

The archipelago is actually two separate geological structures divided by the Turk Island Passage, a 22-mile undersea trench, 7000 feet deep, which connects the Caribbean Sea with the Atlantic Ocean. Each of the island groups, the Caicos to the west and the smaller Turks to the east, are essen-tially great mesas rising from either side of the passage, with a water depth rarely exceeding 20 feet. Most of the barrier reef surrounding the islands is undistinguished. But two great wall formations, both running roughly southwest to northeast, provide the impressive diving: one drops into the Turks Passage immediately west of Grand Turk and Salt Cay (discussed in the Turks section below), the other wall abuts the Caicos Passage, just west of Provo and West Caicos.

The Provo dive shops typically visit four different areas. **Grace Bay**, the long sweep of water immediately north of The Bight, features a tapered spur-and-groove barrier reef from 30 feet down to 60, where a mini-wall starts and drops to about 100 feet below the surface; these sites are close to most of the Provo operators. To the north, **Pine Cay** also features a spur-and-groove reef system of rolling undersea mountains that drop from 50 feet down to 150; two easier sites are usually frequented here, **Football Field** and **Meridian Club Reef**. **Northwest Point**, about a 45-minute boat ride from Grace Bay, overlooks the wall, which lies about a third-mile off the Provo west coast. The wall starts 45 to 50 feet below the surface, descends another hundred feet to a ledge or platform only a few feet wide in some places, and then drops for thousands of feet into the abyss. The fourth area lies off uninhabited **West Caicos**, where the wall parallels the island as close as 500 feet from the shore; these sites are over an hour away from the dive shops on Provo, but yield some of the very best diving in the island chain. In winter months, when winds blow from the northeast, the wall sites offer the best visibility, while the barrier reefs are best during the summer as winds come in from the southeast.

There are some sites along **South Caicos**, 40 miles east of Provo, as well as idyllic diving off remote, uninhabited **French Cay**, but these are generally visited only by the several live-aboard boats which troll the waters, and only sporadically at that. Otherwise, neither the Provo operations nor the Turks dive shops visit their counterparts' sites; the distances by sea are much too far for day trips. There are several wreck sites, but the most famous, the W.E., was churned around in a recent storm and slid down the slope it was resting on to a depth below safe diving limits; the other wrecks on the Provo side are mere distractions from the real star of Caicos diving, the splendid wall. A recompression chamber is available at Menzies Medical Practice on Provo.

The Crack

A big vertical cut splits the wall between 50 and 100 feet and draws a variety of unusual creatures, including West Indian spider crabs. Black corals and demure sea fans hide additional cracks which parallel the coastline at Northwest Point.

The Gulley

This West Caicos site begins at 45 feet in a sandy bowl which pours over the edge of the precipice like a waterfall. On each side of the canyon are massive plate coral formations festooned with huge barrel sponges, particularly below 100 feet.

Shark Hotel

Reef sharks sometimes check in, but this site, located off Northwest Point, is also known for excellent sponge growth and giant pillar corals. The mini-wall (45 to 110 feet) offers a chimney and several crevices, while a swim-through arch drips with rope sponges. Bringing a light to this site will help accentuate the dynamic palette of color.

White Face (a k a Anchor)

The limestone bluff rising above the nearby West Caicos shoreline provides the name, but an eight-foot-high anchor embedded in coral at the lip of the wall, is the underwater highlight; it is thought to be from an 18th-century Spanish galleon and is fabulously encrusted. The anchor is reached via a undercut swim-through gulley featuring heavy sponge growth.

Dive Shops

Art Pickering's Provo Turtle Divers

Turtle Cove Marina, ☎ *(800) 887-0477 or (809) 946-4232.*
Turks and Caicos oldest dive shop opened in 1970. Three boats, one with a 20-diver capacity. A PADI outfit, but can do NAUI and SSI referrals. Two tank dive $60.

Dive Provo

Grace Bay, Provo; ☎ *(809) 946-5029.*
Two tank dive, $60. Night dive Wednesday and Friday, $45. Based at Turquoise Reef Resort. Only PADI five-star facility in Turks and Caicos, courses to Divemaster. Kayak rentals.

Flamingo Divers

Turtle Cove Marina; ☎ *(800) 204-9282 or (809) 946-4193.*
Open since 1988, PADI and SSI affiliated, with courses to assistant instructor. Two tank dive price $60. Uses two smaller boats for groups of 14 or less. Trips to French Cay, weather permitting.

Sea Dancer/Peter Hughes Diving

☎ *(800) 932-6237 or (305) 669-9391.*
One of two live-aboard boats plying the Turks and Caicos waters, the *Sea Dancer* visits West Caicos, Great and Little Inagua and Hogsty Reef (the latter islands are in the Bahamas). All-inclusive prices for the seven-day trip, $1395-1595 (based on type of berth selected). The *Sea Dancer* sleeps 18 and departs every Saturday out of Provo (summer trips focus exclusively on the Bahamas). Beginners with referrals may obtain their open water certification on the Sea Dancer ($198).

Turks and Caicos Aggressor

(800) 348-2628 or (809) 946-5600.
Seven-day, all-inclusive live-aboard trips, $1495. Includes five-and-a-half days of diving and all food; trips depart every Saturday from Provo. Instructor available on all dives, and certification courses are $300 (open water certification $150). 16-passenger boat visits West Caicos, French Caye, Provo and South Caicos. Incorporates whale watching itinerary in January and February (additional $100).

Grand Turk

If Provo is an escape from well-known destinations, Grand Turk, which has been dived for only the past decade, is quieter still. The Turks Island Passage serves as a conduit between the Caribbean and Atlantic, providing much of the rich marine life into the region. Summer months draw mantas to the passage, and January through March brings humpback whales, that can swim quite close to Grand Turk and actually hover off Salt Cay on their annual trek to and from their winter breeding grounds off the Dominican Republic. The massive wall plunges from a point only a quarter-mile off Grand Turk's shoreline, and the crest of the wall sits at an average of just 30 to 40 feet below the surface. There are virtually no currents, and the minimal rain runoff allows visibility to average 120 feet year-round, but it can extend much further in the calm summer months. Weather permitting, the Grand Turk dive shops sometimes make the long trip to **Salt Cay**, which features lovely sites, but only Porpoise Divers makes the occasional haul even further south to the **_H.M.S. Endymion_**. Salt Cay is, for now, the last frontier of Turks and Caicos destinations, averaging under 500 dive visitors a year; spectacular snorkeling amid giant coral formations in 15 feet of water is available at **Point Pleasant**.

The Library

Positioned directly in front of the pink stucco Cockburn Town library, this spot is a spectacular night dive when orange ball corallimorphs light up the scenery. The floor is covered with ballast stones, tossed from ships which anchored here, that have become encrusted with coral and have proven ideal for sheltering crabs, lobster, eels and other hiding creatures. The adjacent wall begins at only 18 feet and features sprigs of black coral at its lip.

Mcdonald's

A single impressive coral arch (not, thankfully, gold in color) marks this location, possibly the most popular site off Grand Turk (70 feet). The area is known for huge elephant ear sponges and its resident angels who are chummy with divers; a sheer drop plunges off the edge of the wall nearby. An abundance of invertebrates makes the site colorful at night.

Wreck of the _H.M.S. Endymion_

Located nearly 20 miles south of Salt Cay, Endymion Rock marks the location of the _H.M.S. Endymion_, which went down in a hurricane in 1790. The ship was found in 1992 and has not been salvaged. Although the hull has long been consumed by the reef, four anchors and over a dozen cannons mark the site, and at least two other more recent wrecks lie nearby. The reef that confronted these ships offers excellent diving down to 25 feet, and features huge tunnels.

Dive Shops

Blue Water Divers

Front Street, Cockburn Town; ☎ *(809) 946-2432.*

Two-tank dive, $55; single-tank dive, $30; night dives, $35. Resort courses, $85; PADI training to Divemaster. Largest group size, eight.

Sea Eye Diving

Duke Street, Cockburn Town; ☎ *(809) 946-1407.*

PADI and NAUI instruction to assistant instructor. Largest group size, 12. Two tank dive, $55. Snorkeling trips to Gibbs Cay twice weekly, $40 with lunch.

Porpoise Divers

Salt Cay; ☎ *(809) 946-6927.*

Brian Sheedy started the diving on Salt Cay, opening his shop in 1988; the island now features nine moored sites. PADI affiliated, courses available to Divemaster. Single-tank dives, $25, packages also available. Grand Turk trips on Thursday; visits the Endymion and Grand San Cay once a week, weather permitting.

By Pedal

Cycling is definitely a sport in search of an audience, but Provo provides the best and most varied road network, allowing some touring possibilities. From the Grace Bay area, **North West Point** is about 15 miles, and the road travels through a few of the smaller villages on the island on its way to remote and relatively unvisited territory. The **Lower Bight Road**, which runs along the north coast to the Leeward Marina, is a shorter trip, under five miles to the eastern tip of the island.

Rental Shops

Scooter Rental

Ocean Club, Grace Bay; ☎ *(809) 946-4684.*

Rents single-speed Huffys, $12 per day, $60 for a week.

Grand Turk

Six miles long by one mile across, Grand Turk is the seat of government for the Turks and Caicos. Accommodations here largely take the form of historic hotels dating from the early 1800s. This is an ideal place for divers who don't like places that cater to tourists. Activities here center around diving, or simply lying on the beach and taking it easy.

What to See

Turks and Caicos National Museum, a must-see under the direction of Brian Riggs, gives you a glimpse into the early days of the islands, reaching back to the tribal population. A special exhibit on the **Molasses Reef** wreck, found on the southern reaches of the Caicos Bank, is fascinating. The wreck, dating from the early days of the 16th century, is the first recorded European wreck in the New World.

Museums and Exhibits
Turks

Turks & Caicos National Museum   ★★★

Guinep House, Cockburn Town, ☎ *(809) 946-2160.*
Hours open: 9 a.m.–4 p.m.

This small museum, housed in an old stone building, centers on the nation's people and natural history. The highlight is the wreck of a caravel that sank on Molasses Reef in 1513, believed to be the earliest shipwreck found in the Americas.

Providenciales

Island Sea Center   ★★★

Blue Hills, ☎ *(809) 946-5330.*

Visitors can learn about the ocean and its creatures at this spot, highlighted by the Caicos Conch Farm, where the tasty critters are bred from tiny eggs. You can watch a video on their production and a touch tank allows for up-close inspections. The admission is $6.00 for Adults and $3.00 for Children.

Sports/Recreation
Turks

Watersports

Various locations, Cockburn Town.

These islands are especially known for their excellent beaches and wonderful scuba diving. If your hotel lacks the necessary equipment, try one of these. Grand Turk: **Blue Water Divers** *(Fax: 946-2432)* and **Sea Divers** *(*☎ *946-1407).* Diving on Providenciales can be found at **Dive Provo** *(*☎ *946-5040),* **Provo Turtle Divers** *(*☎ *946-4232),* and **Flamingo Divers** *(*☎ *946-4193).* Boats can be rented at Provo at **Dive Provo** *(9*☎ *46-5040).*

Providenciales

Provo Golf Club

Blue Hills, ☎ *(809) 946-5591.*
Hours open: 7 a.m.–7 p.m.

This challenging course, designed by Karl Litten, just opened in 1991. It has 18 holes and a par of 72. There's a club house, driving range, and pro shop on the premises. Greens fees are about $80, cart included.

Salt Cay

Salt Cay is stuck in time. It's a monument to the days when salt ruled the island—from 1673 until production ceased in 1971. Today you can still see tools lying about, exactly as they were dropped on their final day of use—the great houses along the shoreline are still packed with high-quality sea salt, the final harvest that was never shipped. As a historical testimony to an era long gone, Salt Cay is considered so important it has been named a World Heritage site by UNESCO. The island has only 200 residents, a couple of small hotels, one guest house and a dozen motorized vehicles. There is one professional dive operator who not only specializes in the excellent shallow reef and wall sites along the island but also does whale watching in the winter months and runs to the isolated wreck of the *Endymion*.

FIELDING'S CHOICE:

Both Grand Turk and Salt Cay, down to the Mouchoir and Silver Banks off Hispaniola, are the southern terminus of the migrational route of the Atlantic herd of some 2500 humpback whales. Sightings happen daily from December–April and divers frequently have a chance encounter both in water and from the boat.

Where to Stay

♰	**Fielding's Highest Rated Hotels in Turks & Caicos Islands**	
★★★★★	**Club Med Turkoise**	$121–$235
★★★★★	**Meridian Club**	$395–$575
★★★★	**Grace Bay Club**	$255–$725
★★★	**Le Deck Hotel**	$95–$175
★★★	**Prospect of Whitby**	$90–$460
★★★	**Ramada Turquoise Reef**	$125–$460
★★★	**Turquoise Reef**	$125–$190
★★★	**Windmills Plantation**	$440–$595

♡	**Fielding's Most Romantic Hotels in Turks & Caicos Islands**	
★★★★★	**Meridian Club**	$395–$575
★★★	**Prospect of Whitby**	$90–$460
★★★	**Windmills Plantation**	$440–$595

	Fielding's Budget Hotels in Turks & Caicos Islands	
★	**Turks Head Inn**	$55–$80
★★	**Sunworshippers Pelican Beach Club**	$70–$120
★★	**Coral Reef Beach Club**	$65–$135
★★	**Erebus Inn**	$80–$150
★★★	**Le Deck Hotel**	$95–$175

Most of the rentals on the Turks and Caicos are in Provo, although you ca[n] find a few cottage rentals on the out islands. **Cockburn**, the capital of Gran[d] Turk, caters to small hotels that are personally run by colorful locals. **Turk[s] Head Inn** is an unusually atmospheric 19th-century dwelling with six room[s.] Even the hotels/resorts in North Caicos hardly aspire to their name, but a[t]

erviceable to those who have come to experience the outdoors. Overlook-
ıg the south side of Providenciales are attractive, newly refurbished one and
wo-bedroom apartments in **Casuarina**. The only property that can be faith-
ılly called a resort is the **Meridian Club** in Pine Cay, a private island, where
ou will find 23 private homes and 15 hotel guest rooms. One of the loveli-
st places to stay is the **Windmills Plantation Salt Cay**, a 2.5-square mile isle
ıat was the hub of the salt industry in the '60s. The colonial-style property is
uilt around the plantation great house and is situated on a superb beach.
or information about lodging in the Middle Caicos and South Caicos, con-
ıct the Tourist Board. Sometimes locals open up their homes.

Hotels and Resorts
Grand Turk

The best property here is **Turks Head Inn**, in Cockburn Town, formerly the Govern-
ıent Guest House turned American Consulate, housed in a 19th-century mansion, com-
lete with hardwood floors and antique furnishings.

uanahani Beach Hotel   **$120–$165**   ★ ★

*P.O. Box 178, Guanahani Beach, Cockburn Town, ☎ (800) 468-8752, (809) 946-
2135, FAX (809) 946-1460.*
Single: $120–$165. Double: $120–$165.
This small hotel is a 20-minute walk from Cockburn Town. Guestrooms are simple
and rely on ceiling fans to keep cool. This property attracts mainly divers, and has
an excellent dive shop and resident instructor. There's also great snorkeling right off
the beach. Facilities include a restaurant, bar and pool at this casual spot.

ttina Hotel   **$75–$220**   ★ ★ ★

*Duke Street, Cockburn Town, ☎ (800) 548-8462, (809) 946-2232, FAX (809) 946-
2877.*
Single: $75–$215. Double: $95–$220.
Located on the west side, five minutes from town, this family-owned hotel is across
the street from the beach. Guestrooms are generally pleasant (but could use some
refurbishing), with local art, ceiling fans, and balconies; most are air conditioned.
The newer beachfront suites also have kitchenettes. The grounds include a dive
shop, two bars, a restaurant, and scooter rentals. The Friday night barbecues, held
around the pool, are great fun.

eridian Club   **$395–$575**   ★ ★ ★ ★ ★

Pine Cay, Cockburn Town, ☎ (800) 331-9154, (809) 946-5128, FAX (809) 946-5128.
Single: $395–$520. Double: $400–$575.
This deluxe operation is located on its own 800-acre private island with a very spectacular beach. Accommodations are in colorful and quite pleasant beachfront
rooms; 15 more expensive cottages supply sitting areas, screened porches, and
kitchenettes. The idea here is pure escapism; no TV, newspapers, or radios to
remind guests that there is a world out there. Ceiling fans and trade winds make up
nicely for the lack of air conditioners. There's a bar and restaurant, and active types
are kept happy with a pool, tennis court, watersports and nature trails. Nice.

Prospect of Whitby   **$90–$460**

North Beach, Cockburn Town, ☎ (809) 946-7119, FAX (809) 946-7114.
Single: $90–$195. Double: $145–$460.
Situated on seven miles of beach, this isolated hotel bills itself as perfect for escaping
the outside world. Rooms are spacious and air conditioned, with basic but comfort
able furnishings. There's a pool, tennis court, bar and restaurant on the premises
and they'll handle watersports requests.

Ramada Turquoise Reef   **$125–$460**   ★ ★ ★

Grace Bay Beach, ☎ (800) 228-9898, (809) 946-5555, FAX (809) 946-5522.
Single: $125–$460. Double: $125–$460.
This full-service Ramada is located on a lovely beach and is a good choice for
dependable, consistent lodging and facilities. Guestrooms are air conditioned and
comfortably appointed with modern amenities. There are three restaurants (includ
ing one offering Italian fare, a rare sight on this island), entertainment in the
lounge, a pool, two tennis courts, an exercise room and watersports. The Ramada
also boasts the island's only casino, so bring lots of cash.

Sunworshippers Pelican Beach Club   **$70–$120**   ★ ★

Sapodilla Bay, ☎ (809) 946-4488, FAX (809) 946-4488.
Single: $70–$95. Double: $70–$120.
Located at this island's south end and overlooking a pretty bay, this small hotel i
unique for its wonderful pastry shop, baked fresh each day by the owner himsel
Guestrooms are simple and airy with ceiling fans and ocean views. There's a div
shop on the pleasant beach, a bar and restaurant, and a small pool.

Windmills Plantation   **$440–$595**   ★ ★ ★

North Beach Road, Cockburn Town, ☎ (800) 822-7715, (809) 946-6962, FAX (41
820-9179.
Single: $440–$595. Double: $440–$595.
This all-inclusive resort is located on Salt Cay, nine miles south of Grand Turk. Se
on a 2.5-mile sandy beach, this recreated colonial plantation is a colorful and eclec
tic mix of architectural styles and facades that is as inviting as it is comfortable. Eac
lovely guestroom is uniquely decorated with four-poster beds, antiques, an
porches or verandas. Dinner is served by candlelight in the fine restaurant, and thre
bars keep thirsty throats at bay. There's also a pool and watersports, included in th
rates. Horseback riding and nature trails are nearby. Wonderful!

North Caicos

The finest property out of a small pool of unimpressive fish is the **Ocean Beach Clu**
an apartment complex with units rented when the owner is absent. Kitchens are include
A swimming pool is on the premises.

Pine Cay

The Meridien is romantic and rustic.

Providenciales

This is where some of the premier properties are located in the region. **Club Med** is sy
onymous with great food (a challenge here) as well as unmitigated enthusiasm for a

things sensuous. **Le Deck Hotel & Beach Club** comes in a close second, though the atmosphere is more inn-line.

The new **Grace Bay Club** has been elegantly designed as a Spanish village in stucco the color of the late-afternoon sun, with red-tiled roofs, terra-cotta floors, stone balustrades, wrought-iron balconies, umbrella-covered terraces and lush courtyards. The Canadian chef magically makes use of Caribbean ingredients, including the local spiny lobsters.

Club Med Turkoise $850–$1650 per wk ★★★★★

Blue Hills, ☎ *(800) 258-2633, (809) 946-4491.*

This large Club Med is one of the best in the chain. It is set on 70 acres with a mile-long beach and attracts mainly couples and singles devoted to scuba diving as well as the pleasures of a tropical vacation. Lodging is found in low-rise buildings lining the beach, all with two double beds and ceiling fans. The extensive facilities include three restaurants, a theater complex, a pool, eight tennis courts, a fitness center and a nightclub. The rates include all activities, meals and watersports, though you'll pay extra for diving and golf at a nearby course. Children from age 12 and teens are welcome, though unlike the family-oriented Club Meds, there are no special facilities for them. Rates range from $850 to $1650 per person per week, plus a one-time $30 membership fee and a $50 annual fee.

Grace Bay Club $255–$725 ★★★★

Grace Bay, ☎ *(800) 946-5758, (809) 946-5757, FAX (809) 946-5758.*
Single: $255–$555. Double: $355–$725.

Situated on a 12-mile sandy beach and designed to resemble a Mediterranean village, this deluxe choice pampers guests nicely. Lodging choices range from studios to one- and two-bedroom suites and penthouses, all air conditioned, elegantly appointed, and with kitchens and all the latest creature comforts. On-premise facilities include a gourmet restaurant, bar, pool, two tennis courts and most watersports.

Le Deck Hotel $95–$175 ★★★

Grace Bay, ☎ *(809) 946-5547, FAX (809) 946-5547.*
Single: $95–$175. Double: $95–$175.

This two-story hotel is located on Grace Bay's lovely sandy beach. The air-conditioned guestrooms are clean and simple. Facilities include a pool, watersports and a popular bar and restaurant. Lots of young singles and couples at this informal and popular spot.

Turquoise Reef $125–$190 ★★★

Grace Bay, ☎ *(800) 223-6510, (809) 946-5555, FAX (809) 946-5629.*
Single: $125–$160. Double: $155–$190.

This low-rise resort overlooks 12 miles of white sandy beach that is part of the Princess Alexandra National Marine Park. Accommodations are outfitted with balcony or patio, cable TV, air conditioning and tile floors. Facilities include a PADI dive shop and watersports center, a fitness club, two lit tennis courts, three restaurants and the Provo Golf Course. There's also nightly entertainment, weekly theme parties and the island's only casino. Inquire about dive and golf packages.

Turtle Cove Inn $90–$180   ★★

Blue Hills, ☎ *(800) 633-7411, (809) 946-4203.*
Single: $90–$180. Double: $90–$180.
This hotel, located at the marina, houses guests in air-conditioned rooms with TV,
VCRs, small refrigerators and phones. Sporting facilities include a pool, two clay
tennis courts, bike rentals, and watersports, including diving. Snorkelers can take
advantage of free boat service to a reef and beach. Ramada's casino is nearby and
there's lots within walking distance.

Salt Cay

Windmills Plantation is a five-minute flight from Grand Turk, hardly worth the time
to buckle up your seat belt. You must like small planes.

Apartments and Condominiums
Providenciales

Check with **Prestigious Properties** ☎ *(809) 946-4379* for villas and cottages that
have kitchen facilities. Don't expect any to come with a maid, though you might ask
around if a local is interested. Do audition first.

Ocean Club $125–$390   ★★

Grace Bay, ☎ *(809) 946-5880, FAX (809) 946-5845.*
Single: $125–$390. Double: $125–$390.
This deluxe condominium complex sits on nicely landscaped grounds fronting a
gorgeous beach. Accommodations are found in five buildings housing studios and
units of one to three bedrooms, all air conditioned and quite luxuriously appointed
with modern amenities and full kitchens. There's a bar and grill on-site, as well as a
pool and lighted tennis court. You can walk to the casino at the Ramada and area
restaurants. Very nice.

Grand Turk

Check with the agency **Prestigious Properties, Ltd.** ☎ *(809) 946-2463* for properties
with kitchens. Supplies will be a problem as you are sure not to find what you are accustomed to in this region. Bring whatever you have to have from home, or be willing to
make do.

Coral Reef Beach Club $65–$135   ★★

The Ridge, Cockburn Town, ☎ *(809) 946-2055, FAX (809) 946-2503.*
Single: $65–$135. Double: $65–$135.
This beachfront property accommodates guests in one- and two-bedroom apartments with motel-like furnishings and air conditioners. Recreational amenities
include a dive shop, watersports, a pool and a tennis court. There's also a bar and
restaurant for those not up to cooking in. A good combination of efficiency living
and hotel facilities.

Ocean Beach Hotel/Condos $94–$175   ★

Whitby, Cockburn Town, ☎ *(809) 946-7113.*
Single: $94–$145. Double: $105–$175.
This complex on North Caicos is set right on the beach. The ocean here is calm and
inviting thanks to a protective reef. Guests can choose from standard rooms or
apartments with kitchens, all done in rattan furnishings and with ocean views. Ceil-

ing fans do the job in lieu of air conditioners. Facilities include a bar, restaurant and pool, and they'll help arrange watersports and island tours.

Treasure Beach Villas   **$112–$175**   ★

Bight, Turtle Cove, ☎ (809) 946-4211, FAX (809) 946-4108.
Single: $112–$175. Double: $112–$175.

This complex offers one- and two-bedroom villas sitting on the beach, each with living and dining areas, full kitchens, and ceiling fans in lieu of air conditioners. There's a pool and tennis court on the premises, and restaurants are within a five-minute walk, though you're best off renting a car for true mobility. They'll help arrange watersports and deep-sea fishing.

Inns
Grand Turk

Erebus Inn   **$80–$150**   ★ ★

Turtle Cove Marina, Turtle Cove, ☎ (809) 946-4240, FAX (809) 946-4704.
Single: $80–$150. Double: $80–$150.

Set on a cliff with wonderful views, this cheerful spot accommodates guests in comfortable rooms, bungalows and chalets. All have telephones and TV, and 22 are air-conditioned. There's a restaurant, bar, two pools and two tennis courts on the premises, and they'll shuttle you over to a nearby beach. Unless your heart is set on being right on the sea, this property fills most needs very nicely.

Turks Head Inn   **$55–$80**   ★

Cockburn Town, ☎ (809) 946-2466, FAX (809) 946 2825.
Single: $55. Double: $80.

This Bermuda-style inn dates back to 1849 and was a government guest house and American Consulate in prior years. Guestrooms are simple but very pleasant with antiques, air conditioners, and private baths. Facilities are limited to a bar and restaurant.

Low Cost Lodging
Grand Turk

Anything considered inexpensive will be in the most basic of properties. For up-to-date options, contact the **Castaways Beach House ☎** *(809) 946-6921.*

Provo

In a region where upscale tourists are courted to the demise of the hard-core backpacker, cheap digs are hard to come by. Contact the tourist board for suggestions. Hotel rates drop late April to November.

Pine Cay

Smith's Cottage is about the only place on Pine Cay that has any rates close to low-cost. Again, on these high-priced islands, it's all relative, but rest assured, the surroundings won't be Club Med.

Salt Cay

Contact the Tourist Office for your best help in finding low-cost lodging. **Mount Pleasant Guest House ☎** *(809) 946-6927* has a storied reputation, but reservations must be made in advance.

Where to Eat

Fielding's Highest Rated Restaurants in Turks & Caicos Islands

★★★★★	Anacaona	$10–$32
★★★★	Alfred's Place	$12–$25
★★★★	Hey, Jose	$8–$14
★★★	Top o' the Cove	$5–$12

Fielding's Special Restaurants in Turks & Caicos Islands

| ★★★★★ | Anacaona | $10–$32 |

Fielding's Budget Restaurants in Turks & Caicos Islands

★★★	Top o' the Cove	$5–$12
★★★★	Hey, Jose	$8–$14
★★★★	Alfred's Place	$12–$25
★★★★★	Anacaona	$10–$32

Providenciales

Alfred's Place $$$ ★★★★

Turtle Cove, ☎ *(809) 946-4679.*
International cuisine.
Lunch: Noon–4 p.m., entrees $12–$19.
Dinner: 4–11 p.m., entrees $10–$25.
A French chef and Austrian owner dish out mostly American meals and stiff drinks
to an appreciative crowd. Diners schmooze and munch on a deck set above Turtle
Cove. Prime rib, swordfish, lobster, salads and sandwiches are on the bill of fare.

Anacaona $$$ ★★★★★

Grace Bay Club, ☎ *(809) 946-5950.*
International cuisine.
Lunch: entrees $10–$25.
Dinner: entrees $28–$32.
It's hard not to feel like a god or goddess while dining indolently under one of the
stunningly decorated thatched roofed huts fronting the ocean. Each of the dis

creetly spaced tables within display pristine napery and gleaming glassware and a single candle encased in a hurricane lamp. Ceiling fans cool the air and torches enhance the glow from the star-filled night sky. Succulent seafood straight off the fishing boats are often served tasting redolently of the in-house smoker. Terrific wine list, homemade desserts and Italian coffee drinks.

| ley, Jose | $$ | ★★★★ |

Atlas House, Leeward, ☎ *(809) 946-4812.*
Mexican cuisine.
Lunch: Noon–3 p.m., entrees $8–$13.
Dinner: 6–10 p.m., entrees $8–$14.

This airport area restaurant has a whiz behind the bar who makes the frothiest margaritas on the island. The chef keeps tasty platters of tacos and sizzling fajitas coming out of the kitchen at all hours of the day and night. Housed in a shopping center, it isn't very intimate, but that's not what the boisterous crowds come for. Pizza, burgers and chicken are also available.

| op o' the Cove | $ | ★★★ |

Leeward Highway, ☎ *(809) 946-4694.*
American cuisine.
Lunch: 6:30 a.m.–4 p.m., entrees $5–$12.

Homesick New Yorkers and other big city dwellers appreciate the bagels and deli fare provided by this cozy spot. The mean cups of eye-opening espressos and foamy cappuccinos wake everybody else out of a midday stupor. There's a nice atmosphere despite its location next to an auto parts store. Mostly take-out, but there are a few tables to park the body for an hour or two.

Turks and Caicos Directory

RRIVAL

Travel to and from the Turks and Caicos is made easy by **American Airlines**, the country's primary carrier, which flies into Provo from Miami seven times a week. Transfers to Grand Turk are handled by **Turks and Caicos Airways**, with small, six-passenger planes. TCA also flies a 19-passenger jet, offering alternative service from Nassau and Miami as well as other destinations. Air travel to all other inhabited islands is also offered by TCA as well as several small carriers such as Interisland.

A departure tax of $15 is collected at the airport.

USINESS HOURS

Shops generally open weekdays 8 a.m.–4 p.m. Banks open Monday–Thursday 8:30 a.m.–2:30 p.m. and Friday 8:30 a.m.–12:30 p.m. and 2:30–4:30 p.m.

LIMATE

Temperatures range from 75–85 degrees F. from November -May, spiraling up to the 90s in June through October. Constant trade winds keep the heat bearable. There is no marked rainy season. Hurricane season runs June-October.

DOCUMENTS

Visitors are required to write a valid passport (or proof of citizenship in the form of a birth certificate, voter's registration card plus a photo ID).

ELECTRICITY

Current runs 100 volts, 60 cycles, the same as in the United States.

GETTING AROUND

Those who've come to the Turks and Caicos for watersports and trekking will find that a cab to and from the airport is probably the only transportation they will need. Major hotels are within walking distance of a beach; those which aren't offer a shuttle service. However, restaurants and most attractions to Provo are located about a $10 taxi trip from most hotels, making a scooter or rental car necessary.

Taxis are unmetered, and rates, posted in the taxis, are regulated by the government. A trip between Provo's airport and most major hotels run $15. On Grand Turk, a trip from the airport to town is about $4.; from the airport to the hotels outside town $5–$10.

Rental cars are available on the island. On Provo, **Budget** ☎ *(809) 94-64079* and **Highway** ☎ *(809) 94-52623* offer the lowest rates, which average $40–$50 per day. Scooters are available at **The Honda Sho** ☎ *(809) 94-65585* and **Scooter Rental** ☎ *(809) 94-65585* an ☎ *(809) 94-64684* for $25 per 24-hour day.

Ferry service is available with the **Caicos Express** ☎ *(809) 94-6711* or *(809) 94-67258* with two scheduled interisland ferries between Provo, Pine Cay, Middle Caicos, Parrot Cay and North Caicos daily except Sunday. Tickets cost $15 each way. Caicos Express also offers various guided tours to the out islands.

A bus runs into town from most hotels on Providenciales, running about $2–$4 one-way. A new public bus system on Grand Turk charge 50 cents one-way to any scheduled stop.

LANGUAGE

The official language of the Turks and Caicos is English.

MEDICAL EMERGENCIES

Emergency medical care is provided at the **Provo Health Medical Centre** downtown ☎ *(809) 946-4201*, including eye and dentalwork. The government **Blue Hills Clinic** has a doctor and midwife on call ☎ *(809) 946-4228*. Grand Turk has a hospital on the north side of town. Other islands organize emergency air service to the closest hospital available

MONEY

The official currency of the Turks and Caicos is the U.S. dollar.

TELEPHONE

The area code is *809*. To dial direct from the U.S., dial *011* (international access) + *809* (country code) +local number. To make international calls from the Turks and Caicos, it's best to go to the Cable & Wireless office in Provo ☎ *(809) 94-64499* and Grand Turk ☎ *(809) 94-62200*. These offices are open Monday-Thursday 800 a.m.–4:30 p.m., Friday 8 a.m.–4 p.m. You can make calls from local phones with the use of a credit card purchased in increments of $5, $10 and $20.

TIME

Atlantic Standard Time, meaning one hour earlier than New York. During daylight saving time, it is the same time as New York.

TIPPING AND TAXES

Hotels charge a seven percent government tax and add a 10–15 percent service charge to your bill. In a restaurant, it's appropriate to leave a 10–15 percent tip if it is not added already; check so you don't duplicate efforts. Taxi drivers expect a small tip.

TOURIST INFORMATION

The **Turks and Caicos Islands Tourist Board** has a toll-free number on the islands ☎ *(800) 241-00824*. For hotel information, contact **The Turks & Caicos Resort Association** ☎ *(800) 2 TC-ISLES*.

WATER

Outside of Providenciales, where desalinators have transformed much of the island into a riot of flowers, water remains a precious commodity. Drink only from the decanter of fresh water provided by the hotel, but tap water is safe for brushing your teeth and other hygienic purposes.

WHEN TO GO

Late April to the end of November is off-season, when you can save 15–20 percent on hotel rates.

TURKS & CAICOS ISLANDS HOTELS	RMS	RATES	PHONE	CR. CARDS
Providenciales				
Blue Hills				
★★★★★ **Club Med Turkoise**	400	$850–$1650	(800) 258-2633	A, DC, MC, V
★★ **Turtle Cove Inn**	30	$90–$180	(800) 633-7411	A, D, MC, V
Grace Bay				
★★★★ **Grace Bay Club**	22	$255–$725	(800) 946-5758	A, MC, V
★★★ **Le Deck Hotel**	27	$95–$175	(809) 946-5547	A, D, MC, V
★★★ **Turquoise Reef**	228	$125–$190	(800) 223-6510	A, MC, V
★★ **Ocean Club**	32	$125–$390	(809) 946-5880	A, D, MC, V

TURKS & CAICOS ISLANDS HOTELS	RMS	RATES	PHONE	CR. CARDS
Turks				
Cockburn Town				
★★★★★ **Meridian Club**	28	$395–$575	(800) 331-9154	**None**
★★★ **Prospect of Whitby**	28	$90–$460	(809) 946-7119	A, MC, V
★★★ **Ramada Turquoise Reef**	228	$125–$460	(800) 228-9898	A, MC, V
★★★ **Windmills Plantation**	8	$440–$595	(800) 822-7715	A, V
★★ **Coral Reef Beach Club**	21	$65–$135	(809) 946-2055	A, D, MC, V
★★ **Erebus Inn**	30	$80–$150	(809) 946-4240	A, D, MC, V
★★ **Guanahani Beach Hotel**	16	$120–$165	(800) 468-8752	A, MC, V
★★ **Kittina Hotel**	43	$75–$220	(800) 548-8462	A, MC, V
★★ **Sunworshippers Pelican Beach Club**	25	$70–$120	(809) 946-4488	A, MC, V
★ **Ocean Beach Hotel/ Condos**	10	$94–$175	(809) 946-7113	MC, V
★ **Treasure Beach Villas**	18	$112–$175	(809) 946-4211	A, MC, V
★ **Turks Head Inn**	7	$55–$80	(809) 946-2466	A, MC, V

TURKS & CAICOS ISLANDS RESTAURANTS	PHONE	ENTREE	CR. CARDS
Providenciales			
Blue Hills			
American			
★★★ **Top o' the Cove**	(809) 946-4694	$5–$12•	A, MC, V
International			
★★★★★ **Anacaona**	(809) 946-5950	$10–$32	A, MC, V
★★★★ **Alfred's Place**	(809) 946-4679	$12–$25	A, MC, V
Mexican			
★★★★ **Hey, Jose**	(809) 946-4812	$8–$14	A, MC, V

Note: • Lunch Only

        •• Dinner Only

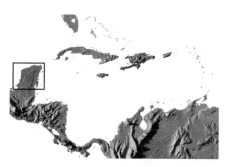

YUCATAN PENINSULA

Watersports of all types are readily available on the Yucatan Peninsula.

Until the 1960s, the Mexican Caribbean was a relatively undeveloped part of the world where people made their living by fishing or making hammocks, slippers, and rope from the henequen plant. Then the Mexican government (with the help of a computer) realized that the humble people of the Yucatan Peninsula were sitting right on top of what just might—with a little help from developers—turn out to be one of the world's most impressive playgrounds for the well-heeled tourists of the U.S. and Europe. So the pristine beaches were turned into hotel zones, cruise ships started making stops, divers started telling their friends that it didn't get much better than this, and—voila!—a few years later, the Mexican Caribbean was rivaling Acapulco as the country's tropical beachside hotspot. The rest, as they say, is history.

Bird's Eye View

The Yucatan Peninsula includes the states of Yucatan, Campeche and Quintana Roo, situated in southeast Mexico and bordered by the Caribbean Sea on the east, the Gulf of Mexico on the west, and Central America (Belize and Guatemala) on the south. Cancun, on the peninsula's northeast tip, and the island of Cozumel, south of Cancun and ten miles offshore, are the best-known resort areas, studded with high-class hotels and scads of tourists—the latter at a peak during the "on" season, which runs from late fall through March or April. Beaches are the main attraction, but the area is also rich in natural lagoons, sheltered bays, and coral reefs that make it a divers' paradise.

Playa del Carmen, approximately 40 miles south of Cancun and across from the island of Cozumel, is also in the process of developing into a major resort area, and is conveniently located partway between Cancun and Tulum. Ferry service connects Playa (as the locals refer to Playa del Carmen) to Cozumel, providing the final link between Playa and all major tourist sites, both coastal and inland.

The five-mile-long Isla Mujeres, located four miles off the coast, can be reached from both Cancun and Cozumel by boat or ferry, and offers lots of opportunities for exploring, as well as a plethora of premiere dive sites—including El Garron Reef—and incredibly gorgeous beaches. There are hotels on the island, but many prefer to visit Isla Mujeres as a day excursion.

Merida, capital of the state of Yucatan, is inland from the sea, but nearer to major archaeological sites such as Chichen Itza and Uxmal. It gets its own share of tourists, many of them on one- or two-day excursions from the resort cities, or as part of cruise ship shore excursions.

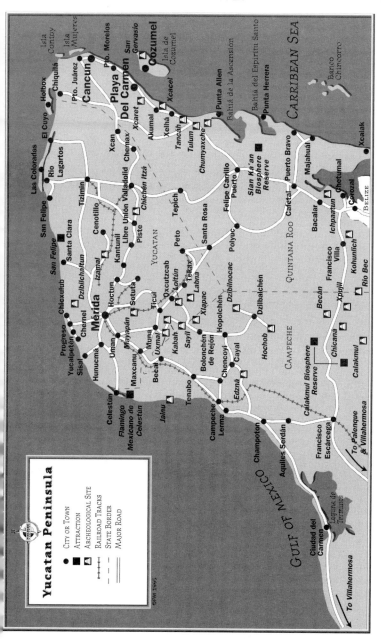

History

Before the Yucatan Peninsula was famous for its beaches, it was known as the land of the Maya, a people that lived in the region for approximately 1500 years, from the first century A.D. until the Spanish conquered Mexico in the early 16th century. By then, many of the Mayan cities had been abandoned, and others were in severe decline. What happened to the Mayan civilizations remains a mystery, but there are plenty of theories, and scientists continue to try and unlock the secrets of the magnificent temples and other buildings left standing—some still completely engulfed by the tropical jungle. The Spanish found that the Yucatan had little to offer in the way of riches, but small populations of people continued to live there, growing sugar cane and raising cattle until Mexico freed itself from Spain's domination in the early 1800s.

By the middle of the 19th century, henequen, a relative of the agave plant became an important cash crop, and was used to make rope, slippers, bags hammocks and many other products. Later, roads (Mexico 186 and 180 were built to connect the peninsula to the rest of Mexico, and the newly "found" area began to grow, a process that ended with the marketing o Cancun and Cozumel as playgrounds for the rich and famous.

People

It's hard to classify the people who live and work on the Mexican Caribbean. The native population of the Yucatan Peninsula consists mostly of descendents of the Maya (Indians) and people who are the result of mixed ancestry (Maya and European). Today, most of the Indians are concentrated in the state of Yucatan, but populations of indigenous peoples are to be found scattered throughout the peninsula. A variety of dialects are spoken but—except in the most remote areas—Indians can generally speak and understand Spanish. In the tourist zones, it is relatively easy to find someone who speaks English. The people of the Yucatan Peninsula are known to b

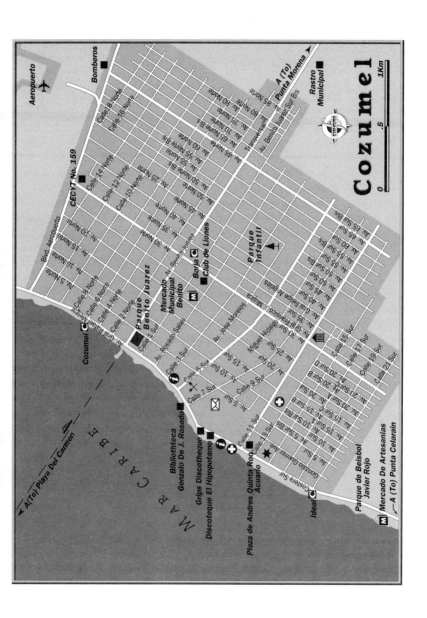

gracious and friendly, but you are still cautioned to be on your toes if you don't speak Spanish; there are those few who will not pass up an opportunity to take advantage of a "gringo" who is completely clueless about financial transactions.

Beaches

All of the beaches on the Mexican Caribbean are gorgeous, some with fine white sand and crystal-clear, turquoise waters, others with a rocky shore and crashing surf. (In contrast, the beaches on the Gulf of Mexico side of the peninsula are quite unimpressive.) Overcrowding is one of the biggest problems, especially in the hotel zones, and some hotels advertise that their beaches are private in order to make them seem less crowded and more exclusive. In fact, all beaches are public, so a "private" beach is no guarantee that you won't be inundated with other beach-goers. Vendors add to the confusion at popular beaches, loudly hawking their wares and pestering tourists to buy. On many beaches, sand flies are as pesky as the vendors, so you may have to add a little insect repellent on top of that sunscreen.

Popular beaches in Cancun include **Playa Chac-Mool**, a lovely beach that's not associated with a hotel; and **Playa Delfines**, which is slightly off the beaten path south of the Hotel Zone. In Cozumel, try **Playa San Francisco**, **Playa Chen Rio**, or the beach at **Palancar National Park**. On Isla Mujeres, **Playa Norte** has a generous stretch of beach and calm waters for swimming.

Not all of the Caribbean waters are as calm as they may look from shore, and unless you're swimming in a bay or along the inner coast, you may be at risk from strong undertows or large, hard-hitting waves. (Watch for the black and red flags that warn swimmers away.) Because of these dangerous conditions, calm, sheltered lagoons are often the destination of choice for swimmers and divers. In Cancun, **Nichupte Lagoon** beckons, and in Cozumel, **Chancanaab Bay** is a favorite spot for swimming and diving (the Chancanaab Lagoon is protected by the government and swimming is not allowed).

Underwater

Cozumel

You've read about it time and again, and your friends have raved for years. The waters are gin clear, drifting—no, soaring past a wall which drops 3000 feet—and it all costs less than virtually any other Caribbean destination. Cozumel beckons. What are you waiting for?

Cozumel's drift diving, possibly the best assortment in the world, is legendary—a true "e-ticket ride." However, those expecting simple or gentle currents may be in for a surprise. The **Palancar Reef**, which lies just off the island's southern tip, is not for the inexperienced. Another site, **Barracuda**, which sits at the north end of the island, can whip up drifts of five or six knots potentially hijacking divers straight out to sea (which is why the harbor master sometimes "shuts down" this area for divers). In fact, Cozumel is the only major Caribbean dive destination that has no use for permanent mooring sites; the dive boats just follow the trail of bubbles along the surface to keep track of divers. As a rule, a two-to-four knot current heads south to north along the island's west coast, but the speed varies and, even within a single area, it's not uncommon for the drift to spin divers around in a new direction. This makes communication between divers and divemaster unusually important. Although the area has been overfished, summer months draw Hawksbill and other turtles into the channel, while December brings eagle rays. Visibility averages 150 feet year round, with summer months clearing to a crystalline 200 feet or more.

Unfortunately, during the research for this chapter, the mood on Cozumel was decidedly glum. Talk to any local diver, and you'll hear bitter resignation about the construction of the new International Pier. Despite fierce opposition from most local dive operators, and intervention from no less than Jean-Michel Cousteau, Greenpeace and even "60 Minutes," the pier will tragically extend over Paradise Reef, long-renowned as one of the great night dives of the Caribbean. Paradise is no more and, lamentably, a few other adjoining beauties will be ruined by the construction as well. Diving has been big business for decades on Cozumel, but it has obviously been eclipsed by the burgeoning cruise ship industry, which will now pay up to $10,000 per day to dock one of their behemoths at the new facility. Money talks.

Divers visiting Cozumel may encounter one other annoying local phenomenon, and that is the high turnover of staff, and even ownership of the island's countless dive shops. It's difficult, therefore, to make unqualified recommendations about most of the local operators. Although some or even most of them are professional outfits, you are best advised to work with an American-based dive-packager and to solicit the opinions of others who have visited the island recently. There is a recompression chamber available in San Miguel. Snorkeling from shore is not ideal, although the inner area of **Chancanaab Park** will tantalize beginners. More avid snorkelers should hitch up with one of the dive boats, preferably one heading for the spellbinding **Palancar Gardens**.

Palancar Reef

Cozumel's most famous site is actually at least four different dives, spread over a spectacular mile-long reef; Palancar Gardens, Palancar Caves, Deep Palancar and Horseshoe Reef are the best-known attractions. The area features astounding mountains of coral climbing above the sandy bottom like a miniature Grand Canyon, with all the requisite channels and drop-offs. While the ride Palancar's current provides will keep your head spinning, there is plenty of fish life to be glimpsed, along with giant deep water fans, vibrant tube sponges and forests of black coral. The spectacle of Horseshoe Reef is probably the most dramatic of the dives, but you'll want to try them all.

Punta Sur

This is the newer site locals love to visit, but it's strictly for very advanced divers. The location lies off the island's southern tip and features coral spires and a dynamic, intimidating tunnel, the Devil's Throat, which drops vertically through the top of the reef (80 feet), turns horizontally, and exits onto the outside of the wall 120 feet down.

Santa Rosa

Immediately next to Palancar, the immensely popular Santa Rosa Wall begins at 80 feet, and features lovely passages topped by striking, yellow and orange sponge-covered coral heads. The dramatic wall and fantasy architecture are what people talk about, but everyone falls in love with the delightful big black groupers that dog divers as they whoosh through the moderate depths.

Tormentos

Split into three sections, the Upper, Middle and Lower Tormentos Reefs surround a mini-wall and are separated by wide channels of sand (40–60 feet). Reef life is more concentrated than at other sites, including French, queen and blue angels, and spotted morays. Some people can take in all three sections in a single dive, but why rush it? This is a beautiful reef you'll want to revisit.

Dive Shops

Dive House
Main Plaza, San Miguel; ☎ *(52) 987-21953.*

Dive House started in 1987, and has a bilingual, safety-conscious staff; PADI, NAUI and SSI affiliated. Maximum group size, 12; two-tank dive, $50.

Fantasia Divers Cozumel

San Miguel; ☎ *(800) 336-3483 or (52) 987-23009.*
Stable, 17-year-old PADI operation, run by American instructor. Two-tank dive, $50. Maximum group size, 16, with a ratio of one divemaster per eight divers.

Papa Hog's Scuba Emporium

San Miguel; ☎ *(52) 987-21651.*
Proclaims to be the "only 100% foreign-owned dive shop on the island," a four-year-old business affiliated with PADI (NAUI referrals), courses to Instructor level. Runs small, six-passenger dive boats

Cancun/Isla Mujeres

Real divers don't go to Cancun, they go to Cozumel. It's not that the reef shared by Cancun and Island Mujeres doesn't feature good diving, in fact, there's a greater abundance of fish life here than on Cozumel. It's just that Cancun has become known as the place where resort courses are taught to neophytes. Cozumel is the island where they haven't figured out how to install seatbelts for the dive ride. As one marine biologist pointed out, rather enthusiastically, the wall off Cozumel may be a great experience, but on Cancun's shallow reefs, you can see the bottom dwellers. Still, the area is good for beginners, offering gentle coastal diving featuring barracudas, moray eels and occasional nurse sharks. Divers, new or old, should steer clear of the cattle operations run by some resorts; you'll enjoy your diving more if you stick to a boat limited to 10 or 12. The **Cave of the Sleeping Sharks** is an unusual site, made famous by Jacques Cousteau many years ago, where a brackish coldwater spring lulls sharks to a sort of slumber. Unfortunately, a combination of substantial diver interest and locals armed with harpoons has greatly reduced the number of sharks. The nearby Ultra Freeze is a cargo ship that went down in 1989. The advanced wreck dive lies 100 feet down, is completely hollow and overflowing with tuna.

Dive Shops

Blue Peace Divers

Royal Plaza Marina, Cancun; ☎ *(52) 988-51497.*
The only NAUI Pro facility in Cancun, also handles PADI referrals. Two-tank dive, $50. Weekly trips to the cenotes ($135 via van including an ocean and a cave dive); Cozumel trips via sea plane ($165 including lunch and two dives), and beginning to arrange trips to Chinchorro. Caters to certified divers, but also features a resort course ($80).

Manta Divers

Playa Tortugas, Cancun; ☎ *(52) 988-34050.*

PADI International Dive Resort facility, opened in 1994. Two-tank dive, $55; one-tank night dive, $50; also offers a two-tank "twilight" dive for $75. Resort course scheduled daily, $85. Dive safaris to the cenotes scheduled twice weekly.

Quicksilver Diving Services

Playa Linda, Cancun; ☎ *(52) 988-34632.*

PADI five-star facility; handles NAUI referrals. Trips for groups of certified divers limited to 10. Two-tank dive, $55, or $65 including all equipment. Resort course, $80. Thursday trip to cenotes, $105 (including lunch and two dives).

Caribbean Coast

An increasingly popular, and unusual Caribbean dive destination is the **cenotes**—limestone sinkholes—which dot the Yucatan coastline facing Cozumel. Unlike their famous saline-submerged cousin in Belize, the Great Blue Hole, the cenotes access underwater rivers which flow through a maze of tunnels and chambers. While many divers regard freshwater diving as an anathema, cave divers consider this region, the largest underwater cave system in the world, a sort of holy grail (the ancient Maya regarded them as sacred locations, too). The huge rooms and tunnels are filled with both stalagmites and stalactites, but it's like soaring midair (rather than traipsing down a well-worn path) through Carlsbad Caverns. The area features the three biggest underwater caves in the world, with the largest of the surveyed cenotes yielding over 24 miles of passages. Obviously, the fresh water environment creates a different collection of fish than is found on the ocean reefs less than a mile away: tetras, mollies, cichlids are among the more common varieties. The caverns actually do have a quantity of salt water, creating a holocline, but it sits at the bottom of the cenotes, beginning about 38 feet below the surface. A special sight here is the Shearer Effect, the curious visual produced where the salt and fresh water currents collide; it's said to appear like gazing into a mirror from a distance, and swimming through it is like passing between worlds. Although the cenotes are found throughout inland Yucatan, the coastal town of Akumal serves as a sort of unofficial base for the dives (a number of the Cancun outfits also visit the area); most of the entrances are located two or three miles inland from the coast. **Carwash** is probably the most popular site, but **Temple of Doom**, **El Grande Cenote** and **Dos Ojos** are also thrilling.

At the base of the Yucatan Peninsula, 100 miles due south of Tulum, lies the last dive frontier of Mexico, the pristine **Banco Chinchorro**. If you haven't heard about Chinchorro, you're not alone, but talk to an older Mexican diver about Chinchorro and you'll see a smile, and his eyes will glaze over with that faraway look. This oval-shaped atoll, which stretches almost 40 miles north-to-south, serves as the final resting place for a striking quantity of wrecks (160 by one count), from Spanish galleons to modern cargo ships, all foiled by the unexpected shallows. Chinchorro's west wall is virtually on-par with Cozumel, featuring the same 3000-foot-deep trench and brisk south-to-north currents for drift diving. But wreck lovers will really be in heaven, particularly since so much of the area remains uncharted at this writing. The galleons have been excavated to some extent, and the atoll is protected by Mexican law, but there is plenty of exploring still possible. The swirling currents through the atoll cause visibility to vary wildly, but it averages 75–85 feet; good days will bring on clarity approaching 150 feet.

There are three tiny islands within the Chinchorro reef structure, all uninhabited except for occasional fishermen, otherwise you are unlikely to see anyone for miles. The Banco Chinchorro is usually accessed out of quiet Xcalak (population: 250), where a few small dive operators are based, and there is also good, isolated diving available on the barrier reef which continues south into Belize waters. All entertainment in undeveloped Xcalak is of the "make do" kind (we are sternly warned to advise readers that there is no disco). The Banco Chinchorro is close enough to San Pedro (Belize), that one can charter a boat from there, although you are still technically obliged to go through customs formalities in Xcalak. Needless to say, a diving accident would be quite serious here; the nearest medical facilities to Xcalak are reached via many kilometers of unpaved roads.

Dive Shops

Aquatech

Aventuras Akumal; ☎ *(52) 987-41271.*
The original cenote explorers, PADI- and NAUI-certified, Aquatech has been diving the region's caverns for eight years. Single-tank cenote dives, $45, including cavern dive briefing and transportation. Also dives the (salt water) Akumal coastline, where the offshore reef drops to about 120 feet and features canyons and sea mounts less than a mile from shore; the area is more peaceful and relaxed than either Cozumel or Cancun. Single-tank boat dives, $25; night dives, $40. Resort course, $80.

Aventuras Chinchorro

Xcalak; ☎ *(800) 480-4505 or (52) 983-80404.*
A PADI training facility at the most remote edge of Mexico. Two-tank dive on barrier reef, $45; the full-day trip to Chinchorro is $85-95 and includes three dives, lunch, and beer on the two-hour trip back to Xcalak.

On Foot

Dry and scrubby in the region around Cancun, the flat Yucatan becomes wetter, greener and more dense as you travel south. Perhaps the best area for exploring the jungle is the **Sian Ka'an Biosphere Reserve**, a 1.3 million-acre protected area along the coastline, about midway between Tulum and Belize. The reserve encompasses a vast area, including tropical forests, mangrove swamps, and a marine belt that extends to the barrier reef. The wildlife protected within Sian Ka'an includes a variety of cats, including jaguars and ocelots, monkeys, manatees and crocodiles. Unfortunately, trekking through the area on your own is quite difficult; the road entry points are rugged and few and there is little printed information to serve as a guide to Sian Ka'an. Your best bet is:

Los Amigos De Sian Ka'an
Plaza Americana, Cancun; ☎ *(52) 988-49583.*
Organizes long day-trips as well as overnight excursions, which include some combination of hiking, birdwatching, snorkeling, cenote-exploring and more.

By Pedal

If you want to spend an afternoon resort-hopping, a bike in Cancun can be handy, but ambitious cyclists will need to head for the mainland, where mile after mile of flat roads spread out over the peninsula. Perhaps the best destination is **Tulum**, on the road which parallels the eye-filling coastline south of Cancun, but keep in mind that you'll be riding on a highway, which carries its own unique thrill. Southbound traffic on the 307—tourists in cars and buses—is heavy in the morning as people head for Tulum and other nearby sights, but picks up in the opposite direction as the afternoon wears on. You'll need to locate an overnight location en route or, if you can make the entire 80-mile haul in a day, in Tulum. Biking on Cozumel is appealing; it's easy to escape the west coast resort crowd on treks to the lighthouses at either end, but plan on a long day to circuit the entire island.

What Else to See

After you've seen all the ruins and done all the watersports, you could be overwhelmed with a "been there, done that" attitude—except that you'll probably want to do it all again. If you have your fill of the major stuff, try venturing inland into some of the smaller towns to see the real Mexico. Many places on the peninsula have their own charming celebrations, usually with a historical or religious bent (Tizimin, in Yucatan, holds the Fair of the Three Kings in early January; the first week of May, the Ceremony of the Holy Incense in Kohunlich, Quintana Roo, includes a reenactment of sacred Mayan rituals). There are also lots of lesser-known ruins scattered throughout the peninsula along the Maya Route, so get a map and go exploring.

City Celebrations
Cancun

Cancun Jazz Festival ★★★

Cancun.

This May celebration brings musicians of international renown to the resort town, and lots of festivities take place in conjunction with the great music.

Carnaval ★★★

Cancun.

It's Mardi Gras-cum-Cancun in this annual festival held on the three days before Ash Wednesday. Everything you'd expect from a Mardi Gras-style bash happens here, from parades to masked balls to dancing in the streets in authentic regional costumes. Hotels book up fast, so reserve early.

Cozumel

Carnaval ★★★

Cozumel.

There's a party going on in many parts of Mexico in conjunction with Carnaval, which happens on the three days before Ash Wednesday. Lots of colorful costumes, parades and dances mark the celebration in Cozumel.

Historical Sites
Cancun

Chichen Itza ★★★★★

125 miles east of Cancun, Merida.
Hours Open: 8 a.m.–5 p.m.

Not everyone is intrigued by ancient ruins, but Chichen Itza is the most famous Maya archaeological site on the Yucatan Peninsula—and maybe in the world. The nearly four-square-mile area encompasses hundreds of buildings, some still buried in the jungle or in a state of partial restoration. About 30 have been completely restored, and they are stunning. Stop at the visitors center before you explore the ruins; films and pamphlets will set the stage and explain the historical context of the buildings. And speaking of that stage, there's an impressive sound and light show presented nightly that bathes the ruins in eerie light and recounts the legends of the ancient inhabitants. Check the schedule to be sure you're there for the English-speaking version. There are charges for parking, admission, the sound and light show and for use of a video camera—though admission is free to all on Sundays. Guided tours are very big here, so you won't have any trouble arranging one. Call Mayaland Resorts (☎ *(800) 235-4079)* to arrange tours or lodging—which has been strategically placed in the center of Chichen Itza. If you're going on your own, try to get there early in the morning, wear sturdy shoes and bring water.

Teatro Peon Contreras   ★★

Calle 60, Merida.

Built in the early 20th century, this ornate Italianate-style theater still hosts various performances. It's also the site of Merida's tourist information center, so you can check out what else there is to see in the area after you tour the theater.

Tulum   ★★★

Merida.

Although it's a bit of a drive (more than 70 miles from Cancun), it's easy to snag a guided tour (from a cruise ship or otherwise) to Tulum, one of the area's best-known archaeological sites. It sits on the coast in what is probably the most stunning setting of any of the ancient Maya ruins. There are dozens of buildings that are quite well preserved, the largest of which is the Castle (El Castillo), perched above the limestone cliffs.

Uxmal   ★★★★

50 miles south of Merida.
Hours Open: 8 a.m.–5 p.m.

The ruins at Uxmal are almost as famous as those of Chichen Itza, and are known for the beauty of the restored buildings. Highlights include the House of the Governor, the single largest structure in the Maya Empire, made up of a mosaic facade containing more than 25,000 hand-cut stones; and the Pyramid of the Magician, supposedly constructed by a mystical dwarf who hatched out of an egg. Like the ruins at Chichen Itza, Uxmal hosts a light and sound show every night that is designed to conjure up an ancient ambience of myth and magic. There is a charge for parking, admission, the sound and light show and for the use of a video camera—but come on Sunday, when it's free to all.

Cozumel

Balancanche Caves   ★★★

three miles east of Chichen Itza.

Explore what is believed to be an ancient underground worship site of the Maya. The caves are lighted for convenience, but there's some rough going (and some crawling) required to get through them, so you may want to pass if that "closed-in" feeling gives you the creeps. Inside are various carved artifacts from the Maya era, probably used in religious ceremonies. Wear sturdy shoes and expect to get dirty.

Celarain Lighthouse

South end of Cozumel Island, Cozumel.

You'll have to drive several miles on a dirt road to the southern tip of the island (a four-wheel drive vehicle is recommended), but the views for the top of the lighthouse are grand—so bring your camera.

San Gervasio Ruins ★★★

11 miles east of San Miguel on trans-island hwy., Cozumel.

San Gervasio isn't on par with Chichen Itza, but it's one of the best-preserved archaeological sites on the island. Several small shrines and temples honoring the Maya goddess of fertility and childbirth, Ixchel, date from more than 1000 years ago. Guided tours are available. There's an admission charge plus a road access fee and an extra charge for using a video camera. Closed on holidays.

Museums and Exhibits
Cancun

CEDAM Museum

Puerto Aventuras Resort, Playa del Carmen.

This small museum near Cancun salutes the members and finds of the Club de Exploraciones y Deportes Acuaticos de Mexico—in other words, local divers. Treasures retrieved from sunken ships, diving gear and other interesting exhibits are on display.

Museo Regional de Antropologia e Historia

Paseo Montejo y Calle 43, Centro, Merida.

Maya art recovered from the ruins at Chichen Itza is on display at this regional museum, which focuses on gold and jade artifacts, stone carvings and pottery. The historic home that houses the museum is also of interest. Admission charged.

Cozumel

Museum of the Island of Cozumel

Ave. Rafael Melgar, San Miguel.

Housed in a turn-of-the-century hotel building, this two-story museum chronicles the anthropological, cultural and natural history of the island of Cozumel. Exhibits show local flora and fauna, sea creatures and history from the Maya civilization to present day. Guided tours are available. Admission charged.

Parks and Gardens
Cancun

Centenario Zoo

Along Ave. Itzaes from Calle 95, Merida.

This modest zoo provides a look at animals native to the Yucatan Peninsula as well as displays of more exotic animals and birds. The kids will particularly like the miniature train ride.

Cozumel

Chankanaab Lagoon & Botanical Gardens

six miles south of San Miguel, Cozumel.

You can't go swimming or diving in the saltwater lagoon, which is a protected habitat, but the diving is great offshore, where there's a sunken ship to explore. The Botanical Garden is wonderful, containing more than 300 kinds of tropical plants and trees from 22 countries around the world. Wander on the trail that leads into the botanical "jungle," then stop at the small museum or beachside restaurant for refreshments.

Palancar National Park

south end of Cozumel Island, Cozumel.

The main attraction here is the Palancar Reef, a divers' paradise and the second-longest reef in the world. Marked by stunning coral formations, underwater caves and brightly colored fish, the reef is perfect for both snorkeling and scuba diving, which can be arranged as a shore excursion from a cruise ship or from your hotel. Non-divers can lounge on the excellent beach. From May to September, ask about guided nighttime excursions to watch sea turtles lay their eggs on the island's eastern shore.

Rio Lagartos National Park

End of Mexico 295 North.

Well off the beaten path, this national park, which includes more than 100,000 acres of protected habitat, sits in the middle of the Yucatan's northern coast. Home of one of Mexico's largest flamingo sanctuaries, the park is a birder's paradise, hosting many other species besides the big pink birds, which breed here from April into June.

Sian Ka'an Biosphere Reserve ★ ★ ★

South of Tulum, East of Mexico 307.

In 1986, the Mexican government set aside more than a million acres of native rain forest to form this preserve, which also includes offshore coral reefs and other precious habitat. There are more than 1000 varieties of plants here, many native animal species, birds and preserved archaeological sites. Much of the area is off-limits to tourists, but the outer buffer zone is accessible to those who want to explore the jungle habitat eihter on foot or by boat. Call for information and to arrange a guided tour—and bring insect repellent!

Theme/Amusement Parks
Cancun

Xcaret

35 miles south of Cancun.

Historical sites and natural wonders combine here to form the Yucatan's first-ever "eco-archaeological" theme park, although it's tame by Disney standards. There are real Maya ruins here, augmented by reproductions of other ruins, lagoons, dolphin ponds, dive sites, underground rivers, botanical gardens, a large aviary, horseback riding and other diversions. Facilities include picnic areas, restaurants, a visitor cen ter, museum and changing rooms. Unlike Disneyland, most of this scenery is the real thing. Admission charged.

Sports

Watersports reign supreme in the Mexican Caribbean, but there are plenty of other recreational opportunities to keep you busy. Cancun boasts the 18-hole championship **Pok-Ta-Pok** golf course (☎ *(98) 830871)*, designed by Robert Trent Jones and situated in a stunning setting. Watch out for the Maya ruins, a definite hazard on this course! Tennis is always an option at the big resort hotels, which will also arrange horseback riding, or you can arrange your own ride by calling ☎ *(98) 840861.* In the way of spectator sports, jai ali is played every evening at the fronton at Km. 4.5 *(☎ (98) 839304)*, and bullfights (cruel but popular nonetheless) take place at the bull ring in Cancun City on Wednesday afternoons during the winter.

The island of Cozumel is almost exclusively a watersports resort, with tennis available at major hotels.

Watersports

Swimming, snorkeling, scuba diving, waterskiing, boating, parasailing, windsurfing and fishing await you at almost any port in the Mexican Caribbean. The most highly touted watersport is diving, and dive companies abound, all competing for the millions of tourist dollars that flow into Mexico each year. Hotels are usually set up to provide both diving instruction and diving excursions, but they may come at a premium. An independent dive shop may save you money, so ask around. In Cancun, call **Scuba Cancun** (☎ *(98) 831011);* in Cozumel, try **Chino's Scuba Shop** *(☎ 987-24487)*.

Fishing can be arranged at the Cancun Yacht Club or the Pok-Ta-Pok Marina in Cancun, and in the harbor at San Miguel in Cozumel. Marlin, swordfish, sailfish, wahoo, barracuda, and tuna are all found in local waters, and in May, the billfish migration is celebrated with an International Billfish Tournament held in Cozumel. If you want to go shark fishing, it's best in **Laguna Yalahau**, at the northern tip of Quintana Roo. Get a boat in Chiquila, and head out for a day of trying to outsmart those sneaky denizens of the deep. Piers are obvious at all the large tourist areas, and offer boat trips to various local destinations. Get aboard on a scheduled fishing trip, or rent a boat and head out on your own.

Windsurfing and parasailing sites are generally clustered around the major tourist areas, and operators provide equipment and instruction. (There's a windsurfing school on **Playa Tortugas** in Cancun, ☎ *98-842023*). Waterskiing is excellent on the **Nichupte Lagoon** in Cancun, and there are various places to rent boats and other equipment everywhere along the Mexican Caribbean. Your hotel should be able to provide information on all nearby watersports, but the small hassle of arranging your watersports itinerary yourself can almost always save you money.

Where to Stay

Highest Rated Hotels on the Yucatan Peninsula

★★★★★	Casa Turquesa	$350–$500
★★★★★	Ritz-Carlton Cancun	$195–$425
★★★★	Camino Real	$130–$290
★★★★	Cancun Sunset Club & Suites	$140–$900
★★★★	Fiesta Americana Cancun	$145–$250
★★★★	Fiesta Americana Coral Beach	$200–$290
★★★★	Hyatt Cancun Caribe Resort	$155–$290
★★★★	Marriott Casa Magna Cancun	$225–$275
★★★★	Presidente Inter-Continental	$150–$260
★★★★	Westin Golf Resort	$180–$280

Most Romantic Hotels on the Yucatan Peninsula

★★★★★	Casa Turquesa	$350–$500
★★★★	Camino Real	$130–$290
★★★★	Cancun Sunset Club & Suites	$140–$900

Fielding's Best Budget Hotels on the Yucatan Peninsula

★★	Barracuda Hotel	$40–$50
★★	Days Inn Villa Del Rey	$50–$80
★★	Best Western Plaza Caribe	$50–$90
★★	Suites Turquesa	$40–$100
★★	Casa Del Mar Resort	$70–$75

Cancun

Most of the resort hotels are smashed together along Blvd. Kukulcan in the Hotel Zone (Zona Hotelera), which is right on the beach at Cancun's northeast shore. Big, splashy, expensive, crowded—you'll find all of these conditions and more in the Hotel Zone, but this is where most of the touristy types stay. The real values are situated in and around the downtown area of San Miguel, which isn't all that far from the beach—maybe three or four blocks. Note that all hotel prices—on both Cancun and Cozumel—nearly double during the winter season when most of the tourists arrive.

If your main concern is saving money, you can stay on Isla Mujeres (about four miles out to sea from Cancun), which is less developed and has cheaper lodging than the heavily-trafficked tourist areas (try Perla del Caribe, (☎ *98-820444*), or Posada del Mar (☎ *98-820044*). This is a terrific option if your main interest is diving or lolling around on the gorgeous beaches, but you'll have to take the ferry or hydrofoil to get to the main resort towns.

If you're extremely interested in staying near the Maya ruins, consider Merida, the capital of the state of Yucatan, situated on the Maya Route in the northwest corner of the peninsula. It's 30-plus miles to the coast, but Merida has an international airport with short flights to the resort areas offered several times a day. The city also has a charm of its own and is quite hospitable to tourists, offering several chain hotels such as the **Best Western** (☎ *99-239133*), **Hyatt Regency** (☎ *99-421234*), **Holiday Inn** (☎ *99-256877*), and **Park Plaza International** (☎ *99-239500*), plus the new **Fiesta Americana Merida** (☎ *99-421111*) and a host of other properties. **Mayaland Resorts** (☎ *800-235-4079*) has hotels located in Chichen Itza and Uxmal, putting you at the center of the ancient Mayan cities, and will arrange tour packages that include airport pickup, lodging, and guided tours to the ruins.

Hotels and Resorts

Beach Palace   **$220–$300**   ★ ★ ★

Blvd. Kukulcan Km 11.5, ☎ *(800) 346-8225, (98) 831177, FAX (98) 850439.*
Single: $220–$300. Double: $220–$300.

Families may find the Beach Palace an extremely attraction option with its spacious suites (complete with kitchenette) and all-inclusive pricing. There are lots of things for kids to do, including a Kitz Club program of supervised activities for those aged 5 to 12. There are two pools (one with a swim-up bar), a tennis court, fitness center and above-ground scuba tank on the premises.

Best Western Playa Blanca   **$80–$140**   ★ ★

Blvd. Kukulcan Km 3.5, ☎ *(800) 523-1234, (98) 830344, FAX (98) 830904.*
Single: $80–$140. Double: $80–$140.

Located across the street from a golf course, the Best Western offers the chain's basic rooms (bathrooms have only showers) and service. There is a pool and one lighted tennis court on site, plus a restaurant and coffeehouse. Watersports are available nearby.

Calida Cancun   **$100–$150**   ★ ★

Playa Linda Km 4, ☎ *(800) 221-2222, (98) 831600, FAX (98) 831857.*
Single: $100–$150. Double: $110–$150.

This Quality Inn property offers what you might expect from the chain: adequate, comfortable rooms (the ones in the newer tower are best), average service and moderate prices. The wide, sandy beach is a plus, and the hotel has a couple of large pools (and pools for the kiddies), two lighted tennis courts, several hot tubs and all local watersports. Dining options are limited and not all that special.

Calinda Viva   **$100–$150**   ★★

Blvd. Kukulcan Km 8.5, ☎ *(800) 221-2222, (98) 830800, FAX (98) 832087.*
Single: $100–$150. Double: $100–$150.

The Calinda doesn't have all the bells and whistles of some of the swankier resorts, but it's good value for the money—and it has a great beach. All rooms have ocean views and satellite TV, and there's a bar and restaurant on site. The recreational opportunities revolve around the pool and one tennis court, but you can find lots else to do nearby.

Camino Real   **$130–$290**   ★★★★

Punta, ☎ *(800) 722-6466, (98) 830100, FAX (98) 831730.*
Single: $130–$290. Double: $130–$290.

This resort, situated in a dramatic setting on the northern tip of Cancun, is surrounded by water and includes a full-service marina, two secluded beaches and deluxe accommodations with private lanais, minibars and satellite TV. There are both rooms and suites available here, and honeymoon packages are extremely popular. Facilities include three lighted tennis courts, a nearby championship golf course designed by Robert Trent Jones, three restaurants, six bars and a disco.

Cancun Clipper Club   **$100–$135**   ★★

Blvd. Kukulcan Km 8.5, ☎ *(98) 831366, FAX (98) 831731.*
Single: $100–$135. Double: $100–$135.

All rooms (including studios and suites) at the recently renovated Clipper Club have refrigerators, safes and cable TV; some have private Jacuzzis and/or kitchens as well. There's a wading pool for the kids, another with a swim-up bar for the adults and a coffeeshop and bar for dining and cocktails. The hotel overlooks a lagoon, but is across the street from the beach.

Cancun Palace   **$150–$250**   ★★★

Blvd. Kukulcan Km 14.5, ☎ *(800) 346-8225, (98) 850533, FAX (98) 851244.*
Single: $150–$250. Double: $150–$250.

Part of the Palace Resort chain, the Cancun Palace is a beachfront hive of activity. In addition to the requisite large pool (pools in this case, including one for wading and one with a swim-up bar), there are tennis courts (two lighted), an exercise room and lots of watersports. Accommodations include rooms and suites (some with kitchenettes) equipped with hair dryers, purified water, cable TV and patio or balcony. Several decent bars and restaurants are on site.

Cancun Sunset Club & Suites   **$140–$900**   ★★★★

Blvd. Kukulcan Km 10, ☎ *(800) 843-3841, (98) 830861, FAX (98) 830868.*
Single: $140–$200. Double: $140–$900.

One of the newest kids on the block, the all-suite Cancun Sunset offers one-, two- and three-bedroom suites, some with coffeemakers, kitchens and/or private whirlpools. All suites in the eight-story building have views of the ocean or Nichupte Lagoon and come equipped with minibar, safe and satellite TV. There's a special play area for the kids, a large pool, Jacuzzi, lighted tennis court, marina, exercise room and a spectacular lobby aquarium. If you really want to pamper yourself, book the Presidential Suite—which will set you back about a thousand bucks a night.

Caribbean Village Cancun $120–$180   ★★★

Blvd. Kukulcan Km 10.5, ☎ *(98) 850112, FAX (98) 850999.*
Single: $120–$180. Double: $120–$180.
The name of this eight-story resort (formerly a Radisson) may imply an exotic island village ambience, but in actuality this is just your basic, moderately priced hotel. A pool and two lighted tennis courts are available for guests, who can also pay to engage in various watersports nearby.

Carrousel Hotel Cancun $100–$130   ★★

Blvd. Kukulcan Km 3.5, ☎ *(98) 830388, FAX (98) 832312.*
Single: $100–$130. Double: $100–$130.
This older, apartment-style beachfront hotel was renovated in the early '90s and occurs ocean views from every room. Recreational facilities include a pool, wading pool, Jacuzzi with room for a party-sized group of soakers, tennis court and all local watersports, including boat rentals. There are two restaurants in the hotel, or you can order room service if you feel like eating in. The Carrousel tends to host the young and the restless, so if you're the more quiet and secluded type, you may wish to stay elsewhere.

Casa Maya $105–$180   ★★★

Ave. Kukulcan Km 5.5, ☎ *(800) 336-5454, (98) 830555, FAX (98) 831188.*
Single: $105–$180. Double: $105–$180.
The ambience is "ancient Maya pyramid" at this all-suite hotel that offers one- and two-bedroom units. The hotel is perfect for families looking for a bargain, and most of the suites have kitchens to cut down on the tab of eating out. (If you're not in the mood for cooking, there's also a restaurant on site.) All suites have an ocean view, private balcony and fully stocked bar. Recreational facilities include two pools, three lighted tennis courts, watersports and supervised programs for kids.

Casa Turquesa $350–$500   ★★★★★

Blvd. Kukulcan Km 13.5, ☎ *(800) 525-4800, (98) 852924, FAX (98) 852922.*
Single: $350–$500. Double: $350–$500.

Casa Turquesa is an elegant, Mexican mansion-style all-suites hotel affiliated with Small Luxury Hotels of the World. In other words, this is a really nice place. You'll pay for it, but the suites are spacious and beautiful and the service shines. Each contains extras such as hair dryers, two phones, TV with VCR, CD player, minibar, in-room safe and a balcony with private Jacuzzi. There's also a great restaurant, private beach and nearby golf course. If you can't keep your mind off the office, you'll have access to a computer and FAX machine for making deals from paradise.

Club Lagoon $80–$120   ★★★

Blvd. Kukulcan Km 5.9, ☎ *(98) 831101, FAX (98) 831197.*
Single: $80–$120. Double: $80–$120.

This older motel is a good value, and you can walk in or sail in as it has its own marina. The kids will enjoy the playground and supervised programs, and there are boats to rent if you get tired of paddling around in the pool. Lots to do, plus a restaurant, bar and coffeeshop.

Continental Villas Plaza Cancun $155–$250   ★★★

Blvd. Kukulcan km 11.5, ☎ (98) 831022, FAX (98) 832270.
Single: $155–$250. Double: $155–$250.
This large, Mediterranean-style resort complex includes standard rooms, 26 villas and more than 100 junior suites. Each unit comes equipped with hair dryer, in-room safe, cable television (some in-room movies are free) and terraces. Recreational amenities include three pools, two lighted tennis courts, racquetball and squash courts and a variety of watersports. Two restaurants and two coffeeshops are open most of the day.

Fiesta Americana Cancun $145–$250

Blvd. Kukulcan Km 11, ☎ (98) 831400, FAX (98) 832502.
Single: $145–$250. Double: $145–$250.
Another in the chain of Fiesta Americanas, this one was built in 1981 and renovated in 1991. It's near the convention center and shopping, and has a large pool. Most everything else you can think of to do is located nearby. Accommodations are pleasant—if basic—and include balconies, minibars and in-room movies. Three restaurants and bars offer a variety of cuisine and nightlife.

Fiesta Americana Condesa Cancun $140–$220   ★★★★

Blvd. Kukulcan Km 16.5, ☎ (98) 851000, FAX (98) 851800.
Single: $140–$170. Double: $180–$220.
This beachfront property is known for its lush tropical setting and variety of activities. All rooms have minibars, balconies and ocean views, and some suites have private Jacuzzis. There's a large pool, three indoor tennis courts, a game room, jogging path, and access to nearby golf and watersports. There are also four restaurants, three bars and Latin entertainment. Nice.

Fiesta Americana Coral Beach $200–$290

Blvd. Kukulcan Km 8.5, ☎ 98) 832900, FAX (98) 833084.
Single: $200–$290. Double: $200–$290.
This 11-story resort is one of the best in Cancun, a deluxe, all-suite property dedicated to keeping you active and entertained from morning to night. On-site sports options include swimming at the large, landscaped pool, tennis on one of three indoor courts, a health club with all amenities and boat rental for diving and fishing. A championship golf course is nearby. Junior suites are large and have balconies overlooking the sea. There's four restaurants and a handful of bars on site.

Hotel America $65–$100   ★

Ave. Tulum and Calle Brisa, ☎ (98) 847500, FAX (98) 841953.
Single: $65–$100. Double: $65–$100.
Located more than a mile from the beach, the Americana provides free transfers to its beach club, but unless you're doing business or are more interested in shopping

than sunning, you may wish to choose lodging closer to the sea. The obvious attraction here is the price.

Hotel Aristos $70–$100   ★★

Blvd. Kulkulcan Km 9.5, ☎ *(98) 830011, FAX (98) 830078.*
Single: $70–$100. Double: $70–$100.
This moderately priced property sits on Chacmol Beach and is frequented by younger types on a budget. Decent rooms (not air conditioned, and not all have ocean views), a couple of tennis courts, a pool and a bar and restaurant round out the offerings.

Hyatt Cancun Caribe Resort $155–$290   ★★★★

Blvd. Kukulcan Km 10.5, ☎ *(800) 233-1234, (98) 830044, FAX (98) 831514.*
Single: $155–$290. Double: $155–$290.
There's a wide selection of lodging options here, with 140 standard guestrooms and 58 rooms and suites located in the Regency Club Villas. All have ocean views, private balconies, hair dryers, and access to in-room movies; some have in-room safes and private whirlpools as well. The hotel has its own marina and dock for easy access to watersports, and there are three pools, a Jacuzzi, three tennis courts and a putting green. Built in 1974, the hotel is known for its excellent service and comparatively nonfrenetic atmosphere.

Hyatt Regency Cancun $150–$300   ★★★

Blvd. Kukulcan, ☎ *(98) 831234, FAX (98) 831349.*
Single: $150–$300. Double: $150–$300.
This 12-story oceanfront hotel is adjacent to the Cancun Convention Center, so attracts lots of business travelers. Rooms and suites (there are six) are nicely furnished and each has a balcony, minibar, satellite TV and an ocean view. The hotel boasts a large pool, Jacuzzi, access to two tennis courts, a health club, shops and a car rental desk—plus a variety of restaurants and bars.

Krystal Cancun $120–$185   ★★★

Paseo Kukulcan Lote 9, ☎ *(800) 231-9860, (98) 831133, FAX (98) 831790.*
Single: $120–$185. Double: $120–$185.
Located on the beach at Punta Cancun, the Hotel Krystal caters to all tastes with its assortment of rooms, suites and club-level amenities. Facilities include tennis and racquetball courts, a romantic landscaped pool, a health club and nearby golf, boat rentals and watersports. With four restaurants, a variety of bars and a dance club, the Krystal keeps the fun alive until well into the night—which is just what the mostly younger clientele looks forward to.

Marriott Casa Magna Cancun $225–$275   ★★★★

Blvd. Kukulcan, Retorno Chac Lote 41, ☎ *(98) 851385, FAX (98) 851385.*
Single: $225–$275. Double: $225–$275.
The guestrooms and 38 suites in this modern hotel have marble floors, cable TV, minibar, in-room safe, a water purification system, hair dryer and individual climate control. Not that you're going to want to spend too much time in your room. There's lots to do here, including use of the outdoor pool, Jacuzzi, health club (get a massage after the aerobics class), two lighted tennis courts and all watersports.

There are three restaurants, a bar and an oldies nightclub where you can listen to music from the '50s and '60s, and where the brave (although not necessarily talented) can try their hand at karaoke.

Melia Turquesa $130–$200   ★★★

Blvd. Kukulcan Km 12, ☎ *(800) 336-3542, (98) 832544, FAX (98) 851029.*
Single: $130–$170. Double: $140–$200.

Built to resemble an ancient Maya temple, the Melia rises up out of a lush garden setting on North Cancun Beach. The excellent guestrooms and suites (one to three bedrooms) are equipped with minibar, balcony, marble fixtures and a hair dryer; some also have a private Jacuzzi. There are some serious conference facilities here, but the family may just want to hang out at the large pool, the smaller one for kids, or try some of the local watersports available nearby. Three restaurants, two bars and a nightclub give you lots to do in the evening, and there's a babysitting service for the kids.

Miramar Mision Park Plaza $125–$150   ★★

Blvd. Kukulca Km 9.5, ☎ *(800) 437-7275, (98) 831755, FAX (98) 831136.*
Single: $125–$150. Double: $125–$150.

The large pool is the highlight of this moderately priced, nine-story beachfront hotel, which is otherwise short on sports facilities (although most are available nearby). Rooms have ocean views, safes, minibars, hairdryers, cable TV and free movies. Dining and entertainment options range from eating in (room service is available) to hitting the hotel's restaurants, bars and clubs. Overall, this place is unremarkable, but the price makes it a tempting option.

Omni Cancun Hotel & Villas $100–$275   ★★★★

Blvd. Kukulcan Km 16.5, ☎ *(800) 843-6664, (98) 850714, FAX (98) 850184.*
Single: $100–$200. Double: $150–$275.

The sprawling Omni isn't the newest hotel in Cancun, but it has definitely retained its dignity, especially after renovations in 1992. In addition to the standard rooms, there are 34 suites and 36 villas, some with kitchenettes. There are several dining options, and sports facilities include six tennis courts (four indoor), four pools, and a health club with gym, sauna, steam, solarium and massage services. A car rental desk is on site, as well as laundry facilities and a beauty salon. Good conference and business services, too.

Presidente Inter-Continental Cancun $150–$210

Blvd. Kukulcan Km 7.5, ☎ *(800) 447-6147, (98) 830200, FAX (98) 832515.*
Single: $150–$210. Double: $150–$210.

Close to Plaza Caracol for shopping and the Pok-Ta-Pol golf course designed by Robert Trent Jones, the Presidente, overlooking Nichupte Lagoon, has much to offer. In addition to the guestrooms, there are 15 suites on the club level, with special amenities offered to guests who stay there. Recreational facilities include two pools situated in a striking pyramid-shaped area, one lighted tennis court, Jacuzzis, sauna and a marina where you can rent kayaks or canoes. The hotel's several restaurants and bars provide a plethora of dining and entertainment options. A serious nod to conference and business services makes this hotel the choice for those who want to work while they play.

Radisson Sierra Plaza Cancun $85–$240   ★★★★

Blvd. Kukulac Km 10, ☎ *(800) 333-3333, (98) 832444, FAX (98) 833486.*
Single: $85–$240. Double: $85–$240.
This large resort—recently renovated—sits on the white sandy beach and boasts its own marina and private lagoon. Rooms are spacious and well furnished with hand-crafted Mexican furniture. Everything is provided for the perfect family vacation: two pools, tennis courts, watersports, shops, restaurants—and babysitting service.

Ritz-Carlton Cancun $195–$425   ★★★★★

Retorno del Ray 36, ☎ *(98) 850808, FAX (98) 851015.*
Single: $195–$355. Double: $275–$425.
If you want to escape to the Caribbean in style, it doesn't get much better than the Ritz-Carlton, which opened in 1993 and added a true touch of elegance (not to mention sootiness) to the Hotel Zone. Rooms and suites are spacious and elegantly furnished, each with marble bath, stocked minibar and ocean view. The multilingual staff will see to your every need, and there are excellent business and fitness centers, pools, three tennis courts, gift shops and a beauty salon.

Sheraton Resort & Towers $120–$170   ★★★★

Blvd. Kukulcan Km 12.5, ☎ *(800) 325-3535, (98) 831988, FAX (98) 850083.*
Single: $120–$170. Double: $120–$170.
As you might expect, this large Sheraton is extremely busy with both conference-goers and vacationers. It has a great beach, a plethora of restaurants, bars and entertainment options and a huge assortment of recreational facilities. There are three large pools (one for kids), lighted tennis courts, miniature golf, a health club and a playground. Accommodations (beachfront and tower rooms are the best) have refrigerators, cable TV and views of the ocean or lagoon; guests staying in suites (some which have private Jacuzzis) and tower rooms get extra amenities. All runs smoothly here.

Westin Golf Resort $180–$280   ★★★★

Blvd. Kukulcan, ☎ *(800) 228-3000, (98) 850086, FAX (98) 850666.*
Single: $180–$280. Double: $180–$280.
This golf resort includes 90 beachfront cabanas along with its standard rooms. A championship golf course is at the back door, and nongolfers can enjoy the pool, fitness center, tennis courts and watersports. A shopping arcade is also on site.

Westin Regina Resort $150–$200   ★★★★

Paseo Kukulcan Km 20, ☎ *(800) 228-3000, (98) 850537, FAX (98) 850074.*
Single: $150–$200. Double: $150–$200.
There's a lagoon on one side and the sparkling Caribbean on the other at this deluxe resort, formerly the Regina Hotel. The rooms and seven suites provide all the extras, including hair dryer, bathrobe, minibar, climate control and satellite TV. (If you want a room with a balcony or terrace, request this when you reserve.) There are activities galore offered at the Westin, including a supervised children's program,

tours to Maya ruins and nearby golfing and watersports. The resort itself has five swimming pools, sauna, health club, two lighted tennis courts and its own beach.

Apartments and Condominiums

Kin-Ha Condos **$90–$160** ★★★

Blvd. Kukulcan Km 8, ☎ *(98) 832155, FAX (98) 832147.*
Single: $90–$160. Double: $90–$160.
Kin-Ha is a budget option for self-caterers. The three-story beachfront property isn't fancy, but does provide the basics and access to local watersports. Some accommodations include kitchens. On-site facilities include a restaurant, pool and boat rentals.

Low Cost Lodging

Best Western Plaza Caribe **$50–$90** ★★

Ave. Tulum y Uxmal, ☎ *(800) 523-1234, (98) 841377, FAX (98) 846352.*
Single: $50–$90. Double: $50–$90.
The Plaza Caribe is located downtown, across from the main bus terminal. It's not all that far to the beach, but if you don't feel like walking you can play in the pool or talk someone into a game of tennis. There aren't many amenities here, but rooms are decent enough with in-room safes and movies, and there's a restaurant and coffeeshop for dining.

Cozumel

Cozumel is an island, located approximately 12 miles off the coast of the Yucatan Peninsula. Most of the hotels are located on the beach on the western side of the island, with the interior of the island remaining largely untouched. Lodging is not cheap on Cozumel, although you can find some bargains, especially in the hotels that cater to divers (who are mainly interested in a clean bed, a shower, and a place to hang their wetsuits at the end of the day).

Across from Cozumel on the mainland is Playa del Carmen, an area that offers slightly less expensive lodging than both Cozumel and Cancun, even though it will eventually be overrun with hotels and even now has a couple of upscale resorts that are expensive. Try the **Blue Parrot Inn** (☎ *(800) 634-3547*), which is reasonably priced and gives you a lot for your money, or the **Continental Plaza Playacar** (☎ *987-30100*), which is a big and expensive resort hotel, reminiscent of those in the Hotel Zone and (perhaps) reflecting the state of things to come at Playa del Carmen.

Hotels and Resorts

Club Cozumel Caribe **$110–$170** ★★★

San Juan Beach Km 4.5, ☎ *(800) 327-2254, (987) 20100, FAX (987) 20255.*
Single: $110–$170. Double: $110–$170.
This all-inclusive, family-oriented hotel offers 260 beachfront rooms and its own snorkeling beach. One price covers lodging, meals, drinks, island cruises, supervised programs for kids, scuba and other watersports and entertainment with a local flavor. There's a small pool on site, as well as a dive shop, shopping arcade, and windsurfing, kayaking, sailing, snorkeling and aerobics classes. Good for the active set.

El Cozumeleno **$120–$140** ★★★★

Playa Santa Pilar, ☎ *(800) 388-8364, (987) 20149, FAX (987) 20381.*

Single: $120–$130. Double: $130–$140.

Considered one of the better family-style lodging options in Cozumel, El Cozume-leno is an all-inclusive property that opened in the fall of 1994. Guestrooms are spacious at this oceanfront hotel, and all have a view of the sea and beach, which is one of the best on the island. Included in the price are all meals, drinks, a glass-bottom boat trip, a supervised children's program and access to all the hotel's game and sports facilities.

Fiesta Americana Cozumel Reef $130–$170   ★★★

Carretera Chankanaab Km 7.5, ☎ *(987) 22622, FAX (987) 22666.*
Single: $130–$170. Double: $130–$170.

Formerly a Holiday Inn, this newer property changed hands but retains the standard Holiday Inn style. The hotel's location near Palancar Reef is good news for divers, and its large, free-form pool will satisfy the non-beach crowd. Most of the 166 rooms have ocean views (be sure to request one).Other amenities include two lighted tennis courts, a jogging trail and access to a dive shop and watersports. Two restaurants, a beach bar and a shopping boutique complete the picture. Service sometimes lags.

Fiesta Inn $100–$120   ★★

Costera Sur Km 1.7, ☎ *(800) 343-7821, (987) 22811, FAX (987) 22154.*
Single: $100. Double: $120.

Located about a mile south of San Miguel and across the street from the beach, the Fiesta reflects the chain's typical architecture and style. Only half of the rooms have a view of the sea, so be sure to request one when reserving. There's a large free-form pool and a wading pool, two bars and two restaurants on site. The hotel also has a tennis court, and everything you need for watersports, pus bike and moped rentals, can be found at the beach club across the street.

La Ceiba Beach Resort $60–$120   ★★

Carretera Chankanaab Km 4.5, ☎ *(800) 877-4383, (987) 20844, FAX (987) 20065.*
Single: $60–$110. Double: $85–$120.

La Ceiba, located two miles south of San Miguel, caters to divers and vacationers looking for solid value. There's an undersea snorkeling trail just offshore, with snorkeling and diving equipment available to guests. Rooms in the high-rise hotel are clean and bright, if rather ordinary, but you actually get a little more than you pay for. Unfortunately, the hotel's location near the cruise ship pier causes a bit of milling around, but there's lots of compensate for occasional inconvenience: two restaurants, a lighted tennis court, weight room, Jacuzzi, sauna and large pool with swim-up bar.

Melia Mayam Cozumel $105–$155   ★★★

Carretera Costera Norte Km 5.8, ☎ *(800) 336-3542, (987) 20411, FAX (987) 21599.*
Single: $105–$155. Double: $115–$155.

This is the northernmost of the island's hotels, and one of the most isolated. About 80 percent of the standard rooms have ocean views; there are also suites and one-bedroom units set in a newer high-rise. Amenities include satellite TV, minibars and balconies in each room. There's two pools on the grounds—one with that requisite swim-up bar—as well as two tennis courts, watersports and a restaurant and coffee-shop.

Plaza Las Glorias   **$120–$265**   ★ ★ ★

Carretera Chankanaab Km 2.5, ☎ *(987) 22411, FAX (987) 21937.*
Single: $120–$155. Double: $200–$265.
Just south of San Miguel, this is one of the island's newer resorts, and reflects the standard Plaza Les Glorias look in its four-story, pueblo-style building. All accommodations are in suites, some with one or two bedrooms and kitchenettes. All have balconies or patios with an ocean view. The grounds include a large pool with swim-up bar, two restaurants (including one that specializes in steak and seafood), three bars and a dive shop.

Presidente Inter-Continental   **$150–$260**   ★ ★ ★ ★

Carretera Chankanaab Km 6.5, ☎ *(800) 447-6147, (987) 20322, FAX (987) 21360.*
Single: $150–$260. Double: $150–$260.
This property has a lot going for it, including a secluded setting, a great snorkeling beach and 253 rooms and suites with ocean views. The hotel is large enough to accommodate conferences and offers a lot of extras such as game rooms, a video bar and car and moped rentals. All rooms are brightly furnished and have balconies and minibars. Two lighted tennis courts, watersports and two restaurants and two bars round out the facilities.

Sol Cabanas del Caribe   **$100–$110**   ★

Costera Norte Km 5.1, ☎ *(800) 336-3542, (987) 20411, FAX (987) 21599.*
Single: $100–$110. Double: $100–$110.
Thirty-nine rooms and nine cabanas make up this modest hotel on the beach. Most rooms have balconies and an ocean view; cabanas have shared patios. The pool is small, but there are lots of watersports to choose from.

Sol Caribe   **$110–$180**   ★ ★ ★

Playa Paraiso Km 3.5, ☎ *(987) 20700, FAX (987) 21301.*
Single: $110–$180. Double: $110–$180.
This large resort hotel is located two miles south of San Miguel. Although the beach is across the street, access is easy and diving facilities are nearby. If you'd rather not take the short walk, relax in the hotel's large, lagoon-like pool or play tennis on one of three courts. Each room as a TV, minibar and small balcony, and a restaurant and bar are located off the lobby.

Apartments and Condominiums

Coral Princess Club   **$85–$200**   ★ ★ ★

Zona Hotelera Norte Km 2.5, ☎ *(800) 253-2702, (987) 23200, FAX (987) 22800.*
Single: $85–$125. Double: $125–$200.
This newer resort offers modern studios and one- and two-bedroom suites with complete kitchens and living areas. All units have ocean views, marble combination baths and satellite TV. The premises includes a pool, restaurant, bar and dive shop.

Suites Turquesa   **$40–$100**   ★ ★

Playa Turquesa, ☎ *(987) 21113, FAX (987) 21135.*
Single: $40–$100. Double: $40–$100.

This small facility offers two-bedroom suites with kitchenettes and living areas. It's near a marina, so watersports are accessible. Amenities are limited to a pool.

Low Cost Lodging

Barracuda Hotel   **$40–$50**   ★★

Ave. Rafael Melgar 628, ☎ *(987) 21243, FAX (987) 20884.*
Single: $40–$45. Double: $45–$50.
Obviously at these rates the Barracuda is not exactly upscale, but it won't take a bite out of your vacation budget, either. Only rooms on the upper floors have ocean views, but all have small refrigerators. Guests are mostly divers who decorate the hotel's exterior with their wetsuits liberally draped over balconies and terraces.

Cantarell   **$60–$105**   ★★

Carretera San Juan Km 3, ☎ *(987) 21779, FAX (987) 20016.*
Single: $60–$100. Double: $65–$105.
This is one of the oldest hotels on Cozumel, but its rooms, suites and villas have recently been renovated, and a new pool overlooking the beach has been added. All rooms have an ocean view, and there are two restaurants, a bar, dive shop and other watersports on site.

Casa Del Mar Resort   **$70–$75**   ★★

Costera Sur Km 4, ☎ *(800) 877-4383, (987) 21900, FAX (987) 21855.*
Single: $70. Double: $75.
One of the best things going for this former Howard Johnson property is its affordability. Its primary emphasis is on diving (services are provided by the Del Mar Aquatics Dive Shop), but non-divers will enjoy the pool and Jacuzzi. You can rent a bike or moped for excursions to nearby ruins or local beaches.

Galapago Inn   **$70–$100**   ★

Carretera Costera Sur Km 1.5, ☎ *(800) 847-5708, (987) 20663.*
Single: $70–$100. Double: $75–$100.
If you're planning to spend most of your time diving and don't care about a fancy resort, the Galapago may be for you. The main attraction is the complete dive school, including its own equipment, boats and dock. The rooms are basic without a lot of extras; a pool is about it. If you're not a diver, pass. Ask about dive packages.

Plaza Azul   **$55–$90**   ★

Carretera San Juan Km 4, ☎ *(987) 20033, FAX (987) 20110.,*
Single: $55–$70. Double: $60–$90.
This small oceanfront hotel doesn't have the flash or sophistication of a large resort, but it has a friendly staff and the basic amenities, including a pool, private beach, tennis courts and nearby watersports. Decent enough for the price.

San Miguel

Days Inn Villa Del Rey   **$50–$80**   ★★

Ave. 11, Sur 460, ☎ *(987) 21600, FAX (987) 21692.*
Single: $50–$80. Double: $50–$80.
Located in downtown San Miguel, the Days inn offers solid value as long as you don't mind not being on the beach. Six of the rooms have kitchenettes, and there's a lovely pool area and Jacuzzi. A nice alternative to the touristy hotels on the sand.

Where to Eat

★★★★	Fielding's Highest Rated Restaurants on the Yucatan Peninsula	
★★★★	Donatello	$5–$25
★★★★	La Joya	$1–$9
★★★★	Mirage	$1–$9
★★★	Acuario	$1–$9
★★★	Blue Bayou	$15–$35
★★★	Bogart's	$1–$9
★★★	Lorenzillo''s	$1–$9

	Fielding's Special Restaurants on the Yucatan Peninsula	
★★★★	Donatello	$5–$25
★★★★	La Joya	$1–$9
★★★	Bogart's	$1–$9

Almost every large, tourist-oriented hotel on the Yucatan Peninsula has at least one (usually expensive) restaurant, and many have several, so you can opt to eat at your own hotel's dining room, or go restaurant hopping until you find something you like at another hotel; or, an independent restaurant that appeals to you. No longer the secluded, exotic place it once was, the peninsula now caters to just about any taste, with its own pizza parlors, Mediterranean-style eateries, chain restaurants, and Americanized Mexican dishes. Middle Eastern cuisine is also to be found here, largely due to the influx of Lebanese and other Middle Easterners in recent years. There are still a few places to get authentic local cuisine, but you may have to get off the beaten path to find regional food that hasn't been dressed up to suit the American palate.

Cozumel

As is the case with Cancun, check out the restaurants in yours and the surrounding hotels, where you can probably find whatever cuisine you have a hankering for. Hotel food is always more expensive than the average, of course. The next obvious place to look is in San Miguel, which has plenty of culinary options and many restaurants that are moderately priced.

Acuario $ ★★★

Beach Road, ☎ (987) 21097.
Seafood cuisine.

This casual seafood restaurant has its own aquarium so that you can watch relatives of your meal swim by as you eat. Moderately priced seafood and a lively bar. The beach club is open from 10:00 to 6:00, offering swimming, sunning and dining. Open for lunch and dinner.

Carlos 'n Charlie's $ ★★

Ocean Promenade, Ave. Rafael, ☎ (987) 20191.
American cuisine.

The Mexico City chain strikes again. Dining (Mexican and American fare) is always a party here, with a happening bar and lots of decent seafood. No air conditioning—but have a few drinks and you may not notice. Open for lunch and dinner.

Donatello $ ★★★★

Ave. Melgar Sur 131, ☎ (987) 22586.
Italian cuisine.

This is one of the best restaurants on Cozumel, and it's all dressed up in Renaissance-style ambience—but you don't have to dress up. In fact, Donatello gives a nod to families with a children's menu and an attractive patio where you can corner the junior-sized spaghetti-flingers among you. This restaurant is extremely popular, which means you'd better make reservations during the high season.

Karen's Pizza and Grill $ ★★

Ave. 5 Norte.
Italian cuisine.

Pizza is the main thing here, and it's done well and delivered with a smile. Best of all, nearly everything on the menu is extremely affordable—so go for those extra toppings.

La Yucatequita $ ★★

9 C Sur y 10 Ave. Sur.
Local cuisine.

One of the best places in town to get real Maya food, La Yucatequita is a favorite for local cuisine at reasonable prices. Open only for dinner.

The Sports Page $ ★★

Calle 2 Norte 7 Ave. 5.
American cuisine.

When you get a hankering for a burger and fries—or just want to hang out and watch sports on satellite TV—come to this happening spot, which also caters to Americans with currency exchange. Open for breakfast, lunch and dinner.

Cancun

Bellini's New York Deli $ ★

Plaza Caracol Mall, 2nd level, ☎ (98) 830459.
Mexican cuisine.

It's New York-cum Mexico in this casual deli where Americans looking for a taste of home can order sandwiches and salads, or just hang out at the bar. There's no air conditioning, so dress lightly. Open for breakfast, lunch and dinner.

Blue Bayou $ ★★★

Blvd. Kukulcan Km 10.5, ☎ (98) 830044.
Cajun cuisine.

You're back on the bayou at this snappy Cajun restaurant located just off the lobby in the Hyatt Cancun Caribe. Expect all your spicy favorites, a lively bar scene and lots of mellow jazz. Very cool, but a bit pricey.

Bogart's $ ★★★

On the beach at Punta Cancun, ☎ (98) 831133.
Middle Eastern cuisine.

You'll think you've died and gone to Morocco at this upbeat spot. Most of the Middle Eastern cuisine is prepared at your table, and the music and ambience set an exotic mood. Open for dinner only.

Carlos'n Charlie's $ ★★

Km 5.5 at the lagoon, ☎ (98) 830846.
American cuisine.

Carlos and Charlie have an incongruous mix here, with American and Mexican specialties served in a party atmosphere. The restaurant, situated overlooking a marina, is part of a chain originating in Mexico City and features a decent variety of seafood at moderate prices. Open for lunch and dinner.

La Joya $ ★★★★

Blvd. Kukulcan Km 15, ☎ (98) 832900.
Mexican cuisine.

"Nouvelle" is the byword here, and Mexican cuisine goes upscale and sophisticated to suit the traveling gourmet. Evidence of the food-as-art fad lingers (at least until you eat it) on every plate, and you can expect to pay a pretty penny for dinner, but it will probably be worth it. Dress up, take advantage of the valet parking, and you'll soon be feeling like you're at some chi-chi L.A. hotspot.

Lorenzillo's $ ★★★

Hotel Zone, Km 10.5, ☎ (98) 831254.
Mexican cuisine.

Look out over the lagoon as you dine on regional specialties at Lorenzillo's, which does an especially good job with seafood. Open for lunch and dinner.

Los Huaraches $ ★★

Ave. Uxnal y Yaxchilian.
Mexican cuisine.

Located in Cancun City, this casual restaurant gives you an inexpensive taste of regional food and offers specials on empanadas and other local fare. Open for lunch and dinner.

Mikado $ ★★

Blvd. Kukulcan Km 16, ☎ (98) 852000.
Japanese cuisine.

This casual restaurant—a Japanese steakhouse that bears little or no resemblance to anything Mexican in either decor or cuisine—offers some good values, especially if you go for the early-bird specials. Open for dinner only.

Mirage   **$**   ★ ★ ★ ★

Blvd. Kukulcan Km 15.5, ☎ *(98) 851000.*
Upscale cuisine.
One of the fanciest restaurants in Cancun—and one of four restaurants at the Fiesta Americana Condesa—the Mirage is open for dinner only, serving such upscale dishes as smoked salmon and other refined choices. The view is great, the surroundings sophisticated, the food excellent and the prices high.

Piemonte Pizzeria   **$**   ★ ★

Ave. Yaxchilan 52.
Italian cuisine.
Pizza and other Italian specialties are served in this modest restaurant in Cancun City. Good value. Open for lunch and dinner.

Playa del Carmen

Playa Caribe   **$**   ★ ★

Ave. 5.
Seafood cuisine.
If you're hanging out at the Plaza, stop in at this nearby casual spot for cheap eats and friendly service. Seafood is a specialty.

Where to Shop

Cancun

Cancun is a duty-free zone packed with tourists, so you probably have a good idea of what the shopping is all about: everything from the "My-mom-went-to-Cancun-and-all-I-got-was-this-lousy-T-shirt!" souvenirs to pricey jewelry and Mexican crafts. There are big shopping malls located in the Hotel Zone and large areas of shops in Cancun City *(Plaza Canzun, on Avenida Tulum)*, but if you're smart, you'll head for the open-air market *(Ave. Tulum 23)*, where you can have a ball dickering over the price on absolutely everything. There are especially good values to be had on jewelry, leather, locally-made clothing and other crafts, so don't chicken out—bargain!

If you take an excursion to Merida, visit the huge downtown market district or the government-run crafts market *(Mercado de Artesanias)*. Both of these areas can be crowded, and the vendors can be pushy and not always honest about what you're getting, so being able to speak (and understand) Spanish and knowing exactly what you're looking for is helpful. Be selective, look around, and comparison shop for the best deals. The most popular items for sale in Merida are hammocks, silver jewelry, sandals, leather goods and locally made clothing.

Cozumel

The main street in San Miguel—**Ave. Rafael Melgar**—is where most of the shops are situated on Cozumel. Although they are not as hoity-toity as the Hotel Zone shops in Cancun, shops along the Malecon are aimed at getting tourists to spend money on everything from junk souvenirs to jewelry and designer clothing. Get off the avenue even a block or two and you'll get better prices. No matter where you shop, remember that bargaining is a way of life in Mexico, so don't pay the asking price.

Yucatan Directory

ARRIVAL AND DEPARTURE

Vacationers usually arrive on the Yucatan Peninsula via one of the international airports located in Cancun, Cozumel, or Merida. Best deals are on flights with a four- or seven-day turnaround. From any of the major airports, you can take commuter flights to Isla Mujeres, Chichen Itza and many other destinations on the peninsula. **Aerocaribe**, **Aerocozumel**, and **Taesa** are the airlines most often used to fly between Cozumel, Cancun and Merida.

Cruise ship passengers arrive at ports of call in Cozumel (near the town of San Miguel), Playa del Carmen (10 miles west of Cozumel) and Cancun. A constant parade of bus tours, sailing excursions and ferries branches out from the major ports to local archaeological and recreational sites, shopping, and beaches. Check your ship's listing of shore excursions—which are more expensive but always get you back to the ship on time—if you're unfamiliar with the area.

When you leave Mexico by plane, a $12 departure tax is added to the price of your ticket. No matter what your mode of transportation, you must also present proof of U.S. citizenship, preferably in the form of a U.S. passport, and return your tourist card. Customs officials will check everything you have, so be sure you can present proof that expensive personal items, cameras, binoculars, etc. that you brought with you into Mexico were not purchased there, or you will have to pay duty on them. Duty must also be paid on all items exceeding the $400 duty-free limit, including gifts. Agricultural products must also be declared, and some may be prohibited from being brought into the U.S. Duty is assessed at 10 percent of fair retail value for the first $1000 in merchandise over the $400 exemption.

And just in case you're thinking how cool it would be to smuggle back some ancient artifact, be warned that doing so will put you in BIG trouble with the Mexican government, which legally owns all national treasures.

BUSINESS HOURS

Stores open Monday–Saturday 10 a.m.–7 p.m.; many in the tourist areas are also open later in the evening and on Sunday. Banks are open weekdays 9 a.m.–1:30 p.m. and generally exchange foreign currency only from 10:30 a.m.–12:30 p.m.

CLIMATE

The Yucatan Peninsula is dry compared to the eastern Caribbean, but there's still lots of heat and humidity and the temperature consistently hovers at around 80 degrees F., peaking in the summer months at an average of 82 or 83, and dipping in the winter to the mid-70s. Rainfall is at its peak (an average of eight or so inches at Cancun) in the summer and early fall (the "off" season in the Caribbean), which means it's muggier than usual then. Hurricanes do occasionally spin in a direction that affects the Mexican Caribbean (Isla Mujeres took an especially nasty hit from Hurricane Gilbert), so pay at least moderate attention to the weather if you're traveling during the hurricane season (late summer—October).

DOCUMENTS

U.S. and Canadian citizens need proof of citizenship in the form of a valid passport or certified (not a photocopy) birth certificate. A Mexican tourist card should be obtained at the port of entry (or will be supplied by your cruise line) and carried with you while you are in Mexico. The card is valid for up to 90 days, and should be returned to Mexican officials when leaving the country. A valid drivers' license from either the U.S. or Canada is valid in Mexico.

ELECTRICITY

The current runs at 110 volts/AC 60.

GETTING AROUND

If you want to tour the area on your own, your cheapest transportation options are buses and taxis, which are all over the place. Bus travel is recommended if you are taking a tour to a specific destination, or if you can obtain "deluxe" service—buses on these jaunts tend to be comfortable and air-conditioned. Bus rides on a lower-class bus are exceedingly cheap, but are not always the most comfortable way to travel, as conditions are hot, crowded, smoky (smoking is allowed on buses)—and small farm animals may also be aboard.

Taxis get you where you're going without extra stops, but be sure to settle on the price beforehand, or you could be gouged for more money than you planned to spend. Dickering over fares is a way of life, so don't be hesitant about negotiating. The fee for several hours of local touring can run anywhere from $35 to $50.

Ferries are also a popular mode of transportation, especially between Cozumel and Playa del Carmen, Cozumel and Puerto Morelos, Cancun and Isla Mujeres, Kukulcan and Isla Mujeres, and Punta Sam and

Isla Mujeres. Some of these trips can be long and uncomfortable; be sure to check schedules before departing, and realize that schedules are not always adhered to, especially during bad weather.

Several major car rental companies (including Avis, Budget and Hertz) offer cars for rent in major cities, but prices tend to be exorbitant ($50/ day and up). (If you're big on the ruins at Chichen Itza, book a stay at the **Hotel Mayaland** and the hotel provides you with free use of a VW "sedan" with unlimited free mileage. Call the resort at ☎ *(800) 235-4079* for information—and a probable reality check. If you do rent a car, be sure it has air conditioning, and stay on main highways—such as the toll road that runs from Cancun to Merida—to avoid bad roads and those maddening little speed bumps called "topes," which are nearly always an annoyance when you take the surface streets through small towns.

If you find that car rental rates are prohibitive, consider renting a moped for tooling around town. It's a popular mode of transportation, and is about half as expensive as renting a car.

LANGUAGE

Obviously, Spanish is the language of Mexico, and it helps if you can speak it. If not, remember that the economy of the Yucatan Peninsula is dependent on hosting lots of American tourists, so it's not difficult to find someone who speaks English in the resort areas. Once you get off the beaten track, you're on your own. No matter where you stay in the Mexican Caribbean, beware of being taken advantage of—especially if you don't speak English.

MEDICAL EMERGENCIES

There is no Mexican equivalent of the 911 call, but English-speaking emergency service is available by dialing 06. You can be directed to an English-speaking hospital by the Red Cross (called the "Cruz Roja" in Mexico), which also has clinics in several areas of the Yucatan (☎ *987-21058 in Cozumel; 98-841616 in Cancun)*, and there is an American Hospital in Cancun (☎ *98-846430)*.

MONEY

Mexico's monetary unit is the New Peso ("Nuevo Peso"), which replaced the "old" peso in 1993. The exchange rate varies from day to day, and you are likely to get the best exchange rate from banks (even though they charge a service fee) or downtown currency exchange booths; airports, hotels, and expensive shops in areas heavily traveled by tourists are generally not the most beneficent when exchanging currency.

You may take U.S. currency and traveler's checks into Mexico, but you should exchange small denominations of traveler's checks or U.S. dollars into Mexican currency as needed. Large Mexican banks generally have English-speaking personnel who can advise you on the exchange rate and help you with the conversion process. Most banks have limited hours during which they will exchange foreign currency, usually between 10:30 a.m. and 12:30 p.m. Regular banking hours are Monday-Friday, 9 a.m.–1:30 p.m., with banks in larger cities open in late afternoon and/or on Saturday mornings. Banks close on all national holidays, and smaller banks close for local celebrations.

TELEPHONE

The Mexican telephone system can be frustrating, and suffers from a lack of consistency, with phone numbers varying between five and seven digits, depending on where you are calling. The international code, to be used when calling Mexico from another country, is *011*, and the country code is *52*. (You can reach an English-speaking international operator by dialing *09*; a long-distance operator within Mexico with *02*.) Local area codes (*98* for Cancun; *987* for Cozumel, Playa del Carmen and Isla Mujeres; *99* for Merida and Uxmal) are used both when calling from another country or when calling within Mexico. If you plan on making a lot of calls, invest in a prepaid LADATEL phone card, which can be used at designated public phones throughout Mexico. Make as few phone calls as possible from your hotel, which will charge you plenty for the privilege.

TIME

The Yucatan Peninsula is in the Central Standard Time Zone.

TIPPING AND TAXES

Expect a 10 percent service charge to be added to your bill for basically all goods and services (including your hotel tab). Some restaurants also add a service charge, so check before you tip to be sure you aren't paying twice. The amount to be left for a tip is roughly consistent with what is expected in the U.S., and you should plan on tipping just about everyone who does a service for you. The exception is cab drivers, who don't really expect it unless they have gone beyond the call of duty enough to warrant a reward.

TOURIST INFORMATION

In Cancun, visit the State Tourism Office—open daily from 9 a.m. to 9 p.m.—in downtown Cancun City *(Ave. Tulum adjacent to the Municipal Palace;* ☎ *98-848073)*, or stop in at one of the information booths at Plaza Caracol in the Hotel Zone, at the airport, and in Cancun City where English is spoken. In Cozumel, the State Tourism Office—open Monday–Friday—is on the *Plaza Cozumel (*☎ *987-20972)*. As in Cancun, there are information kiosks around the main square and in the resort areas.

WHEN TO GO

The best time to visit the Mexican Caribbean is from late fall to spring—unless you are a diver, in which case you should consider coming during the summer, when diving is best and hotel rates are lowest.

Non-divers can also save lots of money by planning a trip in summer, but the heat and humidity associated with the rainy season can make your stay extremely uncomfortable. As far as what's happening, things are pretty much always a party in the tourist zones, so things are rockin' and rollin' at just about any time of year. Those interested in being around for Carnaval, celebrated in both Cancun and Cozumel, should plan to arrive the weekend before Ash Wednesday to get in on the celebration.

YUCATAN HOTELS		RMS	RATES	PHONE	CR. CARDS
Cancun					
★★★★★	**Casa Turquesa**	31	$350–$500	(800) 525-4800	A, CB, DC, MC, V
★★★★★	**Ritz-Carlton Cancun**	370	$195–$425	(98) 850808	A, CB, DC, MC, V
★★★★	**Camino Real**	381	$130–$290	(800) 722-6466	A, DC, MC, V
★★★★	**Cancun Sunset Club & Suites**	218	$140–$900	(800) 843-3841	A, CB, D, DC, MC, V
★★★★	**Fiesta Americana Cancun**	281	$145–$250	(98) 831400	A, DC, MC, V
★★★★	**Fiesta Americana Condesa Cancun**	502	$140–$220	(98) 851000	A, D, MC, V
★★★★	**Fiesta Americana Coral Beach**	602	$200–$290	(98) 832900	A, D, MC, V
★★★★	**Hyatt Cancun Caribe Resort**	198	$155–$290	(800) 233-1234	A, D, MC, V
★★★★	**Marriott Casa Magna Cancun**	450	$225–$275	(98) 851385	A, CB, DC, MC, V
★★★★	**Omni Cancun Hotel & Villas**	328	$100–$275	(800) 843-6664	A, CB, DC, MC, V
★★★★	**Presidente Inter-Continental Cancun**	294	$150–$210	(800) 447-6147	A, CB, D, MC, V
★★★★	**Radisson Sierra Plaza Cancun**	260	$85–$240	(800) 333-3333	A, DC, MC, V
★★★★	**Sheraton Resort & Towers**	622	$120–$170	(800) 325-3535	A, CB, D, MC, V
★★★★	**Westin Golf Resort**	450	$180–$280	(800) 228-3000	A, CB, DC, MC, V
★★★★	**Westin Regina Resort**	385	$150–$200	(800) 228-3000	A, DC, MC, V
★★★	**Beach Palace**	160	$220–$300	(800) 346-8225	A, CB, D, DC, MC, V
★★★	**Cancun Palace**	417	$150–$250	(800) 346-8225	A, D, MC, V
★★★	**Caribbean Village Cancun**	300	$120–$180	(98) 850112	A, D, MC, V
★★★	**Casa Maya**	350	$105–$180	(800) 336-5454	A, CB, D, MC, V
★★★	**Club Lagoon**	89	$80–$120	(98) 831101	A, CB, D, MC, V

YUCATAN HOTELS		RMS	RATES	PHONE	CR. CARDS
★★★	Continental Villas Plaza Cancun	626	$155–$250	(98) 831022	A, CB, D, MC, V
★★★	Hyatt Regency Cancun	300	$150–$300	(98) 831234	A, CB, D, MC, V
★★★	Kin-Ha Condos	150	$90–$160	(98) 832155	A, MC, V
★★★	Krystal Cancun	316	$120–$185	(800) 231-9860	A, CB, D, DC, MC, V
★★★	Melia Turquesa	444	$130–$200	(800) 336-3542	A, DC, MC, V
★★	Best Western Playa Blanca	150	$80–$140	(800) 523-1234	A, D, MC, V
★★	Best Western Plaza Caribe	140	$50–$90	(800) 523-1234	A, D, MC, V
★★	Calida Cancun	470	$100–$150	(800) 221-2222	A, DC, MC, V
★★	Calinda Viva	210	$100–$150	(800) 221-2222	A, CB, D, DC, MC, V
★★	Cancun Clipper Club	142	$100–$135	(98) 831366	A, D, MC, V
★★	Carrousel Hotel Cancun	150	$100–$130	(98) 830388	A, D, MC, V
★★	Hotel Aristos	222	$70–$100	(98) 830011	
★★	Miramar Mision Park Plaza	225	$125–$150	(800) 437-7275	A, CB, D, MC, V
★	Hotel America	177	$65–$100	(98) 847500	A, D, MC, V

Cozumel

★★★★	El Cozumeleno	94	$120–$140	(800) 388-8364	A, D, MC, V
★★★★	Presidente Inter-Continental	253	$150–$260	(800) 447-6147	A, D, MC, V
★★★	Club Cozumel Caribe		$110–$170	(800) 327-2254	A, MC, V
★★★	Coral Princess Club	48	$85–$200	(800) 253-2702	A, MC, V
★★★	Fiesta Americana Cozumel Reef	162	$130–$170	(987) 22622	A, CB, D, DC, MC, V
★★★	Melia Mayam Cozumel	200	$105–$155	(800) 336-3542	A, MC, V
★★★	Plaza Las Glorias	170	$120–$265	(987) 22411	A, MC
★★★	Sol Caribe	322	$110–$180	(987) 20700	A, CB, MC, V
★★	Barracuda Hotel	50	$40–$50	(987) 21243	A, D, MC, V
★★	Cantarell		$60–$105	(987) 21779	A, MC, V
★★	Casa Del Mar Resort	106	$70–$75	(800) 877-4383	A
★★	Fiesta Inn	180	$100–$120	(800) 343-7821	A, MC, V
★★	La Ceiba Beach Resort	113	$60–$120	(800) 877-4383	A, MC

YUCATAN HOTELS		RMS	RATES	PHONE	CR. CARDS
★★	Suites Turquesa	18	$40–$100	(987) 21113	A, MC, V
★	Galapago Inn		$70–$100	(800) 847-5708	MC, V
★	Plaza Azul		$55–$90	(987) 20033	A, MC, V
★	Sol Cabanas del Caribe		$100–$110	(800) 336-3542	A, MC, V

San Miguel

★★	Days Inn Villa Del Rey	43	$50–$80	(987) 21600	A, CB, D, DC, MC, V

YUCATAN RESTAURANTS		PHONE	ENTREE	CR. CARDS

Cancun

American				
★★	Carlos 'n Charlie's	(98) 830846	$1–15	A, MC, V

Cajun				
★★★	Blue Bayou	(98) 830044	$15–$35	A, D, DC, MC, V

Continental				
★★★★	Mirage	(98) 851000	$1–$9	A, D, DC, MC
★★★	Bogart's	(98) 831133	$1–$9	

Italian				
★★	Piemonte Pizzeria		$1–$9	

Japanese				
★★	Mikado	(98) 852000	$1–$9	A, CB, D, MC, V

Mexican				
★★★★	La Joya	(98) 832900	$1–$9	A, D, DC, MC, V
★★★	Lorenzillo's	(98) 831254	$1–$9	A, D, MC, V
★★	Los Huaraches		$1–$9	
★	Bellini's New York Deli	(98) 830459	$1–$9	A, MC, V

Cozumel

American				
★★	Carlos 'n Charlie's	(987) 20191	$1–$15	A, MC, V
★★	The Sports Page		$1–$15	

Continental				
★★	La Yucatequita		$1–$20	

YUCATAN RESTAURANTS	PHONE	ENTREE	CR. CARDS
Italian			
★★★★ **Donatello**	(987) 22586	$5–$25	A, MC, V
★★ **Karen's Pizza and Grill**		$1–$9	
Seafood			
★★★ **Acuario**	(987) 21097	$1–$9	D, MC, V

Playa del Carmen

Seafood			
★★ **Playa Caribe**		$1–$9	

INDEX

Order Your Guide to Travel and Adventure

Title	ISBN	Price
Fielding's Alaska Cruises/Inside Passage	1-56952-068-2	$17.95
Fielding's Amazon	1-56952-000-3	$16.95
Fielding's Australia '96	1-56952-097-6	$16.95
Fielding's Bahamas '96	1-56952-081-X	$15.95
Fielding's Belgium '96	1-56952-078-X	$16.95
Fielding's Bermuda '96	1-56952-082-8	$15.95
Fielding's Borneo	1-56952-026-7	$18.95
Fielding's Brazil	1-56952-027-5	$18.95
Fielding's Britain '96	1-56952-083-6	$16.95
Fielding's Budget Europe '96	1-56952-084-4	$17.95
Fielding's Caribbean '96	1-56952-085-2	$18.95
Fielding's Caribbean Cruises '96	1-56952-070-4	$18.95
Fielding's Eastern Caribbean '96	1-56952-071-2	$17.95
Fielding's Europe '96	1-56952-087-9	$18.95
Fielding's European Cruises '96	1-56952-074-7	$17.95
Fielding's Far East '95/96	1-56952-032-1	$18.95
Fielding's France	1-56952-033-X	$16.95
Fielding's Freewheelin' USA	1-56952-067-4	$17.95
Fielding's Hawaii '96	1-56952-090-9	$17.95
Fielding's Holland '96	1-56952-086-0	$16.95
Fielding's Italy '96	1-56952-091-7	$17.95
Fielding's Guide to Kenya's Best Hotels, Lodges & Homestays	1-56952-038-0	$17.95
Fielding's Las Vegas Agenda	1-56952-075-5	$14.95
Fielding's London Agenda	1-56952-039-9	$14.95
Fielding's Los Angeles Agenda	1-56952-040-2	$14.95
Fielding's Malaysia and Singapore	1-56952-041-0	$17.95
Fielding's Mexico	1-56952-092-5	$18.95
Fielding's New York Agenda	1-56952-044-5	$12.95
Fielding's New Zealand	1-56952-101-8	$16.95
Fielding's Paris Agenda	1-56952-045-3	$14.95
Fielding's Portugal '96	1-56952-102-6	$16.95
Fielding's Rome Agenda	1-56952-077-1	$14.95
Fielding's San Diego Agenda	1-56952-088-7	$14.95
Fielding's Scandinavia	1-56952-103-4	$16.95
Fielding's Southeast Asia '96	1-56952-065-8	$18.95
Fielding's Southern Vietnam on Two Wheels	1-56952-064-X	$15.95
Fielding's Spain	1-56952-094-1	$17.95
Fielding's Guide to Thailand Including Cambodia, Laos, Myanmar	1-56952-069-0	$18.95
Fielding's Vacation Places Rated	1-56952-062-3	$19.95
Fielding's Vietnam	1-56952-095-X	$17.95
Fielding's Western Caribbean '96	1-56952-072-0	$15.95
Fielding's Guide to the World's Most Dangerous Places	1-56952-031-3	$19.95
Fielding's Worldwide Cruises '96	1-56952-073-9	$18.95
The Indiana Jones Survival Guide	1-56952-076-3	$18.95

To place an order: call toll-free 1-800-FW-2-GUIDE
(VISA, MasterCard and American Express accepted)
or send your check or money order to:
Fielding Worldwide, Inc., 308 S. Catalina Avenue, Redondo Beach, CA 90277
add $2.00 per book for shipping & handling (sorry, no COD's), allow 2–6 weeks for delivery

Favorite People, Places & Experiences

ADDRESS:	NOTES:

Name

Address

Telephone

Name

Address

Telephone

Name

Address

Telephone

Name

Address

Telephone

Name

Address

Telephone

Name

Address

Telephone

Favorite People, Places & Experiences

ADDRESS:	NOTES:

Name

Address

Telephone

Name

Address

Telephone

Name

Address

Telephone

Name

Address

Telephone

Name

Address

Telephone

Name

Address

Telephone

Favorite People, Places & Experiences

ADDRESS:	NOTES:

Name

Address

Telephone

Name

Address

Telephone

Name

Address

Telephone

Name

Address

Telephone

Name

Address

Telephone

Name

Address

Telephone

Favorite People, Places & Experiences

ADDRESS:	NOTES:

Name

Address

Telephone

Name

Address

Telephone

Name

Address

Telephone

Name

Address

Telephone

Name

Address

Telephone

Name

Address

Telephone

Favorite People, Places & Experiences

ADDRESS: **NOTES:**

Name

Address

Telephone

Name

Address

Telephone

Name

Address

Telephone

Name

Address

Telephone

Name

Address

Telephone

Name

Address

Telephone

Favorite People, Places & Experiences

ADDRESS:	NOTES:

Name

Address

Telephone

Name

Address

Telephone

Name

Address

Telephone

Name

Address

Telephone

Name

Address

Telephone

Name

Address

Telephone

Favorite People, Places & Experiences

ADDRESS:	NOTES:

Name

Address

Telephone

Name

Address

Telephone

Name

Address

Telephone

Name

Address

Telephone

Name

Address

Telephone

Name

Address

Telephone

Favorite People, Places & Experiences

ADDRESS:	NOTES:

Name

Address

Telephone

Name

Address

Telephone

Name

Address

Telephone

Name

Address

Telephone

Name

Address

Telephone

Name

Address

Telephone